THE GREAT BIG PRESSURE COOKER BOOK

THE GREAT BIG
PRESSURE
COOKER
BOOK

500 Easy Recipes for Every Machine, Both Stovetop and Electric

BRUCE WEINSTEIN AND **MARK SCARBROUGH**

Photographs by Tina Rupp

Clarkson Potter/Publishers
New York

Copyright © 2015 by Mark Scarbrough and
Bruce Weinstein
Photographs copyright © 2015 by Tina Rupp

Published in the United States by Clarkson Potter/
Publishers, an imprint of the Crown Publishing Group,
a division of Random House LLC, a Penguin Random
House Company, New York.
www.crownpublishing.com
www.clarksonpotter.com

CLARKSON POTTER is a trademark and
POTTER with colophon is a registered trademark
of Random House LLC.

Library of Congress Cataloging-in-Publication Data
Weinstein, Bruce, author.
The great big pressure cooker book: 500 easy
recipes for every machine, both stovetop and electric /
Bruce Weinstein and Mark Scarborough; photographs
by Tina Rupp.—First edition.
Includes index.
1. Pressure cooking. I. Scarbrough, Mark, author. II. Title.
TX840.P7W45 2015
641.5'87—dc23 2014022862

ISBN 978-0-8041-8532-5
eBook ISBN 978-0-8041-8533-2

Printed in the United States of America

Book design by Jan Derevjanik
Cover design by Gabriel Levine
Cover illustrations: Shutterstock/Studio_G

11

First Edition

ACKNOWLEDGMENTS

There came a day when ten cookers were going at once in our kitchen.
No, there came many days. We couldn't have done it without great pressure cookers
from Instant Pot (through Robert Wang), Fagor America (through Sarah de la Hera),
Calphalon (through Rachel McLennan at Carmichael Lynch Spong), Cuisinart (through
Mary Rodgers), Sitram (through Katie Hlavinka King at Avalon Communications), and
Kuhn Rikon (through Kristyn Fuller at Field Marketing & Media). Almost every one of
the twenty-five books we've written has also been generously supported with tools and
gadgets from OXO (through Emily Forrest and Gretchen Holt).

They say that the least-used words in modern publishing are "thank you." Not by us.
Thank you, thank you, thank you. Here's where else the gratitude goes:

At Clarkson Potter: to Jessica Freeman-Slade, our editor (again!); Doris Cooper, our
editorial director (and our champion); Aaron Wehner, our publisher; Kevin Garcia, the
book's production manager; Mark McCauslin, its production editorial director; Jane
Treuhaft, the art director; Marysarah Quinn, the head of design; Jan Derevjanik, the
book's designer; Gabriel Levine, the cover designer; Kate Tyler, the book's publicity director; and Meredith McGinnis, its marketing director.

At Writers' House: to Susan Ginsburg, our agent (again and again and again), and
Stacy Testa.

And elsewhere: to Pam Krauss for acquiring this book; Tina Rupp for shooting the
photos; Paige Hicks for the prop styling; and the entire towns of Colebrook and Norfolk,
Connecticut, for testing and tasting these dishes, as well as feeding us and keeping us so
happy in a very quiet part of New England.

CONTENTS

INTRODUCTION

Your grandmother knew this day would come. She knew you'd come back to her favorite kitchen tool, the pressure cooker, to make four-star-but-fast braises, stews, soups, and casseroles. She just didn't know how you'd get here.

About twenty years ago, there was a pressure cooker renaissance in America, sparked mostly by author Lorna Sass. Her recipes offered comfort food in far less time. Perhaps like us, you bought a stovetop pressure cooker and became an unabashed advocate of savory braises or whole grains from the pot.

Meanwhile, a second pressure cooker renaissance was going on right alongside us. The cooker also morphed into a countertop appliance: electric models started showing up on the best foodie sites and in the finest cooking stores. Americans snapped them up in increasing numbers, a testament to both our love of gadgets and our desire for quicker, better meals.

Voilà: two culinary renaissances, happening simultaneously. It sounds like a dream. But there's a problem. Stuck in the past, pressure cooker recipes assume that the stovetop cooker is the only form this appliance takes. Unfortunately, recipes have to be differentiated between the two types. They cook at different pressures and require different timings—and sometimes even different liquid levels. No cookbook has ever been written for both halves of the renaissance.

Until now. All our recipes can be made in a stovetop or an electric pot. They're also geared for today's changing tastes, with bolder flavors, fewer processed ingredients, and more innovative combinations. No, we haven't forgotten the classics: we've got some terrific chicken-and-rice casseroles, fine vegetarian main courses, great chilis, and full-flavored ways to use economical cuts like ground chuck. As we developed these recipes, we made a pact that we wouldn't use anything we couldn't find in our rural New England supermarket, yet we still took advantage of the astounding array there. We've felt free to bring in a wide range of international flavors, to use the full span of *real* ingredients our modern supermarkets afford.

You've probably heard that the pressure cooker is the European answer to the American slow cooker. Swiss households own three on average! But even that divide is false. Time was, almost every U.S. household had one, and more and more do so today. Stats also show that the electric models often outsell the stovetop ones. These gadgets fly off the shelves. We may even catch up to the Swiss. See, your grandmother has been waiting a long time for you to get here.

NO MORE CULINARY DIVIDES

We Americans think about cooking in one of two ways: fast or gourmet. We either want dinner on the table in record time or we want to spend a leisurely afternoon preparing a four-star meal for friends and family. TV shows, cookbooks, magazine articles—they're perched on either side of this divide.

It's high time somebody built a bridge. With a stovetop or an electric pressure cooker, we can create a weekend-worthy pot roast on a weeknight *and* in minutes. Then, come Saturday, we can whip up a fine cacciatore or fricassee for a dinner party without sacrificing our day off. Both will taste as if they've braised all day. In fact, the intense pressure in the pot helps retain complex flavors, as well as a wide range of natural sugars that don't break down as they do during long braising. Our meals may well taste better.

So welcome to the sophisticated braises, the homey stews, and the hearty soups, as well as breakfast porridges and the best cheesecakes around. No, we can't deep-fry or make cookies, but we can indeed get a caramelized crust on a roast. And we can turn out some of the finest comfort imaginable: layered flavors with minimal effort.

Welcome, too, to one-pot meals. We can brown, deglaze, build the sauce, and create a gorgeous dinner without a second saucepan or skillet. (Okay, there are a couple of recipes among these that do indeed call for a second cooking vessel. But really, only a few.) Because we have to set a stovetop pot over the heat or warm up an electric one, we're able to caramelize our proteins or sweeten our aromatics before they undergo the pressured cooking.

Most of us are trying to cook fresher, even if the modern busyness epidemic rages unchecked. If there ever was a ripe moment for the pressure cooker to become a cookware warhorse again, it's now. We all want delectable, innovative, fake-free meals—in minutes. Yep, fake-free. As we did in *The Great American Slow Cooker Book*, we've 86'd the faux vinaigrettes and bottled sauces, the cream of this and fat-free that. Instead, we've used real ingredients that bring the most flavor to the meal. Sure, we use canned broth and tomatoes because good-quality versions are close to what we'd make on our own. But we skip a bottle of fat-free ranch dressing or a can of gloppy enchilada sauce and come out with better meals that take very little time. Buy the best you can comfortably afford—with few other ingredients listed on the label and no "artificial" (or even added "natural") flavorings. Dare to go fake-free.

Yes, a pressure cooker works best for braises and stews. But don't just think of getting out the pot in the cold months. We've calibrated these recipes with lots of citrus notes, with the bright flavors of fresh vegetables, and often with the best summer produce in mind. We've altered the cooking method to make sure the asparagus is crisp and the green beans are snappy. This appliance can keep your kitchen cooler in the summer *and* warmer in the winter.

THE FOUR PRESSURE COOKER PERSONALITY TYPES

Maybe you're already a disciple. Or maybe you're just curious about the fuss. The way we see it, there are four distinct types of people when it comes to pressure cookers. Let's figure out which you are.

The Ingénue

or *I have no idea what you're talking about. Oh, look: a butterfly.*

For those of you unfamiliar with the pressure cooker's magic powers, let's have a primer: The pressure cooker is perhaps the best way to cook economical, luscious cuts—chicken thighs, chuck roasts, briskets, pork shoulders, and country-style ribs. But it's also a fast and efficient way to keep lean chicken breasts moist, to turn a healthy pork loin into a delectable meal, and to make a fine sauce for shrimp or mussels in a couple of minutes (or less).

A pressure cooker works this way: Liquids come to a boil under a locked lid. Steam is trapped; the pressure rises. If you remember your high school physics, as the pressure rises, so does the temperature. In fact, both rise enough in tandem to alter what we perceive as set constants. Soon, the boiling point of water is no longer 212°F; it's around 250°F. Other liquids, even the melted fat from meat, begin simmering away at higher temperatures than their stated boiling points. Those liquids are now superheating the food, cooking it in less time. But that's not all. There are five benefits beyond mere speed.

1. The liquid (and its steam) can't escape from the sealed environment, so everything's cooked with much less moisture loss.

2. The intense pressure softens the fibers in meats and vegetables more quickly.

3. Vitamins and minerals are not dispersed to the air, so the food retains more of its whole food nutrition.

4. Because vegetables are not exposed to large quantities of oxygen during cooking, they retain their essential color, making for a more visually appealing meal.

5. Since you're cooking at a higher temperature and pressure, you'll have up to a 75 percent energy savings over conventional methods of cooking.

But hang back a bit. Before you start down the road of pressure cooking, here are two important things you ingénues (and everyone else) must do:

- Read the manufacturer's instruction booklet. Each model has its own quirks (a.k.a. features), so familiarize yourself with these *before* you proceed. You cannot use the introductory material in this book as an instruction manual for your pot. How does the pressure release valve work? How do you lock the lid in place? How do you do a quick release of pressure? There's no way we can account for the myriad differences among individual cookers. You'll need to know your model.

- Follow the recipe. A recipe for a standard nonpressurized braise in a covered pot in the oven almost always includes some leeway: add a little more broth, double the carrots, or swap out the wine for apple juice. With a pressure cooker recipe, you've got far less play. Sure, you can alter herbs, double the garlic, or swap out minor flavorings (honey for maple syrup, for example). But you can't willy-nilly omit 2 tablespoons of white wine vinegar. Even that small amount may be crucial to creating the right amount of steam and pressure in the closed pot.

Now you know why pressure cookers create disciples. Simply put, there's no gadget like it: for speed, yes; but also for better cooking. But read on. There's more to learn.

The Nervous Nellie

or *Are you crazy? That thing's dangerous. I knew a woman who . . .*

Stop. We've heard it all. Some ancient relative of yours had a pot that blew her to Oz and back. Your great-aunt had one that shellacked her ceiling with stewed chicken. Your mother's friend got a new bay window out of her pot. These people don't have pressure cooker tragedies in common. They're all just old or they used outdated equipment. Do you still scrub your clothes on a washboard? We

thought not. Modern pressure cookers have two basic safety features to dispel these fears.

- First, there's a pressure release valve or mechanism on the lid. Back in the day, a funky weight rotated back and forth as steam sizzled from inside. These days, the valves are not just a piece of lead over a vent. Instead, they're engineered to release varying amounts of steam (and thus pressure) based on your specifications. These newfangled valves or other mechanisms sit in place and work in either smaller, more frequent bursts or in a prolonged, gentle release. In electric cookers, the release is so small and so controlled that you might not even notice it.

  By the way, this valve is not only necessary for safety but also crucial to the recipe's success. The pressure should come up to a stated level—*and then stay there.* It must not climb and climb. Otherwise, everything in the pot will begin to break down into mush. In other words, the pressure release valve is a safety feature that guarantees a good meal.

- There's a rubber gasket around the inside rim of a heavy lid. This gasket will eventually make the pot airtight after (a) the lid has been locked in place (usually by flanges, sometimes by a more complex spring mechanism) and (b) the internal pressure has risen to the right point as the cooker sits over high heat. As the pressure expands, the pot itself actually increases in size, pulling the gasket taut and forming a perfect seal.

  However, this gasket has a second (and perhaps more important) safety function: it's the main release if something catastrophic happens inside the pot. If you leave the flame too high for too long, or if the pressure vent becomes hopelessly clogged, or if there's a technical malfunction in an electric pot, this rubber gasket will give way, causing the contents to cascade down the outside of the pot. You'll end up with a mess on your stove or your counter—but not your ceiling. And the lid will have stayed in place.

Electric pots have programmed controls. These effectively take over and run the pot once you lock the lid in place and select both the level of pressure and the cook time. By contrast, stovetop pots have to be babied a bit: you need to drop the heat under the pot, then watch to make sure that high pressure is maintained, usually indicated by the calm release of steam, often by various buttons or knobs that engage or elevate because of the pressure. (Again, read your manufacturer's instruction booklet to learn the exact visual and auditory cues.)

You must not leave the pot unattended. Stick around. Listen for one of two warning signs: (a) a complete cessation of any steam from the pot, particularly in a stovetop model or (b) a high-pitched, sustained whistle, not just the siss-siss-siss of the steam from the

THE PROBLEM WITH ELECTRIC STOVES

The burners on an electric stove stay hotter longer with less control. When you drop the heat from high to control the pressure in the pot, the pot itself is resting right on the burner, insulating it. So the heat doesn't come down quickly enough to control the pressure in the pot. You solve this by either moving the pot from its current burner to a second one already turned to low or by buying a heat diffuser to set between the pot and the burner.

Always move the pot off an electric burner when you want it to come back to normal pressure naturally. Again, it can insulate the burner, keeping the pressure high longer than would be expected.

valve (in electric or stovetop models). Either the liquid inside has boiled away (you're in danger of a scorched mess) or the pressure has continued to climb exponentially (you're in danger of a stovetop mess).

No matter the cause, shut off the heat immediately. If you're working with a stovetop model, put on heat-safe mitts, get it to the sink, and run cold water over it until it comes back to normal pressure and you can disengage the lid. If you're working with an electric pot, unplug it and set it aside until it naturally returns to normal pressure, perhaps up to 40 minutes.

As you're working with either sort of cooker, use these rules as a safety checklist:

1. Never cook without a liquid of some sort in the pot. You're not at risk for an explosion; you'll end up with a burned mess—*just like in any saucepan.*

2. Check the rubber gasket before you begin. It should be soft, springy, and supple, not stiff, cracked, or ripped. The gasket will wear out after repeated use but manufacturers sell replacements. Order a spare and have it around in case. And use only the rubber gasket made for your pot.

3. Never try to force the lid open. If the rubber gasket blows, remove the stovetop pot from the heat and get it into the sink as quickly as possible so you can run cold water over it to bring the pressure back to normal—or unplug the electric pot and let it come back to normal pressure naturally. Don't open the lid until the pressure locks disengage naturally.

4. Never fill the cooker above the "max fill" line indicated inside the pot. And watch out for "foamy" foods: apples, oats, barley, spinach, pasta. You cannot even minimally increase (much less double) these ingredients over the amounts stated in a recipe.

Throughout, we've made some assumptions about ingredients. Here's the list:

- All vegetables are washed and usually dried (some greens need water to adhere to them for proper cooking).
- Carrots, turnips, beets, and other root vegetables are trimmed of their greens and any rooty bits unless otherwise stated. Carrots need not be peeled after careful washing if used in soups, stews, or braises.
- Onions, shallots, and garlic cloves are peeled unless otherwise stated.
- Scallions and leeks are trimmed of their wiry roots.
- Fresh ginger is peeled.
- Meat is trimmed of any large blobs of fat or hanging skin unless otherwise stated.
- Shrimp are always deveined—and peeled if stated.
- Both smoked and regular paprika are the mild (sometimes called *sweet*) versions.
- Rice vinegar is unseasoned (no sugar in the mix).
- Olive oil is a moderately priced, sturdy, first-cold-pressed cooking oil unless a high-end finishing olive oil is called for.

5. Never cook pasta *on its own* in water under pressure. You're setting yourself up for a frothy mess.

6. Never bring a pressure cooker to pressure in the oven.

7. Never deep-fry under pressure.

8. Don't fiddle with the pressure release valve while cooking under pressure. And don't use the pressure release valve as a stovetop hand warmer. You'll get a nasty burn when it lets off steam.

9. After cooking, wash the rubber gasket separately and rub a little vegetable oil on it to increase its longevity. While you're at it, clean the vents and pressure gauges.

Now you know the basic safety features of modern pressure cookers. There's no reason for fear. There's just the expectation of a better meal in minutes—which you'll get through these recipes. Read on to discover how.

The Doubting Thomas

or *Oh, yeah, I got one of those in the cabinet somewhere. They're always using one on* Iron Chef, *aren't they? I should try it again.*

Chefs the world over know the secrets of this powerful tool. It gets meat tenderized quickly, makes a killer risotto in no time flat, and builds complex sauces for service later in the evening. True, you're not here to become a chef. You're here for dinner. Still, that doesn't mean you can't steal their secrets.

To take full advantage of that impulse, you'll want to use the various features of this book. At the start of each recipe, we list the following:

- The **effort** required (*not much, a little*, or *a lot*, based on the number of ingredients, the prep of those ingredients, and the various steps required to complete the dish).

- The level of the **pressure** (usually *high*, but sometimes a split between cookers: *low* for a stovetop one and *high* for an electric one, for example).

- The **time under pressure.**

- The **release** method (quick or natural—more on that below).

- The number of **servings** (most assume this is what you're eating and nothing else).

Note that the cooking time is for how long the pot *stays at pressure*; it does not count the time it takes the pot to get to that pressure, which is somewhere between 5 and 20 minutes depending on the ingredients, their ratios, their internal moisture, their internal temperature, your kitchen's elevation from sea level, and even the day's high- or low-pressure weather systems.

After each recipe, there are *notes* based on our and others' recipe testing, some information about more esoteric ingredients, and even possible substitutions. Read these *before* you start cooking.

Before we move on to our last personality type, we should address one concern common among you Doubting Thomases. Maybe you've still got a first-generation cooker, the kind our grandmothers had. Yes, you can use it—but with many precautions. Check to see if there's (1) a removable, rubber gasket (2) under flanges (3) on an oversized lid. If the pot does not have or cannot accommodate all three features, buy a new pressure cooker. If there is said gasket, check to make sure it's supple, without tears or nicks. If not, buy a new gasket *made for your model*. (In fact, buy a new gasket if you're the least bit unsure.) Check the valves and locks to make sure they're clean and in good working order. You'll probably need to use this old-fashioned cooker only for high-liquid recipes like soups and stews. Older models let off a lot more steam; you'll end up burning low-moisture dishes like our buttery vegetable soups. When you've got the pot rocking and rolling on the stove, pay close attention to its noise level. If you notice a significant amount of hissing or a high-pitch whistle, take the pot off the heat immediately—*and go buy a new pot*. Finally, you may notice even soups and stews scorch, ingredients stuck to the bottom of the pot. It's most likely a fault of the metal: it's just too thin. Buy a heat diffuser to put between the pot and the heat source. Or

as we've said, just buy a new pressure cooker and stop doubting entirely.

FAT-FREE INGREDIENTS

Fat-free dairy products can pose a problem for pressure cooker recipes because the loss of fat is often made up with other ingredients, even chemical thickeners, many of which will not perform well under pressure. We always give you a low-fat option *whenever possible*. But don't mistake low-fat for fat-free. Only use fat-free alternatives when the recipe specifically says you can.

The Culinary Apostle
or *I have seen the Promised Land and it's a shiny pot.*

Hello, fellow traveler. You probably bought this book for new and innovative recipes. We set it up to accommodate your needs, too. Inside the following seven chapters, the individual recipes are grouped together by specific cuts of meat or types of produce. Like attracts like—all the ground beef recipes are together, all the shrimp, all the rice, all the cheesecakes. You'll note that the recipes are generally ordered from the most straightforward to greater and greater culinary inventiveness (although not necessarily effort). For example, we start out with bone-in chicken breasts braised in white wine and orange juice and end up with them braised in tequila and tomatillos.

Along the way, we've offered substitutions so that even some of the more inventive recipes remain within a weeknight reach. If you're not interested in buying a bottle of clam juice, we offer ways to use wine or broth to get similar (if less briny) results. We also offer serving suggestions. You'll probably be interested in how to use this fast and efficient tool to create a larger meal, balancing what's happening in the pot with a simple side dish. We've also included suggestions for garnishes and finishing touches to take your meal to new heights.

Consider us Aslan in Lewis's *Chronicles of Narnia*—we encourage you always to go "further up and further in." Try some of the more inventive recipes even with our substitution suggestions. Expanding your palate (and the meal's palette) is the reason you don't order in. You want fresh, hot food on the table, maybe beyond the expected. We've got you covered.

A SIX-QUART STANDARD—WITH WAYS TO CHEAT

Every recipe here is designed for a 6-quart pressure cooker because (1) it's the most common one sold in North America, and (2) most electric pressure cookers are 6-quart models. You can of course use these recipes for a 5½-quart model. Or you can cut most recipes by a third and use them in a 4-quart model. Just be sure to keep that max-fill line sacred and never go over it. You'll also need to adjust the timing for these smaller units, usually *adding* a minute or two because the cooker will come to pressure faster (and so have less "regular" boiling time). But you cannot halve or double some of these recipes for other sizes of cookers without the risk scorching low-moisture or heavily-stocked stews and braises, as well as almost all casseroles. Yes, you can cook a high-liquid soup or stew in an 8-quart pot, but you will have to shave a few minutes off the cook time since it will take longer to come up to high pressure (and so include more "regular" boiling time before it hits high pressure).

RECIPE KNOW-HOW

In general, here's how these recipes work:

1. Brown something.
Yes, there are some recipes here in which you simply dump everything into the pot, lock the lid in place, and bring on the pressure. But in many cases, the onions are softened, the pork chops are browned, or the garlic is infused into the broth. Don't shortchange this step—you want to get as much flavor into the dish as possible. This is one-pot cooking, so you might as well use that heat source under the pot, especially since you'll end up with an exponentially better meal.

- With a stovetop cooker, simply heat the oil or melt the butter over medium heat and then carry on.

- With an electric pot, turn it to its browning mode, usually a setting of higher temperature than its simmer mode, then add the fat and wait for it to heat through before you carry on.

In either case, never cover the pot while browning or sautéing unless specially told to do so. And keep this in mind: at this stage of the game, an electric pot offers you less control than a stovetop one. (Later, the advantage of the electric model will become more apparent.) You cannot raise or lower its heat; you cannot move it off the heat if the onion starts to burn. You need to pay close attention to what's happening inside an electric pot and stir more frequently than you might think.

2. Scrape up the browned stuff on the bottom of the pot.
Yes, deglazing is a culinary cliché. You probably know it's all about getting bits of caramelized flavor dissolved in the sauce. But there's a second, more important reason you must stir the liquids until the browned stuff gets unstuck: scorching.

Those burned-on bits will continue to sear and turn bitter against the super-hot surface once the pot comes to high pressure. There's often not enough time for them to become unstuck on their own. Plus, the high pressure is pushing the other ingredients down toward the bottom of the pot. Those brown bits of flavor can act like glue, holding items against the hot surface. If there is none left when the pot goes under pressure, there's far less chance of scorching—and a much better flavor in the sauce.

3. Lock the lid onto the pot.

Every machine has its own locking mechanism: a twist over flanges, a push button that brings out side bars, a large round button that screws the lid tight. You'll need to look at your manufacturer's instructions to determine exactly how your pot works.

Make sure you pay attention to the recipe's subtleties: sometimes, you need to bring the liquid to a boil and *then* get the lid onto the pot; other times, you lock the lid onto the pot and let the pressure build *with* the boil.

After that step, all the recipes move into a chart that differentiates between the stovetop and the electric cooker.

4. Bring the pot to high (or low) pressure.

With a stovetop model, you raise the heat under the pot to high to bring it to the desired pressure. With an electric model, you set the pressure on the pot's keypad.

But that's not all. We just can't stress this enough: *read the instruction manual.* It'll tell you exactly what high or low pressure is for your appliance. In general, high pressure for a stovetop pot is between 14.7 and 15 psi (that is, pounds per square inch). We've felt free to round up and call it 15 psi. By contrast, most electric models operate at a high-pressure mark that's *lower* than stovetop models—somewhere between 9 and 11 psi.

You must know what *high pressure* means for your pot. In fact, there are a few stovetop brands that use 10 psi as their high-pressure mark. And there are a couple of electric pots

that get up to 15 psi. If so, you'll need to follow the directions for the pressure your pot reaches, not necessarily the type of pot it is. In other words, in these rare cases, the stovetop pot will follow the instructions for electric pots and the electric pots will follow those for stovetop pots. Confusing? Sure. But you'll know for certain once you know the exact pressure specifications of your appliance.

5. Reduce the heat.

This step is for stovetop pots only. Electric models do this work for you. (And thus, their advantage becomes apparent.)

Reduce the heat under the stovetop pot to low so that the pressure holds at 15 psi. Again, you'll know by various indicators, idiosyncratic to each appliance. Some have a valve that jumps up and registers the pressure with gauge lines; others have a small indicator in the pressure valve itself that turns red or green. And there are even other methods.

Don't walk away while the dish cooks. If the pressure continues to fall below high, as indicated by your valve or mechanism, raise the heat under the pot to medium-low to compensate. If the pressure continues to rise above high or if the valve begins to emit a high-pitched whistle, immediately turn off the heat.

You will need to learn to balance the heat to get the right pressure. Although they take longer to cook, this jockeying of the heat back and forth with a stovetop model is the primary reason people buy electric cookers. It's not onerous, but you'll have to get used to it. Practice makes perfect.

6. Set the timer.

With a stovetop pot, you'll want to set a kitchen timer *once you see the pot's at high pressure*. You must remember this: the time under pressure does not take into account the time it takes to get to said pressure.

With an electric model, by contrast, you set the timer on the pot's digital panel when you switch the machine to cook at high pressure. This timer is calibrated to hold steady while the pot comes up to high pressure and then *begin counting down once the pot reaches high pressure.*

Remember that there are no visual cues to indicate when the food is done: you have to go by the minutes given. And sometimes you have to adjust. We tested a beef stew for this book that was done in 15 minutes, 16 minutes, and 18 minutes—*in the same stovetop pot.* In cases like this, we erred on the high side because, really, what will it hurt if some chewy stew meat goes a little longer under pressure? But because of a variety of factors—the animal's diet, the water density of the root vegetable, the length of time an ingredient has sat on the shelf—your stew may sometimes be slightly underdone. If so, lock the lid back onto the pot, bring it back to high pressure, and cook for another minute or two.

7. Release the pressure.
There are two distinct ways to do this. Use the one stated in the recipe.

- Quick release. Turn off the heat or unplug the machine. If you're working on a stovetop, turn the oven vent to high. With either type of pot, figure out which way the pot's release mechanism vents its steam and make sure it's headed away from you so you don't (1) fog your glasses, (2) ruin your clothes, and worst of all, (3) burn your fingers. Use the pressure release valve on the pot's lid to bring the pressure back to normal—by twisting, turning, or removing it, based on your manufacturer's guidelines. *Do not open the pot without first bringing the pressure back to normal.* Once there is no more steam escaping from the release valve or

mechanism and the lid is unlocked, open the pot.

If you have a *stovetop* pot and you don't like the idea of turning some valve to emit a geyser of steam, you can bring the pressure back to normal quickly another way. Get the (extremely hot!) pot in the sink and run it under cold water until the pressure falls to normal and the locks disengage. Remember to take the pot out of the sink and put it back on the stove (but not over the heat) before you open it so no water gets inside. (And, of course, never run water over or immerse an electric pressure cooker.)

- Natural release. For a stovetop pot, set it aside off the heat. For an electric pot, turn it off or unplug it (some electric pots do not have an "off" switch). Then wait for the pressure to come back to normal. You'll hear the locking mechanism click free or you'll see the pressure valve disengage when it's safe to open the pot. Even so, press the quick-release valve before opening just to make sure there's not a millibar of pressure left inside.

WARNING

If any non-steam (food, broth, sauce, etc.) begins to spew out of the valve after a quick release of pressure, instantly re-engage the lid and set the pot aside—off the heat or unplugged—until the pressure has returned to normal naturally, until the locking mechanism clicks off or releases in some way and the lid can be opened. There has been a failure inside the pot, probably caused by improperly soaked beans, too-old beans, foamy grains without enough liquid and with too much heat, or mucky bits of leafy greens getting stuck in the release valve.

8. Open the pot.

It's hot inside that pot. Liquids have been simmering above their usual boiling points. They're probably still boiling. Do not reach inside; set the pot aside for a few minutes to cool down. If you dish it up right away, the food may be too hot to eat. After a few minutes, stir before serving to make sure everything's back to a uniform state, the sauce luscious and even.

Remember, too, that the insert to an electric pot is just as hot as the exterior of a stovetop pot. You cannot remove that insert without silicone oven mitts. Even kitchen towels are dangerous because they can pick up steam, turn wet, and conduct the heat right to your fingertips. You'll have to dish up the food or even serve it right out of the unplugged pot.

SO NOW YOU KNOW THE SCORE: the mechanics and safety features of the cookers, as well as the way these specific recipes work. What's left? Just a few tips, a specialty piece of equipment required by a few of these recipes, and then dinner.

HIGH-ALTITUDE MATTERS

If you live well above sea level, you know that water boils at a lower temperature than it does in the flatlands, mostly because there's less atmosphere pushing down on it (and so less ambient pressure). To make the necessary adjustments for a pressure cooker, increase the cooking time in these recipes by 5 *percent* (not five minutes) for every 1,000 feet of elevation gain above 2,000 feet. So if you live at 7,000 feet above sea level in Estes Park, Colorado, you'll need to increase the cooking time by 25 percent.

BASIC TROUBLESHOOTING

Here are four of the most common concerns for pressure cooker users.

1. Foods scorch.

There's probably not enough liquid in the pot, maybe because the pressure escaped too quickly or because the heat was too high. Check your gauges and gaskets to make sure they're tight and in good working order. And reduce the heat more dramatically after the pot comes to high pressure.

2. The pot won't stay at high pressure.

Any stovetop pot can drop below high pressure because of drafts, uneven flames or coils, or loosened valves. (Always check these last before you start.) You may well have to adjust the heat repeatedly, particularly when you're just learning how to use the cooker: up it a bit to bring the pressure back to high, then drop the heat again to keep it at high.

If an electric pot won't stay at high pressure, there's probably a malfunction in the machine. Check with your manufacturer for repair details.

3. Things are unevenly done.

It's either a prep or an ingredient problem. If the former, you may have left ingredients in larger bits than the recipe requires. In general, here's the rule:

Roughly chopped = 1½-inch pieces

Chopped = 1-inch pieces

Finely chopped = ½-inch pieces

Diced = ¼-inch cubes

Minced = ⅛-inch bits or even smaller

Or you may have measured the liquids inaccurately. Make sure you're using liquid measuring cups, not ones meant for dry ingredients. Or you may have used partially frozen ingredients. Everything must be fully thawed unless otherwise stated in the recipe.

Your rice and dried beans may well be old. Replace pantry staples frequently: about every six months for whole grains and rice, about every nine months for beans. And if your supermarket is selling old beans and rice, take your money elsewhere!

4. Everything's not quite ready.
Either set the stovetop pot over medium heat, bring it to a simmer, and cook a few minutes more; or turn the electric model to its simmer function, bring the sauce or stew to a bubble, and cook a few minutes more. It's just a matter of a little extra softening, 5 minutes at most (probably less). Stir as necessary to prevent scorching.

However, if things are really not done, the chicken is tough or the carrots are hard, lock the lid back onto the pot, bring it back to high pressure, and cook for another minute or so before following the recipe again. These things can happen because of ambient factors beyond a recipe's control. But what's another minute or so when a great meal is in the offing?

ONE NECESSITY: A FOIL SLING

Our cheesecakes, as well as several casseroles and a few dips, all require some sort of baking dish inside the pressure cooker, always set on the cooker's rack. The challenge is how to get the superheated dish out of the cooker without burning yourself. You can't really use silicone baking mitts because they're too cumbersome; you can't use traditional hot pads or kitchen towels because they'll turn damp and channel the heat right to your skin. You often can't even get your fingers between the walls of the pot and the sides of the baking dish.

We remedy this problem by using an *aluminum foil sling*. To make one, set two 2-foot-long pieces of foil on top of each other. Fold them together in half the long way (it's now a four-ply strip of foil). Put this sling on the counter as close to the cooker as possible, then set the baking dish or pan right in the center of the sling. Fold over its two ends several times to create secure handles. Lift the whole contraption by these handles and put it inside the pressure cooker. Crimp the ends down so the lid will fit securely on the pot but also so you can grab them later to lift the baking dish or pan back out of the cooker.

When the dish has been cooked to the necessary time, pressure, and release method, set a wire cooling rack as close to the pot as possible. Open it as directed, wait a little for the steam to dissipate, then uncrimp those handles so you can lift the dish or pan and put it on the cooling rack. Carry on with the recipe as directed.

OKAY, YOU'RE FINALLY READY

We've got so many recipes ahead: whole-grain porridges to terrific chilis, cheesy casseroles to easy pasta sauces, mussels aplenty to side dishes for the holidays. Everyone needs to be cooking under pressure. Now, no matter which model you have, you can. And you should. In fact, get two cookers—you won't regret it. And let us hear from you: on Facebook, through Twitter (@markscarbrough, @bruceweinstein), or at bruceandmark.com. We're always eager to meet more pressure cooker mavens.

BREAKFAST

WHO DIGS A PRESSURE COOKER OUT OF THE CABINET ON A BUSY
Tuesday morning? Not us—but we *do* get it out for a Saturday mid-morning breakfast or any time we have weekend guests in from New York City. Or on the holidays when we've got a house full of family. Or during busy photo shoots when we want a hot breakfast. Come to think of it: we've probably pulled out the pressure cooker on a Tuesday morning.

Using a pressure cooker for breakfast isn't just about faster cooking; it's also about better cooking. Toast is fast. A pressure cooker layers depths of flavor in breakfast casseroles and compotes, hashes, and even porridges, all without much effort.

Take steel-cut oats. Yes, they're done in minutes under pressure, as opposed to a long simmer in a saucepan. But they're also done better: they not only take on the vaunted creaminess that long-cooking affords but also pick up more flavor from the surrounding liquid and dried fruit.

Retaining a bit of firmness underneath the velvety luxury, they end up with better texture *and* a more intense flavor. They're definitely more satisfying than any microwave fare.

You may also be surprised at how pressure cooks eggs: the whites stay creamy and delicate; the yolks, set to your preference. At this point, we can't imagine making soft-boiled eggs any other way.

Of course, there's a "but" or two: pay attention to the stated release in these recipes and follow the instructions carefully. Some grains get foamy under pressure and will spurt out of the pressure valve if you attempt a quick release when a natural one is called for. Others need a bit of time under a natural release so they can absorb moisture and get tender without going gummy.

Most whole grains need to be presoaked. And be prepared to eat when breakfast is ready. Many of these dishes aren't forgiving: bread puddings can get dry; eggs can turn tough. So make the coffee, set the table, and prepare the breakfast recipe as the last task in the list. Listen, that's not a bad thing. If ever a meal called for efficiency, it's breakfast. The day awaits!

One more thing: we've adjusted the Effort label in this first chapter. That is, recipes that might have been marked "a little" in a subsequent chapter are labeled "a lot" of effort here. Given that we stumble around half blind before our second cup of coffee, we sometimes think melting butter in the morning qualifies as heroic.

So here are some fine hot cereals, breakfast bread puddings, potato hashes, and fruit compotes. We've even got a fine and fast sausage gravy, a sweet breakfast version of polenta, and an innovative top-of-the-morning risotto for a special treat. You provide the toast and coffee; the pressure cooker will do the rest.

APPLE MAPLE OATMEAL

EFFORT: **NOT MUCH** • PRESSURE: **HIGH** • TIME UNDER PRESSURE: **12 OR 18 MINUTES** • RELEASE: **NATURAL** • SERVES: **4**

$1/2$ **cup steel-cut oats**
$1/2$ **cup chopped dried apples**
$1/4$ **cup maple syrup**
$1/4$ **cup sliced almonds**
$1/4$ **teaspoon ground cinnamon**
$1/4$ **teaspoon salt**

1 Mix everything with $2 1/4$ cups water in a 6-quart stovetop or electric pressure cooker.

2 Lock the lid onto the pot.

STOVETOP: Set the pot over high heat and bring it to high pressure (15 psi). Once the pressure has been reached, reduce the heat as much as possible while keeping this pressure constant. Cook for 12 minutes.
······················· **OR** ·······················
ELECTRIC: Set the machine to cook at high pressure (9–11 psi). Set the machine's timer to cook at this pressure for 18 minutes.

3 Reduce the pressure.

STOVETOP: Set the pot off the heat and let its pressure return to normal, about 10 minutes.
······················· **OR** ·······················
ELECTRIC: Turn off the machine or unplug it so it doesn't jump to its keep-warm setting. Allow the pot's pressure to return to normal, 10 to 12 minutes.

If the pressure in the pot hasn't come back to normal within 12 minutes, use the quick-release method to bring it back to normal.

4 Unlock and open the pot; stir well before serving.

TESTERS' NOTES
• This is a whole-grain breakfast in minutes! It's one of the perks of owning a pressure cooker.
• Use only steel-cut oats (also called "pinhead oats" or "Irish oats"), not rolled oats and not the more ground Scottish oats, and certainly not instant oats. Steel-cut oats are the whole groats (bran, germ, and endosperm), cut into smaller pieces.
• Don't even think about using anything but real maple syrup in this recipe.
• You can substitute chopped dried pears, nectarines, peaches, or apricots for the apples.

Serve It Up! Warm some milk, half-and-half, or cream in a small saucepan over low heat or in the microwave for a couple of minutes on high (but do not boil). Pour over each serving.

CREAMY BANANA OATMEAL

EFFORT: **NOT MUCH** • PRESSURE: **HIGH** • TIME UNDER PRESSURE: **12 OR 18 MINUTES** • RELEASE: **NATURAL** • SERVES: **4**

$1/2$ **cup steel-cut oats**
$1/2$ **cup packed light brown sugar**
2 ripe bananas, chopped
2 teaspoons vanilla extract
$1/2$ **teaspoon ground cinnamon**
$1/4$ **teaspoon salt**
$1/4$ **cup heavy cream**

1 Mix the oats, brown sugar, bananas, vanilla, cinnamon, and salt with $2 1/4$ cups water in a 6-quart stovetop or electric pressure cooker until the brown sugar dissolves.

2 Lock the lid onto the pot.

STOVETOP: Set the pot over high heat and bring it to high pressure (15 psi). Once this pressure has been reached, reduce the heat as much as possible while maintaining this pressure. Cook for 12 minutes.

·······································OR·······································

ELECTRIC: Set the machine to cook at high pressure (9–11 psi). Set the machine's timer to cook at high pressure for 18 minutes.

3 Reduce the pressure.

STOVETOP: Set the pot off the heat and let its pressure fall to normal naturally, about 10 minutes.

·······································OR·······································

ELECTRIC: Turn off the machine or unplug it so it doesn't flip to its keep-warm setting. Allow the pot's pressure to come to normal naturally, 10 to 12 minutes.

If the pot's pressure hasn't returned to normal within 12 minutes, use the quick-release method to bring it back to normal.

4 Unlock and open the cooker. Stir in the cream and set aside for 1 minute to warm before serving.

TESTERS' NOTES
• Don't double the amount of oats in any of these porridges: the grains are stocked with a sticky starch that will rise up and clog the pressure release valve. If you've got more than four persons for breakfast, make two batches.
• For the best flavor, the bananas should be quite ripe, their skins mottled with plenty of brown spots. Look for the ones just about to be discounted: these are the best candidates.
• You can substitute light cream, half-and-half, regular evaporated milk, or almond milk for the heavy cream.

BULGUR, OAT, AND WALNUT PORRIDGE

EFFORT: **A LITTLE** • PRESSURE: **HIGH** • TIME UNDER PRESSURE: **16 OR 24 MINUTES** • RELEASE: **QUICK** • SERVES: **6 TO 8**

½ **cup steel-cut oats**
½ **cup bulgur**
½ **cup chopped walnuts**
½ **cup maple syrup**
½ **teaspoon ground cinnamon**
½ **teaspoon salt**

1 Mix everything with 4 cups water in a 6-quart stovetop or electric pressure cooker.

2 Lock the lid onto the pot.

STOVETOP: Set the pot over high heat and bring it to high pressure (15 psi). Once this pressure has been reached, reduce the heat as much as possible while keeping the pressure constant. Cook for 16 minutes.

·······································OR·······································

ELECTRIC: Set the machine to cook at high pressure (9–11 psi). Set the machine's timer to cook at high pressure for 24 minutes.

3 Use the quick-release method to bring the pot's pressure back to normal.

4 Unlock and remove the lid. Set the stovetop cooker over medium heat or turn the electric cooker to its browning function. Bring to a simmer, stirring often. Cook, stirring constantly, until slightly thickened, about 2 minutes.

TESTERS' NOTES
• Because of the way bulgur absorbs water, there may be a little liquid left in the cereal after cooking—a good thing, since it can otherwise scorch. So we advise simmering the

(continued)

cereal after cooking under pressure. That said, if you open the pot and find the porridge has a consistency to your liking, there's no need for that extra work in step 4.

- Bulgur is sold by grinds—fine, medium-coarse, and extra-coarse. However, those grinds are often not labeled on the packaging except in certain brands sold at health-food or gourmet stores. Any grind will work here, although fine (sometimes labeled "instant") is probably the least successful, more like Cream of Wheat.
- Maple syrup is sold by grades, with some packagers using letters and others using numbers: A or 1 is the lighter in flavor. Grade A or 1 is further broken down into light amber, medium amber, and dark amber. While many people like Grade A or 1 for pancakes, we prefer Grade B or 2 because of its more assertive flavor, including darkly herbaceous notes to pair against the other intense flavors.
- Substitute chopped pecans or pistachios for the walnuts.

Serve It Up! Put a pat of butter and some freshly grated nutmeg on each serving.

CHEESY GRITS

EFFORT: **A LOT** • PRESSURE: **HIGH** • TIME UNDER PRESSURE: **12 OR 18 MINUTES** • RELEASE: **MODIFIED NATURAL** • SERVES: **4 TO 6**

1 cup corn grits (not instant)

2 tablespoons unsalted butter, cut into very small bits

$1/2$ teaspoon salt

1 cup finely grated Cheddar cheese, preferably white (about 4 ounces)

Bottled hot red pepper sauce, such as Tabasco, to taste

1 Set the pressure cooker rack inside a stovetop or electric cooker; pour in 2 cups water. Make an aluminum foil sling (see page 19) and set a 2-quart, high-sided, round baking or soufflé dish on it. Mix the grits, butter, and salt with $2^{1}/_{2}$ cups water in the baking dish until smooth.

2 Use the foil sling to lower the uncovered dish onto the rack in the cooker. (Do not cover the baking dish.) Fold the ends of the sling so they'll fit inside the cooker.

3 Lock the lid onto the pot.

STOVETOP: Set the pot over high heat and bring it to high pressure (15 psi). Once this pressure has been reached, reduce the heat as much as possible while keeping this pressure constant. Cook for 12 minutes.

··· OR ·····························

ELECTRIC: Set the machine to cook at high pressure (9–11 psi). Set the machine's timer to cook at this pressure for 18 minutes.

4 Turn off the heat and or unplug the machine. Set aside for 5 minutes, then use the quick-release method to drop the pot's pressure back to normal.

5 Unlock and remove the lid. Lift the baking dish out of the cooker with its sling, steadying it as necessary to get it to a cutting board. Stir in the cheese and hot red pepper sauce; set aside for 1 minute to melt the cheese before serving.

TESTERS' NOTES

- If you've never had cheese grits from a pressure cooker, you're missing the creamiest cheese grits available. The intense cooking environment forces just the right amount of moisture into the bits of corn, and even without stirring, it's perfect every time.
- There's no reason to use a run-of-the-mill hot red pepper sauce here. Check out versions with smoky chipotles or even fiery habanero chiles.

Serve It Up! Spoon the grits onto a plate and top each serving with a fried egg; serve bacon on the side.

APPLE, HAM, AND GRITS CASSEROLE

EFFORT: **A LOT** • PRESSURE: **HIGH** • TIME UNDER PRESSURE: **15 OR 22 MINUTES** • RELEASE: **QUICK** • SERVES: **4 TO 6**

2 tablespoons unsalted butter, plus more for buttering the dish

8 ounces Canadian bacon, chopped

1 medium tart green apple, such as Granny Smith, peeled, cored, and chopped

4 medium scallions, green and white parts, trimmed and sliced into thin bits

1 teaspoon dried thyme

¾ cup quick-cooking or instant grits

2 large eggs, lightly beaten

½ cup shredded Cheddar cheese (about 2 ounces)

1 Melt the butter in a 6-quart stovetop pressure cooker set over medium heat or in a 6-quart electric pressure cooker turned to the browning function. Add the Canadian bacon; cook, stirring often, for 1 minute. Add the apple, scallions, and thyme; cook for 1 more minute, stirring constantly. Scrape the contents of the cooker into a large bowl. Wipe out the cooker with a damp paper towel.

2 Set the stovetop model back over medium heat or turn the electric one back to its browning or simmer mode. Add 3 cups water and bring to a boil. Whisk in the grits and cook, whisking all the while, until thickened, about 5 minutes. Scrape the grits into the bowl with the bacon mixture; cool for 10 minutes. Wash and dry the cooker.

3 Set the pressure cooker rack inside the cooker and pour in 2 cups water. Make a foil sling (see page 19) and set a 2-quart, high-sided, round baking or soufflé dish on top of it. Lightly butter the inside of the dish.

4 Stir the eggs and cheese into the grits mixture until uniform and well combined. Spread the mixture in the prepared baking dish; cover and seal with foil. Lower the dish onto the rack in the cooker with the sling. Fold the ends of the sling so they'll fit inside the cooker.

5 Lock the lid onto the pot.

STOVETOP: Set the pot over high heat and bring it to high pressure (15 psi). Once this pressure has been reached, reduce the heat as much as possible while keeping this pressure constant. Cook for 15 minutes.

·· OR ··

ELECTRIC: Set the machine to cook at high pressure (9–11 psi). Set the machine's timer to cook at this pressure for 22 minutes.

6 Use the quick-release method to bring the pot's pressure back to normal.

7 Unlock and open the cooker. Use the sling to transfer the baking dish to a wire cooling rack, steadying the dish as necessary. Uncover, cool a couple of minutes, and spoon the casserole onto individual plates to serve.

TESTERS' NOTES
• Here's the perfect brunch dish: a creamy, cheesy casserole with big flavors. You just need the mimosas.
• Be careful: the cooker will be hot as you wipe it out between steps of this recipe.
• You can make the recipe through step 3 up to 1 hour in advance.
• Try substituting one ripe Bosc pear for the apple. You can also substitute Monterey jack or Swiss for the Cheddar.

Serve It Up! For breakfast, garnish with maple syrup. For lunch, offer a tossed green salad on the side. For dinner, pour a glass of Sauvignon Blanc.

BREAKFAST POLENTA WITH PINE NUTS AND HONEY

EFFORT: **NOT MUCH** • PRESSURE: **HIGH** • TIME UNDER PRESSURE: **8 OR 12 MINUTES** • RELEASE: **QUICK** • SERVES: **6**

1/2 cup honey

1/4 cup pine nuts

1/4 teaspoon almond extract

1 cup polenta (not quick-cooking)

1/2 cup heavy cream or half-and-half

1 Mix the honey, pine nuts, and almond extract with 5 cups water in a 6-quart stovetop pressure cooker set over medium heat or in a 6-quart electric pressure cooker turned to the browning function. Bring to a boil, stirring often. Stir in the polenta.

2 Lock the lid onto the cooker.

STOVETOP: Raise the heat to high and bring the pot to high pressure (15 psi). Once this pressure has been reached, reduce the heat as much as possible while keeping this pressure constant. Cook for 8 minutes.

····················· **OR** ·····················

ELECTRIC: Set the machine to cook at high pressure (9–11 psi). Set the machine's timer to cook at this pressure for 12 minutes.

3 Use the quick-release method to bring the pressure in the pot back to normal.

4 Unlock and remove the lid. Stir in the cream or half-and-half; set aside for 1 minute to warm through.

TESTERS' NOTES

• We modeled this recipe on pignoli cookies, an Italian bakery favorite; they're soft little mounds made with almond paste and studded with pine nuts.

• This dish isn't a stiff polenta; rather, it's a little soupy, as befits a breakfast porridge.

• Stir in the polenta in step 1 but don't let it cook for too long. You need as much water in the pot as possible as the mixture comes to pressure.

• You can find extra-coarse, organic polenta at larger supermarkets or from online suppliers. Consider using this for even more corn flavor in each spoonful.

Serve It Up! Remove breakfast sausage from its casings and fry it up in a large skillet, then crumble it over each serving.

BREAKFAST RISOTTO WITH STRAWBERRIES AND CREAM

EFFORT: **A LITTLE** • PRESSURE: **HIGH** • TIME UNDER PRESSURE: **7 OR 11 MINUTES** • RELEASE: **QUICK** • SERVES: **6**

2 tablespoons unsalted butter

1 pint fresh strawberries, hulled and sliced (about 2 cups)

1 1/2 cups medium-grain white rice, such as Arborio

1/2 teaspoon ground cinnamon

1/2 teaspoon salt

2 cups unsweetened apple juice

1/2 cup heavy or light cream

2 tablespoons honey

1 Melt the butter in a 6-quart stovetop pressure cooker set over medium heat or in a 6-quart electric pressure cooker turned to the browning function. Stir in about 1 cup strawberries; cook for 2 minutes, stirring often, to soften.

2 Pour in the rice; add the cinnamon and salt. Stir over the heat for 1 minute until the rice begins to turn translucent. Pour in the apple juice and 1¾ cups water; stir well.

3 Lock the lid onto the pot.

STOVETOP: Raise the heat to high and bring the pot to high pressure (15 psi). Once this pressure has been reached, reduce the heat as much as possible while maintaining this pressure. Cook for 7 minutes.

······························ **OR** ·····························

ELECTRIC: Set the machine to cook at high pressure (9–11 psi). Set the machine's timer to cook at this pressure for 11 minutes.

4 Use the quick-release method to bring the pot's pressure back to normal.

5 Unlock and open the cooker. Set the stovetop cooker over medium heat or turn the electric cooker to its browning mode. Stir in the cream, honey, and the remaining cup (or so) of strawberries; bring to a simmer, stirring constantly. Simmer until thickened, about 3 minutes, stirring frequently but gently so as not to break down the strawberries.

6 Turn off the heat or unplug the machine, cover loosely with its lid, and set aside for 5 minutes to blend the flavors in the rice.

TESTERS' NOTES
• Risotto for breakfast! You bet—especially when it doesn't involve much stirring.

• Use only medium-grain white rice. No other type will work in this breakfast concoction.
• The bland and dry strawberries available in winter may not be worth the trouble. You'd be better off buying frozen whole berries and thawing them in the fridge for a day. They'll give off a lot of liquid but don't discard it: use it and decrease the apple juice by an equivalent amount.

CONGEE
(SAVORY RICE PORRIDGE)

EFFORT: **NOT MUCH** • PRESSURE: **HIGH** • TIME UNDER PRESSURE: **35 OR 55 MINUTES** • RELEASE: **NATURAL** • SERVES: **6**

1 cup long-grain white rice, such as jasmine

1 medium shallot, minced

4 medium garlic cloves, minced

2 tablespoons mirin

2 tablespoons minced fresh ginger

1 teaspoon salt

1 Mix all the ingredients with 7 cups water in a 6-quart stovetop or electric pressure cooker.

2 Lock the lid onto the pot.

STOVETOP: Set the pot over high heat and bring it to high pressure (15 psi). Once this pressure has been reached, reduce the heat as much as possible while maintaining this pressure. Cook for 35 minutes.

······························ **OR** ·····························

ELECTRIC: Set the machine to cook at high pressure (9–11 psi). Set the machine's timer to cook at this pressure for 55 minutes.

(continued)

3 Reduce the pressure.

STOVETOP: Remove the pot from heat and let its pressure return to normal, about 15 minutes.

·· **OR** ··

ELECTRIC: Turn off the machine or unplug it so it doesn't flip to its keep-warm setting. Let its pressure fall to normal, 18 to 20 minutes.

4 Unlock and remove the lid. Stir the porridge before serving.

TESTERS' NOTES

• This savory breakfast is modeled on a porridge served at Chinese restaurants. It's rather addictive: a big bowl of warm comfort, great on a winter weekend.

• The technique involves cooking the rice longer (and with more water) than you would if you were making a side dish, so that the grains begin to break down and thicken the liquid. There's no real reason to stop it short when you turn off the heat or unplug the machine—just let the pressure return to normal before you open the cooker. The more it sits under the reducing pressure, the richer the porridge will be.

• You can substitute 2 tablespoons dry white wine and 2 teaspoons sugar for the mirin.

Serve It Up! Top the finished bowlfuls with sliced shiitake mushroom caps softened in a little sesame oil over medium heat, shelled peanuts, minced scallions, sesame seeds, garlic oil, and/or toasted sesame oil. Or go all out and add chopped chicken, shrimp, or even lump crabmeat.

FRENCH TOAST BREAD PUDDING

EFFORT: **A LOT** • PRESSURE: **HIGH** • TIME UNDER PRESSURE: **10 OR 15 MINUTES** • RELEASE: **QUICK** • SERVES: **4 TO 6**

2 large eggs, at room temperature
1 cup whole or low-fat milk
¼ cup sugar
¼ cup orange marmalade
2 teaspoons vanilla extract
½ teaspoon ground cinnamon
5 cups of 1-inch bread cubes (about 7 ounces)
¼ cup raisins

1 Lightly butter a 2-quart, high-sided, round baking or soufflé dish; set aside. Place the pressure cooker rack inside a 6-quart stovetop or electric cooker; pour in 2 cups water.

2 Whisk the eggs, milk, sugar, marmalade, vanilla, and cinnamon in a big bowl until smooth, with no bits of egg visible. Add the bread cubes and raisins; toss well to soak up the liquids. Pour the entire mixture into the prepared baking dish; cover and seal the dish with aluminum foil. Make a foil sling (see page 19), set the filled baking dish on it, and lower the baking dish in the sling onto the rack. Fold the ends of the sling so they'll fit inside the cooker.

3 Lock the lid onto the cooker.

STOVETOP: Set the pot over high heat and bring to high pressure (15 psi). Once this pressure has been reached, reduce the heat as much as possible while maintaining this pressure. Cook for 10 minutes.

·· **OR** ··

ELECTRIC: Set the machine to cook at high pressure (9–11 psi). Set the machine's timer to cook at high pressure for 15 minutes.

4 Use the quick-release method to bring the pot's pressure back to normal.

5 Unlock the lid and open the cooker. Use the foil sling to transfer the hot baking dish to a wire rack. Uncover and cool for 5 minutes before dishing it up by the big spoonful.

TESTERS' NOTES
• This brunch casserole is modeled on those classic baked French toast recipes that involve soaking the bread overnight. However, because the pressure forces so much of the liquid and flavor into the bread, we can skip the overnight fandango.
• The bread cubes can have crusts or not, depending on your preference. If you buy a 14-ounce loaf of bread and cut off the crust before cubing it up, you'll have to take the loss of crust into your calculation of how much bread you cut up. You can also look for fresh cubes at the bakery counter of many large supermarkets.
• You can substitute strawberry, apricot, or raspberry preserves for the marmalade. (Just don't use jams or jellies.)

Serve It Up! Warm some maple syrup and drizzle over each serving. A little melted butter would also be welcome.

BACONY BREAD PUDDING

EFFORT: **A LOT** • PRESSURE: **HIGH** • TIME UNDER PRESSURE: **12 OR 18 MINUTES** • RELEASE: **QUICK** • SERVES: **4**

6 thin slices of bacon

Six ¼-inch-thick slices of country-style white bread, cut into quarters

3 large eggs, at room temperature

1½ cups whole or low-fat milk

2 tablespoons maple syrup

¼ teaspoon grated nutmeg

1 Butter a 2-quart, round, high-sided baking or soufflé dish; set aside. Place the pressure cooker rack in a stovetop or electric cooker; pour in 2 cups water.

2 Set a large skillet over medium heat for a few minutes. Add the bacon and fry until crisp, 3 or 4 minutes, turning occasionally. Transfer to a cutting board; chop the bacon into bits. Toss these in a large bowl with the bread pieces.

3 Whisk the eggs, milk, syrup, and nutmeg in a second bowl until smooth. Pour over the bread mixture and toss well to coat. Pile the mixture into the prepared baking dish; press down to compact somewhat, submerging all the bread into the liquid. Cover the baking dish with a piece of parchment paper, then seal with aluminum foil. Make a foil sling for the baking dish (see page 19), then lower the sealed dish onto the rack in the pressure cooker. Fold the ends of the sling so they'll fit inside the cooker.

4 Lock the lid onto the pot.

STOVETOP: Set the pot over high heat and bring it to high pressure (15 psi). Once this pressure has been reached, reduce the heat as much as possible while maintaining this pressure. Cook for 12 minutes.

······································· **OR** ·······································

ELECTRIC: Set the machine to cook at high pressure (9–11 psi). Set the machine's timer to cook at this pressure for 18 minutes.

5 Use the quick-release method to bring the pot's pressure back to normal.

6 Unlock and open the cooker. Use the foil sling to transfer the hot baking dish to a wire rack. Uncover the baking dish, cool a few minutes, then scoop out servings in big spoonfuls.

(continued)

• We almost ate the whole batch the first time we tested this recipe! (And we'd already had lunch.) It's like a full breakfast plate in every spoonful: toast, bacon, syrup, and butter.
• Don't stint on buttering that baking dish. It'll keep the casserole intact when you serve it.

SOFT-, MEDIUM-, AND HARD-BOILED EGGS

EFFORT: **NOT MUCH** • PRESSURE: **HIGH** • TIME UNDER PRESSURE: **1 TO 3 MINUTES** • RELEASE: **VARIOUS** • SERVES: **1 TO 12**

1–12 cold, large eggs (straight from the refrigerator)

1 Set a large metal vegetable steamer in a 6-quart stovetop or electric pressure cooker. Add about 2 inches of water to the cooker—not so much that it comes through the holes of the steamer. Set one or more eggs in the steamer.

2 For soft-boiled eggs—Lock the lid onto the pot.

STOVETOP: Set the pot over high heat and bring it to high pressure (15 psi). Once this pressure has been reached, reduce the heat as low as possible while maintaining this pressure. Cook for 1 minute.
·················· **OR** ··················
ELECTRIC: Set the machine to cook at high pressure (9–11 psi). Set the machine's timer to cook at this pressure for 1½ minutes.

3 Use the quick-release method to bring the pressure in the pot back to normal.

2 For medium-boiled eggs—Lock the lid onto the pot.

STOVETOP: Set the pot over high heat and bring it to high pressure (15 psi). Once this pressure has been reached, reduce the heat as much as possible while maintaining this pressure. Cook for 2 minutes.
·················· **OR** ··················
ELECTRIC: Set the machine to cook at high pressure (9–11 psi). Set the machine's timer to cook at this pressure for 3 minutes.

3 Use the quick-release method to bring the pot's pressure back to normal—but do not open the pot. Set the cooker aside, covered, for 1 minute. Use the quick-release method to bring the pot's pressure fully back to normal.

2 For hard-boiled eggs—Lock the lid onto the pot.

STOVETOP: Set the pot over high heat and bring it to high pressure (15 psi). Immediately lower the heat as much as possible while maintaining this pressure. Cook for 2 minutes.
·················· **OR** ··················
ELECTRIC: Set the machine to cook at high pressure (9–11 psi). Set the machine's timer to cook at this pressure for 3 minutes.

3 Reduce the pressure.

STOVETOP: Set the pot off the heat for 7 minutes. Use the quick-release method to bring the pot fully back to normal pressure.
·················· **OR** ··················
ELECTRIC: Turn off the machine or unplug it; set aside for 8 minutes. Use the quick-release method to bring the pot fully back to normal pressure.

4 For all eggs—Unlock and remove the lid. Transfer the eggs to a large bowl. Cut the top off a soft-boiled egg and serve it in an egg cup; peel the other kinds of eggs while still warm.

• A pressure cooker yields great cooked eggs every time. What's more, the even but intense heat makes the process easy and convenient.
• The cooking times are based on large eggs right out of a standard refrigerator, 40°–42°F. Room-temperature eggs or even medium cold eggs will cook more quickly.
• In terms of their set, soft-boiled eggs have set whites but runny yolks; the medium-boiled eggs have silky whites and jammy, thickened yolks; and hard-boiled eggs have fully set whites and yolks.
• If you peel the hard-boiled eggs while warm, the shells should come off cleanly. Work in the sink, putting the egg in and out of a stream of tap water to loosen the shell.

SAUSAGE GRAVY

EFFORT: **A LITTLE** • PRESSURE: **HIGH** • TIME UNDER PRESSURE: **4 OR 6 MINUTES** • RELEASE: **QUICK** • SERVES: **6**

1¹/₂ pounds lean ground pork
1 teaspoon dried sage
1 teaspoon dried thyme
Up to 1 teaspoon ground black pepper
¹/₂ teaspoon grated nutmeg
¹/₂ teaspoon salt
¹/₄ teaspoon cayenne
¹/₄ teaspoon celery seeds
³/₄ cup chicken broth
2¹/₄ cups whole or low-fat milk
6 tablespoons all-purpose flour

1 Crumble the pork into a 6-quart stovetop pressure cooker set over medium heat or a 6-quart electric pressure cooker turned to the browning function; cook, stirring occasionally, until lightly browned, about 4 minutes.

2 Stir in the sage, thyme, pepper, nutmeg, salt, cayenne, and celery seeds; cook for

1 minute, until aromatic. Pour in the broth; stir well to get any browned bits up off the bottom of the cooker.

3 Lock the lid onto the pot.

STOVETOP: Raise the heat to high and bring the pot to high pressure (15 psi). Once this pressure has been reached, reduce the heat as much as possible while maintaining this pressure. Cook for 4 minutes.

·····················OR·····················

ELECTRIC: Set the machine to cook at high pressure (9–11 psi). Set the machine's timer to cook at this pressure for 6 minutes.

4 Use the quick-release method to bring the pot's pressure back to normal.

5 Unlock and open the cooker. Set the stovetop pot over medium heat or turn the electric one to its browning mode; bring the gravy to a simmer, stirring often. Whisk the milk and flour in a medium bowl until the flour dissolves, then whisk the mixture into the pot of simmering gravy. Continue cooking, whisking all the while, until thickened and bubbling, about 2 minutes. Serve at once.

TESTERS' NOTES
• This rich gravy is a perfect topper for toast, scrambled eggs, or biscuits. Of course, if you have a piece of chicken-fried steak, it'd go pretty well over that, too.
• Use lean ground pork, nothing fatty. Because the pressure cooker doesn't allow much evaporation, the fat will end up an unappealing slick on the gravy.
• We like a lot of black pepper in our gravy, but you can lower the amount at will.
• You can substitute 2 to 3 teaspoons Italian seasoning spice blend for all the spices.

Serve It Up! To make **Biscuits** for the gravy, mix 2¹/₄ cups all-purpose flour, 4 teaspoons

(continued)

baking powder, and ½ teaspoon salt in a large bowl; cut in 5 tablespoons cold, unsalted butter or lard until the mixture resembles coarse sand. Stir in ¾ cup plus 1 tablespoon whole milk and mix just until a dough forms. Press the dough to a 1-inch-thick slab on a cleaned, floured surface and cut into 2½-inch-wide rounds. Bake on a rimmed baking sheet in a 425°F oven for 13 to 15 minutes, or until golden brown and puffed. Cool on a wire rack for a couple of minutes before serving.

TORTILLA BREAKFAST CASSEROLE

EFFORT: **A LOT** • PRESSURE: **HIGH** • TIME UNDER PRESSURE: **12 OR 18 MINUTES** • RELEASE: **QUICK** • SERVES: **4 TO 6**

1 cup drained and rinsed canned black beans

1 cup shredded Cheddar cheese (about 4 ounces)

One 4½-ounce can chopped mild green chiles (about ½ cup)

½ teaspoon dried oregano

Four 6-inch flour tortillas

1 cup whole milk

2 large eggs, at room temperature

1 Butter the inside of a 2-quart, high-sided, round baking or soufflé dish. Make an aluminum foil sling (see page 19) and set the baking dish on it. Mix the beans, cheese, chiles, and oregano in a medium bowl; set aside.

2 Place 1 tortilla in the bottom of the prepared baking dish; spread a generous ½ cup of the bean mixture on top. Repeat this three more times, ending with the bean mixture. Whisk the milk and eggs in the used bowl

until smooth, then pour the combined liquid over the casserole.

3 Cover the baking dish with parchment paper, then seal it with a piece of aluminum foil. Set the pressure cooker rack in a 6-quart stovetop or electric cooker; pour in 2 cups water. Use the sling to lower it onto the rack in the pressure cooker. Fold the ends of the sling so they'll fit inside the cooker.

4 Lock the lid onto the pot.

STOVETOP: Set the pot over high heat and bring it to high pressure (15 psi). Once this pressure has been reached, reduce the heat as much as possible while maintaining this pressure. Cook for 12 minutes.

······················ O R ·······················

ELECTRIC: Set the machine to cook at high pressure (9–11 psi). Set the machine's timer to cook at high pressure for 18 minutes.

5 Use the quick-release method to bring the pot's pressure back to normal.

6 Unlock and open the cooker. Use the foil sling to transfer the baking dish to a wire rack. Uncover and cool for 5 minutes, then serve by scooping up by big spoonfuls.

TESTERS' NOTES
• This hearty but easy-to-make casserole is perfect brunch fare for the weekend.
• Layer the casserole up through step 3 the night before. Cover the baking dish and set it in the fridge; let it come back to room temperature on the counter for 20 minutes the next day before proceeding.
• You can use canned pinto beans instead of black beans, or Monterey jack or smoked Cheddar for the cheese.

Serve It Up! Buy some pico de gallo or fresh salsa, and use it as a garnish with a little sour cream on each serving.

BREAKFAST CUP CUSTARDS

EFFORT: **A LITTLE** • PRESSURE: **HIGH** • TIME UNDER PRESSURE:
5 OR 7 MINUTES • RELEASE: **QUICK** • SERVES: **4**

4 cold large eggs
2 cups whole or low-fat milk
1/4 cup sugar
2 teaspoons vanilla extract
1/8 teaspoon salt
1/4 teaspoon grated nutmeg

1 Set the pressure cooker rack in a 6-quart stovetop or electric pressure cooker; pour in 2 cups water.

2 Whisk the eggs in a large bowl until smooth, then whisk in the milk, sugar, vanilla, and salt. Divide the mixture among four 1-cup heat-safe ramekins; sprinkle the nutmeg over the tops. Cover the ramekins with foil and set them on the rack, stacking them as necessary so they fit.

3 Lock the lid onto the pot.

STOVETOP: Set the pot over high heat and bring it to high pressure (15 psi). Once this pressure has been reached, reduce the heat as much as possible while maintaining this pressure. Cook for 5 minutes.

·················· **OR** ··················

ELECTRIC: Set the machine to cook at high pressure (9–11 psi). Set the machine's timer to cook at this pressure for 7 minutes.

4 Use the quick-release method to bring the pot's pressure back to normal.

5 Unlock and open the pot. Transfer the ramekins to a wire rack and uncover. Serve warm or chill in the fridge for up to 2 days, covering after a couple of hours to protect them from ambient odors in the fridge.

TESTERS' NOTES
• Who said you can't have custard for breakfast?
• Make sure you're using heat-safe ramekins, such as those you'd use in the oven. They should also be fairly sturdy pottery, not bone china. Pyrex glass ramekins will conduct heat more quickly than ceramic ones; reduce the cooking time by 1 minute in either pot.
• You can substitute any pumpkin pie-style spice—cinnamon, mace, allspice, or ginger—for the nutmeg.

POTATO AND SAUSAGE HASH

EFFORT: **A LITTLE** • PRESSURE: **HIGH** • TIME UNDER PRESSURE:
10 OR 15 MINUTES • RELEASE: **QUICK** • SERVES: **4 TO 6**

1 tablespoon olive oil
1/2 pound bulk sweet Italian sausage meat
1 large yellow onion, chopped
1 1/2 pounds medium white potatoes (about 4), peeled, quartered, and thinly sliced
2 tablespoons Worcestershire sauce
1/2 teaspoon ground black pepper
1/4 teaspoon salt
One 14-ounce can diced tomatoes with chiles (about 1 3/4 cups)
1/4 cup chicken broth

1 Heat the oil in a 6-quart stovetop pressure cooker set over medium heat or in a 6-quart electric pressure cooker turned to the browning function. Crumble in the sausage and cook, stirring often, until browned, about 4 minutes. Use a slotted spoon to transfer it to a bowl.

(continued)

2 Add the onion; cook, stirring often, until browned, not just softened, even a little sweet, about 8 minutes. Stir in the potatoes, Worcestershire sauce, pepper, and salt, as well as the browned sausage meat. Toss well.

3 Sprinkle the tomatoes and any juice in the can over the ingredients in the cooker; drizzle with the broth.

4 Lock the lid onto the pot.

STOVETOP: Raise the heat to high and bring the pot to high pressure (15 psi). Immediately reduce the heat as low as you can while keeping this pressure constant. Cook for 10 minutes.

·············· **OR** ··············

ELECTRIC: Set the machine to cook at high pressure (9–11 psi). Set the machine's timer to cook at this pressure for 15 minutes.

5 Use the quick-release method to bring the pot's pressure back to normal.

6 Unlock and remove the lid. Set the stovetop cooker over medium-high heat or turn the electric cooker to its browning or simmer function; bring to a full simmer. Cook without stirring until any liquid in the pot boils away and the bottom of the hash browns a bit, 5 to 7 minutes. Turn the hash out of the pot onto a serving platter, browned side up.

TESTERS' NOTES

• You can make a pretty fine hash in a pressure cooker, given the way the appliance renders the potatoes velvety. But there's one drawback: no crunchy, browned bits for those of us drawn to such things. Thus, we brown the hash after it's undergone high pressure. Take it as far as you want, even burning a little onto the bottom of the pot. You can always soak the pot later before boiling water in it to remove pesky bits.

• Canned, diced tomatoes with chiles are almost impossible to find in a reduced-sodium version. If you're concerned about the amount of sodium here (there's plenty in the Worcestershire sauce, too), omit the salt.

• Don't use Russet or baking potatoes; they'll be too starchy and will stick to the pot. Look for waxy white potatoes in bags in the produce section. Or search out more esoteric varietals like Irish Cobblers, Cascades, or Snowdens.

Serve It Up! Lay a fried egg over each serving.

CORNED BEEF HASH

EFFORT: **A LITTLE** • PRESSURE: **HIGH** • TIME UNDER PRESSURE: **10 OR 15 MINUTES** • RELEASE: **QUICK** • SERVES: **4 TO 6**

3 tablespoons unsalted butter

1 medium yellow onion, chopped

1 pound cooked deli corned beef, diced

2 teaspoons minced garlic

1 pound yellow potatoes, such as Yukon Gold, diced

1 small red bell pepper, stemmed, cored, and diced

1/2 teaspoon dried thyme

1/2 teaspoon celery seeds

Up to 1/4 teaspoon cayenne

1/2 cup chicken broth

1 Melt the butter in a 6-quart stovetop pressure cooker set over medium heat or in a 6-quart electric pressure cooker turned to the browning function. Add the onion and cook, stirring often, until softened, about 3 minutes. Add the corned beef and garlic; stir over the heat for 2 minutes.

2 Stir in the potatoes, bell pepper, thyme, celery seeds, and cayenne. Sprinkle the broth over everything.

3 Lock the lid onto the pot.

STOVETOP: Raise the heat to high and bring the pot to high pressure (15 psi). Once this pressure has been reached, reduce the heat as much as possible while maintaining this pressure. Cook for 10 minutes.

·····························**OR**·····························

ELECTRIC: Set the machine to cook at high pressure (9–11 psi). Set the machine's timer to cook at high pressure for 15 minutes.

4 Use the quick-release method to bring the pot's pressure back to normal.

5 Unlock and remove the lid. Set the stovetop pot over medium heat or turn the electric cooker to its browning function. Lightly press the mixture down with the back of a wooden spoon, compacting it without mashing the potatoes. Cook without stirring until the cooker is dry and the bottom of the potato mixture begins to brown, about 5 minutes. Turn the contents of the cooker browned side up onto a serving platter.

TESTERS' NOTES
• Buy a chunk of corned beef right from the deli counter, so you don't have to purchase a ginormous slab and only use a small bit. (You can substitute pastrami for the corned beef if you like.)
• Yukon Golds are starchier than red-skinned potatoes but not as starchy as baking potatoes. They'll have just the right amount of stickiness to create a satisfying hash without becoming dry or gummy.

Serve It Up! Have a selection of pickles and pickle relishes on the table.

SWEET POTATO HASH WITH TURKEY SAUSAGE AND CRANBERRIES

EFFORT: **A LITTLE** • PRESSURE: **HIGH** • TIME UNDER PRESSURE: **5 OR 8 MINUTES** • RELEASE: **QUICK** • SERVES: **4 TO 6**

2 tablespoons unsalted butter
3/4 pound bulk mild Italian turkey sausage
1/2 small red onion, chopped
1/2 cup dried cranberries
1/4 cup shelled green pumpkin seeds (pepitas)
1/2 teaspoon ground cumin
1/2 teaspoon mild paprika
1/2 teaspoon dried sage
1/2 teaspoon salt
Up to 1/4 teaspoon cayenne
2 medium sweet potatoes (about 1 1/2 pounds total), peeled, halved lengthwise, and cut widthwise into 1/2-inch-thick slices
1/2 cup chicken broth

1 Melt the butter in a 6-quart stovetop pressure cooker set over medium heat or in a 6-quart electric pressure cooker turned to the browning function. Crumble in the sausage, add the onion, and cook together, stirring occasionally, until the meat is lightly browned, about 5 minutes.

2 Stir in the cranberries, pumpkin seeds, cumin, paprika, sage, salt, and cayenne; cook until aromatic, less than a minute, stirring occasionally. Add the sweet potatoes and stir over the heat for 1 minute. Sprinkle the broth over the ingredients.

(continued)

3 Lock the lid onto the pot.

STOVETOP: Raise the heat to high and bring the pot to high pressure (15 psi). Once this pressure has been reached, lower the heat as much as possible while maintaining this pressure. Cook for 5 minutes.

························ **OR** ························

ELECTRIC: Set the machine to cook at high pressure (9–11 psi). Set the machine's timer to cook at this pressure for 8 minutes.

4 Use the quick-release method to bring the pot's pressure back to normal.

5 Unlock and open the cooker. Set the stovetop pot over medium heat or turn the electric pot to its browning function. Cook until the liquid has evaporated out of the cooker and the bottom of the sweet potato mixture has begun to brown, 3 to 4 minutes. Turn out onto a serving platter, browned side up.

TESTERS' NOTES
• Since sweet potato hash can be cloyingly sweet, we balance this dish with savory spices as well as tart dried cranberries.
• Beyond breakfast, you might want to consider this a side dish for roast turkey.

CINNAMON HONEY APPLESAUCE

EFFORT: **NOT MUCH** • PRESSURE: **HIGH** • TIME UNDER PRESSURE: **4 OR 6 MINUTES** • RELEASE: **NATURAL** • SERVES: **6 TO 8**

3 pounds medium-tart baking apples, such as McIntosh, cored, peeled, and roughly chopped

³/₄ cup unsweetened apple juice

¹/₃ cup honey

1 tablespoon fresh lemon juice

¹/₂ teaspoon ground cinnamon

¹/₂ teaspoon salt

1 Mix everything in a 6-quart stovetop or electric pressure cooker.

2 Lock the lid onto the pot.

STOVETOP: Set the pot over high heat and bring it to high pressure (15 psi). Once this pressure has been reached, reduce the heat as much as possible while maintaining this pressure. Cook for 4 minutes.

························ **OR** ························

ELECTRIC: Set the machine to cook at high pressure (9–11 psi). Set the machine's timer to cook at this pressure for 6 minutes.

3 Reduce the pressure.

STOVETOP: Set the pot off the heat and let its pressure fall to normal, about 12 minutes.

························ **OR** ························

ELECTRIC: Turn off the machine or unplug it so it doesn't flip to its keep-warm setting. Let its pressure return to normal, 12 to 15 minutes.

4 Unlock and open the cooker. Use an immersion blender or a potato masher right in the pot to puree the apples into a thick sauce.

Serve warm, or spoon into a container, seal, and refrigerate for up to 5 days.

TESTERS' NOTES
• If you like a chunkier applesauce, skip the blender or potato masher and just use the back of a spoon to break the cooked apples against the side of the pot.
• Peeling an apple before you make applesauce is like peeling a potato before you make mashed potatoes—it's a matter of preference. Clearly, we prefer a sauce without bits of peel.
• You can use Gala or Rome apples for a sweeter sauce, or Northern Spy or Granny Smith apples for a tarter one.

CHERRY APRICOT COMPOTE

EFFORT: **NOT MUCH** • PRESSURE: **HIGH** • TIME UNDER PRESSURE: **8 OR 12 MINUTES** • RELEASE: **NATURAL** • SERVES: **6 TO 8**

3/4 **pound dried apricots, preferably Turkish, halved**

1 **pound fresh sweet cherries, pitted, or frozen pitted sweet cherries, thawed**

1 **cup sugar**

2 **tablespoons fresh lemon juice**

One 4-inch cinnamon stick

1/4 **teaspoon vanilla extract**

1/4 **teaspoon salt**

1 Mix everything in a 6-quart stovetop or electric pressure cooker with 1¼ cups water, stirring until the sugar dissolves.

2 Lock the lid onto the pot.

STOVETOP: Set the pot over high heat and bring it to high pressure (15 psi). Once this pressure has been reached, reduce the heat as much as possible while keeping this pressure constant. Cook for 8 minutes.

······· **OR** ·······
ELECTRIC: Set the machine to cook at high pressure (9–11 psi). Set the machine's timer to cook at this pressure for 12 minutes.

3 Reduce the pressure.

STOVETOP: Set the pot off the heat and let its pressure fall to normal naturally, about 12 minutes.
······· **OR** ·······
ELECTRIC: Turn off the machine or unplug it so it doesn't flip to its keep-warm setting. Allow its pressure to return to normal naturally, 14 to 15 minutes.

4 Unlock and open the cooker. Discard the cinnamon stick. Cool the compote for 15 minutes and serve warm, or ladle into a large container, seal well, and store in the refrigerator for up to 5 days.

TESTERS' NOTES
• Dried Turkish apricots are a lighter color and have a more sour flavor than dried California apricots, so they'll provide a better contrast to the other sweet flavors.
• Dried Turkish apricots are sold whole and need to be halved for proper cooking in this sauce. Cutting the apricots with kitchen shears is much easier than using a knife!
• Because of the sugar boiling inside the pot, do not attempt a quick-release—the sauce can bubble up through the vent hole. If this happens, simply move the pot off the heat or unplug it to bring the pressure back down.

Serve It Up! For a decadent breakfast, serve this compote warm over toasted slices of pound cake. (Toast the slices 4 to 6 inches from a heated broiler for 2 minutes, until lightly browned, without turning.)

SOUPS

YOU'RE PROBABLY READING THIS BECAUSE IT'S CHILLY OUTSIDE.
You're also probably reading this because you don't have all day to make soup. Let's face it: soup takes time. A pot of chicken soup needs several hours at a low bubble on the stovetop . . . or it needs a few minutes in a pressure cooker. That's a great reason to break out this appliance: you can create a layered and textured palette with little effort.

Right up front, let's get down a few overall tips for success. First, don't stint on the browning or reducing before you lock the lid onto the pot. While a pressure cooker speeds up the cooking time, it won't cut down the time you spend caramelizing meat or sweating onions. Well-seared meat and translucent onions are essential to a soup's success; those natural sugars and more intense flavors will melt into the broth under pressure, giving you a far finer meal.

Second, never overfill the cooker. Inside the pot, there's a line marked as "max fill" or just "maximum." The total volume of ingredients *must not* go over this line. But individual ingredients can. In other words, if there's a cup or so of liquid in the pot and two or three beef rib bones, these bones may well stand up above the line. However, if you were able to submerge them in the liquid, the total volume then must not come above this line. We've calibrated these recipes to work for modern cookers, but you may have an older pot with a different fill line that's slightly lower. Or you may get exuberant and think, *What's one more fennel bulb?* Don't do it, unless you're looking for a reason to clean up your stove.

Remember, too, that this appliance super-heats liquids, so a soup out of the cooker will be ridiculously hot, even if it has naturally come down from high pressure for 30 minutes. It's not necessarily above the boiling point, but it's near enough to it to give you a nasty burn. It's easy to get fooled: *Oh, I let this sit off the heat for a good while so it can't be scalding.* It is and will be for a while longer after you open the pot—because the fats in there are also super-heated, like cheese on a pizza. In fact, you may find the liquid still bubbling when you take the lid off. So let the soup cool a bit before you serve it. Or at least dish it up in room-temperature bowls.

Finally, plan on leftovers. These soups are hearty and our serving sizes are large, often over 3 cups a pop. If you've got a side salad or some bread on the table, you and yours probably won't eat the whole batch. But that's not a bad thing, since many of these soups freeze well. Dish up leftovers into small, sealable containers and freeze them for a few months. You'll have a microwave-ready lunch when you need it.

Talk of leftovers brings us to one last thought: if you've got a busy household where everyone's out of the door early and returns home late, consider batch-cooking soup on the weekends. With a pressure cooker, you can prepare two or three recipes in relatively little time on a Sunday, then have some choices for dinner that night *and* lunches and suppers during the week. If you plan ahead, you can have a homemade dinner ready in minutes on a weeknight. Need we say more?

Main-Course Soups

Skip the starters; all you need are these one-pot recipes, stocked with meat, poultry, or fish. The pressure cooker can brown, simmer, and finish a soup without dirtying another pan.

A few things to keep in mind: For one, follow the instructions as to the size of the protein—diced (about ¼-inch cubes), chopped (about ½-inch cubes), roughly chopped (½- to 1-inch pieces). The pressure cooker works in a quick, carefully timed burst, so you need to fit the size to the specification.

Two, watch out for substitutions, particularly when it comes to vegetables. Although these are protein-rich soups, most have plenty of vegetables—not just for their flavors but also for their natural moisture. While you can swap out an herb or spice, or even occasionally use ground beef instead of ground lamb, the vegetables were chosen partly for the amount of liquid forced from them under pressure—moisture that creates the soup base. You can't swap out a turnip for a tomato without compromising the recipe. Funny, that: meaty soups rely on veggies for their success.

Finally, watch the stated release time, particularly if there's a tough cut of meat in the mix or if there's any rice or pasta. Short-cutting a natural release with a quick one or not letting the pot sit to the side, covered, for 10 minutes can lead to tough short ribs or underdone rice. It's not the worst thing: just cover the pot and bring it back to high pressure, then set it aside and let it return to normal pressure. It's a hassle, though, so try to avoid it.

As a general rule, a soup has more liquid than a stew (which has more liquid than a braise). However, we offer several dishes that cross the soup/stew line, mostly because we wanted more vegetables in the pot. We also think that comfort food—soup in all its stripes—is best when well stocked. We hope you'll forgive our culinary irreverence.

BEEF AND VEGETABLE SOUP

EFFORT: **NOT MUCH** • PRESSURE: **HIGH** • TIME UNDER PRESSURE:
10 OR 15 MINUTES • RELEASE: **QUICK** • SERVES: **6**

4 cups (1 quart) beef broth

One 28-ounce can diced tomatoes (about 3^1/$_2$ cups)

1 pound boneless beef bottom round, diced

1 medium yellow onion, chopped

2 medium carrots, diced

^{1}/$_2$ teaspoon mild paprika

^{1}/$_2$ teaspoon dried marjoram

^{1}/$_2$ teaspoon salt

^{1}/$_2$ teaspoon ground black pepper

12 ounces green beans, trimmed and cut into ^{1}/$_2$-inch pieces

1 cup shelled fresh peas, or frozen peas, thawed

1 Mix the broth, tomatoes, beef, onion, carrots, paprika, marjoram, salt, and pepper in a 6-quart stovetop or electric pressure cooker.

2 Lock the lid onto the pot.

STOVETOP: Set the pot over high heat and bring to high pressure (15 psi). Once this pressure has been reached, reduce the heat as much as possible while maintaining this pressure. Cook for 10 minutes.

·················· **OR** ··················

ELECTRIC: Set the machine to cook at high pressure (9–11 psi). Set the machine's timer to cook at high pressure for 15 minutes.

3 Use the quick-release method to bring the pressure in the pot back to normal.

4 Unlock and open the pot. Stir in the green beans and peas. Cover and lock on the lid; set aside for 5 minutes to warm up and blanch the vegetables. If necessary, use the quick-release method once again to bring the pressure back to normal. (It may have built up because the soup is still hot.) Open the lid and stir well before serving.

TESTERS' NOTES

• For this American classic, the beef and carrots should be diced into small bits, no more than ¼ inch each. The onion pieces can be a bit larger, maybe ½-inch pieces, so these don't melt into the soup as it cooks under pressure.

• Beef bottom round is fairly lean, so the little bit of marbling inside the cut is much appreciated in this soup. However, if there's a strip of fat along the outer edge or any large bits of interior fat, remove it so the soup doesn't have a grease slick on its surface.

• You can substitute rump roast, boneless arm roast, or boneless shoulder roast.

Serve It Up! Float big croutons in each bowlful. To make your own, cut day-old bread into 1-inch cubes, drizzle with olive oil, and toast on a baking sheet in a 350°F oven, tossing occasionally, until brown and crunchy, about 12 minutes.

BEEF, BARLEY, AND MUSHROOM SOUP

EFFORT: **A LITTLE** • PRESSURE: **HIGH** • TIME UNDER PRESSURE: **25 OR 40 MINUTES** • RELEASE: **NATURAL** • SERVES: **6**

1 tablespoon canola, corn, or vegetable oil

1½ pounds beef shank rounds, trimmed of any large globs of fat

1 large yellow onion, chopped

2 medium celery stalks, chopped

1 teaspoon minced garlic

6 cups beef or chicken broth

1 cup pearl (perlato) barley

1 ounce dried porcini mushrooms

1 tablespoon stemmed thyme leaves

½ teaspoon ground allspice

½ teaspoon salt

½ teaspoon ground black pepper

1 Warm the oil in a 6-quart stovetop pressure cooker set over medium heat or in a 6-quart electric pressure cooker turned to the browning function. Add the meat and brown on all sides, turning occasionally, about 5 minutes. Transfer to a large bowl.

2 Add the onion and celery to the cooker; cook, stirring often, until the onion has softened, about 3 minutes. Add the garlic, stir for a few seconds, then stir in the broth, barley, mushrooms, thyme, allspice, salt, and pepper. Return the meat and any juices in its bowl to the cooker.

3 Lock the lid onto the pot.

STOVETOP: Raise the heat to high and bring the pot to high pressure (15 psi). Once this pressure has been reached, reduce the heat as much as possible while maintaining this pressure. Cook for 25 minutes.

··········· **OR** ···········

ELECTRIC: Set the machine to cook at high pressure (9–11 psi). Set the machine's timer to cook at this pressure for 40 minutes.

4 Reduce the pressure.

STOVETOP: Set the pot off the heat and allow the pressure to return to normal, about 30 minutes.

··········· **OR** ···········

ELECTRIC: Turn off the machine or unplug it so it doesn't flip to its keep-warm setting. Let the pot's pressure return to normal, 30 to 40 minutes.

5 Unlock and open the pot. Transfer the shank or short ribs to a cutting board. Cool for a couple of minutes, then slice the meat off the bones. Discard the bones and tough cartilage. Chop the meat and stir it into the soup before serving.

TESTERS' NOTES

• There's nothing like the flavor a bone brings to soup—and the pressure cooker is sure to extract every drop of goodness!

• Beef shank rounds are cut from the cow's leg, sort of like beef osso buco, except usually in only ½-inch to 1-inch slices. (You can substitute bone-in beef short ribs if desired.)

• The dried mushrooms actually hold their shape during the long cooking, keeping them a bit firm and whole when the soup is served. This long under pressure, fresh mushrooms would almost melt into the broth. (You can also use dried shiitake or portobello mushrooms in lieu of the shiitake.)

• Chicken broth in a beef soup? You bet! It makes the dish a little lighter and even a little more velvety. Of course, the best bet would be your own homemade stock. (But you'd expect food writers to say that, wouldn't you?)

HAMBURGER SOUP

EFFORT: **NOT MUCH** • PRESSURE: **HIGH** • TIME UNDER PRESSURE:
5 OR 8 MINUTES • RELEASE: **QUICK** • SERVES: **6**

3 cups beef broth

One 14-ounce can diced tomatoes (about 1³/₄ cups)

3 tablespoons tomato paste

1 large yellow onion, diced

2 medium green bell peppers, stemmed, cored, and chopped

2 medium celery stalks, thinly sliced

2 medium carrots, thinly sliced

1 large yellow potato (about 12 ounces), such as Yukon Gold, diced

¹/₄ cup loosely packed fresh parsley leaves, finely chopped

1 tablespoon loosely packed fresh oregano leaves, finely chopped

¹/₂ teaspoon salt

¹/₂ teaspoon ground black pepper

1¹/₂ pounds lean ground beef (93% lean or better)

1 Whisk the broth, tomatoes, and tomato paste in a 6-quart stovetop pressure cooker or electric pressure cooker until the tomato paste dissolves. Stir in the onion, bell peppers, celery, carrots, potato, parsley, oregano, salt, and pepper. Crumble in the ground beef in small clumps.

2 Lock the lid onto the pot.

STOVETOP: Set the pot over high heat and bring it to high pressure (15 psi). Once this pressure has been reached, lower the heat as much as possible while maintaining this pressure. Cook for 5 minutes.

········· OR ·········
ELECTRIC: Set the machine to cook at high pressure (9–11 psi). Set the machine's timer to cook at this pressure for 8 minutes.

3 Use the quick-release method to bring the pot's pressure back to normal.

4 Unlock and open the pot; stir well before serving. (If desired, use a flatware spoon to skim off some or most of the surface fat before serving.)

TESTERS' NOTES
• Talk about a kid-friendly recipe. Yes, this one's a little more stocked with vegetables than some versions. Consider it an easy meal on the nights with after-school activities.
• Keep the ground beef in small clumps, rather than crumbling it further. The clumps will stay together under pressure, sort of like small meatballs in the soup.
• You want those onions, carrots, and celery cut into small, thin pieces so they begin to dissolve, offering lots of flavor but not a lot of texture in each spoonful.

Serve It Up! Spoon a little pickle relish in the middle of each serving or grate some Cheddar over each bowlful. And make sure you offer toasted hamburger bun halves, rather than bread!

CHEESEBURGER SOUP

EFFORT: **A LITTLE** • PRESSURE: **HIGH** • TIME UNDER PRESSURE: **5 OR 8 MINUTES** • RELEASE: **QUICK** • SERVES: **4 TO 6**

3 tablespoons unsalted butter

1 large yellow onion, chopped

1 medium yellow bell pepper, stemmed, cored, and chopped

2 tablespoons all-purpose flour

3 cups chicken broth

1/4 cup dry white wine, such as Chardonnay

1 teaspoon dried thyme

1/2 teaspoon dried marjoram

1/2 teaspoon salt

1/2 teaspoon ground black pepper

1 pound lean ground beef (at least 93% lean)

1/2 cup heavy cream, light cream, or half-and-half

2 cups shredded Cheddar cheese, preferably sharp Cheddar (about 8 ounces)

1 Melt the butter in a 6-quart stovetop pressure cooker set over medium heat or in a 6-quart electric pressure cooker turned to the browning function. Add the onion and bell pepper; cook, stirring often, until the onion softens, about 4 minutes.

2 Whisk in the flour and cook for 1 minute, whisking all the while, just until the vegetables are thoroughly coated but not until the flour browns. Pour in the broth in a slow, steady stream, whisking constantly to dissolve the flour. Add the wine and whisk until bubbling and thickened, about 2 minutes. Stir in the thyme, marjoram, salt, and pepper. Crumble in the ground beef, leaving it in little chunks.

3 Lock the lid onto the pot.

STOVETOP: Raise the heat to high and bring the pot to high pressure (15 psi). Once this pressure has been reached, reduce the heat as much as possible while maintaining this pressure. Cook for 5 minutes.

··················· **OR** ···················
ELECTRIC: Set the machine to cook at high pressure (9–11 psi). Set the machine's timer to cook at high pressure for 8 minutes.

4 Use the quick-release method to bring the pot's pressure back to normal.

5 Unlock and open the pot. Set the stovetop pot over medium heat or turn the electric cooker to its browning function. Stir in the cream or half-and-half; simmer for 1 minute, stirring all the while. Add the cheese and stir just until it melts. Serve at once.

TESTERS' NOTES
• Surprisingly complex, this soup may rid you of the need to turn on the grill for burgers this winter.
• Even though there are pieces of vegetable in the pot, it's important to whisk in step 2, not just stir. You need to keep the flour from browning—and make sure it dissolves evenly.
• Do you have to add the cream? Of course not—you can use whole or low-fat milk instead. But you won't know what you're missing.
• You can substitute 2¼ cups frozen chopped onion and bell pepper, thawed, for the fresh onion and bell pepper.

BARBECUE BRISKET SOUP

EFFORT: **NOT MUCH** • PRESSURE: **HIGH** • TIME UNDER PRESSURE:
45 OR 75 MINUTES • RELEASE: **NATURAL** • SERVES: **6 TO 8**

1 pound beef brisket, preferably the flat
    or first cut, cut against the grain into
    $1/2$-inch-thick slices

4 cups (1 quart) beef or chicken broth

One 28-ounce can diced tomatoes (about
    $3^1/2$ cups)

One 12-ounce bottle light-colored beer,
    preferably an amber ale

1 large carrot, chopped

1 large sweet potato, peeled and chopped
    into $1/2$-inch pieces

$1/4$ cup packed dark brown sugar

$1/4$ cup apple cider vinegar

2 tablespoons Worcestershire sauce

1 teaspoon ground coriander

$1/2$ teaspoon ground allspice

$1/2$ teaspoon dry mustard

$1/2$ teaspoon salt

$1/4$ teaspoon ground cloves

$1/4$ teaspoon ground black pepper

1 Combine everything in a 6-quart stovetop
or electric pressure cooker, stirring until the
brown sugar dissolves.

2 Lock the lid onto the pot.

STOVETOP: Set the pot over high heat and bring
it to high pressure (15 psi). Once this pressure has
been reached, reduce the heat as much as possible while maintaining this pressure. Cook for
45 minutes.

·····························**OR**·····························

ELECTRIC: Set the machine to cook at high pressure (9–11 psi). Set the machine's timer to cook at
high pressure for 75 minutes.

3 Reduce the pressure.

STOVETOP: Set the pot off the heat and let the
pressure in the pot fall back to normal naturally,
about 30 minutes.

·····························**OR**·····························

ELECTRIC: Turn off the machine or unplug it. Let
the pot's pressure return to normal naturally, 35 to
40 minutes.

4 Unlock and open the pot. Stir well before
serving.

TESTERS' NOTES

• You don't need a backyard barbecue to make a great
brisket. The pressure cooker will tenderize the meat and
blend the flavors without much effort.

• The brisket should be as lean as possible so it doesn't
leave a slick of fat on top of the soup. Thus, we call for a
first-cut or flat-cut section, the leanest part of the brisket.
However, even it will have a thin layer of fat on the exposed
surface. Leave this small amount for better flavor.

• To tell which way the brisket's grain lies, run your cleaned
fingers over the cut to pull it into its various fibers. Slice
across this grain, not with it.

• You can substitute chopped seeded and peeled butternut
squash (from about 1 pound) for the sweet potato and 2 to
3 teaspoons of your favorite bottled dry barbecue seasoning blend for all the dried spices.

Serve It Up! Open up a hot baked potato
and put it in the bottom of each bowl before
ladling the soup on top.

BEEF AND ONION SOUP

EFFORT: **A LOT** • PRESSURE: **HIGH** • TIME UNDER PRESSURE: **33 OR 50 MINUTES** • RELEASE: **QUICK, THEN QUICK AGAIN** • SERVES: **6**

2 tablespoons unsalted butter

1 tablespoon olive oil

2 pounds yellow onions, sliced into very thin half-moons and rings separated

3 tablespoons cognac

2 beef ribs with plenty of meat on them

6 cups beef broth

$\frac{1}{2}$ cup moderately dry white wine, such as Pinot Grigio

1 teaspoon salt

$\frac{1}{2}$ teaspoon ground black pepper

$\frac{1}{4}$ teaspoon ground allspice

1 tablespoon potato starch

Twelve 1-inch-thick baguette slices

6 ounces shredded Gruyère cheese (about 1$\frac{1}{2}$ cups)

1 Melt the butter in the oil in a 6-quart stovetop pressure cooker set over medium heat or in a 6-quart electric pressure cooker turned to the browning function. Add all the onions and cook, stirring almost constantly, until the onions are golden brown, 12 to 16 minutes. Pour in the cognac; scrape up any browned bits in the pot as the liquid comes to a simmer. Scrape the onions and any juices into a large bowl.

2 Combine the beef, broth, wine, salt, pepper, and allspice in the cooker.

3 Lock the lid onto the pot.

STOVETOP: Set the pot over high heat and bring it to high pressure (15 psi). Once this pressure has been reached, reduce the heat as much as possible while maintaining this pressure. Cook for 30 minutes.

····················· **OR** ·····················

ELECTRIC: Set the machine to cook at high pressure (9–11 psi). Set the machine's timer to cook at high pressure for 45 minutes.

4 Use the quick-release method to bring the pot's pressure back to normal.

5 Unlock the lid and open the pot. Remove the beef ribs and transfer them to a cutting board. Cool for a few minutes, then remove and discard the bones and any bits of cartilage. Chop the meat and stir it back into the pot. Stir the onions and any juices in their bowl into the cooker.

6 Lock the lid back onto the pot.

STOVETOP: Set the pot back over high heat and bring it back to high pressure (15 psi). Once this pressure has been again reached, reduce the heat as much as possible while maintaining this pressure. Cook for 3 minutes.

····················· **OR** ·····················

ELECTRIC: Set the machine to cook at high pressure (9–11 psi). Set the machine's timer to cook at high pressure for 5 minutes.

7 Use the quick-release method to return the pot to normal pressure.

8 Unlock and remove the lid. Set the stovetop pot over medium heat or turn the electric one to its browning function; bring to a simmer. Whisk the potato starch with 1 tablespoon water in a small bowl to create a smooth slurry. Stir the slurry into the soup until thickened, less than 1 minute. Turn off the heat or turn off the machine, cover loosely with the lid, and set aside.

9 Position the oven rack 4 to 6 inches from the broiler; heat the broiler. Lay the baguette slices on a large, rimmed baking sheet. Top them with the cheese, then broil until melted and a little browned, about 1 minute. Serve by ladling the soup into bowls and topping each with two cheesy toast rounds.

TESTERS' NOTES

• This is as close as a pressure cooker can get to traditional French onion soup, since we can't really caramelize onions in such a tall pot. But what flavors! The sweetened onions permeate the soup. We remove them from the cooker so they'll retain their texture during the first cooking, then add them later to bring their flavors to the soup.

• We've left some bits of beef in it, rather than the usual clear beef broth, because we wanted a robust meal-in-a-bowl, not just a first-course soup.

• You needn't thicken the soup in the final step if you don't feel like it; the soup will be more watery but will certainly taste as good. And you can use cornstarch in lieu of potato starch if you do decide to thicken the soup.

• You can also use brandy in lieu of the cognac.

PEPPERY BEEF, POTATO, AND BEER SOUP

EFFORT: **A LITTLE** • PRESSURE: **HIGH** • TIME UNDER PRESSURE: **12 OR 18 MINUTES** • RELEASE: **QUICK, THEN QUICK AGAIN** • SERVES: **4 TO 6**

1¹/₂ pounds boneless beef sirloin, trimmed and cut into 1-inch pieces

1 medium red onion, chopped

3 cups beef broth

Two 12-ounce bottles light-colored beer, preferably an amber ale

2 tablespoons Worcestershire sauce

2 tablespoons balsamic vinegar

Up to 1 tablespoon ground black pepper

¹/₂ teaspoon salt

2 bay leaves

1 pound baby carrots, halved widthwise

1 pound small yellow potatoes, such as Yukon Gold, cut into 1-inch pieces

1 Stir the beef, chopped onion, broth, beer, Worcestershire sauce, vinegar, pepper, salt, and bay leaves in a 6-quart stovetop or electric pressure cooker.

2 Lock the lid onto the pot.

STOVETOP: Set the pot over high heat and bring it to high pressure. Once this pressure has been reached, reduce the heat as much as possible while maintaining this pressure. Cook for 5 minutes.

························ **OR** ························

ELECTRIC: Set the machine to cook at high pressure (9–11 psi). Set the machine's timer to cook at high pressure for 8 minutes.

3 Use the quick-release method to bring the pot's pressure back to normal.

4 Unlock and remove the lid. Stir in the carrots and potatoes.

5 Lock the lid back onto the pot.

STOVETOP: Set the pot back over high heat and bring it back to high pressure (15 psi). Once this pressure has been reached, reduce the heat as much as you can while maintaining this pressure. Cook for 7 minutes.

························ **OR** ························

ELECTRIC: Set the machine to cook once again at high pressure (9–11 psi). Set the machine's timer to cook at high pressure for 10 minutes.

6 Use the quick-release method to return the pressure in the pot to normal.

(continued)

7 Unlock and open the pot, remove the bay leaves, and stir well before serving.

TESTERS' NOTES
• Look no further for a filling, satisfying dinner on a cold night! This meal's a combo of sweet and sour, savory and salty—and frankly, so well stocked it's somewhere between a stew and a soup. You don't even need bread!
• The potatoes needn't be peeled. Make sure they're well scrubbed to remove any dirt.
• There's plenty of ground black pepper to give the soup a real kick. Reduce the amount if you prefer a milder meal.

Serve It Up! Garnish with sour cream, particularly if you added the full amount of black pepper.

ASIAN BEEF SOUP
with RICE NOODLES

EFFORT: **A LITTLE** • PRESSURE: **HIGH** • TIME UNDER PRESSURE: **11 OR 17 MINUTES** • RELEASE: **QUICK, THEN QUICK AGAIN** • SERVES: **4 TO 6**

6 cups chicken broth

1½ pounds boneless beef sirloin, trimmed and cut against the grain into ¼-inch-thick strips

½ cup soy sauce

1 small yellow onion, halved and sliced into thin half-moons

8 dried shiitake mushrooms, stemmed, the caps broken into small bits

2 tablespoons rice vinegar

1 tablespoon minced fresh ginger

Up to 1 tablespoon sambal oelek

¼ cup mirin

4 ounces dried rice stick noodles, about as wide as fettuccini

1 Mix the broth, beef, soy sauce, onion, mushrooms, rice vinegar, ginger, and sambal in a 6-quart stovetop or electric pressure cooker.

2 Lock the lid onto the pot.

STOVETOP: Set the pot over high heat and bring to high pressure (15 psi). Once this pressure has been reached, reduce the heat as much as possible while maintaining this pressure. Cook for 10 minutes.
⋯⋯⋯⋯⋯⋯⋯⋯ **OR** ⋯⋯⋯⋯⋯⋯⋯⋯
ELECTRIC: Set the machine to cook at high pressure (9–11 psi). Set the machine's timer to cook at high pressure for 15 minutes.

3 Use the quick-release method to bring the pot's pressure to normal.

4 Unlock and open the pot. Stir in the mirin and rice stick noodles.

5 Lock the lid back onto the pot.

STOVETOP: Set the pot back over high heat and bring it back to high pressure (15 psi). Once this pressure has been reached, reduce the heat as much as possible while maintaining this pressure. Cook for 1 minute.
⋯⋯⋯⋯⋯⋯⋯⋯ **OR** ⋯⋯⋯⋯⋯⋯⋯⋯
ELECTRIC: Set the machine to cook once again at high pressure (9–11 psi). Set the machine's timer to cook at high pressure for 2 minutes.

6 Use the quick-release method to bring the pot's pressure back to normal.

7 Unlatch and remove the lid; stir the soup before serving.

TESTERS' NOTES
• If you don't have Chinese takeout, this soup is the next best thing. Actually, because the flavors are so well layered and because it's made with ingredients you know, it may

be *the* best thing. Eat the soup with a fork (or chopsticks) in one hand and a big spoon in the other.
• For even more flavor, add either a whole garlic clove with the beef or a star anise pod with the mirin—or both. Discard both before serving.
• In North America, rice stick noodles are so labeled no matter the thickness, from angel hair to almost fettuccini-wide strands. Choose the widest noodles you can find.
• The noodles will continue to absorb liquid if you save any leftovers. You may need to thin these out with additional beef broth.
• You can substitute ¼ cup dry white wine plus 1 tablespoon sugar for the mirin; and you can substitute bottled hot red pepper sauce, preferably one with vinegar in the mix, for the sambal oelek.

HAM AND CORN CHOWDER

EFFORT: **A LITTLE** • PRESSURE: **HIGH** • TIME UNDER PRESSURE: **5 OR 10 MINUTES** • RELEASE: **NATURAL** • SERVES: **4 TO 6**

2¹/₂ cups chicken broth

3 tablespoons all-purpose flour

3 tablespoons unsalted butter

12 ounces smoked ham, chopped

1 medium yellow onion, chopped

3 cups fresh corn kernels, or frozen kernels, thawed

1 medium white potato (about 8 ounces), diced

1 teaspoon dried oregano

¹/₂ teaspoon celery seeds

¹/₂ teaspoon ground black pepper

³/₄ cup light, dry white wine, such as Sauvignon Blanc

¹/₂ cup heavy or light cream

1 Whisk the broth and flour in a small bowl until the flour has dissolved; set aside.

2 Melt the butter in a 6-quart stovetop pressure cooker set over medium heat or in a 6-quart electric pressure cooker turned to the browning function. Add the ham and cook, stirring often, until well browned, even crisp at the edges, about 4 minutes.

3 Add the onion and corn; cook, stirring frequently, until the onion turns translucent, about 3 minutes. Stir in the potato, oregano, celery seeds, and pepper until aromatic, less than a minute. Pour in the wine and scrape up any browned bits in the bottom of the cooker as it comes to a simmer. Stir in the broth mixture.

4 Lock the lid onto the pot.

STOVETOP: Raise the heat to high and bring the pot to high pressure (15 psi). Once this pressure has been reached, reduce the heat as much as possible while maintaining this pressure. Cook for 5 minutes.

.... **OR** ....

ELECTRIC: Set the machine to cook at high pressure (9–11 psi). Set the machine's timer to cook at high pressure for 10 minutes.

5 Reduce the pressure.

STOVETOP: Set the pot off the heat and let its pressure fall to normal naturally, about 20 minutes.

.... **OR** ....

ELECTRIC: Turn off the machine or unplug it so it doesn't flip to its keep-warm setting. Allow its pressure to return to normal naturally, 20 to 30 minutes.

6 Unlock and open the pot; stir in the cream. Cover without engaging the pressure lock. Set aside for about 5 minutes to warm the cream.

(continued)

HAM, BLACK-EYED PEA, AND CHILE SOUP

EFFORT: **A LITTLE** • PRESSURE: **HIGH** • TIME UNDER PRESSURE: **10 OR 15 MINUTES** • RELEASE: **NATURAL** • SERVES: **6**

2 tablespoons peanut oil

1 medium yellow onion, chopped

1 medium green bell pepper, stemmed, cored, and chopped

1 tablespoon minced garlic

1 pound smoked ham, any glaze or spice rub removed from its exterior, chopped

1 teaspoon dried oregano

1 teaspoon ground coriander

$1/2$ teaspoon dried sage

5 cups chicken broth

One 14-ounce can diced tomatoes (about $1^3/4$ cups)

1 cup dried black-eyed peas

One $4^1/2$-ounce can chopped mild green chiles (about $1/2$ cup)

1 Heat the oil in a 6-quart stovetop pressure cooker set over medium heat or in a 6-quart electric pressure cooker turned to the browning function. Add the onion and bell pepper; cook, stirring often, until the onion softens, about 4 minutes. Add the garlic and cook until aromatic, less than a minute, stirring constantly.

2 Add the ham, oregano, coriander, and sage; cook for 2 minutes, stirring quite often. Pour in the broth, tomatoes, black-eyed peas, and chiles. Stir to get any browned bits off the bottom of the pot.

3 Lock the lid in place.

STOVETOP: Raise the heat to high and bring the pot to high pressure (15 psi). Once this pressure has been reached, reduce the heat as much as possible while maintaining this pressure. Cook for 10 minutes.

······· **OR** ·······

ELECTRIC: Set the machine to cook at high pressure (9–11 psi). Set the machine's timer to cook at high pressure for 15 minutes.

4 Reduce the pressure.

STOVETOP: Set the pot off the heat and let its pressure return to normal naturally, about 30 minutes.

······· **OR** ·······

ELECTRIC: Turn off the machine or unplug it so it doesn't flip to its keep-warm setting. Allow the pot's pressure to fall back to normal naturally, 30 to 40 minutes.

5 Unlock and remove the lid; stir well before serving.

holiday table. When your guests go home, you've got an easy weekend meal ahead.

• If you want to make this meal without a holiday in sight, buy smoked ham at the deli counter at your supermarket. Ask for a 1-pound chunk that you can chop into ½- to 1-inch pieces. (Prepackaged thin slices will lose too much texture here.)

• The black-eyed peas actually retain their shape and texture better under pressure if they are *not* soaked in advance.

Serve It Up! Set bread slices on a baking sheet, top them with shredded Cheddar, and melt 4 to 6 inches from a heated broiler to serve alongside.

SPLIT PEA AND HAM BONE SOUP

EFFORT: **A LITTLE** • PRESSURE: **HIGH** • TIME UNDER PRESSURE: **26 OR 39 MINUTES** • RELEASE: **QUICK, THEN QUICK AGAIN** • SERVES: **6 TO 8**

1 smoked ham bone with plenty of meat attached (about 1½ pounds)

2 cups dried green split peas

3 medium carrots, cut into ½-inch-thick coins

1 small yellow onion, chopped

1 teaspoon dried thyme

½ teaspoon celery seeds

½ teaspoon ground black pepper

2 bay leaves

1 Place the ham bone in a 6-quart stovetop or electric pressure cooker. Pour 8 cups of water into the stovetop model or 7 cups into the electric one.

2 Lock the lid onto the pot.

STOVETOP: Set the pot over high heat and bring it to high pressure (15 psi). Once this pressure has been reached, reduce the heat as much as possible while maintaining this pressure. Cook for 20 minutes.

························ **OR** ························

ELECTRIC: Set the machine to cook at high pressure (9–11 psi). Set the machine's timer to cook at high pressure for 30 minutes.

3 Use the quick-release method to bring the pot's pressure back to normal.

4 Unlock and open the pot. Stir in the split peas, carrots, onion, thyme, celery seeds, pepper, and bay leaves.

5 Lock the lid back onto the cooker.

STOVETOP: Set the pot back over high heat and bring it back to high pressure (15 psi). Once this pressure has been reached, lower the heat as much as possible while maintaining this pressure. Cook for 6 minutes.

························ **OR** ························

ELECTRIC: Set the machine to cook once again at high pressure (9–11 psi). Set the machine's timer to cook at this pressure for 9 minutes.

6 Use the quick-release method once again to drop the pressure in the pot to normal.

7 Unlatch and remove the lid. Discard the bay leaves. Transfer the ham bone to a large cutting board; cool for a few minutes before shredding the meat off it.

8 Set the stovetop cooker over medium heat or turn the electric cooker to its browning function. Stir the meat back into the soup. Simmer for 5 minutes, stirring quite often, until slightly thickened.

(continued)

TESTERS' NOTES

• We've got a lot more carrots than onions because we like the way their natural sweetness balances the earthiness of the split peas.

• If you're using a leftover ham bone from a holiday feast, make sure you cut any glaze off the meat so those flavors do not compete with these.

• If desired, brighten the flavors by adding up to 1 tablespoon lemon juice along with the meat in step 8.

• The time you simmer the soup in step 8 is actually a matter of taste. You certainly don't want it to be thick as paste, but you might like yours slightly thicker (or thinner) than we do ours. By all means simmer it another few minutes if you want to, but remember that the soup will continue to thicken as it sits off the heat.

SOUTHWESTERN PINTO BEAN AND HAM BONE SOUP

EFFORT: **A LOT** • PRESSURE: **HIGH** • TIME UNDER PRESSURE: **33 OR 50 MINUTES** • RELEASE: **QUICK, THEN QUICK AGAIN** • SERVES: **6**

2 cups dried pinto beans

3 small fresh poblano chiles

2 tablespoons olive oil

1 medium red onion, chopped

2 teaspoons minced garlic

1 teaspoon ground cumin

1 teaspoon dried oregano

4 cups (1 quart) chicken broth

1 smoked ham bone with plenty of meat still on it (about 1½ pounds)

1 large sweet potato (about 1 pound), peeled and diced

Up to ½ cup loosely packed fresh cilantro leaves, minced

2 tablespoons fresh lime juice

1 Soak the beans in a big bowl of water on the counter overnight, for at least 12 hours or up to 16 hours. Drain them in a colander set in the sink.

2 Roast the chiles over an open gas flame, turning them occasionally with kitchen tongs until blackened, about 5 minutes. (If you don't have a gas flame on your stove, broil them on a large baking sheet 4 to 6 inches from the heated broiler element until blackened, turning occasionally, about 4 minutes.) Set the chiles in a large bowl, seal with plastic wrap, and set aside for 15 minutes. Uncover the bowl and pull the blackened skin off the chiles. Stem, core, and chop the flesh.

3 Heat the oil in a 6-quart stovetop pressure cooker set over medium heat or in a 6-quart stovetop pressure cooker turned to the browning function. Add the onion and cook, stirring often, until translucent, about 4 minutes. Stir in the garlic, cumin, and oregano until aromatic, less than 1 minute. Pour in the broth and 3 cups water; stir well. Nestle the ham bone into the soup.

4 Lock the lid onto the pot.

STOVETOP: Raise the heat to high and bring the pot to high pressure. Once this pressure has been reached, reduce the heat as much as possible while maintaining this pressure. Cook for 23 minutes.

······················· OR ·······················

ELECTRIC: Set the machine to cook at high pressure (9–11 psi). Set the machine's timer to cook at high pressure for 35 minutes.

5 Use the quick-release method to bring the pot's pressure back to normal.

6 Unlock and open the pot. Stir in the drained beans and potato.

7 Lock the lid back onto the pot.

STOVETOP: Set the pot over high heat and bring it back to high pressure (15 psi). Once this pressure has been reached, lower the heat as much as possible while maintaining this pressure. Cook for 10 minutes.

·················· **OR** ··················

ELECTRIC: Set the machine to cook once again at high pressure (9–11 psi). Set the machine's timer to cook at high pressure for 15 minutes.

8 Use the quick-release method to return the pot's pressure to normal.

9 Unlock and remove the lid. Transfer the ham bone to a large cutting board. Cool for a few minutes, then shred the meat off the bone. Chop the meat and stir the meat back into the soup. Stir in the cilantro and lime juice before serving.

TESTERS' NOTES

• You don't have to wait for a holiday ham to make this soup. Ask at the deli counter if they'll sell you the ham bone from their in-house roasted ham. You may have to wait for it, but it'll be a lot easier than roasting a ham on your own! Cut off any glazes or spices before adding the bone to the pot.

• We use roasted chiles here, rather than canned chopped chiles, because we wanted a more intense smoky flavor to balance the sweet potatoes, cilantro, and lime juice. For a shortcut, look for canned fire-roasted whole green chiles; drain and chop 1 to 1½ cups.

• This timing renders the beans tender but with a definite chew to them. If you want them meltingly tender, do a natural release in step 8.

TACO SOUP

EFFORT: **NOT MUCH** • PRESSURE: **HIGH** • TIME UNDER PRESSURE: **3 OR 5 MINUTES** • RELEASE: **QUICK** • SERVES: **4 TO 6**

6 cups chicken broth

2 cups jarred tomato salsa

1 cup fresh corn kernels, or frozen kernels, thawed

1 medium red onion, chopped

1 medium green bell pepper, stemmed, cored, and chopped

1 cup drained and rinsed canned black beans

½ cup loosely packed fresh cilantro leaves, chopped

1 pound lean ground pork

1 Mix the broth, salsa, corn, onion, pepper, black beans, and cilantro in a 6-quart stovetop or electric pressure cooker. Crumble in the ground pork.

2 Lock the lid onto the pot.

STOVETOP: Set the pot over high heat and bring to high pressure (15 psi). Once this pressure has been reached, reduce the heat as much as possible while maintaining this pressure. Cook for 3 minutes.

·················· **OR** ··················

ELECTRIC: Set the machine to cook at high pressure (9–11 psi). Set the machine's timer to cook at this pressure for 5 minutes.

3 Use the quick-release method to bring the pot's pressure back to normal.

4 Unlock and remove the lid; stir well before serving.

TESTERS' NOTES

• It doesn't get much simpler than this soup: a family favorite, made in under 15 minutes from opening your refrigerator to sitting down at the table.

(continued)

- Use the leanest ground pork you can find, even asking the butcher for a good selection. If there's nothing on hand, have him or her grind some boneless center-cut pork chops for you.
- There's plenty of salt in the salsa, so there's none added to the pot. Pass more at the table for those who want it.

Serve It Up! Top with shredded pepper jack cheese and crumbled tortilla chips.

HOT AND SOUR SOUP

EFFORT: **A LOT** • PRESSURE: **HIGH** • TIME UNDER PRESSURE: **20 OR 30 MINUTES** • RELEASE: **QUICK** • SERVES: **6**

6 cups chicken broth

One ½-pound smoked ham chunk, any glaze or spice rub removed

4 pork spare ribs

6 medium scallions, green and white parts

6 dried shiitake mushrooms, stemmed

2 medium garlic cloves, peeled

One 2-inch fresh ginger piece, peeled

¼ cup soy sauce

¼ cup rice vinegar

One 8-ounce can sliced bamboo shoots, drained and rinsed (about ½ cup)

Up to 1 tablespoon sambal oelek

2 tablespoons cornstarch

8 ounces firm, silken tofu, cut into ½-inch pieces

1 Mix the broth, ham, spare ribs, scallions, mushrooms, garlic, and ginger in a 6-quart stovetop or electric pressure cooker.

2 Lock the lid onto the pot.

STOVETOP: Set the pot over high heat and bring it to high pressure (15 psi). Once this pressure has been reached, reduce the heat as much as possible while maintaining this pressure. Cook for 20 minutes.

···························· OR ····························

ELECTRIC: Set the machine to cook at high pressure (9–11 psi). Set the machine's timer to cook at high pressure for 30 minutes.

3 Use the quick-release method to drop the pot's pressure back to normal.

4 Unlock and open the pot. Transfer the ham and spare ribs to a large cutting board. Cool for a few minutes, then shred the meat off the spare rib bones. Chop the rib meat and ham into ½-inch bits. Scrape all the meat into a large bowl.

5 Use a strainer or tongs to transfer the mushrooms to the cutting board; slice the caps into thin strips. Place the mushrooms in the bowl with the meat, then use a strainer to remove and discard the scallions, ginger, and garlic from the cooker.

6 Set the stovetop cooker over medium heat or turn the electric cooker to the browning function; bring the broth to a simmer. Stir in the soy sauce, vinegar, bamboo shoots, and sambal. Simmer, stirring occasionally, for 2 minutes to blend the flavors.

7 Whisk the cornstarch with 2 tablespoons water in a small bowl until smooth, then whisk the mixture into the soup. Cook about 1 minute, stirring all the while, until thickened. Stir in the meat and mushrooms, then gently stir in the tofu. Turn off the heat or unplug the machine; cover without engaging the lid and set aside for 2 minutes to further blend the flavors.

TESTERS' NOTES
- This recipe is a fairly authentic version of the Chinese favorite. You start by making a rich, aromatic soup, letting

the cooker extract every drop of flavor from the ingredients; then you doctor that broth to turn it into a hearty meal, rather than just a first-course soup.

• Some restaurant versions of this soup are also a tad sweet. If desired, add up to 2 teaspoons sugar with the soy sauce and other ingredients.

Serve It Up! Serve with crispy wontons. To make your own, buy wonton wrappers, coat both sides with nonstick spray, and bake on a large, rimmed baking sheet at 400°F for 10 minutes, or until crisp and browned. Break these over each bowlful.

WHITE BEAN AND PANCETTA SOUP

EFFORT: **A LITTLE** • PRESSURE: **HIGH** • TIME UNDER PRESSURE: **10 OR 15 MINUTES** • RELEASE: **QUICK** • SERVES: **6 TO 8**

2 cups dried great northern beans (about 1 pound)
One 4-ounce pancetta chunk, chopped
1 small yellow onion, chopped
4 cups (1 quart) chicken broth
One 4-inch rosemary sprig
1/2 teaspoon ground black pepper
Up to 1/2 cup heavy cream (optional)

1 Soak the beans in a big bowl of water on the counter for at least 12 hours or up to 16 hours. Drain in a colander set in the sink.

2 Put the pancetta and onion in a 6-quart stovetop pressure cooker set over medium heat or in a 6-quart electric pressure cooker turned to the browning mode; fry until the pancetta is crisp at the edges and the onion has softened, about 4 minutes, stirring often.

3 Stir in the broth, rosemary, and pepper, as well as the drained beans.

4 Lock the lid onto the pot.

STOVETOP: Raise the heat to high and bring the pot to high pressure (15 psi). Once this pressure has been reached, reduce the heat as much as possible while maintaining this pressure. Cook for 10 minutes.

······················ OR ·····························

ELECTRIC: Set the machine to cook at high pressure (9–11 psi). Set the machine's timer to cook at high pressure for 15 minutes.

5 Use the quick-release method to return the pot's pressure to normal.

6 Unlock and open the pot; discard the rosemary sprig. Mash some of the beans against the walls of the cooker with a wooden spoon to create a thick paste to thicken the soup. Stir well, adding the cream, if desired.

TESTERS' NOTES
• It's hard to imagine a more satisfying meal from so few ingredients, like trattoria fare at home.
• Don't be tempted to use canned beans. Dried beans will hold their texture much better.
• Use a chunk of pancetta that you can cut into bits, rather than prepackaged thin slices that will get lost in the soup.
• For a smoky flavor, substitute slab bacon for the pancetta—or use 2 ounces of pancetta and 2 ounces of slab bacon for a more sophisticated finish.

Serve It Up! Drizzle lemon-infused olive oil over each helping.

CHEESE SAUSAGE SOUP

EFFORT: **A LITTLE** • PRESSURE: **HIGH** • TIME UNDER PRESSURE: **5 OR 8 MINUTES** • RELEASE: **QUICK** • SERVES: **6**

1 tablespoon olive oil

2 pounds mild Italian sausage, cut into ¹⁄₂-inch pieces

1 large yellow onion, chopped

3 tablespoons all-purpose flour

4 cups (1 quart) chicken broth

¹⁄₂ teaspoon dried sage

¹⁄₂ teaspoon dried thyme

¹⁄₄ teaspoon grated nutmeg

1 cup finely grated Parmesan cheese (about 2 ounces)

¹⁄₂ cup shredded Monterey jack cheese (about 2 ounces)

¹⁄₄ cup heavy or light cream

1 Warm the oil in a 6-quart stovetop pressure cooker set over medium heat or in a 6-quart electric pressure cooker turned to the browning function. Add the sausage pieces and brown on all sides, turning occasionally, about 5 minutes. Transfer to a large bowl.

2 Add the onion and cook, stirring often, until translucent, about 4 minutes. Add the flour and whisk just until it has combined with the residual fat in the cooker, but don't let it brown. Whisk in the broth in a slow, steady stream to dissolve the flour.

3 Stir in the sage, thyme, and nutmeg; then return the sausage and any juices in the bowl to the cooker and stir well.

4 Lock the lid onto the pot.

STOVETOP: Raise the heat to high and bring the pot to high pressure (15 psi). Once this pressure has been reached, lower the heat as much as possible while maintaining this pressure. Cook for 5 minutes.

························ **OR** ························

ELECTRIC: Set the machine to cook at high pressure (9–11 psi). Set the machine's timer to cook at high pressure for 8 minutes.

5 Use the quick-release method to bring the pot's pressure back to normal.

6 Unlock and remove the lid. Stir in both cheeses and the cream until smooth. Serve without delay.

TESTERS' NOTES

• The combination of sage, thyme, and nutmeg gives the soup a more savory finish than some deli incarnations. (Plus, there's no added sugar.)

• The onion should be in 1-inch bits so that it doesn't melt into the soup.

• Make sure you whisk the flour into the rendered sausage fat, then whisk in the broth until the flour dissolves. You need to get the mixture as smooth as possible for a silky finish. If you don't whisk enough, some of the flour may fall out of suspension and burn on the bottom of the pot.

• We prefer mild Italian (pork) sausage, but you can substitute spicy sausage, smoked sausage, even turkey sausage. Just don't choose any sausage that's so highly flavored that it'll compete with the other ingredients.

LAMB SOUP WITH TOMATOES, CINNAMON, AND DILL

EFFORT: **A LITTLE** • PRESSURE: **HIGH** • TIME UNDER PRESSURE:
10 OR 15 MINUTES • RELEASE: **MODIFIED NATURAL** • SERVES: **6**

**1 pound boneless leg of lamb, trimmed of
fat and cut into 1-inch pieces**

1 teaspoon ground coriander

$1/2$ teaspoon ground cinnamon

$1/2$ teaspoon salt

2 tablespoons olive oil

**1 cup fresh pearl onions, peeled, or frozen
onions, thawed**

**One 28-ounce can diced tomatoes (about
$3^1/2$ cups)**

2 cups chicken broth

**2 tablespoons loosely packed minced dill
fronds**

$1/4$ cup heavy cream

1 Toss the lamb, coriander, cinnamon, and salt in a large bowl until the spices thoroughly coat the meat.

2 Heat the oil in a 6-quart stovetop pressure cooker set over medium heat or in a 6-quart electric pressure cooker set on the browning mode. Add the pearl onions and cook, stirring often, until lightly browned, about 4 minutes.

3 Scrape the meat and every last bit of the spices into the cooker. Stir until fragrant, less than a minute. Add the tomatoes, broth, and dill.

4 Lock the lid onto the pot.

STOVETOP: Raise the heat to high and bring the pot to high pressure (15 psi). Once this pressure has been reached, reduce the heat as much as possible while maintaining this pressure. Cook for 10 minutes.

·····················OR·····················

ELECTRIC: Set the machine to cook at high pressure (9–11 psi). Set the machine's timer to cook at high pressure for 15 minutes.

5 Reduce the pressure.

STOVETOP: Set the pot off the heat for 10 minutes.
·····················OR·····················
ELECTRIC: Turn off the machine or unplug it; set aside for 12 minutes.

After 10 or 12 minutes, use the quick-release method to drop the pressure fully back to normal.

6 Unlock and open the pot; stir in the cream. Set aside for a couple of minutes to warm through, then stir again before serving.

TESTERS' NOTES
• This warming soup is quite savory, mostly from the way the dill and cinnamon balance (and even mitigate) the natural sweetness of the tomatoes.
• You can substitute light cream or half-and-half for the heavy cream.

LAMB, WHITE BEAN, AND DRIED CRANBERRY SOUP

EFFORT: **A LOT** · PRESSURE: **HIGH** · TIME UNDER PRESSURE: **40 OR 60 MINUTES** · RELEASE: **QUICK, THEN QUICK AGAIN** · SERVES: **6**

2 cups dried great northern or cannellini beans

1 lamb shank (12–16 ounces)

6 cups (1½ quarts) chicken broth

1 large yellow onion, chopped

2 medium carrots, cut into ½-inch slices

1 medium celeriac (about 14 ounces), peeled and diced

¼ cup dried cranberries

1 teaspoon dried sage

¼ teaspoon red pepper flakes

2 bay leaves

2 tablespoons tomato paste

½ teaspoon salt

½ teaspoon ground black pepper

1 Soak the beans in a large bowl of water on the counter for at least 12 hours or up to 16 hours.

2 Place the shank in a 6-quart stovetop or electric pressure cooker. Pour in the broth.

3 Lock the lid onto the pot.

STOVETOP: Set the pot over high heat and bring it to high pressure (15 psi). Once this pressure has been reached, reduce the heat as much as possible while maintaining this pressure. Cook for 30 minutes.

···················· **OR** ····················

ELECTRIC: Set the machine to cook at high pressure (9–11 psi). Set the machine's timer to cook at high pressure for 45 minutes.

4 Use the quick-release method to bring the pot's pressure to normal.

5 Unlock and open the cooker. Stir in the onion, carrots, celeriac, cranberries, sage, red pepper flakes, and bay leaves. Drain the beans in a colander set in the sink; add them to the pot as well.

6 Lock the lid back onto the cooker.

STOVETOP: Set the pot back over high heat and bring it back to high pressure (15 psi). Once this pressure has been reached, lower the heat as much as possible while maintaining this pressure. Cook for 10 minutes.

···················· **OR** ····················

ELECTRIC: Set the machine to cook once again at high pressure (9–11 psi). Set the machine's timer to cook at high pressure for 15 minutes.

7 Use the quick-release method to drop the pot's pressure to normal.

8 Unlock and remove the lid. Transfer the shank to a cutting board. Cool for a couple of minutes. Remove and chop the meat, discarding the bone and any tough cartilage. Stir the meat back into the soup.

9 Set the stovetop cooker over medium heat or turn the electric cooker to its browning function. Bring the soup to a simmer. Stir in the tomato paste until dissolved, as well as the salt and pepper. Simmer, stirring occasionally, for 5 minutes to toast the tomato paste and incorporate it into the soup. Discard the bay leaves and serve.

TESTERS' NOTES

• This soup has a fairly innovative palette that you might not have tried before: slightly sour dried cranberries, earthy celery root, sweet carrots, and a little bit of heat from the red pepper flakes. It all adds up to a new take on comfort food.

- Celeriac (celery root) can be tough to peel. Use a paring knife rather than a vegetable peeler, to get every last thread and brown bit off the vegetable. If you're going to prep it more than 10 minutes in advance of cooking, drop the pieces in a big bowl of water so they don't turn brown.
- The beans will be firm in texture. If you like softer beans, turn off the machine and give the soup 10 minutes at a natural release before using the quick release to bring the pressure back to normal. However, be warned: the other vegetables will be softer, too.

GARLICKY LAMB SHANK SOUP

EFFORT: **A LOT** • PRESSURE: **HIGH** • TIME UNDER PRESSURE: **33 OR 50 MINUTES** • RELEASE: **NATURAL, THEN QUICK** • SERVES: **6**

6 cups (1$\frac{1}{2}$ quarts) chicken broth

1 lamb shank (12–16 ounces)

2 medium garlic heads, broken into individual cloves and peeled

1 large yellow onion, quartered

4 medium celery stalks, chopped

12 fresh sage sprigs

4 fresh thyme sprigs

1 teaspoon salt

$\frac{1}{2}$ teaspoon ground black pepper

6 medium carrots, thinly sliced

Up to 1 tablespoon fresh lemon juice

1 Pour the broth into a 6-quart stovetop or electric pressure cooker. Add the lamb, garlic, onion, celery, sage, thyme, salt, and pepper.

2 Lock the lid onto the pot.

STOVETOP: Set the pot over high heat and bring to high pressure (15 psi). Once this pressure has been reached, reduce the heat as much as possible while maintaining this pressure. Cook for 30 minutes.

······················· **OR** ·······················
ELECTRIC: Set the machine to cook at high pressure (9–11 psi). Set the machine's timer to cook at high pressure for 45 minutes.

3 Reduce the pressure.

STOVETOP: Set the pot off the heat and let its pressure come back to normal naturally, about 30 minutes.

······················· **OR** ·······················
ELECTRIC: Turn off the machine or unplug it so it doesn't flip to its keep-warm setting. Allow its pressure to fall to normal naturally, 30 to 40 minutes.

4 Unlock and remove the lid. Transfer the shank to a cutting board. Cool for a few minutes, then shred the meat off the bone. Discard the bone and any cartilage; chop the meat and set aside.

5 Pour the soup through a colander and into a large bowl, straining out all the solids. Pour the strained soup into the cooker and add the carrots.

6 Lock the lid onto the pot.

STOVETOP: Set the pot again over high heat and bring it back to high pressure (15 psi). Immediately reduce the heat as much as possible while maintaining this pressure. Cook for 3 minutes.

······················· **OR** ·······················
ELECTRIC: Set the machine to cook one more time at high pressure (9–11 psi). Set the machine's timer to cook at this pressure for 5 minutes.

7 Use the quick-release method to drop the pot's pressure back to normal.

8 Unlock and open the pot. Stir in the chopped meat and lemon juice. Cover loosely and set aside for a few minutes to warm through before serving.

(continued)

• If you're a garlic lover, you've come to the right recipe. Those cloves will get soft over the long cooking. Fish them out and spread them like butter onto bread at the table.
• Lamb shanks have a more pronounced flavor than the meat on the leg. As such, they need to be balanced with bolder tastes. Yes, it's more work to take the meat off the bones, chop it, and add it back, but the shank delivers the flavor of the bone right into the soup and so give a very hearty, satisfying finish.
• This soup is actually a two-step ordeal, mostly to keep the carrots moderately crunchy in the soup, a good match against the soft, sweet lamb.

CHICKEN SOUP

EFFORT: **NOT MUCH** • PRESSURE: **HIGH** • TIME UNDER PRESSURE: **10 OR 15 MINUTES** • RELEASE: **QUICK** • SERVES: **4**

2 tablespoons unsalted butter

1 large yellow onion, chopped

2 medium carrots, diced

2 medium celery stalks, thinly sliced

1 pound boneless and skinless chicken breasts, diced

1/2 teaspoon dried dill

1/2 teaspoon dried thyme

1/2 teaspoon salt

1/2 teaspoon ground black pepper

6 cups chicken broth

1 Melt the butter in a 6-quart stovetop pressure cooker set over medium heat or in a 6-quart electric pressure cooker turned to the browning function. Add the onion, carrots, and celery; cook, stirring often, for 4 minutes, until the onion has softened.

2 Stir in the chicken, dill, thyme, salt, and pepper; cook for 1 minute, stirring all the while. Pour in the broth.

3 Lock the lid onto the pot.

STOVETOP: Raise the heat to high and bring the pot to high pressure (15 psi). Once this pressure has been reached, reduce the heat as much as you can while maintaining this pressure. Cook for 10 minutes.

·····**OR**·····

ELECTRIC: Set the machine to cook at high pressure (9–11 psi). Set the machine's timer to cook at high pressure for 15 minutes.

4 Use the quick-release method to bring the pot's pressure back to normal.

5 Unlock and open the pot; stir well.

• Because of the way the pressure cooker holds essential moisture inside meat, we can actually use white-meat chicken to make a tasty, fast, and healthy version of chicken soup. (We wouldn't dare do that at a stovetop simmer!)
• Dice the carrots and chicken into 1/4-inch pieces so you can get both on a spoon at once.
• For a brighter finish, stir in 1 tablespoon white wine vinegar or fresh lemon juice after cooking.
• You can swap in olive oil for the butter, and dried oregano or rosemary for the dill.

CHICKEN NOODLE SOUP

EFFORT: **A LITTLE** • PRESSURE: **HIGH** • TIME UNDER PRESSURE:
15 OR 22 MINUTES • RELEASE: **QUICK, THEN QUICK AGAIN** •
SERVES: **4 TO 6**

2 tablespoons olive oil

2 large bone-in skinless chicken breasts
   (about 1 pound each)

6 cups chicken broth

1 medium red onion, halved

2 medium carrots

1/2 teaspoon salt

2 fresh thyme sprigs

2 fresh sage sprigs

2 medium garlic cloves, peeled

4 ounces wide egg noodles

1 tablespoon minced fresh dill fronds

1 Heat the oil in a 6-quart stovetop pressure cooker set over medium heat or in a 6-quart electric pressure cooker turned to the browning function. Add the chicken and brown well on both sides, about 4 minutes in all, turning once.

2 Pour in the broth; add the onion, carrots, salt, thyme, sage, and garlic.

3 Lock the lid onto the cooker.

STOVETOP: Raise the heat to high and bring the pot to high pressure (15 psi). Once this pressure has been reached, reduce the heat as much as possible while keeping this pressure constant. Cook for 12 minutes.

································ OR ································

ELECTRIC: Set the machine to cook at high pressure (9–11 psi). Set the machine's timer to cook at high pressure for 18 minutes.

4 Use the quick-release method to return the pot's pressure to normal.

5 Unlock and open the cooker. Transfer the chicken to a cutting board. Cool for a few minutes, then debone and chop the meat into bite-size bits; set aside.

6 Discard the onion, carrots, thyme, sage, and garlic from the pot. Stir in the noodles and dill. Lock the lid onto the cooker.

STOVETOP: Set the pot back over high heat and bring it to high pressure (15 psi). Once this pressure has been reached, lower the heat as much as possible while maintaining this pressure. Cook for 3 minutes.

································ OR ································

ELECTRIC: Set the machine to cook once again at high pressure (9–11 psi). Set the machine's timer to cook at high pressure for 4 minutes.

7 Use the quick-release method to return the pot's pressure to normal.

8 Unlock and open the cooker. Stir in the chopped chicken. Cover loosely and set aside for a couple of minutes to warm through.

TESTERS' NOTES

• Here's the classic soup with a lighter finish because we can use white-meat chicken rather than the standard (and fattier) dark meat.

• For a brighter flavor, stir in 1 tablespoon fresh lemon juice just before serving.

• Substitute an equivalent amount of dried no-yolk noodles but reduce the second cooking to 3 minutes for a stovetop model or 4 minutes for an electric one.

COCONUT CHICKEN SOUP

EFFORT: **NOT MUCH** • PRESSURE: **HIGH** • TIME UNDER PRESSURE: **5 OR 8 MINUTES** • RELEASE: **QUICK** • SERVES: **6**

2 boneless skinless chicken breasts (about 6 ounces each), thinly sliced

1 medium red bell pepper, stemmed, cored, and chopped

4 cups (1 quart) chicken broth

1¹⁄₂ cups coconut milk

One 15-ounce can straw mushrooms, drained and rinsed

One 8-ounce can sliced bamboo shoots, drained and rinsed

Up to 1 serrano chile, stemmed and thinly sliced

1 tablespoon minced fresh ginger

¹⁄₂ teaspoon salt

¹⁄₄ cup fresh lime juice

2 teaspoons sugar

¹⁄₄ cup loosely packed fresh cilantro leaves, chopped

1 Stir the chicken, bell pepper, broth, coconut milk, mushrooms, bamboo shoots, chile, ginger, and salt in a 6-quart stovetop pressure cooker or electric pressure cooker.

2 Lock the lid onto the pot.

STOVETOP: Set the pot over high heat and bring it to high pressure (15 psi). Once this pressure has been reached, reduce the heat as much as possible while maintaining this pressure. Cook for 5 minutes.

·····················OR·····················

ELECTRIC: Set the machine to cook at high pressure (9–11 psi). Set the machine's timer to cook at high pressure for 8 minutes.

3 Use the quick-release method to bring the pot's pressure back to normal.

4 Unlock and open the pot. Set the stovetop model over medium heat or turn the electric one to its browning function. Bring the soup to a simmer, then stir in the lime juice and sugar. Simmer for 1 minute, stirring frequently. Stir in the cilantro just before serving.

TESTERS' NOTES
• Here's an Asian version of chicken soup, fiery and aromatic. Tame the burn by seeding those chile rings at will.
• If you want to pump up your foodie creds, substitute galangal for the ginger and grated palm sugar for the white sugar.
• For a richer flavor, add up to 1 tablespoon fish sauce in step 1. If so, omit the salt.

Serve It Up! Offer on the side bowls of short-grain white rice (sushi rice), tossed with a little toasted sesame oil and minced scallion.

CHICKEN AND LIME SOUP

EFFORT: **A LITTLE** • PRESSURE: **HIGH** • TIME UNDER PRESSURE: **12 OR 18 MINUTES** • RELEASE: **QUICK** • SERVES: **4**

1 tablespoon olive oil

2 large bone-in, skin-on chicken breasts (about 1 pound each)

1 teaspoon salt

1 teaspoon ground black pepper

1 large yellow onion, chopped

Up to 2 tablespoons minced garlic

Up to 1 medium fresh jalapeño chile, stemmed and minced

1 tablespoon minced oregano leaves

6 cups (1½ quarts) chicken broth

¼ cup fresh lime juice

2 ripe Hass avocados, halved, pitted, peeled, and diced

1 Heat the oil in a 6-quart stovetop pressure cooker set over medium heat or in a 6-quart electric pressure cooker turned to the browning function. Season the chicken with the salt and pepper; brown on both sides, turning once, about 4 minutes. Transfer to a large bowl.

2 Add the onion; cook, stirring often, until translucent, about 4 minutes. Add the garlic, jalapeño, and oregano; cook for about 1 minute, until aromatic, stirring all the while.

3 Pour in the broth; scrape up any browned bits on the bottom of the cooker. Return the chicken and any juices in its bowl to the cooker.

4 Lock the lid onto the pot.

STOVETOP: Raise the heat to high and bring the pot to high pressure (15 psi). Once this pressure has been reached, reduce the heat as much as possible while maintaining this pressure. Cook for 12 minutes.

·············· **OR** ··············

ELECTRIC: Set the machine to cook at high pressure (9–11 psi). Set the machine's timer to cook at high pressure for 18 minutes.

5 Use the quick-release method to drop the pot's pressure to normal.

6 Unlock and open the pot. Transfer the chicken to a large cutting board. Cool for a couple of minutes, then skin the breasts. (Discard the skins.) Debone the meat and chop it into small bits. Stir the meat, lime juice, and avocados into the soup; set aside for 1 minute to warm through.

TESTERS' NOTES

• We've adapted this soup, a favorite in the Yucatán peninsula of Mexico, to the North American supermarket so it can be a spiky, hot, and sour meal in the spring or summer.

• Seed the chile if you're worried about the heat—or use less, perhaps just a quarter of it.

• The avocados will soften slightly as they warm through. If you want a firmer texture, put them into the bowls and ladle the soup over them.

• We used the skin here for a big hit of flavor in the soup against the lime juice, though we remove it after cooking. For a real treat, fry the cooked skin until crisp in a little oil in a skillet set over medium-high heat, then shard it over the servings, chicharonnes-style.

Serve It Up! Crumble tortilla chips over each helping.

ROASTED TURKEY SOUP

EFFORT: **NOT MUCH** • PRESSURE: **HIGH** • TIME UNDER PRESSURE: **15 OR 22 MINUTES** • RELEASE: **QUICK** • SERVES: **6**

6 cups (1½ quarts) chicken broth

2 roasted turkey legs, or 1 roasted turkey leg and 1 roasted bone-in turkey thigh

1 medium yellow onion, chopped

2 large parsnips, peeled and chopped

1 large turnip (about 8 ounces), peeled and chopped

1 tablespoon finely chopped sage leaves

2 teaspoons packed fresh thyme leaves

½ teaspoon salt

½ teaspoon ground black pepper

1 bay leaf

1 Mix everything in a 6-quart stovetop or electric pressure cooker.

(continued)

2 Lock the lid onto the pot.

STOVETOP: Set the pot over high heat and bring to high pressure (15 psi). Once this pressure has been reached, reduce the heat as much as possible while maintaining this pressure. Cook for 15 minutes.

······················· **OR** ·······················

ELECTRIC: Set the machine to cook at high pressure (9–11 psi). Set the machine's timer to cook at high pressure for 22 minutes.

3 Use the quick-release method to bring the pot's pressure back to normal.

4 Unlock and open the cooker. Discard the bay leaf. Transfer the turkey parts to a large cutting board; cool for a few minutes. Debone and chop the meat, then stir it back into the soup before serving.

TESTERS' NOTES

• If you've got leftover turkey from the holidays, here's the soup for you! If not, look for roasted turkey legs at your supermarket's prepared food counter.
• Turkey legs have more than just a bone: there's plenty of hard cartilage and tendon, too. You'll need to scrape the meat off these bits before chopping it into small pieces.
• Skin on or off? It's a matter of taste. If the skin has a rub or a glaze on it, remove it before putting the legs or thighs in the cooker in step 1 so that those flavors do not complicate the recipe. Otherwise, skin the meat before chopping it in step 4. There's no need to stir it back into the soup after cooking.
• You can substitute 1 cup peeled and chopped salsify, rutabaga (milder), or kohlrabi (sweeter) for the turnip.

TURKEY AND RICE SOUP WITH LEMON AND SAGE

EFFORT: **NOT MUCH** • PRESSURE: **HIGH** • TIME UNDER PRESSURE: **12 OR 18 MINUTES** • RELEASE: **QUICK** • SERVES: **4 TO 6**

6 cups (1½ quarts) chicken broth
1 pound turkey breast cutlets, cut into 1-inch pieces
1 large yellow onion, chopped
2 medium carrots, thinly sliced
2 medium celery stalks, thinly sliced
¾ cup long-grain white rice, such as white basmati
2 tablespoons loosely packed fresh sage leaves, chopped
2 teaspoons minced garlic
2 teaspoons finely grated lemon zest
1 teaspoon ground black pepper
½ teaspoon salt
1 tablespoon fresh lemon juice

1 Combine the broth, turkey, onion, carrots, celery, rice, sage, garlic, lemon zest, pepper, and salt in a 6-quart stovetop or electric pressure cooker.

2 Lock the lid onto the pot.

STOVETOP: Set the pot over high heat and bring it to high pressure (15 psi). Once this pressure has been reached, reduce the heat as low as possible while maintaining this pressure. Cook for 12 minutes.

······················· **OR** ·······················

ELECTRIC: Set the machine to cook at high pressure (9–11 psi). Set the machine's timer to cook at high pressure for 18 minutes.

3 Use the quick-release method to bring the pot's pressure back to normal.

4 Unlock and open the cooker. Stir in the lemon juice before serving.

TESTERS' NOTES
• When it's chilly, we always want to fire up a batch of this comforting soup. Best of all, we can make it with lean turkey cutlets, so it's a healthy meal in almost no time.
• The lemon in the mix sets this soup apart from the run-of-the-mill versions of turkey rice soup. Use only fresh juice for the best flavor.
• You can substitute rinsed blond (or white) quinoa for the rice.

TURKEY NOODLE SOUP

EFFORT: **A LITTLE** • PRESSURE: **HIGH** • TIME UNDER PRESSURE: **3 OR 5 MINUTES** • RELEASE: **MODIFIED NATURAL** • SERVES: **4 TO 6**

8 cups (2 quarts) chicken broth
1 pound turkey breast cutlets, diced
1 small yellow onion, diced
2 medium carrots, thinly sliced
2 medium celery stalks, thinly sliced
1 teaspoon dried sage
½ teaspoon dried thyme
½ teaspoon salt
½ teaspoon ground black pepper
4 ounces dried wide egg noodles

1 Mix the broth, turkey, onion, carrots, celery, sage, thyme, salt, and pepper in a 6-quart stovetop or electric pressure cooker. Gently stir in the egg noodles.

2 Lock the lid onto the pot.

STOVETOP: Set the pot over high heat and bring it to high pressure (15 psi). Once this pressure has been reached, reduce the heat as much as possible while maintaining this pressure. Cook for 3 minutes.

·····················OR·····················

ELECTRIC: Set the machine to cook at high pressure (9–11 psi). Set the machine's timer to cook at high pressure for 5 minutes.

3 Reduce the pressure.

STOVETOP: Set the pot off the heat for 2 minutes.

·····················OR·····················

ELECTRIC: Turn off the machine or unplug it; set aside for 3 minutes.

After 2 or 3 minutes, use the quick-release method to bring the pressure to normal.

4 Unlock and remove the lid. Stir well before serving.

TESTERS' NOTES
• This turkey noodle soup uses white-meat turkey, something you wouldn't use in a long-simmered soup for fear the meat would dry out and turn tough. The results are just as tasty but much healthier!
• We used dried herbs here because they have a slightly earthier and less bright flavor; we wanted a subtle, comforting soup without much effort at all.

CREAMY CLAM CHOWDER

EFFORT: **A LITTLE** • PRESSURE: **HIGH** • TIME UNDER PRESSURE: **5 OR 8 MINUTES** • RELEASE: **QUICK** • SERVES: **6**

1/2 cup dry vermouth

2 tablespoons all-purpose flour

1 tablespoon unsalted butter

2 thin bacon slices, chopped

1 medium yellow onion, chopped

1 medium yellow potato, such as Yukon Gold (about 8 ounces), diced

1 cup fresh corn kernels, or frozen kernels, thawed

2 tablespoons loosely packed fresh sage leaves, minced

1 teaspoon fennel seeds

1 bay leaf

3 cups chicken broth

1/2 cup bottled clam juice

Four 6 1/2-ounce cans chopped clams (do not drain)

Up to 1 cup heavy cream

1 Whisk the vermouth and flour in a small bowl until smooth; set aside.

2 Melt the butter in a 6-quart stovetop pressure cooker set over medium heat or in a 6-quart electric pressure cooker turned to the browning function. Add the bacon and fry until light brown, stirring occasionally, about 2 minutes.

3 Add the onion and potato; cook, stirring often, just until the onion begins to soften, about 2 minutes. Stir in the corn, sage, fennel seeds, and bay leaf; cook until aromatic, less than a minute.

4 Pour in the broth and clam juice; scrape up any browned bits on the bottom of the cooker. Whisk in the vermouth mixture until uniformly incorporated.

5 Lock the lid onto the pot.

STOVETOP: Raise the heat to high and bring the pot to high pressure (15 psi). Once this pressure has been reached, reduce the heat as much as possible while maintaining this pressure. Cook for 5 minutes.

·························· OR ··························

ELECTRIC: Set the machine to cook at high pressure (9–11 psi). Set the machine's timer to cook at high pressure for 8 minutes.

6 Use the quick-release method to bring the pot's pressure back to normal.

7 Unlock and open the pot. Discard the bay leaf. Set the stovetop pot over medium heat or turn the electric cooker to its browning setting. Stir in the clams, any juice in their cans, and the cream; bring to a simmer. Simmer, stirring quite frequently, for 3 to 5 minutes to thicken slightly and blend the flavors.

TESTERS' NOTES

• This New England–style chowder is stocked with vegetables as well as clams—about the way we like it. If you want a more authentic taste, substitute 3½ cups fish stock for the broth and clam juice.

• Make sure the potato is truly diced—that is, in ¼-inch bits. They need to be small to get tender.

• It's important that the flour be evenly whisked and dissolved into the vermouth so it doesn't fall out of suspension in the soup and burn in the cooker.

• Canned clams make this recipe easy, but they can be too salty and their quality may not be the best. If you can find them, look for refrigerated cans of pasteurized clam meat or even fresh-shucked clams in plastic containers on ice near the fish counter.

SHRIMP BISQUE

EFFORT: **A LOT** • PRESSURE: **HIGH** • TIME UNDER PRESSURE: **10 OR 15 MINUTES** • RELEASE: **QUICK** • SERVES: **6**

1½ pounds medium shrimp (30 per pound)
4 cups (1 quart) vegetable or chicken broth
1 large carrot, halved widthwise
1 large yellow onion, halved
2 tablespoons unsalted butter
2 tablespoons olive oil
1 large leek, white and pale green parts only, halved lengthwise, washed, and thinly sliced
Up to 1 tablespoon minced garlic
2 tablespoons all-purpose flour
1 cup heavy cream
¼ cup brandy
2 tablespoons tomato paste

1 Peel and devein the shrimp, reserving the shells. Roughly chop the shrimp and put them in a bowl; chill the chopped shrimp in the fridge.

2 Mix the shrimp shells, broth, carrot, and onion in a 6-quart stovetop or electric pressure cooker.

3 Lock the lid onto the pot.

STOVETOP: Set the pot over high heat and bring to high pressure (15 psi). Once this pressure has been reached, reduce the heat as much as possible while maintaining this pressure. Cook for 10 minutes.

························· **OR** ·························

ELECTRIC: Set the machine to cook at high pressure (9–11 psi). Set the machine's timer to cook at high pressure for 15 minutes.

4 Use the quick-release method to drop the pot's pressure to normal.

5 Unlock and remove the lid. Set a large strainer over a big bowl in the sink. Pour the contents of the cooker through the strainer, catching the soup below. Discard all the solids in the strainer; reserve the soup.

6 Melt the butter in the oil in the stovetop cooker set over medium heat or in the electric cooker turned to the browning function. Add the leek and garlic; cook, stirring often, until softened, about 2 minutes. Whisk in the flour until it coats the vegetables and mixes evenly with the fat.

7 Whisk in the reserved shrimp broth, pouring it in a slow, steady stream at first and whisking constantly to make sure the flour dissolves. Whisk in the cream, brandy, and tomato paste until smooth.

8 Bring to a full simmer, whisking all the while; cook for 2 minutes, whisking constantly. Stir in the shrimp; turn off the heat under the stovetop cooker or unplug the electric cooker. Set the lid loosely over the pot and set aside for 5 minutes, until the shrimp are pink and firm.

TESTERS' NOTES

• We couldn't imagine making a proper bisque without a pressure cooker. The appliance extracts every drop of flavor from the shrimp shells, turning the soup rich and hearty with minimal effort. After that, it's just a matter of minutes to a creamy, luscious meal.

• Look for deveined but unpeeled shrimp in the freezer section of your supermarket to make this recipe even easier. Thaw them completely—about 2 days in a bowl in the fridge before you make the soup.

• For a smoother soup, puree everything in the cooker with an immersion blender at the end of step 7.

• You can use ½ pound peeled and finely chopped shallots in lieu of the leek and garlic.

SHRIMP SOUP WITH CHICKPEAS AND ROASTED RED PEPPERS

EFFORT: **A LITTLE** • PRESSURE: **HIGH** • TIME UNDER PRESSURE: **10 OR 15 MINUTES** • RELEASE: **QUICK** • SERVES: **4 TO 6**

1 pound medium shrimp (about 30 per pound)

6 cups (1½ quarts) vegetable broth

1 small red onion, halved

1 small fennel bulb, trimmed and halved

2 fresh oregano sprigs

1 teaspoon smoked paprika

½ teaspoon ground black pepper

One 15-ounce can chickpeas, drained and rinsed (about 1¾ cups)

1 large jarred roasted red pepper or pimiento, rinsed and chopped

Up to ¼ cup loosely packed fresh parsley leaves, minced

1 Peel and devein the shrimp, reserving the shells. Roughly chop the meat, put it in a bowl, and refrigerate while you proceed.

2 Mix the broth, onion, fennel, oregano, paprika, pepper, and the shrimp shells in a 6-quart stovetop or electric pressure cooker.

3 Lock the lid onto the pot.

STOVETOP: Set the pot over high heat and bring it to high pressure (15 psi). Once this pressure has been reached, reduce the heat as much as possible while maintaining this pressure. Cook for 10 minutes.

············· OR ·············

ELECTRIC: Set the machine to cook at high pressure (9–11 psi). Set the machine's timer to cook at high pressure for 15 minutes.

4 Use the quick-release method to bring the pot's pressure back to normal.

5 Unlock and open the pot. Set a large strainer over a very big bowl in the sink; pour the contents of the cooker through the colander, catching the soup below. Discard the solids.

6 Pour the soup back into the cooker. Set the stovetop cooker over medium heat or turn the electric cooker to its browning function; bring the liquid to a full simmer. Stir in the chickpeas, red pepper, and chopped shrimp. Turn off the heat or unplug the cooker. Loosely cover the pot and set aside for 5 minutes to cook the shrimp and blend the flavors. Stir in the parsley just before serving.

TESTERS' NOTES

• This Spanish-inspired soup offers a wealth of big flavors in every spoonful. Using the shrimp shells to create the rich soup makes the meal efficient and easy.

• We used vegetable broth for a much lighter, brighter finish.

• While you needn't trim the fennel bulb as exactingly as you might for a braise or stew, you should remove most of the feathery fronds, which will come loose and float in the soup. They're perfectly edible, but they ruin the aesthetics.

• The parsley will wilt; some people find that unappealing. If you're one of those, sprinkle it onto each bowl when serving.

COCONUT SHRIMP SOUP

EFFORT: **A LOT** • PRESSURE: **HIGH** • TIME UNDER PRESSURE: **15 OR 23 MINUTES** • RELEASE: **QUICK, THEN QUICK AGAIN** • SERVES: **6**

2 pounds medium shrimp (about 30 per pound)

3 cups vegetable broth

1 cup bottled clam juice

1 small yellow onion, halved

1 medium carrot, halved widthwise

One 2-inch peeled fresh ginger piece, sliced into thin rings

One 14-ounce can diced tomatoes (about 1¾ cups)

1 cup coconut milk

3 tablespoons loosely packed fresh cilantro leaves, minced

1 tablespoon finely grated lime zest

¼ teaspoon red pepper flakes

1 Peel and devein the shrimp, reserving the shells. Chop the meat and set it in a bowl in the fridge.

2 Mix the broth, clam juice, onion, carrot, ginger, and the shrimp shells in a 6-quart stovetop or electric pressure cooker.

3 Lock the lid onto the pot.

STOVETOP: Set the pot over high heat and bring it to high pressure (15 psi). Once this pressure has been reached, reduce the heat as much as possible while maintaining this pressure. Cook for 10 minutes.

···················· **OR** ····················

ELECTRIC: Set the machine to cook at high pressure (9–11 psi). Set the machine's timer to cook at high pressure for 15 minutes.

4 Use the quick-release method to bring the pot's pressure back to normal.

5 Unlock the lid and open the cooker. Set a large strainer over a big bowl in the sink; pour the contents of the cooker into the strainer, catching the soup below. Discard all the solids; pour the soup back into the cooker. Stir in the tomatoes, coconut milk, cilantro, lime zest, and red pepper flakes.

6 Lock the lid back onto the pot.

STOVETOP: Set the pot back over high heat and bring it back to high pressure (15 psi). Once this pressure has been reached, reduce the heat as much as possible while maintaining this pressure. Cook for 5 minutes.

···················· **OR** ····················

ELECTRIC: Set the machine to cook once again at high pressure (9–11 psi). Set the machine's timer to cook at high pressure for 8 minutes.

7 Use the quick-release method to return the pot's pressure to normal.

8 Unlock and remove the lid. Stir in the shrimp. Set the lid loosely on the pot and set it aside for 5 minutes, until the shrimp are pink and firm.

TESTERS' NOTES

• This soup is a simplified version of a Southeast Asian classic. It's got bright, slightly sour flavors, laced with a minimal amount of heat.

• Rather than adding more red pepper flakes if you want more burn, pass sambal oelek at the table to swirl into the bowlfuls.

• If you'd like the flavor a little brighter, squeeze up to 2 tablespoons fresh lime juice into the pot in step 8.

• You can substitute ½ cup chicken broth and ½ cup water for the clam juice.

Serve It Up! Ladle the soup over cooked rice noodles, such as rice sticks or rice vermicelli.

NO-FUSS BOUILLABAISSE

EFFORT: **A LITTLE** • PRESSURE: **HIGH** • TIME UNDER PRESSURE:
11 OR 17 MINUTES • RELEASE: **QUICK, THEN QUICK AGAIN** •
SERVES: **6**

1 pound medium shrimp (about 30 per
    pound), peeled and deveined, the
    shells reserved

1 pound thin-fleshed fish fillets, such as
    snapper or flounder, skinned and the
    skins reserved

4 cups (1 quart) vegetable broth

1 cup bottled clam juice

3 tablespoons olive oil

3 medium shallots, thinly sliced

1 medium fennel bulb, trimmed and chopped

2 teaspoons minced garlic

1/2 pound mussels, scrubbed and debearded

One 14-ounce can diced tomatoes (about
    1 3/4 cups)

1 tablespoon packed stemmed fresh
    thyme leaves

1 tablespoon finely grated orange zest

1/4 teaspoon saffron threads

2 bay leaves

1 Put the shrimp shells, fish skin, broth, and clam juice in a 6-quart stovetop or electric pressure cooker.

2 Lock the lid onto the pot.

STOVETOP: Set the pot over high heat and bring it to high pressure (15 psi). Once this pressure has been reached, reduce the heat as much as possible while maintaining this pressure. Cook for 10 minutes.
············· **OR** ·············
ELECTRIC: Set the machine to cook at high pressure (9–11 psi). Set the machine's timer to cook at high pressure for 15 minutes.

3 Use the quick-release method to bring the pot's pressure back to normal.

4 Unlock and open the cooker. Set a large strainer over a big bowl in the sink. Pour the contents of the cooker through the strainer, catching the soup in the bowl. Discard the solids; set the fish stock aside.

5 Heat the oil in the stovetop cooker set over medium heat or in the electric cooker turned to the browning function. Add the shallots and fennel; cook, stirring often, until the shallots soften, about 3 minutes. Add the garlic and cook for less than a minute, until aromatic. Stir in the mussels, tomatoes, thyme, orange zest, saffron, and bay leaves. Pour in the prepared fish stock.

6 Lock the lid back onto the pot.

STOVETOP: Set the pot back over high heat and bring it back to high pressure (15 psi). Once this pressure has been reached, lower the heat as much as possible while maintaining this pressure. Cook for 1 minute.
············· **OR** ·············
ELECTRIC: Set the machine to cook once again at high pressure (9–11 psi). Set the machine's timer to cook at high pressure for 2 minutes.

7 Use the quick-release method to drop the pot's pressure to normal.

8 Unlock and open the cooker. Discard the bay leaves, as well as any mussels that have not opened.

9 Set the stovetop pot over medium heat or turn the electric pot to its browning function; bring the soup to a full simmer. Stir in the shrimp; lay the fish fillets on top of the hot mixture. Remove the pot from the heat or turn it off. Cover loosely and set aside for 5 minutes, until the shrimp are pink and firm and the fish fillets are cooked through.

Serve It Up! Bouillabaisse is often garnished and even thickened with rouille (French, *roo-EE*), a pepper and breadcrumb–based sauce. For a **Red Pepper Rouille**, place 1 jarred roasted red bell pepper, 2 torn-up slices of day-old bread, 2 tablespoons lemon juice, 1 teaspoon Dijon mustard, 1 teaspoon minced garlic, ½ teaspoon salt, and ½ teaspoon ground black pepper in a food processor fitted with the chopping blade. Cover and process, drizzling in ½ cup olive oil through the feed tube. Spoon the sauce on top of the servings, stirring it in as you eat the soup.

CIOPPINO

EFFORT: **A LITTLE** · PRESSURE: **HIGH** · TIME UNDER PRESSURE: **10 OR 15 MINUTES** · RELEASE: **QUICK** · SERVES: **6**

3 tablespoons olive oil

1 medium yellow onion, chopped

1 medium green bell pepper, stemmed, cored, and chopped

1 tablespoon minced garlic

4 cups (1 quart) chicken broth

One 14-ounce can diced tomatoes (about 1³/₄ cups)

1 cup rosé wine, preferably a California rosé

2 tablespoons tomato paste

2 tablespoons loosely packed fresh basil leaves, minced

1 tablespoon loosely packed fresh oregano leaves, minced

Up to ¹/₂ teaspoon red pepper flakes

2 bay leaves

1 pound skinless snapper fillets, cut into 2-inch pieces

¹/₂ pound medium shrimp (about 30 per pound), peeled and deveined

¹/₂ pound sea scallops, quartered

1 Heat the oil in a 6-quart stovetop pressure cooker set over medium heat or in a 6-quart electric pressure cooker turned to the browning function. Add the onion and bell pepper; cook, stirring occasionally, until the vegetables soften, about 4 minutes. Add the garlic and cook until aromatic, stirring all the while, less than a minute.

2 Stir in the broth, tomatoes, wine, tomato paste, basil, oregano, red pepper flakes, and bay leaves until the tomato paste dissolves and the mixture is uniform.

(continued)

3 Lock the lid onto the pot.

STOVETOP: Raise the heat to high and bring the cooker to high pressure (15 psi). Once this pressure has been reached, reduce the heat as low as possible while maintaining this pressure. Cook for 10 minutes.

·············· OR ··············

ELECTRIC: Set the machine to cook at high pressure (9–11 psi). Set the machine's timer to cook at high pressure for 15 minutes.

4 Use the quick-release method to bring the pressure in the pot to normal.

5 Unlock and open the cooker. Remove the bay leaves and gently stir in the fish, shrimp, and scallops.

6 Cover and lock the lid onto the pot; set the stovetop pot over medium-high heat until the locking mechanism activates or turn the electric pot to high and heat until the locking mechanism activates. Immediately set the stovetop pot off the heat or unplug the electric cooker. Set aside for 5 minutes. If necessary, use the quick-release method to drop the pot's pressure to normal.

7 Unlock and open the pot. Stir very gently as you dish up bowlfuls.

TESTERS' NOTES
• Here's our version of a Bay Area tradition. Believe it or not, the traditional soup's often made with ketchup. But since the pressure cooker lets us extract every drop of flavor from the tomatoes, we don't have to resort to condiments.
• Use a true rosé wine, not a white Zinfandel, which won't have enough oomph to stand up to the other flavors.
• The fish can begin to break apart rather quickly. To keep the pieces whole in the soup, treat it very gently in steps 5 and 7, stirring as little and as slowly as possible.
• You can use skinless halibut, flounder, lake bass, or perch instead of snapper.

Serve It Up! You'll need some **Garlic Bread** on the side: Combine 2 tablespoons unsalted butter, 2 tablespoons olive oil, and 1½ tablespoons minced garlic in a small skillet until warm. Slice an Italian bread in half lengthwise, then brush the cut side with the garlic mixture. Set on a large baking sheet and broil 4 to 6 inches from a heated broiler element until lightly browned and bubbling, 1 to 2 minutes.

HALIBUT AND ORZO SOUP

EFFORT: **A LOT** • PRESSURE: **QUICK, THEN QUICK AGAIN** • TIME UNDER PRESSURE: **13 OR 20 MINUTES** • RELEASE: **NATURAL** • SERVES: **4 TO 6**

5 cups vegetable broth

1 cup bottled clam juice

1 large fennel bulb, trimmed and roughly chopped

1 medium leek, white and pale green parts only, washed and halved lengthwise

3 fresh thyme sprigs

1 pound halibut fillets, skinned and skins reserved, meat cut into 2-inch pieces

³/₄ cup dried orzo

1 Mix the broth, clam juice, fennel, leek, thyme, and halibut skins (not the meat) in a 6-quart stovetop or electric pressure cooker.

2 Lock the lid onto the pot.

STOVETOP: Set the pot over high heat and bring it to high pressure (15 psi). Once this pressure has been reached, reduce the heat as low as possible while maintaining this pressure. Cook for 10 minutes.

·························· OR ··························

ELECTRIC: Set the machine to cook at high pressure (9–11 psi). Set the machine's timer to cook at high pressure for 15 minutes.

3 Use the quick-release method to return the pot's pressure to normal.

4 Unlock and open the cooker. Set a large colander over a very large bowl in the sink; pour the contents of the cooker through the colander, catching the soup in the bowl. Discard the solids. Pour the soup back into the cooker and stir in the orzo.

5 Lock the lid onto the pot.

STOVETOP: Set the pot back over high heat and bring it back to high pressure (15 psi). Once this pressure has been reached, lower the heat as much as possible while maintaining this pressure. Cook for 3 minutes.

·························· OR ··························

ELECTRIC: Set the machine to cook once again at high pressure (9–11 psi). Set the machine's timer to cook at high pressure for 5 minutes.

6 Use the quick-release method to bring the pot's pressure back to normal.

7 Unlock and open the lid, then stir in the fish pieces. Cover the pot loosely and set aside for 5 minutes, until the fish is cooked through.

TESTERS' NOTES

• This soup is quite simple: just an aromatic broth, some fish, and a little pasta. It would take hours to bring it together on the stovetop, but you can pull it off in a few minutes any night of the week.

• You may not be able to find halibut with the skin still attached. If not, you can omit the skin from the soup. It won't be as briny and rich, but it'll make a fine meal anyway.

• If you have good fish stock, take this shortcut: skip steps 1 to 4 and use 6 cups of stock in step 4.

Serve It Up! Finely grate lemon zest over the bowls before serving.

Vegetable and Grain Soups

Get ready for rice, lentil, grain, and barley soups, stocked with all the goodness you can find in your produce section—or better yet, at a farmers' market. No, we haven't banished meat from these recipes; we've just put it in its place, often as a flavoring agent for fresh vegetables. If the first half of this chapter was about sturdy, filling soups, turn to this section in the spring and summer. Yes, some soups here would be welcome on a cold day, including a well-stocked winter vegetable soup. But there are also fresh tomato soups, creamy cauliflower soups, and even three cold soups.

Because we wanted to be vegetable-centric in this section, we've written many of the recipes with either vegetable broth *or* chicken broth in the mix. Choose whichever best suits your tastes: vegetable broth for a cleaner finish or chicken broth for a richer soup.

We've also followed an innovative technique we first learned about from the consummate mad culinary scientist Nathan Myhrvold: braising vegetables in butter. Yep, it's as good as it sounds. Of course, you can't do it stovetop, pressure cooker or no—the butter will burn. Or at least, you *couldn't* until Myhrvold's amazing notion that you can add baking soda to the mix, drop the overall pH of the soup, and keep the milk solids from burning in a pressure cooker. And thus, butter becomes a braising medium. You'll never think of cauliflower soup in the same way.

There are also lots of bean soups here. A warning about pressure cookers and dried beans: both work better together when the beans have been soaked in advance. Beans have less of a chance of foaming up, clogging the valves, and causing a mess. However, that advice doesn't hold true for black-eyed peas and almost all whole grains. These should *not* be soaked in advance—for the same reason. Once soaked, they can foam up and clog the vents. So soak dried beans but almost nothing else. You'll keep the soup in the pot—and get dinner on the table without a mess.

SUMMER VEGETABLE SOUP

EFFORT: **A LITTLE** • PRESSURE: **HIGH** • TIME UNDER PRESSURE: **6 OR 9 MINUTES** • RELEASE: **QUICK, THEN QUICK AGAIN** • SERVES: **6 TO 8**

1 tablespoon unsalted butter

2 tablespoons olive oil

1 medium leek, white and pale green parts only, halved lengthwise, washed, and thinly sliced

6 cups (1½ quarts) vegetable broth

One 14-ounce can diced tomatoes (about 1¾ cups)

1 medium fennel bulb, trimmed and chopped

1 tablespoon stemmed thyme leaves

1 tablespoon finely chopped dill fronds

1 teaspoon salt

2 cups fresh corn kernels (about 2 large ears), or frozen kernels, thawed

¾ pound green beans, trimmed and cut into 1-inch pieces

1 medium zucchini, diced

1 Melt the butter in the oil in a 6-quart stovetop pressure cooker set over medium heat or in a 6-quart electric pressure cooker turned to the browning mode. Add the leek and cook, stirring often, until softened, about 3 minutes. Stir in the broth, tomatoes, fennel, thyme, dill, and salt.

2 Lock the lid onto the pot.

STOVETOP: Raise the heat to high and bring the pot to high pressure (15 psi). Once this pressure has been reached, reduce the heat as much as possible while maintaining this pressure. Cook for 5 minutes.

···············OR···············

ELECTRIC: Set the machine to cook at high pressure (9–11 psi). Set the machine's timer to cook at high pressure for 7 minutes.

3 Use the quick-release method to drop the pot's pressure to normal. Unlock and open the cooker. Stir in the corn, green beans, and zucchini.

4 Lock the lid back onto the pot.

STOVETOP: Set the pot back over high heat and bring it back to high pressure (15 psi). Once this pressure has been reached, lower the heat as much as possible while maintaining this pressure. Cook for 1 minute.

···············OR···············

ELECTRIC: Set the machine to cook once again at high pressure (9–11 psi). Set the machine's timer to cook at high pressure for 2 minutes.

5 Use the quick-release method to bring the pot's pressure back to normal.

6 Unlock and remove the lid. Stir the soup before serving.

TESTERS' NOTES

• Summer vegetables take almost no time to cook—and are too often turned to mush in a stovetop soup. The pressure cooker, however, keeps the cooking fast and efficient, leaving good texture in a soup fit for the deck on a summer evening. Even so, we had to use a two-step pressure process here; otherwise, the more delicate vegetables would disintegrate. But the effort is worth the results.

• To cut the kernels from a fresh ear of corn, husk the ear and remove the silk. Slice a small bit off one end of the ear so it will stand up straight on a cutting board. Run your knife down it to remove the kernels. If you end up with more than 2 cups, just add them to the pot.

• You can substitute 1 small yellow onion, finely chopped (stronger) or 2 medium shallots, finely chopped (more garlicky) for the leek.

Serve It Up! Garnish the bowls with finely chopped basil—or even with a dollop of pesto.

WINTER VEGETABLE SOUP

EFFORT: **A LITTLE** · PRESSURE: **HIGH** · TIME UNDER PRESSURE: **10 OR 15 MINUTES** · RELEASE: **QUICK** · SERVES: **6**

2 tablespoons olive oil

8 ounces baby bella or cremini mushrooms, thinly sliced

1 large yellow onion, chopped

2 medium carrots, diced

2 medium celery stalks, finely chopped

1 tablespoon loosely packed fresh rosemary leaves, minced

1 tablespoon minced garlic

$1/2$ teaspoon ground black pepper

7 cups vegetable broth

1 small butternut squash (about 1 pound), peeled, halved lengthwise, seeded, and diced

$1/4$ cup soy sauce

One 2-inch-long rind from a hunk of Parmesan cheese

2 cups washed, stemmed, and chopped curly kale (about 4 ounces)

1 tablespoon red wine vinegar

1 Heat the oil in a 6-quart stovetop pressure cooker set over medium heat or in a 6-quart electric pressure cooker turned to the browning function. Add the mushrooms and cook, stirring occasionally, until they give off their moisture and it evaporates to a thick glaze, about 5 minutes.

2 Stir in the onion, carrots, celery, rosemary, garlic, and pepper; cook for 1 minute, stirring all the while. Pour in the broth. Add the butternut squash, soy sauce, and cheese rind, then stir well.

3 Lock the lid onto the pot.

STOVETOP: Raise the heat to high and bring the pot to high pressure (15 psi). Once this pressure has been reached, reduce the heat as much as possible while maintaining this pressure. Cook for 10 minutes.

·· OR ··

ELECTRIC: Set the machine to cook at high pressure (9–11 psi). Set the machine's timer to cook at high pressure for 15 minutes.

4 Use the quick-release method to bring the pot's pressure back to normal.

5 Unlock and open the cooker. Stir in the kale.

6 Cover and lock the lid onto the pot; set it aside for 5 minutes to wilt the kale. (If necessary, use the quick-release method to bring the pressure back to normal.)

7 Unlock and remove the lid; discard the cheese rind, and stir in the vinegar just before serving.

TESTERS' NOTES

• Note the small sizes of the carrots and butternut squash. They need to be in ¼-inch bits so the other vegetables can retain some texture as well. If you buy precut butternut squash, be sure to dice those larger chunks.

• The rind from a chunk of Parmesan will give this soup a slightly cheesy, salty flavor, a nice match for the squash and other vegetables. The rind should have about ¼ inch of cheese still adhering to it. For a real treat, scrape off that cheese after cooking and spread it on bread.

• For a creamy soup, stir up to ½ cup heavy cream into the pot with the kale. Omit the vinegar.

TOMATO SOUP

EFFORT: **NOT MUCH** • PRESSURE: **HIGH** • TIME UNDER PRESSURE:
15 OR 25 MINUTES • RELEASE: **NATURAL** • SERVES: **6**

3 tablespoons unsalted butter

1 medium yellow onion, chopped

1 medium carrot, thinly sliced

1 medium yellow potato (about 6 ounces),
    such as Yukon Gold, diced

3 pounds fresh, ripe tomatoes, preferably
    Globe or beefsteak, chopped

2 cups vegetable broth

1 tablespoon minced dill fronds

1 tablespoon loosely packed fresh
    oregano or marjoram leaves, minced

$1/2$ teaspoon salt

$1/2$ teaspoon ground black pepper

1 Melt the butter in a 6-quart stovetop pressure cooker set over medium heat or in a 6-quart electric pressure cooker turned to the browning function. Add the onion, carrot, and potato; cook, stirring often, until the onion turns translucent, about 5 minutes.

2 Stir in the tomatoes, broth, dill, oregano, salt, and pepper.

3 Lock the lid onto the pot.

STOVETOP: Raise the heat to high and bring the pot to high pressure (15 psi). Once this pressure has been reached, reduce the heat as much as possible while maintaining this pressure. Cook for 15 minutes.

························· OR ·····························

ELECTRIC: Set the machine to cook at high pressure (9–11 psi). Set the machine's timer to cook at high pressure for 25 minutes.

4 Reduce the pressure.

STOVETOP: Set the pot off the heat and let its pressure fall back to normal naturally, about 20 minutes.

························· OR ·····························

ELECTRIC: Turn off the machine or unplug it so it doesn't flip to its keep-warm setting. Allow its pressure to return to normal naturally, 25 to 30 minutes.

5 Unlock and open the cooker. Use an immersion blender right in the pot to puree the mixture into a rich, thick soup. (If you don't have an immersion blender, puree the soup in batches in a large blender, removing the knob in the center of the lid to prevent pressure build-ups but loosely covering that opening with a clean kitchen towel to prevent splatters.)

TESTERS' NOTES

• When summer is at its fullest, make several batches of this simple soup to store in containers in the freezer. When January comes, you'll know why.

• The fresh tomatoes provide most of the liquid here. There's only one way to tell if they're tasty: smell the end where the stem would have attached. It should have that characteristic, sweet if slightly acrid, earthy aroma.

• We like plenty of herbs in our tomato soup, but you could nix one (or even both) for a much cleaner, softer palette. There's no garlic here because we feel it compromises the summery sweetness of the tomatoes.

• For a creamy soup, add up to $1/3$ cup heavy cream in step 5 before pureeing the soup. (Of course, you don't need to puree the soup. It's great chunky, too.)

Serve It Up! Go retro and float a pat of butter on each serving.

CREAMY TOMATO BASIL SOUP

EFFORT: **NOT MUCH** • PRESSURE: **HIGH** • TIME UNDER PRESSURE: **15 OR 25 MINUTES** • RELEASE: **NATURAL** • SERVES: **6**

4 pounds fresh, ripe tomatoes, preferably Globe or beefsteak, chopped

1 medium red onion, chopped

1 medium white potato (about 8 ounces), chopped

2 medium garlic cloves

1 tablespoon dried basil

1 teaspoon salt

$^1/_2$ teaspoon celery seeds

Up to $^1/_2$ teaspoon grated nutmeg

$^2/_3$ cup heavy cream

$^1/_4$ cup packed fresh basil leaves

1 Mix the tomatoes, onion, potato, garlic, dried basil, salt, celery seeds, and nutmeg with 1 cup water in a 6-quart stovetop or electric pressure cooker.

2 Lock the lid onto the pot.

STOVETOP: Set the pot over high heat and bring it to high pressure (15 psi). Once this pressure has been reached, reduce the heat as much as possible while maintaining this pressure. Cook for 15 minutes.

·····OR·····

ELECTRIC: Set the machine to cook at high pressure (9–11 psi). Set the machine's timer to cook at high pressure for 25 minutes.

3 Reduce the pressure.

STOVETOP: Set the pot off the heat and let its pressure come back to normal naturally, about 20 minutes.

·····OR·····

ELECTRIC: Turn off the machine or unplug it so it doesn't flip to its keep-warm setting. Let its pressure fall back to normal naturally, 20 to 30 minutes.

4 Unlock and open the pot. Stir in the cream and basil. Use an immersion blender right in the cooker to puree the soup—or use a standard blender but work in batches and remove the center knob from the lid to prevent pressure explosions; cover the opening with a clean kitchen towel to prevent splatters.

TESTERS' NOTES

• Here's a restaurant favorite. Use their secret weapon—a pressure cooker—and yours will be just as tasty.

• We've used two types of basil. The dried basil will offer a slightly savory, earthy flavor while the fresh basil will perk the soup up with summery goodness.

• If you're not used to the flavor of tomatoes and nutmeg—a favorite with us—you should hold back a bit on the nutmeg the first time you make the soup. Or omit it and grate a little over each serving as a garnish.

• You can use light cream or half-and-half instead of the heavy cream.

TOMATO RICE SOUP

EFFORT: **NOT MUCH** • PRESSURE: **HIGH** • TIME UNDER PRESSURE: **10 OR 15 MINUTES** • RELEASE: **QUICK** • SERVES: **4**

$2^1/_2$ pounds fresh, ripe tomatoes, preferably Globe or Roma, chopped

2 cups vegetable or chicken broth

$^1/_2$ cup medium-grain white rice, such as white Arborio

1 tablespoon stemmed fresh thyme leaves

1 tablespoon sugar

1 tablespoon fresh lemon juice

$^1/_2$ teaspoon salt

1 Mix everything in a 6-quart stovetop or electric pressure cooker.

2 Lock the lid onto the pot.

STOVETOP: Set the pot over high heat and bring it to high pressure (15 psi). The moment this pressure is reached, reduce the heat as much as you can while nonetheless keeping the pressure constant. Cook for 10 minutes.

·········· **OR** ··········

ELECTRIC: Set the machine to cook at high pressure (9–11 psi). Set the machine's timer to cook at high pressure for 15 minutes.

3 Use the quick-release method to bring the pot's pressure back to normal.

4 Unlock and open the pot; stir the soup before serving. If desired, crush some of the tomatoes and rice against the inside wall of the pot and then stir again to thicken the soup.

TESTERS' NOTES
• This tomato soup is perhaps best made in the winter when the only tomatoes worth eating are the small Roma (plum) tomatoes. They'll break down into a thick soup with flavors that won't compete with the other ingredients.
• The medium-grain rice will be slightly chewier than long-grain rice and so a better contrast to the soft tomatoes. Look for it next to the more standard long-grain rice.
• Vegetable broth gives the soup a cleaner flavor; chicken broth, more heft.
• For a richer soup, drizzle up to 2 tablespoons olive oil over the ingredients before locking on the lid and cooking the soup.

Serve It Up! Crumble a bit of blue cheese over each helping.

BROCCOLI CHEDDAR SOUP

EFFORT: **A LITTLE** • PRESSURE: **HIGH** • TIME UNDER PRESSURE: **10 OR 15 MINUTES** • RELEASE: **QUICK** • SERVES: **6**

4 tablespoons (1/2 stick) unsalted butter,
  cut into small bits
6 cups 1-inch broccoli florets
1 teaspoon salt
1/4 teaspoon baking soda
3 cups vegetable or chicken broth
2 tablespoons loosely packed basil leaves
1/2 cup finely grated Cheddar cheese
  (about 2 ounces)
1/4 cup heavy cream

1 Melt the butter in a 6-quart stovetop pressure cooker set over medium heat or in a 6-quart electric pressure cooker turned to the browning function. Stir in the broccoli, salt, and baking soda along with 1/2 cup water.

2 Lock the lid onto the pot.

STOVETOP: Raise the heat to high and bring the cooker to high pressure (15 psi). Once this pressure has been reached, lower the heat as much as you can while keeping this pressure constant. Cook for 10 minutes.

·········· **OR** ··········

ELECTRIC: Set the machine to cook at high pressure (9–11 psi). Set the machine's timer to cook at high pressure for 15 minutes.

3 Use the quick-release method to drop the pot's pressure to normal.

4 Unlock and remove the lid. Stir in the broth and basil. Use an immersion blender to puree the soup right in the cooker (or work in batches to puree the soup in a blender,

(continued)

removing the knob in the blender's lid but covering the opening with a clean kitchen towel). Transfer the puree back to the cooker.

5 Set the stovetop model over medium heat or turn the electric one to its browning function. Stir in the cheese and cream; bring to a simmer, stirring almost constantly. Cook and stir for 1 minute before serving.

TESTERS' NOTES

• Here's where high-school chemistry comes in handy: by stirring in that baking soda, you can use butter as the cooking "liquid" because the higher pH won't let the milk solids burn under pressure.
• Cut the butter into bits so none of it has a chance to brown before it's melted. You don't want any bitter or nutty notes from browned butter in this classic soup.
• You can substitute Colby, Jack, or American cheese for the Cheddar, or light cream or half-and-half for the heavy cream.

CREAM OF CARROT SOUP

EFFORT: **A LITTLE** • PRESSURE: **HIGH** • TIME UNDER PRESSURE: **10 OR 15 MINUTES** • RELEASE: **QUICK** • SERVES: **6**

8 tablespoons (1 stick) unsalted butter, cut into small bits

1¼ pounds carrots, peeled and cut into 2-inch pieces

1 teaspoon salt

¼ teaspoon baking soda

2½ cups vegetable or chicken broth

½ cup heavy cream

Up to 2 tablespoons minced fresh dill fronds

1 Melt the butter in a 6-quart stovetop pressure cooker set over medium heat or in a 6-quart electric pressure cooker turned to the browning function. Stir in the carrots, salt, and baking soda along with ¼ cup water.

2 Lock the lid onto the pot.

STOVETOP: Raise the heat to high and bring the pot to high pressure (15 psi). Once this pressure has been reached, reduce the heat as much as possible while maintaining this pressure. Cook for 10 minutes.

···················· **OR** ····················

ELECTRIC: Set the machine to cook at high pressure (9–11 psi). Set the machine's timer to cook at high pressure for 15 minutes.

3 Use the quick-release method to bring the pot's pressure back to normal.

4 Unlock and open the pot. Stir in the broth, cream, and dill. Use an immersion blender to puree the soup right in the cooker; or ladle the soup in batches into a standard blender, remove the center knob from the lid, cover the hole with a clean kitchen towel, and blend until smooth.

TESTERS' NOTES

• We like a lot of dill in our carrot soup, particularly because it's a summery accent to carrots poached directly in butter and pureed into a smooth, luscious soup.
• This soup freezes exceptionally well, particularly in small containers that you can reheat for lunch.

Serve It Up! Serve the soup warm, or chill it and offer it cold. For an easy lunch dish, lay shrimp or lump crabmeat on each serving.

CARROT GINGER SOUP

EFFORT: **A LITTLE** · PRESSURE: **HIGH** · TIME UNDER PRESSURE:
7 OR 10 MINUTES · RELEASE: **NATURAL** · SERVES: **6**

**1½ pounds carrots, peeled and chopped
(about 10 medium)**

3½ cups vegetable or chicken broth

**3 tablespoons chopped crystallized
(candied) ginger**

½ cup dry vermouth

2 tablespoons all-purpose flour

1 cup plain regular or low-fat yogurt

½ teaspoon salt

½ teaspoon ground black pepper

1 Mix the carrots, broth, and ginger in a
6-quart stovetop or electric pressure cooker.
Whisk the vermouth and flour in a small bowl
until smooth, then stir the mixture into the
cooker.

2 Lock the lid onto the pot.

STOVETOP: Set the pot over high heat and bring
it to high pressure (15 psi). Once this pressure has
been reached, reduce the heat as much as possible while maintaining this pressure. Cook for
7 minutes.

·················· **OR** ··················

ELECTRIC: Set the machine to cook at high pressure (9–11 psi). Set the machine's timer to cook at
high pressure for 10 minutes.

3 Reduce the pressure.

STOVETOP: Set the pot off the heat and let its
pressure fall back to normal naturally, about
18 minutes.

·················· **OR** ··················

ELECTRIC: Turn off the machine or unplug it so it
doesn't flip to its keep-warm setting. Let its pressure return to normal naturally, 20 to 25 minutes.

4 Unlock and open the pot. Stir in the
yogurt, salt, and pepper. Use an immersion blender to puree the soup right in the
cooker—or working in batches, puree the
soup in a blender, removing the center knob
in the lid and covering the hole with a clean
kitchen towel.

TESTERS' NOTES

• Crystallized (candied) ginger gives this soup a sweet
pop, a little less intense than fresh ginger. Look for crystallized ginger in the spice rack.

• Dry vermouth will give the soup a slightly savory, even
herbaceous edge, certainly less sweet than even the driest
white wine. Best of all, leftover dry vermouth can be re-
stoppered and kept in a cool, dark place for months. If you
want to substitute wine, choose a very dry Chardonnay.

• Make sure the flour is whisked into the vermouth until
the flour has dissolved so no bits of it burn on the bottom
of the cooker under pressure.

MUSHROOM SHALLOT SOUP

EFFORT: **A LITTLE** · PRESSURE: **HIGH** · TIME UNDER PRESSURE:
10 OR 15 MINUTES · RELEASE: **QUICK** · SERVES: **6**

8 tablespoons (1 stick) unsalted butter

3 large shallots, thinly sliced

**1 pound baby bella or cremini
mushrooms, thinly sliced**

1 teaspoon salt

¼ teaspoon baking soda

2½ cups vegetable or chicken broth

½ cup heavy cream

**2 tablespoons loosely packed fresh
tarragon leaves, minced**

½ teaspoon ground black pepper

1 Cut 4 tablespoons (½ stick) of the butter
into small bits and melt them in a 6-quart
stovetop pressure cooker set over medium
heat or in a 6-quart electric pressure cooker
turned to the browning function. Add the
shallot and cook, stirring often, until softened, about 2 minutes.

2 Add the mushrooms and cook, stirring occasionally, until they give off their liquid and
it evaporates to a thick glaze, about 5 minutes. Add the remaining 4 tablespoons butter
and melt it into the mixture, stirring often.
Stir in the salt and baking soda along with
¼ cup water.

3 Lock the lid onto the pot.

STOVETOP: Raise the heat to high and bring it to
high pressure (15 psi). Once this pressure has been
reached, reduce the heat as much as possible while
maintaining this pressure. Cook for 10 minutes.

·· **OR** ··
ELECTRIC: Set the machine to cook at high pres-
sure (9–11 psi). Set the machine's timer to cook at
high pressure for 15 minutes.

4 Use the quick-release method to bring the
pot's pressure back to normal.

5 Unlock and remove the lid. Stir in the
broth, cream, tarragon, and pepper. Puree
the soup with an immersion blender right
in the pot—or working in batches, use a
blender but remove the center knob from
the lid and cover the opening with a clean
kitchen towel.

TESTERS' NOTES

• Consider this soup the best cream of mushroom you've
ever tasted. The tarragon and cream give it a French bistro
feel. However, you can also substitute fresh thyme leaves
for the tarragon.

• It's important that the mushrooms "dry out" so their
excess moisture doesn't waterlog the soup. Cook and stir
until you can drag a wooden spoon through the liquid in
the cooker and the line you make does not instantly flow
back into place.

• You can use light cream or half-and-half in lieu of the
heavy cream.

Serve It Up! Sprinkle garlic croutons over
each serving.

BUTTERY CAULIFLOWER SOUP

EFFORT: **A LITTLE** • PRESSURE: **HIGH** • TIME UNDER PRESSURE: **10 OR 15 MINUTES** • RELEASE: **QUICK** • SERVES: **6**

**8 tablespoons (1 stick) unsalted butter,
   cut into bits**
**1 medium cauliflower head (about
   1½ pounds), cored, trimmed, and
   broken into 2-inch pieces**
1 teaspoon salt
½ teaspoon ground caraway
¼ teaspoon baking soda
2½ cups vegetable or chicken broth

1 Melt the butter in a 6-quart stovetop pressure cooker set over medium heat or in a 6-quart electric pressure cooker turned to the browning function. Stir in the cauliflower, salt, caraway, and baking soda until well combined. Pour ¼ cup water over everything.

2 Lock the lid onto the pot.

STOVETOP: Raise the heat to high and bring the pot to high pressure (15 psi). Once this pressure has been reached, reduce the heat as much as possible while maintaining this pressure. Cook for 10 minutes.

·························· **OR** ··························

ELECTRIC: Set the machine to cook at high pressure (9–11 psi). Set the machine's timer to cook at high pressure for 15 minutes.

3 Use the quick-release method to return the pot's pressure to normal.

4 Unlock and remove the lid. Stir the broth into the soup. Use an immersion blender to puree the soup in the pot—or transfer it in

batches to a blender and puree it, taking the knob out of the center of the blender's lid and covering the hole with a clean kitchen towel.

TESTERS' NOTES
• Poaching cauliflower in butter? The results are ridiculously creamy, probably the best cauliflower soup we've ever had.
• You can use precut cauliflower, available in the produce section of many supermarkets, though you'll need to slice larger chunks down to the appropriate size. You'll need about 1¼ pounds.
• If you don't want to buy ground caraway but have some caraway seeds on hand, grind them in a small food processor, spice blender, or even coffee grinder to make a powder. Clean out the coffee grinder by grinding some white rice to a powder, then wiping out the grinder with a damp paper towel. You can also substitute ¼ teaspoon dried dill and ⅛ teaspoon grated nutmeg for the ground caraway.

CAULIFLOWER AND ALMOND SOUP

EFFORT: **A LITTLE** • PRESSURE: **HIGH** • TIME UNDER PRESSURE: **10 AND 15 MINUTES** • RELEASE: **QUICK** • SERVES: **8**

3 tablespoons unsalted butter
1 large yellow onion, chopped
¼ cup sliced almonds
1 tablespoon minced garlic
1 teaspoon ground turmeric
½ teaspoon ground fenugreek
½ teaspoon ground ginger
**6 cups (1½ quarts) chicken or vegetable
   broth**
**One 3-pound cauliflower head, cored,
   trimmed, and broken into 1½-inch
   florets**
½ cup heavy cream

(continued)

1 Melt the butter in a 6-quart stovetop pressure cooker set over medium heat or in a 6-quart electric pressure cooker turned to the browning function. Add the onion and almonds; cook, stirring often, until the onion softens, about 4 minutes.

2 Stir in the garlic, turmeric, fenugreek, and ginger; cook for 1 minute, until aromatic, stirring all the while. Pour in the broth; stir in the cauliflower florets.

3 Lock the lid onto the cooker.

STOVETOP: Raise the heat to high and bring the pot to high pressure (15 psi). Once this pressure has been reached, reduce the heat as much as possible while maintaining this pressure. Cook for 10 minutes.

························· OR ·····························

ELECTRIC: Set the machine to cook at high pressure (9–11 psi). Set the machine's timer to cook at high pressure for 15 minutes.

4 Use the quick-release method to bring the pot's pressure back to normal.

5 Unlock and remove the lid, and stir in the cream. Puree the soup with an immersion blender right in the pot or in batches with a standard blender, removing the center knob and covering the hole in the lid with a clean kitchen towel.

TESTERS' NOTES

• Although we suggest pureeing this soup for a creamy texture, you can skip it and enjoy a rather chunky soup. If so, simmer the soup for a minute or so after adding the cream to make sure you take off any of its raw taste.

• The almonds will add much sweetness to the pot—and brown a bit in the butter with the onion.

• Substitute ¼ teaspoon dry mustard for the fenugreek.

Serve It Up! Garnish each bowlful with jarred diced pimientos (or roasted red peppers).

CREAM OF SWEET POTATO SOUP

EFFORT: **A LITTLE** • PRESSURE: **HIGH** • TIME UNDER PRESSURE: **10 OR 15 MINUTES** • RELEASE: **QUICK** • SERVES: **4 TO 6**

8 tablespoons (1 stick) unsalted butter, cut into small pieces

2 pounds sweet potatoes (about 2 large), peeled and cut into 2-inch pieces

1 teaspoon salt

½ teaspoon ground cinnamon

½ teaspoon ground ginger

¼ teaspoon baking soda

2½ cups chicken broth

½ cup heavy cream

1 Melt the butter in a 6-quart stovetop pressure cooker set over medium heat or in a 6-quart electric pressure cooker turned to the browning function. Stir in the sweet potatoes, salt, cinnamon, ginger, and baking soda. Pour ½ cup water over everything.

2 Lock the lid onto the cooker.

STOVETOP: Raise the heat to high and bring the pot to high pressure (15 psi). Once this pressure has been reached, reduce the heat as much as possible while maintaining this pressure. Cook for 10 minutes.

························· OR ·····························

ELECTRIC: Set the machine to cook at high pressure (9–11 psi). Set the machine's timer to cook at high pressure for 15 minutes.

3 Use the quick-release method to bring the pot's pressure back to normal.

4 Unlock and open the pot. Stir in the broth and cream. Use an immersion blender to puree the soup in the pot; or ladle the soup in batches into a blender, remove the knob from the blender's lid, cover the hole with a clean kitchen towel, and blend until smooth.

TESTERS' NOTES

• So creamy and comforting, this soup would be a great starter to a Thanksgiving meal. It also freezes well: seal in small containers and store in the freezer for up to 6 months.

• Because the baking soda allows us to poach the sweet potatoes in butter, they get ridiculously caramelized without burning. The result is a rich, satisfying, and sweet soup, perhaps more sweet potato-y than you've ever had.

• You can use light cream or half-and-half in lieu of the heavy cream.

Serve It Up! Crunchy bread is a necessity to sop up every drop.

CHUNKY POTATO AND CELERY SOUP

EFFORT: **NOT MUCH** • PRESSURE: **HIGH** • TIME UNDER PRESSURE: **10 OR 15 MINUTES** • RELEASE: **QUICK** • SERVES: **6**

6 tablespoons unsalted butter

1 pound Russet or baking potatoes, peeled and cut into 1-inch pieces

1 small celery root (celeriac—about 8 ounces), peeled and cut into 1-inch pieces

1 teaspoon salt

1/2 teaspoon celery seeds

1/2 teaspoon ground pepper, preferably white pepper

4 cups (1 quart) chicken or vegetable broth

1 Melt the butter in a 6-quart stovetop pressure cooker set over medium heat or in a 6-quart electric pressure cooker turned to the browning function. Stir in the potatoes, celery root, salt, celery seeds, and pepper; cook for 2 minutes, stirring often. Pour in the broth and stir well.

2 Lock the lid onto the cooker.

STOVETOP: Raise the heat to high and bring the pot to high pressure (15 psi). Once this pressure has been reached, reduce the heat as much as possible while maintaining this pressure. Cook for 10 minutes.

·················· **OR** ··················

ELECTRIC: Set the machine to cook at high pressure (9–11 psi). Set the machine's timer to cook at high pressure for 15 minutes.

3 Use the quick-release method to bring the pot's pressure back to normal.

4 Unlock and remove the lid; stir well before serving.

TESTERS' NOTES

• Russet potatoes have the right amount of starch to stay fluffy—almost light as air—in this comforting vegetable soup.

• You *can* puree the soup with an immersion blender or in a standard blender after cooking under pressure, but we prefer it chunkier.

• You can also add 1/2 cup heavy cream after cooking. Bring the soup to a simmer, stir it in, and cook for a minute or so, stirring often, to blend the flavors.

THAI-INSPIRED POTATO, COCONUT, AND BASIL SOUP

EFFORT: **NOT MUCH** · PRESSURE: **HIGH** · TIME UNDER PRESSURE:
10 OR 15 MINUTES · RELEASE: **QUICK** · SERVES: **6**

1 tablespoon olive oil

1 medium leek, white and pale green
    parts only, halved lengthwise, washed
    and thinly sliced

1 large red bell pepper, stemmed, cored,
    and chopped

2 teaspoons minced garlic

2 teaspoons minced fresh ginger

Up to 2 teaspoons green Thai curry paste

4 cups (1 quart) chicken broth

1³/₄ cups canned coconut milk

6 medium yellow potatoes (about
    2¹/₄ pounds), cut into ¹/₂-inch pieces

1 cup fresh corn kernels (about 1 large
    ear), or frozen kernels, thawed

¹/₄ cup packed light brown sugar

¹/₄ cup loosely packed fresh basil leaves,
    chopped

1 Heat the oil in a 6-quart stovetop pressure cooker set over medium heat or in a 6-quart electric pressure cooker turned to the browning function. Add the leek and bell pepper; cook, stirring often, until softened, about 4 minutes. Stir in the garlic, ginger, and curry paste; cook until fragrant, less than a minute.

2 Stir in the broth, coconut milk, potatoes, corn, and brown sugar.

3 Lock the lid onto the pot.

STOVETOP: Raise the heat to high and bring the pot to high pressure (15 psi). Once this pressure has been reached, reduce the heat as much as possible while maintaining this pressure. Cook for 10 minutes.

································· **OR** ·································

ELECTRIC: Set the machine to cook at high pressure (9–11 psi). Set the machine's timer to cook at high pressure for 15 minutes.

4 Use the quick-release method to bring the pot's pressure back to normal.

5 Unlock and open the cooker. Stir in the basil before serving.

TESTERS' NOTES

• This fiery soup is like a Southeast Asian chowder. Have some oyster crackers on hand for a culinary fusion experience! (For more authenticity, use grated palm sugar rather than brown sugar.)

• Thai green curry paste can be searingly hot, so use far less if you're concerned about the heat. Look for the green paste in the international aisle of almost all supermarkets.

• To make your own **green curry paste**, process two 2-inch pieces of lemongrass, 5 stemmed and halved serrano or green Thai hot chiles, 3 medium garlic cloves, 2 teaspoons black peppercorns, 2 teaspoons cumin seeds, and 1 teaspoon ground coriander in a mini food processor or a large spice grinder until you have a wet, coarse paste. Use the requisite amount here and store the rest in a sealed container in the freezer for up to 1 year.

Serve It Up! Top each helping with a handful of bean sprouts and a squeeze of lime juice.

PARSNIP SOUP WITH BUTTERY SHALLOTS AND PECANS

EFFORT: **A LITTLE** • PRESSURE: **HIGH** • TIME UNDER PRESSURE:
5 OR 8 MINUTES • RELEASE: **QUICK** • SERVES: **4 TO 6**

2 tablespoons unsalted butter

6 medium shallots, thinly sliced

1/2 cup chopped pecans

4 1/2 cups vegetable or chicken broth

3 tablespoons all-purpose flour

1 1/2 pounds parsnips, peeled and thinly sliced

1/2 teaspoon salt

1/2 teaspoon ground black pepper

1/4 teaspoon grated nutmeg

1/2 cup heavy cream

1 Melt the butter in a skillet set over medium-low heat. Add the shallots, reduce the heat to low, and cook, stirring frequently, until browned, not just softened, about 10 minutes. Add the pecans and cook for 1 minute, stirring often, until aromatic. Set aside.

2 Pour the broth into a 6-quart stovetop or electric pressure cooker; whisk in the flour until dissolved and smooth.

3 Add the sliced parsnips, salt, pepper, and nutmeg.

4 Lock the lid onto the cooker.

STOVETOP: Set the pot over high heat and bring it to high pressure (15 psi). Once this pressure has been reached, lower the heat as much as possible while maintaining this pressure. Cook for 5 minutes.

⋯⋯⋯⋯⋯⋯⋯⋯⋯⋯ **OR** ⋯⋯⋯⋯⋯⋯⋯⋯⋯⋯

ELECTRIC: Set the machine to cook at high pressure (9–11 psi). Set the machine's timer to cook at high pressure for 8 minutes.

5 Use the quick-release method to return the pot's pressure to normal.

6 Unlock and open the pot. Stir in the cream. Puree the soup right in the cooker with an immersion blender or puree it in batches in a standard blender, removing the knob from the lid and covering the hole with a clean kitchen towel. Serve the soup with a quarter of the pecan/shallot mixture sprinkled onto each bowlful.

TESTERS' NOTES

• Sophisticated enough to impress your foodie friends, this soup could also be served in half portions as the first course at a more formal meal.

• If you've never tried them, parsnips are very sweet with an earthy but herbaceous aroma. This recipe would be a crash course since they become even more so under pressure!

EASY PASTA FAGIOLE

EFFORT: **NOT MUCH** · PRESSURE: **HIGH** · TIME UNDER PRESSURE: **5 OR 8 MINUTES** · RELEASE: **QUICK** · SERVES: **6**

One 28-ounce can whole tomatoes, cut into chunks (and with their juice—about 3½ cups)

One 15-ounce can small red beans, drained and rinsed (about 1¾ cups)

1 medium green bell pepper, stemmed, cored, and chopped

1 small yellow onion, chopped

1 cup dried whole wheat ziti (about 3 ounces)

1 teaspoon dried oregano

1 teaspoon dried thyme

¼ teaspoon grated nutmeg

¼ teaspoon red pepper flakes

¼ teaspoon salt

1 Mix everything in a 6-quart stovetop or electric pressure cooker.

2 Lock the lid onto the pot.

STOVETOP: Set the pot over high heat and bring it to high pressure (15 psi). Once this pressure has been reached, reduce the heat as low as possible while maintaining this pressure. Cook for 5 minutes.

·············· OR ··············

ELECTRIC: Set the machine to cook at high pressure (9–11 psi). Set the machine's timer to cook at high pressure for 8 minutes.

3 Use the quick-release method to drop the pot's pressure back to normal.

4 Unlock and open the lid; stir the soup before serving.

TESTERS' NOTES

• Since there are only two fresh ingredients in this recipe, stock up on the rest for your pantry and consider this your go-to lunch on busy weekends. Or use frozen chopped bell pepper (about 1 cup) and frozen chopped onion (¾ cup), thawed first.

• The whole wheat pasta will have a slight amount of chew after cooking. If you want it softer, use a natural-release method for 5 minutes after cooking, then use the quick-release method to bring the pressure back to normal.

Serve It Up! For a hearty meal, poach large eggs and set them in the bowls before ladling the soup on top.

MINESTRONE IN MINUTES

EFFORT: **A LITTLE** · PRESSURE: **HIGH** · TIME UNDER PRESSURE: **10 OR 15 MINUTES** · RELEASE: **QUICK** · SERVES: **8**

2 cups dried cannellini beans

2 tablespoons olive oil

1 medium yellow onion, chopped

2 medium celery stalks, chopped

1 medium carrot, chopped

2 medium yellow potatoes, diced

1 tablespoon minced garlic

4 cups (1 quart) chicken broth

One 28-ounce can diced tomatoes (about 3½ cups)

1 cup dried macaroni (about 2 ounces), preferably whole wheat macaroni

1 tablespoon loosely packed fresh rosemary leaves, minced

1 tablespoon loosely packed fresh oregano leaves, minced

½ teaspoon salt

Up to ½ teaspoon grated nutmeg

1 Soak the beans in a large bowl of water on the counter overnight, for at least 12 hours or up to 16 hours. Drain in a colander set in the sink.

2 Heat the oil in a 6-quart stovetop pressure cooker set over medium heat or in a 6-quart electric pressure cooker turned to the browning function. Add the onion, celery, and carrot; cook, stirring often, until the onion turns translucent, about 4 minutes.

3 Add the potatoes and garlic; cook for about 1 minute, stirring all the while, until the garlic is aromatic. Dump in the soaked beans, broth, tomatoes, macaroni, rosemary, oregano, salt, and nutmeg. Stir well.

4 Lock the lid onto the cooker.

STOVETOP: Raise the heat to high and bring the pot to high pressure (15 psi). Once this pressure has been reached, lower the heat as much as possible while maintaining this pressure. Cook for 10 minutes.

························ **OR** ························

ELECTRIC: Set the machine to cook at high pressure (9–11 psi). Set the machine's timer to cook at high pressure for 15 minutes.

5 Use the quick-release method to bring the pot's pressure back to normal.

6 Unlock and open the pot; stir the soup before serving.

TESTERS' NOTES
• Since this classic soup is ready in minutes, soaking the beans beforehand is a small price to pay.
• If you really want to skip soaking the beans, do a quick-soak with the pressure cooker. Pour the beans into the pot and add enough water so that the beans are covered by 2 to 3 inches. Bring to a boil by setting the stovetop pot over high heat or turning the electric pot to its browning function. Once the water is boiling, lock the lid onto the pot and cook at high pressure for 2 minutes in the stovetop model, or 3 minutes in the electric one. Use the quick-release method to bring it back to normal pressure, then open the pot and drain the beans in a colander set in the sink. Proceed with the recipe from step 2.
• Whole-wheat macaroni will hold its shape better than regular pasta under pressure.
• If the beans are still too firm for your taste, lock the lid onto the pot and bring it back to high pressure. The moment it hits high pressure, turn off the heat or unplug the machine and allow the pressure to fall back to normal naturally, about 10 minutes.
• You can substitute dried white kidney beans for the cannellini beans.

SOUTHWESTERN PINTO BEAN SOUP

EFFORT: **A LOT** • PRESSURE: **HIGH** • TIME UNDER PRESSURE: **12 OR 18 MINUTES** • RELEASE: **QUICK** • SERVES: **6**

2 cups dried pinto beans

6 cups (1½ quarts) vegetable broth

1 medium red onion, chopped

1 medium red bell pepper, stemmed, cored, and chopped

Up to 2 canned chipotles in adobo sauce, stemmed and chopped

2 teaspoons minced garlic

2 teaspoons ground cumin

2 teaspoons dried oregano

¼ cup tomato paste

3 tablespoons fresh lime juice

1 teaspoon salt

1 Soak the beans in a big bowl of water set on the counter for at least 12 hours or up to 16 hours. Drain in a colander set in the sink.

(continued)

2 Pour the beans into a 6-quart stovetop or electric pressure cooker. Add the broth, onion, bell pepper, chipotles, garlic, cumin, and oregano.

3 Lock the lid onto the pot.

STOVETOP: Set the pot over high heat and bring it to high pressure (15 psi). Once this pressure has been reached, lower the heat as much as possible while maintaining this pressure. Cook for 12 minutes.

························· **OR** ····························

ELECTRIC: Set the machine to cook at high pressure (9–11 psi). Set the machine's timer to cook at high pressure for 18 minutes.

4 Use the quick-release method to bring the pot's pressure back to normal.

5 Unlock and open the cooker. Transfer 2 cups of the soup with beans to a blender; add the tomato paste, lime juice, and salt. Cover the blender, removing the knob from the center of the lid but covering the hole with a clean towel. Blend until smooth, scraping down the inside of the canister at least once.

6 Pour the puree into the soup in the cooker. Set the stovetop model over medium heat or turn the electric one to its browning or simmer function; bring the soup to a simmer. Cook for 3 minutes, stirring almost constantly, to meld the flavors and heat the tomato mixture.

TESTERS' NOTES
• Get this match-up: the sweetness in the tomatoes, the sour of the lime juice, the heat from the chiles, and the earthiness of the beans.
• If you can find the more esoteric (but authentic) *and* creamier bolita beans, use those instead of pinto beans.
• Remember: it's up to two canned chipotles, not two *whole* cans of chipotles.

KIDNEY BEAN SOUP WITH DRIED PEARS AND POTATOES

EFFORT: **A LITTLE** • PRESSURE: **HIGH** • TIME UNDER PRESSURE: **10 OR 15 MINUTES** • RELEASE: **QUICK** • SERVES: **6**

2 cups dried red kidney beans

2 tablespoons olive oil

2 small leeks, white and pale green parts only, halved lengthwise, washed and thinly sliced

1 large yellow potato (about 10 ounces), diced

3 dried pear halves, chopped

2 teaspoons minced garlic

1 teaspoon dried sage

¼ teaspoon ground cloves

¼ teaspoon celery seeds

1 star anise pod (optional)

5 cups chicken or vegetable broth

1 Soak the beans in a big bowl of water on the counter overnight, for at least 12 hours or up to 16 hours. Drain in a colander set in the sink.

2 Heat the oil in a 6-quart stovetop pressure cooker set over medium heat or in a 6-quart electric pressure cooker turned to the browning function. Add the sliced leeks; cook, stirring often, until softened, about 2 minutes.

3 Stir in the potato, pears, garlic, sage, cloves, celery seeds, and the star anise, if using; cook for about a minute, until aromatic. Pour in the broth and soaked beans. Stir well.

4 Lock the lid onto the cooker.

STOVETOP: Raise the heat to high and bring the pot to high pressure (15 psi). Once this pressure has been reached, reduce the heat as much as possible while maintaining this pressure. Cook for 10 minutes.

·············· **OR** ··············

ELECTRIC: Set the machine to cook at high pressure (9–11 psi). Set the machine's timer to cook at high pressure for 15 minutes.

5 Use the quick-release method to bring the pot's pressure back to normal.

6 Unlock and open the pot. Discard the star anise pod, if necessary. Stir well before serving.

TESTERS' NOTES

• The combination of sweet pears and dried beans is irresistible: mellow, aromatic, and satisfying.
• The star anise pod will add a slightly Asian, five-spice flavor to the soup. Without it, the soup is a bit more American comfort food—perhaps not quite as sophisticated but a great meal nonetheless.
• You can use dried adzuki (creamier, sweeter) or dried cranberry beans (earthier) in place of the kidney beans.

CRANBERRY BEAN AND BREAD SOUP

EFFORT: **A LOT** · PRESSURE: **HIGH** · TIME UNDER PRESSURE: **8 OR 12 MINUTES** · RELEASE: **QUICK** · SERVES: **6**

1 cup dried cranberry or borlotti beans
6 cups bread cubes
1/4 cup olive oil
1 large yellow onion, chopped
1 large zucchini, diced
1 tablespoon minced garlic
1 tablespoon minced rosemary leaves
Up to 1/2 teaspoon grated nutmeg
6 ounces kale, washed, stemmed, and chopped (about 3 cups)
Half a small savoy cabbage head, cored and shredded (about 2 cups)
1/2 cup dry white wine, such as Pinot Grigio
6 cups (1 1/2 quarts) chicken or vegetable broth
One 14-ounce can crushed tomatoes (about 1 3/4 cups)

1 Soak the beans in a big bowl of water on the counter overnight, for at least 12 hours or up to 16 hours. Drain in a colander set in the sink.

2 Position the rack in the center of the oven; heat the oven to 350°F. Spread the bread cubes on a large, rimmed baking sheet; bake until golden brown, about 15 minutes, stirring and turning often. Set the cubes aside on their baking sheet.

3 Heat the oil in a 6-quart stovetop pressure cooker set over medium heat or in a 6-quart electric pressure cooker turned to the browning function. Add the onion and zucchini; cook, stirring often, until the onion softens, about 4 minutes.

(continued)

4 Stir in the garlic, rosemary, and nutmeg until aromatic, less than a minute. Add the kale and cabbage; cook, stirring often, until wilted, about 3 minutes. Pour in the wine and scrape up any browned bits in the bottom of the pot as it comes to a simmer. Pour in the broth, tomatoes, and drained beans.

5 Lock the lid onto the pot.

STOVETOP: Raise the heat to high and bring the pot to high pressure (15 psi). Once this pressure has been reached, reduce the heat as much as possible while maintaining this pressure. Cook for 8 minutes.

························· **OR** ·····························

ELECTRIC: Set the machine to cook at high pressure (9–11 psi). Set the machine's timer to cook at high pressure for 12 minutes.

6 Use the quick-release method to return the pot's pressure to normal.

7 Unlock and open the cooker. Stir in the bread cubes. Cover loosely and set aside for 10 minutes, until the bread absorbs some of the soup—which will also thicken it a bit.

TESTERS' NOTES
• This recipe is our streamlined take on ribollita, a renowned Tuscan soup perfect with a glass of red wine on a chilly evening.
• The bread will continue to soak up more soup—so leftovers aren't all that great. You can thin out the soup with more broth or invite enough people over to finish the soup in one sitting.

Serve It Up! Sprinkle finely grated Parmesan cheese and balsamic vinegar over each bowlful of soup.

LIMA BEAN AND TOMATO SOUP

EFFORT: **A LITTLE** • PRESSURE: **HIGH** • TIME UNDER PRESSURE: **3 OR 5 MINUTES** • RELEASE: **NATURAL** • SERVES: **6**

1 cup dried regular lima beans (do not use baby lima beans)
4 cups (1 quart) vegetable or chicken broth
One 14-ounce can diced tomatoes (about 1³/₄ cups)
1 small red onion, diced
¹/₄ cup chopped fresh dill fronds
2 tablespoons fresh lemon juice
2 tablespoons honey
¹/₂ teaspoon salt
¹/₂ teaspoon ground black pepper

1 Soak the beans in a large bowl of water on the counter for at least 12 hours or up to 16 hours.

2 Drain the beans in a colander set in the sink, then pour them into a 6-quart stovetop or electric pressure cooker. Stir in the remaining ingredients.

3 Lock the lid onto the pot.

STOVETOP: Set the pot over high heat and bring it to high pressure (15 psi). Immediately reduce the heat as far as you can while maintaining this pressure. Cook for 3 minutes.

························· **OR** ·····························

ELECTRIC: Set the machine to cook at high pressure (9–11 psi). Set the machine's timer to cook at high pressure for 5 minutes.

4 Reduce the pressure.

STOVETOP: Set the pot off the heat and let its pressure fall back to normal naturally, about 20 minutes.

ELECTRIC: Turn off the machine or unplug it so it doesn't flip to its keep-warm setting. Allow its pressure to return to normal naturally, 20 to 30 minutes.

5 Unlock and open the cooker. Stir the soup before serving.

TESTERS' NOTES
• Here's one of the heartiest soups in this chapter. The natural release will get the lima beans tender without turning them mushy.
• The dill balances the sweet and sour flavors in the soup, but we know some people like a more sour lima bean soup. If you're one of them, squeeze in extra lemon juice.

CHICKPEA AND LEMON SOUP WITH ROASTED GARLIC

EFFORT: **A LOT** • PRESSURE: **HIGH** • TIME UNDER PRESSURE: **6 OR 9 MINUTES** • RELEASE: **NATURAL** • SERVES: **6**

1¹⁄₂ cups dried chickpeas
1 medium garlic head
2¹⁄₂ tablespoons olive oil
1 small yellow onion, chopped
2 medium celery stalks, thinly sliced
2 medium carrots, thinly sliced
1 tablespoon finely grated lemon zest
¹⁄₂ tablespoon dried thyme
¹⁄₂ tablespoon minced garlic
¹⁄₂ teaspoon ground turmeric
¹⁄₂ teaspoon salt
¹⁄₂ teaspoon ground black pepper
8 cups (2 quarts) chicken broth
¹⁄₂ cup loosely packed fresh cilantro leaves, minced
2 tablespoons fresh lemon juice

1 Soak the chickpeas in a big bowl of water set on the counter for at least 8 hours or up to 12 hours. Drain the chickpeas in a colander set in the sink.

2 Position the rack in the center of the oven and heat the oven to 375°F. Cut the top third off the head of garlic, thereby exposing almost all the cloves. Rub ¹⁄₂ tablespoon olive oil over the garlic, then seal in a small aluminum foil packet. Roast on a baking sheet until soft, about 1 hour.

3 Heat the remaining 2 tablespoons oil in a 6-quart stovetop pressure cooker set over medium heat or in a 6-quart electric pressure cooker turned to the browning function. Add the onion, celery, and carrots; cook, stirring often, until softened, about 4 minutes. Add the zest, thyme, garlic, turmeric, salt, and pepper; cook until aromatic, stirring all the while, less than a minute.

4 Pour in the broth and drained chickpeas; stir well. Open the foil packet and squeeze the soft garlic cloves into the soup.

5 Lock the lid onto the pot.

STOVETOP: Raise the heat to high and bring the pot to high pressure (15 psi). Once this pressure has been reached, lower the heat as much as possible while maintaining this pressure. Cook for 6 minutes.

······················OR······················
ELECTRIC: Set the machine to cook at high pressure (9–11 psi). Set the machine's timer to cook at high pressure for 9 minutes.

(continued)

6 Reduce the pressure.

STOVETOP: Set the pot off the heat and let its pressure return to normal naturally, about 20 minutes.

·················· **OR** ··················

ELECTRIC: Turn off the machine or unplug it so that it doesn't flip to its keep-warm setting. Allow its pressure to fall to normal naturally, 20 to 30 minutes.

7 Unlock and open the cooker. Stir in the cilantro and lemon juice before serving.

TESTERS' NOTES
• You want big flavors? This recipe has them! The roasted garlic becomes impossibly sweet, a mellow, aromatic thickener in the soup.
• For a little heat, add up to ¼ teaspoon red pepper flakes with the spices.
• Substitute fresh parsley leaves for the cilantro.

SPLIT PEA SOUP WITH CRANBERRIES AND APPLE CIDER

EFFORT: **NOT MUCH** • PRESSURE: **HIGH** • TIME UNDER PRESSURE: **12 OR 18 MINUTES** • RELEASE: **QUICK** • SERVES: **6**

2 cups green split peas, sifted for any debris and rinsed

6 cups (1½ quarts) vegetable or chicken broth

1 cup unsweetened apple cider

4 medium carrots, thinly sliced

1 small yellow onion, chopped

½ cup dried cranberries

2 teaspoons dried thyme

1 teaspoon celery seeds

½ teaspoon salt

½ teaspoon ground black pepper

1 Pour the split peas into a 6-quart stovetop or electric pressure cooker; stir in everything else.

2 Lock the lid onto the pot.

STOVETOP: Set the pot over high heat and bring it to high pressure (15 psi). Once this pressure has been reached, reduce the heat as much as you can while maintaining this pressure. Cook for 12 minutes.

·················· **OR** ··················

ELECTRIC: Set the machine to cook at high pressure (9–11 psi). Set the machine's timer to cook at high pressure for 18 minutes.

3 Use the quick-release method to drop the pot's pressure back to normal.

4 Unlock and open the cooker; stir the soup before serving.

TESTERS' NOTES
• Split-pea soup just got easier! And healthier: no oil, no added fat, not much salt, just those velvety smooth split peas. Plus, we've gussied up the traditional with spiky cranberries and sweet apple cider.
• You'll be surprised how the pressure cooker keeps the split peas together. Wallpaper paste no more! But the soup will tighten up if leftovers are saved in the fridge. Thin it out with extra broth when reheating.
• For a more traditional split pea soup, see Split Pea and Ham Bone Soup on page 51.

Serve It Up! Squeeze fresh lemon juice over the servings or even crumble crisp bacon over the top.

YELLOW SPLIT PEA SOUP WITH SAUERKRAUT

EFFORT: **NOT MUCH** • PRESSURE: **HIGH** • TIME UNDER PRESSURE:
7 OR 12 MINUTES • RELEASE: **NATURAL** • SERVES: **6**

8 cups (2 quarts) vegetable or chicken broth

2 cups yellow split peas

1 cup drained bagged sauerkraut, chopped

1 medium yellow onion, chopped

2 medium celery stalks, chopped

1 tablespoon minced garlic

1 teaspoon dried thyme

1 teaspoon Dijon mustard

$1/2$ teaspoon caraway seeds

$1/4$ teaspoon ground turmeric

Up to $1/4$ teaspoon cayenne

1 Mix everything in a 6-quart stovetop or electric pressure cooker.

2 Lock the lid onto the pot.

STOVETOP: Set the pot over high heat and bring it to high pressure (15 psi). Immediately reduce the heat as much as possible while maintaining this pressure. Cook for 7 minutes.

·····OR·····

ELECTRIC: Set the machine to cook at high pressure (9–11 psi). Set the machine's timer to cook at this pressure for 12 minutes.

3 Reduce the pressure.

STOVETOP: Set the pot off the heat and let its pressure fall to normal naturally, about 20 minutes.

·····OR·····

ELECTRIC: Turn off the machine or unplug it so it doesn't flip to its keep-warm setting. Allow its pressure to return to normal naturally, 20 to 30 minutes.

4 Unlock and open the pot. Stir well before serving.

TESTERS' NOTES

• Despite the sauerkraut, this soup is quite mild with the earthy, sweet split peas and all those spices. In fact, the pressure cooker even takes much of the edge off the sauerkraut.

• Don't confuse chana dal (small chickpea lentils) for yellow split peas. The latter are smaller and will melt down a bit during cooking to make a more velvety soup.

• Although this is a vegetarian soup, you can add 1 smoked pork chop to the mix and cook under pressure as directed. After opening the pot, scrape the meat off the bone, chop the meat into small bits, and stir them into the soup before serving.

LENTIL, CHICKPEA, AND RICE SOUP

EFFORT: **A LITTLE** • PRESSURE: **HIGH** • TIME UNDER PRESSURE:
15 OR 23 MINUTES • RELEASE: **QUICK** • SERVES: **6**

1 cup dried chickpeas

$1/4$ cup olive oil

1 large yellow onion, chopped

1 teaspoon finely grated lemon zest

1 teaspoon caraway seeds

1 teaspoon salt

1 teaspoon ground black pepper

1 cup white long-grain rice, such as white basmati

1 cup brown lentils

8 cups (2 quarts) chicken or vegetable broth

2 tablespoons fresh lemon juice

1 Soak the chickpeas in a big bowl of water set on the counter overnight, for at least 12 hours or up to 16 hours. Drain in a colander set in the sink.

(continued)

2 Heat the oil in a 6-quart stovetop pressure cooker set over medium heat or in a 6-quart electric pressure cooker turned to the browning function. Add the onion and cook, stirring often, until softened, about 4 minutes.

3 Stir in the lemon zest, caraway seeds, salt, and pepper. Cook about 30 seconds, until aromatic, then stir in the rice and lentils. Cook, stirring often, about 2 minutes, to coat the rice in the fat. Pour in the broth and add the drained chickpeas.

4 Lock the lid onto the cooker.

STOVETOP: Raise the heat to high and bring the pot to high pressure (15 psi). Once this pressure has been reached, reduce the heat as much as possible while maintaining this pressure. Cook for 15 minutes.

······································ **OR** ·······························

ELECTRIC: Set the machine to cook at high pressure (9–11 psi). Set the machine's timer to cook at high pressure for 23 minutes.

5 Use the quick-release method to bring the pot's pressure back to normal.

6 Unlock and open the cooker. Stir in the lemon juice before serving.

TESTERS' NOTES
• There's a terrifically satisfying balance here among the earthy lentils, the nutty brown rice, and the sweet chickpeas.
• Although this dish can be vegetarian fare with vegetable broth in the mix, we prefer chicken broth for a more luxurious texture—as well as some deeper savory notes underneath the other, earthy flavors.

Serve It Up! Serve with a stack of warmed or even grilled whole wheat pita.

CREAMY RED LENTIL AND SQUASH SOUP

EFFORT: **A LITTLE** • PRESSURE: **HIGH** • TIME UNDER PRESSURE: **14 OR 20 MINUTES** • RELEASE: **NATURAL** • SERVES: **6**

3 pounds butternut or buttercup squash, peeled, seeded, and cubed (about 8 cups)
6 cups (1½ quarts) chicken broth
½ cup red lentils
2 tablespoons honey
1 tablespoon minced fresh ginger
1 canned chipotle in adobo sauce, stemmed and minced
One 4-inch cinnamon stick
½ teaspoon ground cardamom
½ teaspoon salt
½ teaspoon ground black pepper

1 Mix everything in a 6-quart stovetop or electric pressure cooker.

2 Lock the lid onto the pot.

STOVETOP: Set the pot over high heat and bring it to high pressure (15 psi). As soon as this pressure has been reached, reduce the heat as much as possible while keeping the pressure constant. Cook for 14 minutes.

······································ **OR** ·······························

ELECTRIC: Set the machine to cook at high pressure (9–11 psi). Set the machine's timer to cook at high pressure for 20 minutes.

3 Reduce the pressure.

STOVETOP: Set the pot off the heat and let its pressure come back to normal naturally, about 18 minutes.

ELECTRIC: Turn off the machine or unplug it so it doesn't flip to its keep-warm setting. Allow its pressure to fall to normal naturally, 18 to 26 minutes.

4 Unlock and open the pot. Remove the cinnamon stick. Puree the soup with an immersion blender right in the cooker; or ladle the soup in batches into a standard blender, remove the center knob from the lid, cover the hole with a clean towel, and puree until smooth.

TESTERS' NOTES

• No, there's no cream in this rich soup. Instead, the red lentils and squash become creamy as they cook under pressure—and are then pureed for a smooth texture and big flavors.

• The soup will continue to thicken as it sits, particularly when you save leftovers in the fridge. The next day, thin it out with canned coconut milk.

Serve It Up! Garnish with chopped roasted cashews.

RED LENTIL AND BULGUR SOUP

EFFORT: **A LOT** • PRESSURE: **HIGH** • TIME UNDER PRESSURE: **7 OR 10 MINUTES** • RELEASE: **QUICK** • SERVES: **6**

3 tablespoons olive oil
2 medium yellow onions, chopped
1 tablespoon minced garlic
1 teaspoon caraway seeds
1 teaspoon coriander seeds
1 teaspoon cumin seeds
$1/2$ teaspoon salt
6 cups ($1^1/2$ quarts) vegetable broth

$1^1/2$ cups red lentils
$1/3$ cup bulgur, preferably medium grind
1 bay leaf
2 tablespoons tomato paste
2 tablespoons fresh lemon juice
$1/2$ tablespoon sweet paprika
Up to $1/2$ teaspoon cayenne

1 Heat 1 tablespoon oil in a 6-quart stovetop pressure cooker set over medium heat or in a 6-quart electric pressure cooker turned to the browning function. Add the onion and cook, stirring often, until softened, about 4 minutes.

2 Stir in the garlic, caraway, coriander, cumin, and salt; cook about 30 seconds, until fragrant. Add the broth, lentils, bulgur, and bay leaf; stir in the tomato paste until dissolved.

3 Lock the lid onto the pot.

STOVETOP: Raise the heat to high and bring the pot to high pressure (15 psi). Once this pressure has been reached, reduce the heat as much as possible while maintaining this pressure. Cook for 7 minutes.

························ **OR** ························

ELECTRIC: Set the machine to cook at high pressure (9–11 psi). Set the machine's timer to cook at high pressure for 10 minutes.

4 Use the quick-release method to bring the pot's pressure back to normal.

5 Unlock and open the cooker. Discard the bay leaf and stir in the lemon juice. Scoop 2 cups of the soup into a blender. Remove the center knob from the lid, return the lid to the blender, covering the hole with a clean towel, and blend until smooth, scraping down the inside of the canister at least once. Stir the mixture back into the cooker, cover loosely, and set aside.

(continued)

6 Heat the remaining 2 tablespoons oil in a medium skillet over low heat. Add the paprika and cayenne; cook until aromatic, about 10 seconds. Remove from the heat. Serve by ladling the soup into bowls and drizzling the spicy oil over each serving.

TESTERS' NOTES

• We became fanatical about this soup when we were testing recipes! We kept making it over and over again—it's so satisfying, a great mix of grains and spices.

• If you can find whole-grain bulgur from an artisanal producer, by all means use it.

• The red lentils will break down quite a bit, thickening the soup and giving it a pleasantly sweet, slightly earthy flavor, a good contrast to the many spices.

BEEFY WHEATBERRY AND TOMATO SOUP

EFFORT: **A LITTLE** • PRESSURE: **HIGH** • TIME UNDER PRESSURE: **25 OR 40 MINUTES** • RELEASE: **NATURAL** • SERVES: **6**

1 tablespoon olive oil

1 meaty beef rib bone

One 28-ounce can whole tomatoes, cut into chunks, but with their juice (about 3¹/₂ cups)

2 cups chicken broth

1 medium yellow onion, chopped

1 medium green bell pepper, stemmed, cored, and chopped

¹/₂ cup dried wheatberries, preferably soft white wheatberries

1 tablespoon dried sage

¹/₂ teaspoon celery seeds

¹/₂ teaspoon salt

¹/₂ teaspoon ground black pepper

1 Heat the oil in a 6-quart stovetop pressure cooker set over medium heat or in a 6-quart electric pressure cooker turned to the browning function. Add the beef rib and brown on all sides, about 4 minutes, turning occasionally.

2 Add the tomatoes, broth, onion, bell pepper, wheatberries, sage, celery seeds, salt, and pepper to the pot.

3 Lock the lid onto the cooker.

> **STOVETOP:** Raise the heat to high and bring the pot to high pressure (15 psi). Once this pressure has been reached, reduce the heat as low as possible while maintaining this pressure. Cook for 25 minutes.
> ·············· OR ··············
> **ELECTRIC:** Set the machine to cook at high pressure (9–11 psi). Set the machine's timer to cook at high pressure for 40 minutes.

4 Reduce the pressure.

> **STOVETOP:** Set the pot off the heat; let its pressure fall to normal naturally, about 30 minutes.
> ·············· OR ··············
> **ELECTRIC:** Turn off the machine or unplug it so it doesn't flip to its keep-warm setting. Allow its pressure to return to normal naturally, 30 to 40 minutes.

If the pressure hasn't returned to normal within 40 minutes, use the quick-release method to bring it back to normal.

5 Unlock and open the pot. Transfer the beef rib to a cutting board. Cool a few minutes, then slice the meat off the bone and chop into small bits. Discard the bone and stir the meat back into the soup before serving.

• Not only does the single beef rib give the soup some meaty bits, the flavor from its bone and cartilage will soak into the soup under pressure.

• Why don't we just use canned diced tomatoes? Because the bits are too small and will dissolve under pressure. By cutting whole tomatoes into chunks, some tomato texture remains in the soup. The easiest tool for the task is kitchen shears: just open the can and cut up the tomatoes right inside. If you don't own kitchen shears, use your hands to break them up into chunks in a bowl.

• If you can only find hard red wheatberries at your market, let the soup cook an extra 5 minutes to ensure they're tender. If you can't find wheatberries at all, use dried spelt berries, Kamut berries, rye berries, or triticale berries (just add 5 minutes to the time under pressure).

Serve It Up! You'll need some warm dinner rolls and lots of butter to go alongside this soup.

WHEATBERRY AND ZUCCHINI SOUP

EFFORT: **A LITTLE** • PRESSURE: **HIGH** • TIME UNDER PRESSURE: **25 OR 41 MINUTES** • RELEASE: **QUICK, THEN QUICK AGAIN** • SERVES: **6**

6 cups (1½ quarts) chicken or vegetable broth

¾ cup dried wheatberries, preferably soft white wheatberries

2 large zucchini (about 8 ounces each), chopped

1 small yellow onion, chopped

2 tablespoons finely chopped fresh dill fronds

2 teaspoons minced garlic

2 teaspoons minced fresh oregano leaves

2 teaspoons finely grated lemon zest

½ teaspoon salt

½ teaspoon ground black pepper

1 Mix the broth and wheatberries in a 6-quart stovetop or electric pressure cooker.

2 Lock the lid onto the pot.

STOVETOP: Set the pot over high heat and bring it to high pressure (15 psi). Once this pressure has been reached, lower the heat as much as you can while maintaining this pressure. Cook for 23 minutes.

·············· **OR** ··············

ELECTRIC: Set the machine to cook at high pressure (9–11 psi). Set the machine's timer to cook at high pressure for 38 minutes.

3 Use the quick-release method to drop the pot's pressure to normal.

4 Unlock and open the cooker. Stir in the zucchini, onion, dill, garlic, oregano, zest, salt, and pepper.

5 Lock the lid back onto the cooker.

STOVETOP: Set the pot back over high heat and bring it back to high pressure (15 psi). Once this pressure has been reached, reduce the heat as much as possible while maintaining this pressure. Cook for 2 minutes.

·············· **OR** ··············

ELECTRIC: Set the machine to cook once again at high pressure (9–11 psi). Set the machine's timer to cook at high pressure for 3 minutes.

6 Use the quick-release method to bring the pot's pressure to normal.

7 Unlock and open the pot. Stir the soup before serving.

TESTERS' NOTES

• This Italian-inspired soup gets much of its flavor from the way the vegetable release their essential moisture into the broth—after the wheatberries have cooked. Were they

(continued)

to be cooked together, the vegetables would be mushy and the wheatberries themselves would absorb too much of the vegetables' flavor, leaving the broth tasteless.

• Check the wheatberries for tenderness after the first cooking under pressure. They should be almost ready, just a little firm at the center. If they're not, lock the lid back onto the pot, bring it back to high pressure, leave it there 1 to 2 minutes, and then use the quick-release to reopen the pot.

• Substitute fresh sage or thyme for the oregano.

Serve It Up! Drizzle about 1 tablespoon olive oil over each bowlful.

BARLEY AND RICE SOUP WITH YOGURT AND MINT

EFFORT: **A LOT** • PRESSURE: **HIGH** • TIME UNDER PRESSURE: **18 OR 25 MINUTES** • RELEASE: **QUICK** • SERVES: **6**

2 tablespoons unsalted butter

2 medium yellow onions, chopped

1/2 cup pearled (perlato) barley

1/4 cup long-grain white rice, such as white basmati or Texmati

2 teaspoons dried oregano

1 teaspoon dried dill

1/2 teaspoon salt

1/2 teaspoon ground black pepper

5 cups vegetable broth

1 cup plain Greek yogurt

3 tablespoons loosely packed fresh parsley leaves, minced

2 tablespoons loosely packed fresh mint leaves, minced

2 large egg yolks

1 Melt the butter in a 6-quart stovetop pressure cooker set over medium heat or in a 6-quart electric pressure cooker turned to the browning mode. Add the onion; cook, stirring often, until golden and soft, about 5 minutes.

2 Add the barley, rice, oregano, dill, salt, and pepper. Cook, stirring often, until fragrant, less than 1 minute. Pour in the broth.

3 Lock the lid onto the cooker.

STOVETOP: Raise the heat to high and bring the pot to high pressure (15 psi). Once this pressure has been reached, reduce the heat as much as possible while maintaining this pressure. Cook for 18 minutes.

⋯⋯⋯⋯⋯⋯⋯⋯⋯ **OR** ⋯⋯⋯⋯⋯⋯⋯⋯⋯

ELECTRIC: Set the machine to cook at high pressure (9–11 psi). Set the machine's timer to cook at high pressure for 25 minutes.

4 Use the quick-release method to bring the pot's pressure back to normal.

5 Unlock and open the pot. Set the stovetop cooker over medium heat or turn the electric cooker to the browning function. Stir in the yogurt, parsley, and mint. Bring to a simmer; cook for 2 minutes, stirring frequently.

6 Whisk the egg yolks in a large bowl. Whisk about 2 cups of the soup into the eggs until fairly smooth, then whisk the combined mixture back into the soup. Serve at once.

TESTERS' NOTES

• Here's our egg-enriched soup: the egg gives the soup a beautifully smooth finish; the yogurt gives the soup a slightly sour edge, balanced a bit by the sweet rice and barley.

• Use pearled barley, not semi-perlato or whole-grain barley. You want this soup as creamy and smooth as possible.

• Although there will be bits of barley and rice in the soup added to the egg yolk, make sure the broth itself is as smooth as possible after whisking, with no little bits of egg yolk visible anywhere.

CHILLED PEA AND LEEK SOUP

EFFORT: **A LITTLE** • PRESSURE: **HIGH** • TIME UNDER PRESSURE:
2 OR 3 MINUTES • RELEASE: **QUICK** • SERVES: **6**

3 tablespoons olive oil

2 medium leeks, white and pale green
    parts only, halved lengthwise, washed
    and thinly sliced

2 medium celery stalks, thinly sliced

1 teaspoon minced garlic

5 cups chicken or vegetable broth

4$\frac{1}{2}$ cups shelled fresh peas, or frozen
    peas, thawed

$\frac{1}{4}$ cup packed fresh parsley leaves

1 teaspoon stemmed fresh thyme leaves

$\frac{1}{2}$ teaspoon salt

$\frac{1}{2}$ teaspoon ground pepper, preferably
    white pepper

$\frac{1}{2}$ cup heavy cream

1 Heat the oil in a 6-quart stovetop pressure cooker set over medium heat or in a 6-quart electric pressure cooker turned to the browning function. Add the leeks, celery, and garlic; cook just until softened, not in the least bit browned, about 2 minutes, stirring almost constantly. Stir in the broth, peas, parsley, thyme, salt, and pepper.

2 Lock the lid onto the pot.

STOVETOP: Raise the heat to high and bring the pot to high pressure (15 psi). Once this pressure has been reached, reduce the heat as much as you can while maintaining this pressure. Cook for 2 minutes.

·····················**OR**·····················

ELECTRIC: Set the machine to cook at high pressure (9–11 psi). Set the machine's timer to cook at high pressure for 3 minutes.

3 Use the quick-release method to bring the pot's pressure back to normal.

4 Unlock and open the pot. Stir in the cream and puree with an immersion blender right in the pot or ladle the soup into a blender in batches, removing the center knob in the blender's lid and covering the hole with a clean towel. Blend the soup until smooth.

5 Pour the pureed soup into a large container, seal well, and chill in the refrigerator for at least 6 hours or up to 3 days. Serve cold.

TESTERS' NOTES
• A chilled soup is a perfect summer quencher. This one's a little more savory than you might expect: a velvety vegetable mélange. We prefer it with chicken broth because it gives the soup more body, but using vegetable broth will yield a lighter finish.
• Turn the soup into shots. Put a small jigger of vodka into iced shot glasses, add the soup, stir gently, and serve at once.

Serve It Up! Ladle the soup into bowls, then top each serving with a small mound of lump crabmeat or chopped shrimp.

COLD PLUM SOUP

EFFORT: **A LITTLE** • PRESSURE: **HIGH** • TIME UNDER PRESSURE: **3 OR 5 MINUTES** • RELEASE: **QUICK** • SERVES: **6**

2 pounds ripe black or red plums, halved and pitted

1/4 teaspoon ground cloves

1/4 teaspoon grated nutmeg

One 4-inch cinnamon stick

1/2 cup sugar

1/2 cup sour cream

1/2 cup full-bodied red wine, such as Rioja

1 Mix the plums, cloves, nutmeg, and cinnamon stick with 2 cups water in a 6-quart stovetop or electric pressure cooker.

2 Lock the lid onto the pot.

STOVETOP: Set the pot over high heat and bring to high pressure (15 psi). Once this pressure has been reached, reduce the heat as much as possible while maintaining this pressure. Cook for 3 minutes.

·······················OR·······················

ELECTRIC: Set the machine to cook at high pressure (9–11 psi). Set the machine's timer to cook at high pressure for 5 minutes.

3 Use the quick-release method to bring the pot's pressure back to normal.

4 Unlock and remove the lid. Discard the cinnamon stick. Cool the soup in the pot for 30 minutes.

5 Stir the sugar, sour cream, and wine into the soup until the sugar dissolves. Use an immersion blender to puree the soup right in the cooker—or ladle it in batches into a blender and puree, removing the center knob from the lid but covering the hole with a clean towel.

6 Pour the puree into a large container, seal well, and store in the refrigerator for at least 6 hours or up to 3 days.

TESTERS' NOTES

• Serve small bowls of this soup right before the meat comes off the barbecue. The spiced plum mixture— a little sour but mostly sweet—will perk up everyone's appetite.

• The plums should be fairly ripe but not mushy. Even hard winter plums will work in this soup because the pressure cooker softens them so quickly.

Serve It Up! Garnish the bowls with minced mint leaves.

COLD PEAR GINGER SOUP

EFFORT: **A LITTLE** • PRESSURE: **HIGH** • TIME UNDER PRESSURE: **7 OR 10 MINUTES** • RELEASE: **QUICK** • SERVES: **6**

2 pounds ripe, firm pears, such as Anjou, stemmed, cored, and chopped

1 tablespoon minced fresh ginger

One 4-inch cinnamon stick

$^1/_2$ cup packed light brown sugar

$^1/_2$ cup heavy cream

$^1/_4$ cup orange-flavored liqueur, such as Grand Marnier or Cointreau

1 Place the pears, ginger, and cinnamon stick with 2 cups water in a 6-quart stovetop or electric pressure cooker.

2 Lock the lid onto the pot.

STOVETOP: Set the pot over high heat and bring it to high pressure (15 psi). Once this pressure has been reached, reduce the heat as much as possible while maintaining this pressure. Cook for 7 minutes.

········· **OR** ·········

ELECTRIC: Set the machine to cook at high pressure (9–11 psi). Set the machine's timer to cook at high pressure for 10 minutes.

3 Use the quick-release method to bring the pot's pressure back to normal.

4 Unlock and open the cooker. Discard the cinnamon stick. Cool the soup in the pot for 30 minutes.

5 Stir in the brown sugar, cream, and liqueur until the brown sugar dissolves. Puree the soup with an immersion blender right in the pot—or working in batches, puree it in a standard blender, removing the center knob from the lid and covering the hole with a clean towel.

6 Transfer the puree to a large container, seal well, and chill in the fridge for at least 6 hours or up to 3 days.

TESTERS' NOTES
• Although you could offer this soup as a cold summer dessert, it's even better as an appetite pick-me-up in the middle of a larger meal any time of year. Consider it a necessity at Thanksgiving, sometime between the appetizers and the turkey.
• The pears should be firm but ripe. Too soft and they'll lose all texture, even in a pureed soup.

Serve It Up! Float toasted pine nuts in the servings.

MEAT

ON WEEKNIGHTS, MOST OF US LOOK FOR QUICK-COOKING MEALS:
perhaps a steak to throw on the grill, some ground beef for burgers, or a lean piece of loin for a quick stir-fry. We save the bigger, tougher, richer cuts for the weekends: briskets, pot roasts, and pork butts.

Not anymore! The pressure cooker puts a pot roast within reach on a Tuesday night. You can brown a few ingredients, toss the meat into the pot, and plate a braise by the time you pour the second glass of wine. We just turned weeknights into weekends. You can thank us later.

In the meantime, welcome to our recipes for beef, pork, veal, lamb, and even rabbit, probably the very reasons you bought this appliance (and maybe this book) in the first place. Well, okay, not for the rabbit. But we'll get to that later.

Don't worry: not everything's a giant brisket or breast of veal. Because of the way the pressure cooker works, there are plenty of ground beef dishes—even some cheesy casseroles—as well as recipes that use various sorts of lean pork chops. There are also short ribs and country-style ribs. And you don't think we'd forget about meatballs, do you?

In all these recipes, work with evenly sized pieces of meat. When you're making a braise in the oven, you can be less exacting—if you've got a quarter pound more than the recipe requires, another 20 minutes isn't going to kill the thing. But here, the cuts need to be more exactingly sized to cook correctly. And if you've put a few hunks of meat together in the cooker, they also need to be similarly sized. Otherwise, some will end up tough and others, tender—or some will be tender and others, mushy (a worse fate to our minds). And that advice even goes for smaller, individual cuts like pork chops. Four boneless pork chops need to be similarly sized so they cook evenly.

Almost every recipe in this chapter asks you to brown the meat in the pot before you lock on the lid. Listen, the pot's already over the heat—you might as well take advantage

of it. We even ask that you brown roasts and larger cuts so the dish gains more flavor at every turn. Some pressure cooker mavens insist on setting roasts on a rack in the cooker. Apparently, they fear a little too much brown on the exterior of the cut as it sits directly against the hot cooker. *We* never fear brown and adore the deeper flavor the roast gets as it sits right against the hot surface.

The recipes in this chapter start pretty easy, then build to more complex offerings. Even among the recipes themselves, when we're dealing with a specific cut, we begin with fairly simple preparations for pork loin chops, beef sirloin tips, or leg of lamb. Then we get more creative, calling in a bigger array of spices, flavorings, aromatics, and liquids. We move from broth to ginger beer, from onions to leeks, from two spices to four. If you're new to pressure cooking or want a simpler meal, always go for the earlier recipes in the set.

So here's to Saturday suppers on Tuesday nights. We still haven't figured out how to turn Tuesday mornings into Saturday mornings. But we're working on it.

Beef

Yes, we've got plenty of ground beef in this chapter. But no tenderloin, rib-eyes, or strip steaks. After the ground stuff, brisket, top round, bottom round, chuck roasts, and short ribs are the best bets in a pressure cooker. More economical than the quick-cookers, they're also stocked with chewy and fatty bits that soften and melt under pressure, rendering them gorgeously tender and savory.

You might be surprised at how savory these beef dishes are. Sure, some include honey or other sweeteners; but most tip toward the *umami,* largely because of the way that collagen and other interstitial goodness melt under pressure. In other words, the beef is bathed in the essence of its meatiness without evaporation or the collapse of more savory flavors into simpler sugars that would occur under long cooking. Any of those natural sugars have less time to caramelize and have a bigger range of sour and salty notes. So these dishes are well suited to a glass of beer, wine, or even unsweetened iced tea.

Most of these recipes make four or six servings. Unfortunately, you can't double them at will. For one thing, you might overfill the cooker; for another, larger cuts will not get tender evenly. If you need to cook for more people, buy a second cooker and double the recipe that way.

You may well need a second pot: these beef stews and braises will make your cooking the talk of the town. Sure, there's a lot here for a typical weeknight: meatballs, ground beef casseroles, and even a fine reinterpretation of Swiss steak, that old-time cafeteria classic. But there are also recipes fit to impress even finicky in-laws: try braising sirloin tips in port, chuck roast in coffee, and short ribs in white (yep, white) wine. Stock up on sales at the butcher counter, store these typically slow-cooking cuts in the freezer, and get ready for some of the most savory fare in the book.

GROUND BEEF (AND WHOLE GRAIN!) SLOPPY JOES

EFFORT: **A LITTLE** • PRESSURE: **HIGH** • TIME UNDER PRESSURE:
7 OR 11 MINUTES • RELEASE: **QUICK** • SERVES: **8**

1/2 **cup white or red quinoa**

2 **tablespoons olive oil**

1 **large yellow onion, chopped**

1 **large cubanelle (Italian frying pepper),**
   stemmed, seeded, and chopped

2 **pounds lean ground beef (preferably**
   93% lean)

2 **teaspoons minced garlic**

One 28-ounce **can crushed tomatoes**
   (about 31/2 **cups)**

1/4 **cup old-fashioned rolled oats**

1/4 **cup packed dark brown sugar**

2 **tablespoons Dijon mustard**

2 **tablespoons Worcestershire sauce**

2 **tablespoons apple cider vinegar**

2 **tablespoons sweet paprika**

1/4 **teaspoon ground cloves**

1 Pour the quinoa into a 6-quart stovetop or electric pressure cooker; fill the cooker with water until the grains are submerged by 2 inches.

2 Lock the lid in place.

STOVETOP: Set the pot over high heat and bring it to high pressure (15 psi). Once this pressure has been reached, reduce the heat as much as possible to maintain this pressure. Cook for 2 minutes.
·················· **OR** ··················
ELECTRIC: Set the pot to cook at high pressure (9–11 psi). Set the pot's timer to cook for 3 minutes.

3 Use the quick-release method to bring the pressure back to normal.

4 Unlock and open the pot. Drain the quinoa in a fine-mesh sieve set in the sink.

5 Heat the oil in the stovetop cooker set over medium heat or in an electric cooker turned to its browning function. Add the onion and pepper; cook, stirring often, until the onion softens, about 4 minutes. Crumble in the ground beef and stir in the garlic. Cook, stirring often, until the beef is no longer pink, about 6 minutes.

6 Stir in the tomatoes, oats, brown sugar, mustard, Worcestershire sauce, vinegar, paprika, cloves, and the drained quinoa until well combined.

7 Lock the lid onto the pot.

STOVETOP: Raise the heat to high; bring the pot to high pressure (15 psi). Once this pressure has been reached, reduce the heat as much as possible while maintaining this pressure. Cook for 5 minutes.
·················· **OR** ··················
ELECTRIC: Switch the machine to cook once again at high pressure (9–11 psi). Set the machine's timer to cook at this pressure for 8 minutes.

8 Use the quick-release method to bring the pressure back to normal in the pot.

9 Unlock and open the lid; stir well before serving. If the quinoa is not tender enough for your taste, particularly in the electric pot, lock on the lid and cook at high pressure for 1 additional minute.

TESTERS' NOTES
• Quinoa and oats add a wonderful texture to sloppy joes. That texture provides a culinary service as well. Without the grains to absorb moisture and add a firm bite, the meat can take on an unpleasant, boiled taste. As a bonus, your family will be eating whole grains and may not even realize it!

(continued)

• Use only old-fashioned rolled oats, not quick-cooking oats or steel-cut oats. The quick-cooking will foam up in the pot; the steel-cut will never get tender in time.

• Rinse the quinoa if its package directs you to, in case there are any little bits of a bitter chemical still adhering to the grains. If you use a standard colander to drain the quinoa, line it with cheesecloth, a layer of strong paper towels, or even a very large coffee filter so the tiny grains don't drain away.

• Use 1 small green bell pepper, cored and finely chopped, instead of the cubanelle pepper.

Serve It Up! Break out the spread: toasted whole wheat buns (to match the flavors in the filling), as well as chopped lettuce, sliced tomatoes, bread-and-butter pickles, pickled jalapeño rings, chow-chow, or pickle relish. Even try creamy cole slaw as a topper. Or serve this beef mixture in steamed or roasted acorn squash halves topped with a little sour cream.

GROUND BEEF CHILI

EFFORT: **NOT MUCH** • PRESSURE: **HIGH** • TIME UNDER PRESSURE: **5 OR 8 MINUTES** • RELEASE: **QUICK** • SERVES: **6**

1 tablespoon olive oil

1 large yellow onion, chopped

1 large green bell pepper, stemmed, seeded, and chopped

2 teaspoons minced garlic

2 pounds lean ground beef (preferably 93% lean)

One 28-ounce can diced tomatoes (about 3$\frac{1}{2}$ cups)

Two 15-ounce cans red kidney beans, drained and rinsed (about 3$\frac{1}{2}$ cups)

6 tablespoons chili powder

2 teaspoons ground cumin

2 teaspoons dried oregano

Up to $\frac{1}{2}$ cup chicken broth

1 Heat the oil in a 6-quart stovetop pressure cooker set over medium heat or in a 6-quart electric pressure cooker set to the browning function. Add the onion and bell pepper; cook, stirring often, until the onion softens, about 4 minutes. Stir in the garlic; cook for 30 seconds.

2 Crumble in the ground beef; cook, stirring often, until the meat loses all its raw color. Stir in the tomatoes, beans, chili powder, cumin, and oregano. Stir $\frac{1}{2}$ cup broth into a stovetop pressure cooker or $\frac{1}{4}$ cup broth into an electric pressure cooker.

3 Lock the lid onto the pot.

STOVETOP: Raise the heat to high and bring the pot to high pressure (15 psi). Once this pressure has been reached, reduce the heat as much as possible while still maintaining this pressure. Cook for 5 minutes.

································· OR ·······························

ELECTRIC: Set the machine to cook at high pressure (9–11 psi). Set the machine's timer to cook at high pressure for 8 minutes.

4 Use the quick-release method to drop the pot's pressure to normal.

5 Unlock and open the pot. Stir well before serving.

TESTERS' NOTES

• Nothing could be simpler than this chili. No, it won't satisfy the mavens who claim authenticity has to be this way or that, but they can make their own meal.

• Because a pressure cooker traps most of the moisture in a dish and cooks so quickly, there's little time for excess fat to lose its moisture and break down. Using lean ground beef isn't (necessarily) a health concern, but more of a taste and texture factor.

• Browning the ground beef is as much about giving it better texture as about giving the meat a head start on cooking under pressure. After browning, the bits stay distinct and don't take on an unappealing "boiled" squishiness.

• Shorten this recipe by using frozen chopped onion and bell peppers. There's no need to thaw them; cook a couple of minutes longer to make sure they've lost any chill.

CHEESY CHILI MAC CASSEROLE

EFFORT: **A LITTLE** · PRESSURE: **HIGH** · TIME UNDER PRESSURE: **5 OR 8 MINUTES** · RELEASE: **MODIFIED NATURAL** · SERVES: **6 TO 8**

2 tablespoons olive oil

2 small yellow onions, chopped

Two 4$\frac{1}{2}$-ounce canned chopped mild green chiles (about 1 cup)

1 tablespoon minced garlic

1$\frac{1}{2}$ pounds lean ground beef

$\frac{1}{4}$ cup chili powder

1 teaspoon ground cumin

$\frac{1}{2}$ teaspoon salt

One 28-ounce can crushed tomatoes (about 3$\frac{1}{2}$ cups)

Two 15-ounce cans small red beans, drained and rinsed (about 3$\frac{1}{2}$ cups)

2 cups chicken broth

8 ounces dried ziti pasta

1 cup shredded Cheddar cheese (about 4 ounces)

1 Heat the oil in a 6-quart stovetop pressure cooker set over medium heat or in a 6-quart electric pressure cooker turned to the browning function. Add the onion, chiles, and garlic; cook, stirring often, until the onions soften a bit, about 3 minutes. Add the ground beef and stir until it loses its raw color, about 3 minutes.

2 Stir in the chili powder, cumin, and salt; cook until aromatic, about a minute. Stir in the crushed tomatoes, beans, broth, and pasta.

3 Lock the lid onto the pot.

STOVETOP: Raise the heat to high and bring the pot to high pressure (15 psi). Once this pressure has been reached, reduce the heat as much as possible while maintaining this pressure. Cook for 5 minutes.

·····················OR·····················

ELECTRIC: Set the machine to cook at high pressure (9–11 psi). Set the machine's timer to cook at this pressure for 8 minutes.

4 Reduce the pressure.

STOVETOP: Set the pot off the heat for 5 minutes.

·····················OR·····················

ELECTRIC: Turn off the machine or unplug it; set aside for 7 minutes.

Use the quick-release method to bring the pot's pressure fully to normal.

5 Unlock and open the pot. Sprinkle the cheese on top, set the lid loosely on the cooker, and set aside for 2 minutes to melt the cheese. Uncover and stir well before serving.

TESTERS' NOTES

• You won't believe how easy it is to make a real chili mac without any fake ingredients or cream-of-something-unknown. This meal's a robust one for a chilly evening. You can also use Colby, Jack, or mild American cheese instead of the Cheddar.

• There's quite a bit of chili powder here, not only to flavor the sauce but also to thicken it. To save money, look for large bottles of chili powder in the bulk aisle of your supermarket or from suppliers online.

GROUND BEEF AND SWEET POTATO STEW

EFFORT: **NOT MUCH** • PRESSURE: **HIGH** • TIME UNDER PRESSURE: **3 OR 5 MINUTES** • RELEASE: **QUICK** • SERVES: **4**

1 tablespoon olive oil

1½ pounds lean ground beef (about 93% lean)

1 large yellow onion, chopped

1 large sweet potato (about 1 pound), peeled and shredded through the large holes of a box grater

1 teaspoon ground cinnamon

1 teaspoon ground cumin

½ teaspoon dried sage

½ teaspoon dried oregano

½ teaspoon salt

½ teaspoon ground black pepper

2 tablespoons yellow cornmeal

2 tablespoons honey

2½ cups beef broth

1 Heat the oil in a 6-quart stovetop pressure cooker set over medium heat or in a 6-quart electric pressure cooker turned to the browning function. Crumble in the ground beef; cook, stirring occasionally, until it loses its raw color and browns a bit, about 5 minutes. Add the onion; cook, stirring often, until softened, about 3 minutes.

2 Stir in the sweet potato, cinnamon, cumin, sage, oregano, salt, and pepper. Cook for 1 minute, stirring constantly. Stir in the cornmeal and honey; cook for 1 minute, stirring often, to dissolve the cornmeal. Stir in the broth.

3 Lock the lid onto the pot.

STOVETOP: Raise the heat to high and bring the pot to high pressure (15 psi). Once this pressure has been reached, reduce the heat as low as possible while maintaining this pressure. Cook for 3 minutes.

······························ OR ·····························

ELECTRIC: Switch the machine to cook at high pressure (9–11 psi). Set the machine's timer to cook at high pressure for 5 minutes.

4 Use the quick-release method to drop the pot's pressure to normal.

5 Unlock and open the lid. Stir well and set aside, loosely covered, for 5 minutes before serving.

TESTERS' NOTES
• The sweet potatoes melt into this stew, thickening it quite a bit (along with the cornmeal).
• This stew has a Southwestern flavor palette, but without extra heat. If desired, you could either add up to ½ teaspoon cayenne with the dried spices or pass hot red pepper sauce at the table.
• Cinnamon has a distinct shelf life, no more than about a year in cool, dry conditions. After that, it loses much of its buzz.
• Use a standard, medium-grind cornmeal, the kind found in most supermarkets.

Serve It Up! Offer warmed corn tortillas on the side and dollop servings with chunky cranberry relish.

BEEF, MAC, AND BEAN CASSEROLE

EFFORT: **NOT MUCH** • PRESSURE: **HIGH** • TIME UNDER PRESSURE:
5 OR 8 MINUTES • RELEASE: **QUICK** • SERVES: **4**

1 tablespoon olive oil

1 medium yellow onion, chopped

1 medium green bell pepper, stemmed,
    seeded, and chopped

1 tablespoon minced garlic

1 pound lean ground beef (about 93%
    lean)

One 28-ounce can diced tomatoes (about
    3$\frac{1}{2}$ cups)

2 cups fresh corn kernels (about 2 large
    ears), or frozen kernels, thawed

One 15-ounce can kidney beans, drained
    and rinsed (aboue 1$\frac{3}{4}$ cups)

One 12-ounce bottle dark beer, preferably
    a brown ale

2 tablespoons sweet paprika

1 teaspoon dried oregano

1 teaspoon ground cumin

$\frac{1}{2}$ teaspoon pure chile powder, preferably
    chipotle

$\frac{1}{2}$ teaspoon salt

8 ounces dried medium pasta shells

1 Heat the oil in a 6-quart stovetop pressure cooker set over medium heat or in a 6-quart electric pressure cooker turned to the browning function. Add the onion, bell pepper, and garlic; cook, stirring often, until the onion becomes translucent, about 4 minutes.

2 Crumble in the ground beef. Cook, stirring often, until it has browned a bit, about 4 minutes. Add the tomatoes, corn, beans, beer, paprika, oregano, cumin, chile powder, and salt, stirring until most of the beer's foam dies down. Stir in the pasta until coated in the sauce.

3 Lock the lid onto the pot.

STOVETOP: Raise the heat to high and bring the pot to high pressure (15 psi). Once this pressure has been reached, lower the heat as much as possible while maintaining this pressure. Cook for 5 minutes.

································ **OR** ································

ELECTRIC: Set the machine to cook at high pressure (9–11 psi). Set the machine's timer to cook at high pressure for 8 minutes.

4 Use the quick-release method to bring the pot's pressure back to normal.

5 Unlock and remove the lid. Stir well before serving.

TESTERS' NOTES
• Here's a family favorite, sort of like a chili-mac casserole, but without any cheese and a little more like a stew. Look for pure ground chipotle (much smokier than regular chili powder) in the spice aisle.

• If you want to save time, look for pre-chopped onion and bell pepper on the salad bar or in the produce section at your supermarket.

• Do not use jumbo pasta shells or tiny mini-shells. The right ones should be between 1 and 1½ inches in length.

• For a non-alcoholic version, use 1½ cups beef broth plus 1 teaspoon sugar for the beer.

Serve It Up! Place a large spoonful of ricotta cheese in each of the serving bowls, then ladle the hot casserole on top. Garnish with chopped parsley leaves and/or finely grated lemon zest.

CHEESY BEEF AND TORTILLA CASSEROLE

EFFORT: **A LOT** · PRESSURE: **HIGH** · TIME UNDER PRESSURE: **20 OR 30 MINUTES** · RELEASE: **NATURAL** · SERVES: **6**

2 tablespoons olive oil

1 small yellow onion, chopped

One 4^1/$_2$-ounce can chopped mild green chiles (do not drain)

1 tablespoon minced garlic

1^1/$_4$ pounds lean ground beef (preferably 93% lean)

1^1/$_2$ tablespoons chili powder

^{1}/$_2$ teaspoon ground cumin

One 14-ounce can crushed tomatoes (about 1^3/$_4$ cups)

^{1}/$_4$ cup loosely packed fresh cilantro leaves, chopped

6 corn tortillas

2 cups shredded Cheddar cheese (about 8 ounces)

1 Set a large saucepan over medium heat for a couple of minutes. Swirl in the oil, then add the onion. Cook, stirring often, until softened, about 3 minutes. Add the chiles and garlic; cook for 1 minute.

2 Crumble in the ground beef. Cook, stirring often, until lightly browned, about 4 minutes. Stir in the chili powder and cumin; cook until aromatic, less than a minute. Add the tomatoes and cilantro. Cook another 2 minutes, stirring often. Remove the pan from the heat.

3 Set the pressure cooker rack in a 6-quart stovetop or electric cooker; pour in 2 cups water. Smooth ^{1}/$_2$ cup of the ground beef sauce into a 2-quart, high-sided, round casserole or soufflé dish. Add a tortilla, then a

heaping ^{1}/$_2$ cup of the sauce and ^{1}/$_3$ cup of the cheese, creating even layers of each. Repeat five more times; cover the casserole tightly with a layer of parchment paper and then of aluminum foil. Set the casserole on an aluminum sling (page 19) and use this sling to transfer the baking dish to the rack in the pressure cooker. Crimp the ends of the sling onto the pot.

4 Lock the lid onto the pot.

STOVETOP: Set the pot over high heat and bring it to high pressure (15 psi). Once this pressure has been reached, reduce the heat as much as possible while maintaining this pressure. Cook for 20 minutes.

·············· OR ··············

ELECTRIC: Set the machine to cook at high pressure (9–11 psi). Set the machine's timer to cook at this pressure for 30 minutes.

5 Reduce the pressure.

STOVETOP: Set the pot off the heat and allow its pressure to fall back to normal naturally, about 12 minutes.

·············· OR ··············

ELECTRIC: Turn off the machine or unplug it so it doesn't jump to its keep-warm setting. Let the pot's pressure return to normal naturally, 15 to 18 minutes.

6 Unlock and remove the lid. Set the cooker aside for 5 minutes to cool, then use the sling to lift the (hot!) casserole dish out of the pot. Uncover and cool for another 5 minutes before scooping out servings by the spoonful.

TESTERS' NOTES
• An old-fashioned Tex-Mex supper, this hearty dish will be a winner on a winter night.
• Note that the meat sauce additions to the baking dish are fairly small, only ^{1}/$_2$ cup at a time.

• Make the meat sauce (steps 1 and 2) up to 2 days in advance; store in the covered saucepan in the refrigerator. Set over medium heat and bring back to a bubble before building the casserole.

Serve It Up! Garnish the casserole with pickled jalapeño rings.

ITALIAN-STYLE GROUND BEEF AND PASTA CASSEROLE

EFFORT: **A LITTLE** • PRESSURE: **HIGH** • TIME UNDER PRESSURE: **5 OR 8 MINUTES** • RELEASE: **MODIFIED NATURAL** • SERVES: **4**

2 tablespoons olive oil

1 pound lean ground beef (preferably 93% lean)

1 medium yellow onion, chopped

1 medium green bell pepper, stemmed, cored, and chopped

1 medium yellow bell pepper, stemmed, cored, and chopped

2 teaspoons dried basil

1 teaspoon dried oregano or marjoram

1 teaspoon dried thyme

1/2 teaspoon fennel seeds

1/2 teaspoon salt

1/4 teaspoon red pepper flakes

3/4 cup dry, fruit-forward red wine, such as Zinfandel

One 28-ounce can crushed tomatoes (about 3 1/2 cups)

8 ounces dried ziti

1 Heat the oil in a 6-quart stovetop pressure cooker set over medium heat or in a 6-quart electric pressure cooker turned to the browning function. Add the ground beef; cook, stirring often, until browned, about 5 minutes. Use a slotted spoon to transfer the beef to a bowl.

2 Add the onion and chopped peppers to the pot; cook, stirring often, until the onion softens, about 5 minutes. Stir in the basil, oregano or marjoram, thyme, fennel seeds, salt, and red pepper flakes. Pour in the wine and scrape up any browned bits in the pot as the mixture comes to a simmer. Return the ground beef to the pot along with the crushed tomatoes and pasta. Stir well.

3 Lock the lid onto the pot.

STOVETOP: Raise the heat to high and bring the pot to high pressure (15 psi). Once this pressure has been reached, reduce the heat as low as possible while maintaining this pressure. Cook for 5 minutes.

································ **OR** ································

ELECTRIC: Switch the machine to cook at high pressure (9–11 psi). Set the machine's timer to cook for 8 minutes.

4 Reduce the pressure.

STOVETOP: Set the pot off the heat for 5 minutes.

································ **OR** ································

ELECTRIC: Turn off or unplug the machine; set aside for 5 minutes.

Use the quick-release method to bring the pot's pressure back to normal.

5 Unlock and open the lid. Stir well before serving

TESTERS' NOTES

• This pasta casserole, stocked with big flavors, should be served in bowls so you can catch every drop of the sauce.

(continued)

- For an easier preparation, omit all the spices and use up to 1½ tablespoons dried Italian seasoning blend.
- We allow the pressure to fall naturally for 5 minutes since there's little extra liquid here (only the wine and the tomato juices). That extra time lets the vegetables break down, providing more moisture to the sauce without extra broth bogging it down.

Serve It Up! Grate Parmesan cheese or aged Asiago over the servings.

CLASSIC MEATLOAF WITH BARBECUE GRAVY

EFFORT: **A LITTLE** • PRESSURE: **HIGH** • TIME UNDER PRESSURE: **20 OR 30 MINUTES** • RELEASE: **NATURAL** • SERVES: **6**

1 cup canned crushed tomatoes

³/₄ cup chicken broth

1 small sweet potato (about 8 ounces), shredded through the large holes of a box grater

2 tablespoons packed dark brown sugar

1 tablespoon white wine vinegar

2 teaspoons sweet paprika

1 teaspoon chili powder

¹/₂ teaspoon ground cloves

¹/₂ teaspoon celery seeds

¹/₂ teaspoon salt

2 pounds lean ground beef (preferably 93% lean)

¹/₂ cup Italian-seasoned dry breadcrumbs

1 large egg, at room temperature

¹/₄ cup loosely packed fresh parsley leaves, minced

1 tablespoon Worcestershire sauce

2 teaspoons minced garlic

2 teaspoons dried thyme

1 Mix the tomatoes, broth, sweet potato, brown sugar, vinegar, paprika, chili powder, cloves, celery seeds, and ¼ teaspoon salt in a 6-quart stovetop or electric pressure cooker until the brown sugar dissolves.

2 Mix the ground beef, breadcrumbs, egg, parsley, Worcestershire sauce, garlic, thyme, and the remaining ¼ teaspoon salt in a large bowl until the breadcrumbs and herbs are evenly distributed throughout the mixture. Form this into a large half-dome, like a sphere cut in half. Set into the sauce in the cooker; spoon and smear some of the tomato sauce over the meatloaf.

3 Lock the lid onto the pot.

STOVETOP: Raise the heat to high and bring the pot to high pressure (15 psi). Once this pressure has been reached, reduce the heat as much as possible while maintaining this pressure. Cook for 20 minutes.

·····················OR·····················

ELECTRIC: Set the machine to cook at high pressure (9–11 psi). Set the machine's timer to cook at high pressure for 30 minutes.

4 Reduce the pressure.

STOVETOP: Set the pot off the heat and allow its pressure to fall to normal naturally, 15 minutes.

·····················OR·····················

ELECTRIC: Turn off the machine or unplug it. Do not let it flip to its keep-warm setting. Let the pot's pressure return to normal naturally, 15 to 20 minutes.

5 Unlock and open the lid. Set aside to cool for 5 minutes. Use a sharp knife to cut the meatloaf into ½-inch slices while it's still in the cooker; remove these slices to plates. Dress the slices with the sauce.

• This sweet and salty meatloaf will be just the thing when you don't want to wait for one to bake in the oven. Imagine Italian flavors combined with American barbecue sauce, where the sweet potatoes melt into the rich, thick sauce.

• It's hard to lift a whole meatloaf out of a pressure cooker. Yes, you *can* do it, provided you have a large metal spatula in one hand, a flexible rubber spatula in the other (for balance), and strong nerves. In our opinion, it's easier to use a nonstick-safe spatula or knife and cut the meatloaf into slices right in the cooker, lifting them out one by one.

• Leftovers make amazing sandwiches. Skip the cold sauce and smear the bread with deli mustard.

MEATBALLS WITH ORZO, ARTICHOKES, AND TOMATOES

EFFORT: **A LITTLE** • PRESSURE: **HIGH** • TIME UNDER PRESSURE: **5 OR 8 MINUTES** • RELEASE: **QUICK** • SERVES: **4**

1¹/₂ **pounds lean ground beef (preferably 93% lean)**

¹/₂ **cup dried orzo**

1 medium shallot, peeled and shredded through the large holes of a box grater

1 tablespoon minced fresh dill fronds

2 teaspoons finely grated lemon zest

1 teaspoon minced garlic

1 large egg, at room temperature

2 tablespoons olive oil

One 28-ounce can diced tomatoes (about 3¹/₂ cups)

One 9-ounce box frozen artichoke heart quarters, thawed (about 2 cups)

¹/₂ **cup rosé wine, such as Bandol**

¹/₄ **cup loosely packed fresh basil leaves, minced**

2 tablespoons loosely packed fresh oregano leaves, minced

¹/₂ **teaspoon salt**

¹/₂ **teaspoon ground black pepper**

1 Mix the ground beef, orzo, shallot, dill, lemon zest, garlic, and egg in a large bowl until uniform. Form into twelve 2-inch balls.

2 Heat the oil in a 6-quart stovetop pressure cooker set over medium heat or in a 6-quart electric pressure cooker set to the browning function. Add the meatballs, just as many as will fit without crowding. Brown on all sides, turning occasionally, about 8 minutes. Transfer to a bowl and repeat with the rest of the meatballs.

3 Add the tomatoes, artichokes, wine, basil, oregano, salt, and pepper to the cooker; stir well to get any browned bits off the bottom of the pot. Return the meatballs and their juices to the sauce.

4 Lock the lid onto the pot.

STOVETOP: Raise the heat to high and bring the pot to high pressure (15 psi). Once this pressure has been reached, reduce the heat as much as possible while maintaining this pressure. Cook for 5 minutes.

·······················**OR**·······················

ELECTRIC: Switch the machine to cook at high pressure (9–11 psi). Set the machine's timer to cook at high pressure for 8 minutes.

5 Use the quick-release method to drop the pot's pressure back to normal.

6 Unlock and open the pot. Stir gently before scooping the meatballs into serving bowls; ladle the sauce over them.

TESTERS' NOTES
• The pasta in the meatballs keeps them tender and juicy under pressure, allowing them a firm texture despite the extreme conditions in the pot. Don't use whole wheat pasta here; you'll want the softer bite of the more standard stuff.

(continued)

- There are quite a few herbs in the mix. They'll add subtle notes to the overall dish. Don't stint: you need a fair amount to withstand the onslaught of the pressure and make a successful dinner.
- Frozen artichoke heart quarters can be hard to track down. You can use canned or jarred artichoke hearts (packed in water). Cut these in half, not quarters, in an effort to keep them more intact during cooking.

Serve It Up! Serve the meatballs and their sauce on a bed of wilted, stemmed spinach or chard.

HERB-STOCKED MINI MEATBALLS WITH RADIATORI

EFFORT: **A LITTLE** • PRESSURE: **HIGH** • TIME UNDER PRESSURE: **5 OR 8 MINUTES** • RELEASE: **QUICK** • SERVES: **4**

1 pound lean ground beef (preferably 93% lean)

1 tablespoon dried basil

1 teaspoon dried marjoram

1/2 teaspoon dried thyme

2 tablespoons olive oil

1 large fennel bulb, trimmed and chopped

1 medium yellow onion, chopped

1 medium red bell pepper, stemmed, cored, and chopped

8 ounces dried radiatori

One 28-ounce can diced tomatoes (about 3 1/2 cups)

1 cup chicken broth

1/2 cup dry white wine, such as Chardonnay

1 tablespoon dried oregano

1/2 teaspoon dried rosemary

1/2 teaspoon grated nutmeg

1/4 teaspoon salt

1 Mix the beef, basil, marjoram, and thyme in a medium bowl until the spices are evenly distributed throughout. Form the mixture into twenty 1-inch meatballs.

2 Heat the oil in a 6-quart stovetop pressure cooker set over medium heat or in a 6-quart electric pressure cooker turned to the browning function. Add the fennel, onion, and bell pepper; cook, stirring often, until the onion turns translucent, about 5 minutes.

3 Stir in the pasta, tomatoes, broth, wine, oregano, rosemary, nutmeg, and salt. Submerge the meatballs in the sauce.

4 Lock the lid onto the pot.

STOVETOP: Raise the heat to high and bring the pot to high pressure (15 psi). Once this pressure has been reached, reduce the heat as much as possible while maintaining this pressure. Cook for 5 minutes.

···················· **OR** ····················

ELECTRIC: Set the machine to cook at high pressure (9–11 psi). Set the machine's timer to cook at high pressure for 8 minutes.

5 Use the quick-release method to bring the pot's pressure back to normal.

6 Unlock and open the lid. Stir gently before serving.

TESTERS' NOTES
- Radiatori are small, crunched pieces of pasta that look like old-fashioned steam radiators. They'll stay firm in this quick meal, offering good texture against the soft meatballs.
- Make sure the meatballs are submerged or well coated in the sauce before you lock the lid in place. They need to pick up as many of its flavors as possible.

MEATBALL, CABBAGE, AND RICE CASSEROLE

EFFORT: **A LITTLE** · PRESSURE: **HIGH** · TIME UNDER PRESSURE:
7 OR 12 MINUTES · RELEASE: **QUICK** · SERVES: **4**

1 small green cabbage, cored and shredded

6 tablespoons raisins

1 tablespoon minced fresh dill fronds

1 teaspoon fennel seeds

1½ pounds lean ground beef (preferably 93% lean)

¾ cup *cooked* long-grain brown rice, roughly chopped

1 medium shallot, minced

1 large egg plus 1 large egg yolk, at room temperature

¼ cup finely chopped fresh parsley leaves

1 teaspoon minced garlic

½ teaspoon salt

½ teaspoon ground black pepper

One 28-ounce can crushed tomatoes (about 3½ cups)

3 tablespoons fresh lemon juice

2 tablespoons packed dark brown sugar

1 Mix the cabbage, raisins, dill, and fennel seeds in a large bowl. Use half this mixture to make an even bed in the bottom of a 6-quart stovetop or electric pressure cooker.

2 Mix the beef, rice, shallot, egg, egg yolk, parsley, garlic, salt, and pepper in a second large bowl until uniform, the parsley even throughout the mixture. Form into twelve 2-inch balls. Lay half these balls over the cabbage mixture, then top with an even layer of the remaining cabbage mixture. Nestle the remainder of the balls in this cabbage mixture.

3 Whisk the tomatoes, lemon juice, and brown sugar with ½ cup water in a large bowl until the brown sugar dissolves. Pour over the top of the ingredients in the pressure cooker.

4 Lock the lid onto the pot.

STOVETOP: Set the pot over high heat and bring it to high pressure (15 psi). Once this pressure has been reached, reduce the heat as low as possible while maintaining this pressure. Cook for 7 minutes.

·············· **OR** ··············

ELECTRIC: Set the machine to cook at high pressure (9–11 psi). Set the machine's timer to cook at high pressure for 12 minutes.

5 Use the quick-release method to bring the pot's pressure back to normal.

6 Unlock and open the lid. Dish up in large spoonfuls, dividing the sauce, cabbage, and meatballs among the serving bowls.

TESTERS' NOTES

• This is a deconstructed version of stuffed cabbage. It's really more of a one-pot meal than a standard meatball dish that needs other sides.

• The cabbage will begin to melt into the sauce, turning it rich and aromatic. Make sure you slice the cabbage into thin threads to get the desired effect. (You can also use 6 cups bagged, shredded cabbage.)

• The rice must be cooked: if you used raw rice, the cabbage would be squishy by the time the rice was tender.

JALAPEÑO MEATBALLS

EFFORT: **A LITTLE** • PRESSURE: **HIGH** • TIME UNDER PRESSURE: **5 OR 8 MINUTES** • RELEASE: **QUICK** • SERVES: **4 TO 6**

1 pound lean ground beef (preferably 93% lean)

³/₄ pound ground pork

¹/₂ cup plain panko breadcrumbs

1 large egg, at room temperature

Up to 2 tablespoons minced pickled jalapeño rings

Up to 2 teaspoons brine from the pickled jalapeños

1¹/₄ teaspoons ground cumin

¹/₂ teaspoon ground cinnamon

1 medium yellow onion

One 28-ounce can crushed tomatoes (about 3¹/₂ cups)

¹/₂ cup loosely packed fresh cilantro leaves, finely chopped

2 teaspoons minced garlic

Up to 1 teaspoon red pepper flakes

1 Mix both meats, breadcrumbs, egg, minced jalapeño, jalapeño brine, cumin, and cinnamon in a large bowl until even and uniform. Use clean, dry hands to form into twelve 2-inch meatballs.

2 Grate the onion into a 6-quart stovetop or electric pressure cooker, using the large holes of a box grater. Squeeze the grated onion by the handful over the sink to remove its excess liquid; put it back into the cooker. Stir in the tomatoes, cilantro, garlic, and red pepper flakes. Nestle the meatballs in the sauce.

3 Lock the lid onto the pot.

STOVETOP: Set the pot over high heat and bring it to high pressure (15 psi). Once this pressure has been reached, reduce the heat as low as possible while maintaining this pressure. Cook for 5 minutes.

·························· **OR** ··························

ELECTRIC: Set the machine to cook at high pressure (9–11 psi). Set the machine's timer to cook at high pressure for 8 minutes.

4 Return the pot's pressure to normal with the quick-release method.

5 Unlock and open the lid. Stir gently before serving.

TESTERS' NOTES
• Skip the standard recipes and cook up a batch of these flavorful meatballs, simmered in an aromatic tomato sauce.
• Pressure cookers dull a chile's heat but bring out its spiky, fruity notes. If you're spice-averse, use half the stated amounts of jalapeños, their brine, and red pepper flakes. You can always pass more at the table.
• The egg is at room temperature so it will better mix with and coat the meat. To get an egg to the right temperature, either set it out on the counter for 20 minutes or submerge it in a bowl of warm (not hot) tap water for 4 or 5 minutes.

Serve It Up! Rather than serving these meatballs and their sauce over pasta, offer them over a mix of long-grain white rice and black beans.

BEEF-AND-BULGUR STUFFED CABBAGE

EFFORT: **A LOT** • PRESSURE: **HIGH** • TIME UNDER PRESSURE: **10 OR 15 MINUTES** • RELEASE: **QUICK, THEN QUICK** • SERVES: **6**

½ cup quick-cooking bulgur

½ cup boiling water

12 large savoy cabbage leaves

1 medium yellow onion

1 pound lean ground beef (preferably 93% lean)

1 teaspoon salt

One 28-ounce can crushed tomatoes (about 3½ cups)

½ cup chicken broth

3 tablespoons red wine vinegar

2 tablespoons honey

1 tablespoon minced fresh dill fronds

1 tablespoon loosely packed fresh oregano leaves, minced

½ teaspoon red pepper flakes

1 Mix the bulgur and boiling water in a large bowl; cover and set aside for 30 minutes.

2 Fill a 6-quart stovetop pressure cooker or electric pressure cooker two-thirds full of water. Set the stovetop pot over high heat or turn the electric cooker to the browning function; bring the water to a simmer. Immerse the cabbage leaves one by one in the water, pressing down each with the back of a wooden spoon before adding the next.

3 Lock the lid onto the pot.

STOVETOP: Turn off the heat without bringing the pot to high pressure. Set aside for 3 minutes.
························· **OR** ·····························
ELECTRIC: Turn off or unplug the machine without bringing it to high pressure. Set aside for 3 minutes.

4 Use the quick-release method to return the pot's pressure to normal.

5 Unlock and open the pot. Drain the leaves into a large colander set in the sink; rinse them with cold tap water to stop the cooking. Drain well and transfer the leaves to paper towels to dry.

6 Grate the onion through the large holes of a box grater into a small bowl. Squeeze the onion dry by the handful over the sink to remove excess liquid before returning it to the bowl.

7 Fluff the bulgur with a fork; add half the grated onion, the meat, and ½ teaspoon salt. Mix until uniform, then form into twelve 1½-inch meatballs. Trim the tough central stems from the cabbage leaves. Set one meatball in each leaf; roll the leaves closed, folding in the sides to make even packages.

8 Whisk the tomatoes, broth, vinegar, honey, dill, oregano, red pepper flakes, the remaining grated onion, and the remaining ½ teaspoon salt in the pressure cooker. Nestle the stuffed cabbage packets into the sauce.

9 Lock the lid onto the pot.

STOVETOP: Set the pot over high heat; bring it to high pressure (15 psi). Once this pressure has been reached, reduce the heat as much as possible while maintaining this pressure. Cook for 7 minutes.
························· **OR** ·····························
ELECTRIC: Set the machine to cook at high pressure (9–11 psi). Set the machine's timer to cook at high pressure for 12 minutes.

10 Use the quick-released method to drop the pot's pressure back to normal.

11 Unlock and remove the lid. Scoop out the stuffed cabbage rolls with a very large spoon,

(continued)

setting two in each bowl with plenty of sauce ladled over the top.

TESTERS' NOTES

• An Old World favorite, this classic comfort food is done in minutes with a pressure cooker—and so the texture of the cabbage is somewhat firmer and a better match for the beef.

• By using meatballs, rather than a looser stuffing, the packages have a better chance of staying together under intense pressure.

• You can use ground turkey instead of ground beef.

SMOKY PORTER SIRLOIN TIP STEW

EFFORT: **A LITTLE** • PRESSURE: **HIGH** • TIME UNDER PRESSURE: **18 OR 30 MINUTES** • RELEASE: **NATURAL** • SERVES: **6**

2 pounds sirloin tips, cut into 1$\frac{1}{2}$-inch pieces

1 tablespoon smoked paprika

2 teaspoons dried marjoram

1 teaspoon dried thyme

8 ounces slab bacon, preferably double-smoked, cut into $\frac{1}{2}$-inch pieces

1 medium yellow onion, chopped

Up to 2 canned chipotle chiles in adobo sauce, stemmed, seeded, and chopped

Up to 2 tablespoons adobo sauce from the can

1 teaspoon minced garlic

1 tablespoon unsulfured molasses

Up to $\frac{3}{4}$ cup dark beer, preferably a smoky porter

One 28-ounce can diced tomatoes, drained (about 3$\frac{1}{2}$ cups)

$\frac{1}{4}$ cup golden raisins

1 Mix the beef, smoked paprika, marjoram, and thyme in a large bowl until the pieces of meat are evenly coated in the spices.

2 Put the bacon in a 6-quart stovetop pressure cooker set over medium heat or in a 6-quart electric pressure cooker turned to the browning function; fry, stirring often, until crisp, about 6 minutes. Use a slotted spoon to transfer the bacon to a big bowl.

3 Add the spiced beef to the cooker and brown on all sides, stirring and turning occasionally, about 8 minutes. Transfer the beef to the bowl with the bacon.

4 Add the onion, chipotles, adobo sauce, and garlic to the cooker; stir until the onion begins to soften, about 3 minutes. Stir in the molasses until bubbling, then add $\frac{3}{4}$ cup beer to a stovetop cooker or $\frac{1}{2}$ cup beer to an electric model. Stir in the tomatoes and raisins, scraping up some of the browned bits in the pot. Add the beef and bacon, plus any juices in their bowl, and stir well.

5 Lock the lid onto the pot.

STOVETOP: Raise the heat to high and bring the pot to high pressure (15 psi). Once this pressure has been reached, reduce the heat as much as possible while maintaining this pressure. Cook for 18 minutes.

················· OR ·················

ELECTRIC: Set the machine to cook at high pressure (9–11 psi). Set the machine's timer to cook at high pressure for 30 minutes.

6 Reduce the pressure.

STOVETOP: Set the pot off the heat and allow its pressure to fall back to normal naturally, about 15 minutes.

················· OR ·················

ELECTRIC: Turn the machine off or unplug it so it doesn't flip to its keep-warm setting. Let its pressure fall to normal naturally, 15 to 20 minutes.

If the pressure has not returned to normal within 20 minutes, use the quick-release method to drop it back to normal.

7 Unlock and open the pot; stir well before serving.

TESTERS' NOTES
• Sirloin tips make a flavorful (and economical) addition to this stew. They are a tougher cut of beef, better for braising. (You can also use beef top round roast or round-tip steaks.)
• There are plenty of chiles here. Adjust the amounts to suit your taste—the upper range will be quite a mouth-burner.
• You don't have to drain the tomatoes. You can add all their liquid, but then you'll end up with a well-stocked soup, rather than a stew.
• You can use honey (for a sweeter finish) in lieu of the molasses.

SIRLOIN TIPS WITH PORT, SHALLOTS, AND CHERRIES

EFFORT: **A LITTLE** • PRESSURE: **HIGH** • TIME UNDER PRESSURE: **18 OR 30 MINUTES** • RELEASE: **NATURAL** • SERVES: **6**

2 pounds sirloin tips, cut into 1¹/₂-inch pieces

¹/₂ teaspoon salt

¹/₂ teaspoon ground black pepper

2 tablespoons olive oil

8 medium shallots, peeled and lobes separated

2 medium garlic cloves, halved lengthwise

1 tablespoon packed dark brown sugar

1 tablespoon packed fresh rosemary leaves, finely chopped

2 tablespoons balsamic vinegar

¹/₂ cup non-vintage ruby port

1 cup chicken broth

¹/₂ cup dried sour cherries

12 baby carrots, halved widthwise

1 star anise pod

1 Season the meat with the salt and pepper. Heat the oil in a 6-quart stovetop pressure cooker set over medium heat or in a 6-quart electric pressure cooker set to the browning function. Add as many beef pieces as will fit without crowding; brown well on all sides, stirring occasionally, about 8 minutes. Transfer to a large bowl and finish browning the remaining pieces before getting them into that bowl.

2 Add the shallots and garlic to the pressure cooker; cook, stirring often, until the shallots begin to brown a bit at the edges, about 3 minutes. Stir in the brown sugar and rosemary; then pour in the vinegar. Stir until bubbling, then add the port. Scrape up any browned bits in the pot, then pour in the broth. Add the dried cherries, carrots, and star anise pod, as well as the meat and any juices in the bowl. Stir well.

3 Lock the lid onto the pot.

STOVETOP: Raise the heat to high and bring the pot to high pressure (15 psi). Once this pressure has been reached, reduce the heat as much as possible while maintaining this pressure. Cook for 18 minutes.

·······················**OR**·······················

ELECTRIC: Set the machine to cook at high pressure (9–11 psi). Set the machine's timer to cook at high pressure for 30 minutes.

(continued)

4 Reduce the pressure.

STOVETOP: Set the pot off the heat and allow its pressure to fall back to normal naturally, about 15 minutes.

················· **OR** ·················

ELECTRIC: Switch off the machine or unplug it. (Do not let it move to its keep-warm setting.) Let the pressure fall back to normal naturally, 15 to 20 minutes.

If the pressure has not returned to normal within 20 minutes, use the quick-release function to drop it back to normal.

5 Unlock and open the pot. Stir well; discard the star anise pod before serving.

TESTERS' NOTES
• By combining sour cherries and port, as well as balsamic vinegar and brown sugar, you'll be able to make a sweet-and-sour beef stew that needs little more than a glass of Syrah on the side.
• If the shallots you've got are not double-lobed, double the amount of single-lobed shallots.
• You can use beef top round instead of the sirloin tips, and pomegranate juice for the port.

SHREDDED BARBECUE SKIRT STEAK

EFFORT: **A LITTLE** • PRESSURE: **HIGH** • TIME UNDER PRESSURE: **25 OR 42 MINUTES** • RELEASE: **NATURAL** • SERVES: **6**

¼ cup unsweetened apple juice

¼ cup fresh lime juice

Up to 3 canned chipotles in adobo sauce, stemmed, seeded, and chopped

1 medium shallot, chopped

1 tablespoon minced garlic

1 tablespoon packed fresh oregano leaves, finely chopped

1 tablespoon ground cumin

½ teaspoon salt

¼ teaspoon ground cloves

4 juniper berries (optional)

2 tablespoons rendered bacon fat

3 pounds beef skirt steak, cut into 6-inch-long pieces

1 Place the apple juice, lime juice, chipotles, shallot, garlic, oregano, cumin, salt, cloves, and juniper berries, if using, in a large blender or food processor; cover and blend or process until smooth, stopping the machine a couple of times to scrape down the inside of the canister.

2 Melt the bacon fat in a 6-quart stovetop pressure cooker set over medium heat or in a 6-quart electric pressure cooker turned to the browning function. Add one or two of the steaks and brown on both sides, about 4 minutes, turning once. Transfer to a plate and continue browning until you've worked your way through all the steak pieces.

3 Return the meat and any juices on its plate to the cooker. Pour the pureed sauce over the beef; stir well.

4 Lock the lid onto the pot.

STOVETOP: Raise the heat to high and bring the pot to high pressure (15 psi). Once this pressure has been reached, reduce the heat as much as possible while maintaining this. Cook for 25 minutes.

·······················OR·······················

ELECTRIC: Set the pot to cook at high pressure (9–11 psi). Set the machine's timer to cook at high pressure for 42 minutes.

5 Reduce the pressure.

STOVETOP: Set the pot off the heat and allow its pressure to return to normal naturally, about 15 minutes.

·······················OR·······················

ELECTRIC: Turn off the machine or unplug it. Allow its pressure to fall to normal naturally, 15 to 20 minutes.

6 Unlock and open the lid. Transfer the meat to a large cutting board; shred with two forks. Return the meat to the sauce in the cooker; stir well before serving.

TESTERS' NOTES
• Smoky and spicy, this dish is a cross between Caribbean barbacoa and a Southwestern stew. The juniper berries give it an herbaceous earthiness.
• Skirt steak is a long, trimmed cut from the underside of the cow. Because ruminants like cows use the muscle a lot, a skirt steak is in need of good tenderizing under pressure. (Do not substitute flank steak.)
• You can use unsalted butter instead of the bacon fat (if desired, also add ½ teaspoon smoked paprika to the barbecue sauce).

Serve It Up! Offer this hearty concoction on open-faced Kaiser rolls with cole slaw and dill pickles on the side.

FLANK STEAK WITH SWEET POTATO GRAVY

EFFORT: **A LITTLE** · PRESSURE: **HIGH** · TIME UNDER PRESSURE: **40 OR 60 MINUTES** · RELEASE: **NATURAL** · SERVES: **4**

1 tablespoon unsalted butter

1 tablespoon olive oil

2 pounds flank steak, cut into 4 equal chunks

1 medium yellow onion, chopped

1 large sweet potato (about 1 pound), peeled and grated through the large holes of a box grater

1 tablespoon sweet paprika

2 teaspoons packed stemmed fresh thyme leaves

1/2 teaspoon salt

1/4 teaspoon ground cloves

1/4 teaspoon cayenne

1 cup beef broth

3 tablespoons tomato paste

1 Melt the butter in the oil in a 6-quart stovetop pressure cooker set over medium heat or in a 6-quart electric pressure cooker turned to the browning function. Add the beef, probably just two pieces to avoid crowding, and brown well, about 6 minutes, turning once. Transfer the beef to a big bowl and repeat with the remaining pieces.

2 Add the onion; cook, stirring often, until softened, about 3 minutes. Add the sweet potato, paprika, thyme, salt, cloves, and cayenne. Cook for 1 minute, then pour in the broth and stir well.

3 Stir in the tomato paste as the mixture comes to a simmer, scraping up any browned bits in the pot. Stir the meat and any juices back into the pot.

(continued)

4 Lock the lid in place.

STOVETOP: Raise the heat to high and bring the pot to high pressure (15 psi). Once this pressure has been reached, reduce the heat as much as possible while maintaining this pressure. Cook for 40 minutes.

·························· **OR** ··························

ELECTRIC: Set the machine to cook at high pressure (9–11 psi). Set the machine's timer to cook at this pressure for 60 minutes.

5 Reduce the pressure.

STOVETOP: Turn off the heat and allow the pressure in the pot to return to normal naturally, about 18 minutes.

·························· **OR** ··························

ELECTRIC: Unplug the machine or turn it off. (Do not let it flip to its keep-warm setting.) Allow the pressure to fall to normal naturally, 18 to 22 minutes.

6 Unlock and open the lid. Transfer the chunks of meat to four serving bowls; ladle the sauce and vegetables around the beef in each bowl.

TESTERS' NOTES

• This fairly simple one-pot supper offers earthy flavors from the spices plus a lot of sweetness from the tomatoes, onions, and sweet potatoes, all to accent the beef.
• The only surprise may well be the ground cloves. Paired with the cayenne, the two spices put a slightly sophisticated twist on American comfort food.
• The meat will be so tender, serve it in bowls with a fork and spoon. Everyone can shred the meat in their bowls, making a rustic version of pulled beef.

Serve It Up! Garnish each bowl with shelled fresh peas (or frozen that have been thawed and warmed in the microwave).

FLANK STEAK AND BROCCOLI "STIR-FRY"

EFFORT: **A LITTLE** • PRESSURE: **HIGH** • TIME UNDER PRESSURE: **7 OR 10 MINUTES** • RELEASE: **QUICK** • SERVES: **4**

1 tablespoon toasted sesame oil
1 medium yellow onion, chopped
2 teaspoons minced fresh ginger
2 teaspoons minced garlic
1¼ pounds flank steak, cut into ¼-inch-thick slices against the grain
Up to ¼ cup chicken broth
2 tablespoons soy sauce
2 tablespoons dry sherry
2 tablespoons rice vinegar
½ tablespoon cornstarch
4 cups small broccoli florets

1 Heat the oil in a 6-quart stovetop pressure cooker set over medium heat or in a 6-quart electric pressure cooker turned to the browning function. Add the onion, ginger, and garlic; stir-fry for 2 minutes, tossing and stirring all the while. Add the meat; stir-fry just until it has lost its raw color, approximately 2 minutes.

2 Stir in ¼ cup broth in a stovetop pressure cooker or 2 tablespoons broth in an electric model, along with the soy sauce, sherry, and vinegar.

3 Lock the lid onto the pot.

STOVETOP: Raise the heat to high and bring the pot to high pressure (15 psi). Once this pressure has been reached, reduce the heat as much as possible while maintaining this pressure. Cook for 7 minutes.

4 Use the quick-release method to return the pot's pressure to normal.

5 Unlock and open the lid. Set the stovetop model back over medium-high heat or turn the electric model to its browning function. Whisk the cornstarch and 2 teaspoons water in a small bowl, then stir the slurry into the bubbling sauce in the cooker. Cook, stirring often, until thickened, about 20 seconds.

6 Stir in the broccoli and lock the lid onto the pot. Set the stovetop model off the heat or turn off the electric model. Set aside for 10 minutes. Unlock the lid and stir again before serving.

TESTERS' NOTES

• No, of course you can't make an authentic stir-fry in a pressure cooker. But you can replicate the flavors for a close approximation that's quick and satisfying.
• By just steaming the broccoli at the end, it retains much of its crunchy texture. The pot will most likely drop to normal pressure over the 10 minutes you set it aside. If it doesn't, use the quick-release method to bring the pressure back to normal.
• For a spicier dish, add up to 1 teaspoon sambal oelek with the rice vinegar.
• You can use tri-tip steak or skirt steak instead of the flank steak, 1 tablespoon white wine vinegar and 1 additional tablespoon chicken broth for the rice vinegar, and dry vermouth or dry white wine and a pinch of sugar instead of the sherry.

Serve It Up! Serve over rice noodles (sometimes called *rice stick noodles*).

STUFFED FLANK STEAK with BACON and PICKLES

EFFORT: **A LOT** • PRESSURE: **HIGH** • TIME UNDER PRESSURE: **50 OR 70 MINUTES** • RELEASE: **NATURAL** • SERVES: **6**

3 thick-cut bacon strips, halved crosswise
2 pounds beef flank steak
2 tablespoons prepared horseradish
3 small dill pickles, halved lengthwise (about ¹/₂ inch in width)
¹/₂ cup beef broth
¹/₂ cup unsweetened apple juice
1 teaspoon dried thyme
¹/₄ teaspoon ground cloves
¹/₄ teaspoon celery seeds
¹/₄ teaspoon ground black pepper
¹/₂ tablespoon potato starch or cornstarch

1 Fry the bacon in a 6-quart stovetop pressure cooker set over medium heat or in a 6-quart electric pressure cooker turned to the browning function, just until browned but still soft, about 3 minutes. Transfer the bacon to a cutting board; take the stovetop pot off the heat or turn off the electric pressure cooker.

2 Set the flank steak on a cutting board flatter side up; smear the top surface with horseradish. Alternate the bacon strips and pickles down the steak, setting them widthwise to the meat and leaving a third of the steak open at one end. Starting at the other end, roll the steak closed, folding the bacon and pickles inside it. Tie the flank steak closed with three pieces of butcher's twine, each about 16 inches long. Wrap one piece widthwise around the middle of the roast; tie securely but not so tight that it cuts into the meat. Then tie the roll in two more places: about 1 inch from each end.

(continued)

3 Set the stovetop pressure cooker back over medium heat or turn the electric cooker back to its browning mode. Melt any bacon fat inside, then add the steak roll. Brown on all sides, turning gently, about 6 minutes. Transfer to the cutting board.

4 Add the broth, apple juice, thyme, cloves, celery seeds, and pepper to the cooker. Stir well to scrape up any browned bits in the pot, then nestle the meat into the sauce.

5 Lock the lid onto the pot.

STOVETOP: Raise the heat to high and bring the pot to high pressure (15 psi). Once this pressure has been reached, reduce the heat as much as possible while maintaining this pressure. Cook for 50 minutes.

······················ **OR** ·······················

ELECTRIC: Set the machine to cook at high pressure (9–11 psi). Set the machine's timer to cook at high pressure for 70 minutes.

6 Reduce the pressure.

STOVETOP: Set the pot off the heat and let its pressure return to normal naturally, about 18 minutes.

······················ **OR** ·······················

ELECTRIC: Turn off the machine or unplug it. Do not let it flip to its keep-warm setting. Allow its pressure to fall back to normal naturally, 18 to 22 minutes.

7 Unlock and open the lid; transfer the meat roll to a carving board. Set the stovetop model back over medium-high heat or turn the electric one to its browning mode; bring the sauce to a simmer.

8 Whisk the potato starch or cornstarch into 2 teaspoons water in a small bowl; stir the slurry into the pressure cooker. Cook,

stirring constantly, until thickened and bubbling, about 30 seconds. Remove the cooker from the heat or turn off the electric model. Cut the beef roll into 1-inch slices; serve in bowls with the sauce ladled on top.

TESTERS' NOTES
• This hearty supper is German beer house food: the vinegar in the pickles and the horseradish mellow beautifully under pressure.
• Don't worry if the bacon and pickles hang out of the roll a bit. They'll hold together when the beef is tied.
• If desired, place thin slices of Havarti cheese on the beef on top of the horseradish.

OLD SCHOOL SWISS STEAK WITH MUSHROOM GRAVY

EFFORT: **A LITTLE** • PRESSURE: **HIGH** • TIME UNDER PRESSURE: **50 OR 75 MINUTES** • RELEASE: **NATURAL** • SERVES: **6**

1$\frac{1}{2}$ cups beef broth

2 tablespoons Worcestershire sauce

2 tablespoons all-purpose flour

$\frac{1}{2}$ teaspoon ground black pepper

2 tablespoons olive oil

2$\frac{1}{2}$ pounds eye of round roast, tied widthwise in three places with butcher's twine

8 ounces white button mushrooms, thinly sliced

8 medium scallions, green and white parts, thinly sliced

1 Whisk the broth, Worcestershire sauce, flour, and pepper in a large bowl until the flour dissolves; set aside.

2 Heat the oil in a 6-quart stovetop pressure cooker set over medium heat or in a 6-quart electric pressure cooker turned to the browning function. Add the meat; brown on all sides, turning occasionally, about 6 minutes. Transfer to a large bowl.

3 Add the mushrooms and scallions to the cooker; cook, stirring often, until softened, about 4 minutes. Whisk the broth mixture one more time, then pour it into the cooker. Stir until bubbling and slightly thickened, scraping up any browned bits on the bottom of the pot. Return the meat to the gravy.

4 Lock the lid onto the pot.

STOVETOP: Raise the heat to high and bring the pot to high pressure (15 psi). Once this pressure has been reached, reduce the heat as much as possible while maintaining this pressure. Cook for 50 minutes.

·························· **OR** ··························

ELECTRIC: Set the machine to cook at high pressure (9–11 psi). Set the machine's timer to cook at high pressure for 75 minutes.

5 Reduce the pressure.

STOVETOP: Set the pot off the heat and allow its pressure to drop back to normal naturally, about 18 minutes.

·························· **OR** ··························

ELECTRIC: Turn off or unplug the machine. Do not let it flip to its keep-warm setting. Allow its pressure to fall to normal naturally, 18 to 22 minutes.

6 Unlock and open the pot. Transfer the meat to a cutting board; let stand for 5 minutes. Snip off and discard the twine. Slice the roast into ½-inch-thick rounds. Serve the rounds in the gravy.

TESTERS' NOTES

• Cafeteria food? No way! This is a hearty supper for those chilly weeknights when you've got a little extra time. Yes, it takes quite a long while in the pressure cooker but far less time than it would in a standard stovetop braise.

• If you don't have a bottle of Worcestershire sauce in your fridge, you should. It's a chef's secret, the little bit of umami and salt added to so many dishes for a depth of flavor.

• The butcher at your supermarket may be willing to tie the roast for you.

Serve It Up! You'll need mashed potatoes but don't mash them with butter and milk; instead, try a combination of chicken broth and sour cream, garnished with a little grated nutmeg.

SWISS STEAKS WITH TOMATOES AND CREAM

EFFORT: **A LITTLE** • PRESSURE: **HIGH** • TIME UNDER PRESSURE: **20 OR 30 MINUTES** • RELEASE: **NATURAL** • SERVES: **6**

2 tablespoons olive oil

2 pounds beef eye of round, cut into 6 equal steaks

½ teaspoon salt

½ teaspoon ground black pepper

2 tablespoons minced garlic

½ cup moderately dry red wine, like Zinfandel

One 15-ounce can diced tomatoes (about 1¾ cups)

3 tablespoons packed fresh oregano leaves, minced

¼ cup heavy cream

(continued)

1 Heat the oil in a 6-quart stovetop pressure cooker set over medium heat or in a 6-quart electric pressure cooker. Season the steaks with the salt and pepper, then brown them in batches in the cooker, about 5 minutes per batch, turning once. Transfer them to a large plate.

2 Add the garlic to the cooker; cook for about 30 seconds, just until aromatic. Pour in the wine and scrape up any browned bits on the bottom of the pot as the wine comes to a simmer. Continue simmering until the wine has been reduced to about half its original volume, about 3 minutes. Stir in the tomatoes and oregano; return the steaks to the cooker.

3 Lock the lid onto the pot.

STOVETOP: Raise the heat to high and bring the pot to high pressure (15 psi). Once this pressure has been reached, reduce the heat as low as possible while maintaining this pressure. Cook for 20 minutes.

················**OR**················

ELECTRIC: Set the machine to cook at high pressure (9–11 psi). Set the machine's timer to cook at high pressure for 30 minutes.

4 Reduce the pressure.

STOVETOP: Set the pot off the heat and allow its pressure to fall to normal naturally, about 18 minutes.

················**OR**················

ELECTRIC: Turn off the machine or unplug it so it doesn't switch to its keep-warm setting. Allow its pressure to fall to normal naturally, 18 to 22 minutes.

5 Unlock and open the lid. Transfer the steaks to serving plates or a platter. Set the stovetop cooker over medium heat or turn the electric cooker to its browning function.

Stir in the cream and bring the sauce to a simmer, stirring occasionally. Simmer for 1 minute, then ladle the sauce over the steaks.

TESTERS' NOTES
• They're called "steaks," but they're actually mini-roasts, one per bowl. They're so tender you can serve them with a fork and spoon.
• The pressure cooker excels at making sauces: they come out complex but vibrant with surprisingly layered flavors. With cream, this one's even better!
• Don't be tempted to use dried oregano here. The fresh leaves will give a spiky lightness to the sauce.
• For a more complex flavor profile, add one 4-inch cinnamon stick with the tomatoes and cream. Remove it before serving.
• Substitute beef rump roast for the eye of round roast.

SWISS STEAK CASSEROLE WITH ONIONS AND TOMATOES

EFFORT: **A LOT** • PRESSURE: **HIGH** • TIME UNDER PRESSURE: **18 OR 27 MINUTES** • RELEASE: **NATURAL** • SERVES: **6**

One 28-ounce can diced tomatoes (about 3¹/₂ cups)

3 tablespoons olive oil

2 large yellow onions, halved and thinly sliced

One 4¹/₂-ounce can diced mild green chiles (about ¹/₂ cup)

1 tablespoon minced garlic

2 teaspoons dried basil

2 teaspoons dried oregano

1 teaspoon dried thyme

¹/₂ teaspoon salt

¹/₂ teaspoon ground black pepper

2 pounds beef eye of round, cut into ½-inch-thick slices

½ cup dry, hearty red wine, such as Syrah

2 tablespoons tomato paste

2 tablespoons all-purpose flour

1 Drain the tomatoes in a colander set over a large bowl; set the tomatoes and the liquid aside separately.

2 Heat the oil in a 6-quart stovetop pressure cooker set over medium heat or in a 6-quart electric pressure cooker set to the browning function. Add the onions and cook, stirring often, until very soft, even browned, about 10 minutes.

3 Use a slotted spoon to transfer the onions to a large bowl; stir the drained tomatoes, the chiles, garlic, basil, oregano, thyme, salt, and pepper into the bowl with the onions. Layer this mixture and the beef slices in the cooker, starting and ending with a layer of the onion mixture. Overlap the meat slices as little as possible.

4 Whisk the wine, tomato paste, and flour in the bowl with the tomato juice until the flour dissolves, then pour the mixture over the layers in the pot.

5 Lock the lid into place.

STOVETOP: Raise the heat to high and bring the pot to high pressure (15 psi). Once the pressure has been reached, reduce the heat as low as possible while maintaining the pressure. Cook for 18 minutes.

·············· **OR** ··············

ELECTRIC: Switch the machine to high pressure (9–11 psi). Set the timer to cook at that pressure for 27 minutes.

6 Reduce the pressure.

STOVETOP: Set the pot off the heat and allow its pressure to fall to normal naturally, about 18 minutes.

·············· **OR** ··············

ELECTRIC: Turn off the machine or unplug it so it doesn't flip to its keep-warm setting. Allow the pressure to fall back to normal naturally, 18 to 22 minutes.

If the pressure has not returned to normal in 22 minutes, use the quick-release method to drop it to normal.

7 Unlock and open the lid. Dish up into bowls, ladling the sauce over the meat.

TESTERS' NOTES

• By layering the steak with the onion mixture, you'll end up with a comforting, one-pot casserole.

• To prepare the onion properly, slice it in half through its root end, then set both halves cut side down on your cutting board. Starting at one side of the onion, slice thin strips across the onion, thereby creating little half-moons. Separate the rings before cooking.

TOP ROUND WITH BOURBON, BACON, AND POTATOES

EFFORT: **A LOT** • PRESSURE: **HIGH** • TIME UNDER PRESSURE: **50 OR 70 MINUTES** • RELEASE: **QUICK, THEN NATURAL** • SERVES: **6**

2 teaspoons coarsely ground black
    pepper or cracked black peppercorns

3-pound beef top round roast

4 thick-cut bacon slices, chopped

1 large green bell pepper, stemmed,
    cored, and chopped

1½ cups beef broth

¼ cup bourbon

One 6-inch rosemary sprig

1½ pounds small yellow potatoes, such
    as Yukon Gold

1 Spread the ground pepper on a large cutting board; roll the roast in the pepper to coat evenly and thoroughly. Set aside.

2 Fry the bacon crisp in a 6-quart stovetop pressure cooker set over medium heat or in a 6-quart electric pressure cooker turned to the browning function, stirring often, about 4 minutes. Use a slotted spoon to transfer the bacon to a big bowl.

3 Add the roast to the pot; brown on all sides, turning often, about 6 minutes. Transfer the roast to the bowl with the bacon. Add the bell pepper; stir over the heat until softened a bit, about 3 minutes.

4 Pour the broth into the pot, then the bourbon; scrape up any browned bits on the bottom of the pot as the liquids come to a simmer. Tuck the rosemary into the sauce; return the bacon and the roast to the pot, as well as any juices in their bowl.

5 Lock the lid onto the pot.

STOVETOP: Raise the heat to high and bring the pot to high pressure (15 psi). Once this pressure has been reached, reduce the heat as much as possible while maintaining this pressure. Cook for 40 minutes.

········· OR ·········

ELECTRIC: Set the machine to cook at high pressure (9–11 psi). Set the machine's timer to cook at high pressure for 55 minutes.

6 Use the quick-release method to return the pot's pressure to normal.

7 Unlock and remove the lid. Add the potatoes.

8 Lock the lid back onto the pot.

STOVETOP: Raise the heat again to high and bring the pot back once again to high pressure (15 psi). Once this pressure has been reached, reduce the heat as much as possible while maintaining pressure. Cook for 10 minutes.

········· OR ·········

ELECTRIC: Set the machine to cook once again at high pressure (9–11 psi). Set the machine's timer to cook at high pressure for 15 minutes.

9 Reduce the pressure.

STOVETOP: Set the pot off the heat and let its pressure drop back to normal naturally, about 15 minutes.

········· OR ·········

ELECTRIC: Turn the machine off or unplug it to keep it from switching to its keep-warm setting. Allow its pressure to drop back to normal naturally, 15 to 20 minutes.

If the pressure has not returned to normal within 20 minutes, use the quick-release method to return it to normal.

10 Unlock and open the cooker. Transfer the roast to a cutting board; let stand for 5 minutes. Discard the rosemary. Carve the beef into ½-inch-thick slices. Serve in bowls with the potatoes and sauce.

TESTERS' NOTES
• Pot roast has never been faster—or more economical, since you'll use top round rather than a more expensive cut. The bourbon adds a smoky sweetness to the sauce, no more than a whisper of its more assertive self in drink form.
• Some supermarkets sell top round roasts tied. You can leave it tied for this preparation but remove the twine before slicing and serving.
• Make sure you use top round, not fattier bottom round. This recipe was calibrated for the leaner cut; more fat would weigh down the sauce, muting the subtler flavors.
• The potatoes should be no more than 2 inches long. Slice larger potatoes into 2–inch chunks.
• For the best texture, carve the finished roast against the grain. It's often hard to tell the grain's direction in a top round roast, so make one slice: if you see the meat fibers running in long strips along the slice, you've got it wrong; rotate the roast 90 degrees. If you see them in small circular or ragged bits, as if you stacked up chopsticks and made a slice off the end, you got it right the first time.

TEXAS-STYLE BEEF CHILI

EFFORT: **A LITTLE** • PRESSURE: **HIGH** • TIME UNDER PRESSURE: **10 OR 15 MINUTES** • RELEASE: **NATURAL** • SERVES: **6**

12 dried New Mexican red chiles, stemmed, seeded, and torn into small bits
4 medium garlic cloves, chopped
Up to ¼ cup loosely packed fresh oregano leaves
2 teaspoons cumin seeds
1 teaspoon salt
½ teaspoon ground cinnamon
2 tablespoons lard or bacon fat
2 large yellow onions, chopped
3 large green bell peppers, stemmed, seeded, and chopped
3 pounds top or bottom round, diced
Up to 1 cup dark beer, such as brown ale

1 Place the chile bits in a big bowl; cover with boiling water. Soak for 20 minutes. Set a fine-mesh sieve or a lined colander over a bowl; drain the chiles, catching the soaking liquid below.

2 Put the chile bits in a large blender; add the garlic, oregano, cumin, salt, and cinnamon. Cover and blend, adding dribs and drabs of the soaking liquid just to get a thick, rich sauce, turning off the machine and scraping down the inside of the canister occasionally.

3 Melt the lard or bacon fat in a 6-quart stovetop pressure cooker set over medium heat or a 6-quart electric pressure cooker set to the browning function. Add the onions and peppers; cook, stirring often, until softened, about 5 minutes. Scrape the chile paste into the pot; stir over the heat for 2 minutes.

(continued)

4 Add the meat; toss well to coat. Pour 1 cup beer into a stovetop pressure cooker or ⅔ cup beer into an electric model; scrape up any browned bits in the pot.

5 Lock the lid onto the pot.

STOVETOP: Raise the heat to high and bring the pot to high pressure (15 psi). Once this pressure has been reached, reduce the heat as much as possible while maintaining this pressure. Cook for 10 minutes.

························ OR ························

ELECTRIC: Set the machine to cook at high pressure (9–11 psi). Set the machine's timer to cook at high pressure for 15 minutes.

6 Reduce the pressure.

STOVETOP: Set the pot off the heat and allow its pressure to fall to normal naturally, about 15 minutes.

························ OR ························

ELECTRIC: Unplug the machine or turn it off—just don't let it switch to its keep-warm setting. Let its pressure return to normal naturally, 15 to 20 minutes.

If the pressure has not returned to normal in 20 minutes, use the quick-release method to drop the pressure to normal.

7 Unlock and open the pot. Stir well before serving.

TESTERS' NOTES
• Texans swear proper chili has no beans or tomatoes. This one's made according to those specifications—and with an authentic chile paste, to boot.
• Some of the smallest chile bits may slip through the larger holes of a colander. Lining it with a single layer of paper towels should take care of the problem.
• Add the soaking liquid to the blender in increments no larger than 1 tablespoon. You want as dry a sauce as possible, just enough liquid to blend the ingredients.

• If you're not comfortable using lard or bacon fat, substitute vegetable oil.
• Make sure the meat is truly diced into little ¼-inch bits. Although labor-intensive, such effort will help the beef become soft and luxurious in a fairly short amount of time.
• There's a lot of oregano here. Its flavor is muted under pressure, but use less if you're not quite sure you want such an aromatic hit.

Serve It Up! Have warmed corn tortillas on hand, as well as diced avocado, diced tomatoes, sour cream, minced scallions, and/or grated Cheddar cheese.

BEEF BOTTOM ROUND CASSEROLE WITH CURRANTS AND CINNAMON

EFFORT: **A LITTLE** • PRESSURE: **HIGH** • TIME UNDER PRESSURE: **20 OR 33 MINUTES** • RELEASE: **QUICK, THEN MODIFIED QUICK** • SERVES: **4 TO 6**

¼ **cup olive oil**

2 **large yellow onions, halved and thinly sliced**

2 **pounds beef bottom round, cut into 1½-inch pieces**

½ **teaspoon salt**

½ **teaspoon ground black pepper**

Up to 8 green or white cardamom pods

6 **whole cloves**

One 4-inch cinnamon stick

Up to 2 cups beef broth

1 **cup long-grain white rice, preferably white basmati**

¼ **cup dried currants**

¼ **cup loosely packed fresh cilantro leaves, chopped**

2 **tablespoons minced fresh dill fronds**

1 Heat 2 tablespoons oil in a 6-quart stovetop pressure cooker set over medium heat or in a 6-quart electric pressure cooker switched to the browning function. Add the onions and cook, stirring quite often, until light brown, about 20 minutes. Use a slotted spoon to transfer the onions to a large bowl.

2 Season the meat with the salt and pepper. Add the remaining 2 tablespoons oil to the cooker. Add the meat and brown well, about 8 minutes, stirring once in a while.

3 Add the cardamom pods, cloves, and cinnamon stick. Stir for 30 seconds, until fragrant. Pour 2 cups broth into the stovetop pressure cooker or 1¾ cups into an electric model.

4 Lock the lid onto the pot.

STOVETOP: Raise the heat to high and bring the pot to high pressure (15 psi). Once this pressure has been reached, reduce the heat as much as possible while maintaining this pressure. Cook for 13 minutes.

·················· **OR** ··················

ELECTRIC: Set the machine to cook at high pressure (9–11 psi). Set the machine's timer to cook at high pressure for 22 minutes.

5 Use the quick-release method to bring the pot's pressure back to normal.

6 Unlock and open the lid. Stir in the onions and any juices in their bowl, as well as the rice, currants, cilantro, and dill.

7 Lock the lid back on the pot.

STOVETOP: Raise the heat again to high and bring the pot back to high pressure. Once this pressure has been reached, reduce the heat as much as possible while maintaining this pressure. Cook for 7 minutes.

·················· **OR** ··················

ELECTRIC: Set the machine to cook once again at high pressure (9–11 psi). Set the machine's timer to cook at high pressure for 11 minutes.

8 Use the quick-release method to drop the pressure back to normal but leave the lid in place.

9 Set aside off the heat for 10 minutes with the pressure valve open to steam the rice.

10 Unlock and open the pot. Stir gently. Discard the cinnamon stick, cloves, and cardamom pods before serving.

TESTERS' NOTES

• This recipe makes hearty servings—you may even find yourself with leftovers. Thin out what's left the next day with plenty more broth, then heat it up as a stew.

• The onions are not cooked the full time so they retain some of their texture and flavor. However, you'll want to brown them more than you might for a standard casserole, since that slight bitterness works well against the sweet rice and beef.

• The cloves and cardamom pods are fully edible, but they may offer too big a pop of flavor for some. Thus, remove all you find.

FAST SAUERBRATEN

EFFORT: **A LOT** • PRESSURE: **HIGH** • TIME UNDER PRESSURE: **50 TO 80 MINUTES** • RELEASE: **NATURAL** • SERVES: **6**

1 cup dry red wine, such as Syrah

$\frac{1}{2}$ cup red wine vinegar

$\frac{1}{4}$ cup packed dark brown sugar

2 teaspoons minced garlic

1 teaspoon salt

1 teaspoon ground black pepper

$\frac{1}{2}$ teaspoon ground cloves

$3\frac{1}{2}$ pounds beef bottom round roast

3 thin bacon slices, chopped

3 large carrots, halved lengthwise

$\frac{1}{2}$ cup crushed gingersnap cookies

1 Whisk the wine, vinegar, brown sugar, garlic, salt, pepper, and cloves in a large bowl. Add the beef; turn to coat. Cover and refrigerate for 48 hours, turning every 12 hours.

2 Remove the meat from the marinade; pat dry with paper towels. Reserve the marinade.

3 Fry the bacon in a 6-quart stovetop pressure cooker set over medium heat or in a 6-quart electric pressure cooker turned to the browning function, about 5 minutes, stirring occasionally, until crisp. Use a slotted spoon to transfer the bacon to a bowl.

4 Place the carrots on the bottom of the pressure cooker and set the roast on top. Pour the reserved marinade over everything; return the bacon to the pot.

5 Lock the lid in place.

STOVETOP: Raise the heat under the pot to high and bring the pressure to high (15 psi). Once this pressure has been reached, reduce the heat as much as possible while maintaining this pressure. Cook for 50 minutes.

·················· **OR** ··················

ELECTRIC: Set the machine to cook at high pressure (9–11 psi). Set the machine's timer to cook at high pressure for 1 hour 20 minutes.

6 Reduce the pressure.

STOVETOP: Set the pot off the heat off and let its pressure fall to normal naturally, about 25 minutes.

·················· **OR** ··················

ELECTRIC: Turn the machine off. (Do not let it flip to its keep-warm setting.) Allow its pressure to return to normal naturally, 25 to 35 minutes.

7 Unlock and open the cooker. Transfer the roast to a carving board.

8 Stir the gingersnaps into the sauce. Use an immersion blender in the pot to puree the carrots and sauce in the cooker until fairly smooth if a little grainy (rustic is better than velvety for this sauce). Set the stovetop model over medium heat or turn the electric model to its browning function. Bring the sauce to a simmer and cook, stirring often, until thickened, about 5 minutes. Slice the roast into $\frac{1}{2}$-inch-thick slices against the grain; ladle the sauce over them to serve.

TESTERS' NOTES

• Okay, this recipe is *relatively* fast—certainly faster than a stovetop or oven braise. And it's a tasty rendition of a German favorite, still popular in beer halls in the Midwest.

• The bacon must be removed and then added back on top of the meat and carrots; otherwise, it will burn.

• If you don't have an immersion blender, you'll need to puree the sauce in batches in a large blender. Make sure you remove the center knob from the lid and cover the hole with a clean kitchen towel so pressure doesn't build in the canister and cause a mess on your cabinets.

Serve It Up! Serve over no-yolk noodles, tossed with unsalted butter and poppy seeds.

PICADILLO-STYLE BEEF BOTTOM ROUND STEW

EFFORT: **A LITTLE** · PRESSURE: **HIGH** · TIME UNDER PRESSURE: **10 OR 15 MINUTES** · RELEASE: **NATURAL** · SERVES: **6**

2 tablespoons olive oil

1 large yellow onion, chopped

2 teaspoons minced garlic

1/2 tablespoon cumin seeds

1/2 teaspoon coriander seeds

2 bay leaves

One 4-inch cinnamon stick

2 1/2 pounds beef bottom round, diced

Up to 1 1/2 cups beef broth

1 pound yellow potatoes, such as Yukon Gold, diced

1/2 cup golden raisins

1/2 cup sliced pitted green olives

1/4 cup tomato paste

1 tablespoon packed fresh oregano leaves, finely chopped

1 teaspoon drained capers, rinsed and finely chopped

1/2 cup packed fresh cilantro leaves, chopped

1 Heat the oil in a 6-quart stovetop pressure cooker set over medium heat or in a 6-quart electric pressure cooker turned to the browning function. Add the onion; cook, stirring often, until somewhat softened, about 4 minutes. Add the garlic, cumin seeds, coriander seeds, bay leaves, and cinnamon stick; cook for 1 minute, stirring constantly.

2 Add the beef and cook, stirring occasionally, until it loses its raw color. Pour 1 1/2 cups broth into the stovetop cooker or 1 1/4 cups broth into the electric model; stir well to get any of the browned bits off the bottom of the cooker. Stir in the potatoes, raisins, olives, tomato paste, oregano, and capers.

3 Lock the lid onto the cooker.

STOVETOP: Raise the heat to high and bring the pot to high pressure (15 psi). Once this pressure has been reached, reduce the heat as much as possible while maintaining this pressure. Cook for 10 minutes.

············ **OR** ············

ELECTRIC: Set the machine to cook at high pressure (9–11 psi). Set the machine's timer to cook at high pressure for 15 minutes.

4 Reduce the pressure.

STOVETOP: Set the pot off the heat and allow its pressure to drop to normal naturally, about 15 minutes.

············ **OR** ············

ELECTRIC: Turn the machine off or unplug it without letting it flip to its keep-warm setting. Let its pressure fall to normal naturally, 15 to 20 minutes.

If the pressure has not fallen back to normal in 20 minutes, use the quick-release method to lower it instantly.

5 Unlock and open the lid. Discard the bay leaves. Add the cilantro and stir well. Set the lid partially ajar over the cooker and set aside for 5 minutes to blend the flavors. Stir again before serving.

TESTERS' NOTES

• This Latin American–inspired dish is traditionally made with ground beef. We opt for bottom round for better texture and flavor. Plus, we like the slightly soupy consistency here, rather than the drier texture of traditional picadillo.

• Cut the beef into small bits, no more than 1/4 inch each, about the size of a raisin. The same goes for those potatoes. You want a big variety in every spoonful.

(continued)

• You can substitute beef rump roast for the bottom round roast.

Serve It Up! Mix cooked long-grain white rice, canned black beans, and pico de gallo for an easy side dish. Make it even easier by picking up a container of rice from a Chinese restaurant on your way home.

DELI-STYLE BRISKET

EFFORT: **NOT MUCH** • PRESSURE: **HIGH** • TIME UNDER PRESSURE: **50 OR 80 MINUTES** • RELEASE: **NATURAL** • SERVES: **6**

3 pounds flat- or first-cut brisket, well trimmed

2 tablespoons minced garlic

2 teaspoons Dijon mustard

1 teaspoon onion powder

1 large yellow onion, halved and sliced into thin half-moons

¼ cup tomato paste

1 Set the brisket flatter side down on a cutting board. Mix the garlic, mustard, and onion powder in a small bowl. Rub the paste all over the exposed surface of the meat.

2 Line the bottom of a 6-quart stovetop pressure cooker or electric cooker with the onion; set the brisket coated side up in the cooker. Whisk 3 cups water with the tomato paste in a medium bowl until smooth; pour around (but not on) the brisket in the cooker. Add more water as necessary so that the liquid comes halfway up the sides of the meat.

3 Lock the lid onto the pot.

STOVETOP: Set the pot over high heat and bring to high pressure (15 psi). Adjust the heat as low as possible to maintain that pressure. Cook for 50 minutes.

·················· **OR** ··················

ELECTRIC: Set the machine to cook at high pressure (9–11 psi). Set the timer to cook at this pressure for 80 minutes.

4 Reduce the pressure.

STOVETOP: Set the pot off the heat; let its pressure fall back to normal naturally, about 35 minutes.

·················· **OR** ··················

ELECTRIC: Turn off the machine or unplug it, so it doesn't jump to its keep-warm setting. Allow its pressure to fall to normal naturally, 35 to 45 minutes.

5 Unlock and remove the lid. Transfer the brisket to a large carving board; cool for 10 minutes. (Discard everything in the pot.) Run your fingers across the surface of the meat to tell which way its fibers are placed; cut ¼-inch-thick slices from the brisket at a 90 degree angle to these fibers.

TESTERS' NOTES

• A brisket is a large cut of beef; the first-cut section is the leanest piece—and best for the pressure cooker because the rendered fat will not overwhelm other flavors.
• Take off any big pockets of yellow or white fat along the exterior of the beef. You needn't trim it down to just pink meat—a translucent coating of fat will keep the cut moist under pressure. Run the knife parallel to the meat to slice off bits of fat, as if you were shaving the brisket.
• Cut as many slices as you need, then seal the cooled brisket in plastic wrap to store in the refrigerator (on a platter to catch any drips) for up to 4 days. Or freeze the larger chunk, tightly wrapped, for up to 4 months.

Serve It Up! Have slices of rye bread on hand, as well as plenty of deli mustard.

"BARBECUED" BRISKET

EFFORT: **NOT MUCH** • PRESSURE: **HIGH** • TIME UNDER PRESSURE:
50 OR 80 MINUTES • RELEASE: **NATURAL** • SERVES: **6**

1 cup canned crushed tomatoes

2 tablespoons packed dark brown sugar

2 tablespoons cider vinegar

1½ tablespoons tomato paste

1½ tablespoons smoked paprika

1 teaspoon Worcestershire sauce

1 teaspoon ground coriander

½ teaspoon ground allspice

½ teaspoon ground cloves

¼ teaspoon dry mustard

1 tablespoon olive oil

3 pounds flat- or first-cut brisket, well
   trimmed

1 Whisk the tomatoes, brown sugar, cider vinegar, tomato paste, smoked paprika, Worcestershire sauce, coriander, allspice, cloves, and mustard in a large bowl until the brown sugar and tomato paste have dissolved.

2 Heat the oil in a 6-quart stovetop pressure cooker set over medium heat or in a 6-quart electric pressure cooker turned to the browning function. Add the brisket and brown on both sides, 3 to 4 minutes per side. Pour the tomato mixture on and all around the meat.

3 Lock the lid onto the pot.

STOVETOP: Raise the heat to high and bring the pot to high pressure (15 psi). Once this pressure has been reached, reduce the heat as much as possible while maintaining this pressure. Cook for 50 minutes.

·········· OR ··········

ELECTRIC: Set the machine to cook at high pressure (9–11 psi). Set the machine's timer to cook at high pressure for 80 minutes.

4 Reduce the pressure.

STOVETOP: Set the pot off the heat and allow its pressure to return to normal naturally, about 25 minutes.

·········· OR ··········

ELECTRIC: Turn off the machine or unplug it, so it doesn't switch to its keep-warm setting. Allow its pressure to return to normal naturally, 25 to 35 minutes.

5 Unlock and open the cooker. Transfer the brisket to a carving board and let stand for 10 minutes. Discard the liquid in the pot. Run your fingers across the meat to determine the direction of the fibers; carve ¼-inch slices at a 90 degree angle against the grain.

TESTERS' NOTES

• Although hardly cooked on a barbecue, this brisket takes on the taste of the long-roasted Texas classic.

• Not only does the pressure cooker keep all the moisture in the pot, it even keeps it in the cut itself. The result is the juiciest brisket you've ever had. True, there's no concentration of flavors due to evaporation and dehydration—so we've pumped up the spices in the sauce.

Serve It Up! For the authentic Texas brisket experience, serve with sliced white sandwich bread, sliced white onions, pickled jalapeño rings, pickle relish, and baked beans. If you want to be truly authentic, nix the plates and serve on wax paper sheets.

BLACK PEPPER BEEF BRISKET WITH MARMALADE CARAMEL

EFFORT: **A LITTLE** · PRESSURE: **HIGH** · TIME UNDER PRESSURE: **50 OR 80 MINUTES** · RELEASE: **NATURAL** · SERVES: 6

3 pounds flat- or first-cut beef brisket, well trimmed

1 tablespoon coarsely ground black pepper or crushed black peppercorns

1 tablespoon almond oil

1 medium yellow onion, chopped

6 tablespoons orange marmalade

2 tablespoons soy sauce

3/4 cup beef broth

1 Coat the brisket in the pepper; set aside. Heat the oil in a 6-quart stovetop pressure cooker set over medium heat or in a 6-quart electric pressure cooker turned to the browning mode. Add the beef; brown well on both sides, 3 to 4 minutes per side. Transfer the meat to a cutting board.

2 Add the onion to the pot; cook, stirring often, until translucent, about 4 minutes. Stir in the marmalade, soy sauce, and broth until the marmalade has dissolved. Return the brisket to the pot.

3 Lock the lid in place.

STOVETOP: Raise the heat to high and bring the pot to high pressure (15 psi). Once this pressure has been reached, reduce the heat as much as possible while maintaining this pressure. Cook for 50 minutes.

·········· OR ··········
ELECTRIC: Set the machine to cook at high pressure (9–11 psi). Set the machine's timer to cook at high pressure for 80 minutes.

4 Reduce the pressure.

STOVETOP: Set the pot off the heat and allow its pressure to return to normal naturally, about 30 minutes.

·········· OR ··········
ELECTRIC: Turn the machine off or unplug it—just don't let it switch to its keep-warm setting. Let the pressure return to normal naturally, 30 to 40 minutes.

5 Unlock and open the pot. Transfer the brisket to a carving board; set aside for 10 minutes. Defat the sauce in the cooker by skimming a spoon along its surface. Bring the sauce to a boil by setting the stovetop pot over medium-high heat or turning the electric model to the browning mode. Boil, stirring quite often, until the sauce has reduced to a thick glaze, about 7 minutes. Carve the brisket against the grain into 1/4-inch-thick slices and serve with the sauce on the side.

TESTERS' NOTES

• The orange marmalade will slowly melt and start to darken in the intense heat and pressure—thus giving you that vaunted caramel. All that black pepper will balance the sweetness considerably.

• Don't use a thick-cut or chunky marmalade here. You want one without huge chunks of fruit in the jar. Feel free to substitute lemon or grapefruit marmalade, if you prefer.

• In step 5, the sauce should be reduced and thickened until a wooden spoon can make a clean line in it. Turn off the heat or unplug the machine the moment you see this happen.

• Substitute canola or vegetable oil (more savory) for the almond oil.

CHIPOTLE-BRAISED BEEF BRISKET AND BUTTERNUT SQUASH

EFFORT: **A LOT** • PRESSURE: **HIGH** • TIME UNDER PRESSURE: **50 OR 80 MINUTES** • RELEASE: **QUICK, THEN NATURAL** • SERVES: **6**

2 tablespoons olive oil

3½ pounds flat- or first-cut beef brisket, well trimmed

1 small red onion, chopped

1 medium red bell pepper, stemmed, seeded, and chopped

Up to 2 canned chipotles in adobo sauce, stemmed and chopped

1 tablespoon minced garlic

1 tablespoon Worcestershire sauce

1 tablespoon sweet paprika

1 teaspoon ground cumin

1 teaspoon dried oregano

One 4-inch cinnamon stick

Up to 1¼ cups beef broth

3 cups peeled, seeded, and cubed butternut squash

1 Heat the oil in a 6-quart stovetop pressure cooker set over medium heat or in a 6-quart electric pressure cooker turned to the browning function. Add the brisket; brown on both sides, 3 to 4 minutes per side. Transfer to a cutting board.

2 Add the onion and bell pepper; cook, stirring often, until the onion turns translucent, about 4 minutes. Add the chipotles and garlic; cook until aromatic, about 20 seconds.

3 Stir in the Worcestershire sauce, paprika, cumin, oregano, and cinnamon stick; cook for 1 minute, stirring constantly. Pour 1¼ cups broth into a stovetop pressure cooker or 1 cup broth into an electric model; scrape up any browned bits in the pot with a wooden spoon. Slip the brisket into the sauce.

4 Lock the lid onto the pot.

STOVETOP: Raise the heat to high and bring the pot to high pressure (15 psi). Once this pressure has been reached, reduce the heat as much as possible to maintain this pressure. Cook for 40 minutes.

·············· OR ··············

ELECTRIC: Set the machine to cook at high pressure (9–11 psi). Set the machine's timer to cook at high pressure for 65 minutes.

5 Use the quick-release method to return the pot's pressure to normal.

6 Unlock and open the pot. Sprinkle the squash pieces all around.

7 Lock the lid in place again.

STOVETOP: Raise the heat back to high and bring the pot back to high pressure (15 psi). Once this pressure has been reached, reduce the heat as much as possible while maintaining this pressure. Cook for 10 minutes.

·············· OR ··············

ELECTRIC: Set the machine to cook once again at high pressure (9–11 psi). Set the machine's timer to cook at high pressure for 15 more minutes.

8 Reduce the pressure.

STOVETOP: Set the pot off the heat and allow the pressure to return to normal naturally, about 15 minutes.

·············· OR ··············

ELECTRIC: Turn off the machine or unplug it without letting it flip to its keep-warm setting. Allow the pressure to return to normal naturally, 15 to 20 minutes.

(continued)

9 Unlock and open the pot. Transfer the brisket to a cutting board; let stand for 10 minutes. Discard the cinnamon stick. Carve the brisket into ¼-inch-thick slices against the grain; serve in bowls with the squash and sauce.

TESTERS' NOTES

• Smoky and sweet, this braised brisket may take the place of turkey at your Thanksgiving table. Or how about a nontraditional, Southwest-inspired Rosh Hashanah supper?

• There's no wine here, so the sauce will be more savory. If you want a sweeter finish, substitute a pale ale or amber lager for half the beef broth used.

• You can defat the sauce, particularly if you didn't trim the brisket very well. Use a slotted spoon to transfer the vegetables to a serving bowl; pour the sauce into a fat separator and wait about 5 minutes for the fat to rise to the top. Discard the fat and pour off the bottom liquid as the sauce.

• The success of this dish lies in the browning. Make sure the brisket is truly browned, not just grayed over the heat. The flavors will be more intense, a better counterpoint to the chiles and squash.

CORNED BEEF AND CABBAGE IN SPICED CIDER

EFFORT: **A LITTLE** • PRESSURE: **HIGH** • TIME UNDER PRESSURE: **55 OR 88 MINUTES** • RELEASE: **NATURAL, THEN QUICK** • SERVES: **6**

1½ cups unsweetened apple cider

One 4-inch cinnamon stick

8 whole cloves

3½ pounds corned beef, rinsed, any spice packet or spices discarded

¼ cup honey mustard

1 large green cabbage, cored and cut into 6 wedges

6 large carrots, halved widthwise

1 Put the cider, cinnamon stick, and cloves in a 6-quart stovetop or electric pressure cooker; set the pressure cooker rack inside the cooker. Set the brisket on the rack flatter side down; rub the exposed surface with the mustard.

2 Lock the lid onto the pot.

STOVETOP: Set the pot over high heat and bring the pot to high pressure (15 psi). Once this pressure has been reached, reduce the heat as much as possible while maintaining this pressure. Cook for 50 minutes.

························· OR ·························

ELECTRIC: Set the machine to cook at high pressure (9–11 psi). Set the machine's timer to cook at high pressure for 80 minutes.

3 Reduce the pressure.

STOVETOP: Set the pot off the heat and allow its pressure to fall to normal naturally, about 30 minutes.

························· OR ·························

ELECTRIC: Turn the machine off or unplug it so it doesn't flip to the keep-warm setting. Allow its pressure to fall back to normal naturally, 30 to 40 minutes.

4 Unlock and open the lid. Transfer the brisket to a cutting board; set aside. Remove the rack as well as the cinnamon and cloves from the cooker. Add the cabbage wedges and carrots.

5 Lock the lid once again onto the pot.

6 Return the pot's pressure to normal with the quick-release method.

7 Unlock and open the lid. Carve the meat against the grain into ½-inch-thick slices. Ladle the cabbage wedges and carrots into bowls. Add the sliced meat and spoon lots of broth around the servings.

TESTERS' NOTES
- Forget that horrid corned beef boiled in water! This braised version in apple cider is far tastier and faster.
- We like thicker slices for corned beef, since the meat is already so thoroughly tenderized by its brine.
- By cooking the vegetables separately, we ensure they stay juicy and even a little firm.
- Some corned beef briskets are way too salty, so look for a reduced-sodium packaging at your supermarket.

CLASSIC POT ROAST AND POTATOES

EFFORT: **A LOT** · PRESSURE: **HIGH** · TIME UNDER PRESSURE: **60 OR 90 MINUTES** · RELEASE: **QUICK, THEN NATURAL** · SERVES: **6**

1 tablespoon olive oil

One 3- to 3½-pound boneless beef chuck roast

1 teaspoon salt

½ teaspoon ground black pepper

1 large yellow onion, chopped

2 teaspoons minced garlic

Up to 1½ cups beef broth

3 tablespoons tomato paste

One 4-inch rosemary sprig

½ ounce dried mushrooms, preferably porcini

1½ pounds small white or yellow potatoes

1 Heat the oil in a 6-quart stovetop pressure cooker set over medium heat or in a 6-quart electric pressure cooker turned to the browning function. Season the roast with the salt and pepper; brown it on both sides, turning once, about 10 minutes. Transfer the meat to a large bowl.

2 Add the onion; cook, stirring often, until translucent, about 4 minutes. Add the garlic; cook, stirring constantly, until aromatic, about 30 seconds. Pour 1½ cups broth into the stovetop pressure cooker or 1¼ cups broth in an electric model. Add the tomato paste and stir well until dissolved. Tuck the rosemary into the sauce and crumble in the mushrooms. Nestle the meat into the sauce, adding any juices in the bowl.

3 Lock the lid onto the pot.

4 Use the quick-release method to drop the pot's pressure back to normal.

(continued)

5 Unlock and open the cooker; sprinkle the potatoes around the meat.

6 Lock the lid back onto the pot.

STOVETOP: Again raise the heat to high and bring the pot back to high pressure (15 psi). Once this pressure has been reached, reduce the heat as much as possible while maintaining this pressure. Cook for 20 minutes.

·············· **OR** ··············

ELECTRIC: Set the machine to cook once again at high pressure (9–11 psi). Set the machine's timer to cook at high pressure for 35 minutes.

7 Reduce the pressure.

STOVETOP: Set the pot off the heat and allow its pressure to fall to normal naturally, about 20 minutes.

·············· **OR** ··············

ELECTRIC: Turn off the machine or unplug it. Let its pressure fall back to normal naturally, 20 to 30 minutes.

If the pressure has not returned to normal in 30 minutes, use the quick-release method to return it to normal.

8 Unlock and remove the lid. Transfer the roast to a cutting board; set aside for 5 minutes. Discard the rosemary sprig. Slice the meat into 2-inch irregular chunks and serve these in bowls with the vegetables, mushrooms, and broth.

TESTERS' NOTES

• Fairly straightforward, this pot roast is comfort food deluxe, a '50s favorite made quicker and simpler.
• Bones require space; the pressure cooker doesn't have much to spare. A bone-in chuck roast will fill the pot too full, especially once you add vegetables. However, because the pressure cooker so efficiently traps essential juices inside the cut, there's less call for the bone's added flavor. So we can call for boneless chuck roasts.

• We don't tie our chuck roast for the pressure cooker, as the meat doesn't collapse much in the (relatively) quick cooking time. However, if you want perfect aesthetics, you can wrap butcher's twine securely around the perimeter of the roast to hold its shape as it cooks, resulting in a perkier, more upright cut of beef.
• Do not use baking or Russet potatoes; they'll leach too much starch into the sauce. Use small potatoes like Irish Cobblers, white fingerlings, or even small Yukon Gold potatoes, each about 3 inches in length.

Serve It Up! For a richer sauce, transfer the meat to a cutting board and use a slotted spoon to remove all the vegetables and mushrooms to a large bowl. Set the stovetop cooker over medium heat or turn the electric cooker to its browning function; bring the sauce to a full simmer. Mash 2 tablespoons softened unsalted butter with 1½ tablespoons all-purpose flour into a paste; whisk the paste in small bits into the bubbling sauce to thicken.

CHUCK ROAST WITH HORSERADISH AND PARSNIPS

EFFORT: **A LOT** • PRESSURE: **HIGH** • TIME UNDER PRESSURE: **60 OR 90 MINUTES** • RELEASE: **NATURAL** • SERVES: **6**

2 tablespoons olive oil
One 3½-pound boneless beef chuck roast
2 medium yellow onions, halved and
    sliced into thin half-moons
2 teaspoons minced garlic
1 teaspoon dried sage
1 teaspoon dried thyme
½ teaspoon ground allspice
½ teaspoon salt
½ teaspoon ground black pepper
½ cup red vermouth (sweet vermouth)

¾ cup beef broth

2 bay leaves

4 medium parsnips, peeled and cut into
  3-inch pieces

3 tablespoons jarred prepared white
  horseradish

2 teaspoons potato starch or cornstarch

1 Heat the oil in a 6-quart stovetop pressure cooker set over medium heat or in a 6-quart electric pressure cooker turned to the browning mode. Add the chuck roast; brown on both sides, turning once, about 10 minutes in all. Transfer to a large bowl.

2 Add the onions; cook, stirring often, until translucent, about 5 minutes. Stir in the garlic, sage, thyme, allspice, salt, and pepper; cook about 20 seconds. Pour in the vermouth and scrape any browned bits up off the bottom of the pot as everything comes to a simmer.

3 Pour in the broth, then tuck the meat back into the sauce, adding any extra juice in its bowl. Slip the bay leaves into the sauce; arrange the parsnips around the roast. Spread the horseradish on the exposed surface of the meat.

4 Lock the lid onto the pot.

STOVETOP: Raise the heat to high and bring the pot to high pressure (15 psi). Once this pressure has been reached, reduce the heat as much as possible while maintaining this pressure. Cook for 1 hour.

···················· OR ····················

ELECTRIC: Set the machine to cook at high pressure (9–11 psi). Set the machine's timer to cook at high pressure for 1½ hours.

5 Reduce the pressure.

STOVETOP: Set the pot off the heat and let its pressure return to normal naturally, about 15 minutes.

···················· OR ····················

ELECTRIC: Turn off the machine or unplug it so it doesn't jump to its keep-warm setting. Allow its pressure to return to normal naturally, 15 to 20 minutes.

If the pressure has not returned to normal in 20 minutes, use the quick-release method to bring it back to normal.

6 Unlock and remove the lid. Transfer the roast to a cutting board, transfer the parsnips to a serving bowl, and discard the bay leaves.

7 Skim the sauce of excess fat by running a flatware spoon along its surface. Set the stovetop cooker over medium-high heat or turn the electric cooker to its browning function. Bring the sauce to a simmer.

8 Whisk the potato starch or cornstarch into 2 teaspoons water in a small bowl, then whisk the slurry into the simmering sauce. Cook until somewhat thickened, about 1 minute, whisking constantly. Remove the pot from the meat or turn off the electric cooker. Slice the meat into 2-inch irregular chunks; serve in bowls with the parsnips and sauce.

TESTERS' NOTES

• You may not have known it, but a chuck roast is the whole reason you got a pressure cooker. The cut makes a moist and flavorful pot roast, a better choice than brisket (though you can substitute boneless beef arm or blade roast).

• We prefer parsnips here for their more aromatic flavor, less sweet and more in keeping with the beef. However, if you find them too aromatic, substitute carrots.

• The horseradish will mellow as the meat cooks, becoming a somewhat sweet glaze on the beef.

Serve It Up! Top the servings with dollops of sour cream or crème fraîche.

COFFEE-BRAISED CHUCK ROAST WITH BALSAMIC VINEGAR

EFFORT: **A LITTLE** • PRESSURE: **HIGH** • TIME UNDER PRESSURE: **50 OR 75 MINUTES** • RELEASE: **NATURAL** • SERVES: **4**

1½ tablespoons peanut oil

1 large yellow onion, halved and thinly sliced into half-moons

½ teaspoon cumin seeds

One 2-pound boneless beef chuck roast

1 cup very strong coffee

2 tablespoons balsamic vinegar

1 tablespoon finely grated orange zest

½ teaspoon ground allspice

½ teaspoon salt

½ teaspoon ground black pepper

1 Heat the oil in a 6-quart stovetop pressure cooker set over medium heat or in a 6-quart electric pressure cooker turned to the browning mode. Add the onion and cumin seeds; cook, stirring quite often, until the onion begins to brown a bit at the edges, about 7 minutes.

2 Push the onion and seeds to the sides of the cooker; add the beef and brown on both sides, turning once, about 8 minutes. Pour in the coffee and vinegar; sprinkle in the zest, allspice, salt, and pepper.

3 Lock the lid onto the pot.

STOVETOP: Raise the heat to high and bring the pot to high pressure (15 psi). Once this pressure has been reached, reduce the heat as much as possible while maintaining this pressure. Cook for 50 minutes.

··· **OR** ·······························

ELECTRIC: Set the machine to cook at high pressure (9–11 psi). Set the machine's timer to cook at high pressure for 75 minutes.

4 Reduce the pressure.

STOVETOP: Set the pot off the heat and allow its pressure to fall back to normal naturally, about 25 minutes.

··· **OR** ·······························

ELECTRIC: Turn off the machine or unplug it so it doesn't flip to its keep-warm setting. Let its pressure fall back to normal naturally, 25 to 35 minutes.

5 Unlock and remove the lid. Transfer the roast to a cutting board; use a slotted spoon to transfer the onions to a small serving bowl. Defat the sauce, either by using a fat separator or skimming it with a small spoon.

6 Bring the sauce to a simmer in the stovetop pot by setting it over medium-high heat or in the electric cooker by turning it to the browning function. Boil, stirring once in a while, until the sauce has reduced to half its original volume, about 7 minutes. Slice the roast into 2-inch, irregular chunks, then serve with the sauce and onions.

TESTERS' NOTES

• If you've never had beef braised in coffee, you're in for a treat. The sauce is mellow, sweet-and-sour, and sophisticated.

• Use a cup of very strong coffee (half again as much ground coffee as you would use for a standard cup), rather than espresso.

Serve It Up! Grate peeled celeriac (celery root) through the large holes of a box grater. Blanch in a large pot of boiling water for 2 minutes, then drain in a colander set in the sink. Toss with a little unsalted butter, divide it among the serving bowls, and top with the meat, onion, and sauce.

SUNDAY BEEF STEW WITH SWEET POTATOES AND RUTABAGA

EFFORT: **A LITTLE** · PRESSURE: **HIGH** · TIME UNDER PRESSURE: **25 OR 40 MINUTES** · RELEASE: **NATURAL** · SERVES: **6**

Up to 1½ cups beef broth

1½ tablespoons all-purpose flour

2 teaspoons stemmed fresh thyme leaves

2 teaspoons sweet paprika

¼ teaspoon red pepper flakes

8 ounces slab bacon, diced

3 pounds boneless beef chuck, cut into 2-inch pieces

1 large yellow onion, chopped

2 medium Roma (plum) tomatoes, chopped

2 teaspoons minced garlic

1 medium rutabaga (about 1½ pounds), peeled and cut into 1½-inch pieces

1 large sweet potato (about 1 pound), peeled and cut into 1½-inch pieces

1 Using 1½ cups broth for a stovetop pressure cooker or 1¼ cups broth for an electric pressure cooker, whisk the broth, flour, thyme, paprika, and red pepper flakes in a bowl until the flour dissolves. Set aside.

2 Fry the bacon crisp, stirring often, in a 6-quart stovetop pressure cooker set over medium heat or in a 6-quart electric pressure cooker turned to the browning function. Use a slotted spoon to transfer the bacon bits to a large bowl.

3 Add the beef; brown on all sides, turning occasionally with kitchen tongs, about 8 minutes. Transfer the browned beef to the bowl with the bacon.

4 Add the onion; cook, stirring occasionally, until softened, about 5 minutes. Add the tomatoes and garlic; stir over the heat for 1 minute. Pour the broth mixture into the cooker; bring to a boil, scraping up any browned bits with a wooden spoon.

5 Return the beef and bacon to the pot, along with any juices in their bowl. Add the rutabaga and sweet potato; stir well.

6 Lock the lid on the pot.

STOVETOP: Raise the heat to high and bring the pressure in the pot to high (15 psi). Once this pressure has been reached, reduce the heat as much as possible while maintaining this pressure. Cook for 25 minutes.

········· **OR** ·········

ELECTRIC: Set the machine to cook at high pressure (9–11 psi). Set the machine's timer to cook at high pressure for 40 minutes.

7 Reduce the pressure.

STOVETOP: Set the pot off the heat and allow its pressure to return to normal naturally, about 20 minutes.

········· **OR** ·········

ELECTRIC: Turn off the machine or unplug it so it doesn't jump to its keep-warm setting. Let its pressure fall back to normal naturally, 20 to 25 minutes.

(continued)

If the pressure has not returned to normal within 25 minutes, use the quick-release method to draw off the excess pressure.

8 Unlock and open the lid. Skim the stew for excess fat before serving in bowls, chunks of meat and lots of vegetables surrounded by the sauce.

TESTERS' NOTES

• Here's the first of our big beef stews. Trim the meat as you cut it up. You'll have less work at the end since you won't need to skim the stew.

• Yes, you can use beef stew meat for any of the following beef stews. However, the quality of meat is often marginal, a selection of less-than-perfect bits taken from various parts of the cow, some things connected by tough fibers that won't get tender. If you want to avoid extra work, ask the butcher to cut a boneless chuck roast into 2-inch chunks for you.

• The meat and vegetables must be in fairly hefty chunks, larger than what you'd use if you were cooking this stew stovetop. If they're not fairly large, they'll break apart under high pressure.

BISTRO BEEF STEW WITH RED WINE, CARROTS, AND FIGS

EFFORT: **A LITTLE** • PRESSURE: **HIGH** • TIME UNDER PRESSURE: **20 OR 30 MINUTES** • RELEASE: **NATURAL** • SERVES: **6**

3 tablespoons olive oil

3 pounds boneless beef chuck, cut into 1½-inch pieces

2 cups frozen pearl onions, thawed

1½ cups dry, big red wine, such as Syrah

1 pound baby or small carrots, cut into 2-inch sections

6 dried figs, stemmed

One 6-inch fresh rosemary sprig

One 4-inch fresh thyme sprig

½ teaspoon salt

½ teaspoon ground black pepper

1 teaspoon potato starch or cornstarch

1 Heat the oil in a 6-quart stovetop pressure cooker set over medium heat or in a 6-quart electric pressure cooker set on the browning mode. Add the beef and brown, turning occasionally, about 10 minutes. Transfer to a large bowl.

2 Add the onions; cook, stirring often, until translucent, about 5 minutes. Pour in the wine, scraping up any browned bits in the pot; then stir in the carrots, figs, rosemary, thyme, salt, and pepper. Return the beef and any juices to the cooker; stir well.

3 Lock the lid on the pot.

STOVETOP: Raise the heat to high and bring the pot to high pressure (15 psi). Once this pressure has been reached, reduce the heat as much as possible while maintaining this pressure. Cook for 20 minutes.

·····················OR·····················
ELECTRIC: Set the machine to cook at high pressure (9–11 psi). Set the machine's timer to cook at high pressure for 30 minutes.

4 Reduce the pressure.

STOVETOP: Set the pot off the heat and let its pressure fall to normal naturally, about 20 minutes.
·····················OR·····················
ELECTRIC: Turn off the machine or unplug it so it doesn't flip to its keep-warm setting. Let its pressure in the pot return to normal naturally, 20 to 25 minutes.

If the pressure has not returned to normal in 25 minutes, use the quick-release method to bring it back to normal.

5 Unlock and remove the lid. Discard the rosemary and thyme sprigs. Turn the heat to medium under the stovetop cooker or set the electric model to its browning mode. Bring the stew to a simmer.

6 Whisk the potato starch or cornstarch with 2 teaspoons water in a small bowl until smooth. Stir the mixture into the stew; cook, stirring constantly, until thickened, about 1 minute.

TESTERS' NOTES
• A fairly straightforward recipe, this stew gets an added boost of sweetness from the dried figs. It's like comfort food from a neighborhood French bistro.
• Beef chuck will get tender at its own rate, which is sometimes longer than the timings we've given. If you open the pot and find that the meat is not fork-tender, lock the lid back in place and cook at high pressure for another 5 to 7 minutes. But be forewarned: the vegetables may get very soft.

Serve It Up! Cut a day-old loaf of Italian bread into 2-inch squares, then toast these on a large, rimmed baking sheet placed 4 to 6 inches from a heated broiler until browned on all sides, about 5 minutes, turning occasionally. Transfer from the baking sheet to a wire rack to cool and crisp. Place these in the serving bowls before you ladle in the stew.

PROVENÇAL-STYLE BEEF STEW WITH OLIVES, BRANDY, AND BACON

EFFORT: **A LOT** • PRESSURE: **HIGH** • TIME UNDER PRESSURE: **25 OR 37 MINUTES** • RELEASE: **QUICK, THEN NATURAL** • SERVES: **6**

1 tablespoon olive oil

2 ounces slab bacon, chopped

3 pounds boneless beef chuck, cut into 2-inch pieces

1 teaspoon ground black pepper

2 tablespoons brandy

1½ cups dry, fruit-forward red wine, such as Zinfandel

½ cup beef broth

2 tablespoons all-purpose flour

1 cup pitted green olives

1 tablespoon stemmed fresh thyme leaves

1 tablespoon packed fresh sage leaves, minced

2 bay leaves

1 tablespoon unsalted butter

2 cups frozen pearl onions (about 8 ounces—do not thaw)

12 ounces cremini mushrooms, thinly sliced

2 tablespoons tomato paste

1 Heat the oil in a 6-quart pressure cooker set over medium heat or in a 6-quart electric pressure cooker turned to the browning function. Add the bacon; fry until crisp, stirring often, about 5 minutes. Use a slotted spoon to transfer the bacon to a large bowl. Set aside.

(continued)

2 Add the beef to the pot, season it with the pepper, and cook, stirring occasionally, until browned, about 8 minutes. Transfer the beef to the bowl with the bacon.

3 Pour the brandy into the pot and stir up any browned bits on the bottom. Add the wine; return the beef, bacon, and any meat juices to the cooker.

4 Whisk the broth and flour in the now-empty beef bowl until the flour dissolves, then stir it into the pot. Stir in the olives, thyme, sage, and bay leaves.

5 Lock the lid onto the pot.

STOVETOP: Raise the heat to high and bring the pot to high pressure (15 psi). Once this pressure has been reached, reduce the heat as much as possible while maintaining this pressure. Cook for 20 minutes.

···OR···

ELECTRIC: Set the machine to cook at high pressure (9–11 psi). Set the machine's timer to cook at high pressure for 30 minutes.

6 As the stew cooks, melt the butter in a large, high-sided skillet set over medium-low heat. Add the onions and cook, stirring occasionally, until they are soft and lightly browned, about 10 minutes. Add the mushrooms, raise the heat to medium, and cook, stirring, until they give off their moisture and it reduces to a thick glaze, about 7 minutes. Stir in the tomato paste until dissolved. Set the skillet off the heat.

7 Use the quick-release method to bring the pot's pressure back to normal.

8 Unlock and open the pot. Scrape the contents of the skillet into the stew and stir well.

9 Lock the lid back in place.

STOVETOP: Raise the heat once again to high and bring the pot back to high pressure (15 psi). Once this pressure has been reached, reduce the heat as much as possible while maintaining this pressure. Cook for 5 minutes.

···OR···

ELECTRIC: Set the machine to cook once again at high pressure (9–11 psi). Set the timer to cook at high pressure for 7 minutes.

10 Reduce the pressure.

STOVETOP: Set the pot off the heat and allow its pressure to return to normal naturally, about 15 minutes.

···OR···

ELECTRIC: Turn off the machine or unplug it so it doesn't jump to its keep-warm setting. Let its pressure fall back to normal naturally, 15 to 20 minutes.

11 Unlock and open the lid. Remove the bay leaves and stir the stew before serving.

TESTERS' NOTES

• This stew is a pressure cooker riff on a classic from southern France: *boeuf en daube,* a rich supper stocked with plenty of aromatics.

• If you keep the pearl onions frozen, they'll brown more evenly before they begin to burn. Those onions will add a long-braised character to the sauce.

• A pressure cooker pot is so tall that there's little chance of the brandy igniting. That said, should it ignite, quickly cover the pot and set it aside off the heat for a couple minutes. If you've accidentally locked the lid onto the pot, you'll need to use the quick-release method to lower the pressure and open the cooker.

TUSCAN-STYLE BEEF STEW WITH PRUNES AND PANCETTA

EFFORT: **A LITTLE** • PRESSURE: **HIGH** • TIME UNDER PRESSURE:
25 OR 40 MINUTES • RELEASE: **NATURAL** • SERVES: **4**

Up to 1 cup chicken broth

1 tablespoon all-purpose flour

1 tablespoon unsalted butter

1 tablespoon olive oil

One 4-ounce pancetta chunk, diced

**2 pounds boneless beef chuck, cut into
    2-inch pieces**

**1 cup frozen pearl onions (about
    4 ounces—do not thaw)**

¹/₂ ounce dried porcini mushrooms

12 pitted prunes

**2 tablespoons loosely packed fresh sage
    leaves, minced**

**1 tablespoon loosely packed fresh
    rosemary leaves, minced**

1 Using 1 cup broth for a stovetop cooker or ²/₃ cup broth for an electric cooker, whisk the broth with the flour in a small bowl until the flour dissolves; set aside.

2 Melt the butter in the oil in a 6-quart stovetop pressure cooker set over medium heat or in a 6-quart electric pressure cooker turned to the browning mode. Add the pancetta; cook until brown and crisp, about 6 minutes, stirring often. Use a slotted spoon to transfer the pancetta to a large bowl.

3 Add the meat; brown on all sides, turning occasionally, about 8 minutes. Transfer the meat to the bowl with the pancetta.

4 Add the pearl onions; cook, stirring often, until lightly browned, about 4 minutes. Crumble in the dried mushrooms, then return the beef, pancetta, and any juices in their bowl to the pot. Stir in the prunes, sage, and rosemary, then stir in the broth mixture.

5 Lock the lid onto the pot.

STOVETOP: Raise the heat to high and bring the pot to high pressure (15 psi). Once this pressure has been reached, reduce the heat as much as possible while maintaining this pressure. Cook for 25 minutes.

·····OR·····

ELECTRIC: Set the machine to cook at high pressure (9–11 psi). Set the machine's timer to cook at high pressure for 40 minutes.

6 Reduce the pressure.

STOVETOP: Set the pot off the heat and let its pressure fall to normal naturally, about 20 minutes.

·····OR·····

ELECTRIC: Turn off the machine or unplug it. Do not let it jump to its keep-warm setting. Let its pressure return to normal naturally, 20 to 25 minutes.

If the pressure has not returned to normal in 25 minutes, use the quick-release method to get rid of the excess pressure.

7 Unlock and open the pot; stir well before serving.

TESTERS' NOTES

• Prunes and pancetta are a match made in heaven: salty with sweet, soft with chewy. Here, they truly complement the sweet savoriness of the beef chuck.

• A stew like this is more traditionally made with veal. But the stronger flavor of beef is a better balance to the flavors, allowing the meat to be the focus and the other ingredients more in the background. However, to keep that original

(continued)

veal "feel," we used chicken broth, which gives the stew a lighter, velvety finish.

• Dried mushrooms hold more flavor and texture under pressure. Fresh mushrooms simply melt, especially after a long time under pressure. You can use dried portobellos (milder) or dried shiitake (muskier) instead of porcini.

VENETIAN-STYLE BEEF STEW WITH ONIONS AND VINEGAR

EFFORT: **A LOT** • PRESSURE: **HIGH** • TIME UNDER PRESSURE: **22 OR 33 MINUTES** • RELEASE: **QUICK, THEN NATURAL** • SERVES: **6**

1 tablespoon unsalted butter

2 tablespoons olive oil

2¹/₂ pounds boneless beef chuck, cut into 1¹/₂-inch pieces

4 large yellow onions, thinly sliced

¹/₂ teaspoon salt

¹/₄ cup balsamic vinegar

2 tablespoons tomato paste

1 cup beef broth

1¹/₂ tablespoons all-purpose flour

One 6-inch fresh rosemary sprig

1 Melt the butter in the oil in a 6-quart stovetop pressure cooker set over medium heat or in a 6-quart electric pressure cooker turned to the browning mode. Add the meat and brown on all sides, turning occasionally, about 10 minutes. Transfer to a large bowl.

2 Add the onions and salt; reduce the heat to medium-low under the stovetop pot. Cook, stirring often, until very soft, about 20 minutes (or less, if using an electric cooker).

3 Whisk the vinegar and tomato paste in a small bowl until smooth; stir into the cooker.

4 Lock the lid onto the pot.

STOVETOP: Raise the heat to high and bring the pot to high pressure (15 psi). Once this pressure has been reached, reduce the heat as much as possible while still maintaining this pressure. Cook for 2 minutes.

·······**OR**·······

ELECTRIC: Set the machine to cook at high pressure (9–11 psi). Set the machine's timer to cook at high pressure for 3 minutes.

5 Use the quick-release method to bring the pot's pressure back to normal.

6 Unlock and open the cooker. Set the stovetop pot over medium heat or turn the electric model to its browning function. Cook, stirring all the while, for 5 more minutes, until thickened.

7 Whisk the broth and flour in a small bowl until the flour dissolves; stir the mixture into the pot. Return the beef chunks and any juices to the pot. Tuck the rosemary sprig into the sauce.

8 Lock the lid back onto the pot.

STOVETOP: Raise the heat to high and bring the pot back to high pressure (15 psi). Once this pressure has been reached, reduce the heat as much as possible while maintaining this pressure. Cook for 20 minutes.

·······**OR**·······

ELECTRIC: Set the machine to cook at high pressure (9–11 psi). Set the machine's timer to cook at this pressure for 30 minutes.

9 Reduce the pressure.

STOVETOP: Set the pot off the heat and allow its pressure to return to normal naturally, about 15 minutes.

10 Unfasten and open the pot. Discard the rosemary sprig. Stir well before serving.

TESTERS' NOTES
• A riff on a Venetian classic, this sweet-and-sour stew is hearty comfort food almost any night of the week and especially welcome at a Sunday supper.
• The electric cooker will cook hotter on its brown setting than the stovetop model will over medium-low heat. You'll need to stir the onions in the electric pot quite often.
• For a more classic flavor, add a minced anchovy fillet with the onions in step 2.

UKRAINIAN-STYLE BEEF STEW WITH BEETS AND PICKLES

EFFORT: **A LITTLE** · PRESSURE: **HIGH** · TIME UNDER PRESSURE: **20 OR 30 MINUTES** · RELEASE: **NATURAL** · SERVES: **6**

1 tablespoon almond oil

3 thin slices of bacon, chopped

1 large yellow onion, halved and thinly sliced into half-moons

3 pounds boneless beef chuck, cut into 1½-inch pieces

2 pounds red beets (about 4 large), peeled and cut into 1-inch pieces

2 small dill pickles, diced

1 tablespoon minced fresh dill fronds

1 teaspoon minced garlic

1 teaspoon ground black pepper

½ teaspoon caraway seeds

One 14-ounce can diced tomatoes (about 1¾ cups)

1 cup beef broth

1 Heat the oil in a 6-quart stovetop pressure cooker set over medium heat or in a 6-quart electric pressure cooker turned to the browning function. Add the bacon; cook, stirring often, until lightly browned, about 2 minutes. Add the onion; cook, stirring often, until translucent, about 4 minutes.

2 Add the beef; cook, stirring occasionally, just until the pieces lose their raw color, about 3 minutes. Stir in the beets, pickles, dill, garlic, pepper, and caraway seeds. Cook, stirring often, for 1 minute, until aromatic.

3 Stir in the tomatoes and broth, scraping up the browned bits on the bottom of the cooker as the sauce comes to a simmer.

4 Lock the lid onto the pot.

STOVETOP: Raise the heat to high and bring the pot to high pressure (15 psi). Once this pressure has been reached, reduce the heat as much as possible while maintaining this pressure. Cook for 20 minutes.
·····························OR····························
ELECTRIC: Set the machine to cook at high pressure (9–11 psi). Set the machine's timer to cook at high pressure for 30 minutes.

5 Reduce the pressure.

STOVETOP: Set the pot off the heat and allow its pressure to return to normal naturally, about 15 minutes.
·····························OR····························
ELECTRIC: Turn off the machine or unplug it so it doesn't flip to its keep-warm setting. Let its pressure fall to normal naturally, 15 to 20 minutes.

(continued)

6 Unlock and open the lid. Stir the stew well before serving.

TESTERS' NOTES

• This dish is modeled on the Ukrainian version of borscht, a vinegary beet soup with beef in the mix. But the recipe is really a bit of whimsy with a delicious sweet-and-sour combination at the base of the stew.

• The beets can stain your hands. Wear rubber gloves—or rub them with soap and coarse salt to remove some of the stains. (You'll need to moisturize your hands afterward.)

Serve It Up! Mix 2 tablespoons prepared white horseradish into 1 cup regular or low-fat sour cream; spoon on top of each serving.

TAMARIND BEEF STEW

EFFORT: **A LOT** • PRESSURE: **HIGH** • TIME UNDER PRESSURE: **25 OR 40 MINUTES** • RELEASE: **NATURAL** • SERVES: **4**

1 cup sugar

2 pounds boneless beef chuck, cut into 2-inch pieces

1 tablespoon ground cumin

1 teaspoon ground allspice

1 teaspoon sweet paprika

1/2 teaspoon cayenne

1/2 teaspoon salt

2 tablespoons olive oil

1 medium yellow onion, chopped

1 medium red bell pepper, stemmed, seeded, and chopped

1 large globe or beefsteak tomato, chopped

1 1/2 tablespoons tamarind concentrate

2 teaspoons minced garlic

Up to 3/4 cup light lager beer, such as Pilsner

1/2 cup loosely packed fresh cilantro leaves, minced

1 Mix the sugar and 1 cup water in a large saucepan set over low heat until the sugar dissolves. Raise the heat to medium and continue cooking, stirring occasionally, until dark amber, about 7 minutes. Remove the saucepan from the heat; stir in 1 cup water. (Take care; the mixture will froth.) Set the pan back over low heat and stir until the sugar has dissolved. Set aside to cool to room temperature while you prepare the stew. (You'll have around 1 1/4 cups caramel sauce.)

2 Mix the beef, cumin, allspice, paprika, cayenne, and salt in a large bowl until the meat is completely and evenly coated.

3 Heat the oil in a 6-quart stovetop pressure cooker set over medium heat or in a 6-quart electric pressure cooker turned to the browning function. Add the meat and the spices; cook, stirring, until lightly browned, about 5 minutes. Transfer the beef back to its bowl.

4 Add the onion and bell pepper; cook, stirring often, until the onion turns translucent, about 5 minutes. Stir in the tomato, tamarind concentrate, and garlic; cook until very aromatic, about 2 minutes, stirring occasionally.

5 Add 3/4 cup beer to the stovetop pressure cooker or 1/2 cup beer to the electric machine; stir well to get any browned bits off the bottom of the pot. Stir in the meat and any juices in its bowl as well as the cilantro.

6 Lock the lid onto the machine.

STOVETOP: Raise the heat to high and bring the pot to high pressure (15 psi). Once this pressure has been reached, reduce the heat as much as possible while still maintaining this pressure. Cook for 25 minutes.

·············· OR ··············
ELECTRIC: Set the machine to cook at high pressure (9–11 psi). Set the machine's timer to cook at high pressure for 40 minutes.

7 Reduce the pressure.

STOVETOP: Set the pot off the heat and let its pressure return to normal naturally, about 18 minutes.

·············· OR ··············
ELECTRIC: Turn off the machine or unplug the pot. Do not let it flip to its keep-warm setting. Allow its pressure in the pot to return to normal naturally, 18 to 25 minutes.

8 Unlock and open the pot. Stir 3 tablespoons of the caramel syrup into the stew before serving.

TESTERS' NOTES
• This tangy and spicy stew is also very aromatic. The recipe is based on any number of Latin American stews, but we've reinvented those flavors with a North American supermarket in mind.
• You'll make more caramel syrup than you need for this dish. Pour the remainder into a glass jar, seal well, and refrigerate for up to 6 months. Use it in frozen drinks or even as a sauce over chocolate ice cream.
• For a more authentic flavor, substitute ground annatto seeds for the paprika, giving the stew more earthy sourness.
• Tamarind paste is a reduced, sticky, sour-sweet sauce made from the tamarind fruit, a culinary star across the southern hemisphere. Look for the paste in the international aisle of almost all supermarkets.

Serve It Up! Add peeled, boiled small white potatoes or peeled, steamed yucca chunks to the bowls.

HOT PAPRIKA BEEF STEW

EFFORT: **A LITTLE** • PRESSURE: **HIGH** • TIME UNDER PRESSURE: **25 OR 40 MINUTES** • RELEASE: **NATURAL** • SERVES: **6**

1 small yellow onion, quartered
3 medium garlic cloves, peeled
1 tablespoon hot Hungarian paprika
1 tablespoon sweet paprika
2 tablespoons olive oil
3 pounds boneless beef chuck, cut into 2-inch pieces
1/2 teaspoon salt
4 medium globe or beefsteak tomatoes, chopped (about 4 cups)
2 medium green bell peppers, stemmed, seeded, and chopped
1 cup dry white wine, such as Chardonnay

1 Combine the onion, garlic, and both paprikas in a mini food processor or a blender; process or blend until you have a coarse paste, scraping down the inside of the bowl or canister occasionally.

2 Heat the oil in a 6-quart stovetop pressure cooker set over medium heat or in a 6-quart electric pressure cooker turned to the browning function. Add about half the meat; season with half the salt. Cook, stirring occasionally, until very well browned, even dark in places, about 12 minutes. Transfer the beef chunks to a large bowl. Repeat with the remaining beef and salt.

3 Add the onion paste to the cooker; cook, stirring often, for 2 minutes, until aromatic. Add the tomatoes, peppers, and wine; scrape up any browned bits in the bottom as the wine comes to a simmer. Return the meat and its juices to the cooker; stir well.

(continued)

4 Lock the lid onto the pot.

STOVETOP: Raise the heat to high and bring the pot to high pressure (15 psi). Once this pressure has been reached, reduce the heat as much as possible while still maintaining this pressure. Cook for 25 minutes.

·············· **OR** ··············

ELECTRIC: Set the machine to cook at high pressure (9–11 psi). Set the machine's timer to cook at high pressure for 40 minutes.

5 Reduce the pressure.

STOVETOP: Set the pot off the heat and allow its pressure to return to normal naturally, about 18 minutes.

·············· **OR** ··············

ELECTRIC: Turn off the machine or unplug it, all to keep it from jumping to its keep-warm setting. Let its pressure in the pot fall back to normal naturally, 18 to 25 minutes.

6 Unlock and remove the lid. Stir the stew before serving.

TESTERS' NOTES

• Fiery hot, this stew is a dairy-free take on paprikash, sort of a Hungarian chili. The tomatoes will break down into a rich red sauce, thickened with the paprika.

• Cool that culinary fire with fat, not liquids. The hot chemicals (capsaicin) are fat-soluble, so take down the burn with a buttered slice of bread. (For a less hot stew, cut down the hot paprika as much as you like and fill out the remainder with sweet paprika.)

Serve It Up! Top the servings with a dollop of corn relish.

SESAME SHORT RIBS WITH PEANUT BUTTER AND BROWN SUGAR

EFFORT: **A LITTLE** · PRESSURE: **HIGH** · TIME UNDER PRESSURE: **35 OR 50 MINUTES** · RELEASE: **NATURAL** · SERVES: **6**

2 tablespoons toasted sesame oil

3 pounds boneless beef short ribs, trimmed

1 large leek, white and pale green parts only, halved, washed, and thinly sliced

1 tablespoon minced fresh ginger

1 tablespoon minced garlic

1/2 teaspoon red pepper flakes

1/4 cup packed dark brown sugar

1/2 cup beef broth

1/2 cup soy sauce

2 tablespoons smooth natural-style peanut butter

3 medium scallions, green part only, thinly sliced

1 tablespoon white sesame seeds

1 Heat the oil in a 6-quart stovetop pressure cooker set over medium heat or in a 6-quart electric pressure cooker turned to the browning setting. Add the short ribs, in batches to prevent crowding, and brown on all sides, turning occasionally, about 8 minutes. Transfer to a large bowl and brown more as necessary, transferring them to the bowl when you're done.

2 Add the leek, ginger, garlic, and red pepper flakes; cook, stirring constantly, until the leek begins to soften and the garlic to brown, about 3 minutes. Add the brown sugar and cook for 30 seconds until melted, stirring all the while.

3 Stir in the broth, soy sauce, and peanut butter until the latter dissolves, scraping up any browned bits on the bottom of the pot. Return the meat to the pot, along with any juices in the bowl.

4 Lock the lid onto the cooker.

STOVETOP: Raise the heat to high and bring the pot to high pressure (15 psi). Once this pressure has been reached, reduce the heat as much as possible while maintaining this pressure. Cook for 35 minutes.

································**OR**································

ELECTRIC: Set the machine to cook at high pressure (9–11 psi). Set the machine's timer to cook at high pressure for 50 minutes.

5 Reduce the pressure.

STOVETOP: Set the pot off the heat and allow its pressure to fall to normal naturally, about 20 minutes.

································**OR**································

ELECTRIC: Turn off the machine or unplug it so it doesn't flip to its keep-warm setting. Let its pressure return to normal naturally, 20 to 25 minutes.

6 Unlock and open the lid. Transfer the short rib chunks to serving bowls. Skim the fat from the sauce, then ladle the sauce over the pieces. Sprinkle each serving with sliced scallions and sesame seeds.

TESTERS' NOTES
• This sweet-and-salty sauce is a riff on certain Southeast Asian sauces, perhaps most common in Thai cooking.
• We're great fans of bones in all cuts of beef; however, we discovered that only 3 bone-in short ribs fit comfortably in most modern pressure cookers. What's more, the bone falls away from the meat during the intense cooking—so much of the benefit of that bone flavor is lost. To compensate, we cranked up the number of servings with boneless short ribs and increased the flavorings in the sauce.

• Although you'll never be able to trim beef short ribs completely, you should remove any thick fat caps that sit on top of the meat.
• Toast the sesame seeds in a dry skillet set over medium-low heat for a few minutes, stirring occasionally. Since the seeds can pick up static electricity and become impossible to scrape into a bowl, leave them in the skillet at room temperature until you're ready to serve.
• You can substitute 3 medium shallots, thinly sliced, for the leek and garlic.

Serve It Up! Serve over cooked and drained udon noodles.

TWICE-COOKED CRISPY SHORT RIBS

EFFORT: **A LOT** • PRESSURE: **HIGH** • TIME UNDER PRESSURE: **35 OR 50 MINUTES** • RELEASE: **NATURAL** • SERVES: **6**

1 tablespoon sweet paprika
1 tablespoon cocoa powder, preferably natural
2 teaspoons dried oregano
1 teaspoon red pepper flakes
1 teaspoon ground cumin
1 teaspoon onion powder
1/2 teaspoon ground coriander
1/2 teaspoon garlic powder
1/2 teaspoon salt
3 1/2 pounds boneless beef short ribs, trimmed
1 tablespoon sugar
1 tablespoon balsamic vinegar
2 tablespoons olive oil

1 Mix the paprika, cocoa powder, oregano, red pepper flakes, cumin, onion powder, coriander, garlic powder, and salt in a

(continued)

6-quart stovetop or electric pressure cooker. Add the beef and stir well until the spice mixture evenly coats the beef. Add water to the cooker to come halfway up the meat.

2 Lock the lid onto the pot.

STOVETOP: Set the pot over high heat and bring the pressure in the pot to high (15 psi). Once this pressure has been reached, reduce the heat as much as possible while maintaining this pressure. Cook for 35 minutes.

······················ **OR** ····························

ELECTRIC: Set the machine to cook at high pressure (9–11 psi). Set the machine's timer to cook at high pressure for 50 minutes.

3 Reduce the pressure.

STOVETOP: Set the pot off the heat and let its pressure return to normal naturally, about 20 minutes.

······················ **OR** ····························

ELECTRIC: Turn off the machine or unplug it, so it doesn't switch to a keep-warm setting. Allow its pressure to fall back to normal naturally, 20 to 25 minutes.

4 Unlock and open the lid. Transfer the meat to a platter; pour the sauce and juices in the cooker into a small bowl. Refrigerate the meat and sauce separately for at least 2 hours or up to 2 days, covering when cool.

5 Take the beef out of the fridge for 20 minutes. Skim any congealed fat from the sauce; pour and scrape the skimmed sauce into a small saucepan. Stir in the sugar and vinegar; bring to a boil over high heat, stirring occasionally. Boil until the sauce thickens, about 10 minutes, stirring once in a while.

6 Heat the oil in a large skillet set over medium heat. Add the short ribs and fry until crisp, turning occasionally, about 3 minutes per side, maybe less as the skillet continues to heat up. Transfer to serving plates or a platter and pour the sauce over the beef.

TESTERS' NOTES
• This may be the best way to gussy up barbecue for a dinner party.
• For a smoky flavor, substitute smoked paprika for the sweet paprika.
• Cooling the meat after cooking allows the fibers to set up so they can be fried to perfection—so you can make this dish a few days in advance of the feast.

Serve It Up! Shred a peeled jicama through the large holes of a box grater. Toss with a little lime juice and a pinch of salt. Place a pile of the salad on each short rib after you've sauced them.

SHORT RIBS BRAISED WITH WHITE WINE AND MUSHROOMS

EFFORT: **A LITTLE** • PRESSURE: **HIGH** • TIME UNDER PRESSURE: **35 OR 50 MINUTES** • RELEASE: **NATURAL** • SERVES: **6**

4 ounces slab bacon, chopped

3¹/₂ pounds boneless beef short ribs, well trimmed

1 medium yellow onion, chopped

1 pound baby bella or cremini mushrooms, thinly sliced (about 5 cups)

¹/₂ ounce dried mushrooms, preferably porcini

2 tablespoons jarred prepared white horseradish

2 teaspoons dried thyme

½ teaspoon ground black pepper

Up to 1 cup light, dry white wine, such as Sauvignon Blanc

1 tablespoon all-purpose flour

1 tablespoon unsalted butter, softened to room temperature

1 Fry the bacon until crisp in a 6-quart stovetop pressure cooker set over medium heat or in a 6-quart electric pressure cooker turned to the browning function. Transfer the bits to a large bowl.

2 Add the short ribs and brown on all sides in the bacon fat, about 8 minutes, turning occasionally. Transfer to the bowl with the bacon.

3 Add the onion and cook, stirring often, until it turns translucent, about 4 minutes. Add the fresh mushrooms; cook, stirring once in a while, until they give off their internal moisture and the mixture reduces to a thick glaze, about 7 minutes.

4 Crumble in the dried mushrooms, then add the horseradish, thyme, and pepper. Cook for 1 minute, stirring all the while. Pour 1 cup wine into a stovetop pressure cooker or ¾ cup into an electric pressure cooker. Nestle the meat into the sauce, pouring in any juices in the bowl.

5 Lock the lid onto the pot.

STOVETOP: Raise the heat to high and bring the pot to high pressure (15 psi). Once this pressure has been reached, reduce the heat as much as possible to maintain this pressure. Cook for 35 minutes.

········· **OR** ·········

ELECTRIC: Set the pot to cook at high pressure (9–11 psi). Set the machine's timer to cook at this pressure for 50 minutes.

6 Reduce the pressure.

STOVETOP: Set the pot off the heat and allow its pressure to return to normal naturally, about 20 minutes.

········· **OR** ·········

ELECTRIC: Turn off the machine or unplug it without letting it flip to its keep-warm setting. Let its pressure return to normal naturally, 20 to 25 minutes.

7 Unlock and open the cooker. Transfer the meat to serving bowls or a serving platter; defat the sauce in the pan by skimming it with a spoon.

8 Set the stovetop pressure cooker over medium heat or turn the electric cooker to its browning function. Bring the sauce to a simmer, stirring occasionally. Mash the flour with the butter into a thick paste in a small bowl; whisk small bits of the paste into the sauce to thicken it, cooking about 2 minutes and whisking constantly. Ladle the sauce over the short ribs to serve.

TESTERS' NOTES

• The horseradish will mellow over the heat, melting into the sauce to create a sweet and aromatic finish that's balanced by the butter at the end.

• The butter and flour mixture (a *beurre manié*—French, *burh mahn-YAY*) should be whisked into the sauce only in the smallest bits so that each has a chance to dissolve before the next is added.

Serve It Up! For a quick side dish, toss small trimmed Brussels sprouts with olive oil in a large roasting pan and bake at 375°F until lightly browned and tender, about 15 minutes, stirring occasionally. Toss with a bit of maple syrup and pecan pieces while still hot.

SHORT RIBS BRAISED WITH SAFFRON AND OLIVES

EFFORT: **A LITTLE** • PRESSURE: **HIGH** • TIME UNDER PRESSURE: **35 OR 50 MINUTES** • RELEASE: **NATURAL** • SERVES: **6**

1¼ cups chicken broth

½ teaspoon saffron threads

2 tablespoons olive oil

3½ pounds boneless beef short ribs, trimmed

1 large leek, white and pale green parts only, halved lengthwise, washed and thinly sliced

2 teaspoons dried oregano

¼ teaspoon red pepper flakes

½ cup dry sherry

¾ cup pitted green olives

¾ cup pitted black olives

¾ cup drained and chopped jarred roasted red pepper or pimiento

1 Warm the broth and saffron in a small saucepan over low heat until the liquid is just steaming, about 3 minutes. Set aside.

2 Heat the oil in a 6-quart stovetop pressure cooker set over medium heat or a 6-quart electric pressure cooker set to the browning mode. Add the short ribs, as many as will fit without crowding, and brown on all sides, about 8 minutes, turning occasionally. Transfer to a large bowl and brown more if necessary.

3 Add the leek and cook, stirring often, until softened, about 2 minutes. Add the oregano and red pepper flakes; cook a few seconds, stirring constantly, until aromatic. Pour in the sherry and scrape up any browned bits in the pot with a wooden spoon.

4 Stir in both kinds of olives and the roasted red peppers. Return the meat and any juices in the bowl to the pot. Pour in the broth mixture.

5 Lock the lid onto the pot.

STOVETOP: Raise the heat to high and bring the pot to high pressure (15 psi). Once this pressure has been reached, reduce the heat as much as possible to maintain this pressure. Cook for 35 minutes.

·············· **OR** ··············

ELECTRIC: Set the machine to cook at high pressure (9–11 psi). Set the machine's timer to cook at high pressure for 50 minutes.

6 Reduce the pressure.

STOVETOP: Set the pot off the heat and allow its pressure to fall to normal naturally, about 20 minutes.

·············· **OR** ··············

ELECTRIC: Turn the machine off or unplug it so it doesn't jump to its keep-warm setting. Let its pressure return to normal naturally, 20 to 25 minutes.

7 Unlock and open the cooker. Transfer the short ribs to serving bowls or a serving platter. Defat the sauce in the cooker by skimming it with a flatware spoon. Spoon the sauce over the short ribs to serve.

TESTERS' NOTES

• This luxurious dish would be fantastic for a New Year's Eve party or any time you want to show off your mad skills. It's Spanish-influenced in its palette and quite savory, a good dish to serve with beer.

• The secret, as always, lies in browning the beef. Don't skimp—color is flavor, and you can't overcook short ribs in this recipe.

Serve It Up! Make an easy brown rice pilaf by mixing cooked long-grain brown rice and chickpeas, sliced almonds, and dried currants.

Drizzle with sherry vinegar and olive oil, add a pinch of salt, toss well, and pour into a baking dish. Cover and bake at 325°F until warm, 15 to 20 minutes.

CURRIED BEEF SHORT RIBS AND POTATOES

EFFORT: **A LOT** • PRESSURE: **HIGH** • TIME UNDER PRESSURE: **45 OR 50 MINUTES** • RELEASE: **QUICK, THEN NATURAL** • SERVES: **6**

1 tablespoon canola or vegetable oil

2 tablespoons Thai red curry paste

One 4-inch cinnamon stick

6 green cardamom pods

1 teaspoon whole cloves

3 pounds boneless beef short ribs, trimmed

1 cup coconut milk

2 tablespoons packed dark brown sugar

1½ pounds small white potatoes (no more than 2 inches in length), halved

1 Heat the oil in a 6-quart stovetop pressure cooker set over medium heat or a 6-quart electric pressure cooker set on the browning mode. Add the curry paste, cinnamon stick, cardamom pods, and cloves; stir until aromatic, about 1 minute. Add the beef and toss well to coat in the spices. Pour in the coconut milk and stir in the brown sugar until dissolved.

2 Lock the lid onto the pot.

STOVETOP: Raise the heat to high and bring the pot to high pressure (15 psi). Once this pressure has been reached, reduce the heat as much as possible while maintaining this pressure. Cook for 35 minutes.

················ OR ················

ELECTRIC: Set the machine to cook at high pressure (9–11 psi). Set the machine's timer to cook at high pressure for 35 minutes.

3 Use the quick-release method to return the pot's pressure to normal.

4 Unlock and open the cooker. Sprinkle the potatoes into the sauce around the meat.

5 Lock the lid back onto the pot.

STOVETOP: Raise the heat to high and bring the pot back to high pressure (15 psi). Once this pressure has been reached, reduce the heat as much as possible while maintaining this pressure. Cook for 10 minutes.

················ OR ················

ELECTRIC: Set the machine to cook once again at high pressure (9–11 psi). Set the machine's timer to cook at high pressure for 15 minutes.

6 Reduce the pressure.

STOVETOP: Set the pot off the heat and allow its pressure to fall to normal naturally, about 15 minutes.

················ OR ················

ELECTRIC: Turn off the machine or unplug it to keep it from jumping to its keep-warm setting. Let its pressure fall back to normal naturally, 15 to 20 minutes.

If the pressure has not returned to normal in 20 minutes, use the quick-release method to bring it back to normal.

7 Unlatch and open the pot; stir well before serving.

(continued)

- This is our take on massaman curry from Southeast Asia. Make sure you have soup spoons to catch every drop of the sauce.
- Red curry paste is most often available in the Asian aisle at large supermarkets. Look for a brand that's not just a searing mix of chiles, but instead includes plenty of aromatics.
- To make your own **chile paste**, toast 2 dried New Mexican red chiles in a dry skillet over medium heat until aromatic, about 3 minutes, turning often. Set them in a large bowl and cover with boiling water. Soak for 15 minutes, then drain in a colander. Stem and seed the drained chiles; place them in a mini food processor with two 1-inch pieces of peeled lemongrass, 3 halved garlic cloves, half a small shallot, 1 tablespoon finely grated lime zest, and ½ teaspoon salt. Cover and process until you have a coarse paste, adding a few drops of water as necessary. Save the paste in a covered jar in the fridge for up to 1 week or in the freezer for up to 4 months.

TZIMMES WITH FLANKEN

EFFORT: **A LITTLE** · PRESSURE: **HIGH** · TIME UNDER PRESSURE:
23 OR 35 MINUTES · RELEASE: **NATURAL, THEN QUICK** · SERVES: **4**

2 cups chicken broth

3 medium garlic cloves, peeled and quartered

1 teaspoon whole cloves

One 4-inch cinnamon stick

1 pound flanken-cut beef short ribs (about ½ inch thick)

¼ cup honey

½ teaspoon salt

1½ pounds sweet potatoes (about 3 medium), peeled and cut into 1-inch pieces

½ pound carrots (about 4 medium), cut into 1-inch chunks

1 cup pitted prunes

1 Mix the broth, garlic, cloves, and cinnamon stick in a 6-quart stovetop or electric pressure cooker. Slip the flanken strips into the sauce.

2 Lock the lid onto the pot.

STOVETOP: Set the cooker over high heat and bring it to high pressure (15 psi). Once this pressure has been reached, reduce the heat as much as you can while maintaining this pressure. Cook for 15 minutes.

································· OR ·································

ELECTRIC: Set the machine to cook at high pressure (9–11 psi). Set the machine's timer to cook at high pressure for 23 minutes.

3 Reduce the pressure.

STOVETOP: Set the pot off the heat and allow its pressure to return to normal naturally, about 15 minutes.

································· OR ·································

ELECTRIC: Turn off the machine or unplug it. Allow its pressure to fall back to normal naturally, 15 to 20 minutes.

4 Unlock and open the cooker. Stir the honey and salt into the sauce; sprinkle the sweet potatoes, carrots, and prunes around the cooker.

5 Lock the lid back on the pot.

STOVETOP: Set the pot back over high heat and bring it back to high pressure (15 psi). Once this pressure has been reached, reduce the heat as much as possible while maintaining this pressure. Cook for 8 minutes.

································· OR ·································

ELECTRIC: Set the machine to cook once again at high pressure (9–11 psi). Set the machine's timer to cook at high pressure for 12 minutes.

6 Use the quick-release method to bring the pot's pressure back to normal.

7 Unlock and open the cooker; spoon the stew into serving bowls.

TESTERS' NOTES
• This dish is a sweetened root vegetable side dish with a specific cut of short ribs (see below). It's a traditional side at Rosh Hashanah but also makes a great main course. The meat is mostly a flavor for the vegetables, turning their natural sweetness a bit savory.
• Flanken-cut short ribs—sometimes called "Korean-cut short ribs"—are an Old World specialty that find their way into markets around the Jewish holidays in the fall. They're short ribs that have been cut across the bones, several round bits of rib in a line down the strip of meat.
• The bones can fall out of the meat under high pressure. Make sure you check the bowls of those going to children to remove any small bits of bone.

Serve It Up! Make sure you have thick slices of challah or egg bread for dipping into the sauce.

COLA-INFUSED BEEF RIBS

EFFORT: **A LOT** • PRESSURE: **HIGH** • TIME UNDER PRESSURE: **25 OR 40 MINUTES** • RELEASE: **NATURAL** • SERVES: **4**

1 tablespoon sweet paprika

1 tablespoon smoked paprika

2 teaspoons dry mustard

1 teaspoon ground black pepper

1/2 teaspoon salt

1/2 teaspoon onion powder

1/4 teaspoon garlic powder

One 3 1/2-pound rack of beef ribs, cut into individual ribs

1 cup cola-flavored soda

1 Mix both paprikas, the dry mustard, pepper, salt, onion powder, and garlic powder in a small bowl. Massage the mixture into the ribs.

2 Pour the cola in a 6-quart stovetop or electric pressure cooker; set the pressure cooker basket inside the cooker. Lay the ribs in the basket.

3 Lock the lid on the pot.

STOVETOP: Set the cooker over high heat and bring it to high pressure (15 psi). Once this pressure has been reached, reduce the heat as low as possible while maintaining this pressure. Cook for 25 minutes.

······················· **OR** ·······················

ELECTRIC: Set the machine to cook at high pressure (9–11 psi). Set the machine's timer to cook at high pressure for 40 minutes.

4 Reduce the pressure.

STOVETOP: Set the pot off the heat and allow its pressure to drop to normal naturally, about 6 minutes.

······················· **OR** ·······················

ELECTRIC: Unplug the machine or turn it off, either way keeping it from jumping to its keep-warm setting. Let its pressure fall to normal naturally, 5 to 9 minutes.

5 Unlock and open the pot. Transfer the ribs to a large baking sheet. Defat the sauce in the pot, either by pouring it into a fat separator and then pouring the skimmed sauce back into the cooker or by skimming the sauce with a flatware spoon.

6 Set the stovetop cooker over medium heat or turn the electric cooker to its browning function. Bring the sauce to a simmer, stirring occasionally; cook, stirring often, until

(continued)

the sauce reduces to about half its original volume, about 5 minutes.

7 Set the broiler rack 4 to 6 inches from the heat source; heat the broiler. Brush the sauce evenly over the ribs. Broil until glazed and hot, about 3 minutes, turning once and basting again. Cool for 5 minutes before serving.

TESTERS' NOTES
• Beef ribs are the meaty bones that lie under a standing rib roast. Steaming them in cola is a Southern tradition. They take on a light, sweet flavor—and are even better when crisped under the broiler.
• You may have a hard time separating the rack into its ribs at home without big cleavers, so ask the butcher at your supermarket to do it for you. Make sure you buy beef ribs with quite a bit of meat still adhering to them.
• Don't use a diet soda. You need the sugar for an effective sauce.
• Some pressure cookers do not come equipped with a steaming basket; if yours lacks this attachment, use the cooker's steaming rack, laying the ribs right on top.

OXTAILS STEWED WITH MUSHROOMS AND HERBS

EFFORT: **A LITTLE** • PRESSURE: **HIGH** • TIME UNDER PRESSURE: **50 OR 75 MINUTES** • RELEASE: **NATURAL** • SERVES: **6**

1 tablespoon olive oil

One 4-ounce pancetta chunk, diced

3 pounds beef oxtails

1 medium yellow onion, chopped

2 large cubanelle peppers, stemmed, seeded, and chopped

2 fresh hot cherry peppers, seeded and chopped

1 ounce dried mushrooms, preferably portobellos

2 teaspoons minced garlic

1 teaspoon dried thyme

1 teaspoon dried sage

1 cup dry white wine, such as Chardonnay

3 tablespoons tomato paste

1/2 cup beef broth

1 tablespoon balsamic vinegar

1 Heat the oil in a 6-quart stovetop pressure cooker set over medium heat or in a 6-quart electric pressure cooker turned to the browning function. Add the pancetta; cook, stirring occasionally, until well browned, about 4 minutes. Use a slotted spoon to transfer the pancetta to a large bowl.

2 Add the oxtails; brown well on all sides, stirring occasionally, about 5 minutes. Transfer to that same large bowl. Add the onion, cubanelles, and cherry peppers; cook, stirring often, until the onion softens, about 4 minutes.

3 Crumble in the dried mushrooms; stir in the garlic, thyme, and sage. Cook for less than a minute, stirring a lot, until aromatic. Pour in the wine; scrape up any browned bits in the pot.

4 Add the tomato paste; stir until dissolved. Stir in the broth and vinegar. Return the oxtails and pancetta to the pot, as well as any juices in the bowl. Stir well.

5 Lock the lid onto the pot.

STOVETOP: Raise the heat to high and bring the pot to high pressure (15 psi). Once this pressure has been reached, reduce the heat as much as possible while maintaining this pressure. Cook for 50 minutes.

········OR········

ELECTRIC: Set the machine to cook at high pressure (9–11 psi). Set the machine's timer to cook at high pressure for 75 minutes.

6 Reduce the pressure.

STOVETOP: Set the pot off the heat and allow its pressure to fall to normal naturally, about 25 minutes.

········OR········

ELECTRIC: Turn off the machine or unplug it so it doesn't flip to its keep-warm setting. Let its pressure return to normal naturally, 25 to 35 minutes.

7 Unlock and remove the lid. Transfer the oxtails to serving bowls. Skim the sauce for fat with a flatware spoon. Ladle the sauce over the oxtails to serve.

TESTERS' NOTES

• Oxtails are from the tail of the *cow* (not an ox), sliced into individual segments. They make a fantastic meal: rich, sticky, and extraordinarily beefy. If you have a hard time tracking down oxtails, ask your butcher to order them for you. Our butcher in rural New England takes about a week, but urban stores may have a quicker response.

• You really don't want anything else in the bowl: no rice, no mashed potatoes. These are luscious, indulgent bits—and anything else will just get in the way.

• You can substitute 1 large green bell pepper, stemmed, cored, and diced, for the cubanelle peppers, and 1 fresh medium jalapeño chile, stemmed and thinly sliced, for the fresh cherry peppers.

OXTAILS STEWED WITH BACON, CHILES, AND ROASTED GARLIC

EFFORT: **A LOT** • PRESSURE: **HIGH** • TIME UNDER PRESSURE: **50 OR 75 MINUTES** • RELEASE: **NATURAL** • SERVES: **4**

2 tablespoons olive oil

4 ounces slab bacon, cut into 1/2-inch pieces

4 pounds beef oxtails

1 medium yellow onion, chopped

2 medium Roma (plum) tomatoes, chopped

1 medium carrot, chopped

1/4 cup shelled raw green pumpkin seeds (pepitas)

2 tablespoons chopped pickled jalapeños

1 tablespoon chili powder

2 teaspoons dried oregano

2 teaspoons honey

1/2 teaspoon ground cinnamon

1/2 teaspoon ground cumin

1/2 teaspoon ground black pepper

1/2 cup dry sherry

1 cup beef broth

1 medium garlic head

1 Heat the oil in a 6-quart stovetop pressure cooker set over medium heat or in a 6-quart electric pressure cooker set to the browning mode. Add the bacon; fry until crisp on all sides, stirring occasionally, about 5 minutes. Use a slotted spoon to transfer the bacon to a large bowl.

2 Add as many oxtails as will fit without crowding; brown well on both sides, about 6 minutes, turning once. Transfer the oxtails

(continued)

to the bowl with the bacon, then repeat with the remaining oxtails.

3 Add the onion to the pot; cook, stirring often, until softened, about 4 minutes. Stir in the tomatoes, carrot, pumpkin seeds, and jalapeño. Stir over the heat for about 2 minutes, then add the chili powder, oregano, honey, cinnamon, cumin, and black pepper. Stir over the heat about 30 seconds, then pour in the sherry. Scrape up any browned bits in the bottom of the pot as it comes to a simmer.

4 Add the broth, stir well, and return all the oxtails and bacon as well as any juices in the bowl to the pot.

5 Lock the lid onto the pot.

STOVETOP: Raise the heat to high and bring to high pressure (15 psi). Once this pressure has been reached, reduce the heat as much as possible to maintain that pressure. Cook for 50 minutes.
························ OR ························
ELECTRIC: Set the machine to cook at high pressure (9–11 psi). Set the machine's timer to cook at high pressure for 75 minutes.

6 As the stew cooks, position the rack in the center of the oven and heat the oven to 375°F. Cut the top third off the head of garlic, exposing most of the cloves below. Seal the trimmed head in a small aluminum foil packet. Bake until very soft, about 45 minutes. Open the packet and cool a bit as you prepare the stew.

7 Reduce the pressure.

STOVETOP: Turn the heat off under the cooker; let the pressure fall in the pot back to normal naturally, 25 to 35 minutes.
························ OR ························
ELECTRIC: Turn off the electric model; let the pressure fall in the pot back to normal naturally, 25 to 35 minutes.

8 Unlock and open the cooker. Transfer the oxtails to a large serving bowl or serving bowls. Use a spoon to skim the sauce of excess fat. Set the stovetop cooker over medium-high heat or turn the electric cooker to its browning mode; bring the sauce to a simmer, stirring occasionally. Squeeze the soft garlic out of the head, whisking the cloves one by one into the sauce. Ladle or pour the sauce over the oxtails to serve.

TESTERS' NOTES
• There will be much slurping at the table. Cut off as much meat as you can, then pick up the bone and start gnawing. The best part is the soft, luscious center at the top and bottom of each bone.
• The roasted garlic acts as a sort of thickener in the sauce. It brings a mellow, savory bite to the other flavors.
• Substitute dry vermouth (less sweet) for the sherry, and unsalted sunflower seeds for the pumpkin seeds.

Serve It Up! Have a baguette on the table to tear into chunks. Dress a salad of chopped Boston lettuce and sliced celery with a lemon vinaigrette: 3 parts olive oil to 1 part lemon juice, whisked until smooth, then seasoned with a pinch of salt and sugar.

Pork

Although we had to use smaller cuts of beef in the pressure cooker, we can make up for the lack of big-batch cooking with pork. Indeed, we can use larger cuts of pork all around and feed more people (or save leftovers for lunches). Because of its wealth of both interstitial fat and savory connective tissue, a four-pound pork shoulder can withstand the onslaught of prolonged cooking and still remain ridiculously moist. (By contrast, a four-pound beef chuck roast would cook unevenly.) While beef is usually left with a chunky texture and definite chew, pork is often prepared until it falls off the bone.

Pay special attention in this section to whether the cut of pork is bone-in or bone-less. Yes, the bone takes up precious space, but it's sometimes necessary to add flavor and moisture. You'll notice, for example, that the recipes for *bone-in* country-style pork ribs have a more neutral palette, the better to let the flavor come through. Those recipes for *boneless* country-style pork ribs, however, are more highly flavored, with a more extensive range of sweet, sour, and bitter accents. With bone-in cuts we felt obliged to honor the meat in the mix; with boneless, we felt freer to push the flavor combinations.

Those bones also increase cooking times: they take up more space in the closed environment and alter the pressure dynamics by their sheer weight. They also bring more tough bits to the game. Don't be fooled into using bone-in cuts when boneless are called for or the meat may not be ready in the estimated time. And don't use boneless when bone-in cuts are the stated ingredient: the meat may well be squishy.

If you follow the cut called for, you'll get some of the best stews and braises in this book. The moist environment inside the pot aids in the breakdown of all those juicy bits. In many ways, pork represents the best that a pressure cooker can do. But we suspect you already know that—or if you don't, you're about to discover it.

PORK CHOPS WITH BUTTERY APPLES

EFFORT: **NOT MUCH** • PRESSURE: **HIGH** • TIME UNDER PRESSURE:
6 OR 10 MINUTES • RELEASE: **QUICK** • SERVES: **4**

3 tablespoons unsalted butter

**Four 1/2-inch-thick bone-in pork loin or rib
chops (6–8 ounces each)**

1/2 teaspoon ground allspice

1/2 teaspoon salt

1/2 teaspoon ground black pepper

1 cup frozen pearl onions, thawed

**2 large firm green apples, such as Granny
Smith, peeled, cored, and each cut into
6 wedges**

4 fresh thyme sprigs

3/4 cup chicken broth

1 Melt 1 tablespoon butter in a 6-quart
stovetop pressure cooker set over medium
heat or in a 6-quart electric pressure cooker
turned to the browning mode. Season the
chops with the allspice, salt, and pepper. Slip
two into the pot and brown on both sides,
turning once, about 4 minutes. Transfer the
browned chops to a plate, melt 1 more tablespoon butter in the cooker, and repeat with
the remaining chops.

2 Melt the remaining tablespoon butter in
the cooker. Add the pearl onions; cook, stirring often, until lightly browned, about
3 minutes. Add the apples and thyme; pour
in the broth. Nestle the pork chops among
the apples and onions; pour any juice
from the plate into the cooker.

3 Lock the lid onto the pot.

STOVETOP: Raise the heat to high and bring the
pot to high pressure (15 psi). Once this pressure
has been reached, reduce the heat as much as possible while maintaining this pressure. Cook for
6 minutes.

························· **OR** ·····························

ELECTRIC: Set the machine to cook at high pressure (9–11 psi). Set the machine's timer to cook at
high pressure for 10 minutes.

4 Use the quick-release method to bring the
pot's pressure back to normal.

5 Unlock and remove the lid. Transfer the
chops to serving plates or a serving platter;
spoon the apples and pearl onions among the
chops. Discard the thyme sprigs and spoon
the sauce over the servings.

TESTERS' NOTES

• The only trick in this easy supper is to brown the chops
well, with plenty of golden color. Any effort will have a big
payoff in the final dish.

• The apples should be firm so they'll hold up to high pressure. If they're spongy, they'll break down into applesauce.

• Use only bone-in pork chops—and slightly thicker than
the standard (although not those gigantic steakhouse pork
chops). The bone will partially protect the meat under
pressure and offer more fat to keep the chop moist and
tender.

Serve It Up! Warm oven-safe serving bowls
at 175°F for 15 minutes, then shred trimmed
Brussels sprouts into them through the large
holes of a box grater. Spoon the pork chops,
vegetables, and sauce over the shredded
Brussels sprouts and set aside for 5 minutes
while the threads soften (the warm bowls will
keep the food hot).

PORK CHOPS WITH ACORN SQUASH AND MAPLE SYRUP

EFFORT: **NOT MUCH** • PRESSURE: **HIGH** • TIME UNDER PRESSURE: **6 OR 10 MINUTES** • RELEASE: **QUICK** • SERVES: **4**

2 tablespoons unsalted butter

Four $^{1}/_{2}$-inch-thick bone-in pork loin or rib chops (6–8 ounces each)

$^{1}/_{2}$ teaspoon salt

$^{1}/_{2}$ teaspoon ground black pepper

2 medium acorn squash, peeled, seeded, and cut into eighths

3 tablespoons maple syrup

$^{1}/_{2}$ teaspoon dried sage

$^{1}/_{2}$ teaspoon dried thyme

$^{1}/_{2}$ teaspoon ground cinnamon

$^{3}/_{4}$ cup chicken broth

1 Melt 1 tablespoon butter in a 6-quart stovetop pressure cooker set over medium heat or in a 6-quart electric pressure cooker turned to the browning function. Season the chops with the salt and pepper, then brown two of them in the butter, turning once, about 4 minutes. Transfer these two chops to a plate, melt the remaining tablespoon butter, and brown the remaining chops. Arrange all four chops so they're in one layer as much as possible in the cooker, thin ends over thicker as necessary.

2 Add the squash to the cooker. Sprinkle the maple syrup, sage, thyme, and cinnamon over everything. Gently pour in the broth so that some of the spices stay on the chops.

3 Lock the lid onto the pot.

STOVETOP: Raise the heat to high and bring the pot to high pressure (15 psi). Once this pressure has been reached, reduce the heat as much as possible while maintaining this pressure. Cook for 6 minutes.

············ **OR** ············

ELECTRIC: Set the machine to cook at high pressure (9–11 psi). Set the machine's timer to cook at high pressure for 10 minutes.

4 Use the quick-release method to bring the pot's pressure to normal.

5 Unlock and open the pot. Transfer the chops to a serving platter; mound the squash around them. Ladle any sauce over the chops.

TESTERS' NOTES
• Particularly in a fairly simple recipe like this one, be sure to measure the spices and big-flavor ingredients like the maple syrup correctly. Small increases or decreases will greatly affect the success of the dish, particularly under pressure where there's less condensation.
• Bone-in pork chops will stay together better under high pressure—and the flavor of the bone will infuse the meat, resulting in a better meal.

Serve It Up! Plate the servings over cooked whole grains: wheatberries, quinoa, whole-grain bulgur, or brown rice.

ASIAN-STYLE PORK CHOPS AND BROCCOLI

EFFORT: **A LITTLE** • PRESSURE: **HIGH** • TIME UNDER PRESSURE:
6 OR 10 MINUTES • RELEASE: **QUICK** • SERVES: **4**

1½ tablespoons toasted sesame oil

Four ½-inch-thick bone-in pork loin or rib
 chops (6–8 ounces each)

6 medium scallions, thinly sliced

1 teaspoon minced garlic

½ cup chicken broth

¼ cup soy sauce

2 tablespoons packed dark brown sugar

1 tablespoon rice vinegar

4 cups small broccoli florets

1 Heat the oil in a 6-quart stovetop pressure cooker set over medium heat or in a 6-quart electric pressure cooker turned to the browning function. Add two of the chops and brown on both sides, turning once, about 4 minutes. Transfer to a plate and repeat with the remaining chops.

2 Add the scallions and garlic; cook until aromatic, about 1 minute, stirring all the while. Stir in the broth, soy sauce, brown sugar, and vinegar until the sauce begins to bubble.

3 Return the chops to the cooker, pouring in any juices from the plate and arranging the chops so that there's little overlap.

4 Lock the lid in place.

STOVETOP: Raise the heat to high to bring the pot to high pressure (15 psi). Once this pressure has been reached, reduce the heat as much as possible while maintaining this pressure. Cook at high pressure for 6 minutes.

⋯⋯⋯⋯⋯⋯⋯⋯⋯⋯**OR**⋯⋯⋯⋯⋯⋯⋯⋯⋯⋯

ELECTRIC: Set the machine to cook at high pressure (9–11 psi). Set the machine's timer to cook at high pressure for 10 minutes.

5 Use the quick-release method to bring the pot's pressure back to normal.

6 Unlock and open the pot. Sprinkle the broccoli florets over the chops.

7 Lock the lid on the pot and set aside for 5 minutes to steam the florets.

8 Unlock and open the cooker (using the quick-release method as necessary) and serve the chops and broccoli with the pan sauce ladled on top.

TESTERS' NOTES
• Even in a wok, you can't stir-fry whole pork chops. Too bad, because they take well to Asian flavors. Here's a terrific compromise: a braise that tastes like a stir-fry.
• The broccoli will still be crisp, even after steaming for a bit. If you like it a bit softer, bring the pot back to high pressure after you add the florets, then immediately turn off the heat or unplug the machine and let the pressure in the pot fall back to normal pressure naturally, about 5 minutes.
• Rice vinegar comes in two forms: unseasoned (unsweetened) and seasoned (with sugar or even corn syrup). Only the former is called for in this book. Look for it among the vinegars at the supermarket or in the international aisle with the Chinese condiments. (You can substitute ½ tablespoon white wine vinegar and ½ tablespoon broth if necessary.)
• For some heat in the dish, add up to ½ teaspoon red pepper flakes with the broth.

Serve It Up! You'll need rice—and lots of it! Try a short-grain white rice, sometimes called "sushi rice," a sticky, fragrant bed to hold the chops, sauce, and vegetables.

TOMATO-CHILE PORK CHOPS AND RICE

EFFORT: **A LITTLE** · PRESSURE: **HIGH** · TIME UNDER PRESSURE:
7 OR 10 MINUTES · RELEASE: **MODIFIED QUICK** · SERVES: **4**

2 tablespoons olive oil

**Four 1/2-inch-thick bone-in pork loin or rib
  chops (6–8 ounces each)**

1 large yellow onion, chopped

**One 41/2-ounce canned chopped mild
  green chiles (about 1/2 cup)**

1/2 tablespoon dried oregano

**One 14-ounce can diced tomatoes (about
  13/4 cups)**

**1 cup long-grain white rice, such as white
  basmati rice**

11/2 cups chicken broth

1 Heat the oil in a 6-quart stovetop pressure
cooker set over medium heat or in a 6-quart
electric pressure cooker set on the browning mode. Add two chops and brown on both
sides, about 4 minutes. Transfer the browned
chops to a plate and repeat with the remaining chops.

2 Add the onion to the pot; cook, stirring
often, until softened, about 4 minutes. Stir in
the chiles and oregano; cook until aromatic,
stirring constantly, less than 1 minute. Stir in
the diced tomatoes and rice, then stir in the
chicken broth.

3 Nestle the pork chops into the cooker, taking care to get the chops and rice submerged
as much as possible in the liquid. Pour any
juice from the plate into the cooker.

4 Lock the lid onto the pot.

STOVETOP: Raise the heat to high and bring the
pot to high pressure (15 psi). Once this pressure
has been reached, reduce the heat as much as possible while maintaining this pressure. Cook for
7 minutes.

·· **OR** ··

ELECTRIC: Set the machine to cook at high pressure (9–11 psi). Set the machine's timer to cook at
high pressure for 10 minutes.

5 Use the quick-release method to bring the
pot's pressure back to normal, but do not
open the pot. Set the cooker aside for 10 minutes to steam the rice.

6 Unlock the lid and open the pot. Dish up
the pork chops and rice onto plates.

TESTERS' NOTES

• The rice in this one-pot casserole will get tender without turning mushy if you use the modified quick-release
method, so the grains can continue steaming without any
added pressure. (You can use jasmine rice for a more aromatic finish.)

• The pork chops need to be immersed in the liquid as
much as possible to flavor the rice as it cooks. However,
the important thing is that the rice itself be submerged so
that the grains cook evenly.

HOMINY, PEPPERS, AND PORK STEW

EFFORT: **NOT MUCH** • PRESSURE: **HIGH** • TIME UNDER PRESSURE:
8 OR 12 MINUTES • RELEASE: **QUICK** • SERVES: **4**

2 tablespoons olive oil

1 large yellow or white onion, chopped

1 large green bell pepper, stemmed, cored, and cut into 1/4-inch-thick strips

1 large red bell pepper, stemmed, cored, and cut into 1/4-inch-thick strips

2 teaspoons minced garlic

2 teaspoons minced, seeded fresh jalapeño chile

2 teaspoons dried oregano

2 1/2 cups canned hominy, drained and rinsed

One 14-ounce can diced tomatoes, drained (about 1 3/4 cups)

1 cup chicken broth

1 pound boneless center-cut pork loin chops, cut into 1/4-inch-thick strips

1 Heat the oil in a 6-quart stovetop pressure cooker set over medium heat or in a 6-quart electric pressure cooker turned to the browning function. Add the onion and both bell peppers; cook, stirring often, until the onion softens, about 4 minutes.

2 Add the garlic, jalapeño, and oregano; stir well until aromatic, less than 20 seconds. Add the hominy, tomatoes, broth, and pork; stir over the heat for 1 minute.

3 Lock the lid onto the cooker.

STOVETOP: Raise the heat to high and bring the pot to high pressure (15 psi). Once this pressure has been reached, reduce the heat as much as possible while maintaining this pressure. Cook for 8 minutes.

·····OR·····
ELECTRIC: Set the machine to cook at high pressure (9–11 psi). Set the machine's timer to cook at high pressure for 12 minutes.

4 Use the quick-release method to bring the pot's pressure back to normal.

5 Unlock and open the cooker. Stir well before serving.

TESTERS' NOTES
• This down-home stew couldn't be easier—just soften a few ingredients and add the rest. You'll need a fork and spoon at each place.
• Make sure you drain the canned tomatoes; otherwise the excess liquid will turn the stew too soupy.
• Substitute minced pickled jalapeño rings for a slightly brighter finish to the dish.

Serve It Up! Have lime wedges on hand to squeeze over each bowlful, as well as a stack of warm corn tortillas.

BONELESS PORK LOIN CHOPS AND PEARS

EFFORT: **NOT MUCH** • PRESSURE: **HIGH** • TIME UNDER PRESSURE:
8 OR 12 MINUTES • RELEASE: **MODIFIED NATURAL** • SERVES: **4**

2 tablespoons unsalted butter

Four 3/4- to 1-inch-thick boneless center-cut pork loin chops (5–7 ounces each)

1/2 teaspoon salt

1/2 teaspoon ground black pepper

2 medium yellow onions, peeled and cut into 8 wedges each

2 large, firm Bosc pears, peeled, cored, and cut into 4 wedges each

¹/₂ **cup unsweetened pear cider**

¹/₂ **teaspoon ground allspice**

Several dashes of hot red pepper sauce

1 Melt 1 tablespoon butter in a 6-quart stovetop pressure cooker set over medium heat or in a 6-quart electric pressure cooker turned to the browning function. Season the chops with the salt and pepper, then brown two of them in the cooker, about 4 minutes, turning once. Transfer to a large plate, melt the remaining tablespoon of butter in the pot, and repeat with the remaining chops.

2 Add the onions and pears; cook, stirring occasionally, until the pears are lightly browned, about 3 minutes. Pour in the cider and stir in the allspice and red pepper sauce. Nestle the chops into the sauce, placing them as evenly as possible to make neat but not compact layers. Pour any juices from the plate over them.

3 Lock the lid onto the cooker.

STOVETOP: Raise the heat to high and bring the pot to high pressure (15 psi). Once this pressure has been reached, reduce the heat as much as possible while maintaining this pressure. Cook for 8 minutes.

································ **OR** ································

ELECTRIC: Set the machine to cook at high pressure (9–11 psi). Set the machine's timer to cook at high pressure for 12 minutes.

4 Reduce the pressure.

STOVETOP: Set the pot off the heat for 5 minutes.

······················· **OR** ·······················

ELECTRIC: Turn off the machine or unplug it; set aside for 5 minutes.

Use the quick-release method to bring the pressure back to normal.

5 Unlock and open the lid. Serve the chops with the pears and sauce ladled on each.

TESTERS' NOTES

• You can indeed make boneless pork chops in the pressure cooker but they need to be slightly thicker to protect them from the onslaught. As a result, they also take a little longer to get tender.

• We don't want the pears to get mushy. So we modified the natural-release method, giving them 5 minutes under slowly decreasing pressure before stopping the process and opening the lid.

• Rather than chopped or sliced onions, you want fairly big chunks to match the pear wedges.

• Use unsweetened pear cider, not hard pear cider. You can also use unsweetened apple juice in lieu of the pear cider.

Serve It Up! You'll need a loaf of crunchy bread at the table.

THICK PORK CHOPS WITH BASIL, GARLIC, AND PINE NUTS

EFFORT: **NOT MUCH** • PRESSURE: **HIGH** • TIME UNDER PRESSURE: **12 OR 18 MINUTES** • RELEASE: **NATURAL** • SERVES: **4 TO 6**

2 tablespoons olive oil

Four 1¹/₄- to 1¹/₂-inch-thick bone-in pork loin chops (about 12 ounces each), trimmed

¹/₂ **teaspoon salt**

¹/₂ **teaspoon ground black pepper**

2 tablespoons pine nuts

1¹/₂ tablespoons minced garlic

³/₄ **cup chicken broth**

2 tablespoons packed fresh basil leaves, minced

1 tablespoon white wine vinegar

(continued)

1 Heat the oil in a 6-quart stovetop pressure cooker set over medium heat or in a 6-quart electric pressure cooker turned to the browning function. Season the chops with the salt and pepper, then slip two of them into the cooker. Brown on both sides, turning once, about 4 minutes. Transfer to a plate and repeat with the remaining chops.

2 Add the pine nuts and garlic to the cooker; cook, stirring often, until aromatic, about 1 minute. Pour in the broth and scrape up any browned bits in the cooker while the liquid comes to a simmer. Stir in the basil and vinegar. Return the chops to the cooker, stacking them evenly and with as little overlap as possible. Pour any juice on the plate over the chops.

3 Lock the lid onto the pot.

STOVETOP: Raise the heat to high to bring the pot to high pressure (15 psi). Once this pressure has been reached, reduce the heat as much as possible while maintaining this pressure. Cook for 12 minutes.

················· **OR** ·················

ELECTRIC: Set the machine to cook at high pressure (9–11 psi). Set the machine's timer to cook at high pressure for 18 minutes.

4 Reduce the pressure.

STOVETOP: Set the pot off the heat and allow its pressure to fall back to normal naturally, about 10 minutes.

················· **OR** ·················

ELECTRIC: Turn off the machine or unplug it so it doesn't jump to its keep-warm setting. Let its pressure come back to normal naturally, 10 to 13 minutes.

5 Unlock and open the pot. Transfer the chops to individual plates or a large platter; spoon the sauce over them to serve.

TESTERS' NOTES

• This hearty supper is based on a deconstructed pesto, without the goopy mess that pesto would make in the cooker.

• The servings are steakhouse size. You might be able to divide the dish into 6 (or even 8) servings if you don't have big eaters at the table. However, don't halve the recipe for smaller numbers, since it was calibrated to work at this time with this amount of liquid. Plan on leftovers—a glorious thing, indeed.

• There's no need to go crazy trimming these chops. Just make sure any thick layer of fat is removed. A small layer will add flavor without weighing down the sauce.

• The chops won't fit in one layer, and maybe not in two. The point is to get them fairly level in the cooker, even if some are not fully submerged. You might also consider lining them up on their sides, bones down.

• For a spark of more flavor, add 1 teaspoon finely grated lemon zest with the basil.

THICK PORK CHOPS WITH CARROTS AND DILL

EFFORT: **NOT MUCH** • PRESSURE: **HIGH** • TIME UNDER PRESSURE: **12 OR 15 MINUTES** • RELEASE: **MODIFIED NATURAL** • SERVES: **4 TO 6**

2 tablespoons unsalted butter

1 tablespoon olive oil

Four 1¼- to 1½-inch-thick bone-in pork loin chops (about 12 ounces each), trimmed

½ teaspoon salt

½ teaspoon ground black pepper

16 baby carrots

1 tablespoon minced fresh dill fronds

½ cup dry white wine, such as Chardonnay

½ cup chicken broth

1 Melt 1 tablespoon of the butter in the oil in a 6-quart stovetop pressure cooker set over medium heat or in a 6-quart electric pressure cooker turned to the browning function. Season the chops with the salt and pepper, then brown two of them in the cooker, turning once, about 4 minutes. Transfer to a large plate and repeat with the remaining chops.

2 Add the remaining 1 tablespoon butter, then the carrots and dill; stir over the heat for 1 minute. Pour in the wine and scrape up any browned bits in the pot as the liquid comes to a boil. Stir in the broth. Return the chops to the cooker, arranging them as evenly as possible in layers.

3 Lock the lid onto the pot.

STOVETOP: Raise the heat to high and bring the pot to high pressure (15 psi). Once this pressure has been reached, reduce the heat as much as possible while maintaining pressure. Cook for 12 minutes.

························· **OR** ·························

ELECTRIC: Set the machine to cook at high pressure (9–11 psi). Set the machine's timer to cook at high pressure for 18 minutes.

4 Reduce the pressure.

STOVETOP: Set aside off the heat for 8 minutes.

························· **OR** ·························

ELECTRIC: Turn off the machine or unplug it; set aside for 8 minutes.

Use the quick-release method to return the pot's pressure to normal.

5 Unlock and open the pot. Transfer the pork chops to individual plates or a large platter; spoon the sauce and carrots over them to serve.

TESTERS' NOTES
• The grassy taste of the fresh dill will balance the sweetness in the carrots and pork. Dried dill has a much heavier flavor that doesn't work nearly so well.
• We don't mean true baby carrots but, rather, those 3- to 4-inch cut-down carrots sold as "baby" carrots in bags in the produce section.
• The release here is a modified natural one to keep the carrots from turning mushy.
• You can use ¼ cup unsweetened apple juice and ¼ cup broth instead of the wine.

SUPER-THICK PORK CHOPS WITH ARTICHOKE AND LEMON

EFFORT: **A LITTLE** • PRESSURE: **HIGH** • TIME UNDER PRESSURE: **16 OR 24 MINUTES** • RELEASE: **QUICK** • SERVES: **4 TO 6**

1 tablespoon unsalted butter

One 3-ounce pancetta chunk, diced

Two 1¾- to 2-inch-thick bone-in pork loin chops (1–1¼ pounds each), trimmed

2 teaspoons ground black pepper

1 medium shallot, minced

Four 2-inch lemon zest strips

2 teaspoons minced garlic

1 teaspoon dried rosemary

One 9-ounce box frozen artichoke heart quarters, thawed (about 2 cups)

½ cup moderately dry white wine, such as Pinot Gris

¼ cup chicken broth

1 Melt the butter in a 6-quart stovetop pressure cooker set over medium heat or in a 6-quart electric pressure cooker turned to the browning mode. Add the pancetta; cook

(continued)

until crisp and brown, about 5 minutes, stirring often. Use a slotted spoon to transfer the pancetta to a plate.

2 Season the chops with the pepper, then slip one of them into the cooker. Brown well, turning once, about 4 minutes. Transfer to the plate with the pancetta and repeat with the remaining chop.

3 Add the shallot to the cooker; stir for 1 minute, until slightly softened. Add the lemon zest, garlic, and rosemary; stir until aromatic, less than a minute. Stir in the artichokes, wine, and broth.

4 Sprinkle the pancetta back into the cooker; add the chops, overlapping as little as possible. Pour any juices on the plate into the cooker.

5 Lock the lid in place.

STOVETOP: Raise the heat to high and bring the pot to high pressure (15 psi). Once this pressure has been reached, reduce the heat as much as possible while maintaining this pressure. Cook for 16 minutes.

·························· **OR** ··························

ELECTRIC: Set the machine to cook at high pressure (9–11 psi). Set the machine's timer to cook at high pressure for 24 minutes.

6 Use the quick-release method to bring the pot's pressure back to normal.

7 Unlock and open the cooker. Transfer the chops to a carving board. Slice the eye of meat off the bones and then slice the meat into strips; divide among the serving plates or bowls. Ladle the sauce and vegetables over the servings.

TESTERS' NOTES

• These are steakhouse-sized pork chops, each easily serving two people. You can also use 2-inch rib chops, as double-boned chops. The cooking time will not have these falling-off-the-bone tender; you'll need a knife and fork.

• Frozen artichoke hearts are loaded with excess moisture—which will build a simple sauce.

• Make lemon zest strips with a vegetable peeler, running it along the length of the fruit. Take off only the yellow zest, leaving as much of the white pith on the fruit as possible. Those strips are perfectly edible after cooking under pressure.

• Mince the shallot into fine bits, preferably around $1/8$ inch each, so they can melt into the sauce.

• If you've got bone lovers at the table, cut a portion of the meat off the bone, giving one person a large boneless chop and the other a bone with plenty of meat still on it.

Serve It Up! This Italian-inspired supper would be best next to some noodles, particularly fettuccini. The sauce and vegetables in the pot should go right on top of the noodles—maybe with a little extra butter in the noodles for good measure.

SUPER-THICK SPICED PORK CHOPS WITH CHERRY SAUCE

EFFORT: **A LITTLE** • PRESSURE: **HIGH** • TIME UNDER PRESSURE: **16 OR 24 MINUTES** • RELEASE: **QUICK** • SERVES: **4 TO 6**

$1/2$ **teaspoon ground cinnamon**

$1/4$ **teaspoon ground cardamom**

$1/4$ **teaspoon ground coriander**

$1/4$ **teaspoon ground ginger**

$1/4$ **teaspoon salt**

Two 1³/₄- to 2-inch-thick bone-in pork loin chops (1–1¹/₄ pounds each), trimmed

1 tablespoon unsalted butter

2 tablespoons olive oil

1 cup fresh pearl onions, peeled, or frozen pearl onions, thawed

¹/₂ cup cherry jam, preferably sour cherry jam

¹/₄ cup medium-dry red wine, such as Shiraz

1 Mix the cinnamon, cardamom, coriander, ginger, and salt in a small bowl; massage onto each side of each pork chop.

2 Melt the butter in the olive oil in a 6-quart stovetop pressure cooker set over medium heat or in a 6-quart electric model set to the browning function. Add one chop and brown lightly on both sides, about 3 minutes, turning once. Transfer to a large plate when done and repeat with the remaining chop.

3 Add the pearl onions to the cooker. Stir until lightly browned, about 4 minutes. Stir in the jam and wine until the jam melts, scraping up all the browned bits in the bottom of the pot. Return the chops and any juices on their plate to the cooker, overlapping them as necessary or standing them up bone side down.

4 Lock the lid onto the pot.

STOVETOP: Raise the heat to high and bring the cooker to high pressure (15 psi). Once this pressure has been reached, reduce the heat as much as possible while maintaining this pressure. Cook for 16 minutes.

········· OR ·········

ELECTRIC: Set the machine to cook at high pressure (9–11 psi). Set the machine's timer to cook at this pressure for 24 minutes.

5 Use the quick-release method to bring the pot's pressure to normal.

6 Unlock and open the cooker. Transfer the chops to a carving board. Slice the meat off the bone and slice into strips; divide among the serving plates or bowls. Ladle the sauce over the servings.

TESTERS' NOTES
• We don't brown the chops as long in this recipe because we don't want the spice rub to burn.
• If you can't find appropriately sized chops at the supermarket, ask the butcher to slice some off a rack of pork.
• Although jam will make a smoother sauce, you can substitute sour cherry preserves for small bits of fruit throughout.
• For more flavor, swirl 2 tablespoons of unsalted butter into the sauce before spooning it over the chops.

Serve It Up! Make **Coriander Rice** as a bed for the chops: Heat 1¹/₂ tablespoons olive oil in a large nonstick skillet over medium heat. Add ¹/₂ tablespoon coriander seeds and ³/₄ teaspoon cumin seeds; cook 2 minutes, stirring all the while, until the seeds pop. Stir in 2 teaspoons minced garlic until heated through, then 2 cups cooked long-grain white rice. Toss well; remove from the heat; and stir in ¹/₄ cup chopped cilantro leaves, 1 tablespoon lemon juice, and ¹/₄ teaspoon salt.

PORK TENDERLOIN WITH BLACK BEANS AND COCONUT RICE

EFFORT: **A LITTLE** • PRESSURE: **HIGH** • TIME UNDER PRESSURE:
10 OR 15 MINUTES • RELEASE: **MODIFIED QUICK** • SERVES: **4**

2 tablespoons peanut oil

1 pound pork tenderloin, cut into 4 pieces

1 small leek, white and pale green parts
   only, halved lengthwise, washed and
   thinly sliced

One 4½-ounce can chopped mild green
   chiles (about ½ cup)

1 teaspoon dried thyme

1 teaspoon ground cumin

½ teaspoon ground coriander

¼ teaspoon salt

¼ teaspoon ground black pepper

One 15-ounce can black beans, drained
   and rinsed (about 1¾ cups)

1 cup chicken broth

1 cup regular or low-fat canned coconut
   milk

1 cup white long-grain rice, such as white
   basmati rice

2 tablespoons packed light brown sugar

1 Heat the oil in a 6-quart stovetop pressure
cooker set over medium heat or in a 6-quart
electric pressure cooker turned to the
browning function. Add the pork tenderloin
pieces; brown on all sides, turning occasionally, about 6 minutes. Transfer to a plate.

2 Add the leek and chiles; cook, stirring
often, until the leek softens, about 2 minutes.
Stir in the thyme, cumin, coriander, salt, and
pepper; cook until aromatic, less than half
a minute. Stir in the beans, broth, coconut
milk, rice, and brown sugar until the brown
sugar dissolves.

3 Nestle the pieces of pork in the sauce, submerging the meat and rice as much as possible in the liquid; pour any juices from the
meat's plate into the cooker.

4 Lock the lid onto the pot.

STOVETOP: Raise the heat to high and bring the
pot to high pressure (15 psi). Once this pressure
has been reached, reduce the heat as much as possible while maintaining this pressure. Cook for
10 minutes.

·· **OR** ··

ELECTRIC: Set the machine to cook at high pressure (9–11 psi). Set the machine's timer to cook at
high pressure for 15 minutes.

5 Use the quick-release method to bring the
pot's pressure back to normal, but do not
open the cooker. Set the pot aside for 10 minutes to steam the rice.

6 Unlock and open the cooker. Transfer the
pork pieces to four serving plates; spoon the
rice and beans around them.

TESTERS' NOTES

• An easy take on a Caribbean dish, this one-pot meal is
perhaps the best way to cook a pork tenderloin in the pressure cooker. In fact, this cut is such a quick-cooker that
a pressure cooker can turn it stringy or dry. However, by
burying tenderloin chunks in the broth and rice, we protect
it and keep it moist.

• Coconut solids can separate from the milk in cans; stir
those solids back into the liquid before using.

• For more heat, rather than using chopped canned *hot*
green chiles, use the mild ones as requested but also add
up to 1 stemmed, seeded, and minced fresh jalapeño with
the leek. Or go insane and add a stemmed, seeded, and
minced habanero chile.

Serve It Up! Drizzle each serving with bottled
Thai sweet chile sauce, then sprinkle with
minced scallions and cilantro leaves.

PORK LOIN WITH APPLES AND RED ONIONS

EFFORT: **A LITTLE** • PRESSURE: **HIGH** • TIME UNDER PRESSURE:
20 OR 30 MINUTES • RELEASE: **QUICK** • SERVES: **6 TO 8**

2 tablespoons unsalted butter

One 3-pound boneless pork loin roast

1 large red onion, halved and thinly sliced

2 medium tart green apples, such as
   Granny Smith, peeled, cored, and
   thinly sliced

4 fresh thyme sprigs

2 bay leaves

1/2 cup moderately sweet white wine,
   such as Riesling

1/4 cup chicken broth

1/2 teaspoon salt

1/2 teaspoon ground black pepper

1 Melt the butter in a 6-quart stovetop pressure cooker set over medium heat or in a 6-quart electric model set on the browning function. Add the pork loin and brown it on all sides, turning occasionally, about 8 minutes in all. Transfer to a large plate.

2 Add the onion to the pot; cook, stirring often, until softened, about 3 minutes. Stir in the apple, thyme, and bay leaves. Pour in the wine and scrape up any browned bits on the bottom of the pot.

3 Pour in the broth; stir in the salt and pepper. Nestle the pork loin into this apple mixture; pour any juices from the plate into the pot.

4 Lock the lid onto the pot.

STOVETOP: Raise the heat to high and bring the pot to high pressure (15 psi). Once this pressure has been reached, reduce the heat as much as possible while maintaining this pressure. Cook for 20 minutes.

·············· OR ··············

ELECTRIC: Set the machine to cook at high pressure (9–11 psi). Set the machine's timer to cook at high pressure for 30 minutes.

5 Use the quick-release method to bring the pot's pressure to normal.

6 Unlock and open the cooker. Discard the bay leaves. Transfer the pork to a cutting board; let stand for 5 minutes while you dish the sauce into serving bowls or onto a serving platter. Slice the loin into 1/2-inch-thick rounds and lay these over the sauce.

TESTERS' NOTES

• For the best flavor, buy a center-cut pork loin, one that's solidly pink, rather than a mix of pink and gray bits.

• For a less complex but more savory dish, use sweet firm apples like Gala or Northern Spy, and use a dry white wine like an American Chardonnay.

• To thicken the sauce, mix 2 teaspoons potato starch or cornstarch with 1 teaspoon water, then whisk it into the sauce (after the pork has been removed) with the stovetop cooker set over medium heat or the electric cooker turned to the browning function. Stir until simmering and thickened, less than 1 minute.

SPICED BEER-BRAISED PORK LOIN

EFFORT: **A LITTLE** • PRESSURE: **HIGH** • TIME UNDER PRESSURE:
20 OR 30 MINUTES • RELEASE: **QUICK** • SERVES: **6 TO 8**

2 tablespoons unsalted butter

One 3-pound boneless pork loin

1 cup frozen pearl onions, thawed

2 medium moderately tart baking apples,
    such as Northern Spy or McIntosh,
    peeled, cored, and chopped

1¼ cups light-colored beer, preferably
    Pilsner

¼ cup packed light brown sugar

1 teaspoon ground cinnamon

½ teaspoon ground ginger

½ teaspoon ground black pepper

¼ teaspoon ground cardamom

¼ teaspoon salt

1 Melt the butter in a 6-quart stovetop pressure cooker set over medium heat or in a 6-quart electric pressure cooker turned to the browning function. Add the pork loin; brown on all sides, turning occasionally, about 8 minutes in all. Transfer to a large plate.

2 Add the pearl onions and apples; cook, stirring often, until the onion softens, about 4 minutes. Pour in the beer; stir in the brown sugar, cinnamon, ginger, pepper, cardamom, and salt. Stir just to get any browned bits off the bottom of the pot, then nestle the pork loin into the sauce.

3 Lock the lid in place.

STOVETOP: Raise the heat to high and bring the pot to high pressure (15 psi). Once this pressure has been reached, reduce the heat as much as possible while maintaining this pressure. Cook for 20 minutes.

·····································OR·····································

ELECTRIC: Set the machine to cook at high pressure (9–11 psi). Set the machine's timer to cook at high pressure for 30 minutes.

4 Use the quick-release method to return the pot's pressure to normal.

5 Unlock and remove the lid. Transfer the pork loin to a cutting board while you finish the sauce.

6 Set the stovetop cooker over medium-high or switch the electric cooker to the browning or simmer function; bring the sauce to a boil. Boil for 10 minutes, stirring often, until thickened to a jam-like consistency.

7 Slice the loin into ½-inch-thick rounds. Serve these on individual plates or a large platter by ladling the sauce on top.

TESTERS' NOTES

• There's really no benefit to using fresh pearl onions here, since they're subjected to high pressure for so long. The frozen ones are already peeled and much more convenient. Thaw them by putting them in a bowl in the fridge all day or on the counter for a couple of hours.

• Some pork loins have a fair amount of fat clinging to their outside surface. Trim this off for a less oily meal.

• If desired, add minced garlic, up to 1½ teaspoons, with the dried spices.

• Make the sauce richer by swirling up to 2 tablespoons unsalted butter into it after it has reduced.

Serve It Up! Mash potatoes with a little chicken broth, sour cream, and Dijon mustard to serve alongside.

PORK LOIN WITH CRANBERRIES, GINGER, AND HONEY

EFFORT: **A LITTLE** · PRESSURE: **HIGH** · TIME UNDER PRESSURE:
18 OR 27 MINUTES · RELEASE: **QUICK** · SERVES: **4 TO 6**

2 tablespoons olive oil
One 2¹/₂-pound boneless pork loin
¹/₂ cup frozen pearl onions, thawed
¹/₂ cup whole fresh cranberries
2 tablespoons minced fresh ginger
1 tablespoon honey
1 tablespoon apple cider vinegar
1 cup chicken broth
¹/₂ teaspoon ground cinnamon
¹/₂ teaspoon salt
¹/₂ teaspoon ground black pepper
¹/₄ teaspoon ground cloves

1 Heat the oil in a 6-quart stovetop pressure cooker set over medium heat or in a 6-quart electric pressure cooker turned to the browning mode. Add the pork loin and brown on all sides, turning occasionally, about 6 minutes. Transfer to a large plate.

2 Add the onions and cranberries; cook, stirring often, until the onions begin to brown a bit, about 3 minutes. Stir in the ginger, honey, and vinegar; cook about 1 minute, until fragrant. Pour in the broth and scrape up any browned bits on the bottom of the pot.

3 Stir in the cinnamon, salt, pepper, and cloves. Return the pork to the pot as well as any juices on its plate.

4 Lock the lid onto the cooker.

STOVETOP: Raise the heat to high and bring the pot to high pressure (15 psi). Once this pressure has been reached, reduce the heat as much as possible while maintaining this pressure. Cook for 18 minutes.

·······································OR·······································

ELECTRIC: Set the machine to cook at high pressure (9–11 psi). Set the machine's timer to cook at high pressure for 27 minutes.

5 Use the quick-release method to drop the pot's pressure back to normal.

6 Unlock and open the cooker. Transfer the pork loin to a cutting board; cool for 5 minutes. Slice into ¹/₄-inch-thick rounds to serve in bowls with plenty of the pan sauce and vegetables ladled onto each serving.

TESTERS' NOTES
• Aromatic and light, this may well be the best pork loin dinner for a spring evening, despite the cranberries and fall flavors. The pearl onions and ginger balance these spices to create a sweet-and-sour sauce for the pork.
• The only real trick here is to brown that pork loin well, for lots of good color and flavor.
• If you're making this dish in the spring or summer, look for frozen cranberries in the supermarket's freezer case. There's no need to thaw them before using.

Serve It Up! Serve the dish over roasted sweet potatoes, skinned and mashed with a little milk, some white wine, some butter, and a pinch of salt.

PORK LOIN WITH MUSTARD AND CREAM

EFFORT: **A LITTLE** · PRESSURE: **HIGH** · TIME UNDER PRESSURE:
18 OR 27 MINUTES · RELEASE: **QUICK** · SERVES: **4 TO 6**

1 tablespoon unsalted butter

1 tablespoon olive oil

One 2½-pound boneless pork loin

4 large shallots, peeled and halved

¼ cup dry, light white wine, such as
    Sauvignon Blanc

½ cup chicken broth

2 tablespoons Dijon mustard

1 teaspoon dried dill

½ teaspoon ground black pepper

⅓ cup heavy cream

1 Melt the butter in the oil in a 6-quart stovetop pressure cooker set over medium heat or in a 6-quart electric pressure cooker turned to the browning function. Add the pork loin; brown on all sides, turning occasionally, about 6 minutes. Transfer to a large plate.

2 Add the shallots to the pot; cook, stirring once in a while, until lightly browned, about 5 minutes. Pour in the wine and scrape up any browned bits in the pot as it comes to a simmer. Add the broth; stir in the mustard, dill, and pepper. Set the pork loin in the sauce; pour any juices from its plate into the cooker.

3 Lock the lid onto the pot.

STOVETOP: Raise the heat to high and bring the pot to high pressure (15 psi). Once this pressure has been reached, reduce the heat as much as possible while maintaining this pressure. Cook for 18 minutes.

·························· **OR** ··························

ELECTRIC: Set the machine to cook at high pressure (9–11 psi). Set the machine's timer to cook at high pressure for 27 minutes.

4 Use the quick-release method to bring the pot's pressure to normal.

5 Unlock and open the cooker. Transfer the pork to a cutting board; cool for 5 minutes. Place the lid loosely over the cooker to keep the sauce warm. Slice the pork loin into ¼-inch-thick rounds.

6 Gently warm the cream in a small saucepan over very low heat. Whisk the cream into the sauce in the cooker. Serve the rounds in bowls with the shallots and plenty of the sauce ladled onto each serving.

TESTERS' NOTES
• There's nothing like cream to set off braised pork. However, that cream will break under pressure, so we add it at the end—and just a touch of it for good measure. (You can use light cream or half-and-half if you prefer.)
• Dried dill actually has a slightly savory edge, a little less bright and summery than its fresh kin. As such, it pairs better with the shallots and wine in this sauce.

Serve It Up! Toss boiled small potatoes with kosher salt, butter, and minced parsley leaves to serve alongside.

WHITE-WINE BRAISED PORK LOIN

EFFORT: **A LITTLE** • PRESSURE: **HIGH** • TIME UNDER PRESSURE:
18 OR 27 MINUTES • RELEASE: **QUICK** • SERVES: **4 TO 6**

$^1/_2$ **cup chicken broth**

$1^1/_2$ **tablespoons all-purpose flour**

1 tablespoon unsalted butter

1 tablespoon olive oil

One 2$^1/_2$-pound boneless pork loin

$^1/_2$ **teaspoon salt**

$^1/_2$ **teaspoon ground black pepper**

1 medium yellow onion, chopped

1 ounce dried mushrooms, preferably porcini

1 tablespoon Worcestershire sauce

1 teaspoon dried thyme

$^1/_2$ **cup dry white wine, such as Chardonnay**

1 Whisk the broth and flour in a small bowl until smooth; set aside.

2 Melt the butter in the oil in a 6-quart stovetop pressure cooker set over medium heat or in a 6-quart electric pressure cooker turned to the browning function. Season the loin with salt and pepper, then place it in the cooker and brown on all sides, turning occasionally, about 6 minutes. Transfer to a large plate.

3 Add the onion to the pot; cook, stirring often, until softened, about 4 minutes. Crumble in the dried mushrooms; add the Worcestershire sauce and thyme. Cook, stirring all the while, until fragrant, about 30 seconds. Pour in the wine and scrape up any browned bits in the bottom of the cooker as it comes to a simmer.

4 Whisk the broth once more to make sure the flour is still dissolved, then pour it into the cooker and stir well. Set the loin in the sauce; pour any juices from its plate into the cooker.

5 Lock the lid in place.

STOVETOP: Raise the heat to high and bring the pot to high pressure (15 psi). Once this pressure has been reached, reduce the heat as much as possible while maintaining this pressure. Cook for 18 minutes.

····················· **OR** ·····················

ELECTRIC: Set the machine to cook at high pressure (9–11 psi). Set the machine's timer to cook at high pressure for 27 minutes.

6 Use the quick-release method to drop the pot's pressure to normal.

7 Unlock and remove the lid. Transfer the loin roast to a carving board; cool for 5 minutes. Slice the roast into $^1/_4$-inch-thick rounds; serve these in bowls with plenty of the sauce ladled on each.

TESTERS' NOTES

• Although the sauce is rich on its own, you could stir another tablespoon or so of butter into it at the end. You could even add ¼ cup heavy cream.

• For the best flavor, make sure the dried mushrooms are well crumbled into the sauce.

• Because the flour also thickens the broth—and thus the sauce—it's crucial that it be properly dissolved in the broth and then the sauce. Otherwise, bits will fall out of suspension and burn on the bottom of the pot.

PORK LOIN CHILI WITH CHICKPEAS AND SAFFRON

EFFORT: **A LOT** • PRESSURE: **HIGH** • TIME UNDER PRESSURE: **7 OR 10 MINUTES** • RELEASE: **QUICK** • SERVES: **6**

12 dried New Mexican red chiles

3 tablespoons stemmed fresh thyme leaves

2 tablespoons packed fresh oregano leaves, chopped

2 tablespoons smoked paprika

1 tablespoon minced garlic

1/2 teaspoon salt

Up to 1/2 teaspoon saffron threads

3 tablespoons olive oil

2 medium green bell peppers, stemmed, cored, and chopped

One 2 1/2-pound boneless pork loin, cut into 1/2-inch pieces

One 15-ounce can chickpeas, drained and rinsed (about 1 3/4 cups)

1 cup chicken broth

1/2 cup dry sherry

1 tablespoon yellow cornmeal

1 Stem and seed the chiles; tear them into small bits. Place these in a medium bowl and cover with boiling water. Set aside to soak for 20 minutes, until softened.

2 Drain the chiles into a colander set in the sink; transfer them to a blender. Add the thyme, oregano, smoked paprika, garlic, salt, and saffron. Cover and blend until smooth, turning off the machine once in a while to scrape down the inside of the canister.

3 Heat the oil in a 6-quart stovetop pressure cooker set over medium heat or in a 6-quart electric model turned to the browning function. Add the bell peppers; cook, stirring often, until softened, about 3 minutes. Add the pork and stir until it loses its raw color, about 6 minutes.

4 Scrape the chile paste into the pot; stir over the heat until aromatic, less than a minute. Add the chickpeas, broth, sherry, and cornmeal; stir well to get any browned bits off the bottom of the pot.

5 Lock the lid onto the pot.

STOVETOP: Raise the heat to high and bring the pot to high pressure (15 psi). Once this pressure has been reached, reduce the heat as much as possible while maintaining this pressure. Cook for 7 minutes.

······································ OR ····································

ELECTRIC: Set the machine to cook at high pressure (9–11 psi). Set the machine's timer to cook at high pressure for 10 minutes.

6 Use the quick-release method to bring the pot's pressure back to normal.

7 Unlock and open the cooker. Stir the chili before serving.

TESTERS' NOTES
• Hardly a traditional chili, this one's a version of a North African tagine sieved through the American Southwest. You won't believe what saffron does for the dish: a musky sweetness that's a great foil to the pork.
• While you don't have to blow the budget on a fine sherry, use a bottling you'd drink on its own after dinner, something better than mere "cooking sherry." Or try an Amontillado for darker, earthier notes. (You can also substitute dry vermouth plus 2 teaspoons sugar, if you've got it on hand.)

Serve It Up! Offer sour cream or crème fraîche to dollop on the bowlful, as well as minced red onion and chopped pistachios for garnish.

BONE-IN PORK LOIN ROAST

EFFORT: **A LITTLE** • PRESSURE: **HIGH** • TIME UNDER PRESSURE: **35 OR 55 MINUTES** • RELEASE: **NATURAL** • SERVES: **4 TO 6**

1 tablespoon sweet paprika

1 teaspoon dried sage

1 teaspoon ground black pepper

1/2 teaspoon dried thyme

1/2 teaspoon dry mustard

1/2 teaspoon salt

2 tablespoons olive oil, plus a little more for rubbing on the roast

One 3-pound bone-in pork loin rib roast

2 medium leeks, white and pale green parts only, halved lengthwise, washed and thinly sliced

1 tablespoon minced garlic

1 cup chicken broth

1 Mix the paprika, sage, pepper, thyme, mustard, and salt in a small bowl. Smear a very light coating of olive oil over the pork roast, then massage the spice mixture across its surface, particularly on any exposed bits of meat without bone.

2 Heat 2 tablespoons olive oil in a 6-quart stovetop pressure cooker set over medium heat or in a 6-quart electric pressure set on the browning mode. Add the roast and brown on all sides, turning occasionally, about 8 minutes. Transfer to a large plate.

3 Add the leeks and garlic; cook, stirring all the while, just until the leeks begin to soften, about 1 minute. Pour in the broth and scrape up any browned bits in the bottom of the cooker as the broth comes to a simmer. Place the roast in the cooker bone side down; pour in any juices from its plate.

4 Lock the lid onto the pot.

STOVETOP: Raise the heat to high and bring the pot to high pressure (15 psi). Once this pressure has been reached, reduce the heat as much as possible while maintaining this pressure. Cook for 35 minutes.

······················ **OR** ······························

ELECTRIC: Set the machine to cook at high pressure (9–11 psi). Set the machine's timer to cook at high pressure for 55 minutes.

5 Reduce the pressure.

STOVETOP: Set the pot off the heat and let its pressure fall to normal naturally, about 15 minutes.
······················ **OR** ······························
ELECTRIC: Turn off the machine or unplug it so it doesn't jump to its keep-warm setting. Let its pressure return to normal naturally, 16 to 18 minutes.

6 Unlock the lid and open the pot. Transfer the roast to a large carving board; let stand for 5 minutes before carving into chops.

TESTERS' NOTES

• Yep, you can indeed cook a whole bone-in pork roast in a pressure cooker. You'll end up with ridiculously luxurious meat, something like pork confit.

• Look for a bone-in roast with a large, coherent eye of meat at the ribs on both sides of the cut. Avoid those with shoulder bones that begin to stick into the thick round of meat or those with large pockets of fat that break up the meat.

• Brown the roast well, searing caramelized flavors onto the pork before it undergoes its intense cooking.

• The pan juices are pretty fatty. You can strain and defat them for a sauce or you can have condiments like chutney and coarse-ground mustard on the table.

• When carving the roast, you actually have two choices: slice between the rib bones to make thick, bone-in pork chops; or slice the big eye of meat off the bones and cut this into 1/2-inch-thick rounds—then cut the bones apart and give one to each person who wants to gnaw.

PORK STEAKS AND POTATOES

EFFORT: **NOT MUCH** • PRESSURE: **HIGH** • TIME UNDER PRESSURE:
12 OR 18 MINUTES • RELEASE: **MODIFIED NATURAL** • SERVES: **4**

1 tablespoon olive oil

Four ¹/₂-inch-thick, 8-ounce boneless pork
  sirloin steaks

¹/₂ teaspoon salt

¹/₂ teaspoon ground black pepper

Four 6-ounce white potatoes, quartered
  lengthwise

1 tablespoon packed fresh sage leaves,
  minced

1 teaspoon sweet paprika

¹/₂ cup chicken broth

1 Heat the oil in a 6-quart stovetop pressure cooker set over medium heat or in a
6-quart electric pressure cooker turned to
the browning function. Season the steaks
with salt and pepper, then brown two of them
in the cooker, turning once, about 5 minutes
in all. Transfer to a large plate and brown the
remaining two steaks.

2 Place all the steaks in the cooker, then lay
the potatoes on top of them. Sprinkle with
sage and paprika, then pour in the broth.

3 Lock the lid onto the pot.

STOVETOP: Raise the heat to high and bring the
pot to high pressure (15 psi). Once this pressure
has been reached, reduce the heat as much as possible while maintaining this pressure. Cook for
12 minutes.

·····················OR·····················

ELECTRIC: Set the machine to cook at high pressure (9–11 psi). Set the machine's timer to cook at
high pressure for 18 minutes.

4 Reduce the pressure.

STOVETOP: Set the pot off the heat for 5 minutes.

·····················OR·····················

ELECTRIC: Turn off the machine or unplug it; set
aside for 5 minutes.

5 Use the quick-release method to bring the
pot to normal pressure.

6 Unlock the lid and open the cooker. Dish up
the steaks and potatoes onto serving plates.

TESTERS' NOTES
• A fairly economical cut of pork, the sirloin contains some
of the eye of loin and also bits of the tenderloin. Time was,
the cut was sold with the backbone or hip bone attached.
These days, they're sold boneless—and sometimes as a
larger 3 to 4-pound roast. If you can only find these larger
roasts, ask your butcher to cut the larger roast into sirloin
steaks.
• Since this is a lean dish, feel free to drizzle a
cold-pressed olive oil over each serving. Or spritz each
serving with lemon juice. Or do both!

Serve It Up! Serve with **Caesar Salad:** Whisk
1 large egg yolk, 2 tablespoons lemon juice, 2
teaspoons Dijon mustard, ¹/₂ teaspoon ground
black pepper, ¹/₂ teaspoon sugar, and ¹/₄ teaspoon salt in a large bowl until smooth. Whisk
in ¹/₃ cup olive oil in a slow, steady stream until
the dressing is creamy and thick. Add 6 cups
chopped romaine and radicchio; toss well before serving.

BARBECUED PORK SIRLOIN

EFFORT: **NOT MUCH** • PRESSURE: **HIGH** • TIME UNDER PRESSURE:
12 OR 18 MINUTES • RELEASE: **QUICK** • SERVES: **4**

**One 14-ounce can crushed tomatoes
(about 1³/₄ cups)**

²/₃ cup canned tomato paste

¹/₃ cup packed dark brown sugar

¹/₃ cup cider vinegar

**¹/₄ cup molasses, preferably unsulfured
molasses**

2 teaspoons minced garlic

1 teaspoon salt

1 teaspoon ground black pepper

¹/₂ teaspoon celery seeds

¹/₂ teaspoon ground cloves

**One 2-pound boneless pork sirloin roast,
cut into ¹/₂-inch-wide strips against the
grain**

**2 large sweet potatoes (about 1 pound
each), peeled and cut into 2-inch
chunks**

**1 medium red onion, halved and thinly
sliced**

1 Whisk the tomatoes, tomato paste, brown
sugar, vinegar, molasses, garlic, salt, pepper,
celery seeds, and cloves in a 6-quart stovetop
or electric slow cooker until the brown sugar
dissolves. Stir in the pork, sweet potato
chunks, and sliced onion.

2 Lock on the lid.

STOVETOP: Set the pot over high heat and bring
it to high pressure (15 psi). Once this pressure has
been reached, reduce the heat as much as possible while maintaining this pressure. Cook for
12 minutes.

··················· OR ···················
ELECTRIC: Set the machine to cook at high pressure (9–11 psi). Set the machine's timer to cook at
high pressure for 18 minutes.

3 Use the quick-release method to return
the pot's pressure to normal.

4 Unlock the lid and open the pot. Stir well
before serving.

TESTERS' NOTES
• This isn't pulled pork. Instead, the strips of pork sirloin
will still have plenty of firm, steak-like texture.
• To slice the pork sirloin into strips, run your fingers over the
top of the meat to discover which way the fibers lay. Rotate
the piece so you're slicing across those fibers—that is, at a
90 degree angle to their direction, or "against the grain."
• The sweet potatoes are in large chunks so that they
won't break down into the sauce.

Serve It Up! Offer pickled jalapeño rings as a
garnish.

CHINESE-STYLE ROAST PORK

EFFORT: **A LOT** • PRESSURE: **HIGH** • TIME UNDER PRESSURE: **12 OR
18 MINUTES** • RELEASE: **QUICK** • SERVES: **6**

¹/₂ cup unsweetened applesauce

¹/₄ cup soy sauce

¹/₄ cup mirin

¹/₄ cup packed dark brown sugar

1 tablespoon minced garlic

Up to 2 teaspoons sambal oelek

¹/₄ teaspoon five-spice powder

**Two 1-pound, 1-inch-thick boneless pork
sirloin steaks**

(continued)

1 Stir the applesauce, soy sauce, mirin, brown sugar, garlic, sambal, and five-spice powder in a 6-quart stovetop pressure cooker or a 6-quart electric pressure cooker until the brown sugar dissolves. Set the sirloins in the mixture; turn to coat.

2 Lock the lid onto the pot.

STOVETOP: Set the cooker over high heat and bring it to high pressure (15 psi). Once this pressure has been reached, reduce the heat as much as possible while maintaining this pressure. Cook for 12 minutes.

························ **OR** ························

ELECTRIC: Set the machine to cook at high pressure (9–11 psi). Set the machine's timer to cook at high pressure for 18 minutes.

3 Use the quick-release method to bring the pot's pressure to normal.

4 Unlock and remove the lid. Transfer the steaks to a large rimmed baking sheet. Position the oven rack 4 to 6 inches from the broiler and heat the broiler. Broil the steaks for 8 minutes, turning once after 4 minutes, until crisp and browned.

5 Pour the liquid in the cooker into a large saucepan. Bring the sauce to a boil over high heat; reduce the heat to medium and boil until reduced to a thick glaze, 2 to 4 minutes.

6 Transfer the steaks to a carving board; slice against the grain into ¼-inch-thick strips. Pour the glaze over the pork to serve.

TESTERS' NOTES
• Chinese restaurants use pork belly or other fatty bits for their roast pork, but we can make a leaner version that's equally satisfying because the pressure cooker won't let the meat dry out.
• The glaze here is not the typical red stuff found in most Chinese restaurants; we've adapted the ingredients to those in standard American supermarkets and offer a cleaner, brighter finish on the meat. However, if you miss the lurid color, add 4 or 5 drops of red food coloring along with the applesauce.
• You can use ¼ cup sake or dry white wine and an additional 1 tablespoon brown sugar for the mirin, or bottled hot red pepper sauce for the sambal oelek.

PORK SIRLOIN STEW WITH DRIED PINEAPPLE AND GREEN CHILES

EFFORT: **A LITTLE** • PRESSURE: **HIGH** • TIME UNDER PRESSURE: **15 OR 24 MINUTES** • RELEASE: **NATURAL** • SERVES: **4**

2 tablespoons peanut oil

1 small leek, white and pale green parts only, halved lengthwise, washed, and minced

Up to 1 small fresh jalapeño chile, stemmed, seeded, and minced

1 tablespoon minced garlic

One 2-pound boneless pork sirloin roast, cut into 4-inch chunks

One 4½-ounce can chopped mild green chiles (about ½ cup)

3 dried pineapple rings, chopped

1½ tablespoons minced crystallized (candied) ginger

1 teaspoon dried thyme

½ teaspoon ground allspice

⅓ cup chicken broth

2 tablespoons apple cider vinegar

1 tablespoon soy sauce

1 Heat the oil in a 6-quart stovetop pressure cooker set over medium heat or in a 6-quart electric pressure cooker turned to the browning function. Add the leek, jalapeño, and garlic; cook about 1 minute, just until aromatic, stirring constantly.

2 Add the pork; cook, turning occasionally, until the pieces are lightly browned, about 3 minutes. Stir in the chiles, pineapple, ginger, thyme, and allspice; cook until aromatic, about 30 seconds.

3 Pour in the broth, vinegar, and soy sauce; scrape up any browned bits at the bottom of the pot while the liquids come to a simmer.

4 Lock the lid onto the cooker.

STOVETOP: Raise the heat to high and bring the pot to high pressure (15 psi). Once this pressure has been reached, reduce the heat as much as possible while maintaining this pressure. Cook for 15 minutes.

·········· **OR** ··········

ELECTRIC: Set the machine to cook at high pressure (9–11 psi). Set the machine's timer to cook at high pressure for 24 minutes.

5 Reduce the pressure.

STOVETOP: Set the pot off the heat and allow its pressure to fall to normal naturally, about 12 minutes.

·········· **OR** ··········

ELECTRIC: Turn off the machine or unplug it so it doesn't flip to its keep-warm setting. Let its pressure come back to normal naturally, 12 to 15 minutes.

6 Unlock and open the pot. Stir well before serving.

TESTERS' NOTES
• This hearty supper is a riff on jerk pork, a Jamaican favorite. Because of the way the pressure cooker holds in every drop of moisture, we can use a far leaner cut. The results aren't as heavy but are far more flavorful.

• For more heat, skip the jalapeño and add up to 1 small, seeded, and minced habanero chile with the leeks.
• Leftovers can dull a bit in storage. Spark them back to life with bottled hot red pepper sauce and a dash of lime juice before reheating.

Serve It Up! Serve this over equal parts cooked long-grain white rice and warmed canned black beans seasoned with thinly sliced scallions and a dash of ground cumin.

PORK SIRLOIN AND BLACK BEAN CHILI

EFFORT: **NOT MUCH** • PRESSURE: **HIGH** • TIME UNDER PRESSURE: **12 OR 18 MINUTES** • RELEASE: **QUICK** • SERVES: **6**

1 tablespoon olive oil

1 small red onion, chopped

3 medium cubanelle peppers (Italian frying peppers), stemmed, seeded, and chopped

3 tablespoons chili powder

1 tablespoon ground cumin

One 2-pound boneless pork sirloin roast, diced

One 15-ounce can black beans, drained and rinsed (about 1³/₄ cups)

One 14-ounce can diced tomatoes (about 1³/₄ cups)

¹/₂ cup chicken broth

2 tablespoons Worcestershire sauce

1 Heat the oil in a 6-quart stovetop pressure cooker set over medium heat or in a 6-quart electric pressure cooker turned to the browning function. Add the onion and peppers; cook, stirring often, until the onion softens, about 4 minutes.

(continued)

2 Stir in the chili powder and cumin; cook until fragrant, less than a minute. Stir in the pork until coated in the spices. Pour in the beans, tomatoes, broth, and Worcestershire sauce; stir well.

3 Lock the lid onto the cooker.

STOVETOP: Raise the heat to high and bring the pot to high pressure (15 psi). Once this pressure has been reached, reduce the heat as much as possible while maintaining this pressure. Cook for 12 minutes.

·············· **OR** ··············

ELECTRIC: Set the machine to cook at high pressure (9–11 psi). Set the machine's timer to cook at high pressure for 18 minutes.

4 Use the quick-release method to drop the pot's pressure back to normal.

5 Unlock and open the pot. Stir well and serve.

TESTERS' NOTES
• Pork sirloin makes a lean, healthy chili, a little less decadent than one made with pork shoulder. This one's particularly savory, without any beer or brown sugar to sweeten it.
• Make sure the pork is cut into small bits, no more than ¼ inch each.
• You can substitute 1 large green bell pepper for the cubanelle peppers.

Serve It Up! Have sour cream, grated cheese, diced avocado, and thinly sliced scallions to garnish each serving.

REALLY FAST ALL-DAY RAGÙ

EFFORT: **A LITTLE** • PRESSURE: **HIGH** • TIME UNDER PRESSURE: **35 OR 50 MINUTES** • RELEASE: **QUICK** • SERVES: **8**

3 tablespoons olive oil

3 pounds pork neck or back bones, with meat attached

1 large yellow onion, chopped

2 medium cubanelle peppers (Italian frying peppers), stemmed, seeded, and chopped

2 teaspoons minced garlic

2 teaspoons dried basil

2 teaspoons dried oregano

1 teaspoon dried rosemary

1 teaspoon dried thyme

1 teaspoon fennel seeds

½ teaspoon red pepper flakes

½ teaspoon salt

1½ cups dry red wine, such as a Montepulciano

One 28-ounce can diced tomatoes (about 3½ cups)

One 28-ounce can crushed tomatoes (about 3½ cups)

½ cup canned tomato paste

1 Heat the oil in a 6-quart stovetop pressure cooker set over medium heat or a 6-quart electric model set to the browning function. Add the pork bits in batches as necessary to avoid crowding and brown them well on all sides, turning occasionally, about 8 minutes per batch. Transfer to a plate and repeat with the remaining pork pieces.

2 When all the pork has been browned, add the onion and peppers to the pot; cook, stirring often, until softened and aromatic, about 4 minutes. Stir in the garlic for a few seconds, then add the basil, oregano, rosemary, thyme, fennel seeds, red pepper flakes, and salt. Stir well, then pour in the wine and scrape up any browned bits in the pot. Stir in the diced and crushed tomatoes; nestle the pork in the sauce.

3 Lock the lid in the place.

STOVETOP: Raise the heat to high and bring the pot to high pressure (15 psi). Once this pressure has been reached, reduce the heat as much as possible while maintaining this pressure. Cook for 35 minutes.

···································· OR ····································

ELECTRIC: Set the machine to cook at high pressure (9–11 psi). Set the machine's timer to cook at high pressure for 50 minutes.

4 Use the quick-release method to drop the pot's pressure to normal.

5 Unlock and open the cooker. Remove the pork to a cutting board and cool for a few minutes. Remove as much meat as you can from the bones; discard the bones. Chop the meat and return it to the pressure cooker.

6 Stir the tomato paste into the meat in the cooker until dissolved. Set the stovetop pot over medium heat and bring to a simmer or turn the electric model to its browning function and bring the mixture to a simmer. Simmer uncovered for 15 minutes, stirring occasionally, to thicken the sauce.

TESTERS' NOTES
• You don't need to spend all day to make a fabulous Old World ragù. That may be the best news we have in this entire book!
• Pork neck bones can fall apart under high pressure. Fish around in the sauce with a spoon to see if you can locate small bits but always warn your friends and family that there may be little bits of bone left in the sauce. (If you

can't find pork neck or back bones, substitute a bone-in pork shoulder cut into 2- to 3-inch chunks.)
• Because some electric pressure cookers hold every drop of steam inside, you may end up with a slightly soupier sauce than in a stovetop model. Simmer it an extra 5 to 10 minutes in step 6 to further thicken the sauce; or reduce the wine used to 1 cup plus 3 tablespoons up front for a thicker sauce with less reduction time.
• Substitute 1 medium green bell pepper for the cubanelle.

Serve It Up! Good ragù usually needs good pasta. We prefer fresh fettuccini or pappardelle for this sauce. Or look for fresh chestnut pasta, a real treat available at high-end supermarkets or Italian grocery stores.

HONEST-TO-GOD PULLED PORK

EFFORT: **A LOT** • PRESSURE: **HIGH** • TIME UNDER PRESSURE: **1 HOUR OR 1 HOUR 20 MINUTES** • RELEASE: **NATURAL** • SERVES: **8 TO 10**

2 tablespoons smoked paprika

2 tablespoons packed dark brown sugar

1 tablespoon ground cumin

2 teaspoons ground black pepper

$1/2$ tablespoon dry mustard

1 teaspoon ground coriander

1 teaspoon dried thyme

1 teaspoon onion powder

1 teaspoon salt

$1/2$ teaspoon garlic powder

$1/2$ teaspoon ground cloves

$1/2$ teaspoon ground cinnamon

One 4- to $4^{1}/_{2}$-pound bone-in skinless pork shoulder, preferably pork butt

Up to $1^{1}/_{2}$ cups light-colored beer, preferably a pale ale or amber lager

(continued)

1 Mix the smoked paprika, brown sugar, cumin, pepper, mustard, coriander, thyme, onion powder, salt, garlic powder, cloves, and cinnamon in a small bowl. Massage the mixture all over the pork.

2 Set the pork in a 6-quart stovetop or electric pressure cooker. Pour 1½ cups beer into the stovetop model or 1 cup beer into the electric model without knocking the spices off the meat.

3 Lock the lid onto the pot.

STOVETOP: Set the pot over high heat and bring it to high pressure (15 psi). Once this pressure has been reached, reduce the heat as much as possible while maintaining this pressure. Cook for 1 hour.

·············· **OR** ··············

ELECTRIC: Set the machine to cook at high pressure (9–11 psi). Set the machine's timer to cook at this pressure for 80 minutes.

4 Reduce the pressure.

STOVETOP: Set the pot off the heat and allow its pressure to fall to normal naturally, about 25 minutes.

·············· **OR** ··············

ELECTRIC: Turn off or unplug the machine. (Do not let it flip to its keep-warm setting.) Let its pressure fall to normal naturally, 25 to 35 minutes.

5 Unlock and open the cooker. Transfer the meat to a large cutting board. Let stand for 5 minutes. Use a spoon to skim as much fat off the sauce in the pot as possible.

6 Set the stovetop pressure cooker back over medium-high heat or turn the electric model to the browning function. Bring the sauce to a simmer, stirring occasionally; continue boiling the sauce, stirring often, until reduced by half, 7 to 10 minutes.

7 Use two forks to shred the meat off the bones; discard the bones and any attached cartilage. Pull any large chunks of meat apart with the forks and stir the meat back into the simmering sauce to reheat.

TESTERS' NOTES
• Who knew a pork shoulder could get tender in an hour or so? Pulled pork was never easier.
• Add heat to the dish by using hot smoked paprika or adding up to ½ teaspoon cayenne to the spice blend.
• Pick through the meat to make sure you've removed all the tiny bones before you stir in the sauce.

Serve It Up! The pulled pork needs buns for serving, though it'll be a messy concoction—have plenty of napkins on hand. We like mustard and pickle relish on those buns, though we've also been known to make an Alabama barbecue sauce for this dish: half mayonnaise, half white vinegar, a little sugar to taste, and tons of ground black pepper.

DRIED FRUIT-LACED PULLED PORK

EFFORT: **A LITTLE** • PRESSURE: **HIGH** • TIME UNDER PRESSURE: **55 OR 78 MINUTES** • RELEASE: **NATURAL** • SERVES: **6**

One 28-ounce can whole tomatoes, drained (about 3½ cups)
½ cup whole-berry cranberry sauce
¼ cup packed dark brown sugar
2 tablespoons apple cider vinegar
1 tablespoon sweet paprika
1 tablespoon Worcestershire sauce
½ teaspoon ground allspice
½ teaspoon ground coriander
½ teaspoon salt
¼ teaspoon ground cloves

¹/₄ teaspoon celery seeds

¹/₄ teaspoon dry mustard

One 3-pound skinless bone-in picnic ham

²/₃ cup dried apricots (about 4 ounces)

¹/₄ cup golden raisins

1 Pour the tomatoes, cranberry sauce, brown sugar, vinegar, paprika, Worcestershire sauce, allspice, coriander, salt, cloves, celery seeds, and dry mustard into a large blender. Cover and blend until smooth, scraping down the inside of the canister at least once. Pour the mixture into a 6-quart stovetop or electric pressure cooker.

2 Add the pork, apricots, and raisins. Turn the meat over several times to coat well, then position the ham so that the meat is mostly submerged in the sauce.

3 Lock the lid onto the cooker.

STOVETOP: Set the pot over high heat and bring it to high pressure (15 psi). Once this pressure has been reached, reduce the heat as much as possible while maintaining this pressure. Cook for 55 minutes.

·········· **OR** ··········

ELECTRIC: Set the machine to cook at high pressure (9–11 psi). Set the machine's timer to cook at high pressure for 78 minutes (1 hour 18 minutes).

4 Reduce the pressure.

STOVETOP: Set the pot off the heat and let its pressure come back to normal naturally, about 23 minutes.

·········· **OR** ··········

ELECTRIC: Turn off the machine or unplug it so it doesn't jump to its keep-warm setting. Allow its pressure to fall to normal naturally, about 35 minutes.

5 Unlock and open the pot. Transfer the pork to a big cutting board. Let stand for

5 minutes. Slice the meat off the bone; discard that bone. Chop the pork into bite-sized bits. Skim the sauce for surface fat and stir the meat back into the sauce before serving.

TESTERS' NOTES

• This pulled pork relies on a stocked spice cabinet and lots of dried fruit to punch up the meat. Don't expect a barbecue-sauce flavor; this one has a sweet, fruit-laced sauce and is more like a thick stew. True, the dish is not truly "pulled," but it's in the spirit of the original.

• Make sure the apricots and raisins are fresh—not dried out, still moist and pliable.

Serve It Up! Offer this soupy version of pulled pork in bowls with warmed corn tortillas or pile crunchy corn chips on top of the servings in the bowls.

PORK CARNITAS

EFFORT: **A LOT** • PRESSURE: **HIGH** • TIME UNDER PRESSURE: **30 OR 45 MINUTES** • RELEASE: **NATURAL** • SERVES: **6**

One 3-pound boneless skinless pork shoulder, preferably pork butt, cut into 2-inch pieces

2 tablespoons finely grated orange zest

1 tablespoon minced garlic

1 teaspoon ground cumin

¹/₂ teaspoon pure chipotle chile powder

¹/₂ teaspoon salt

³/₄ cup beef broth

3 tablespoons lard

2 tablespoons fresh lime juice

1 Mix the meat, orange zest, garlic, cumin, chile powder, and salt in a 6-quart stovetop or electric pressure cooker until the meat is evenly coated in the spices. Pour in the broth.

(continued)

2 Lock on the lid.

STOVETOP: Set the pot over high heat and bring it to high pressure (15 psi). Once this pressure has been reached, reduce the heat as much as possible while maintaining this pressure. Cook for 30 minutes.

·············· **OR** ··············

ELECTRIC: Set the machine to cook at high pressure (9–11 psi). Set the machine's timer to cook at high pressure for 45 minutes.

3 Reduce the pressure.

STOVETOP: Set the pot aside off the heat and let its pressure come back to normal naturally, about 20 minutes.

·············· **OR** ··············

ELECTRIC: Turn off or unplug the machine so it doesn't jump to its keep-warm setting. Allow its pressure to fall to normal naturally, 20 to 30 minutes.

4 Unlock and open the pot. Transfer the chunks of pork to a large bowl.

5 Heat a large sauté pan or high-sided skillet over medium-high heat. Melt the lard, then add the pork, as many pieces as will fit without crowding. Fry until crisp, turning often, 6 to 8 minutes. Transfer the pork to a serving platter and continue frying more bits.

6 Use a flatware spoon to defat the sauce in the cooker. Pour the sauce into the hot skillet and stir in the lime juice. Boil until reduced by half over high heat, scraping up any browned bits in the pan about 10 minutes. Pour the sauce over the pork chunks to reheat them before serving.

TESTERS' NOTES
• A crazy-good use for pork shoulder, this simplified version of a Tex-Mex classic would be welcome on a chilly weekend.

• The pork shoulder has plenty of fat to keep it tender under high pressure. Rather than trimming each piece, defat the sauce after cooking.
• You can use olive oil instead of lard.
• You can substitute ¼ teaspoon smoked paprika and ¼ teaspoon cayenne for the chipotle powder.

Serve It Up! Make **Spiced Rice and Lentils:** Mix 1 cup white basmati rice and ½ cup small green lentils (or lentils de Puy) with 2½ cups chicken broth in a large saucepan. Add a cinnamon stick, ½ tablespoon dried oregano, and ¼ teaspoon ground cardamom, then bring to a simmer over high heat. Cover, reduce the heat to low, and simmer until the rice is tender and the liquid has been absorbed, about 22 minutes. Discard the cinnamon stick before serving. Season with salt and pepper to taste.

SPICY PORK SHOULDER AND PEANUT STEW

EFFORT: **A LITTLE** • PRESSURE: **HIGH** • TIME UNDER PRESSURE: **25 OR 40 MINUTES** • RELEASE: **NATURAL** • SERVES: **4**

One 14-ounce can diced tomatoes (about 1³/₄ cups)

½ cup crunchy natural-style peanut butter

1 tablespoon packed fresh oregano leaves, chopped

¼ teaspoon cayenne

¼ teaspoon grated nutmeg

¼ teaspoon salt

2 tablespoons peanut oil

One 2-pound boneless skinless pork shoulder, trimmed of any large bits of fat and cut into 2-inch pieces

1 large yellow onion, halved and thinly sliced

1 tablespoon minced fresh ginger

2 teaspoons minced garlic

¼ cup dry white wine, such as
   Chardonnay

6 medium carrots, cut into 2-inch pieces

2 bay leaves

2 tablespoons fresh lime juice

1 Whisk the tomatoes, peanut butter, oregano, cayenne, nutmeg, and salt in a medium bowl until the peanut butter has loosened; set aside.

2 Heat the oil in a 6-quart stovetop pressure cooker set over medium heat or in a 6-quart electric pressure cooker set to the browning function. Add the meat in batches to prevent crowding; brown on all sides, turning occasionally, about 6 minutes per batch. Transfer to a large bowl and continue browning more as necessary.

3 Add the onion and ginger to the pot; cook, stirring often, until softened, about 4 minutes. Add the garlic and cook for about 10 seconds. Pour in the wine and scrape up any browned bits in the bottom of the pot.

4 Stir in the tomato mixture, then return the pork to the pot along with the juices on its plate, the carrots, and bay leaves. Stir again.

5 Lock the lid onto the cooker.

STOVETOP: Raise the heat to high and bring the pot to high pressure (15 psi). Once this pressure has been reached, reduce the heat as much as possible while maintaining this pressure. Cook for 25 minutes.

············· OR ·············

ELECTRIC: Set the machine to cook at high pressure (9–11 psi). Set the machine's timer to cook at high pressure for 40 minutes.

6 Reduce the pressure.

STOVETOP: Set the pot off the heat and allow its pressure to fall to normal naturally, about 15 minutes.

············· OR ·············

ELECTRIC: Turn off the machine or unplug it so it doesn't flip to its keep-warm setting. Let its pressure fall to normal naturally, 15 to 20 minutes.

7 Unlock and open the cooker. Remove the bay leaves and stir in the lime juice before serving.

TESTERS' NOTES

• Based on a central African ground-nut stew that has been transplanted to the American South, this rich meal is best on a cold night.

• Slice the onion as thinly as possible so the strips dissolve into the sauce.

• Pork shoulder can be particularly fatty. For a (slightly) leaner, less oily sauce, use the oddly named pork butt, a more meaty part of the front shoulder.

Serve It Up! Place baby spinach leaves in the serving bowls, then ladle the hot stew over them. They'll wilt by the time you set the bowls on the table.

PORK GOULASH

EFFORT: **NOT MUCH** • PRESSURE: **HIGH** • TIME UNDER PRESSURE:
25 OR 40 MINUTES • RELEASE: **NATURAL** • SERVES: **4**

1 cup chicken broth

3 tablespoons sweet paprika

1¹/₂ tablespoons all-purpose flour

1 teaspoon dried dill

1 teaspoon dried thyme

¹/₂ teaspoon salt

¹/₂ teaspoon ground black pepper

2 tablespoons olive oil

**One 2¹/₂-pound boneless skinless pork
      shoulder, preferably pork butt, cut into
      2-inch pieces**

1 medium yellow onion, chopped

1 pound baby carrots

**One 14-ounce can diced tomatoes (about
      1³/₄ cups)**

1 Whisk the broth, paprika, flour, dill, thyme,
salt, and pepper in a large bowl until the flour
dissolves; set aside.

2 Heat the oil in a 6-quart stovetop pressure
cooker set over medium heat or in a 6-quart
electric pressure cooker set to the browning
function. Add the pork chunks, as many as
will fit without crowding; brown on all sides,
turning occasionally, about 6 minutes per
batch. Transfer the pork to a bowl and continue browning more as needed.

3 Add the onion to the pot; cook, stirring
often, until softened, about 4 minutes. Stir in
the carrots and tomatoes; pour in the broth
mixture and stir well. Return the meat and
any juices in the bowl to the cooker, stirring
well to coat the pieces in the sauce.

4 Lock the lid into place.

STOVETOP: Raise the heat to high to bring the
pot to high pressure (15 psi). Once this pressure
has been reached, reduce the heat as much as possible while maintaining this pressure. Cook for
25 minutes.

·····································OR·····································

ELECTRIC: Set the machine to cook at high pressure (9–11 psi). Set the machine's timer to cook at
high pressure for 40 minutes.

5 Reduce the pressure.

STOVETOP: Set the pot off the heat and allow
its pressure to return to normal naturally, about
15 minutes.

·····································OR·····································

ELECTRIC: Turn off or unplug the machine—don't
let it jump to its keep-warm setting. Allow its pressure to drop to normal naturally, 15 to 20 minutes.

6 Unlock and open the cooker. Stir the stew
before serving.

TESTERS' NOTES
• You might think beef is the only protein for goulash;
you'd be wrong. Pork adds a luxurious sweetness, taking
retro comfort food to new heights.
• If you want some spice in your goulash, consider substituting up to half the sweet paprika with hot Hungarian
paprika—but be forewarned that you'll quickly turn the
dish fiery. Better to start with ½ teaspoon or so and work
your way up.
• Traditionally, goulash doesn't have sour cream in the
mix—and we can't use it in the cooker without its breaking
under pressure. But you can always garnish the servings
with a dollop of it!

Serve It Up! Cook no-yolk noodles as a bed
for each serving. For an even richer dinner,
toss the hot noodles with a little unsalted butter and some poppy seeds before serving.

RED-WINE BRAISED PORK SHOULDER CHOPS

EFFORT: **A LITTLE** • PRESSURE: **HIGH** • TIME UNDER PRESSURE: **25 OR 40 MINUTES** • RELEASE: **NATURAL** • SERVES: **4 TO 6**

2 tablespoons unsalted butter

3 pounds bone-in pork shoulder chops, each $1/2$ to $3/4$ inch thick

$1/2$ teaspoon salt

$1/2$ teaspoon ground black pepper

$1/2$ cup dry, fruit-forward red wine, such as Zinfandel

2 tablespoons red wine vinegar

4 medium garlic cloves

One 4-inch cinnamon stick

2 bay leaves

1 Melt the butter in a 6-quart stovetop pressure cooker set over medium heat or in a 6-quart electric pressure cooker turned to the browning function. Season the chops with salt and pepper, then brown them in batches, turning once, about 5 minutes per batch. Transfer to a bowl.

2 Add the wine to the cooker and stir it well as it comes to a simmer to scrape up the browned bits on the bottom. Stir in the vinegar; add the garlic, cinnamon stick, and bay leaves. Return the chops and their juices to the cooker; stir well to coat the meat in the sauce.

3 Lock the lid onto the pot.

STOVETOP: Raise the heat to high and bring the cooker to high pressure (15 psi). Once this pressure has been reached, reduce the heat as much as possible while maintaining this pressure. Cook for 25 minutes.

························ **OR** ························

ELECTRIC: Set the machine to cook at high pressure (9–11 psi). Set the machine's timer to cook at high pressure for 40 minutes.

4 Reduce the pressure.

STOVETOP: Set the pot aside off the heat and let its pressure return to normal, about 15 minutes.

························ **OR** ························

ELECTRIC: Turn off the machine or unplug it so it doesn't flip to its keep-warm setting. Let its pressure in the pot fall to normal naturally, 15 to 20 minutes.

5 Unlock and open the cooker. Transfer the chops and garlic cloves to a large serving bowl. Discard the cinnamon stick and bay leaves; skim the fat from the sauce. Pour the sauce over the chops and garlic before serving.

TESTERS' NOTES

• Note that these are not pork chops—rib or loin chops—but instead the bonier, fattier, and more economical pork chops cut from the front shoulder of the pig. This rather classic preparation with red wine and a few aromatics couldn't be easier, a great way to highlight the rich and sweet meat.

• For a bolder sauce, remove the pork and garlic, strain the sauce into a medium saucepan, and bring it to a boil over high heat. Whisk in 2 tablespoons unsalted butter and boil for 1 minute, whisking constantly. Pour over the chops and garlic.

PORK SHOULDER CHOPS WITH SOY SAUCE, MAPLE SYRUP, AND CARROTS

EFFORT: **A LITTLE** • PRESSURE: **HIGH** • TIME UNDER PRESSURE: **25 OR 40 MINUTES** • RELEASE: **NATURAL** • SERVES: **4 TO 6**

1 tablespoon bacon fat

3 pounds bone-in pork shoulder chops, each 1/2 to 3/4 inch thick

6 medium carrots

3 medium garlic cloves

1/3 cup soy sauce

1/3 cup maple syrup

1/3 cup chicken broth

1/2 teaspoon ground black pepper

1 Melt the bacon fat in a 6-quart stovetop pressure cooker set over medium heat or in a 6-quart electric pressure cooker turned to the browning function. Add about half the chops and brown well, turning once, about 5 minutes. Transfer these to a large bowl and brown the remaining chops.

2 Stir the carrots and garlic into the pot; cook for 1 minute, stirring constantly. Pour in the soy sauce, maple syrup, and broth, stirring to dissolve the maple syrup and to get up any browned bits on the bottom of the pot. Stir in the pepper. Return the shoulder chops and their juices to the pot. Stir to coat them in the sauce.

3 Lock the lid onto the cooker.

STOVETOP: Raise the heat to high and bring the pot to high pressure (15 psi). Once this pressure has been reached, reduce the heat as much as possible while maintaining this pressure. Cook for 25 minutes.

························ OR ························

ELECTRIC: Set the machine to cook at high pressure (9–11 psi). Set the machine's timer to cook at high pressure for 40 minutes.

4 Reduce the pressure.

STOVETOP: Set the pot off the heat and let its pressure fall to normal naturally, about 14 minutes.

························ OR ························

ELECTRIC: Turn off the machine or unplug it so it doesn't jump to its keep-warm setting. Let its pressure fall to normal naturally, 14 to 16 minutes.

If the pressure hasn't returned to normal within 16 minutes, use the quick-release method to bring it back to normal.

5 Unlock and open the pot. Transfer the chops, carrots, and garlic cloves to a large serving bowl. Skim the fat off the sauce and ladle it over the servings.

TESTERS' NOTES
• This sweet-and-salty braise is one of the best ways to get economical but flavorful pork shoulder chops on your table. The bacon fat adds a little smoky flavor, but you could substitute a neutral oil like canola oil.
• Use low-sodium soy sauce if you're concerned about the amount of sodium in each serving. The dish braises for so long at high pressure that any difference in taste will be negligible.
• For braises like this one, the darker the maple syrup, the better. In fact, Grade B (2 in Canada) would be best.

Serve It Up! Since the braise is rather sweet, serve it over mashed potatoes made with chicken broth and a little Dijon mustard.

PULLED PORK SLIDERS

EFFORT: **A LITTLE** • PRESSURE: **HIGH** • TIME UNDER PRESSURE:
30 OR 45 MINUTES • RELEASE: **NATURAL** • SERVES: **8**

2 tablespoons peanut oil

3 pounds boneless pork shoulder chops,
    about 1 inch thick

1 large yellow onion, chopped

1 tablespoon minced garlic

2 teaspoons dry mustard

One 12-ounce bottle dark beer, such as
    brown ale

1/3 cup molasses

1/4 cup Worcestershire sauce

1/4 cup canned tomato paste

3 tablespoons apple cider vinegar

2 teaspoons smoked paprika

1 teaspoon dried oregano

1/2 teaspoon ground black pepper

16 small slider buns

1 Heat the oil in a 6-quart stovetop pressure
cooker set over medium heat or in a 6-quart
electric pressure cooker turned to the
browning function. Add about half the chops
and brown them well, turning once, about
5 minutes. Transfer to a large bowl and
brown the remaining chops.

2 Add the onion to the pot; cook, stirring
often, until softened, about 4 minutes. Add
the garlic and dry mustard; cook until fragrant, about 20 seconds. Stir in the beer, molasses, Worcestershire sauce, tomato paste,
vinegar, smoked paprika, oregano, and black
pepper until the molasses and tomato paste
dissolve. Return the chops and their juices to
the cooker; stir to coat well.

3 Lock the lid onto the pot.

STOVETOP: Raise the heat to high and bring the
pot to high pressure (15 psi). Once this pressure
has been reached, reduce the heat as much as possible while maintaining this pressure. Cook for
30 minutes.

·· OR ··

ELECTRIC: Set the machine to cook at high pressure (9–11 psi). Set the machine's timer to cook at
high pressure for 45 minutes.

4 Reduce the pressure.

STOVETOP: Set the pot aside off the heat and
let its pressure return to normal naturally, about
15 minutes.

·· OR ··

ELECTRIC: Turn off the machine or unplug it so it
doesn't jump to its keep-warm setting. Let its pressure fall back to normal naturally, 15 to 20 minutes.

5 Unlock and open the pot. Skim any surface
fat off the sauce. Use two forks to shred the
meat in the pot; stir well to make a uniform
mixture of sauced meat. Divide among the
slider buns to serve.

TESTERS' NOTES

• *Boneless* pork shoulder chops give you that great,
cheeky, fatty flavor without your having to pick the bones
out of the sauce. Plus, the chops' flavor is a tad simpler,
letting the aromatics show through more dramatically.

• You can substitute 3 tablespoons dark brown sugar dissolved in 2½ tablespoons warm water for the molasses.

Serve It Up! Top the filling for these sliders
with **Creamy Cole Slaw**: Whisk ¼ cup mayonnaise, ¼ cup sour cream, 2 tablespoons
lemon juice, 1 tablespoon Dijon mustard,
1 teaspoon sugar, ½ teaspoon salt, ½ teaspoon
ground black pepper, and ¼ teaspoon celery
seeds in a large bowl. Add 4 cups bagged cabbage slaw mix and toss well to coat.

BRAISED PORK BUTT WITH FENNEL AND LEMON

EFFORT: **A LITTLE** • PRESSURE: **HIGH** • TIME UNDER PRESSURE:
1 HOUR OR 1 HOUR 20 MINUTES • RELEASE: **NATURAL** • SERVES:
6 TO 8

2 tablespoons canola oil

One 4- to 4½-pound bone-in skinless pork butt

2 medium yellow onions, chopped

½ tablespoon fennel seeds

1 teaspoon cumin seeds

Up to ¾ cup light but dry white wine,
    such as Sauvignon Blanc

Up to ¾ cup chicken broth

1 tablespoon finely grated lemon zest

½ teaspoon salt

½ teaspoon ground black pepper

1 tablespoon fresh lemon juice

1 teaspoon Dijon mustard

1 Heat the oil in a 6-quart stovetop pressure cooker set over medium heat or in a 6-quart electric pressure cooker set to the browning function. Add the pork roast and brown on all sides, turning occasionally, until darkly colored on each side, about 12 minutes in all. Transfer the meat to a large bowl.

2 Add the onions to the pot; cook, stirring often, until softened, about 4 minutes. Add the fennel and cumin seeds; cook, stirring all the while, for about 30 seconds. Pour the wine and broth into a stovetop cooker, use only ½ cup of each in an electric cooker. Add the zest, salt, and pepper; stir well to get the browned bits off the bottom of the pot. Return the pork and its juices to the pot.

3 Lock the lid in place.

STOVETOP: Raise the heat to high and bring the pot to high pressure (15 psi). Once this pressure has been reached, reduce the heat as much as possible while maintaining this pressure. Cook for 1 hour.

······················ **OR** ·······················

ELECTRIC: Set the machine to cook at high pressure (9–11 psi). Set the machine's timer to cook at high pressure for 80 minutes.

4 Reduce the pressure.

STOVETOP: Set the pot aside off the heat and let its pressure drop to normal naturally, 20 to 25 minutes.

······················ **OR** ·······················

ELECTRIC: Turn off the machine or unplug it. (Do not allow it to flip to the keep-warm setting.) Allow its pressure to drop to normal naturally, 25 to 35 minutes.

5 Unlock and open the cooker. Transfer the meat to a cutting or carving board. Strain the liquid in the cooker through a fine-mesh sieve or a colander lined with a large coffee filter and into a bowl below. Defat the strained sauce by skimming it with a flatware spoon or pouring it into a fat separator.

6 Pour the sauce into a medium saucepan; bring to a simmer over medium-high heat. Stir in the lemon juice and mustard; boil until reduced by half, stirring often, about 7 minutes.

7 Carve the pork into chunks and bits; serve with the sauce on the side.

• Surprisingly light, this pork stew would be a welcome treat at a springtime table, even for Easter.

• Pork shoulders are often sold with the skin still on, particularly bone-in shoulders, and particularly at large supermarket chains. However, even boneless pork shoulders sometimes have the skin attached. Ask the butcher behind the counter to remove it for you, or slice it off yourself, removing a good deal of the fat but leaving a thin layer to protect the meat as it cooks.

• Oven-safe silicone mitts are the easiest way to pick up a hot hunk of meat and get it to a cutting board. Failing those, you'll need a couple of large, sturdy spatulas and the courage of your convictions.

Serve It Up! Consider serving this with a stack of grilled asparagus spears on the side—or even a platter of steamed artichokes, the first of the season.

COUNTRY-STYLE PORK RIBS WITH TARRAGON AND CREAM

EFFORT: **A LITTLE** • PRESSURE: **HIGH** • TIME UNDER PRESSURE: **25 OR 40 MINUTES** • RELEASE: **NATURAL** • SERVES: **4 TO 6**

Up to 1 cup chicken broth

1½ tablespoons all-purpose flour

1 tablespoon unsalted butter

1 tablespoon olive oil

3 pounds bone-in country-style pork ribs, trimmed

1 small yellow onion, chopped

8 ounces white button mushrooms, thinly sliced

½ cup dry white wine, such as Chardonnay

2 tablespoons Dijon mustard

2 tablespoons packed fresh tarragon leaves, minced

2 teaspoons finely grated lemon zest

½ teaspoon pink peppercorns, crushed (optional)

½ teaspoon salt

½ teaspoon ground black pepper

¼ cup heavy cream

1 Using 1 cup broth for a stovetop pressure cooker or ¾ cup for an electric model, whisk the broth and flour in a small bowl until the flour dissolves; set aside.

2 Melt the butter in the oil in a 6-quart stovetop pressure cooker set over medium heat or in a 6-quart electric pressure cooker set to the browning mode. Add the ribs, as many as will fit without crowding; brown on all sides, turning occasionally, about 8 minutes. Transfer the ribs to a bowl and continue browning as necessary.

3 Add the onion to the pot; cook, stirring often, until softened, about 3 minutes. Add the mushrooms; cook until they release their liquid and it evaporates to a glaze, about 6 minutes, stirring frequently.

4 Pour in the wine and scrape up any browned bits in the bottom of the cooker with a wooden spoon. Continue boiling the wine until it reduces to a glaze, about 3 minutes. Stir in the mustard, tarragon, lemon zest, peppercorns (if using), salt, and ground black pepper; then whisk the broth mixture again and pour it into the cooker. Nestle the meat and its juices back into the sauce.

(continued)

5 Lock the lid in place.

STOVETOP: Raise the heat to high and bring the pot to high pressure (15 psi). Once this pressure has been reached, reduce the heat as much as possible while maintaining this pressure. Cook for 25 minutes.

·····························**OR**·····························

ELECTRIC: Set the machine to cook at high pressure (9–11 psi). Set the machine's timer to cook at high pressure for 40 minutes.

6 Reduce the pressure.

STOVETOP: Set the pot off the heat and allow its pressure to return to normal naturally, about 14 minutes.

·····························**OR**·····························

ELECTRIC: Turn off or unplug the machine. (Do not let it flip to its keep-warm setting.) Allow its pressure to fall to normal naturally, 14 to 18 minutes.

7 Unlock and open the cooker. Transfer the ribs to a large bowl. Return the sauce to a simmer in the stovetop cooker by setting it back over medium-high heat; switch the electric machine to its browning function. Boil the sauce until it has reduced to about half its original volume, about 5 minutes, stirring frequently.

8 Stir in the cream; continue boiling for 2 minutes to blend the flavors, stirring almost constantly. Return the ribs to the cooker and toss them in the sauce to coat before serving.

TESTERS' NOTES
• We can elevate a lowly cut of pork to dinner-party elegance. The cream, mustard, and tarragon are a sophisticated mix, satisfying and indulgent.
• Pink peppercorns will give the sauce a sweet bite, a little more aromatic than the dull thud of black peppercorns. You needn't use them, but they're very impressive in the final dish.

• The onion will almost melt into the sauce over pressure, yielding every bit of its aromatic sweetness to the dish.
• Watch carefully in these recipes for country-style pork ribs. Some are for bone-in country-style ribs and some for boneless. The liquids and other ingredients have been calibrated to match the cuts. Country-style pork ribs are not technically ribs at all—they're from the front shoulder of the pig, a very luxurious cut.

SWEET-AND-SOUR COUNTRY-STYLE PORK RIBS

EFFORT: **A LOT** • PRESSURE: **HIGH** • TIME UNDER PRESSURE: **25 OR 40 MINUTES** • RELEASE: **NATURAL** • SERVES: **4 TO 6**

1 tablespoon olive oil

1 medium yellow onion, chopped

1 medium carrot, shredded through the large holes of a box grater

1 tablespoon minced garlic

One 12-ounce bottle light-colored beer, preferably Pilsner

1 tablespoon soy sauce

3 pounds bone-in country-style pork ribs, trimmed

1/4 cup packed light brown sugar

2 tablespoons coarse-grain mustard

1 1/2 tablespoons white wine vinegar

1 Heat the oil in a 6-quart pressure cooker set over medium heat or in a 6-quart electric pressure cooker set to the browning function. Add the onion and carrot; cook, stirring occasionally, until the onion has softened, about 4 minutes. Stir in the garlic and cook for a few seconds. Then stir in the beer and soy sauce, scraping up any browned bits in the cooker. Nestle the ribs into the cooker.

2 Lock the lid in place.

Raise the heat to high and bring the pot to high pressure (15 psi). Once this pressure has been reached, reduce the heat as much as possible while maintaining this pressure. Cook for 25 minutes.

·············· **OR** ··············

ELECTRIC: Set the machine to cook at high pressure (9–11 psi). Set the machine's timer to cook at high pressure for 40 minutes.

3 Reduce the pressure.

STOVETOP: Set the pot off the heat and allow its pressure to return to normal naturally, about 14 minutes.

·············· **OR** ··············

ELECTRIC: Turn off the machine or unplug it so it doesn't jump to its keep-warm setting. Let its pressure return to normal naturally, 14 to 16 minutes.

If the pressure has not returned to normal in 16 minutes, use the quick-release method to drop the pressure back to normal.

4 Unlock and open the lid. Transfer the ribs to a large baking sheet. Return the stovetop model to medium-high heat or set the electric machine to its browning function; bring the sauce to a boil, stirring occasionally, and cook until the sauce has been reduced by about half its original volume, about 10 minutes. Stir in the brown sugar, mustard, and vinegar; continue boiling, stirring more frequently, until thickened, about 10 more minutes.

5 Set the oven rack 4 to 6 inches from the broiler and heat the broiler. Baste the ribs with the sauce, then broil them, basting several more times, until browned and sizzling all around, about 3 minutes per side.

TESTERS' NOTES

- This entails a bit more work than some other country-style rib recipes, mostly because you crisp the ribs under the broiler after cooking them. But this dish is guaranteed to be a crowd-pleaser because of the way the sweet/sticky sauce gets crunchy on the tender ribs. Sure, it's more cleanup, too, but it's so worth it.
- We stop the pot's pressure from coming down naturally after 14 to 16 minutes—and it *should* be down by that point—so that the carrots don't turn too mushy.
- For a (slightly) healthier dinner, skim the fat from the sauce before you boil it down.

COUNTRY-STYLE PORK RIBS WITH GINGER BEER AND HONEY

EFFORT: **A LITTLE** • PRESSURE: **HIGH** • TIME UNDER PRESSURE: **20 OR 30 MINUTES** • RELEASE: **NATURAL** • SERVES: **6**

1 tablespoon unsalted butter

1 tablespoon olive oil

3 pounds boneless country-style pork ribs, trimmed

4 large shallots, halved

4 large garlic cloves

2 tablespoons honey

One 6-inch rosemary sprig

One 12-ounce bottle ginger beer

1/2 teaspoon salt

1/2 teaspoon ground black pepper

1 Melt the butter in the oil in a 6-quart stovetop pressure cooker or in a 6-quart electric pressure cooker set to the browning function. Add the ribs, as many as will fit without crowding, and brown them on all sides, turning occasionally, about 8 minutes.

(continued)

Transfer them to a big bowl and continue browning as necessary.

2 Add the shallots to the pot; cook, stirring often, until they are beginning to brown, about 5 minutes. Stir in the garlic for a few seconds, then add the honey and rosemary. Stir until fragrant, about 10 seconds.

3 Pour in the beer. Stir well to get any browned bits off the bottom of the pot; stir in the salt and pepper. Nestle the ribs into the sauce.

4 Lock the lid in place.

STOVETOP: Raise the heat to high and bring the pot to high pressure (15 psi). Once this pressure has been reached, reduce the heat as much as possible while maintaining this pressure. Cook for 20 minutes.

························ **OR** ····························

ELECTRIC: Set the machine to cook at high pressure (9–11 psi). Set the machine's timer to cook at high pressure for 30 minutes.

5 Reduce the pressure.

STOVETOP: Set the pot off the heat and allow its pressure to drop to normal naturally, about 14 minutes.

························ **OR** ····························

ELECTRIC: Unplug or turn off the machine so it doesn't jump to its keep-warm setting. Let its pressure fall to normal naturally, 14 to 18 minutes.

6 Unlock and open the pot. Discard the rosemary sprig. Stir well before serving.

TESTERS' NOTES
• Ginger beer adds a pleasing sweetness to the pork. Don't use a light or low-calorie bottling; you want the sugars to caramelize a bit in the sauce. (You can use ginger ale for a slightly milder taste.)

• Add heat if desired, up to ½ teaspoon red pepper flakes with the rosemary.
• For a richer sauce, remove the ribs to a platter, swirl in up to 2 tablespoons unsalted butter, and bring the sauce to a simmer before ladling over the meat.
• To skim or not to skim. . . . You'll never get all the fat off that sauce but you don't want so much that your lips are sticky afterward. We prefer some skimming, but make your own choices.

COUNTRY-STYLE PORK RIBS WITH SWEET PEPPERS AND VINEGAR

EFFORT: **A LITTLE** • PRESSURE: **HIGH** • TIME UNDER PRESSURE: **20 OR 30 MINUTES** • RELEASE: **NATURAL** • SERVES: **6**

2 tablespoons olive oil

3 pounds boneless country-style pork ribs, trimmed and cut into 2-inch chunks

3 medium red or orange bell peppers, stemmed, seeded, and cut into ¹/₂-inch strips

1 large yellow onion, halved and thinly sliced

¹/₂ cup dry vermouth

2 tablespoons white wine vinegar

³/₄ cup chicken broth

¹/₄ cup packed fresh basil leaves, chopped

2 tablespoons packed fresh oregano leaves, chopped

1 teaspoon fennel seeds

¹/₂ teaspoon salt

¹/₂ teaspoon ground black pepper

1 Heat the oil in a 6-quart stovetop pressure cooker set over medium heat or in a 6-quart electric pressure cooker switched to the browning function. Add about half the meat and brown, stirring often, about 8 minutes. Transfer the pieces to a large bowl and continue browning as necessary.

2 Add the peppers and onion to the pot; cook, stirring occasionally, until the onion begins to soften, about 4 minutes. Pour in the vermouth and vinegar; scrape up any browned bits in the bottom of the pot.

3 Stir in the broth, basil, oregano, fennel seeds, salt, and pepper. Return the meat and its juices to the pot; stir well.

4 Lock the lid onto the pot.

STOVETOP: Raise the heat to high and bring the pot to high pressure (15 psi). Once this pressure has been reached, reduce the heat as much as possible while maintaining this pressure. Cook for 20 minutes.

···············**OR**···············

ELECTRIC: Set the machine to cook at high pressure (9–11 psi). Set the machine's timer to cook at high pressure for 30 minutes.

5 Reduce the pressure.

STOVETOP: Set the pot off the heat and allow its pressure to fall to normal naturally, about 14 minutes.

···············**OR**···············

ELECTRIC: Turn off the machine or unplug it so it doesn't flip to its keep-warm setting. Let its pressure return to normal naturally, 14 to 16 minutes.

If the pressure hasn't returned to normal within 16 minutes, use the quick-release method to bring it back down.

6 Unlock and open the cooker. Transfer the ribs to a large platter or individual bowls. Use a slotted spoon to scoop up the onion and peppers; lay these on top of the meat. Skim the fat from the sauce before ladling it over the meat and vegetables.

TESTERS' NOTES
• Call this one Italian-American comfort food, a heady blend of aromatics and spices, with some vinegar to give it a little spark.
• Don't use frozen pepper strips. They'll be gummy after so long under high pressure.
• The vermouth will give the dish a slightly savory, herbal edge, a good match to the basil and oregano. However, for a lighter, sweeter finish, substitute a light but dry white wine like a Chenin Blanc.

Serve It Up! You don't have to use bowls; fill hoagie buns with the boneless ribs and top with some of the onion and peppers. Drizzle a little of the sauce on each before digging in.

BARBECUED BABY BACK RIBS

EFFORT: **A LOT** • PRESSURE: **HIGH** • TIME UNDER PRESSURE: **20 OR 32 MINUTES** • RELEASE: **NATURAL** • SERVES: **4**

1/4 cup canned tomato paste

2 tablespoons cider vinegar

1 tablespoon sweet paprika

1/2 tablespoon coriander seeds

1/2 tablespoon fennel seeds

1 teaspoon onion powder

1 teaspoon dried thyme

1/2 teaspoon ground allspice

1/2 teaspoon salt

1/2 teaspoon ground black pepper

1/4 teaspoon celery seeds

One 4-pound rack baby back ribs, cut into 2 or 3 sections to fit in the cooker

(continued)

1 Whisk the tomato paste, vinegar, paprika, coriander and fennel seeds, onion powder, thyme, allspice, salt, pepper, and celery seeds with ¾ cup water in a 6-quart stovetop or electric pressure cooker until the tomato paste dissolves. Add the ribs; toss to coat thoroughly and evenly in the sauce.

2 Lock the lid onto the cooker.

STOVETOP: Set the pot over high heat and bring it to high pressure (15 psi). Once this pressure has been reached, reduce the heat as much as possible while maintaining this pressure. Cook for 20 minutes.

························· OR ·························

ELECTRIC: Set the machine to cook at high pressure (9–11 psi). Set the machine's timer to cook at high pressure for 32 minutes.

3 Reduce the pressure.

STOVETOP: Set the pot aside off the heat and let its pressure come back to normal naturally, about 12 minutes.

························· OR ·························

ELECTRIC: Turn off the machine or unplug it so it doesn't flip to its keep-warm setting. Let its pressure return to normal naturally, 12 to 15 minutes.

4 Unlock and open the pot. Transfer the rib rack sections to a large rimmed baking sheet. Turn the heat to medium-high under the stovetop cooker or set the electric one to its browning function; bring the sauce to a simmer. Cook, stirring occasionally, until the sauce has thickened, 3 to 5 minutes.

5 Position the oven rack 4 to 6 inches from the broiler; heat the broiler. Brush a light coating of the sauce onto the ribs, then broil until glazed and hot, 6 to 8 minutes, turning once. Slice the racks between the bones to make individual ribs. Serve with the extra sauce on the side.

TESTERS' NOTES

• Okay, it's not authentic barbecue, but it's a good approximation and much simpler than manning the grill all day.

• A full rack of ribs won't fit in a pressure cooker, so you'll need to cut it into sections to make it fit. If you don't have a cleaver to do the job, ask the butcher at your supermarket to do it for you.

• For some extra smoke, substitute smoked paprika for the sweet paprika.

SWEET AND TANGY BABY BACK RIBS

EFFORT: **A LITTLE** • PRESSURE: **HIGH** • TIME UNDER PRESSURE: **20 OR 32 MINUTES** • RELEASE: **NATURAL** • SERVES: **4**

4 pounds baby back pork ribs, cut into 2 or 3 sections to fit the cooker

⅓ cup honey, preferably a wildflower honey

⅓ cup fresh lime juice

¼ cup soy sauce

1 Place the rib sections in a 6-quart stovetop or electric pressure cooker. Whisk the honey, lime juice, and soy sauce in a small bowl until the honey dissolves; pour over the ribs. Brush the sauce over the ribs.

2 Lock the lid onto the pot.

STOVETOP: Set the cooker over high heat and bring it to high pressure (15 psi). Once this pressure has been reached, reduce the heat as much as possible while maintaining this pressure. Cook for 20 minutes.

···························· OR ····························
ELECTRIC: Set the machine to cook at high pressure (9–11 psi). Set the machine's timer to cook at high pressure for 32 minutes.

3 Reduce the pressure.

STOVETOP: Set the pot off the heat and let its pressure come back to normal naturally, about 12 minutes.

···························· OR ····························

ELECTRIC: Turn off the machine or unplug it so it doesn't flip to its keep-warm setting. Let its pressure come back to normal naturally, 12 to 15 minutes.

4 Unlock and open the pot. Transfer the ribs to a large rimmed baking sheet. Set the stovetop cooker over high heat or turn the electric cooker to the browning function; bring the sauce to a simmer. Boil until thickened slightly, about 2 minutes. Set aside off the heat.

5 Position the oven rack 4 to 6 inches from the broiler; heat the broiler. Baste the ribs with some of the sauce and broil until bubbling and coated, about 3 minutes. Turn, baste again, and broil another 3 minutes or so. Slice between the bones to create individual ribs. Transfer to a platter; serve with more sauce on the side.

TESTERS' NOTES

• Three simple ingredients create a complex sauce, a great alternative to standard barbecue sauce. Consider making a double or triple batch and saving the rest in the fridge, tightly covered, for up to 2 weeks (for another round of these ribs or to be used for just about anything on the grill).
• If you want to spice up the sauce a bit, whisk up to 2 teaspoons hot Hungarian paprika into it before spreading it on the ribs.

PORK RIBS WITH MEDITERRANEAN SPICES

EFFORT: **A LOT** • PRESSURE: **HIGH** • TIME UNDER PRESSURE: **20 OR 32 MINUTES** • RELEASE: **NATURAL** • SERVES: **4**

2 tablespoons packed fresh rosemary leaves
2 tablespoons packed stemmed fresh thyme leaves
2 tablespoons packed fresh oregano leaves
1 teaspoon fennel seeds
1 teaspoon salt
2 tablespoons olive oil, plus more for brushing the ribs
1 tablespoon minced garlic
1 teaspoon ground black pepper
One 4-pound rack of baby back ribs, cut into 2 or 3 sections to fit in the cooker
1/3 cup red wine vinegar

1 Place the rosemary, thyme, oregano, fennel seeds, and salt on a cutting board; rock a large knife repeatedly through the mixture until it is very finely minced. Scrape the herbs into a small bowl; stir in the olive oil, garlic, and pepper. Smear the paste evenly over the rib sections. Set the ribs on a large plate, cover tightly, and refrigerate for at least 4 hours or up to 24 hours.

2 Place the rib sections in a 6-quart stovetop or electric pressure cooker; sprinkle the vinegar over and around the ribs without knocking off the paste.

(continued)

3 Lock the lid onto the cooker.

STOVETOP: Set the pot over high heat and bring it to high pressure (15 psi). Once this pressure has been reached, reduce the heat as much as possible while maintaining this pressure. Cook for 20 minutes.

·················· **OR** ··················

ELECTRIC: Set the machine to cook at high pressure (9–11 psi). Set the machine's timer to cook at high pressure for 32 minutes.

4 Reduce the pressure.

STOVETOP: Set the pot off the heat and let its pressure drop to normal naturally, about 12 minutes.

·················· **OR** ··················

ELECTRIC: Turn off the machine or unplug it so it doesn't flip to its keep-warm setting. Let its pressure return to normal naturally, 12 to 15 minutes.

5 Unlock the lid and open the pot. Use tongs to transfer the rib sections to a large, rimmed baking sheet. Brush them lightly with a little olive oil on both sides.

6 Position the oven rack 4 to 6 inches from the broiler; heat the broiler. Broil the ribs until bubbling and brown, about 6 minutes, turning once. Slice the rack into individual ribs for serving.

TESTERS' NOTES

• This aromatic rub gives the racks an almost springtime feel. They're steamed in vinegar, a bit of a change from the traditionally sweet preparations, but the sour stuff brings out the meat's natural sweetness.

• Keep as much of the spice coating on the ribs as possible as they go into the cooker.

HAM BONE CHILI

EFFORT: **A LOT** • PRESSURE: **HIGH** • TIME UNDER PRESSURE: **50 MINUTES OR 1 HOUR 15 MINUTES** • RELEASE: **QUICK, THEN QUICK** • SERVES: **6**

2 cups dried pinto beans

1 tablespoon olive oil

1 large yellow onion, chopped

2 medium green bell peppers, stemmed, cored, and chopped

2 teaspoons minced garlic

¼ cup chili powder

One 14-ounce can diced tomatoes (about 1¾ cups)

One 2- to 2½-pound ham bone with plenty of meat still attached

1 Pour the beans into a large bowl and fill it about three-quarters full of water. Set aside to soak overnight, for at least 12 hours or up to 16 hours.

2 Heat the oil in a 6-quart stovetop pressure cooker set over medium heat or in a 6-quart electric pressure cooker turned to the browning function. Add the onion and bell peppers; cook, stirring often, until the onion softens, about 4 minutes. Stir in the garlic and chili powder; cook until aromatic, about 20 seconds.

3 Pour in the diced tomatoes with 4 cups water; stir well. Nestle the ham bone into the sauce.

4 Lock the lid onto the pot.

STOVETOP: Raise the heat to high and bring the pot to high pressure (15 psi). Once this pressure has been reached, reduce the heat as much as possible while maintaining this pressure. Cook for 40 minutes.

5 Use the quick-release method to bring the pot's pressure back to normal.

6 Unlock and open the lid. Transfer the ham bone to a cutting board; cool for 5 minutes. Shred the meat off the bone and remove any excess fat and cartilage. Chop the meat into small bits and stir these back into the stew. Drain the beans in a colander and stir them into the stew.

7 Lock the lid back on the pot.

STOVETOP: Set the cooker over high heat and bring it back to high pressure (15 psi). Once this pressure has been reached, reduce the heat as much as possible while maintaining this pressure. Cook for 10 minutes.

.... **OR** ....

ELECTRIC: Set the machine to cook once again at high pressure (9–11 psi). Set the machine's timer to cook at high pressure for 15 minutes.

8 Use the quick-release method to bring the pot's pressure back to normal.

9 Unlock and open the pot; stir well before serving.

TESTERS' NOTES
• Here's the perfect dish for the days after a holiday meal when you've got a leftover ham bone. But if you want to make it any other time of year, ask the person at your local deli counter if they'll sell you the ham bone from the house-roasted ham.
• Since dried beans take so little time in the pressure cooker, they're a much better alternative to their canned kin in this post-holiday chili.

• Make sure you remove any glaze or coating on the ham bone before adding it to the pot, as well as any large bits of fat.

HAM AND TOMATILLO STEW

EFFORT: **NOT MUCH** • PRESSURE: **HIGH** • TIME UNDER PRESSURE: **10 OR 15 MINUTES** • RELEASE: **QUICK** • SERVES: **4**

1 tablespoon olive oil
1 large yellow onion, chopped
1 large green bell pepper, stemmed, cored, and chopped
1 pound boneless smoked ham, chopped
1 pound yellow potatoes, such as Yukon Gold, diced
2 cups frozen corn kernels, thawed
1 teaspoon dried oregano
1 teaspoon dried thyme
$1/2$ teaspoon ground cumin
$1/2$ teaspoon ground black pepper
$1^1/2$ pounds fresh tomatillos, husked and chopped
1 cup chicken broth

1 Heat the oil in a 6-quart stovetop pressure cooker set over medium heat or in a 6-quart electric pressure cooker turned to the browning function. Add the onion and bell pepper; cook, stirring often, until the onion softens, about 4 minutes.

2 Add the ham, potatoes, corn, oregano, thyme, cumin, and black pepper; stir over the heat for 1 minute, until aromatic. Stir in the tomatillos and broth.

3 Lock the lid onto the cooker.

(continued)

4 Use the quick-release method to drop the pressure to normal.

5 Unlock and open the pot. Stir well before serving.

TESTERS' NOTES

• This simple stew has bright flavors. For the best taste, ask for a chunk of the house-roasted ham at your supermarket and chop this into ½-inch bits at home.

• Cut any glaze or coating off the ham so its flavors don't conflict with the spice blend here.

• Tomatillos can be a bit sticky, especially if they're very fresh. Spray a knife with nonstick spray before chopping.

Serve It Up! Garnish the bowls with sour cream and pickled jalapeño rings.

HAM STEW WITH TOMATOES, SWEET POTATOES, AND WARM SPICES

EFFORT: **NOT MUCH** · PRESSURE: **HIGH** · TIME UNDER PRESSURE: **6 OR 9 MINUTES** · RELEASE: **QUICK** · SERVES: **8**

²/₃ cup canned crushed tomatoes

2 tablespoons Dijon mustard

2 tablespoons Worcestershire sauce

1 tablespoon jarred prepared white horseradish

1 tablespoon packed dark brown sugar

Up to 1 canned chipotle in adobo sauce, stemmed and minced

Up to 1 tablespoon adobo sauce from the can

½ teaspoon ground cinnamon

½ teaspoon ground ginger

¼ teaspoon ground cloves

1 tablespoon peanut oil

1 large yellow onion, chopped

2 medium green bell peppers, stemmed, seeded, and chopped

¼ cup unsweetened apple juice

2½ pounds boneless smoked ham, cut into 1-inch pieces

2 large sweet potatoes (about 1 pound each), peeled and cut into 1-inch cubes

1 Mix the tomatoes, mustard, Worcestershire sauce, horseradish, brown sugar, chipotle, adobo sauce, cinnamon, ginger, and cloves in a large bowl.

2 Heat the oil in a 6-quart stovetop pressure cooker set over medium-high heat or in a 6-quart electric pressure cooker set to the browning function. Add the onion and bell peppers; cook, stirring often, until softened and aromatic, about 5 minutes. Pour in the apple juice and scrape up any browned bits on the bottom of the pot. Stir in the ham, sweet potatoes, and the tomato mixture.

3 Lock the lid onto the pot.

STOVETOP: Raise the heat to high and bring the pot to high pressure (15 psi). Once this pressure has been reached, reduce the heat as much as possible while maintaining this pressure. Cook for 6 minutes.

4 Use the quick-release method to bring the pot's pressure back to normal.

5 Unlock and open the cooker. Stir the stew before serving.

TESTERS' NOTES
• The apple juice adds a bright sweetness to the sauce. For subtler, less assertive flavor, use a dry white wine like a Sauvignon Blanc.
• There's a lot of chipotle here! Seed the chile for less heat. Or use less, even just ¼ teaspoon with no adobo sauce from the can if you fear the burn.
• This stew freezes well; seal it into plastic containers and freeze it for up to 4 months.

KIELBASA AND KRAUT

EFFORT: **NOT MUCH** · PRESSURE: **HIGH** · TIME UNDER PRESSURE: **10 OR 15 MINUTES** · RELEASE: **QUICK** · SERVES: **4**

1 tablespoon peanut oil

1½ pounds kielbasa, cut into 4 pieces

2 pounds sauerkraut, squeezed dry over the sink

½ cup unsweetened apple juice

½ cup chicken broth

1 teaspoon dried dill

½ teaspoon caraway seeds

6 small white potatoes (about 1 pound), halved

1 Heat the oil in a 6-quart stovetop pressure cooker set over medium heat or in a 6-quart electric pressure cooker turned to the browning mode. Add the sausage pieces; brown, turning occasionally, about 5 minutes. Transfer to a large bowl.

2 Add the sauerkraut, apple juice, broth, dill, and caraway seeds. Stir well, then make a loose bed in the pot. Nestle the sausage and potatoes into the sauerkraut.

3 Lock the lid in place.

4 Use the quick-release method to drop the pot's pressure to normal.

5 Unlock and open the lid. Stir well before serving.

TESTERS' NOTES
• Here's a simple beer-house dinner to fit the average weeknight rush. Just bring the brew, preferably something dark and hearty like a brown ale or a porter.
• The best sauerkraut is not found in cans but in refrigerated pouches, sometimes in the deli case and sometimes near the hot dogs. Squeezing it dry by the handful will make the sauce in the pot far less watery, and will remove some of the excess sodium.
• You can use smoked Polish sausage, smoked bratwurst, or smoked turkey sausage instead of kielbasa.

Serve It Up! Have sliced rye bread as well as deli mustard and sliced pickles at the table.

SAUSAGE AND PEPPERS

EFFORT: **NOT MUCH** · PRESSURE: **HIGH** · TIME UNDER PRESSURE:
7 OR 10 MINUTES · RELEASE: **QUICK** · SERVES: **6**

2 tablespoons olive oil

2¹/₂ pounds sweet Italian sausages in
their casings

4 large red bell peppers, stemmed,
seeded, and cut into strips

1 medium red onion, halved and thinly
sliced

2 medium garlic cloves, slivered

1 cup red (sweet) vermouth

2 tablespoons balsamic vinegar

¹/₄ teaspoon grated nutmeg

1 Heat the oil in a 6-quart stovetop pressure
cooker set over medium heat or in a 6-quart
electric pressure cooker turned to the
browning function. Prick the sausages with
a fork, add them to the pot, and brown on all
sides, about 6 minutes. Transfer to a large
bowl.

2 Add the peppers and onion; cook, stirring almost constantly, just until the pepper strips glisten, about 2 minutes. Add the
garlic, cook a few seconds, then stir in the
vermouth, vinegar, and nutmeg. Nestle the
sausages into the mixture.

3 Lock the lid onto the cooker.

STOVETOP: Raise the heat to high and bring the
pot to high pressure (15 psi). Once this pressure
has been reached, reduce the heat as much as possible while maintaining this pressure. Cook for
7 minutes.

················OR················
ELECTRIC: Set the machine to cook at high pressure (9–11 psi). Set the machine's timer to cook at
high pressure for 10 minutes.

4 Use the quick-release method to bring the
pot's pressure back to normal.

5 Unlock and open the pot. Stir well before
serving.

TESTERS' NOTES
• A sweet-and-sour sauce matches the Italian sausages
perfectly—and gives a nice foil to the bright flavor of all
those bell peppers.
• Don't use flavored sausages or ones with any soy
sauce in the mix. You want the full Italian treatment, no
compromises.
• There's no heat here, so pass some bottled hot sauce at
the table to spice things up.
• You can use sweet white wine such as Spätlese or
Auslese instead of the sweet vermouth.

SAUSAGE, KALE, AND MACARONI CASSEROLE

EFFORT: **NOT MUCH** · PRESSURE: **HIGH** · TIME UNDER PRESSURE:
6 OR 9 MINUTES · RELEASE: **QUICK** · SERVES: **4**

1 tablespoon olive oil

1 pound sweet Italian pork sausage, cut
into 1-inch pieces

1 small yellow onion, chopped

1 medium cubanelle pepper (Italian frying
pepper), stemmed, seeded, and chopped

2 teaspoons minced garlic

One 28-ounce can diced tomatoes (about
3¹/₂ cups)

2 cups chicken broth

10 ounces dried whole wheat ziti

4 ounces kale, stemmed, washed, and chopped

1 tablespoon dried basil

1 tablespoon dried oregano

1 teaspoon dried rosemary

1 teaspoon fennel seeds

1 Heat the oil in a 6-quart stovetop pressure cooker set over medium heat or in a 6-quart electric pressure cooker set to the browning function. Add the sausage pieces; brown lightly, stirring occasionally, about 4 minutes.

2 Add the onion, pepper, and garlic; cook, stirring often, for 2 minutes. Add the tomatoes and broth, stir well, then add the ziti, kale, basil, oregano, rosemary, and fennel seeds. Stir once more.

3 Lock the lid in place.

STOVETOP: Raise the heat to high and bring the pot to high pressure (15 psi). Once this pressure has been reached, reduce the heat as much as possible while maintaining this pressure. Cook for 6 minutes.

·······································OR·······································

ELECTRIC: Set the machine to cook at high pressure (9–11 psi). Set the machine's timer to cook at high pressure for 9 minutes.

4 Use the quick-release method to drop the pressure.

5 Unlock and open the cooker. Stir gently before serving.

TESTERS' NOTES

• This one's not a gooey casserole; it's more like a loose sausage and vegetable mélange with pasta in the mix.

• Whole wheat pasta has a firmer bite than standard pasta; your family will be eating a bit healthier without even knowing it.

• Substitute ½ cup diced bell pepper and ⅛ teaspoon red pepper flakes for the cubanelle pepper.

SPICY SAUSAGE AND CHARD PASTA SAUCE

EFFORT: **NOT MUCH** · PRESSURE: **HIGH** · TIME UNDER PRESSURE: **4 OR 6 MINUTES** · RELEASE: **QUICK** · SERVES: **6, WITH PASTA**

2 tablespoons olive oil

1 medium red onion, chopped

Up to 3 small hot chiles, such as cherry peppers or Anaheim chiles, stemmed, seeded, and chopped

1 tablespoon minced garlic

1 pound mild Italian pork sausage meat, any casings removed

½ cup dry red wine, such as Syrah

½ cup canned tomato paste

¼ cup chicken broth

1 tablespoon dried basil

2 teaspoons dried oregano

4 cups stemmed and chopped Swiss chard

1 Heat the oil in a 6-quart stovetop pressure cooker set over medium heat or in a 6-quart electric pressure cooker turned to the browning function. Add the onion and cook, stirring often, until softened, about 4 minutes. Add the chiles and garlic; cook until aromatic, stirring all the while, about 1 minute.

2 Crumble in the sausage meat, breaking up any clumps with a wooden spoon. Stir until it loses its raw color. Stir in the wine, tomato

(continued)

paste, broth, basil, and oregano until the tomato paste dissolves. Add the chard and stir well.

3 Lock the lid onto the cooker.

STOVETOP: Raise the heat to high and bring the pot to high pressure (15 psi). Once this pressure has been reached, reduce the heat as much as possible while maintaining this pressure. Cook for 4 minutes.

·············· **OR** ··············

ELECTRIC: Set the machine to cook at high pressure (9–11 psi). Set the machine's timer to cook at high pressure for 6 minutes.

4 Use the quick-release method to drop the pressure back to normal.

5 Unlock and open the pot. Stir well before serving.

TESTERS' NOTES

• This simple pasta sauce has lots of leafy greens in the mix, a slightly sweet accent to the pork and spices.
• There's actually very little tomato here, just the reduced paste in the sauce. The wine and broth carry much of the weight, delivering a more savory flavor.
• Rather than using hot Italian sausage, we prefer the chiles in this mix, a brighter, slightly more sour heat and thus a better foil to the chard and herbs.

Serve It Up! While spaghetti may seem a natural, try this sauce with rigatoni or other pasta shapes that have some crevasses to hold the tomatoes and greens. Grate pecorino romano cheese or even an aged Asiago over the servings.

SWEDISH MEATBALLS

EFFORT: **A LITTLE** · PRESSURE: **HIGH** · TIME UNDER PRESSURE: **5 OR 8 MINUTES** · RELEASE: **QUICK** · SERVES: **4**

1 cup fresh breadcrumbs
1/4 cup whole or low-fat milk
2 tablespoons unsalted butter
1 small yellow onion, chopped
1 pound ground pork
3/4 pound ground beef, preferably ground chuck
2 large egg yolks, at room temperature
1 teaspoon sugar
1/2 teaspoon ground allspice
1/2 teaspoon ground black pepper
1/4 teaspoon grated nutmeg
1/4 teaspoon salt
2 cups beef broth
1/4 cup all-purpose flour
1 tablespoon Worcestershire sauce
1/4 cup regular or low-fat sour cream

1 Stir the breadcrumbs and milk in a small bowl until the crumbs are thoroughly moistened; set aside until they absorb the milk, about 5 minutes.

2 Melt the butter in a 6-quart stovetop pressure cooker set over medium heat or in a 6-quart electric pressure cooker turned to the browning function. Add the onion and cook, stirring often, until it is soft and golden, almost sweet, about 10 minutes.

3 Transfer the onion and its liquid to a large bowl. Turn the heat off under the stovetop pressure cooker or switch off the electric model; wipe out the cooker. Cool the onion for 10 minutes.

4 Stir the soaked breadcrumbs into the onion. Add the ground meats, egg yolks, sugar, allspice, pepper, nutmeg, and salt; stir well to form a uniform, coherent mixture. With clean, dry hands, form into twelve 2-inch meatballs.

5 Whisk the broth, flour, and Worcestershire sauce in the cooker. Set the stovetop pot over medium heat or turn the electric pot to the browning function; bring the broth mixture to a boil to thicken it, stirring often, about 3 minutes. Place the meatballs in the bubbling sauce.

6 Lock the lid in place.

STOVETOP: Raise the heat to high and bring the pot to high pressure (15 psi). Once this pressure has been reached, reduce the heat as much as possible while maintaining this pressure. Cook for 5 minutes.
···························· **OR** ····························
ELECTRIC: Set the machine to cook at high pressure (9–11 psi). Set the machine's timer to cook at high pressure for 8 minutes.

7 Use the quick-release method to return the pressure to normal.

8 Unlock and open the cooker. Use a slotted spoon or kitchen tongs to transfer the meatballs to a large bowl. Whisk the sour cream into the sauce until smooth. Return the meatballs to the pot, cover, and set aside off the heat (or turned off) for 5 minutes to blend the flavors.

TESTERS' NOTES
• The pressure cooker makes the most tender and the juiciest meatballs around! The even cooking allows the meatballs to cook without soaking up too much sauce.
• A mix of ground pork and ground chuck gives these meatballs the best texture. Use lean ground pork for a slightly healthier meal, but keep the chuck in the mix for the added beef flavor.

Serve It Up! Mix cooked fettuccini with stemmed and wilted Swiss chard to make a bed for the meatballs and sauce.

GROUND PORK, PEANUT, AND PASTA STEW

EFFORT: **A LITTLE** • PRESSURE: **HIGH** • TIME UNDER PRESSURE: **5 OR 8 MINUTES** • RELEASE: **QUICK** • SERVES: **4**

¹⁄₄ **cup creamy natural-style peanut butter**
2 tablespoons soy sauce
2 tablespoons sambal oelek
1¹⁄₂ tablespoons Worcestershire sauce
1¹⁄₂ tablespoons balsamic vinegar
1 tablespoon packed dark brown sugar
2 tablespoons peanut oil
1 pound lean ground pork
1 medium yellow onion, chopped
2 medium celery stalks, chopped
1 tablespoon minced fresh ginger
2 teaspoons minced garlic
8 ounces dried farfalle (bow-tie) pasta
2 cups chicken broth

1 Whisk the peanut butter, soy sauce, sambal oelek, Worcestershire sauce, vinegar, and brown sugar in a medium bowl until smooth; set aside.

(continued)

2 Heat 1 tablespoon oil in a 6-quart stovetop pressure cooker set over medium heat or in a 6-quart electric pressure cooker turned to the browning function. Crumble in the pork and cook, stirring often, until well browned, about 3 minutes. Use a slotted spoon to transfer the pork to a bowl; drain the fat in the cooker.

3 Add the remaining tablespoon oil to the cooker. Add the onion and celery; cook, stirring often, until the onion begins to soften, about 4 minutes. Add the ginger and garlic; cook, stirring all the while, for 1 minute.

4 Return the ground pork to the pot; pour in the peanut sauce mixture. Stir well to coat everything in the sauce. Stir in the pasta until coated, then pour in the broth and stir until incorporated.

5 Lock the lid onto the pot.

STOVETOP: Raise the heat to high and bring the pot to high pressure (15 psi). Once this pressure has been reached, reduce the heat as much as possible while maintaining this pressure. Cook for 5 minutes.

·······················**OR**·······················

ELECTRIC: Set the machine to cook at high pressure (9–11 psi). Set the machine's timer to cook at high pressure for 8 minutes.

6 Use the quick-release method to return the pot to normal pressure.

7 Unlock the lid and open the cooker. Stir gently before serving.

TESTERS' NOTES
• The ground pork is cooked in a spicy peanut sauce with pasta to fill out the meal. It's a new comfort food classic, something you'll want on a Sunday night.
• Draining the excess fat after you brown the pork keeps the dish from tasting too oily. There's still plenty of flavor left, given all the peanut butter and aromatics!

Serve It Up! Nothing matches a spicy casserole like a **Vinegary Salad:** Slice cucumbers and radishes into paper-thin strips, then dress them with a combination of rice vinegar and a splash of sesame oil. Season with salt and a pinch of sugar before serving.

WHOLE-GRAIN PORK LETTUCE WRAPS

EFFORT: **A LITTLE** • PRESSURE: **HIGH** • TIME UNDER PRESSURE: **30 OR 45 MINUTES** • RELEASE: **QUICK** • SERVES: **4**

1 cup dried wheatberries (preferably soft white spring wheatberries)

1 tablespoon peanut oil

1 pound lean ground pork

6 medium scallions, thinly sliced

¼ cup packed fresh cilantro leaves, minced

¼ cup fresh lime juice

2 tablespoons fish sauce (nam pla or nuoc nam)

2 tablespoons packed light brown sugar

Up to 1 teaspoon sambal oelek

2 heads of Boston lettuce, torn into individual leaves, washed and dried

1 Pour the wheatberries into a 6-quart stovetop or electric pressure cooker; add enough cool tap water that they're submerged by 2 inches.

2 Lock the lid onto the cooker.

STOVETOP: Set the pot over high heat and bring it to high pressure (15 psi). Once this pressure has been reached, reduce the heat as much as possible while maintaining this pressure. Cook for 30 minutes.

···················· **OR** ····················

ELECTRIC: Set the machine to cook at high pressure (9–11 psi). Set the machine's timer to cook at high pressure for 45 minutes.

3 Drop the pot's pressure to normal with the quick-release method.

4 Unlock and open the pot. Drain the grains in a colander set in the sink; wipe out the cooker.

5 Heat the oil in the stovetop cooker set over medium heat or in the electric cooker turned to its browning function. Crumble in the ground pork; cook, stirring often, until well browned and cooked through, about 5 minutes. Stir in the scallions, cilantro, lime juice, fish sauce, brown sugar, and sambal oelek until uniform.

6 Remove the stovetop cooker from the heat or turn off the electric cooker. Add the drained wheatberries and stir well.

7 To serve, scoop up about 2 tablespoons of the mixture and put it into a lettuce leaf, folding it over the filling, like a small taco. Continue making more lettuce wraps as desired.

TESTERS' NOTES

• This is a whole-grain version of larb, a national dish of Laos and now quite common in Southeast Asian restaurants. The addition of wheatberries gives the dish great texture and flavor.

• If you have kids at the table, omit the sambal from the mixture and pass it at the table (or offer bottled hot sauce instead).

• You can substitute dried rye berries (murkier), spelt berries (sweeter), or Kamut berries (more buttery) for the wheatberries.

Serve It Up! Either make a platter of these wraps or transfer the filling to a serving bowl and bring it to the table with a platter of lettuce leaves. If desired, heat some olive oil in a large skillet over medium heat and add slivered garlic; fry until crisp and browned, about 3 minutes, stirring often, then transfer the garlic to a paper towel–lined plate. Blot dry and serve as a garnish in the wraps.

Lamb, Veal, and Rabbit

Perhaps you've started in the last section in this chapter because you're in the mood for something out of the ordinary. After well over a hundred beef and pork recipes, you've come to the right place! Lamb is standard in our supermarkets; veal, a bit less so. And rabbit? That may take some looking. But all three are more and more a part of our culinary landscape in the United States. As we've moved out to fresher whole foods, farm-to-table ideals, and fewer processed ingredients, we've actually expanded the possibilities of what we prepare for dinner. Isn't that odd? We've deep-sixed the fake stuff and ended up expanding our choices.

All three of these meats provide big flavors, especially in the pressure cooker—none more so than lamb. If you get lamb, veal, or rabbit home from the store and notice a funky aroma, or a metallic tang, or even a too-gamey odor, take it back for a full refund. There's no sense in spending money on lamb shanks that smell like über-gamy mutton.

Still, the flavor palate among these recipes is considerably broader, with a wide range of dried spices and fresh herbs. Since the pressure cooker forces so much natural flavor out of every cut of meat, these proteins need a bigger set of ingredients than pork or beef to provide good balance. And truth be told, we felt more at liberty to call for a bigger selection of ingredients.

As always, there are no quick-cookers here, but watch the release times carefully. Veal and rabbit can turn tough if left under pressure too long, even with a natural release. And lamb can turn quite strong-tasting. Be even more exacting because you're dealing with culinary powerhouses.

So, welcome to the unusual and exciting. Even if you make only one or two of these recipes, you'll have expanded your range dramatically.

LAMB AND EGGPLANT PASTA CASSEROLE

EFFORT: **A LITTLE** • PRESSURE: **HIGH** • TIME UNDER PRESSURE: **5 OR 8 MINUTES** • RELEASE: **QUICK** • SERVES: **4**

2 tablespoons olive oil

1 medium red onion, chopped

1 tablespoon minced garlic

1¹/₂ pounds lean ground lamb

One small eggplant (about ³/₄ pound), stemmed and diced

³/₄ cup dry red wine, such as Syrah

2¹/₄ cups chicken broth

¹/₂ cup canned tomato paste

1 teaspoon ground cinnamon

¹/₂ tablespoon dried oregano

¹/₂ teaspoon dried dill

¹/₂ teaspoon salt

¹/₂ teaspoon ground black pepper

8 ounces dried spiral-shaped pasta, such as rotini

1 Heat the oil in a 6-quart stovetop pressure cooker set over medium heat or in a 6-quart electric pressure cooker turned to the browning function. Add the onion and cook, stirring often, until softened, about 4 minutes. Add the garlic and cook until aromatic, less than 1 minute.

2 Crumble in the ground lamb; cook, stirring occasionally, until it has lost its raw color, about 5 minutes. Add the eggplant and cook for 1 minute, stirring often, to soften a bit. Pour in the red wine and scrape up any browned bits in the pot as it comes to a simmer.

3 Stir in the broth, tomato paste, cinnamon, oregano, dill, salt, and pepper until everything is coated in the tomato sauce. Stir in the pasta until coated.

4 Lock the lid onto the pot.

STOVETOP: Raise the heat to high and bring the pot to high pressure (15 psi). Once this pressure has been reached, reduce the heat as much as possible while maintaining this pressure. Cook for 5 minutes.

································ **OR** ································

ELECTRIC: Set the machine to cook at high pressure (9–11 psi). Set the machine's timer to cook at high pressure for 8 minutes.

5 Use the quick-release method to bring the pot's pressure back to normal.

6 Unlock and open the pot. Stir well before serving.

TESTERS' NOTES

• What could be simpler than this pasta stew, a real dose of comfort food? There are plenty of spices to balance lamb's more assertive flavor. However, if you're worried about the meat being too strong, skip the pre-ground lamb in the case and ask the butcher to grind boneless leg of lamb for you. Pre-ground lamb is often full of trimmings and other bits that can have a more assertive flavor.

• Although browning brings flavor to many recipes, there's no need to go overboard browning the lamb here because the flavor will become much stronger. Just make sure the ground meat no longer has that raw color.

Serve It Up! Top each serving with chopped parsley leaves and/or crumbled feta.

GROUND LAMB STEW WITH SWEET POTATOES, LEEKS, AND DRIED APRICOTS

EFFORT: **NOT MUCH** · PRESSURE: **HIGH** · TIME UNDER PRESSURE:
5 OR 8 MINUTES · RELEASE: **QUICK** · SERVES: **4 TO 6**

2 tablespoons olive oil

2 large leeks, white and pale green parts
  only, halved, washed, and thinly sliced

2 tablespoons minced fresh ginger

2 teaspoons ground cinnamon

1/2 tablespoon ground coriander

1 teaspoon ground ginger

1/2 teaspoon salt

1/2 teaspoon ground black pepper

2 pounds lean ground lamb

1 large sweet potato (about 1 pound),
  peeled and shredded through the large
  holes of a box grater

1 cup chicken broth

1 cup packed dried apricots, chopped

1/4 cup slivered almonds

1 Heat the oil in a 6-quart stovetop pressure cooker set over medium heat or in a 6-quart electric pressure cooker turned to the browning function. Add the leeks and ginger; cook, stirring occasionally, until the leeks have softened, about 3 minutes.

2 Add the cinnamon, coriander, ginger, salt, and pepper; stir until aromatic, about 30 seconds. Crumble in the ground meat; cook, stirring often, until lightly browned, about 4 minutes. Stir in the sweet potato, broth, dried apricots, and almonds; scrape up any browned bits on the pot's bottom.

3 Lock the lid in place.

STOVETOP: Raise the heat to high and bring the pot to high pressure (15 psi). Once this pressure has been reached, reduce the heat as much as possible while maintaining this pressure. Cook for 5 minutes.

································ OR ································

ELECTRIC: Set the machine to cook at high pressure (9–11 psi). Set the machine's timer to cook at high pressure for 8 minutes.

4 Use the quick-release method to return the pot's pressure to normal.

5 Unlock and open the pot. Stir well before serving.

TESTERS' NOTES
• This North African flavor palette highlights the lamb and sweet potato, balancing their savory and sweet components with plenty of spices.
• Make sure the dried apricots are soft and supple, not dried out or hard. Dried California apricots will offer a stronger pop than Turkish apricots.
• The shredded sweet potato will almost melt into the sauce, thickening it a bit. Substitute a white sweet potato for a less sweet, more savory finish.

LAMB, RICE, AND CHICKPEA CASSEROLE

EFFORT: **A LOT** · PRESSURE: **HIGH** · TIME UNDER PRESSURE:
20 OR 30 MINUTES · RELEASE: **QUICK, THEN MODIFIED QUICK** ·
SERVES: **6**

2 pounds boneless leg of lamb, well
  trimmed and cut into 1 1/2-inch pieces

1 medium yellow onion, halved

1 tablespoon salt

2 teaspoons whole allspice berries

2 teaspoons whole cloves

1 teaspoon black peppercorns

8 green cardamom pods

2 bay leaves

2 tablespoons olive oil

1 large yellow onion, halved and sliced into thin half-moons

1 tablespoon minced garlic

One 15-ounce can chickpeas, drained and rinsed (about 1³/₄ cups)

1 cup long-grain white rice, such as white basmati rice

¹/₂ teaspoon ground allspice

¹/₂ teaspoon ground ginger

Up to ¹/₂ teaspoon saffron threads

1 Combine the lamb, onion halves, salt, allspice berries, cloves, peppercorns, cardamom pods, and bay leaves in a 6-quart stovetop or electric pressure cooker. Add enough tap water to cover all the ingredients.

2 Lock the lid onto the pot.

STOVETOP: Set the pot over high heat and bring it to high pressure (15 psi). Once this pressure has been reached, reduce the heat as much as possible while maintaining this pressure. Cook for 10 minutes.

···············OR···············

ELECTRIC: Set the machine to cook at high pressure (9–11 psi). Set the machine's timer to cook at high pressure for 15 minutes.

3 Use the quick-release method to bring the pot's pressure back to normal.

4 Unlock and open the cooker. Cool for 5 minutes. Transfer the meat from the pot to a large bowl. Set a large bowl underneath a colander and drain the contents of the pot through the colander, catching the broth below. Discard the solids. Rinse out the cooker.

5 Set the stovetop cooker over medium heat or turn an electric cooker to its browning mode. Add the oil, then the onion. Cook, stirring often, until softened, about 4 minutes. Stir the garlic; cook for just 30 seconds or so. Add the chickpeas, rice, allspice, ginger, and saffron; stir over the heat for 1 minute. Return the meat and any juices to the pot; pour in 2¹/₄ cups of the reserved cooking liquid and stir well.

6 Lock the lid onto the pot again.

STOVETOP: Raise the heat again to high and bring the cooker back to high pressure (15 psi). Once this pressure has been reached, reduce the heat as much as possible maintaining this pressure. Cook for 10 minutes.

···············OR···············

ELECTRIC: Set the machine to cook at high pressure (9–11 psi). Set the machine's timer to cook at high pressure for 15 minutes.

7 Use the quick-release method to return the pot's pressure to normal, but do not remove the lid. Set the cooker aside for 5 minutes.

8 Unlock and open the cooker. Stir well before serving.

TESTERS' NOTES

• In this recipe, you make a fragrant lamb stock for the final dish. The lamb needs to cook longer than the rice, so there's no sense in not building a stock with it to use later in the recipe.

• You'll end up with extra lamb stock, probably no more than 2 cups. Save it in small increments so you can add it to other recipes in the future that need a hit of flavor.

Serve It Up! Drizzle the servings with aged, syrupy balsamic vinegar or pomegranate molasses and grind lots of black pepper over each bowlful.

LAMB MEATBALLS WITH SHALLOTS AND WHITE WINE

EFFORT: **A LITTLE** • PRESSURE: **HIGH** • TIME UNDER PRESSURE: **5 OR 7 MINUTES** • RELEASE: **QUICK** • SERVES: **6**

2 pounds lean ground lamb

$1/2$ cup loosely packed fresh parsley leaves, minced

1 large egg, at room temperature

2 tablespoons dried currants

1 tablespoon minced garlic

$1/2$ teaspoon ground allspice

$1/2$ teaspoon ground cinnamon

$1/2$ teaspoon salt

$1/2$ teaspoon ground black pepper

2 tablespoons olive oil

8 medium shallots, peeled, the root still intact, but halved through the root end

1 cup chicken broth

$1/2$ cup dry but light white wine, such as Sauvignon Blanc

10 pitted dates

4 fresh thyme sprigs

2 bay leaves

1 Mix the ground lamb, parsley, egg, currants, garlic, allspice, cinnamon, salt, and pepper in a large bowl until the egg and spices are evenly distributed throughout. Roll the mixture into sixteen $1/2$-inch meatballs. Set aside.

2 Heat the oil in a 6-quart stovetop pressure cooker set over medium heat or in a 6-quart electric pressure cooker turned to the browning function. Add the shallots; cook, stirring occasionally, until lightly browned.

Stir in the broth, wine, dates, thyme sprigs, and bay leaves. Nestle the meatballs into the sauce.

3 Lock the lid onto the pot.

STOVETOP: Raise the heat to high and bring the pot to high pressure (15 psi). Once this pressure has been reached, reduce the heat as much as possible while maintaining this pressure. Cook for 5 minutes.

·· OR ··

ELECTRIC: Set the machine to cook at high pressure (9–11 psi). Set the machine's timer to cook at high pressure for 7 minutes.

4 Use the quick-release method to return the pot's pressure to normal.

5 Unlock and open the pot. Stir gently to coat the meatballs in the sauce. Discard the thyme sprigs and bay leaves before serving.

TESTERS' NOTES

• Because lamb can be so assertive, we balance its flavors with plenty of herbs and spices in this Greek-inspired dish.
• Ground lamb is notoriously fatty. Look for lean ground lamb, preferably from leg of lamb.
• The meatballs should be tightly rolled and quite compact, and as smooth as possible. Wetting your hands while rolling them will make the job easier.

Serve It Up! Dollop some Greek yogurt over bowlfuls of the meatballs and sprinkle them with chopped cilantro leaves and dill fronds.

LAMB RAGÙ

EFFORT: **A LITTLE** • PRESSURE: **HIGH** • TIME UNDER PRESSURE:
10 OR 15 MINUTES • RELEASE: **NATURAL** • SERVES: **6**

3 tablespoons olive oil

1 large yellow onion, chopped

2 medium carrots, chopped

1½ tablespoons minced garlic

1½ pounds boneless leg of lamb,
  trimmed and diced

1 tablespoon all-purpose flour

2 tablespoons packed fresh rosemary
  leaves, minced

2 tablespoons packed fresh sage leaves,
  minced

½ teaspoon salt

½ teaspoon ground black pepper

1 cup beef broth

1½ cups dry, hearty red wine, such as
  Syrah

¼ cup canned tomato paste

1 Heat the oil in a 6-quart stovetop pressure cooker set over medium heat or in a
6-quart electric pressure cooker turned to
the browning function. Add the onion and
carrots; cook, stirring occasionally, until the
onion softens, about 4 minutes. Stir in the
garlic; cook about 20 seconds.

2 Add the lamb and brown evenly, about 5
minutes, stirring often. Add the flour, stir to
coat the meat and vegetables, then stir in the
rosemary, sage, salt, and pepper. Cook about
1 minute, just until aromatic, stirring almost
constantly.

3 Pour in the broth and stir well to dissolve
the flour and scrape up any browned bits on
the bottom of the pot. Stir in the wine and
tomato paste until the latter dissolves.

4 Lock the lid onto the pot.

STOVETOP: Raise the heat to high and bring the
pot to high pressure (15 psi). Once this pressure
has been reached, reduce the heat as much as possible while maintaining this pressure. Cook for
10 minutes.

··· **OR** ·····································

ELECTRIC: Set the machine to cook at high pressure (9–11 psi). Set the machine's timer to cook at
high pressure for 15 minutes.

5 Reduce the pressure.

STOVETOP: Set the pot off the heat and let its pressure drop to normal naturally, about 12 minutes.

··· **OR** ·····································

ELECTRIC: Turn off the machine or unplug it so it
doesn't flip to its keep-warm setting. Let its pressure fall back to normal naturally, 12 to 15 minutes.

If the pressure in the pot is not back to normal within 15 minutes, use the quick-release
method to bring it all the way back down.

6 Unlock and open the pot. Stir well before
serving.

TESTERS' NOTES

• Leg of lamb makes a delicious ragù, bold and satisfying.
Make sure the meat is truly diced into ¼-inch pieces. If the
meat is any larger, it may not get properly tender—and you
won't be able to get lamb and vegetables in each bite.

• Make sure the flour has browned just a bit in step 2, then
dissolved in step 3. It's the main thickener in the meat sauce
but its flavor needs to be dispersed throughout the sauce.

Serve It Up! Toss cooked and drained whole
wheat pasta with a little olive oil and use
it as a bed for the ragù. Use dried pasta; its
firmer bite is a better match to the slightly
chewy meat. Or skip the pasta and spoon over
split-open baked potatoes.

CUMIN LAMB "STIR-FRY"

EFFORT: **A LITTLE** • PRESSURE: **HIGH** • TIME UNDER PRESSURE:
3 OR 5 MINUTES • RELEASE: **QUICK** • SERVES: **4**

**One 2¹/₂-pound butterflied (boneless) leg
of lamb, well trimmed**

1 tablespoon cumin seeds

¹/₂ tablespoon coriander seeds

1 teaspoon ground black pepper

2 tablespoons peanut oil

**12 medium scallions, cut into 1-inch
pieces**

¹/₄ cup chicken broth

3 tablespoons packed dark brown sugar

2 tablespoons soy sauce

**1 tablespoon fish sauce (nam pla or nuoc
nam)**

1 teaspoon cornstarch

1 Spread the lamb out onto a large cutting
board; halve it lengthwise, then slice those
pieces widthwise into ¹/₄-inch-thick strips.
Toss the lamb with the cumin seeds, coriander seeds, and pepper in a large bowl.

2 Heat the oil in a 6-quart stovetop pressure
cooker set over medium-high heat or in a
6-quart electric pressure cooker turned to
the browning mode. Add the lamb and the
spices; stir-fry for 3 minutes, until browned,
tossing constantly.

3 Add the scallions; stir-fry for 1 minute.
Stir in the broth, brown sugar, soy sauce, and
fish sauce until the brown sugar dissolves.

4 Lock the lid onto the pot.

STOVETOP: Raise the heat to high and bring the
pot to high pressure (15 psi). Once this pressure
has been reached, reduce the heat as much as possible while maintaining this pressure. Cook for
3 minutes.

·· OR ··

ELECTRIC: Set the machine to cook at high pressure (9–11 psi). Set the machine's timer to cook at
high pressure for 5 minutes.

5 Use the quick-release method to drop the
pot's pressure back to normal.

6 Unlock and open the pot. Set the stovetop
cooker over high heat or turn the electric
cooker to its browning function; bring the
sauce to a simmer. Whisk the cornstarch
with 2 teaspoons water in a small bowl until
smooth; stir the slurry into the bubbling
sauce. Stir until thickened, about 20 seconds.
Immediately turn off the heat or turn off the
machine and dish the stew into bowls.

TESTERS' NOTES

• No, this isn't a stir-fry, but you should use good
stir-frying technique in steps 2 and 3 to make sure the
ingredients are lightly browned but still crisp before you
set the lid onto the pot. Keep tossing over the heat, stirring
with two wooden spoons if necessary, so nothing softens
as it browns.

• The leg of lamb needs to be trimmed well; it will have
large sections of fat in it, even some big blobs. You may
lose up to ¹/₂ pound of the meat before you begin to slice
it into strips. But it's worth the effort; otherwise, there'll be
an unattractive slick of grease over the whole dish.

• There's no heat in this dish, so the aromatics really poke
through the other flavors. If you want some spike, add up
to 1 teaspoon red pepper flakes with the seeds.

Serve It Up! Use cooked short-grain sushi
rice for the base in the bowls. If desired, toss
the hot rice with a little rice vinegar and a
pinch of sugar before serving.

LAMB STEW WITH BRUSSELS SPROUTS, DRIED APPLES, AND PISTACHIOS

EFFORT: **A LOT** • PRESSURE: **HIGH** • TIME UNDER PRESSURE: **25 OR 38 MINUTES** • RELEASE: **QUICK, THEN QUICK AGAIN** • SERVES: **6**

2 teaspoons ground coriander

1/2 tablespoon ground cinnamon

1 teaspoon ground cumin

1 teaspoon ground black pepper

1/2 teaspoon ground ginger

1/2 teaspoon salt

2 1/2 pounds boneless leg of lamb, well trimmed and cut into 2-inch pieces

2 tablespoons olive oil

1 large yellow onion, halved and sliced into thin half-moons

3 medium garlic cloves, slivered

1 cup chicken broth

1 cup packed dried apples, chopped

1/4 cup shelled unsalted pistachios

1 tablespoon honey

1 pound small Brussels sprouts, stemmed and halved

1 Mix the coriander, cinnamon, cumin, pepper, ginger, and salt in a large bowl. Add the lamb and stir until evenly and well coated in the spices; set aside.

2 Heat the oil in a 6-quart stovetop pressure cooker set over medium heat or in a 6-quart electric pressure cooker turned to the browning mode. Add the onion and cook, stirring often, until softened, about 5 minutes.

3 Add the meat and every drop of spice from the bowl, as well as the garlic. Cook, stirring occasionally, until the meat has browned a bit, about 5 minutes. Add the broth, dried apples, pistachios, and honey; stir to scrape up any browned bits on the pot's bottom.

4 Lock the lid in place.

STOVETOP: Raise the heat to high and bring the pot to high pressure (15 psi). Once this pressure has been reached, reduce the heat as much as possible while maintaining this pressure. Cook for 20 minutes.

·············· **OR** ··············

ELECTRIC: Set the machine to cook at high pressure (9–11 psi). Set the machine's timer to cook at high pressure for 30 minutes.

5 Use the quick-release method to bring the pot's pressure back to normal.

6 Unlock and open the cooker. Stir in the Brussels sprouts.

7 Lock the lid back onto the pot.

STOVETOP: Raise the heat back to high and bring the pot back to high pressure (15 psi). Once this pressure has been reached, reduce the heat as much as possible while maintaining this pressure. Cook for 5 minutes.

·············· **OR** ··············

ELECTRIC: Set the machine to cook once again at high pressure (9–11 psi). Set the machine's timer to cook at high pressure for 8 minutes.

8 Drop the pot's pressure back to normal with the quick-release method.

9 Unlock and open the cooker. Stir well before serving.

(continued)

• The stew's über-fragrant and somewhat sweet flavors are actually a riff on those in Tunisian tagines, a North African casserole cooked in a pot with a conical lid.
• The smaller the Brussels sprouts, the less assertive their flavor. If you've got kids who are vegetable phobes, try shredding the Brussels sprouts with a mandoline or the shredding blade of a food processor. They'll almost melt into the sauce.

Serve It Up! Serve over cooked couscous or wheatberries.

LAMB, DATE, AND WALNUT STEW

EFFORT: **A LITTLE** · PRESSURE: **HIGH** · TIME UNDER PRESSURE: **25 OR 38 MINUTES** · RELEASE: **NATURAL** · SERVES: **4**

1/2 **tablespoon ground cinnamon**

1 **teaspoon ground ginger**

1/2 **teaspoon salt**

1/4 **teaspoon ground allspice**

1/4 **teaspoon grated nutmeg**

2 1/2 **pounds boneless leg of lamb, well trimmed and cut into 2-inch pieces**

2 **tablespoons olive oil**

1 **large red onion, halved and sliced into thin half-moons**

1 **cup pitted dried dates, halved**

1/2 **cup walnuts**

1/2 **cup chicken broth**

1/2 **cup unsweetened apple juice**

1 Mix the cinnamon, ginger, salt, allspice, and nutmeg in a large bowl. Add the lamb and stir until the meat is well coated with the spices.

2 Heat the oil in a 6-quart stovetop pressure cooker set over medium heat or in a 6-quart electric pressure cooker turned to the browning function. Add the onion and cook, stirring occasionally, until softened, about 5 minutes.

3 Scrape the meat and spices into the pot; cook, stirring often, until browned, about 5 minutes. Stir in the dates, walnut pieces, broth, and apple juice, scraping up any browned bits on the bottom of the pot.

4 Lock the lid in place.

STOVETOP: Raise the heat to high and bring the pot to high pressure (15 psi). Once this pressure has been reached, reduce the heat as much as possible while maintaining this pressure. Cook for 25 minutes.

·············· OR ··············

ELECTRIC: Set the machine to cook at high pressure (9–11 psi). Set the machine's timer to cook at high pressure for 38 minutes.

5 Reduce the pressure.

STOVETOP: Set the pot off the heat and allow its pressure to fall to normal naturally, about 14 minutes.

·············· OR ··············

ELECTRIC: Turn off the machine or unplug it so it doesn't flip to its keep-warm setting. Let the pot's pressure return to normal naturally, 14 to 18 minutes.

6 Unlock and open the pot. Stir the stew before serving.

TESTERS' NOTES
• The spice mixture here is reminiscent of that used for pumpkin pie—and gives the stew a wintry warmth, best with a glass of beer.

• For a less sweet stew, use 1 cup broth, rather than the broth–apple juice combo.

Serve It Up! Make mashed potatoes using cooked potatoes and canned pumpkin in equal portions; mash with an electric mixer at medium speed, adding unsalted butter, milk, salt, and pepper.

LAMB STEW WITH EAST INDIAN SPICES

EFFORT: **NOT MUCH** • PRESSURE: **HIGH** • TIME UNDER PRESSURE: **15 OR 25 MINUTES** • RELEASE: **NATURAL** • SERVES: **6**

2 tablespoons peanut oil

3 medium red onions, halved and thinly sliced into half-moons

2 tablespoons minced fresh ginger

1 teaspoon coriander seeds

1 teaspoon fennel seeds

1/2 teaspoon whole cloves

1/2 teaspoon ground cinnamon

1/2 teaspoon salt

1/2 teaspoon ground black pepper

2 3/4 pounds boneless leg of lamb, cut into 1 1/2-inch pieces

1 1/2 tablespoons white wine vinegar

1 tablespoon canned tomato paste

1/2 cup chicken broth

1 Heat the oil in a 6-quart stovetop pressure cooker set over medium heat or in a 6-quart electric pressure cooker turned to the browning mode. Add the onions and ginger; cook, stirring often, until soft and even a little browned, 8 to 10 minutes.

2 Add the coriander and fennel seeds, cloves, cinnamon, salt, and pepper; stir until

aromatic, about 1 minute. Add the lamb all at once and cook, stirring occasionally, until the pieces have lost their raw color, about 5 minutes. Stir in the vinegar and tomato paste until everything's evenly coated. Pour in the broth and stir well.

3 Lock the lid onto the pot.

STOVETOP: Raise the heat to high and bring the pot to high pressure (15 psi). Once this pressure has been reached, reduce the heat as much as possible while maintaining this pressure. Cook for 15 minutes.

························· OR ·························

ELECTRIC: Set the pot to cook at high pressure (9–11 psi). Set the machine's timer to cook at high pressure for 25 minutes.

4 Reduce the pressure.

STOVETOP: Set the pot off the heat and let its pressure fall to normal naturally, about 12 minutes.

························· OR ·························

ELECTRIC: Turn off or unplug the machine so it doesn't flip to its keep-warm setting. Let its pressure fall to normal naturally, 12 to 15 minutes.

5 Unlock and open the pot. Stir the stew before serving.

TESTERS' NOTES
• This curry is based on dopiaza, a classic East Indian dish, usually served with copious amounts of onions—caramelized, just softened, and sometimes even raw on top. The pressure cooker softens and sweetens them all into down-home comfort food.
• You can remove the whole cloves after cooking, although they're perfectly edible.

Serve It Up! Offer buttery grilled bread—or better, grilled na'an, brushed with butter.

BRAISED LAMB SHOULDER WITH HOMINY AND TOMATILLOS

EFFORT: **A LOT** • PRESSURE: **HIGH** • TIME UNDER PRESSURE: **50 OR 75 MINUTES** • RELEASE: **NATURAL** • SERVES: **6**

2 tablespoons olive oil

One 3-pound bone-in lamb shoulder roast

1 large yellow onion, chopped

2 poblano chiles, stemmed, seeded, and chopped

1 pound fresh tomatillos, husked and chopped

2 tablespoons apple cider vinegar

2 teaspoons dried oregano

1 teaspoon ground cumin

1/2 teaspoon ground allspice

11/2 cups chicken broth

3 cups drained and rinsed canned hominy

1/2 cup loosely packed fresh cilantro leaves, finely chopped

1 Heat the oil in a 6-quart stovetop pressure cooker set over medium heat or in a 6-quart electric pressure cooker turned to the browning mode. Add the lamb roast; brown well on all sides, turning occasionally, about 8 minutes in all. Transfer to a large bowl.

2 Add the onion and poblanos to the cooker; cook, stirring occasionally, until the onion turns translucent, about 4 minutes. Add the tomatillos; cook, stirring more often, until they begin to break down, about 5 minutes.

3 Stir in the vinegar, oregano, cumin, and allspice; scrape up any browned bits on the pot's bottom. Pour in the broth, then add the roast and its juices. Stir well.

4 Lock the lid onto the pot.

STOVETOP: Raise the heat to high and bring the pot to high pressure (15 psi). Once this pressure has been reached, reduce the heat as much as possible while maintaining this pressure. Cook for 50 minutes.

································ **OR** ································

ELECTRIC: Set the machine to cook at high pressure (9–11 psi). Set the machine's timer to cook at high pressure for 75 minutes.

5 Reduce the pressure.

STOVETOP: Set the pot off the heat and let its pressure return to normal naturally, about 20 minutes.

································ **OR** ································

ELECTRIC: Turn off the machine or unplug it so it doesn't jump to its keep-warm setting. Let its pressure come back to normal naturally, 18 to 25 minutes.

6 Unlock and open the pot. Transfer the roast to a cutting board; cool for 5 minutes. Pull the meat from the bone(s), discard the bone(s), and chop the meat into small bits. Stir the bits back into the sauce; stir in the hominy and cilantro.

7 Lock the lid back onto the pot.

STOVETOP: Set the pot over high heat and bring it back to high pressure (15 psi).

································ **OR** ································

ELECTRIC: Set the machine to cook at high pressure again (9–11 psi).

The moment the pot reaches high pressure, turn off the heat or turn off the machine. Allow its pressure to fall back to normal naturally, about 10 minutes.

8 Unlock and open the cooker. Stir well before serving.

TESTERS' NOTES
• Cooking a bone-in lamb roast allows the bone's flavor to begin to permeate the meat, sweetening it a bit as it undergoes high pressure.
• You might find one large bone in a lamb shoulder roast—or two (or more) with smaller bits in the roast. Remove any bone you see, as well as any undissolved cartilage still adhering to the bone, particularly near the joints.

Serve It Up! Offer warmed whole wheat flour tortillas on the side.

CREAMY LAMB SHOULDER STEW WITH SPRING VEGETABLES

EFFORT: **A LITTLE** • PRESSURE: **HIGH** • TIME UNDER PRESSURE: **22 OR 35 MINUTES** • RELEASE: **NATURAL** • SERVES: **8**

2 tablespoons unsalted butter

1 tablespoon olive oil

3 pounds boneless lamb shoulder, trimmed and cut into 1¹⁄₂-inch cubes

2 large leeks, white and pale green parts only, halved lengthwise, washed and thinly sliced

2 tablespoons all-purpose flour

1 cup chicken broth

¹⁄₂ cup dry, light white wine, such as Chablis

6 ounces baby carrots, halved widthwise

4 fresh thyme sprigs

1 fresh tarragon sprig

2 bay leaves

¹⁄₄ cup heavy cream

1 cup shelled fresh peas, or frozen peas, thawed

4 ounces snow peas, halved (about 1 cup)

¹⁄₂ teaspoon salt

¹⁄₂ teaspoon ground black pepper

1 Melt the butter in the oil in a 6-quart stovetop pressure cooker set over medium heat or in a 6-quart electric pressure cooker turned to the browning function. Add the meat, working in batches to prevent crowding as necessary; brown on all sides, about 6 minutes. Transfer to a large bowl and continue browning more as necessary.

2 Add the leeks to the cooker; cook, stirring occasionally, until softened, about 4 minutes. Add the flour; stir well over the heat for less than a minute, just enough to get rid of its raw taste.

3 Whisk in the broth in a slow, steady stream to dissolve the flour. Whisk in the wine until the sauce is bubbling, about 1 minute. Add the carrots, thyme, tarragon, and bay leaves, as well as the meat and its juices. Stir well.

4 Lock the lid onto the pot.

STOVETOP: Raise the heat to high and bring the pot to high pressure (15 psi). Once this pressure has been reached, reduce the heat as much as possible while maintaining this pressure. Cook for 22 minutes.

·······································**OR**·······································

ELECTRIC: Set the machine to cook at high pressure (9–11 psi). Set the machine's timer to cook at high pressure for 35 minutes.

(continued)

5 Reduce the pressure.

STOVETOP: Set the pot off the heat and let its pressure return to normal naturally, about 12 minutes.

·····················**OR**·····················

ELECTRIC: Turn off the machine or unplug it so it doesn't flip to its keep-warm setting. Let its pressure return to normal naturally, 12 to 15 minutes.

6 Unlock and open the pot. Discard the bay leaves. Set the stovetop pot over medium heat or turn the electric pot to its browning function. Stir in the cream; bring back to a simmer, stirring constantly. Stir in the peas, snow peas, salt, and pepper.

7 Take the pot off the heat or turn it off, lock its lid in place, and set aside for 5 minutes.

8 Use the quick-release method as necessary to reopen the pot.

9 Unlock and open the pot. Discard the thyme and tarragon sprigs and bay leaves before serving.

TESTERS' NOTES
• Modeled on a classic French navarin, this creamy stew could become a springtime favorite or a fine Easter dinner. The lamb mellows quite a bit in the creamy sauce, spiked with plenty of herbs that offer an earthy counterbalance.
• The peas and snow peas are heated only to a crisp tenderness in the hot stew. You'll end up with a good contrast of textures: meltingly tender lamb and somewhat crunchy spring vegetables.
• If you don't want to buy a whole bag of baby carrots, slice two medium carrots in half lengthwise and then into 3-inch segments.

LAMB SHOULDER STEW WITH JUNIPER BERRIES AND COGNAC

EFFORT: **A LITTLE** • PRESSURE: **HIGH** • TIME UNDER PRESSURE: **25 OR 40 MINUTES** • RELEASE: **NATURAL** • SERVES: **6**

4 thin bacon strips, chopped

3 pounds boneless lamb shoulder, trimmed and cut into 2-inch pieces

1 teaspoon ground black pepper

8 medium scallions, cut into 2-inch pieces

2 medium carrots, thinly sliced

1 tablespoon juniper berries (about 10), crushed

1 tablespoon stemmed fresh thyme leaves

2 bay leaves

1/2 cup dry, fruit-forward red wine, such as Zinfandel

1/2 cup cognac

1 cup beef broth

2 teaspoons potato starch or cornstarch

1 Set a 6-quart stovetop pressure cooker over medium heat or turn a 6-quart electric pressure cooker to the browning mode. Add the bacon; fry until crisp, stirring occasionally, about 4 minutes. Use a slotted spoon to transfer the bacon to a big bowl.

2 Add the lamb in batches to avoid overcrowding, seasoning each batch with some pepper. Brown the meat on all sides, turning occasionally, about 6 minutes. Transfer the lamb to the bowl with the bacon and continue browning as necessary.

3 Add the scallions, carrots, juniper berries, thyme, and bay leaves to the pot. Cook about

1 minute, until aromatic, stirring all the while. Pour in the red wine, then the cognac; scrape up any brown bits in the pot as they come to a simmer. Stir in the broth, browned lamb, bacon, and any juices in their bowl.

4 Lock the lid on the pot.

STOVETOP: Raise the heat to high and bring the pot to high pressure (15 psi). Once this pressure has been reached, reduce the heat as much as possible while maintaining this pressure. Cook for 25 minutes.

····················· **OR** ·····················

ELECTRIC: Set the machine to cook at high pressure (9–11 psi). Set the machine's time to cook at high pressure for 40 minutes.

5 Reduce the pressure.

STOVETOP: Set the pot aside off the heat and let its pressure fall to normal naturally, about 15 minutes.

····················· **OR** ·····················

ELECTRIC: Turn off the machine or unplug it so it doesn't flip to its keep-warm setting. Let its pressure fall back to normal naturally, 15 to 18 minutes.

6 Unlock and open the pot. Skim the surface fat off the stew and discard the bay leaves. Set the stovetop cooker back over medium heat or turn the electric cooker to its browning function; bring the sauce back to a simmer.

7 Whisk the potato starch or cornstarch into 2 teaspoons water in a small bowl until smooth. Stir the slurry into the stew; cook, stirring almost constantly, until thickened and bubbling, about 1 minute.

TESTERS' NOTES
• For the best flavor, make sure you fry the bacon crisp and brown the lamb well. Both need to offer a big punch of flavors to match the other bold tastes.

• Because the pressure cooker pot is so tall, there's almost no chance the cognac will ignite over the heat. But should it suddenly ignite, cover the pot quickly and set it off the heat or turn it off at once. Wait about 5 minutes, then set the pot back over the heat or turn it on to start again. (You can also use brandy or more beef broth instead.)
• Crushed juniper berries can be difficult to find in the stew after cooking; they've certainly softened enough to be edible but they are a big spark of flavor. You'll need to fish around a bit to remove them if you want to mitigate their pop. (Frankly, we enjoy the surprise in some spoonfuls.) If you decide not to use the juniper berries, use gin instead of the cognac.

Serve It Up! Make a bed of buttered egg noodles in the bowls before ladling the stew on top.

LAMB SHANKS WITH GINGER AND FIGS

EFFORT: **A LITTLE** • PRESSURE: **HIGH** • TIME UNDER PRESSURE: **40 OR 60 MINUTES** • RELEASE: **NATURAL** • SERVES: **4**

2 tablespoons toasted sesame oil

Four 12-ounce lamb shanks

1 large leek, white and pale green parts only, halved lengthwise, washed, and thinly sliced

2 tablespoons minced fresh ginger

2 tablespoons soy sauce

1 tablespoon balsamic vinegar

1 tablespoon Worcestershire sauce

1¼ cups chicken broth

8 dried figs, stemmed and halved lengthwise

1 Heat 1 tablespoon oil in a 6-quart stovetop pressure cooker set over medium heat or in a 6-quart electric pressure cooker turned to the browning function. Add two of the

(continued)

shanks; brown them on all sides, turning occasionally, about 8 minutes. Transfer to a large bowl. Add the remaining tablespoon oil, and repeat with the remaining shanks.

2 Add the leek and ginger; cook, stirring often, until softened, about 3 minutes. Stir in the soy sauce, vinegar, and Worcestershire sauce; scrape up any browned bits in the pot. Stir in the broth and figs. Return the shanks and their juices to the cooker.

3 Lock the lid in place.

STOVETOP: Raise the heat to high and bring the pot to high pressure (15 psi). Once this pressure has been reached, reduce the heat as much as possible while maintaining this pressure. Cook for 40 minutes.

·················· **OR** ··················

ELECTRIC: Set the machine to cook at high pressure (9–11 psi); set the timer to cook at that pressure for 1 hour.

4 Reduce the pressure.

STOVETOP: Set the pot off the heat and let its pressure fall to normal naturally, about 20 minutes.

·················· **OR** ··················

ELECTRIC: Turn off the machine or unplug it so it doesn't jump to its keep-warm setting. Let its pressure return to normal naturally, 20 to 30 minutes.

5 Unlock and open the cooker. Transfer each shank to a serving bowl. Skim the surface fat from the sauce in the cooker and ladle the sauce over the shanks.

TESTERS' NOTES

• This sweet-and-salty preparation is good winter warmer fare. It's got an Asian bent, but also includes leeks and dried figs to sweeten the sauce.
• You will not fit four lamb shanks side by side in the bottom of a 6-quart pressure cooker. Position them so that the meatiest part of each shank is at least partially submerged, some of the bones and thinner parts sticking up and out of the liquid.
• Don't let the ginger brown in step 2. Stir almost constantly; cook just until the leek softens. Otherwise, the ginger can take on bitter overtones.

Serve It Up! Make a bed of cooked medium-grain brown rice (like brown Arborio) in each bowl.

LAMB SHANKS WITH PANCETTA AND TOMATOES

EFFORT: **A LITTLE** • PRESSURE: **HIGH** • TIME UNDER PRESSURE: **40 OR 60 MINUTES** • RELEASE: **NATURAL** • SERVES: **4**

2 tablespoons olive oil

One 6-ounce pancetta chunk, chopped

Four 12-ounce lamb shanks

1 small yellow onion, chopped

One 28-ounce can diced tomatoes, drained (about 3¹/₂ cups)

1 ounce dried mushrooms, preferably porcini, crumbled

3 tablespoons packed celery leaves, minced

2 tablespoons minced chives

2 cups dry, light white wine, such as Sauvignon Blanc

2 tablespoons all-purpose flour

¹/₂ teaspoon ground black pepper

1 Heat the oil in a 6-quart stovetop pressure cooker set over medium heat or in a 6-quart electric pressure cooker turned to the browning function. Add the pancetta and brown well, about 6 minutes, stirring often. Use a slotted spoon to transfer the pancetta to a large bowl.

2 Add two of the shanks to the cooker; brown on all sides, turning occasionally, about 8 minutes. Transfer them to the bowl and repeat with the remaining shanks.

3 Add the onion to the pot; cook, stirring often, until softened, about 4 minutes. Stir in the tomatoes, dried mushroom crumbles, celery leaves, and chives. Cook until bubbling, about 2 minutes, stirring often.

4 Whisk the wine, flour, and pepper in a medium bowl until the flour dissolves; stir this mixture into the sauce in the pot. Cook until thickened and bubbling, about 1 minute. Return the shanks, pancetta, and their juices to the cooker.

5 Lock the lid onto the pot.

STOVETOP: Raise the heat to high and bring the pot to high pressure (15 psi). Once this pressure has been reached, reduce the heat as much as possible while maintaining this pressure. Cook for 40 minutes.

·············· **OR** ··············

ELECTRIC: Set the machine to cook at high pressure (9–11 psi). Set the machine's timer to cook at high pressure for 1 hour.

6 Reduce the pressure.

STOVETOP: Set the pot off the heat and let its pressure fall to normal naturally, about 20 minutes.

·············· **OR** ··············

ELECTRIC: Turn off the machine or unplug it so it doesn't jump to its keep-warm setting. Let its pressure return to normal naturally, 20 to 30 minutes.

7 Unlock and open the cooker. Transfer a shank to each serving bowl. Skim any surface fat from the sauce with a flatware spoon. Ladle the sauce and vegetables over the lamb shanks.

TESTERS' NOTES
- Lamb shanks may be the quintessential six-hour oven braise, but a pressure cooker makes them a weeknight supper. The meat becomes quite tender without drying out.
- Make sure you brown both the pancetta and the shanks. Any complexity in the flavors must happen there, rather than through evaporation during long cooking.
- Celery leaves—those inner leaves in a bunch of celery—will give a delicate, grassy flavor to the sauce. If you want to go all out, substitute fresh chervil leaves.

Serve It Up! Serve over toasted sourdough croutons.

VEAL ROAST WITH **PANCETTA, ORANGE,** AND **CREAM**

EFFORT: **A LOT** · PRESSURE: **HIGH** · TIME UNDER PRESSURE: **50 OR 75 MINUTES** · RELEASE: **NATURAL** · SERVES: **6**

3 tablespoons unsalted butter

One 4-ounce pancetta chunk, chopped

One 2¹/₂-pound boneless veal shoulder roast, tied with butcher's twine

2 medium yellow onions, chopped

2 teaspoons minced garlic

2 teaspoons stemmed fresh thyme leaves

2 teaspoons finely grated orange zest

1 bay leaf

Up to ³/₄ cup dry vermouth

¹/₂ cup fresh orange juice, strained of pulp

1 tablespoon all-purpose flour

¹/₄ cup heavy cream

1 tablespoon minced chives

1 Melt the butter in a 6-quart stovetop pressure cooker set over medium heat or in a

(continued)

6-quart electric pressure cooker turned to the browning function. Add the pancetta; cook, stirring often, until browned and crisp, about 6 minutes. Use a slotted spoon to transfer the pancetta to a large bowl.

2 Add the roast to the pot. Brown on all sides, turning occasionally, 6 to 8 minutes. Transfer the roast to the bowl with the pancetta.

3 Add the onions to the pot; cook, stirring often, until softened, about 4 minutes. Stir in the garlic, thyme, orange zest, and bay leaf; cook for 1 minute, stirring constantly. Pour $^3/_4$ cup vermouth into a stovetop cooker or $^1/_2$ cup vermouth into an electric cooker; scrape up any browned bits in the bottom of the pot as it comes to a simmer.

4 Whisk the orange juice and flour in a small bowl until smooth; pour into the pot and stir well until dissolved. Return the pancetta, roast, and their juices to the pot.

5 Lock the lid in place.

STOVETOP: Raise the heat to high and bring the pot's pressure to high (15 psi). As soon as possible, lower the heat as much as possible while keeping this pressure constant. Cook for 50 minutes.

·· **OR** ··

ELECTRIC: Set the machine to cook at high pressure (9–11 psi). Set the timer to cook at high pressure for 75 minutes.

6 Reduce the pressure.

STOVETOP: Set the pot off the heat and let its pressure come back to normal naturally, 20 minutes.

·· **OR** ··

ELECTRIC: Turn off the machine or unplug it so it doesn't jump to its keep-warm setting. Let its pressure return to normal naturally, 20 to 30 minutes.

7 Unlock and open the pot. Transfer the roast to a cutting board; set aside. Discard the bay leaf. Skim the sauce of excess fat.

8 Set the stovetop cooker over medium heat or turn the electric cooker to its browning function; bring the sauce to a simmer. Boil until reduced by half its volume, about 5 minutes. Stir in the cream and chives; continue to boil for 2 minutes, stirring constantly. Slice the twine off the meat, carve the meat into $^1/_2$-inch-thick, irregular rounds, and serve with plenty of the sauce.

TESTERS' NOTES
• Cream, butter—there's no point in going halfway when you're making a veal roast! Best of all, the pressure cooker will morph the recipe's chemistry so the citrus won't break the sauce when the cream is added. It's a rich, indulgent meal, worthy of a dinner party.
• To tie, wrap the meat in butcher's twine to make the roast as cylindrical as possible; the meat may well be more folded than rolled. (Or you can ask the butcher at your supermarket to tie this roast for you.)

VEAL SHOULDER CHOPS STEWED WITH APPLES AND MUSHROOMS

EFFORT: **A LITTLE** • PRESSURE: **HIGH** • TIME UNDER PRESSURE: **30 OR 50 MINUTES** • RELEASE: **NATURAL** • SERVES: **6**

1 tablespoon unsalted butter

1 tablespoon olive oil

One 4-ounce pancetta chunk, chopped

4 pounds bone-in veal shoulder chops, cut into large chunks

1 large yellow onion, chopped

1 cup packed dried apples, chopped

8 ounces cremini mushrooms, thinly sliced

2 teaspoons minced garlic

2 teaspoons packed fresh rosemary leaves, minced

2 teaspoons stemmed fresh thyme leaves

$\frac{1}{2}$ teaspoon grated nutmeg

$\frac{1}{2}$ teaspoon ground black pepper

One 14$\frac{1}{2}$-ounce can diced tomatoes (about 1$\frac{3}{4}$ cups)

1 cup dry white wine, such as a California Chardonnay

1 tablespoon all-purpose flour

1 Melt the butter in the oil in a 6-quart stovetop pressure cooker set over medium heat or in a 6-quart electric pressure cooker turned to the browning mode. Add the pancetta; fry, stirring often, until crisp, about 5 minutes. Use a slotted spoon to transfer the pancetta to a large bowl.

2 Add the veal; cook, stirring often, until browned on both sides, about 6 minutes. Transfer the meat to the bowl with the pancetta. Add the onion and apples; cook, stirring often, until the onion softens, about 4 minutes.

3 Add the mushrooms and garlic; cook, stirring often, until the mushrooms give off their liquid and it reduces to a glaze, about 5 minutes. Add the rosemary, thyme, nutmeg, and pepper; cook for 30 seconds.

4 Pour in the tomatoes, stir well, and bring to a full simmer. Whisk the wine and flour in a small bowl until the flour dissolves, then pour the mixture into the pot. Cook, stirring once in a while, until thickened, about 4 minutes. Return the veal, pancetta, and their juices to the cooker.

5 Lock the lid onto the pot.

STOVETOP: Raise the heat to high and bring the pot to high pressure (15 psi). Once this pressure has been reached, reduce the heat as much as possible while maintaining this pressure. Cook for 30 minutes.

································ **OR** ································

ELECTRIC: Set the machine to cook at high pressure (9–11 psi). Set the machine's timer to cook at high pressure for 50 minutes.

6 Reduce the pressure.

STOVETOP: Set the pot off the heat and let its pressure fall to normal naturally, about 18 minutes.

································ **OR** ································

ELECTRIC: Turn off the machine or unplug it so it doesn't go into keep-warm mode. Let the pressure return to normal naturally, 18 to 25 minutes.

7 Unlock and open the cooker. Stir the stew gently before serving.

TESTERS' NOTES

• There's no point in cooking veal loin or rib chops in the pressure cooker; they'll be overcooked before you know it. But veal shoulder chops have plenty of flavor and need a good long (or here, short) braise to get tender.

• Veal is naturally sweet, so we want accents that won't turn the dish cloying—thus, acidic tomatoes, an oaky wine, and earthy vegetables. We still need balance; so the apples give us a little sweetness.

• Veal shoulder chops have small, thin bones in them, as in lamb or pork shoulder chops. You can chop them into smaller pieces, but you do have to work around those bones to leave them in the meat (and give more flavor to the stew).

CREAMY VEAL STEW WITH PEARL ONIONS AND SAGE

EFFORT: **A LOT** • PRESSURE: **HIGH** • TIME UNDER PRESSURE: **20 OR 35 MINUTES** • RELEASE: **NATURAL** • SERVES: **6**

3 pounds boneless veal shoulder, cut into 1½-inch pieces

1½ cups chicken broth

1 cup frozen pearl onions, thawed

12 ounces white button mushrooms, thinly sliced

2 fresh thyme sprigs

4 large fresh sage leaves

¼ teaspoon ground allspice

¼ teaspoon grated nutmeg

½ cup dry vermouth

1½ tablespoons all-purpose flour

¼ cup heavy cream

1 large egg yolk

¼ teaspoon salt

1 Combine the veal pieces and broth in a 6-quart stovetop or electric pressure cooker. Bring to a boil, either by setting the stovetop cooker over medium-high heat or by turning the electric model to its browning function. Boil for 10 minutes.

2 Set a large colander over a large bowl; strain the meat, catching the broth in the bowl below. Remove the bowl from underneath the colander. Skim any foam from the broth and rinse the veal pieces under cool water. Return both to the pressure cooker.

3 Set the stovetop pot over high heat or turn the electric pot to its browning mode. Stir in the onions, mushrooms, thyme, sage, allspice, and nutmeg. Whisk the vermouth and flour in a small bowl until smooth, then pour into the pot and stir well.

4 Lock the lid in place.

STOVETOP: Raise the heat to high and bring the pot to high pressure (15 psi). Once this pressure has been reached, reduce the heat as much as possible while maintaining this pressure. Cook for 20 minutes.

·························· **OR** ··························

ELECTRIC: Set the machine to cook at high pressure (9–11 psi). Set the machine's timer to cook at high pressure for 35 minutes.

5 Reduce the pressure.

STOVETOP: Set the pot off the heat and let its pressure come back to normal naturally, about 15 minutes.

·························· **OR** ··························

ELECTRIC: Turn off the machine or unplug it so it doesn't flip to its keep-warm setting. Allow its pressure to return to normal naturally, 15 to 20 minutes.

6 Unlock and open the pot. Use a slotted spoon to transfer the meat and all the vegetables to a large serving bowl. Discard the thyme sprigs and sage leaves.

7 Set the stovetop cooker over medium heat or turn the electric cooker to its browning function; bring the sauce inside to a low simmer, stirring occasionally. Whisk the cream, egg yolk, and salt in a medium bowl until smooth. Ladle about 2 cups of the sauce into the cream mixture, whisking nonstop to prevent the sauce from breaking. Whisk the combined mixture back into the sauce in the pot. Whisking all the while, cook just until barely thickened, less than 1 minute. Do not let the sauce return to a boil at this point (you may need to turn off the electric cooker to control the heat). Pour the sauce over the meat and vegetables in the serving bowl.

TESTERS' NOTES
• A streamlined take on the French classic, *blanquette de veau*, this stew has no browning of the meat to ward off any deep, caramelized layers of flavor in favor of a much lighter palette.
• This classic sauce would be enhanced with up to 1 tablespoon cognac added with the cream.
• Although there's little fat on most veal, trim off any bits you see. The fat in this dish should come primarily from the cream and egg yolks.

BREAST OF VEAL WITH FIGS AND CARROTS

EFFORT: **A LITTLE** • PRESSURE: **HIGH** • TIME UNDER PRESSURE: **45 OR 75 MINUTES** • RELEASE: **NATURAL** • SERVES: **4**

2 tablespoons unsalted butter

One 4¹/₂-pound bone-in breast of veal (4-bone roast), cut into two 2-bone pieces

1 large yellow onion, chopped

1 pound medium carrots, cut into 1-inch pieces

4 dried figs, stemmed and halved lengthwise

1 teaspoon dried sage

1 teaspoon dried thyme

1 teaspoon minced garlic

¹/₂ teaspoon salt

¹/₂ teaspoon ground black pepper

³/₄ cup dry, slightly acidic white wine, such as Chablis

1 Melt the butter in a 6-quart stovetop pressure cooker set over medium heat or in a 6-quart electric pressure cooker turned to the browning function. Add one piece of the breast of veal; brown on all sides, even the edges, about 8 minutes, turning occasionally. Transfer to a cutting board and repeat with the other piece.

2 Add the onion to the pot; cook, stirring often, until translucent, about 4 minutes. Add the carrots, figs, sage, thyme, garlic, salt, and pepper; stir in the wine to scrape up any browned bits at the bottom of the pot.

3 Return the meat to the pot, each piece lying on its side so they nestle together in the cooker. (Or set them standing up, leaning against the sides of the pot.)

4 Lock the lid in place.

STOVETOP: Raise the heat to high and bring the pot to high pressure (15 psi). Once this pressure has been reached, reduce the heat as much as possible while maintaining this pressure. Cook for 45 minutes.

························ **OR** ························

ELECTRIC: Set the machine to cook at high pressure (9–11 psi). Set the machine's time to cook at high pressure for 75 minutes.

5 Reduce the pressure.

STOVETOP: Set the pot off the heat and let its pressure come back to normal naturally, about 22 minutes.

························ **OR** ························

ELECTRIC: Turn off the machine or unplug it so it doesn't flip to its keep-warm setting. Let its pressure return to normal naturally, 20 to 30 minutes.

6 Unlock and open the pot. Transfer the veal to a carving board; cool for 5 minutes. Slice each piece into a one-bone section. Transfer these to four serving bowls. Skim the fat from the sauce; serve the meat, vegetables, and sauce in bowls.

(continued)

• A breast of veal is a rich (that is, fatty) cut of meat, loaded with collagen and connective tissue—and thus a prime candidate for a pressure cooker. It'll become meltingly tender and make for a hearty meal.

• The flavor palette here is straightforward: just basic herbs for a little aroma and some carrots to sweeten the sauce. If you've never had a breast of veal, this is probably the first recipe to try.

• The portions are hearty. If you've got smaller appetites, you'll get six servings. Take the meat off the bones, chop it into smaller bits, and serve with the sauce and vegetables like a stew.

OSSO BUCO, ITALIAN STYLE

EFFORT: **A LITTLE** • PRESSURE: **HIGH** • TIME UNDER PRESSURE: **35 OR 50 MINUTES** • RELEASE: **NATURAL** • SERVES: **4**

1 tablespoon unsalted butter

1 tablespoon olive oil

Four 12- to 16-ounce osso buco (veal shank slices), each tied around the circumference

1 small yellow onion, chopped

1 medium celery stalk, thinly sliced

1 large fennel bulb, trimmed and chopped

2 teaspoons minced garlic

One 28-ounce can diced tomatoes, drained (about 3½ cups)

1 tablespoon dried oregano

1 teaspoon dried thyme

½ teaspoon ground black pepper

2 bay leaves

½ cup dry, heavy red wine, such as Syrah

Up to ½ cup beef broth

½ teaspoon salt

2 tablespoons canned tomato paste

1 teaspoon balsamic vinegar

1 Melt the butter in the oil in a 6-quart stovetop pressure cooker set over medium heat or in a 6-quart electric pressure cooker turned to the browning function. Add two of the osso buco pieces and brown them on all sides, turning occasionally, about 8 minutes. Transfer these to a large bowl and repeat with the remaining pieces.

2 Add the onion and celery to the pot; cook, stirring often, until the onion turns translucent, about 5 minutes. Add the fennel and garlic; cook for 1 minute, stirring often.

3 Stir in the tomatoes, oregano, thyme, pepper, and bay leaves. Cook until aromatic, less than a minute; then pour in the wine. Scrape up any browned bits in the bottom of the cooker. Pour in ½ cup broth for a stovetop cooker or ¼ cup broth for an electric model. Stir in the salt. Return the meat and any juices to the pot, stacking the osso buco on their sides like tires.

4 Lock the lid onto the cooker.

STOVETOP: Raise the heat to high and bring the pot to high pressure (15 psi). Once this pressure has been reached, reduce the heat as much as possible while maintaining this pressure. Cook for 35 minutes.

················· **OR** ·················

ELECTRIC: Set the machine to cook at high pressure (9–11 psi). Set the machine's timer to cook at high pressure for 50 minutes.

5 Reduce the pressure.

STOVETOP: Set the pot off the heat and let its pressure fall to normal naturally, about 22 minutes.

················· **OR** ·················

ELECTRIC: Turn off the machine or unplug it so it doesn't flip to its keep-warm setting. Let its pressure return to normal naturally, 22 to 28 minutes.

6 Unlock and uncover the pot. Transfer the osso buco to four serving bowls; snip off the twine. Skim the fat from the sauce. Set the stovetop cooker back over medium-high heat or turn the electric cooker to its browning function; bring the sauce to a simmer. Whisk in the tomato paste and vinegar. Simmer until the sauce is as thick as a loose pasta sauce, about 5 minutes, whisking often. Ladle the sauce over the servings in the bowls.

TESTERS' NOTES

• There may be no more classic veal dish than this Italian favorite, here given a fairly traditional preparation.

• Add pancetta at the beginning if you like: fry 4 ounces diced pancetta in the cooker before you brown the meat, transferring the little bits to a large bowl. Get them back in the pot with the osso buco before locking the lid in place.

• To tie, wrap a piece of butcher's twine around the circumference of each piece of osso buco. Some may come already tied for you.

• Want to take this dish further? Nix the beef broth and use veal stock, available at some high-end markets.

OSSO BUCO, GERMAN STYLE

EFFORT: **A LITTLE** • PRESSURE: **HIGH** • TIME UNDER PRESSURE: **35 OR 50 MINUTES** • RELEASE: **NATURAL** • SERVES: **4**

6 ounces slab bacon, diced

Four 12- to 14-ounce osso buco (veal shank slices), each tied around the circumference

1 medium yellow onion, chopped

1 small red cabbage, cored and shredded (about 4 cups)

1 tablespoon Dijon mustard

1 tablespoon Worcestershire sauce

1 teaspoon caraway seeds

1/2 teaspoon ground allspice

1/2 teaspoon ground black pepper

Up to 1 1/4 cups beef broth

2 teaspoons potato starch or cornstarch

2 teaspoons red wine vinegar

1 Put the bacon in a 6-quart stovetop pressure cooker set over medium heat or a 6-quart electric pressure cooker turned to the browning function. Fry until crisp, about 6 minutes. Use a slotted spoon to transfer the bacon to a large bowl.

2 Add two of the osso buco pieces to the cooker; brown on all sides, about 8 minutes. Transfer them to the bacon bowl and repeat with the remaining shanks.

3 Add the onion to the pot; cook, stirring often, just until softened, about 3 minutes. Add the cabbage; toss constantly over the heat until wilted, 3 to 4 minutes. Stir in the mustard, Worcestershire sauce, caraway seeds, allspice, and pepper; cook for about 1 minute, just until fragrant.

4 Pour 1 1/4 cups broth into the stovetop cooker or 1 cup broth into an electric cooker. Nestle the osso buco and bacon into the cabbage and sauce, stacking the veal rounds on their sides like tires; pour any juices in the bowl over the ingredients.

5 Lock the lid onto the pot.

STOVETOP: Raise the heat to high and bring the pot to high pressure (15 psi). Once this pressure has been reached, reduce the heat as much as possible while maintaining this pressure. Cook for 35 minutes.

············· **OR** ·············

ELECTRIC: Set the machine to cook at high pressure (9–11 psi). Set the machine's timer to cook at this pressure for 50 minutes.

(continued)

6 Reduce the pressure.

STOVETOP: Set the pot off the heat and let its pressure fall to normal naturally, about 22 minutes.

·················· **OR** ··················

ELECTRIC: Turn off the machine or unplug it so it doesn't flip to its keep-warm setting. Let its pressure return to normal naturally, 22 to 28 minutes.

7 Unlock and open the pot. Transfer the osso buco to four serving bowls; cut off the twine. Use a flatware spoon to skim any surface fat off the sauce.

8 Set the stovetop pot over medium-high heat or turn the electric pot to its brown setting; bring the sauce to a simmer. Whisk the potato starch or cornstarch into the vinegar in a small bowl until smooth; then stir the mixture into the sauce with a fork, continuing to stir for about 1 minute, until thickened. Ladle the sauce over the osso buco.

TESTERS' NOTES

• Although osso buco is most often an Italian dish, there's no reason we have to stand on ceremony. So here's a hybrid: a spicy, German-inspired palette to highlight the naturally sweet flavor of the veal.
• To keep the osso buco hot while you prepare the sauce, warm the serving bowls for about 20 minutes in a 175°F or 200°F oven before you set the meat in them.

OSSO BUCO, NORTH AFRICAN STYLE

EFFORT: **A LITTLE** • PRESSURE: **HIGH** • TIME UNDER PRESSURE: **35 OR 50 MINUTES** • RELEASE: **NATURAL** • SERVES: **4**

2 tablespoons olive oil
2 tablespoons finely grated lemon zest
2 tablespoons minced garlic

1 tablespoon dried savory
¹/₂ teaspoon salt
Four 1-pound veal osso buco (veal shank slices), each tied around the circumference
2 tablespoons unsalted butter
1 large yellow onion, halved and sliced into very thin half-moons
¹/₂ teaspoon ground ginger
¹/₂ teaspoon ground cardamom
¹/₂ teaspoon ground allspice
¹/₄ teaspoon grated nutmeg
¹/₄ teaspoon ground turmeric
1 cup fairly light white wine, such as Chenin Blanc
One 14-ounce can diced tomatoes (about 1³/₄ cups)
One 4-inch cinnamon stick
1 medium lemon, cut into quarters and the seeds removed

1 Mix the olive oil, lemon zest, garlic, savory, and salt in a small bowl; rub the paste into the osso buco. Set the meat on a plate, cover with plastic wrap, and refrigerate for at least 4 hours or up to 8 hours.

2 Melt the butter in a 6-quart stovetop pressure cooker set over medium heat or in a 6-quart electric pressure cooker turned to the browning function. Add two veal shanks and brown on all sides, turning occasionally, about 8 minutes. Transfer to a plate and repeat with the remaining two shanks.

3 Add the onion to the cooker; cook, stirring often, until softened, about 4 minutes. Stir in the ginger, cardamom, allspice, nutmeg, and turmeric; cook until aromatic, stirring all the while, about half a minute. Pour in the wine and scrape up any browned bits in the pot as the mixture comes to a boil.

4 Stir in the tomatoes, then return the osso buco and their juices to the cooker, stacking the pieces of meat on their sides. Tuck in the cinnamon stick and lemon quarters.

5 Lock the lid onto the pot.

STOVETOP: Raise the heat to high and bring the pot to high pressure (15 psi). Once this pressure has been reached, reduce the heat as much as possible while maintaining this pressure. Cook for 35 minutes.

·······················OR·······················

ELECTRIC: Set the machine to cook at high pressure (9–11 psi). Set the timer to cook at this pressure for 50 minutes.

6 Reduce the pressure.

STOVETOP: Set the pot off the heat and let its pressure fall to normal naturally, about 22 minutes.

·······················OR·······················

ELECTRIC: Turn off the machine or unplug it so it doesn't flip to its keep-warm setting. Let its pressure return to normal naturally, 22 to 28 minutes.

7 Unlock and open the pot. Transfer the osso buco to serving bowls; cut off the twine. Discard the cinnamon stick. Skim the surface fat from the sauce and ladle the sauce around the shanks.

TESTERS' NOTES

• Although you're not likely to find osso buco in Tunisia, this recipe mimics the spice blends in tagines found in that North African country. It's rich but surprisingly light, thanks to all the lemon in the sauce. Those lemon wedges are perfectly edible, rind and all, after so long under high pressure.

• For the most flavor, scrape any bits of oil and zest into the cooker from the plate that held the osso buco while the pieces marinated in the fridge.

Serve It Up! Serve these shanks over cooked Israeli couscous.

BRAISED RABBIT WITH FENNEL AND OLIVES

EFFORT: **A LITTLE** · PRESSURE: **HIGH** · TIME UNDER PRESSURE: **15 OR 22 MINUTES** · RELEASE: **NATURAL** · SERVES: **6**

2 tablespoons olive oil

One 6-ounce pancetta chunk, chopped

One 3-pound rabbit, cut into 8 or 9 pieces, or 3 pounds rabbit hind legs

1 large fennel bulb, trimmed and chopped

1 medium yellow onion, chopped

2 tablespoons packed fresh oregano leaves, minced

2 teaspoons minced garlic

2 teaspoons finely grated lemon zest

1 cup moderately dry white wine, such as Chenin Blanc

1/2 cup green olives, preferably picholine

1/2 cup chicken broth

1 1/2 tablespoons all-purpose flour

1 Heat the oil in a 6-quart stovetop pressure cooker set over medium heat or in a 6-quart electric pressure cooker turned to the browning function. Add the pancetta; fry until crisp, about 8 minutes, stirring occasionally. Use a slotted spoon to transfer the pancetta to a large bowl.

2 Add the rabbit to the pot, as many pieces as will fit without crowding. Brown on both sides, turning once, about 5 minutes. Transfer those pieces to the bowl with the pancetta and continue browning as necessary.

3 Add the fennel and onion to the pot; cook, stirring often, until the onion has softened, about 5 minutes. Stir in the oregano, garlic, and lemon zest; cook for just under a minute,

(continued)

until aromatic. Pour in the wine and scrape up any browned bits in the bottom of the pot.

4 Nestle the olives, rabbit pieces, and pancetta into the sauce; pour any juices in that bowl into the pot. Whisk the broth and flour in the empty bowl until smooth, then pour the mixture into the pot.

5 Lock the lid onto the cooker.

STOVETOP: Raise the heat to high and bring the pot to high pressure (15 psi). Once this pressure has been reached, reduce the heat as much as possible while maintaining this pressure. Cook for 15 minutes.

·······················**OR**·····························

ELECTRIC: Set the machine to cook at high pressure (9–11 psi). Set the machine's timer to cook at high pressure for 22 minutes.

6 Reduce the pressure.

STOVETOP: Set the pot off the heat and let its pressure return to normal naturally, about 10 minutes.

·······················**OR**·····························

ELECTRIC: Turn off the machine or unplug it so it doesn't jump to its keep-warm setting. Let its pressure fall to normal naturally, 10 to 15 minutes.

If the pressure hasn't returned to normal within 15 minutes, use the quick-release method to bring it to normal.

7 Unlock and open the pot. Transfer the rabbit pieces to serving bowls; stir the sauce well before ladling it over the meat.

TESTERS' NOTES
• Rabbit is an incredibly sweet and mild meat, like a cross between white meat chicken and pork tenderloin. Use extra care with the timings here—rabbit is low enough in fat that it's easily overcooked. Yes, you should brown it

a bit for color and flavor, but you don't want to turn the sauce too dark.
• Picholine olives are almost never pitted. Those pits will, in fact, add a subtle bitterness to the otherwise sweet sauce, about the way the cherry pits do in a classic clafouti. Warn everyone about the pits.
• Rabbit anatomy is difficult to learn. Ask the butcher at your supermarket to cut the rabbit into the required pieces for you.
• You can use 1 cup chopped celery in lieu of the fennel.

RABBIT LEGS WITH PRUNES AND PORT

EFFORT: **A LITTLE** • PRESSURE: **HIGH** • TIME UNDER PRESSURE: **15 OR 22 MINUTES** • RELEASE: **NATURAL** • SERVES: **6**

1/2 **cup chicken broth**
1 1/2 **tablespoons all-purpose flour**
3 thin strips of bacon
6 rabbit hind legs
1 large yellow onion, chopped
1 large carrot, chopped
2 teaspoons minced garlic
3 fresh thyme sprigs
1 bay leaf
3/4 **cup non-vintage ruby port**
12 pitted prunes
1 tablespoon packed dark brown sugar

1 Whisk the broth and flour in a small bowl until the flour dissolves.

2 Lay the bacon in a 6-quart pressure cooker set over medium heat or in a 6-quart electric pressure cooker turned to the browning function; fry until very crisp, turning once or twice, about 5 minutes. Transfer the bacon to a large plate.

3 Brown half the rabbit legs in the bacon fat, turning once, about 5 minutes. Transfer to the plate with the bacon and repeat with the remaining legs.

4 Add the onion and carrot; cook, stirring often, until the onion softens, about 4 minutes. Stir in the garlic, thyme sprigs, and bay leaf; cook until aromatic, less than a minute. Pour in the port and scrape up any browned bits on the pot's bottom while it comes to a simmer.

5 Whisk the broth mixture one more time to combine, pour it into the pot, and stir well. Crumble the bacon into the sauce; return the rabbit and its juices to the sauce. Scatter the prunes into the cooker and sprinkle the brown sugar over everything.

6 Lock the lid onto the pot.

STOVETOP: Raise the heat to high and bring the pot to high pressure (15 psi). Once this pressure has been reached, reduce the heat as much as possible while maintaining this pressure. Cook for 15 minutes.

·························· **OR** ··························

ELECTRIC: Set the machine to cook at high pressure (9–11 psi). Set the machine's timer to cook at high pressure for 22 minutes.

7 Reduce the pressure.

STOVETOP: Set the pot off the heat and let its pressure fall to normal naturally, about 10 minutes.

·························· **OR** ··························

ELECTRIC: Turn off the machine or unplug it so it doesn't flip to its keep-warm setting. Let its pressure return to normal naturally, 10 to 15 minutes.

If the pressure hasn't returned to normal within 15 minutes, use the quick-release method to bring it to normal.

8 Unlock and open the pot. Discard the thyme sprigs and bay leaf. Transfer the rabbit legs to serving bowls; spoon the vegetables and sauce around them.

TESTERS' NOTES

• Many larger supermarkets in North America carry rabbit legs in the freezer case. They're always the meatier hind legs. If you can't find them, use one 3- to 3½-pound rabbit, cleaned and cut into 8 or 9 pieces. Since rabbit anatomy is so difficult to master, it's best to ask the butcher to cut the rabbit into pieces for you.

• The brown sugar shouldn't be stirred into the sauce. Rather, sprinkling it on top will let it caramelize under pressure, providing bits of flavor throughout.

• Since there's no skin on the rabbit, the meat can tear when seared in fat if turned too quickly. You must leave the pieces alone—don't be tempted to turn them too soon. They'll brown nicely, the natural sugars caramelizing until the meat can be popped off the hot surface with minimal tearing. If you find the meat is still tearing, add a little more fat and increase the heat, if possible.

• If you're concerned about the sauce being too sweet, use a salty, double-smoked bacon for even more counterweight among the flavors.

POULTRY

THINK OF PRESSURE COOKERS AS THE MANHATTAN OF APPLIANCES: glamorous (the best chefs use them!), fast, and crowded. Indeed, space is at a premium. So our poultry chapter is full of chicken pieces. Sure, we have a couple of recipes for whole game hens and even one for a whole chicken. But for the most part, we're talking about cooking legs, thighs, wings, and breasts.

Actually, that's the good news. Since we're working with parts, we can also work with the bones in ways we couldn't with many beef and pork recipes. Poultry bones, by and large, are smaller and more flexible. We don't have to use boneless cuts (although we will on occasion). Once we get the bones in the mix, we can then let the pressure do its best work: infuse that intense flavor into the meat.

Many pressure cooker mavens insist on removing the skin from poultry before it's cooked. We disagree. The skin adds flavor, even if you don't intend to eat it after cooking. (It does such amazing things for the sauce!) That skin also protects the meat under pressure, keeping it moist and tender while firm. Finally, the skin can be a delight at the table if—and it's the most important *if*—it's well browned before undergoing pressure or (more rarely) crisped under a broiler afterward.

There's been a lot about salmonella in the news lately and some of it bears restating: poultry must be cooked to an internal temperature of 165°F. There should be no problem with braises or casseroles in which the meat cooks far more intensely than it would, say, on a grill. But if you have any doubt, insert an instant-read meat thermometer into the meat without touching the bone. If the temperature is just a couple of degrees short of the desired mark, set the lid on the pot and set it aside for a couple of minutes. The other ingredients will continue to warm the meat. If it's more than just a few degrees shy of 165°F, lock the lid back onto the cooker and bring it back to high pressure; cook for 1 minute, then use a quick release to open the pot.

Before you start, remember that bad pests are not controlled through rinsing. You're likely to splash contaminated droplets across your work surfaces or onto the faucet. Bacteria are killed by heat, not water. For the best browning, blot a piece of poultry dry with paper towels and get it right into the hot oil or fat in the pot, then cook it to the right temperature. Afterward, wash cutting boards, knives, other utensils, and your hands with hot, soapy water.

And one more thing: if you thaw poultry, you're not obligated to eat it. As long as the thawed meat has sat in a 40°F refrigerator for no more than 1 day, you can refreeze it at will. The chicken will be a bit softer, even spongier, when you thaw it a second time (darn ice crystals), but a pressure cooker braise will turn it into a great dinner in no time.

Yes, we know you'll spend more time with the chicken here than the other birds, but we do hope you'll consider turkey, game hen, and duck. After all, birds of all feathers make excellent meals. And with our supermarkets as stocked as they are, there's no point in not taking advantage of the abundance.

Chicken

These are some of the simplest recipes in the book. No fenugreek here!
Advertising claims notwithstanding, chicken is what's for dinner so very often. It's fast, flavorful, and economical. But let's face it: we all need ideas to spice it up.

While there are a lot of recipes with dark meat (thighs, drumsticks, and leg quarters), we've also got chicken breast ideas aplenty, mostly because the pressure cooker lets us (1) cook cut-up chicken breasts pretty quickly if bathed in a sauce, or (2) bury whole boneless skinless breasts in a salt-seasoned broth, almost brining the meat as it cooks.

Given that emphasis on sauces throughout this section, watch out for chicken that has been pumped "with a solution"—or even kosher chicken, for that matter. Both are sodium-laced. Read those labels. You can certainly use these "enhanced" bits in these recipes, but you'll want to cut out any salt we recommend.

If you're lucky enough to find pasture-raised chickens at a local farmers' market, increase the cooking time under pressure by 10 percent for white meat or 25 percent for dark meat. Pasture-raised chicken means not just "free-range" but also genuinely raised in a pasture. Yes, it's more flavorful, but it also needs a boost to get tender.

There is one thing missing: ground chicken. We found that it developed an unappealing rubbery texture under pressure unless we larded it with way too much fat. In the end, we settled for whole cuts. You also won't find any specific recipes for chicken sausage. If that's what you've got on the counter, feel free to substitute it for turkey sausage in any of those recipes in the next section of this chapter.

But before you turn the page to the turkey recipes, there's still chicken to consider. And lots of it, thighs to wings. We've even got a way to braise a whole chicken in the pressure cooker. Simple but satisfying, familiar but new dinners await. Let's get cooking.

BEER-BRAISED CHICKEN TACOS

EFFORT: **A LITTLE** • PRESSURE: **HIGH** • TIME UNDER PRESSURE:
12 OR 18 MINUTES • RELEASE: **QUICK** • SERVES: **6 TO 8**

2 tablespoons olive oil

2 pounds boneless skinless chicken
   thighs, trimmed

1 small yellow onion, chopped

2 Roma (plum) tomatoes, chopped

1 tablespoon loosely packed fresh
   oregano leaves, chopped

1 tablespoon minced garlic

Up to 1 tablespoon pickled jalapeño rings,
   chopped

One 12-ounce bottle amber beer,
   preferably a Pilsner or an IPA

One 4½-ounce can chopped mild green
   chiles (about ½ cup)

One 4-inch cinnamon stick

12 corn tortillas

1 Heat the oil in a 6-quart stovetop pressure cooker set over medium heat or in a 6-quart electric pressure cooker turned to the browning function. Add half the chicken pieces and brown thoroughly, turning occasionally, about 6 minutes. Use a slotted spoon to transfer the meat to a large bowl. Repeat with the remainder of the chicken.

2 Add the onion to the cooker; cook, stirring frequently, for a couple of minutes to soften the onion; then stir in the tomatoes, oregano, garlic, and jalapeño. Cook for 1 minute to break down the tomatoes a bit, then pour in the beer and stir until the foaming stops. Add the chiles and cinnamon stick; return the thighs and any juices in their bowl to the pot, and stir well.

3 Lock the lid onto the cooker.

STOVETOP: Raise the heat to high and bring the pot to high pressure (15 psi). Once this pressure has been reached, reduce the heat as much as possible while maintaining this pressure. Cook for 12 minutes.

······························ **OR** ······························

ELECTRIC: Set the machine to cook at high pressure (9–11 psi). Set the machine's timer to cook at high pressure for 18 minutes.

4 Use the quick-release method to bring the pot's pressure back to normal.

5 Unlock and open the pot. Discard the cinnamon stick. Set the stovetop model over medium heat or turn the electric model to the browning or simmer function; bring the mixture to a full simmer. Cook, stirring frequently, until thickened and saucy, not soupy, 2 to 5 minutes, depending on the heat source. Use a wooden spoon to break the chicken into clumps. Transfer to a large serving bowl and serve with the tortillas on the side.

TESTERS' NOTES

• If you've got a crowd for football this weekend, you need a pot of this taco meat. Start cooking at halftime and it'll be ready by the time third quarter gets under way.

• You might not be used to cinnamon in the mix, but it's a traditional ingredient in Mexican cooking. Its gentle warmth perks up the tomatoes and balances the spikier heat of the jalapeños.

• Don't forget that pressure cookers eat capsaicin, the fiery chemical in chiles. If you like spicy food, pass more pickled jalapeños at the table—or even jalapeño relish.

• If desired, warm the tortillas by wrapping them tightly in an aluminum foil packet and setting them in a 350°F oven for 15 minutes while you make the taco filling.

Serve It Up! You'll want the usual suspects: salsa, pico de gallo, sour cream, and/or shredded Monterey Jack, as well as chopped iceberg lettuce, diced tomato, and thinly sliced red onion.

CHERRY CHIPOTLE PULLED CHICKEN

EFFORT: **NOT MUCH** • PRESSURE: **HIGH** • TIME UNDER PRESSURE: **15 OR 22 MINUTES** • RELEASE: **QUICK** • SERVES: **6**

One 28-ounce can whole tomatoes, drained (about 3½ cups)

1 cup sour cherry jam

¼ cup packed dark brown sugar

2 tablespoons red wine vinegar

Up to 1 canned chipotle in adobo sauce, stemmed, seeded, and minced

1½ tablespoons smoked paprika

1 tablespoon Worcestershire sauce

1 teaspoon ground cumin

¼ teaspoon ground cinnamon

¼ teaspoon ground cloves

3 pounds boneless skinless chicken thighs, trimmed

¼ cup raisins

1 Place the tomatoes, jam, brown sugar, vinegar, chipotle, smoked paprika, Worcestershire sauce, cumin, cinnamon, and cloves in a large blender. Cover and blend until smooth, stopping the machine at least once to scrape down the inside of the canister.

2 Pour the sauce into a 6-quart stovetop or electric pressure cooker. Stir in the thighs and raisins.

3 Lock the lid onto the pot.

STOVETOP: Set the pot over high heat and bring it to high pressure (15 psi). Once this pressure has been reached, reduce the heat as much as possible while maintaining this pressure. Cook for 15 minutes.

························· OR ·····························

ELECTRIC: Set the machine to cook at high pressure (9–11 psi). Set the machine's timer to cook at high pressure for 22 minutes.

4 Use the quick-release method to return the pot's pressure to normal.

5 Unlock and open the pot. Use two forks to shred the chicken in the pot, stirring it into the sauce before serving.

TESTERS' NOTES

• This isn't your average pulled chicken! The cherry jam and smoky chile combine to make this a bold mix of sweet, savory, salty, sour, and spicy.

• We leave the chicken thighs under pressure longer so they become extraordinarily tender, almost falling apart.

• Remove any globs of fat that adhere to the meat. While some fat adds flavor, too much weighs down the sauce.

• Although there's plenty of heat around the seeds of a canned chipotle in adobo sauce, we prefer to seed the chile but use more of the flesh for a bolder flavor, more earthy and sour notes, rather than just a spike of heat.

• For more cherry flavor, substitute dried cherries for the raisins.

Serve It Up! Serve on buns with plenty of pickle relish on the side. Or try it in whole wheat pita pockets with chopped lettuce and tomato, dressed with a little creamy Ranch or blue cheese dressing.

BALSAMIC AND ORANGE-GLAZED CHICKEN THIGHS

EFFORT: **NOT MUCH** • PRESSURE: **HIGH** • TIME UNDER PRESSURE:
10 OR 15 MINUTES • RELEASE: **QUICK** • SERVES: **4 TO 6**

1/4 cup orange marmalade

3 tablespoons balsamic vinegar

2 tablespoons olive oil

2 pounds boneless skinless chicken
     thighs, trimmed

1/2 teaspoon salt

1/2 teaspoon ground black pepper

One 4-inch fresh rosemary sprig

Up to 4 medium scallions, green and
     white parts, thinly sliced

1 Use a fork to whisk the marmalade and
vinegar in a small bowl until as smooth as
possible; set aside.

2 Heat the oil in a 6-quart stovetop pressure
cooker set over medium heat or in a 6-quart
electric pressure cooker turned to the
browning function. Season the chicken with
salt and pepper, then add half to the pot and
brown well, turning once, about 6 minutes.
Transfer to a bowl and repeat with the remaining chicken. Once everything is cooked,
return all the pieces to the pot.

3 Pour the marmalade mixture over the
meat; tuck in the rosemary sprig.

4 Lock the lid onto the cooker.

STOVETOP: Raise the heat to high and bring the
pot to high pressure (15 psi). Once this pressure
has been reached, reduce the heat as much as possible while maintaining this pressure. Cook for
10 minutes.

························· **OR** ·························

ELECTRIC: Set the machine to cook at high pressure (9–11 psi). Set the machine's timer to cook at
high pressure for 15 minutes.

5 Use the quick-release method to bring the
pot's pressure back to normal.

6 Unlock and open the pot. Discard the rosemary sprig. Stir well, then sprinkle with the
scallions before serving.

TESTERS' NOTES
• Although it may be new to you, orange and rosemary are
a classic combination, dating back centuries. Here, we've
used a single rosemary sprig to make the flavor a bit more
delicate, a little perfume in the sticky, slightly sour glaze.
• There's no call for an expensive balsamic vinegar here. A
sturdy, standard bottling will work best. But avoid flavored
balsamic vinegars (fig, Meyer lemon) that will unduly complicate the dish.
• Boneless skinless chicken thighs have not only a few
globs of fat but also a bit of hard cartilage where the bone
was attached. Trim off all these hard bits for better texture.

Serve It Up! Spoon the chicken and its
glaze over cooked white rice, particularly a
medium-grain white rice like Arborio.

CHICKEN AND RICE CASSEROLE WITH ARTICHOKES AND TOMATOES

EFFORT: **A LITTLE** • PRESSURE: **HIGH** • TIME UNDER PRESSURE:
10 OR 15 MINUTES • RELEASE: **MODIFIED QUICK** • SERVES: **4 TO 6**

2 tablespoons olive oil

1/2 pound mild or hot Italian sausage, cut
  into 1-inch pieces

6 boneless skinless chicken thighs (about
  1 1/2 pounds), trimmed

1 medium yellow onion, chopped

2 small green bell peppers, stemmed,
  cored, and chopped

2 teaspoons minced garlic

1/2 cup rosé wine, preferably Spanish

One 28-ounce can whole tomatoes,
  drained and roughly chopped (about
  3 1/2 cups)

1 1/4 cups chicken broth

1 cup plus 2 tablespoons long-grain white
  rice, such as white basmati or Texmati

One 9-ounce box frozen artichoke heart
  quarters, thawed (about 2 cups)

2 teaspoons smoked paprika

2 teaspoons dried oregano

1/2 teaspoon salt

1/2 teaspoon ground black pepper

1 Heat the oil in a 6-quart stovetop pressure cooker set over medium heat or in a 6-quart electric pressure cooker turned to the browning function. Add the sausage and cook, turning occasionally, until browned, about 4 minutes. Transfer to a large bowl. Add the chicken and brown well, turning once, about 6 minutes. Transfer to the bowl, too.

2 Add the onion and bell peppers to the pot; cook, stirring often, until the onion is translucent, about 4 minutes. Add the garlic and cook until aromatic, less than a minute. Pour in the wine and bring to a simmer, scraping up the browned bits in the pot. Continue simmering until the wine has reduced to a thick glaze (that is, when you drag a wooden spoon through the liquid, it doesn't immediately flow back in place).

3 Stir in the tomatoes, broth, rice, artichoke hearts, smoked paprika, oregano, salt, and pepper. Return the sausage and chicken to the pot, as well as any juices in their bowl. Stir well, making sure all the rice grains are submerged.

4 Lock the lid onto the cooker.

STOVETOP: Raise the heat to high and bring the pot to high pressure (15 psi). Once this pressure has been reached, reduce the heat as much as possible while maintaining this pressure. Cook for 10 minutes.

······················ **OR** ·······················

ELECTRIC: Set the machine to cook at high pressure (9–11 psi). Set the machine's timer to cook at high pressure for 15 minutes.

5 Use the quick-release method to bring the pot's pressure back to normal, but do not open the cooker. Set the cooker aside for 10 minutes to steam the rice.

6 Unlock and open the pot. Stir gently before serving.

TESTERS' NOTES

• This innovative chicken and rice casserole may be good enough for a dinner party—it's a warm and robust meal that can become spicy with hot Italian sausage.

• The rice should absorb almost all the liquid as it steams. If there's some left in the pot when you open it, set the stovetop model over medium heat or turn the electric one to its browning function to boil off that liquid. As a plus,

the heat will form a brown crust on the rice, considered a delicacy in Spain.
• For an earthier, more elegant taste, substitute dry sherry for the rosé wine.

Serve It Up! For a side salad, slice radishes and avocados; drizzle with olive oil, lime juice, a little salt, and a sprinkling of ground cumin.

CHICKEN AND GREEN CHILE STEW

EFFORT: **NOT MUCH** • PRESSURE: **HIGH** • TIME UNDER PRESSURE: **10 OR 15 MINUTES** • RELEASE: **QUICK** • SERVES: **4 TO 6**

2 tablespoons peanut oil

6 boneless skinless chicken thighs (about 1¹/₂ pounds), trimmed and halved

1 large yellow onion, chopped

Three 4¹/₂-ounce cans chopped mild green chiles (about 1¹/₂ cups)

1 tablespoon minced garlic

¹/₂ tablespoon ground cumin

1 teaspoon dried oregano

2 cups chicken broth

6 small white potatoes (about 1¹/₄ pounds), halved

¹/₄ cup loosely packed fresh cilantro leaves, chopped

1 Heat the oil in a 6-quart pressure cooker set over medium heat or in a 6-quart electric pressure cooker turned to the browning function. Add the chicken and cook until lightly browned, about 6 minutes, stirring occasionally. Transfer the chicken pieces to a large bowl.

2 Add the onion to the pot; cook, stirring often, until softened, about 4 minutes. Stir in the chiles, garlic, cumin, and oregano; cook

until aromatic, less than a minute. Pour in the broth and stir well to get any browned bits up off the bottom of the pot. Return the chicken and any juices to the cooker, add the potatoes, and stir well.

3 Lock the lid onto the pot.

STOVETOP: Raise the heat to high and bring the pot to high pressure (15 psi). Once this pressure has been reached, reduce the heat as much as possible while maintaining this pressure. Cook for 10 minutes.

·············· **OR** ··············

ELECTRIC: Set the machine to cook at high pressure (9–11 psi). Set the machine's timer to cook at high pressure for 15 minutes.

4 Use the quick-release method to bring the pot's pressure back to normal.

5 Unlock and open the pot. Stir in the cilantro before serving.

TESTERS' NOTES
• This easy stew is like chicken braised in salsa verde, a bright, slightly sour dish with simple flavors and a refined finish.
• Increase the heat of the dish by using canned chopped *hot* green chiles. We don't recommend using three cans of them—maybe one can of the hot and two of the mild for a better balance.
• The potatoes must be quite small, about 3½ ounces each.

Serve It Up! Garnish the bowls with handfuls of corn chips and some shredded pepperjack cheese.

CHICKEN AND SAUSAGE STEW

EFFORT: **A LITTLE** · PRESSURE: **HIGH** · TIME UNDER PRESSURE:
10 OR 15 MINUTES · RELEASE: **QUICK** · SERVES: **6**

2 pounds boneless skinless chicken
    thighs, trimmed

1 tablespoon minced garlic

1 teaspoon dried oregano

1 teaspoon finely grated orange zest

1 teaspoon smoked paprika

$^1/_2$ teaspoon fennel seeds

$^1/_2$ teaspoon salt

$^1/_2$ teaspoon ground black pepper

Up to $^1/_2$ teaspoon saffron threads

2 teaspoons olive oil

1 small yellow onion, chopped

1 medium celery stalk, chopped

1 large globe or beefsteak tomato,
    chopped

$^1/_2$ cup dry white wine, such as Pinot
    Grigio

$^1/_2$ cup chicken broth

$^3/_4$ pound smoked pork or turkey sausage,
    such as kielbasa, cut into 2-inch
    pieces

8 small red potatoes, halved

1 Mix the chicken, garlic, oregano, zest, smoked paprika, fennel seeds, salt, pepper, and saffron in a large bowl until the meat is evenly coated in the spices. Cover and refrigerate for 4 to 6 hours.

2 Heat the oil in a 6-quart stovetop pressure cooker set over medium heat or in a 6-quart stovetop pressure cooker turned to the browning function. Add half the chicken thighs and brown well, turning once, about 6 minutes. Transfer to a large, clean bowl and repeat with the remainder of the chicken.

3 Add the onion and celery to the pot; cook, stirring often, until the onion turns translucent, about 4 minutes. Add the tomato and stir just until it begins to break down, about 2 minutes. Pour in the wine and broth; scrape up any browned bits in the bottom of the cooker.

4 Return the chicken to the cooker, adding any juices in the bowl and every last speck of the spices. Nestle the sausage and potatoes into the sauce.

5 Lock the lid onto the cooker.

STOVETOP: Raise the heat to high and bring the pot to high pressure (15 psi). Once this pressure has been reached, reduce the heat as much as possible while maintaining this pressure. Cook at high pressure for 10 minutes.

·················· **OR** ··················

ELECTRIC: Set the machine to cook at high pressure (9–11 psi). Set the machine's timer to cook at high pressure for 15 minutes.

6 Use the quick-release method to bring the pot's pressure back to normal.

7 Unlock and open the pot. Stir well before serving.

TESTERS' NOTES

• Although we marinate the chicken in a wet rub, we then use the pressure cooker to force even more flavor into the meat for this hearty stew.

• The quality of the sausage will directly affect the dish's success. Look for a locally made smoked pork sausage, preferably one that's fairly lean with bold flavors.

• You needn't use all that saffron—even a couple of threads will flavor the stew with a characteristic muskiness. But if you use the whole amount, you'll end up with a much earthier, more sophisticated meal.

Serve It Up! Pile a small handful of baby spinach leaves in each bowl, then ladle the stew on top. Set aside for a minute or two, until the heat of the stew has begun to wilt the spinach leaves.

CHICKEN THIGHS
WITH **PEARS** AND
CRANBERRIES

EFFORT: **NOT MUCH** • PRESSURE: **HIGH** • TIME UNDER PRESSURE: **10 OR 15 MINUTES** • RELEASE: **QUICK** • SERVES: **4 TO 6**

2 tablespoons unsalted butter

2 pounds boneless skinless chicken thighs, trimmed

¹/₂ teaspoon salt

¹/₂ teaspoon ground black pepper

1 medium shallot, chopped

2 large, firm Bosc pears, peeled, cored, and cut into ¹/₂-inch-thick slices

¹/₄ cup dried cranberries

2 tablespoons balsamic vinegar

¹/₂ teaspoon dried dill

²/₃ cup chicken broth

1 Melt the butter in a 6-quart stovetop pressure cooker set over medium heat or in a 6-quart electric pressure cooker turned to the browning function. Season the chicken with salt and pepper, then slip half of the thighs into the pot and brown lightly on both sides, about 4 minutes, turning once. Transfer to a large bowl and repeat with the remainder of the chicken.

2 Add the shallot and pears to the pot; cook, stirring often, until the shallot softens, about 2 minutes. Stir in the cranberries, vinegar, and dill until bubbling. Pour in the broth and stir well. Nestle the chicken into the sauce; add any juice in its bowl.

3 Lock the lid onto the pot.

STOVETOP: Raise the heat to high and bring the pot to high pressure (15 psi). Once this pressure has been reached, reduce the heat as much as possible while maintaining this pressure. Cook for 10 minutes.

············ OR ············

ELECTRIC: Set the machine to cook at high pressure (9–11 psi). Set the machine's timer to cook at high pressure for 15 minutes.

4 Use the quick-release method to drop the pot's pressure to normal.

5 Unlock and open the pot. Stir well before serving.

TESTERS' NOTES
• Adding a little balsamic vinegar to this sauce gives a sour complement to the sweet pears and heightens the flavor of the cranberries, all balanced by the small amount of floral dill.
• You needn't go nuts browning the thighs; the meat should be golden, but don't let the butter burn. You want a simpler, cleaner finish.

Serve It Up! Serve over cooked wild rice.

JAMAICAN-STYLE CHICKEN THIGHS WITH PLANTAINS

EFFORT: **NOT MUCH** • PRESSURE: **HIGH** • TIME UNDER PRESSURE:
10 OR 15 MINUTES • RELEASE: **QUICK** • SERVES: **4 TO 6**

2 pounds boneless skinless chicken
   thighs, trimmed

1 teaspoon dried thyme

½ teaspoon ground allspice

½ teaspoon salt

½ teaspoon ground black pepper

¼ teaspoon grated nutmeg

2 tablespoons peanut oil

Up to 1 medium fresh jalapeño chile,
   stemmed, seeded, and diced

6 medium scallions, green and white
   parts, thinly sliced

1 tablespoon minced fresh ginger

1 tablespoon minced garlic

½ cup chicken broth

2 tablespoons red wine vinegar

2 tablespoons packed dark brown sugar

3 large, very ripe plantains, peeled and
   cut into ½-inch sections

1 Mix the chicken, thyme, allspice, salt, pepper, and nutmeg in a large bowl until the meat is coated in the spices; set aside on the counter for 10 minutes.

2 Heat the oil in a 6-quart stovetop pressure cooker set over medium heat or in a 6-quart electric pressure cooker turned to the browning function. Add the jalapeño, scallions, ginger, and garlic; cook, stirring often, until the scallions soften, about 2 minutes.

3 Add the chicken mixture, scraping every speck of spice into the pot; cook about 4 minutes, stirring occasionally, until lightly browned. Pour in the broth and vinegar; stir in the brown sugar until dissolved. Nestle the plantains into the sauce.

4 Lock the lid onto the pot.

STOVETOP: Raise the heat to high and bring the pot to high pressure (15 psi). Once this pressure has been reached, reduce the heat as much as possible while maintaining this pressure. Cook for 10 minutes.

······················· OR ·······················

ELECTRIC: Set the machine to cook at high pressure (9–11 psi). Set the machine's timer to cook at high pressure for 15 minutes.

5 Use the quick-release method to return the pot's pressure to normal.

6 Unlock and open the pot. Stir well before serving.

TESTERS' NOTES
• This recipe is an easy riff on jerk dishes, with a simplified palette of spices.
• The plantains should be quite ripe, their skins soft with black bits. Otherwise, the vegetable will have a mouth-drying metallic flavor even after cooking.
• Jerk dishes traditionally use habanero chiles, not jalapeños. Substitute one at will, based on your stamina.

Serve It Up! Toss cooked long-grain white rice with lots of unsalted butter and serve it under the stew. (The fat will cut the burn!)

SMOKY RED CURRY CHICKEN THIGHS

EFFORT: **A LITTLE** • PRESSURE: **HIGH** • TIME UNDER PRESSURE:
10 OR 15 MINUTES • RELEASE: **QUICK** • SERVES: **4 TO 6**

1 tablespoon packaged Thai red curry paste

1 tablespoon tomato paste

1 tablespoon minced fresh ginger

1 tablespoon smoked paprika

3 tablespoons canola or vegetable oil

2 medium red onions, halved and sliced
    into thin half-moons

2½ pounds boneless skinless chicken
    thighs, trimmed

¾ cup chicken broth

1½ tablespoons packed light brown sugar

1 Use a fork to mash the red curry paste, tomato paste, ginger, and smoked paprika in a small bowl until you have a thick paste; set aside.

2 Heat the oil in a 6-quart stovetop pressure cooker set over medium heat or in a 6-quart electric pressure cooker turned to the browning function. Add the onions and cook, stirring often, until softened, about 5 minutes.

3 Add the spice paste and cook for 1 minute, stirring all the while. Add the thighs and stir until coated in the red paste. Pour in the broth; stir well.

4 Lock the lid onto the pot.

STOVETOP: Raise the heat to high and bring the pot to high pressure (15 psi). Once this pressure has been reached, reduce the heat as much as possible while maintaining this pressure. Cook for 10 minutes.

···················· **OR** ····················

ELECTRIC: Set the machine to cook at high pressure (9–11 psi). Set the machine's timer to cook at high pressure for 15 minutes.

5 Use the quick-release method to bring the pot's pressure back to normal.

6 Unlock and open the pot. Transfer the thighs to a large serving bowl or serving plates. Set the stovetop model over medium heat or turn the electric model to its browning function. Stir in the brown sugar; bring the sauce to a simmer, stirring often. Cook, stirring often, until reduced by half its original volume, 3 to 5 minutes. Pour the sauce over the chicken to serve.

TESTERS' NOTES

• This curry is surprisingly smoky and loaded with aromatics. Although it appears to be a tomato sauce, there's relatively little tomato. Instead, the red sauce is a sweet and hot combination, a great contrast to the milder chicken.

• Red curry pastes can be fiery, so use less if you're concerned. Look for containers of brands like Mae-Ploy in the international aisle of most large supermarkets.

• Make your own **Red Curry Paste**: Toast 2 dried New Mexican red chiles in a dry skillet until aromatic, then put them in a bowl and cover with boiling water. Soak for 20 minutes, then drain. Place them in a food processor with one 3-inch piece of trimmed lemongrass, 4 quartered garlic cloves, 1 tablespoon finely grated lime zest, 1 teaspoon ground coriander, 1 teaspoon ground cumin, and 1 green cardamom pod. Cover and process until a grainy paste, then scrape into a small bowl or plastic container and store, covered, in the refrigerator for up to 1 week or in the freezer for up to 1 year.

Serve It Up! You'll need cooked short-grain white rice to go underneath the curry. Consider using half coconut milk and half water to cook the rice, for a more aromatic side dish.

TIKKA PULLED CHICKEN

EFFORT: **A LITTLE** • PRESSURE: **HIGH** • TIME UNDER PRESSURE:
12 OR 18 MINUTES • RELEASE: **NATURAL** • SERVES: **6**

1/4 **cup plain regular or low-fat yogurt**

1 **teaspoon ground turmeric**

1 **teaspoon sweet paprika**

1 **teaspoon ground coriander**

1 **teaspoon ground ginger**

1/2 **teaspoon salt**

2 **pounds boneless skinless chicken
    thighs, trimmed**

2 **tablespoons peanut oil**

1 **large yellow onion, chopped**

2 **tablespoons minced fresh ginger**

1 **tablespoon minced garlic**

1 **tablespoon garam masala**

**One 14-ounce can diced tomatoes (about
    1**3/4 **cups)**

1/2 **cup chicken broth**

1/4 **cup loosely packed fresh cilantro
    leaves, chopped**

1 Mix the yogurt, turmeric, paprika, coriander, ground ginger, and salt in a large bowl
until smooth. Add the thighs and toss until
well coated. Cover and refrigerate for at least
1 hour or up to 3 hours, stirring occasionally.

2 Heat the oil in a 6-quart stovetop pressure cooker set over medium heat or in a
6-quart electric pressure cooker turned to
the browning function. Add the onion and
cook, stirring often, until translucent, about
3 minutes. Stir in the fresh ginger, garlic,
and garam masala until aromatic, less than a
minute; then stir in the tomatoes, broth, and
cilantro. Pour the thighs and all their marinade into the cooker; stir well.

3 Lock the lid onto the pot.

STOVETOP: Raise the heat to high and bring the
pot to high pressure (15 psi). Once this pressure
has been reached, reduce the heat as much as possible while maintaining this pressure. Cook for
12 minutes.

···**OR**···

ELECTRIC: Set the machine to cook at high pressure (9–11 psi). Set the machine's timer to cook at
high pressure for 18 minutes.

4 Reduce the pressure.

STOVETOP: Set the pot off the heat and let its
pressure fall to normal naturally, about 12 minutes.

···**OR**···

ELECTRIC: Turn off the machine or unplug it so
it doesn't jump to its keep-warm setting. Let its
pressure come back to normal naturally, 12 to
15 minutes.

If the pressure hasn't returned to normal
within 15 minutes, use the quick-release
method to bring it fully back to normal.

5 Unlock and open the pot. Transfer the
chicken thighs to a cutting board, cool for a
couple of minutes, then slice into thin strips.
Stir back into the sauce before serving.

TESTERS' NOTES

• This recipe is a hybrid: pulled chicken in a yogurt curry.
• Do not substitute Greek yogurt. You'll need the higher
liquid content of regular yogurt for a successful dish.
• The meat should be falling-apart tender when you open
the cooker—thus, the natural (rather than quick) release
method here.
• Instead of the dried spices in the yogurt marinade, you
can use up to 1 tablespoon bottled yellow curry powder.

Serve It Up! Offer warmed pitas on the side
with chopped lettuce, diced tomatoes, minced
cucumber, and a few mint leaves.

CHICKEN RAGÙ

EFFORT: **A LITTLE** • PRESSURE: **HIGH** • TIME UNDER PRESSURE:
5 OR 7 MINUTES • RELEASE: **QUICK** • SERVES: **4 TO 6**

1 tablespoon unsalted butter

2 tablespoons olive oil

One 8-ounce pancetta chunk, chopped

1 medium yellow onion, diced

1 medium carrot, diced

2 pounds boneless skinless chicken
   thighs, trimmed and finely chopped

1/2 cup dry, oaky white wine, such as
   Chardonnay

1 1/2 cups chicken broth

6 tablespoons golden raisins

1/4 cup tomato paste

2 tablespoons loosely packed fresh sage
   leaves, minced

1/2 teaspoon ground cloves

1/2 teaspoon ground black pepper

Up to 1/2 teaspoon grated nutmeg

1 pound dried spaghetti, cooked and
   drained

1 Melt the butter in the oil in a 6-quart
stovetop pressure cooker set over medium
heat or in a 6-quart electric pressure cooker
turned to the browning function. Add the
pancetta, onion, and carrot; cook, stirring often, until the onion softens, about
5 minutes.

2 Add the chicken and cook, stirring occasionally, until it has lost its raw color, about
4 minutes. Pour in the wine and scrape up
any browned bits on the bottom of the pot as
it comes to a simmer. Add the broth, raisins,
tomato paste, sage, cloves, pepper, and nutmeg; stir until the tomato sauce dissolves.

3 Lock the lid onto the pot.

STOVETOP: Raise the heat to high and bring the
pot to high pressure (15 psi). Once this pressure
has been reached, reduce the heat as much as possible while maintaining this pressure. Cook for
5 minutes.

···························· **OR** ····························

ELECTRIC: Set the machine to cook at high pressure (9–11 psi). Set the machine's timer to cook at
high pressure for 7 minutes.

4 Use the quick-release method to bring the
pot's pressure back to normal.

5 Unlock and open the pot. Set the stovetop
cooker over medium heat or turn the electric
cooker to its browning or simmer function.
Bring the sauce to a simmer; cook, stirring
often, until slightly thickened, about 5 minutes. Serve over the cooked spaghetti in bowls.

TESTERS' NOTES

• Here's a light but robust pasta sauce, laced with warm
spices that are balanced by sweet raisins.

• If you're adventurous, reduce the chicken thighs to
1½ pounds and dice ½ pound cleaned chicken gizzards to
add to the remaining thighs. Use a natural release after
cooking, rather than the quick, to assure that the gizzards
are tender (but they'll be chewy in any event).

• This sauce freezes well; store it in the freezer for up to
4 months in sealed 1-cup containers for individual servings over pasta. Save it to make a lasagna with shaved
Parmigiano-Reggiano and sliced fresh mozzarella; drizzle
cream in between the layers of pasta before baking.

Serve It Up! Garnish with chopped toasted
pine nuts.

FRENCH ONION SOUP CHICKEN THIGHS

EFFORT: **A LITTLE** • PRESSURE: **HIGH** • TIME UNDER PRESSURE: **12 OR 18 MINUTES** • RELEASE: **NATURAL** • SERVES: **4 TO 6**

1 tablespoon unsalted butter

1 tablespoon olive oil

8 bone-in, skin-on chicken thighs, trimmed (about 3 pounds total weight)

3 large yellow onions, halved and sliced into thin half-moons (about 4 cups)

1/2 teaspoon sugar

1/2 teaspoon salt

1/2 cup dry white wine, such as Chardonnay

1/2 cup beef broth

2 teaspoons stemmed fresh thyme leaves

1/2 teaspoon ground black pepper

1 cup finely grated Gruyère cheese (about 4 ounces)

1 Melt the butter in the oil in a 6-quart stovetop pressure cooker set over medium heat or in a 6-quart electric pressure cooker turned to the browning function. Add half the chicken thighs and brown well, turning once, about 6 minutes. Transfer to a large bowl and repeat with the remainder of the thighs.

2 Add the onions, sugar, and salt; cook, stirring almost constantly, until golden and sweet, even a little browned, about 20 minutes in the stovetop cooker or 12 minutes in the electric model.

3 Pour in the wine and scrape up all the browned bits on the bottom of the pot. Stir in the broth, thyme, and pepper. Return the chicken thighs and any juices in the bowl to the cooker. Stir well.

4 Lock the lid onto the pot.

STOVETOP: Raise the heat to high and bring the pot to high pressure (15 psi). Once this pressure has been reached, reduce the heat as much as possible while maintaining this pressure. Cook for 12 minutes.

················· OR ·····················

ELECTRIC: Set the machine to cook at high pressure (9–11 psi). Set the machine's timer to cook at high pressure for 18 minutes.

5 Reduce the pressure.

STOVETOP: Set the pot off the heat and let its pressure fall to normal naturally, about 12 minutes.

················· OR ·····················

ELECTRIC: Turn off the machine or unplug it so it doesn't flip to its keep-warm setting. Let its pressure return to normal naturally, 12 to 15 minutes.

If the pressure has not returned to normal within 15 minutes, use the quick-release method to bring it fully back to normal.

6 Unlock and open the pot. Sprinkle the cheese evenly over the top of the ingredients. Cover loosely and set aside for 5 minutes to melt the cheese. Dish up the chicken by putting the thighs into bowls and ladling the soupy sauce around them.

TESTERS' NOTES
• What could be better than this cross between a classic bistro soup and a classic bistro braise? The thighs swap their natural moisture with the onions to morph into pure comfort food. It's a bit wetter than a sauced braise, more in keeping with the hybrid nature of the dish.
• We keep the skin on the thighs because it adds so much flavor to the dish. If you want a (slightly) healthier meal, remove the skin after cooking. And don't even think of using boneless thighs here—the bone brings way too many savory notes to the sauce!

CLOCKWISE FROM TOP LEFT:
Breakfast Polenta with Pine Nuts
and Honey (*page 26*), Bacony Bread
Pudding (*page 29*), and Sweet
Potato Hash with Turkey Sausage
and Cranberries (*page 35*).

SOUPS

RIGHT: Parsnip Soup with Buttery
Shallots and Pecans *(page 87)*.

BELOW: Asian Beef Soup with Rice
Noodles *(page 48)*.

Wheatberry and Zucchini Soup
(*page 99*).

CLOCKWISE FROM TOP LEFT: Sunday Beef Stew with Sweet Potatoes and Rutabaga (*page 145*), Cheesy Beef and Tortilla Casserole (*page 112*), Stuffed Flank Steak with Bacon and Pickles (*page 125*), and Twice-Cooked Crispy Short Ribs (*page 155*).

OPPOSITE: Herb-Stocked Mini Meatballs with Radiatori (*page 116*).

CLOCKWISE FROM TOP: Chinese-Style Roast Pork *(page 185)*, Pork Loin with Cranberries, Ginger, and Honey *(page 179)*, and Pork Shoulder Chops with Soy Sauce, Maple Syrup, and Carrots *(page 196)*.

Whole-Grain Pork Lettuce Wraps
(page 214).

CLOCKWISE FROM TOP LEFT: Balsamic-and-Orange-Glazed Chicken Thighs (*page 247*), Jamaican-Style Chicken Thighs with Plantains (*page 252*), and Cajun Wings (*page 286*).

OPPOSITE: Chicken and Rice Casserole with Artichokes and Tomatoes (*page 248*).

ABOVE: Chicken and Cashew "Stir-Fry" (*page 281*). RIGHT: Fruit-Stuffed Turkey Breast with White Wine and Honey (*page 312*).

OPPOSITE: Beer-and-Mustard Pulled Turkey (*page 319*).

RIGHT: Clam Rolls (*page 369*).
BELOW: Crab Risotto with Lemon and
Asparagus (*page 371*).

Warm Potato and Green Bean Salad
(*page 398*).

Beet Tabbouleh *(page 431)*.

CLOCKWISE FROM LEFT: Collard Greens in a Spicy
Tomato Sauce (*page 404*), Brown Rice
and Lentils with Caramelized Onions (*page 423*),
and Black Bean and Corn Salad (*page 455*).

CLOCKWISE FROM ABOVE:
Coconut Flan *(page 484)*, White
Chocolate Cheesecake with
Raspberry Sauce *(page 494)*,
and Pineapple Upside-Down
Cake *(page 488)*.

- Beef broth? It's traditional in French onion soup. It adds heft and body, a less velvety finish than chicken broth.
- You can substitute Cheddar (sweeter) or Jarlsberg (milder) for the Gruyère.

Serve It Up! Serve this chicken over sliced baguette rounds, toasted until dark and crunchy.

CHICKEN THIGHS
WITH **RED WINE** AND **CARROTS**

EFFORT: **A LITTLE** • PRESSURE: **HIGH** • TIME UNDER PRESSURE: **12 OR 18 MINUTES** • RELEASE: **NATURAL** • SERVES: **4 TO 6**

¾ cup chicken broth

1½ tablespoons all-purpose flour

4 thin bacon slices, chopped

8 bone-in, skin-on chicken thighs, trimmed (about 3 pounds total weight)

1 medium yellow onion, chopped

4 medium carrots, cut into 1-inch pieces

2 tablespoons packed fresh rosemary leaves, minced

1 tablespoon stemmed fresh thyme leaves

½ teaspoon ground black pepper

¾ cup dry and bold red wine, such as Syrah

1 Whisk the broth and flour in a medium bowl until the flour dissolves; set aside.

2 Place the bacon in a 6-quart stovetop pressure cooker set over medium heat or in a 6-quart electric pressure cooker turned to the browning function. Fry, stirring occasionally, until crisp, about 3 minutes. Use a slotted spoon to transfer the bacon to a big bowl.

3 Add half the thighs skin side down; brown well, turning once, about 6 minutes. Transfer to the bowl with the bacon and repeat with the remainder of the thighs.

4 Drain all but 1 tablespoon fat from the cooker; add the onion and cook, stirring often, until translucent, about 4 minutes. Add the carrots, rosemary, thyme, and pepper; cook, stirring all the while, until aromatic, about 1 minute.

5 Pour in the wine and scrape up any browned bits in the bottom of the pot as it comes to a simmer. Pour in the broth mixture; stir well. Return the chicken, bacon, and any juices in their bowl to the pot.

6 Lock the lid onto the cooker.

STOVETOP: Raise the heat to high and bring the pot to high pressure (15 psi). Once this pressure has been reached, reduce the heat as much as possible while maintaining this pressure. Cook for 12 minutes.

························· **OR** ·························

ELECTRIC: Set the machine to cook at high pressure (9–11 psi). Set the machine's timer to cook at high pressure for 18 minutes.

7 Reduce the pressure.

STOVETOP: Set the pot off the heat and let its pressure fall to normal naturally, about 12 minutes.

························· **OR** ·························

ELECTRIC: Turn off the machine or unplug it so it doesn't flip to its keep-warm setting. Let its pressure return to normal naturally, 12 to 15 minutes.

If the pressure hasn't returned to normal within 15 minutes, use the quick-release method to bring it fully back to normal.

(continued)

8 Unlock and open the pot. Transfer the chicken and carrots to serving plates or a platter; stir the sauce well before ladling over the servings.

TESTERS' NOTES

• There's not much more classic than this red-wine braise for chicken, morphed from an all-afternoon project in the oven to a weeknight dinner with the pressure cooker.

• Make sure you brown the chicken skin well; it shouldn't be golden but should be truly brown with some dark bits mottled across the surface. Doing so will not only burn some flavorful bits onto the bottom of the cooker, it will also give the chicken a better texture after it's undergone pressure.

Serve It Up! Serve over cooked orzo tossed with minced parsley leaves and unsalted butter.

CHICKEN THIGHS WITH OLIVES AND LEMONS

EFFORT: **NOT MUCH** • PRESSURE: **HIGH** • TIME UNDER PRESSURE: **12 OR 18 MINUTES** • RELEASE: **NATURAL** • SERVES: **4 TO 6**

2 tablespoons unsalted butter

8 bone-in, skin-on chicken thighs, trimmed (3 pounds total weight)

1/2 cup pitted black olives, preferably kalamata olives

2 teaspoons minced garlic

Two 1/4-inch-thick lemon slices, seeded and quartered

Two 4-inch fresh rosemary sprigs

2 fresh thyme sprigs

1/4 teaspoon red pepper flakes

1/2 cup dry but light white wine, such as Pinot Grigio

1 Melt the butter in a 6-quart stovetop pressure cooker set over medium heat or in a 6-quart electric pressure cooker turned to the browning function. Add half the thighs skin side down; brown well, turning once, about 6 minutes. Transfer to a large bowl; repeat with the remaining thighs.

2 Add the olives, garlic, lemon, rosemary, thyme, and red pepper flakes; stir for 1 minute. Pour in the wine and scrape up any browned bits in the bottom of the pot. Return the chicken and any juices in its bowl to the pot.

3 Lock the lid onto the cooker.

STOVETOP: Raise the heat to high and bring the pot to high pressure (15 psi). Once this pressure has been reached, reduce the heat as much as possible while maintaining this pressure. Cook for 12 minutes.

········· OR ·········

ELECTRIC: Set the machine to cook at high pressure (9–11 psi). Set the machine's timer to cook at this pressure for 18 minutes.

4 Reduce the pressure.

STOVETOP: Set the pot off the heat and let its pressure fall to normal naturally, about 12 minutes.

········· OR ·········

ELECTRIC: Turn off the machine or unplug it so it doesn't flip to its keep-warm setting. Let its pressure return to normal naturally, 12 to 15 minutes.

If the pressure hasn't returned to normal within 15 minutes, use the quick-release method to bring it fully back to normal.

5 Unlock and open the pot; discard the rosemary and thyme sprigs. Transfer the chicken thighs to plates or a platter; stir the sauce before serving.

TESTERS' NOTES

- Lemons and olives are a classic Mediterranean combo: sour and salty, a great match to the fairly sweet chicken thighs. The balance comes from the sweet heat of the red pepper flakes: we advise you use the full amount—or even double the amount, if you can handle it.
- Kalamata olives are moderately sized black or brown olives, originally from Greece but now grown elsewhere around the world. They are usually preserved in olive oil and have a meaty texture that matches that of the chicken thighs.
- The lemon (even its rind) will soften and almost melt under high pressure. You can eat every bite—and should, the biggest spike of flavor in the dish.

CHICKEN THIGHS WITH FIGS AND CINNAMON

EFFORT: **NOT MUCH** • PRESSURE: **HIGH** • TIME UNDER PRESSURE: **12 OR 18 MINUTES** • RELEASE: **NATURAL** • SERVES: **4 TO 6**

2 tablespoons unsalted butter

8 bone-in, skin-on chicken thighs, trimmed (about 3 pounds total weight)

1/2 teaspoon salt

1/2 teaspoon ground black pepper

1 medium yellow onion, chopped

6 large dried figs, preferably Turkish or Calimyrna, stemmed and halved

1/2 teaspoon ground cinnamon

3/4 cup dry but fruit-forward red wine, such as Zinfandel

1 Melt the butter in a 6-quart stovetop pressure cooker set over medium heat or in a 6-quart electric pressure cooker turned to the browning function. Season the thighs with salt and pepper; brown half of them in the cooker, turning once, about 6 minutes.

Transfer to a large bowl and repeat with the remaining thighs.

2 Add the onion to the pot; cook, stirring often, until translucent, about 3 minutes. Add the figs and cinnamon; stir for 30 seconds. Pour in the wine, then return the chicken and any juices in its bowl to the cooker.

3 Lock the lid onto the pot.

STOVETOP: Raise the heat to high and bring the pot to high pressure (15 psi). Once this pressure has been reached, reduce the heat as much as possible while maintaining this pressure. Cook for 12 minutes.

····· OR ·····

ELECTRIC: Set the machine to cook at high pressure (9–11 psi). Set the machine's timer to cook at high pressure for 18 minutes.

4 Reduce the pressure.

STOVETOP: Set the pot off the heat and let its pressure come back to normal naturally, about 12 minutes.

····· OR ·····

ELECTRIC: Turn off the machine or unplug it so it doesn't flip to its keep-warm setting. Let its pressure return to normal naturally, 12 to 15 minutes.

If the pressure hasn't returned to normal within 15 minutes, use the quick-release method to bring it fully back to normal.

5 Unlock and open the cooker. Transfer the thighs and figs to serving bowls; ladle the sauce on top.

TESTERS' NOTES

- Red wine and figs are a classic combination—but fresh figs dissolve in a pressure cooker. Dried figs hold up better and have a more intense flavor with caramelized notes that pair perfectly with the wine.

(continued)

- The dried figs should be plump and firm, even a bit juicy, not desiccated or broken. The stems should still be pliable and the fruit should have a decidedly sweet aroma.
- The sauce is a little soupy, but we felt thickening it wasn't in the spirit of a weeknight dinner. However, if you want to, transfer the chicken and figs to a large bowl, then bring the remaining sauce to a simmer in the stovetop pot over medium heat or with the electric cooker turned to the browning function. Whisk ½ tablespoon potato starch into ½ tablespoon water until smooth, then add this mixture to the simmering sauce, whisking until thickened, less than a minute. Pour over the chicken and figs.

CHICKEN THIGHS WITH GREEN CHILES, CUMIN, AND GINGER

EFFORT: **NOT MUCH** • PRESSURE: **HIGH** • TIME UNDER PRESSURE: **12 OR 18 MINUTES** • RELEASE: **NATURAL** • SERVES: **4 TO 6**

2 tablespoons olive oil

8 bone-in, skin-on chicken thighs, trimmed (about 3 pounds total weight)

1 teaspoon cumin seeds

1 medium red onion, chopped

3 tablespoons minced crystallized (candied) ginger

1 teaspoon minced garlic

1 pound baby carrots, halved lengthwise

1 cup canned crushed tomatoes

One 4½-ounce can chopped mild green chiles (about ½ cup)

½ cup chicken broth

1 Heat the oil in a 6-quart stovetop pressure cooker set over medium heat or in a 6-quart electric pressure cooker turned to the browning function. Add half the chicken thighs skin side down; brown well, turning once, about 6 minutes, before transferring

to a large bowl. Repeat with the remaining thighs.

2 Add the cumin seeds; toast, stirring often, for 30 seconds. Stir in the onion, ginger, and garlic; cook, stirring often, until aromatic, about 2 minutes. Stir in the carrots, tomatoes, chiles, and broth. Return the chicken and any juice in the bowl to the cooker.

3 Lock the lid onto the pot.

STOVETOP: Raise the heat to high and bring the pot to high pressure (15 psi). Once this pressure has been reached, reduce the heat as much as possible while maintaining this pressure. Cook for 12 minutes.

························ OR ························

ELECTRIC: Set the machine to cook at high pressure (9–11 psi). Set the machine's timer to cook at this pressure for 18 minutes.

4 Reduce the pressure.

STOVETOP: Set the pot off the heat and let its pressure come back to normal naturally, about 12 minutes.

························ OR ························

ELECTRIC: Turn off the machine or unplug it so it doesn't flip to its keep-warm setting. Let its pressure return to normal naturally, 12 to 15 minutes.

If the pressure hasn't returned to normal within 15 minutes, use the quick-release method to bring it fully back to normal.

5 Unlock and open the pot. Transfer the thighs to serving bowls; stir the sauce and ladle lots over each helping.

TESTERS' NOTES
- This unusual weeknight dinner spikes Southwestern flavors with warming ginger, an innovative kick that's balanced by the sweet carrots and tomatoes.

• The toasted cumin seeds add a sophisticated, slightly bitter edge to the sauce. They're ready to go when they start to pop over the heat.

Serve It Up! Make a tossed salad from shredded Brussels sprouts, chopped pecans, and halved cherry tomatoes, dressed with a bottled balsamic vinaigrette.

SOY SAUCE– BRAISED CHICKEN THIGHS

EFFORT: **NOT MUCH** • PRESSURE: **HIGH** • TIME UNDER PRESSURE: **12 OR 18 MINUTES** • RELEASE: **NATURAL** • SERVES: **4 TO 6**

2 tablespoons peanut oil

8 bone-in, skin-on chicken thighs, trimmed (about 3 pounds total weight)

6 medium scallions, green and white parts, thinly sliced

2 tablespoons minced fresh ginger

1 tablespoon minced garlic

3/4 cup chicken broth

1/4 cup mirin

1/4 cup soy sauce

6 medium carrots, halved widthwise

1 tablespoon rice vinegar

1 teaspoon toasted sesame oil

1 Heat the oil in a 6-quart stovetop pressure cooker set over medium heat or in a 6-quart electric pressure cooker turned to the browning function. Add half the chicken and brown lightly, turning once, about 3 minutes in all. Transfer to a large bowl. Repeat with the remaining chicken.

2 Add the scallions, ginger, and garlic; cook, stirring often, until the scallions have softened, about 2 minutes. Pour in the broth, mirin, and soy sauce. Return the chicken and any juices to the pot, turning the meat to coat in the sauce. Stir well and tuck in the carrots.

3 Lock the lid onto the cooker.

STOVETOP: Raise the heat to high and bring to high pressure (15 psi). Once this pressure has been reached, reduce the heat as much as possible while maintaining this pressure. Cook for 12 minutes.

··········· **OR** ···········

ELECTRIC: Set the machine to cook at high pressure (9–11 psi). Set the machine's timer to cook at high pressure for 18 minutes.

4 Reduce the pressure.

STOVETOP: Set the pot off the heat and let its pressure come back to normal naturally, about 12 minutes.

··········· **OR** ···········

ELECTRIC: Turn off the machine or unplug it so it doesn't flip to its keep-warm setting. Let its pressure return to normal naturally, 12 to 15 minutes.

If the pressure hasn't returned to normal within 15 minutes, use the quick-release method to bring it fully back to normal.

5 Unlock and open the pot. Drizzle the vinegar and oil over the top before serving.

TESTERS' NOTES
• This dish is a simplified version of a traditional Japanese home-cooking braise. The soy sauce actually mellows a bit, taking on an earthy, complex flavor under pressure.
• You can substitute 3 tablespoons dry white wine and 1 tablespoon sugar for the mirin.

Serve It Up! Serve this chicken over cooked and drained soba noodles.

CHICKEN DRUMSTICKS IN CREAMY TOMATO GRAVY

EFFORT: **A LITTLE** • PRESSURE: **HIGH** • TIME UNDER PRESSURE:
10 OR 15 MINUTES • RELEASE: **NATURAL** • SERVES: **4 TO 6**

2 tablespoon unsalted butter

8 skin-on chicken drumsticks (about
　3 pounds)

1 large yellow onion, halved and sliced
　into thin half-moons

1 teaspoon dried thyme

1 teaspoon fennel seeds

1/2 teaspoon salt

1/2 teaspoon ground black pepper

One 14-ounce can crushed tomatoes
　(about 1³/₄ cups)

1/4 cup chicken broth

1/4 cup heavy cream

1 Melt the butter in a 6-quart stovetop pressure cooker set over medium heat or in a 6-quart electric pressure cooker turned to the browning function. Add half the drumsticks; brown them well, turning occasionally, about 5 minutes; and transfer them to a large bowl. Repeat with the remaining drumsticks.

2 Add the onion; cook, stirring occasionally, until softened, about 4 minutes. Stir in the thyme, fennel seeds, salt, and pepper until aromatic, about 20 seconds. Pour in the tomatoes and broth, then nestle the drumsticks into the sauce, pouring any juices from their bowl into the cooker.

3 Lock the lid onto the pot.

STOVETOP: Raise the heat to high and bring the pot to high pressure (15 psi). Once this pressure has been reached, reduce the heat as much as possible while maintaining this pressure. Cook for 10 minutes.

···························· **OR** ····························

ELECTRIC: Set the machine to cook at high pressure (9–11 psi). Set the machine's timer to cook at high pressure for 15 minutes.

4 Reduce the pressure.

STOVETOP: Set the pot off the heat and let its pressure come back to normal naturally, about 11 minutes.

···························· **OR** ····························

ELECTRIC: Turn off the machine or unplug it so it doesn't flip to its keep-warm setting. Let its pressure return to normal naturally, 11 to 14 minutes.

5 Unlock and open the pot. Set the stovetop pot over medium heat or turn the electric model to its browning setting so the sauce comes to a bubble. Stir in the cream and simmer for 1 minute to blend the flavors before serving in bowls.

TESTERS' NOTES
• There's not much to do here, other than brown the chicken and soften the onion.
• The fennel seeds will give the dish a bit of German or Italian flavoring. However, if you've got picky eaters, substitute dried oregano (or omit the spice entirely).
• For a kick, add up to 1/2 teaspoon red pepper flakes with the thyme.
• If you want a somewhat lighter dish, substitute half-and-half or evaporated whole milk for the heavy cream.

Serve It Up! Serve steamed or blanched corn on the cob on the side. You can dip it into the sauce with each bite!

SWEET-SPICY-SALTY CHICKEN DRUMSTICKS

EFFORT: **A LITTLE** · PRESSURE: **HIGH** · TIME UNDER PRESSURE:
10 OR 15 MINUTES · RELEASE: **NATURAL** · SERVES: **4 TO 6**

¼ cup chicken broth

3 tablespoons minced garlic

3 tablespoons packed light brown sugar

3 tablespoons soy sauce

2 tablespoons rice vinegar

1 tablespoon minced fresh ginger

1 tablespoon sambal oelek

2 tablespoons peanut oil

8 skin-on chicken drumsticks (about
    3 pounds)

1 Put the broth, garlic, brown sugar, soy sauce, vinegar, ginger, and sambal oelek in a large blender; cover and blend until smooth, stopping the machine at least once to scrape down the inside of the canister.

2 Heat the oil in a 6-quart stovetop pressure cooker set over medium heat or in a 6-quart electric pressure cooker turned to the browning function. Add half the drumsticks; brown well, turning occasionally, about 5 minutes; then transfer to a large bowl. Repeat with the remaining drumsticks.

3 Return the chicken legs to the cooker; pour the spice puree over them. Toss to coat.

4 Lock the lid onto the pot.

STOVETOP: Raise the heat to high and bring the pot to high pressure (15 psi). Once this pressure has been reached, reduce the heat as much as possible while maintaining this pressure. Cook for 10 minutes.

·······OR·······

ELECTRIC: Set the machine to cook at high pressure (9–11 psi). Set the machine's timer to cook at high pressure for 15 minutes.

5 Reduce the pressure.

STOVETOP: Set the pot off the heat and let its pressure come back to normal naturally, about 11 minutes.

·······OR·······

ELECTRIC: Turn off the machine or unplug it so it doesn't flip to its keep-warm setting. Let its pressure return to normal naturally, 11 to 14 minutes.

6 Unlock and open the cooker. Transfer the drumsticks to a serving bowl or platter. Set the stovetop cooker over medium heat or turn the electric model to its browning function; bring the sauce to a boil. Cook, stirring often, until the sauce in the pot has reduced to ¼ cup, about 6 minutes. Pour over the legs to serve.

TESTERS' NOTES

• These drumsticks may well replace the wings for your next afternoon watching the game. Make sure you've got plenty of napkins. That sauce is sticky!

• Be sure to brown the drumsticks well; it's the only way the skin will be edible after cooking under pressure. (Or remove the skin *after* cooking, if desired.)

• Sambal oelek is a vinegary chile sauce from Indonesia. It's available in the international aisle of almost all supermarkets. (You can also use rooster sauce or a thick, red, Asian hot sauce instead.) If you're not used to the heat, use half as much sambal oelek the first time you make these drumsticks. You can always pass more at the table.

• You can substitute 1 tablespoon white wine vinegar and 1 tablespoon water for the rice vinegar.

CHICKEN DRUMSTICKS WITH CHERRY TOMATOES AND BASIL

EFFORT: **NOT MUCH** • PRESSURE: **HIGH** • TIME UNDER PRESSURE: **10 OR 15 MINUTES** • RELEASE: **NATURAL** • SERVES: **4 TO 6**

2 tablespoons olive oil

8 skin-on chicken drumsticks (about 3 pounds total weight)

½ teaspoon salt

½ teaspoon ground black pepper

2 cups halved cherry tomatoes (about 12)

1 teaspoon minced garlic

Up to 1 medium fresh jalapeño chile, stemmed, seeded, and minced

¼ cup chicken broth

¼ cup loosely packed fresh basil leaves, minced

1 Heat the oil in a 6-quart stovetop pressure cooker set over medium heat or in a 6-quart electric pressure cooker turned to the browning function. Season the chicken legs with the salt and pepper, then set half of them in the cooker. Brown well, turning occasionally, about 5 minutes. Transfer to a large bowl, then repeat with the remaining drumsticks.

2 Add the tomatoes, garlic, and jalapeño; stir over the heat for 1 minute, just until the tomatoes soften without breaking down. Pour in the broth; stir in the basil. Scrape up any browned bits on the bottom of the pot. Nestle the drumsticks into the sauce; pour any juice from their bowl into the pot.

3 Lock the lid onto the cooker.

STOVETOP: Raise the heat to high and bring the pot to high pressure (15 psi). Once this pressure has been reached, reduce the heat as much as possible while maintaining this pressure. Cook for 10 minutes.

························ **OR** ························

ELECTRIC: Set the machine to cook at high pressure (9–11 psi). Set the machine's timer to cook at high pressure for 15 minutes.

4 Reduce the pressure.

STOVETOP: Set the pot off the heat and let its pressure come back to normal naturally, about 11 minutes.

························ **OR** ························

ELECTRIC: Turn off the machine or unplug it so it doesn't flip to its keep-warm setting. Let its pressure return to normal naturally, 11 to 14 minutes.

5 Unlock and open the pot. Transfer the drumsticks to serving bowls; stir the sauce and ladle generously over each helping.

TESTERS' NOTES

• Here's a fresh summery recipe for drumsticks. The jalapeño will mellow the sweet notes from the cherry tomatoes and basil, giving you a sophisticated sauce.

• We season the drumsticks before browning them to dry out the skin a bit more. The skin becomes a little firmer and so has less of a chance of becoming gummy in this wetter sauce.

Serve It Up! You can also offer this dish cold for picnics and summer outings. Lay the cooked legs in a 9 x 13-inch baking dish, pour the sauce over them, cover, and refrigerate for up to 3 days.

CHICKEN DRUMSTICKS WITH HONEY AND GARLIC

EFFORT: **A LITTLE** · PRESSURE: **HIGH** · TIME UNDER PRESSURE: **10 OR 15 MINUTES** · RELEASE: **NATURAL** · SERVES: **4 TO 6**

1/2 cup chicken broth

2 tablespoons honey

1 tablespoon molasses

1 tablespoon packed dark brown sugar

1 tablespoon minced garlic

1 tablespoon white wine vinegar

2 tablespoons unsalted butter

8 skin-on chicken drumsticks (about 3 pounds total weight)

1/2 teaspoon salt

1/2 teaspoon ground black pepper

1 Whisk the broth, honey, molasses, brown sugar, garlic, and vinegar in a large bowl until the molasses and brown sugar dissolve; set aside.

2 Melt the butter in a 6-quart stovetop pressure cooker set over medium heat or in a 6-quart electric pressure cooker turned to the browning function. Season the drumsticks with salt and pepper, then slip half of them into the pot. Brown well, turning occasionally, about 5 minutes. Transfer to a second bowl and repeat with the remaining drumsticks.

3 Return the drumsticks to the cooker; pour the broth mixture over them all and toss to coat.

4 Lock the lid onto the pot.

STOVETOP: Raise the heat to high and bring the pot to high pressure (15 psi). Once this pressure has been reached, reduce the heat as much as possible while maintaining this pressure. Cook for 10 minutes.

······ **OR** ······

ELECTRIC: Set the machine to cook at high pressure (9–11 psi). Set the machine's timer to cook at high pressure for 15 minutes.

5 Reduce the pressure.

STOVETOP: Set the pot off the heat and let its pressure come back to normal naturally, about 11 minutes.

······ **OR** ······

ELECTRIC: Turn off the machine or unplug it so it doesn't flip to its keep-warm setting. Let its pressure return to normal naturally, 11 to 14 minutes.

6 Unlock and open the pot. Use kitchen tongs to transfer the drumsticks to a serving platter or serving bowls. Set the stovetop cooker over medium heat or turn the electric model to its browning or simmer function; bring the sauce to a simmer. Cook, stirring often, until the liquid in the pot has reduced to a syrupy glaze, 1 to 3 minutes. Pour over the drumsticks to serve.

TESTERS' NOTES

- If you've got garlic lovers in your crowd, double the amount of garlic here for a real kick.
- We use both honey and molasses because we want a slightly bitter depth in the sweetness.
- For some heat, whisk up to 1/2 teaspoon red pepper flakes into the broth mixture.

BACON-WRAPPED CHICKEN DRUMSTICKS

EFFORT: **A LITTLE** · PRESSURE: **HIGH** · TIME UNDER PRESSURE:
10 OR 15 MINUTES · RELEASE: **NATURAL** · SERVES: **4 TO 6**

**8 chicken drumsticks, skin removed
(about 3 pounds total weight)**

1/2 teaspoon ground black pepper

8 thin bacon slices

1 tablespoon packed fresh rosemary leaves

2 teaspoons minced garlic

1 tablespoon balsamic vinegar

1/2 cup chicken broth

1 Season the drumsticks with the pepper, then spiral-wrap a strip of bacon around each leg, overlapping the bacon slightly as you wind it around the leg. Set half of them in a 6-quart stovetop pressure cooker set over medium heat or in a 6-quart electric pressure cooker turned to the browning function. Brown well, turning occasionally, about 5 minutes. Transfer to a bowl and repeat with the remaining drumsticks.

2 Return the drumsticks to the cooker. Sprinkle with the rosemary and garlic; drizzle with the vinegar. Pour the broth around the legs without knocking off the spices.

3 Lock the lid onto the cooker.

STOVETOP: Raise the heat to high and bring the pot to high pressure (15 psi). Once this pressure has been reached, reduce the heat as much as possible while maintaining this pressure. Cook for 10 minutes.

·······OR·······

ELECTRIC: Set the machine to cook at high pressure (9–11 psi). Set the machine's timer to cook at this pressure for 15 minutes.

4 Reduce the pressure.

STOVETOP: Set the pot off the heat and let its pressure come back to normal naturally, about 11 minutes.

·······OR·······

ELECTRIC: Turn off the machine or unplug it so it doesn't flip to its keep-warm setting. Let its pressure return to normal naturally, 11 to 14 minutes.

5 Unlock and open the cooker. Transfer the legs to serving plates or a platter; stir the sauce well before ladling on top.

TESTERS' NOTES

• We've taken off the skin so that the meat can absorb some of the bacon's flavor.

• To skin a chicken drumstick, hold the narrow end in one hand and grab the skin at the thick end with a paper towel. Pull the skin toward the narrow end, turning the skin inside out as you pull it up the leg. You may have to cut the skin off right at the end of the leg. Or ask the butcher at your supermarket to do the job for you.

• Kitchen tongs are the best tool for turning the legs so the bacon doesn't come undone as they brown.

• For more flavor, use double-smoked or pepper bacon (but not thick-sliced bacon).

SALSA-BRAISED CHICKEN LEG QUARTERS

EFFORT: **A LITTLE** • PRESSURE: **HIGH** • TIME UNDER PRESSURE:
12 OR 18 MINUTES • RELEASE: **NATURAL** • SERVES: **4 TO 6**

2 tablespoons olive oil

4 skin-on chicken leg-and-thigh quarters
  (3–3½ pounds total weight)

One 14-ounce can diced tomatoes (about
  1¾ cups)

½ cup loosely packed fresh cilantro
  leaves, minced

¼ cup fresh lime juice

1 small white onion, minced

Up to 1 medium fresh jalapeño chile,
  stemmed, seeded, and minced

2 teaspoons minced garlic

½ tablespoon ground cumin

½ teaspoon salt

1 Heat the oil in a 6-quart stovetop pressure cooker set over medium heat or in a 6-quart electric pressure cooker turned to the browning function. Add two of the chicken quarters skin side down and brown them well, turning once, about 6 minutes. Transfer to a large bowl and repeat with the remaining quarters.

2 Pour the tomatoes into the pot; stir in the cilantro, lime juice, onion, jalapeño, garlic, cumin, and salt. Stir well, then nestle the chicken quarters into the sauce.

3 Lock the lid onto the pot.

STOVETOP: Raise the heat to high and bring the pot to high pressure (15 psi). Once this pressure has been reached, reduce the heat as much as possible while maintaining this pressure. Cook for 12 minutes.

······················· **OR** ·······················

ELECTRIC: Set the machine to cook at high pressure (9–11 psi). Set the machine's timer to cook at high pressure for 18 minutes.

4 Reduce the pressure.

STOVETOP: Set the pot off the heat and let its pressure come back to normal naturally, about 12 minutes.

······················· **OR** ·······················

ELECTRIC: Turn off the machine or unplug it so it doesn't jump to its keep-warm setting. Let its pressure return to normal naturally, 12 to 15 minutes.

5 Unlock and open the cooker. Serve the quarters in bowls with the sauce on top.

TESTERS' NOTES

• Leg-and-thigh quarters were made for the pressure cooker: dark meat, a bit of fat, and the ability to withstand intense cooking to tenderize them completely. Here, you build a fresh salsa as a sauce for the meat.

• Leg-and-thigh quarters can have blobs of fat hanging from the meat. Trim these before browning them.

• For more flavor, add ½ teaspoon dried oregano with the "salsa" ingredients. For a smoky salsa, add up to 1 teaspoon sweet smoked paprika.

• Mince the onion into ⅛-inch bits. They must melt into the salsa sauce as it cooks.

Serve It Up! Mix cooked long-grain white rice with drained and rinsed canned black beans and corn kernels; use as a bed for the chicken and sauce in the serving bowls.

HERB-BRAISED CHICKEN LEG QUARTERS

EFFORT: **A LITTLE** • PRESSURE: **HIGH** • TIME UNDER PRESSURE:
12 OR 18 MINUTES • RELEASE: **NATURAL** • SERVES: **4 TO 6**

2 tablespoons olive oil

4 skin-on chicken leg-and-thigh quarters
(3–3¹/₂ pounds total weight)

¹/₂ teaspoon salt

¹/₂ teaspoon ground black pepper

1 medium yellow onion, chopped

4 medium celery stalks, cut into 1-inch
pieces

2 teaspoons minced garlic

2 teaspoons loosely packed fresh
oregano leaves, minced

2 teaspoons loosely packed fresh sage
leaves, minced

2 teaspoons stemmed fresh thyme leaves

¹/₂ cup dry but fruit-forward white wine,
such as Sauvignon Blanc

¹/₂ cup chicken broth

1 Heat the oil in a 6-quart stovetop pressure cooker set over medium heat or in a 6-quart electric pressure cooker turned to the browning function. Season the quarters with salt and pepper, then slip two pieces, skin side down, into the pot. Brown well, turning once, about 6 minutes, and transfer to a bowl. Repeat with the remaining quarters.

2 Add the onion and celery to the pot; cook, stirring often, until the onion softens, about 4 minutes. Add the garlic and stir for about 30 seconds. Stir in the oregano, sage, and thyme; pour in the wine and broth. Scrape up any browned bits on the bottom of the cooker, then nestle the chicken quarters into the sauce.

3 Lock the lid onto the pot.

STOVETOP: Raise the heat to high and bring the pot to high pressure (15 psi). Once this pressure has been reached, reduce the heat as much as you can while maintaining this pressure. Cook for 12 minutes.

······································· **OR** ·······································

ELECTRIC: Set the machine to cook at high pressure (9–11 psi). Set the machine's timer to cook at high pressure for 18 minutes.

4 Reduce the pressure.

STOVETOP: Set the pot off the heat and let its pressure come back to normal naturally, about 12 minutes.

······································· **OR** ·······································

ELECTRIC: Turn off the machine or unplug it so it doesn't jump to its keep-warm setting. Let its pressure return to normal naturally, 12 to 15 minutes.

5 Unlock and open the pot. Serve the chicken in bowls with the sauce on top.

TESTERS' NOTES
• Only fresh herbs will have enough flavor to stand up well in this summery sauce.
• If you don't want the skin in the final dish, remove it *after* cooking. (You can also skim the sauce after cooking, but the bits of floating herbs will make the task a tad maddening.)
• We made the servings adjustable in these chicken quarters recipes. We'd each eat a whole quarter; others would split them into two servings each.

Serve It Up! For a side salad, toss halved cherry tomatoes with toasted bread cubes, thinly sliced red onion, and minced basil; dress with a red wine vinaigrette and season with salt.

CRANBERRY AND MAPLE-GLAZED CHICKEN LEG QUARTERS

EFFORT: **A LITTLE** • PRESSURE: **HIGH** • TIME UNDER PRESSURE: **12 OR 18 MINUTES** • RELEASE: **NATURAL** • SERVES: **4 TO 6**

2 tablespoons unsalted butter

4 skin-on chicken leg-and-thigh quarters (3–3¹/₂ pounds total weight)

¹/₂ teaspoon salt

¹/₂ teaspoon ground black pepper

¹/₂ cup canned whole-berry cranberry sauce

¹/₂ cup maple syrup

¹/₄ cup chicken broth

2 teaspoons loosely packed fresh sage leaves, minced

1 Melt the butter in a 6-quart stovetop pressure cooker set over medium heat or in a 6-quart electric pressure cooker turned to the browning mode. Season the chicken with salt and pepper, then set two of the quarters skin side down in the pot. Brown well, turning once, about 6 minutes, leaving them longer on the skin side than the other. Transfer to a large bowl and repeat with the remaining quarters.

2 Stir in the cranberry sauce, maple syrup, broth, and sage until well combined. Slip the chicken quarters back into the pot; pour in any juices from their bowl.

3 Lock the lid onto the cooker.

STOVETOP: Raise the heat to high and bring the pot to high pressure (15 psi). Once this pressure has been reached, reduce the heat as much as possible while maintaining this pressure. Cook for 12 minutes.

······· **OR** ·······

ELECTRIC: Set the machine to cook at high pressure (9–11 psi). Set the machine's timer to cook at high pressure for 18 minutes.

4 Reduce the pressure.

STOVETOP: Set the pot off the heat and let its pressure come back to normal naturally, about 15 minutes.

······· **OR** ·······

ELECTRIC: Turn off the machine or unplug it so it doesn't jump to its keep-warm setting. Let its pressure return to normal naturally, 15 to 18 minutes.

5 Unlock and open the pot. Serve the chicken quarters in bowls with lots of sauce.

TESTERS' NOTES

• The sauce for the dark-meat chicken is a bit thick, a little syrupy, with just notes from the sage to give it a little depth.

• Whole-berry cranberry sauce will give better texture *and* flavor to the sauce in the pot. The standard, smooth jellied cranberry sauce will add nothing but sugar.

• There's no doubt the glaze is sweet. To mellow it a bit, add up to 1 teaspoon finely grated lemon zest and ½ teaspoon red pepper flakes to the cranberry mixture before pouring it into the cooker.

Serve It Up! Serve over steamed collard or turnip greens to balance the sweet of the sauce.

CHICKEN LEG QUARTERS WITH OKRA AND TOMATOES

EFFORT: **A LOT** • PRESSURE: **HIGH** • TIME UNDER PRESSURE: **12 OR 18 MINUTES** • RELEASE: **QUICK, THEN NATURAL** • SERVES: **4 TO 6**

1 tablespoon unsalted butter

1 tablespoon olive oil

4 skin-on chicken leg-and-thigh quarters (3–3½ pounds total weight)

½ teaspoon salt

1 small yellow or white onion, chopped

2 teaspoons minced garlic

1 teaspoon stemmed fresh thyme leaves

1 teaspoon ground cumin

One 14-ounce can diced tomatoes (about 1¾ cups)

½ cup dry white wine, such as Chardonnay

1 pound frozen sliced okra, thawed

1 tablespoon red wine vinegar

Several dashes of bottled hot red pepper sauce, to taste

1 Melt the butter in the oil in a 6-quart stovetop pressure cooker set over medium heat or in a 6-quart electric pressure cooker turned to the browning function. Season the chicken quarters with the salt, then set two of them skin side down in the pot. Brown well, turning once, about 6 minutes; transfer to a large bowl. Repeat with the remaining quarters.

2 Add the onion; cook, stirring often, until translucent, about 3 minutes. Add the garlic, thyme, and cumin; cook about a minute, until aromatic. Stir in the tomatoes and wine; scrape up any browned bits in the bottom of

the cooker. Return the chicken quarters to the pot as well as any juices in their bowl.

3 Lock the lid onto the cooker.

STOVETOP: Raise the heat to high and bring the pot to high pressure (15 psi). Once this pressure has been reached, reduce the heat as much as possible while maintaining this pressure. Cook for 8 minutes.

·············· **OR** ··············

ELECTRIC: Set the machine to cook at high pressure (9–11 psi). Set the machine's timer to cook at high pressure for 12 minutes.

4 Use the quick-release method to bring the pot's pressure back to normal.

5 Unlock and open the cooker. Stir in the okra, vinegar, and hot red pepper sauce.

6 Lock the lid back onto the pot.

STOVETOP: Turn the heat to high and bring the pot back to high pressure (15 psi). Once this pressure has been reached, reduce the heat as much as possible while maintaining this pressure. Cook for 4 minutes.

·············· **OR** ··············

ELECTRIC: Set the machine to cook once again at high pressure (9–11 psi). Set the machine's timer to cook at this pressure for 6 minutes.

7 Reduce the pressure.

STOVETOP: Set the pot off the heat and let its pressure come back to normal naturally, about 8 minutes.

·············· **OR** ··············

ELECTRIC: Turn off the machine or unplug it so it doesn't jump to its keep-warm setting. Let its pressure return to normal naturally, 8 to 10 minutes.

8 Unlock and open the cooker. Serve the chicken quarters and vegetables in bowls with plenty of sauce.

TESTERS' NOTES

• Here's a Southern supper if we've ever heard of one! The chicken is stewed in the tomato sauce until beautifully tender. It's a two-step process because the okra needs less time to get tender.

• Even if you have lots of fresh okra in your garden, slice it up and freeze it before thawing and using in this recipe. Doing so will cut down on its slimy texture when cooked under pressure.

• The cumin is the secret ingredient: a little savory hit that keeps the flavors from becoming too sweet.

CHICKEN LEG QUARTERS WITH ROSEMARY AND GARLIC

EFFORT: **A LITTLE** • PRESSURE: **HIGH** • TIME UNDER PRESSURE: **12 OR 18 MINUTES** • RELEASE: **NATURAL** • SERVES: **4 TO 6**

2 tablespoons olive oil

2 tablespoons loosely packed fresh rosemary leaves, minced

1 tablespoon mild paprika

1 teaspoon salt

$1/2$ teaspoon ground black pepper

4 chicken leg-and-thigh quarters (3–3$1/2$ pounds total weight), skin removed

$3/4$ cup chicken broth

8 medium garlic cloves

1 Make a paste from the olive oil, rosemary, paprika, salt, and pepper by stirring it in a small bowl with a fork. Rub this paste into the quarters.

2 Pour the broth into a 6-quart stovetop or electric pressure cooker; set the quarters in the pot, overlapping only as necessary. Tuck the garlic cloves around the quarters.

3 Lock the lid onto the pot.

STOVETOP: Set the pot over high heat and bring it to high pressure (15 psi). Once this pressure has been reached, reduce the heat as much as possible while maintaining this pressure. Cook for 12 minutes.

························ OR ························

ELECTRIC: Set the machine to cook at high pressure (9–11 psi). Set the machine's timer to cook at high pressure for 18 minutes.

4 Reduce the pressure.

STOVETOP: Set the pot off the heat and let its pressure come back to normal naturally, about 12 minutes.

························ OR ························

ELECTRIC: Turn off the machine or unplug it so it doesn't jump to its keep-warm setting. Let its pressure return to normal naturally, 12 to 15 minutes.

5 Unlock and open the pot. Transfer the chicken to serving plates; stir the sauce and spoon over the meat.

TESTERS' NOTES

• The liquid in this Italian-inspired braise isn't a thickened sauce. If desired, boil it down to half its original volume, whisk in a few tablespoons of butter until smooth, and spoon it over the dish.

• The quarters are skinless so the paste can sit right against the meat. Mince the rosemary into fine bits so the paste will be fairly smooth, without any large bits in it.

Serve It Up! Steam small white potatoes until tender and serve in the bowls with the chicken and sauce.

CHICKEN MAC-AND-CHEESE

EFFORT: **A LITTLE** • PRESSURE: **HIGH** • TIME UNDER PRESSURE: **5 OR 8 MINUTES** • RELEASE: **QUICK** • SERVES: **4**

1 pound boneless skinless chicken breasts, cut into $1/2$-inch pieces

8 ounces dried elbow macaroni

$1^1/_2$ cups half-and-half

1 tablespoon all-purpose flour

2 teaspoons Dijon mustard

$1/2$ teaspoon dried thyme

$1/2$ teaspoon salt

$1/2$ teaspoon ground black pepper

$1^1/_2$ cups shredded Cheddar cheese (about 6 ounces)

1 Combine the chicken and macaroni with 6 cups water in a 6-quart stovetop or electric pressure cooker.

2 Lock the lid onto the pot.

STOVETOP: Set the pot over high heat and bring it to high pressure (15 psi). Once this pressure has been reached, reduce the heat as much as possible while maintaining this pressure. Cook for 5 minutes.

············ OR ············

ELECTRIC: Set the machine to cook at high pressure (9–11 psi). Set the machine's timer to cook at this pressure for 8 minutes.

3 Use the quick-release method to bring the pot's pressure back to normal.

4 Unlock and open the pot. Drain the contents into a large colander set in the sink. Set the stovetop pot back over medium heat or turn the electric pot to its browning setting. Add the half-and-half, flour, mustard, thyme,

salt, and pepper; whisk over the heat until bubbling and thickened, 2 to 3 minutes.

5 Remove the stovetop model from the heat or turn off the electric machine. Add the cooked pasta and chicken, as well as the cheese, stirring until the cheese has melted. Serve at once.

TESTERS' NOTES

• Look no more for a great mac-and-cheese! The creamy sauce is a velvety match to the pasta and the white-meat chicken is about as healthy as you can get. Best of all, there's no canned this or bottled that in the mix: just real food.

• Substitute whole wheat pasta (but not rice pasta) at will. You can also use Gruyère, Emmentaler, Jarlsberg, Colby, or mild American instead of the Cheddar.

Serve It Up! Give each bowlful **Crunchy Breadcrumb Topping:** Melt 4 tablespoons ($1/2$ stick) unsalted butter in a large skillet over medium-low heat; add 1 cup fresh breadcrumbs, $1/2$ teaspoon salt, and $1/4$ teaspoon ground black pepper. Toss over the heat until light brown and crunchy, about 3 minutes. Spoon over the servings.

WARM CHICKEN AND PASTA SALAD WITH SUN-DRIED TOMATO PESTO

EFFORT: **A LITTLE** • PRESSURE: **HIGH** • TIME UNDER PRESSURE: **5 OR 8 MINUTES** • RELEASE: **QUICK** • SERVES: **4**

1 pound boneless skinless chicken breasts, cut into $1/2$-inch pieces

8 ounces dried farfalle (bow-tie) pasta

16 sun-dried tomatoes packed in oil

1 cup loosely packed fresh basil leaves

1/3 cup finely grated Parmesan cheese (about 3/4 ounce)

1/4 cup olive oil

2 tablespoons pine nuts

1 medium garlic clove

1 Mix the chicken and pasta with 6 cups water in a 6-quart stovetop or electric pressure cooker.

2 Lock the lid onto the pot.

STOVETOP: Set the pot over high heat and bring it to high pressure (15 psi). Once this pressure has been reached, reduce the heat as much as possible while maintaining this pressure. Cook for 5 minutes.

························· OR ·························

ELECTRIC: Set the machine to cook at high pressure (9–11 psi). Set the machine's timer to cook at high pressure for 8 minutes.

3 Use the quick-release method to bring the pot's pressure back to normal.

4 Unlock and open the cooker. Drain the contents in a large colander set in the sink. Shake a couple of times to get rid of excess water, then pour into a large serving bowl and set aside.

5 Process the sun-dried tomatoes, basil, cheese, oil, pine nuts, and garlic in a food processor fitted with the chopping blade until smooth, scraping down the inside of the canister at least once. Pour and scrape the mixture over the chicken and pasta; toss well to coat. Serve while warm.

TESTERS' NOTES

• Sun-dried tomatoes packed in oil are often on the salad bar at large supermarkets—you can buy as many as you need without getting a whole jar.

• Although this dish is a main-course pasta salad, there's no reason you couldn't make it ahead and serve it as part of a barbecue extravaganza. Store at room temperature for 2 hours or in the refrigerator, covered, for up to 2 days.

• If you don't have a food processor, make the sun-dried tomato pesto by hand. Place the sun-dried tomatoes, basil, cheese, nuts, and garlic on a large cutting board, then rock a large knife back and forth through them, gathering them together repeatedly until you have a fairly smooth paste. Scrape the paste into a small bowl and stir in the oil in a slow, steady drizzle until you have a wet but cohesive pesto.

CHICKEN, FARFALLE, AND ARTICHOKE HEART SALAD

EFFORT: **A LITTLE** • PRESSURE: **HIGH** • TIME UNDER PRESSURE: **5 OR 8 MINUTES** • RELEASE: **QUICK** • SERVES: **4**

1 pound boneless skinless chicken breasts, cut into 1/2-inch pieces

8 ounces dried farfalle (bow-tie) pasta

2 tablespoons olive oil

1 small red onion, chopped

8 ounces white button mushrooms, thinly sliced

1/2 cup packed marinated artichoke hearts, chopped

1 tablespoon loosely packed fresh rosemary leaves, minced

2 teaspoons stemmed fresh thyme leaves

1/4 cup dry white wine, such as Chardonnay

1/2 cup finely grated Parmesan cheese (about 1 ounce)

1 Place the chicken and pasta with 6 cups water in a 6-quart stovetop or electric pressure cooker.

(continued)

2 Lock the lid onto the pot.

STOVETOP: Set the pot over high heat and bring it to high pressure (15 psi). Once this pressure has been reached, reduce the heat as much as possible while maintaining this pressure. Cook for 5 minutes.

·······················**OR**·······················
ELECTRIC: Set the machine to cook at high pressure (9–11 psi). Set the machine's timer to cook at high pressure for 8 minutes.

3 Use the quick-release method to return the pot's pressure to normal.

4 Unlock and open the cooker. Drain the contents into a large colander set in the sink. Shake to remove excess water.

5 Heat the oil in the stovetop cooker set over medium heat or in the electric cooker turned to the browning mode. Add the onion and cook, stirring often, until translucent, about 3 minutes. Add the mushrooms and continue cooking, stirring once in a while, until they give off their liquid and it evaporates to a glaze, about 5 minutes.

6 Stir in the artichoke hearts, rosemary, and thyme until aromatic, less than a minute. Pour in the wine as well as the cooked chicken and pasta. Toss over the heat until the wine has been almost completely absorbed. Stir in the cheese to serve.

TESTERS' NOTES
• More like a pasta salad than a casserole, this dish will give you the flavors of summer.
• The wine isn't really part of a sauce; instead, it adds necessary moisture to the pasta and other ingredients. There should only be a little of it left in the pot at the very end.
• Since this has the flavors of an antipasto plate, add other antipasti you like: pitted olives, pepperoncini, sliced roasted red peppers, or mozzarella balls.

SOUTHWESTERN CHICKEN AND ZITI

EFFORT: **NOT MUCH** • PRESSURE: **HIGH** • TIME UNDER PRESSURE: **5 OR 8 MINUTES** • RELEASE: **QUICK** • SERVES: **4**

1 pound boneless skinless chicken breasts, cut into 1/2-inch pieces
One 14-ounce can diced tomatoes (about 1 3/4 cups)
1 1/2 cups chicken broth
1 cup drained and rinsed canned pinto beans
8 ounces dried whole wheat ziti
One 4 1/2-ounce can chopped mild green chiles (about 1/2 cup)
1/3 cup loosely packed fresh cilantro leaves, chopped
1 tablespoon chili powder
1 teaspoon ground cumin (optional)
1/2 teaspoon salt
1/2 teaspoon ground black pepper

1 Mix everything in a 6-quart stovetop or electric pressure cooker.

2 Lock the lid onto the pot.

STOVETOP: Set the pot over high heat and bring it to high pressure (15 psi). Once this pressure has been reached, reduce the heat as low as possible while maintaining this pressure. Cook for 5 minutes.

·······················**OR**·······················
ELECTRIC: Set the machine to cook at high pressure (9–11 psi). Set the machine's timer to cook at high pressure for 8 minutes.

3 Use the quick-release method to bring the pot's pressure back to normal.

4 Unlock and open the pot. Stir well before serving.

• This is like chili mac but with chicken. You can even find chicken breasts already cut up for stir-fry; just slice these strips into ½-inch pieces.
• The cilantro may be sandy, so rinse the leaves carefully. If possible, fill a cleaned sink with cool water, add the leaves, agitate a few times, and then let settle for 5 minutes. Lift the leaves out of the water before draining the sink, then blot dry on paper towels.

Serve It Up! Sprinkle shredded Monterey jack and sliced scallions over each bowlful.

CHICKEN AND PASTA IN A SPICY PEANUT SAUCE

EFFORT: **A LITTLE** • PRESSURE: **HIGH** • TIME UNDER PRESSURE: **5 OR 8 MINUTES** • RELEASE: **QUICK** • SERVES: **4**

2 tablespoons peanut oil

1 medium yellow onion, chopped

1 tablespoon minced fresh ginger

2 teaspoons minced garlic

1 pound boneless skinless chicken breasts, cut into ¹/₂-inch cubes

One 14-ounce can diced tomatoes (about 1³/₄ cups)

6 tablespoons creamy natural-style peanut butter

1 tablespoon packed dark brown sugar

¹/₂ teaspoon ground allspice

¹/₂ teaspoon ground cinnamon

¹/₂ teaspoon ground cloves

¹/₂ teaspoon salt

¹/₄ teaspoon cayenne

2¹/₄ cups chicken broth

8 ounces dried whole wheat ziti

1 Heat the oil in a 6-quart stovetop pressure cooker set over medium heat or in a 6-quart electric pressure cooker turned to the browning function. Add the onion, ginger, and garlic; cook until the onion softens, about 3 minutes, stirring often. Add the chicken and cook until it loses its raw color, about 3 minutes, stirring more frequently.

2 Stir in the tomatoes, peanut butter, brown sugar, allspice, cinnamon, cloves, salt, and cayenne until the peanut butter dissolves. Add the broth and pasta; stir well.

3 Lock the lid onto the pot.

STOVETOP: Raise the heat to high and bring the pot to high pressure (15 psi). Once this pressure has been reached, reduce the heat as much as possible while maintaining this pressure. Cook for 5 minutes.

·······**OR**·······

ELECTRIC: Set the machine to cook at high pressure (9–11 psi). Set the machine's timer to cook at high pressure for 8 minutes.

4 Use the quick-release method to bring the pot's pressure to normal.

5 Unlock and open the pot. Stir well before serving in bowls.

TESTERS' NOTES
• Here's a one-pot meal: the chicken and pasta cook in a fragrant, long-way-from-traditional red sauce.
• Peanut butter is like a ready-made sauce with its dark, complex, roasted flavor. You can also use cashew butter (richer) or almond butter (sweeter).
• If you like spicy food, double the cayenne—or pass bottled hot red pepper sauce at the table.

CREAMY CURRIED CHICKEN AND PASTA

EFFORT: **NOT MUCH** • PRESSURE: **HIGH** • TIME UNDER PRESSURE:
5 OR 8 MINUTES • RELEASE: **QUICK** • SERVES: **4**

3 cups chicken broth

2 tablespoons all-purpose flour

2 tablespoons unsalted butter

1 large yellow onion, chopped

2 teaspoons yellow curry powder

4 medium carrots, shredded through the
    large holes of a box grater

8 ounces dried ziti pasta

1 pound boneless skinless chicken
    breasts, cut into 1/2-inch pieces

1/4 cup heavy cream

1 Whisk the broth and flour in a medium bowl until smooth; set aside.

2 Melt the butter in a 6-quart stovetop pressure cooker set over medium heat or in a 6-quart electric pressure cooker turned to the browning function. Add the onion; cook, stirring often, until softened, about 4 minutes. Stir in the curry powder until aromatic, less than a minute. Then stir in the carrots and cook for 1 minute.

3 Pour in the broth mixture. Add the pasta and chicken; stir well

4 Lock the lid onto the pot.

STOVETOP: Raise the heat to high and bring the pot to high pressure (15 psi). Once this pressure has been reached, reduce the heat as much as possible while maintaining this pressure. Cook for 5 minutes.

·························· OR ··························
ELECTRIC: Set the machine to cook at high pressure (9–11 psi). Set the machine's timer to cook at high pressure for 8 minutes.

5 Use the quick-release method to bring the pot's pressure back to normal.

6 Unlock and open the cooker. Stir in the cream. Put the lid loosely on the pot and set aside for 2 minutes to heat through. Serve in bowls.

TESTERS' NOTES

• There's a vast array of yellow curry powders on the market, many far beyond the bottled standard. You can search for endless varieties at East Indian grocery stores or in specialty spice stores.

• Grate the carrots before you start cooking the dish. By the time they're added to the pot, the cooking is moving along too quickly for you to grate them one by one into the cooker.

• We use regular pasta here, not whole wheat, because the slightly sweeter flavor of the regular pasta balances the curry more effectively.

• You can substitute light cream or half-and-half for the heavy cream.

Serve It Up! Dice peeled cucumbers and seeded tomatoes, then toss them with a little rice vinegar or white wine vinegar. Chill for an hour or so, then serve as a cold garnish on top of the still-warm curry.

CHICKEN BREASTS IN A DIJON CREAM SAUCE

EFFORT: **A LITTLE** • PRESSURE: **HIGH** • TIME UNDER PRESSURE:
9 OR 14 MINUTES • RELEASE: **QUICK** • SERVES: **4**

2 tablespoons unsalted butter

**Four 6- to 8-ounce boneless skinless
    chicken breasts**

1/4 teaspoon salt

1/4 teaspoon ground black pepper

1 small yellow onion, chopped

**1/4 cup dry but fruit-forward white wine,
    such as Pinot Gris**

1/2 cup chicken broth

2 tablespoons Dijon mustard

1 teaspoon dried tarragon

1/4 cup heavy cream

1 Melt the butter in a 6-quart stovetop pressure cooker set over medium heat or in a 6-quart electric pressure cooker turned to the browning function. Season the chicken with salt and pepper, then set the breasts in the pot. Brown the meat well, about 4 minutes, turning once. Transfer to a large bowl.

2 Add the onion to the pot; cook, stirring often, until translucent, about 3 minutes. Pour in the wine and scrape up any browned bits in the cooker as the wine comes to a simmer. Stir in the broth, mustard, and tarragon. Return the breasts and any juices in their bowl to the pot.

3 Lock the lid onto the cooker.

STOVETOP: Raise the heat to high and bring the pot to high pressure (15 psi). Once this pressure has been reached, reduce the heat as much as possible while maintaining this pressure. Cook for 9 minutes.

·······································OR·······································
ELECTRIC: Set the machine to cook at high pressure (9–11 psi). Set the machine's timer to cook at high pressure for 14 minutes.

4 Use the quick-release method to return the pot's pressure to normal.

5 Unlock and open the cooker. Transfer the breasts to a serving platter or individual plates. Set the stovetop cooker over medium heat or turn the electric cooker to its browning function; bring the sauce to a boil. Cook, stirring occasionally, until reduced to half its volume, 2 to 3 minutes. Add the cream and cook for 1 more minute, stirring almost constantly. Pour or ladle the sauce over the chicken breasts.

TESTERS' NOTES

• Here's a classic bistro dish in minutes. The sauce actually has deeper flavors than one made stovetop, thanks to the way the pressure cooker forces more chicken flavor into the liquids.

• While previous recipes can use any sort of chicken breast meat you can find, this one calls for the thick boneless *and* skinless breasts, not fillets, which are thinner slices of chicken breast, or even the tenders, which are strips of chicken breast meat that lie alongside the breastbone. These latter two cuts are too thin to stay tender under pressure.

• Boneless and skinless chicken breasts are really *chicken breast halves*, the meat from one side of the chicken's chest. The terminology is shortened for brevity's sake.

Serve It Up! Serve a **Classic New York Diner Salad** to go on the side: Stir together 3 cups chopped romaine lettuce, 1 cup cored and diced green bell pepper, 1/2 cup thinly sliced celery, and 1/2 cup diced cucumber. Add 3 tablespoons olive oil, 1 1/2 tablespoons red wine vinegar, 1/2 teaspoon dried oregano, 1/4 teaspoon salt, and 1/4 teaspoon ground black pepper. Toss well before serving.

CHICKEN BREASTS WITH PEACH JAM AND BOURBON

EFFORT: **NOT MUCH** • PRESSURE: **HIGH** • TIME UNDER PRESSURE: **9 OR 14 MINUTES** • RELEASE: **QUICK** • SERVES: **4**

2 tablespoons unsalted butter
Four 6- to 8-ounce boneless skinless chicken breasts
1 large shallot, chopped
1 teaspoon minced garlic
¼ cup peach jam
¼ cup chicken broth
¼ cup bourbon
½ teaspoon dried thyme
¼ teaspoon salt
¼ teaspoon ground black pepper

1 Melt the butter in a 6-quart stovetop pressure cooker set over medium heat or in a 6-quart electric pressure cooker turned to the browning function. Add the chicken breasts and brown them well, turning once, about 4 minutes. Transfer to a large bowl.

2 Add the shallot and garlic; cook until softened, about 2 minutes, stirring often. Stir in the jam, broth, bourbon, thyme, salt, and pepper until the jam dissolves. Slip the breasts into the sauce; add any juices from their bowl.

3 Lock the lid onto the cooker.

STOVETOP: Raise the heat to high and bring the pot to high pressure (15 psi). Once this pressure has been reached, reduce the heat as much as possible while maintaining this pressure. Cook for 9 minutes.

···OR···
ELECTRIC: Set the machine to cook at high pressure (9–11 psi). Set the machine's timer to cook at high pressure for 14 minutes.

4 Use the quick-release method to bring the pot's pressure back to normal.

5 Unlock and open the cooker. Transfer the breasts and sauce to large bowls.

TESTERS' NOTES
• This peach-and-bourbon sauce is fairly thin but boldly flavored. If you'd like a thicker sauce, remove the breasts from the cooker and boil the sauce down until it's reduced by about half its volume, 3 to 5 minutes. Whisk in another tablespoon of unsalted butter and spoon over the meat.
• There's little chance the bourbon will ignite, given the size of the pot and the broth added before the liquor. However, if it does, set the lid onto the cooker and take it off the heat for a minute or two. (If you want an alcohol-free version, substitute 3½ tablespoons unsweetened apple juice, 1¼ teaspoons molasses, and ¼ teaspoon vanilla extract for the bourbon.)
• Use peach jam, not peach jelly (which is too loose for a good sauce). Or substitute peach preserves for pieces of fruit in the mix. (Apricot jam is also a good substitute.)

CHICKEN FAJITA STEW

EFFORT: **NOT MUCH** • PRESSURE: **HIGH** • TIME UNDER PRESSURE: **4 OR 6 MINUTES** • RELEASE: **QUICK** • SERVES: **4 TO 6**

1 tablespoon olive oil
1 large yellow onion, halved and cut into thin half-moons
2 medium yellow bell peppers, stemmed, cored, and cut into ½-inch-thick strips
2 teaspoons minced garlic

One 14-ounce can diced tomatoes (about 1³/₄ cups)

¹/₄ cup golden raisins

1 tablespoon loosely packed fresh oregano leaves, minced

¹/₂ teaspoon cumin seeds

¹/₂ teaspoon salt

¹/₄ teaspoon pure chipotle chile powder

One 4-inch cinnamon stick

1¹/₂ pounds boneless skinless chicken breasts, sliced into ¹/₂-inch-wide strips

1 Heat the oil in a 6-quart stovetop pressure cooker set over medium heat or in a 6-quart electric pressure cooker turned to the browning function. Add the onion and bell peppers; cook until the onion softens, about 5 minutes, stirring often. Add the garlic and cook for a few seconds.

2 Pour in the tomatoes; stir in the raisins, oregano, cumin seeds, salt, chipotle powder, and cinnamon stick. Add the chicken strips; stir well.

3 Lock the lid onto the pot.

STOVETOP: Raise the heat to high and bring the pot to high pressure (15 psi). Once this pressure has been reached, reduce the heat as much as possible while maintaining this pressure. Cook for 4 minutes.

.... **OR** ....

ELECTRIC: Set the machine to cook at high pressure (9–11 psi). Set the machine's timer to cook at high pressure for 6 minutes.

4 Use the quick-release method to bring the pot's pressure back to normal.

5 Unlock and open the cooker. Remove and discard the cinnamon stick. Stir well before serving.

TESTERS' NOTES

• No, these are not fajitas. We've taken the flavors of traditional fajitas and turned the dish into a quick, saucy stew for a weeknight.

• Pure chipotle chile powder is available in the spice rack of most supermarkets. (Substitute ¼ teaspoon smoked paprika and ¼ teaspoon cayenne in a pinch.)

Serve It Up! Serve the stew dolloped with sour cream and pico de gallo or guacamole. Top with shredded Monterey jack cheese, too. Offer warmed corn tortillas for sopping up the sauce.

ENCHILADA-BRAISED CHICKEN BREASTS

EFFORT: **A LITTLE** • PRESSURE: **HIGH** • TIME UNDER PRESSURE: **9 OR 14 MINUTES** • RELEASE: **QUICK** • SERVES: **4**

1 teaspoon packed dark brown sugar

1 teaspoon ground cumin

1 teaspoon smoked paprika

¹/₂ teaspoon salt

¹/₂ teaspoon ground black pepper

¹/₂ teaspoon onion powder

¹/₄ teaspoon garlic powder

Four 6- to 8-ounce boneless skinless chicken breasts

2 tablespoons olive oil

One 8-ounce can tomato sauce (1 cup)

¹/₂ cup light-colored beer, preferably a Pilsner or an IPA

2 tablespoons chili powder

2 tablespoons fresh lime juice

1 Mix the brown sugar, cumin, smoked paprika, salt, pepper, onion powder, and garlic powder in a medium bowl. Massage the spice rub onto the chicken breasts.

(continued)

2 Heat the oil in a 6-quart stovetop pressure cooker set over medium heat or in a 6-quart electric pressure cooker turned to the browning function. Set the breasts in the cooker and brown well, turning once, about 6 minutes.

3 Mix the tomato sauce, beer, chili powder, and lime juice in the bowl the spices were in; pour the sauce over the breasts.

4 Lock the lid onto the pot.

STOVETOP: Raise the heat to high and bring the pot to high pressure (15 psi). Once this pressure has been reached, reduce the heat as much as possible while maintaining this pressure. Cook for 9 minutes.

........................**OR**........................

ELECTRIC: Set the machine to cook at high pressure (9–11 psi). Set the machine's timer to cook at high pressure for 14 minutes.

5 Use the quick-release method to bring the pot's pressure back to normal.

6 Unlock and open the cooker. Serve the chicken with the sauce ladled on top.

TESTERS' NOTES
• Making your own enchilada sauce just got easier! You first make a Tex-Mex rub, then an easy sauce to go over the chicken.
• The sugar and spices on the chicken breasts will make them look almost blackened when you're done browning them, but don't worry: they're not burned, just intensely flavored. That coating will melt a bit into the beer and tomato sauce, giving you a much more satisfying (and complexly flavored) meal.

Serve It Up! Sprinkle grated Cheddar or Monterey jack cheese over warm sauce on the cooked chicken. Have warmed flour tortillas on the side.

CHICKEN AND ASPARAGUS "STIR-FRY"

EFFORT: **A LITTLE** • PRESSURE: **HIGH** • TIME UNDER PRESSURE: **2 OR 3 MINUTES** • RELEASE: **QUICK** • SERVES: **4**

2 tablespoons toasted sesame oil

1 large red bell pepper, stemmed, cored, and sliced into $1/2$-inch-thick strips

6 medium scallions, green and white parts, thinly sliced

1 tablespoon minced fresh ginger

2 teaspoons minced garlic

Up to $1/2$ teaspoon red pepper flakes

$1^1/_2$ pounds boneless skinless chicken breasts, sliced into $1/4$-inch-wide strips

6 tablespoons chicken broth

2 tablespoons soy sauce

1 tablespoon balsamic vinegar

1 tablespoon Worcestershire sauce

1 pound thin asparagus spears, woody ends trimmed, cut into 1-inch sections (about $3^1/_2$ cups)

1 Heat the oil in a 6-quart stovetop pressure cooker set over medium heat or in a 6-quart electric pressure cooker turned to the browning function. Add the bell pepper, scallions, ginger, garlic, and red pepper flakes; stir-fry for 2 minutes.

2 Add the chicken and toss until well coated. Pour in the broth, soy sauce, vinegar, and Worcestershire sauce. Stir well.

3 Lock the lid onto the pot.

································· **OR** ·································

4 Use the quick-release method to bring the pot's pressure back to normal.

5 Unlock and open the cooker. Stir in the asparagus. Cover loosely and set aside without heat for 10 minutes to blanch the asparagus in the sauce. Serve in bowls.

TESTERS' NOTES

• No, it's hardly a traditional stir-fry. But you will need good stir-frying technique in steps 1 and 2. Work with two wooden spoons—or better yet, wooden paddles. Keep the ingredients moving over the heat so they sear rather than caramelize.

• For a more authentic taste, use 2 tablespoons Chinese black vinegar instead of the balsamic vinegar and Worcestershire sauce. Look for Chinese black vinegar in Asian markets and at their online sites.

• If desired, substitute up to 1 tablespoon red Asian chile paste for the red pepper flakes.

Serve It Up! Have cooked long-grain white rice to go under the "stir-fry." Or make it easier and pick up a carton or two of cooked white rice at a Chinese restaurant on your way home from work.

CHICKEN AND CASHEW "STIR-FRY"

EFFORT: **A LITTLE** • PRESSURE: **HIGH** • TIME UNDER PRESSURE: **2 OR 3 MINUTES** • RELEASE: **QUICK** • SERVES: **4**

2 tablespoons toasted sesame oil

1 large yellow bell pepper, stemmed, cored, and chopped

6 medium scallions, green and white parts, thinly sliced

3 medium celery stalks, cut into $1/2$-inch sections

1 tablespoon minced fresh ginger

$1^1/2$ pounds boneless skinless chicken breasts, sliced into $1/4$-inch-wide strips

1 cup roasted cashews

$1/4$ cup chicken broth

2 tablespoons soy sauce

2 tablespoons rice vinegar

2 tablespoons hoisin sauce

2 teaspoons arrowroot or cornstarch

1 Heat the oil in a 6-quart stovetop pressure cooker set over medium heat or in a 6-quart electric pressure cooker turned to the browning function. Add the bell pepper, scallions, celery, and ginger; stir-fry for 1 minute. Add the chicken and cashews; stir-fry for another minute.

2 Pour in the broth, soy sauce, rice vinegar, and hoisin sauce; stir well to dissolve the hoisin sauce.

(continued)

3 Lock the lid onto the cooker.

STOVETOP: Raise the heat to high and bring the pot to high pressure (15 psi). Once this pressure has been reached, reduce the heat as much as possible while maintaining this pressure. Cook for 2 minutes.

························ **OR** ························

ELECTRIC: Set the machine to cook at high pressure (9–11 psi). Set the machine's timer to cook at high pressure for 3 minutes.

4 Use the quick-release method to drop the pot's pressure to normal.

5 Unlock and open the pot. Set the stovetop cooker over medium heat or turn the electric cooker to its browning function. Stir the arrowroot or cornstarch with 2 teaspoons water in a small bowl until dissolved. Bring the sauce to a simmer, add this slurry, and stir until thickened, about 30 seconds. Serve in bowls.

TESTERS' NOTES
• This aromatic "stir-fry" is fairly saucy, what with the added broth and other condiments. The vegetables will not be crisp but instead intensely flavored. Consider it a stew with the palette of a stir-fry.
• Use unsalted roasted cashews to cut down on the sodium in the dish.
• Hoisin sauce is a thick, sweet paste traditionally made from sweet potatoes. It's familiar as the sauce in moo-shu pork roll-ups or Peking duck. Look for it in the international aisle of almost all supermarkets. Once opened, it can stay in the refrigerator for up to 1 year. (For a quick substitute, you can also use 1½ tablespoons canned tomato paste plus ½ tablespoon five-spice powder.)

CHICKEN BREASTS with WHITE WINE and ORANGE JUICE

EFFORT: **A LITTLE** • PRESSURE: **HIGH** • TIME UNDER PRESSURE: **12 OR 18 MINUTES** • RELEASE: **QUICK** • SERVES: **4**

3 tablespoons unsalted butter

Four 12-ounce bone-in, skin-on chicken breasts

½ teaspoon salt

½ teaspoon ground black pepper

½ cup fresh orange juice

½ cup dry but light white wine, such as Sauvignon Blanc

One 4-inch fresh rosemary sprig

1 tablespoon honey

½ tablespoon potato starch or cornstarch

1 Melt the butter in a 6-quart stovetop pressure cooker set over medium heat or in a 6-quart electric pressure cooker turned to the browning function. Season the chicken with the salt and pepper, then add two breasts skin side down to the cooker. Brown well, turning once, about 5 minutes; transfer to a large bowl. Brown the remaining breasts, and leave them in the cooker.

2 Return the first two breasts to the cooker, arranging them so that all are skin up but overlapping only as necessary, thinner parts over thick. Pour the orange juice and wine over the chicken. Tuck in the rosemary and drizzle everything with honey.

3 Lock the lid onto the pot.

STOVETOP: Raise the heat to high and bring the pot to high pressure (15 psi). Once this pressure has been reached, reduce the heat as low as you can while maintaining this pressure. Cook for 12 minutes.

·······························**OR**·······························

ELECTRIC: Set the machine to cook at high pressure (9–11 psi). Set the machine's timer to cook at high pressure for 18 minutes.

4 Use the quick-release method to bring the pot's pressure back to normal.

5 Unlock and open the pot. Discard the rosemary sprig. Use kitchen tongs to transfer the chicken breasts to individual serving plates or a serving platter.

6 Dissolve the potato starch or cornstarch with ½ tablespoon water in a small bowl. Set the stovetop pot over medium heat or turn the electric cooker to its browning or simmer function; bring the sauce to a simmer. Add this slurry and cook, stirring all the time, until thickened, about 20 seconds. Ladle the sauce over the chicken to serve.

TESTERS' NOTES

• Any sort of orange juice from concentrate, refrigerated or frozen, will simply not have enough pop to stand out in the dish. Only fresh will work. And for more orange flavor, use orange-blossom honey, as well as 2 teaspoons finely grated orange zest.

• Bone-in chicken breasts—technically, bone-in chicken breast halves—sometimes have a small flap of tiny rib bones hanging from one side. Slice this off if still attached, along with any large globs of fat.

• No, you don't have to thicken the sauce. You could skip step 6 and simply serve the breasts in deep bowls with the more watery sauce spooned around them.

CHICKEN BREASTS WITH SWEET WINE AND HERBS

EFFORT: **A LITTLE** • PRESSURE: **HIGH** • TIME UNDER PRESSURE: **12 OR 18 MINUTES** • RELEASE: **QUICK** • SERVES: **4**

1 tablespoon unsalted butter

1 tablespoon olive oil

Four 12-ounce bone-in, skin-on chicken breasts

¹/₂ teaspoon salt

¹/₂ teaspoon ground black pepper

1 small red onion, chopped

¹/₂ cup sweet white wine, such as a sweet Riesling

¹/₄ cup chicken broth

2 tablespoons loosely packed fresh parsley leaves, chopped

1 teaspoon stemmed fresh thyme leaves

1 bay leaf

¹/₄ cup heavy cream

1 Melt the butter in the oil in a 6-quart stovetop pressure cooker set over medium heat or in a 6-quart electric pressure cooker turned to the browning function. Season the breasts with salt and pepper, then slip two skin side down into the pot. Brown well, turning once, about 5 minutes. Repeat with the remaining breasts.

2 Add the onion to the pot and cook, stirring often, until softened, about 3 minutes. Pour in the wine and scrape up any browned bits in the cooker. Stir in the broth, then the parsley, thyme, and bay leaf. Return the chicken to the pot as well as any juices in the bowl, arranging the pieces skin side up but overlapping as necessary.

(continued)

3 Lock the lid onto the pot.

STOVETOP: Raise the heat to high and bring the pot to high pressure (15 psi). Once this pressure has been reached, reduce the heat as much as possible while maintaining this pressure. Cook for 12 minutes.

·························· **OR** ··························

ELECTRIC: Set the machine to cook at high pressure (9–11 psi). Set the machine's timer to cook at high pressure for 18 minutes.

4 Use the quick-release method to drop the pot's pressure to normal.

5 Unlock and open the cooker. Discard the bay leaf. Use kitchen tongs to transfer the chicken breasts to a large serving platter or individual serving bowls.

6 Set the stovetop cooker over medium heat or turn the electric model to its browning function; bring the sauce to a simmer. Stir in the cream and cook for 1 minute, stirring often, to take the raw flavor off the dairy. Spoon the sauce over the breasts to serve.

TESTERS' NOTES
• When browning the breasts, spend more time with the skin down against the hot surface, since the other side of the breast is arched and will have relatively little contact. Figure on 3 or 4 minutes browning the skin, followed by 1 or 2 minutes browning the other side. Make sure there's deep color on that skin so it stays firm and luscious under pressure.
• Substitute other sweet white wines, such as Spätlese or Auslese. Just don't use a dessert wine, like an Eiswein, which is far too syrupy for this sauce.

Serve It Up! Make a **Nut and Barley Pilaf** to go on the side: Mix warm, cooked barley with thinly sliced scallions and chopped walnuts; toss with melted butter, salt, and pepper.

CHICKEN BREASTS WITH **CHICKPEAS** AND HOT SAUCE

EFFORT: **A LITTLE** • PRESSURE: **HIGH** • TIME UNDER PRESSURE: **12 OR 18 MINUTES** • RELEASE: **QUICK** • SERVES: **4**

3 tablespoons unsalted butter
Four 12-ounce bone-in, skin-on chicken breasts
1/2 teaspoon salt
1 small yellow or white onion, chopped
One 14-ounce can diced tomatoes (about 1³/₄ cups)
One 15-ounce can chickpeas, drained and rinsed (about 1³/₄ cups)
Up to 2 tablespoons bottled hot red pepper sauce
1/2 cup chicken broth

1 Melt 2 tablespoons of the butter in a 6-quart pressure cooker set over medium heat or in a 6-quart electric pressure cooker turned to the browning function. Season the chicken with the salt, then slip two of the breasts into the pot skin side down. Brown well, turning once, about 5 minutes. Transfer to a large bowl, add the remaining tablespoon of butter, and repeat with the other two breasts.

2 Add the onion to the pot and cook, stirring often, until translucent, about 3 minutes. Pour in the tomatoes, chickpeas, and hot red pepper sauce; scrape up any browned bits as the liquid comes to a simmer. Stir in the broth, then return the chicken breasts to the cooker, placing them skin side up but overlapping as necessary. Pour any juices from the chicken bowl into the cooker.

3 Lock the lid onto the pot.

STOVETOP: Raise the heat to high and bring the pot to high pressure (15 psi). Once this pressure has been reached, reduce the heat as much as possible while maintaining this pressure. Cook for 12 minutes.

·· **OR** ··································

ELECTRIC: Set the machine to cook at high pressure (9–11 psi). Set the machine's timer to cook at high pressure for 18 minutes.

4 Use the quick-release method to bring the pot's pressure back to normal.

5 Unlock and open the pot. Stir the sauce gently before serving in deep bowls.

TESTERS' NOTES
• Here's a riff on Buffalo chicken wings with a buttery and spicy sauce.
• The bottled hot sauce can be of any stripe you imagine. Of course, something like Tabasco Sauce is the usual suspect, but there are fruity or intensely hot sauces on the market, too. A chipotle hot sauce would give the dish a smoky edge.

Serve It Up! Make a **Celery and Carrot Salad** for the side: Mix thinly sliced celery and shredded carrots with mayonnaise, a sprinkle of white wine vinegar, a pinch of sugar, a little salt, and some blue cheese crumbles.

CHICKEN BREASTS WITH **TEQUILA** AND TOMATILLOS

EFFORT: **A LITTLE** · PRESSURE: **HIGH** · TIME UNDER PRESSURE: **12 OR 18 MINUTES** · RELEASE: **QUICK** · SERVES: **4**

2 tablespoons olive oil

Four 12-ounce bone-in, skin-on chicken breasts

1 large yellow onion, chopped

1 small green bell pepper, stemmed, cored, and chopped

Up to 1 medium fresh jalapeño chile, stemmed, seeded, and minced

1 pound tomatillos, husked and chopped

1/4 cup tequila

2 teaspoons dried oregano

1 teaspoon ground cumin

1/2 teaspoon ground cinnamon

1 tablespoon fresh lime juice

1/2 teaspoon salt

1 Heat the oil in a 6-quart stovetop pressure cooker set over medium heat or in a 6-quart electric pressure cooker turned to the browning function. Add two of the breasts skin side down; brown well, turning once, about 5 minutes. Transfer to a large bowl. Repeat with the remaining breasts.

2 Add the onion, bell pepper, and jalapeño to the pot; cook, stirring often, until the onion softens, about 4 minutes. Add the tomatillos and cook, stirring frequently, until they begin to break down into a sauce, about 5 minutes. Stir in the tequila, oregano, cumin, and cinnamon until aromatic, less than a minute.

(continued)

3 Return the chicken and its juices to the cooker, setting the breasts skin side up in the sauce but overlapping them as necessary.

4 Lock the lid onto the pot.

STOVETOP: Raise the heat to high and bring the pot to high pressure (15 psi). Once this pressure has been reached, reduce the heat as much as possible while maintaining this pressure. Cook for 12 minutes.

·························· **OR** ··························

ELECTRIC: Set the machine to cook at high pressure (9–11 psi). Set the machine's timer to cook at high pressure for 18 minutes.

5 Use the quick-release method to bring the pot's pressure back to normal.

6 Unlock and open the pot. Add the lime juice and salt; stir well before serving in deep bowls.

TESTERS' NOTES

• If you added up to 2 teaspoons finely grated orange zest, this recipe would be like braising chicken in a margarita with plenty of aromatics.

• We add the salt at the end of cooking so that its flavor is more present, not melded with the other ingredients. If you really want a salty hit, omit it from the pot and sprinkle a little coarse sea salt or even flaked salt over each serving.

• The husks can stick to tomatillos. If necessary, run them under water to remove every bit of the papery shells. (You can also substitute green cherry tomatoes plus 1 teaspoon finely grated lime zest for the tomatillos.)

CAJUN WINGS

EFFORT: **A LITTLE** • PRESSURE: **HIGH** • TIME UNDER PRESSURE: **7 OR 10 MINUTES** • RELEASE: **QUICK** • SERVES: **4 TO 6**

4 medium scallions, thinly sliced

¼ cup light-colored beer, preferably an amber ale

¼ cup ketchup

¼ cup Worcestershire sauce

2 tablespoons packed dark brown sugar

Up to 2 teaspoons bottled hot red pepper sauce

½ teaspoon dried sage

½ teaspoon dried thyme

¼ teaspoon celery seeds

3 pounds chicken wing drumettes and/or wingettes

1 Stir the scallions, beer, ketchup, Worcestershire sauce, brown sugar, hot red pepper sauce, sage, thyme, and celery seeds in a 6-quart stovetop or electric pressure cooker until the brown sugar dissolves. Add the wings and toss until well coated.

2 Lock the lid onto the pot.

STOVETOP: Set the pot over high heat and bring it to high pressure (15 psi). Once this pressure has been reached, reduce the heat as much as possible while maintaining this pressure. Cook for 7 minutes.

·························· **OR** ··························

ELECTRIC: Set the machine to cook at high pressure (9–11 psi). Set the machine's timer to cook at high pressure for 10 minutes.

3 Use the quick-release method to bring the pot's pressure back to normal.

4 Unlock and open the pot. Transfer the wings to a large, rimmed baking sheet. Set the oven rack 4 to 6 inches from the broiler element; heat the broiler. Broil the wings until brown and crisp, turning once, 4 to 6 minutes. Transfer the baking sheet to a wire cooling rack.

5 Set the stovetop cooker over medium heat or turn the electric model to its browning or simmer function; bring the sauce to a full simmer. Cook, stirring occasionally, until reduced to a thick glaze, 2 to 3 minutes. Smear the sauce over the wings to serve.

TESTERS' NOTES
• Chicken wings in the pressure cooker get a bit gummy, so broiling them for a couple of minutes takes care of the problem to render them crunchy (and irresistible).
• The sauce here is quite sticky and sweet. It needs the full hit of hot red pepper sauce to keep it in balance.
• Chicken wings have three parts: the drumette, the wingette, and the little flapper with almost no meat on it. You can often find them sold in separate parts, so pick your favorite. If you find only whole wings, buy 3½ pounds; remove and discard the flappers before slicing the wingette and drumette apart.

LEMONY WINGS

EFFORT: **A LITTLE** • PRESSURE: **HIGH** • TIME UNDER PRESSURE: **7 OR 10 MINUTES** • RELEASE: **QUICK** • SERVES: **4 TO 6**

½ **cup fresh lemon juice**

¼ **cup olive oil**

1 **tablespoon red wine vinegar**

1 **teaspoon minced garlic**

1 **teaspoon dried oregano**

¼ **teaspoon red pepper flakes**

3 **pounds chicken wing wingettes and/or drumettes**

½ **teaspoon salt**

1 Mix the lemon juice, oil, vinegar, garlic, oregano, and red pepper flakes in a 6-quart stovetop or electric pressure cooker. Add the chicken wings and toss well to coat.

2 Lock the lid onto the pot.

STOVETOP: Set the pot over high heat and bring to high pressure (15 psi). Once this pressure has been reached, reduce the heat as much as possible while maintaining this pressure. Cook for 7 minutes.

························· **OR** ·····························

ELECTRIC: Set the machine to cook at high pressure (9–11 psi). Set the machine's timer to cook at high pressure for 10 minutes.

3 Use the quick-release method to drop the pot's pressure to normal.

4 Unlock and open the pot. Transfer the wing parts to a large rimmed baking sheet; sprinkle with salt. Position the oven rack 4 to 6 inches from the broiler element; heat the broiler. Broil the wings until browned and crisp, turning once, 4 to 6 minutes. Transfer to a large serving platter; pour the sauce in the cooker over the wings to serve.

TESTERS' NOTES
• These wings are a sour lover's dream! Use only fresh lemon juice for the best flavor. (But get rid of any pits before using.)
• If desired, substitute dried rosemary or thyme for the oregano.
• The sauce is a bit thin. You can boil it down to create a thicker lacquer on the wings, but we honestly preferred it as a sauce, not a glaze. There's no sugar, so it'll never get sticky.

MAPLE DIJON WINGS

EFFORT: **A LITTLE** • PRESSURE: **HIGH** • TIME UNDER PRESSURE: **7 OR 10 MINUTES** • RELEASE: **QUICK** • SERVES: **4 TO 6**

⅓ cup maple syrup

2 tablespoons Dijon mustard

2 tablespoons soy sauce

1 tablespoon apple cider vinegar

3 pounds chicken wing wingettes and/or drumettes

1 Whisk the syrup, mustard, soy sauce, and vinegar in a 6-quart stovetop or electric pressure cooker until the syrup dissolves. Add the wing parts and toss to coat well.

2 Lock the lid onto the pot.

STOVETOP: Set the pot over high heat and bring to high pressure (15 psi). Once this pressure has been reached, reduce the heat as much as possible while maintaining this pressure. Cook for 7 minutes.
······················ **OR** ·····························
ELECTRIC: Set the machine to cook at high pressure (9–11 psi). Set the machine's timer to cook at high pressure for 10 minutes.

3 Use the quick-release method to drop the pot's pressure to normal.

4 Unlock and open the pot. Transfer the wing parts to a large rimmed baking sheet. Position the oven rack 4 to 6 inches from the broiler element; heat the broiler. Broil until the wings are a bit crunchy, turning once, 4 to 6 minutes. Transfer to a large serving platter.

5 Set the stovetop cooker over medium heat or turn the electric cooker to its browning function; bring the sauce to a simmer. Cook, stirring frequently, until reduced to a thick glaze. Smear the glaze over the chicken wings to serve.

TESTERS' NOTES

• Don't dare use anything but real maple syrup for this sweet and spicy sauce on the wing parts.
• We prefer a thicker glaze on the wings, but you may prefer the sauce thinner. If so, consider defatting it first by skimming its surface with a flatware spoon or by pouring it into a fat separator and waiting a couple of minutes for the fat to ride up on the surface before using what's down below.

SESAME WINGS

EFFORT: **A LITTLE** • PRESSURE: **HIGH** • TIME UNDER PRESSURE: **7 OR 10 MINUTES** • RELEASE: **QUICK** • SERVES: **4 TO 6**

¼ cup soy sauce

¼ cup dry white wine, such as Chardonnay

2 tablespoons granulated white sugar

2 tablespoons packed light brown sugar

2 tablespoons toasted sesame oil

1 tablespoon minced fresh ginger

1 tablespoon sesame seeds

3 pounds chicken wing wingettes and/or drumettes

1 Whisk the soy sauce, wine, sugars, sesame oil, ginger, and sesame seeds in a 6-quart stovetop or electric pressure cooker. Add the wings and toss until well coated.

2 Lock the lid onto the pot.

STOVETOP: Set the pot over high heat and bring it to high pressure (15 psi). Once this pressure has been reached, reduce the heat as much as possible while maintaining this pressure. Cook for 7 minutes.

······················· **OR** ·······················

ELECTRIC: Set the machine to cook at high pressure (9–11 psi). Set the machine's timer to cook at high pressure for 10 minutes.

3 Use the quick-release method to bring the pot's pressure back to normal.

4 Unlock and open the pot. Transfer the wing parts to a large rimmed baking sheet. Position the oven rack 4 to 6 inches from the broiler element; heat the broiler. Broil until the wings are a bit crunchy, turning once, 4 to 6 minutes. Transfer to a large serving platter.

5 Set the stovetop cooker over medium heat or turn the electric cooker to its browning function; bring the sauce to a simmer. Cook, stirring frequently, until reduced to a thick glaze. Paint the glaze over the wings to serve.

TESTERS' NOTES

• If you want an intense sesame flavor on chicken wings, you've come to the right recipe. The pressure cooker does what no oven can: it forces those flavors right into the meat.

• You can use wingettes or drumettes or a combination of the two. Frankly, we prefer the drumettes because they're easier to eat so there's less chance for the sauce to end up on our sofa.

• For even more flavor, toast those sesame seeds in a dry skillet over medium-low heat until golden and aromatic, 2 or 3 minutes, before using them in the sauce.

BRAISED WHOLE CHICKEN

EFFORT: **A LOT** • PRESSURE: **HIGH** • TIME UNDER PRESSURE: **35 OR 50 MINUTES** • RELEASE: **QUICK** • SERVES: **4 TO 6**

One 4-pound whole chicken, any giblets or neck removed
1/2 teaspoon salt
1/2 teaspoon ground black pepper
3 tablespoons unsalted butter
1 1/2 cups dry white wine, such as Chardonnay
2 medium carrots, halved widthwise
1 small onion, halved
1 tablespoon all-purpose flour

1 Use butcher's twine to tie the chicken legs together over the large opening. Wrap the twine around the body to hold the wings against the breast, knotting it securely. Season the outside of the chicken with the salt and pepper.

2 Melt 2 tablespoons butter in a 6-quart stovetop pressure cooker set over medium heat or in a 6-quart electric pressure cooker turned to the browning function. Add the chicken and brown well on all sides, turning occasionally, about 10 minutes. Pour in the wine; tuck the carrots and onion into the pot.

3 Lock the lid onto the cooker.

STOVETOP: Set the pot over high heat and bring it to high pressure (15 psi). Once this pressure has been reached, reduce the heat as much as possible while maintaining this pressure. Cook for 35 minutes.

······················· **OR** ·······················

ELECTRIC: Set the machine to cook at high pressure (9–11 psi). Set the machine's timer to cook at high pressure for 50 minutes.

(continued)

4 Use the quick-release method to bring the pot's pressure back to normal.

5 Unlock and open the pot. Use kitchen tongs and a large spatula to transfer the chicken to a cutting board; snip off the twine. Discard the carrots and onion. Use a flatware fork to mash the remaining tablespoon butter with the flour in a small bowl to create a thick paste.

6 Skim the surface of the juices in the pot with a flatware spoon to defat them or pour them into a fat separator and wait a couple of minutes for the fat to rise to the top of the container before pouring off the juices below. Bring the skimmed or defatted sauce in the cooker to a simmer by placing the stovetop model over medium heat or turning the electric one to its browning setting. Whisk in the butter paste in small bits, making sure each dissolves before adding the next; remove from the heat or turn off the machine the moment you're done. Carve the chicken and serve with the gravy on the side.

TESTERS' NOTES
• A braised chicken may be a bygone dish, but it's due for a comeback. The meat becomes meltingly tender with just a hint of sweetness behind its inherent savory notes.
• You may or may not be inclined to eat the skin. It's not crunchy, but the more brown you can get it before braising, the more flavorful the meat below will be.
• To carve a whole chicken, pull the leg-and-thigh quarters back from the body and slice down at the joint to remove them; pull them open and slice through the joint holding them together. Slice down on either side of the breast bone, then trim off the meatless bits near the back. Slice each of the breast halves into two pieces for serving.
• You can substitute olive oil (more floral) or walnut oil (earthier) for the butter, or chicken broth (more savory) for the wine.

CHICKEN AND RICE CASSEROLE WITH OLIVES AND MUSHROOMS

EFFORT: **A LITTLE** • PRESSURE: **HIGH** • TIME UNDER PRESSURE: **10 OR 15 MINUTES** • RELEASE: **MODIFIED QUICK** • SERVES: **6**

2 tablespoons olive oil

One 4-ounce pancetta chunk, chopped

One 3$^{1}/_{2}$- to 4-pound whole chicken, cut into 8 or 9 pieces, the giblets and neck removed

1 medium yellow onion, chopped

$^{1}/_{2}$ cup pitted black olives

2 teaspoons minced garlic

Two 4-inch fresh rosemary sprigs

1 cup long-grain white rice, such as basmati

$^{1}/_{2}$ ounce dried mushrooms of any sort

$^{1}/_{2}$ cup dry but fruit-forward white wine, such as Sauvignon Blanc

1$^{1}/_{2}$ cups chicken broth

1 Heat the oil in a 6-quart stovetop pressure cooker set over medium heat or in a 6-quart electric pressure cooker turned to the browning function. Add the pancetta; cook, stirring often, until browned and crisp at the edges, about 4 minutes. Use a slotted spoon to transfer the pancetta bits to a big bowl.

2 Add about half the chicken pieces to the pot and brown well, turning once, about 6 minutes. Transfer to the bowl with the pancetta, then repeat with the remaining pieces.

3 Add the onion to the pot and cook, stirring often, until softened, about 4 minutes. Stir in the olives, garlic, and rosemary until aromatic, less than a minute. Add the rice;

crumble in the dried mushrooms. Stir until the rice grains are coated in the fat and juices.

4 Pour in the wine and scrape up any browned bits on the bottom of the cooker. Add the broth and stir well. Nestle the chicken pieces and pancetta into the pot, overlapping the chicken bits as necessary, skin side up as much as possible. Pour any juices from the chicken bowl into the cooker.

5 Lock the lid onto the cooker.

STOVETOP: Raise the heat to high and bring the pot to high pressure (15 psi). Once this pressure has been reached, reduce the heat as much as possible while maintaining this pressure. Cook for 10 minutes.

·····**OR**·····

ELECTRIC: Set the machine to cook at high pressure (9–11 psi). Set the machine's timer to cook at high pressure for 15 minutes.

6 Use the quick-release method to bring the pot's pressure back to normal but do not open the cooker. Set aside for 10 minutes to steam the rice.

7 Open the cooker. Spoon the casserole onto serving plates.

TESTERS' NOTES
• While there are other chicken-and-rice casseroles in this chapter, this is the only one that uses the whole chicken—and so has the most balanced, earthy, but elegant set of flavors to match the mix of dark and white meat. (Those olives, those dried mushrooms!)
• Dried mushrooms are often found in the produce section of a supermarket. You can usually find packages of a mixed assortment or ones with an individual type of mushroom inside. There's no need to spend a fortune on morels or chanterelles for recipes like this one. You simply want the intense flavor dried mushrooms provide, so shiitake, porcini, or portobellos are great choices.

BRAISED HONEY-LEMON CHICKEN

EFFORT: **A LITTLE** • PRESSURE: **HIGH** • TIME UNDER PRESSURE: **12 OR 18 MINUTES** • RELEASE: **QUICK** • SERVES: **4 TO 6**

2 cups all-purpose flour

2 teaspoons salt

1 teaspoon ground black pepper

One 3¹/₂- to 4-pound whole chicken, cut into 8 or 9 parts, the giblets and neck removed

2 tablespoons olive oil

¹/₄ cup fresh lemon juice

2 tablespoons red wine vinegar

1 tablespoon loosely packed fresh oregano leaves, minced

1 teaspoon honey

¹/₄ teaspoon red pepper flakes

¹/₂ cup chicken broth

1 Mix the flour, salt, and pepper in a large, shallow bowl. Dredge the chicken in the flour mixture, coating the pieces evenly and completely. Set the dredged pieces on a cutting board.

2 Heat the oil in a 6-quart stovetop pressure cooker set over medium heat or in a 6-quart electric pressure cooker turned to the browning function. Add half the chicken pieces and brown lightly, just until golden, turning once, about 4 minutes. Transfer to a large bowl. Repeat with the remainder of the chicken.

3 Pour in the lemon juice and vinegar; scrape up any browned bits on the bottom of the pot. Add the oregano, honey, and red pepper flakes; stir well. Pour in the broth, then return the chicken pieces to the pot, arranging them skin side up as much as possible.

(continued)

4 Lock the lid onto the cooker.

STOVETOP: Raise the heat to high and bring the pot to high pressure (15 psi). Once this pressure has been reached, reduce the heat as much as possible while maintaining this pressure. Cook for 12 minutes.

························ **OR** ··························

ELECTRIC: Set the machine to cook at high pressure (9–11 psi). Set the machine's timer to cook at high pressure for 18 minutes.

5 Use the quick-release method to bring the pot's pressure back to normal.

6 Unlock and open the pot. Serve the chicken pieces in bowls with the sauce spooned over them.

TESTERS' NOTES
• This flavorful braise takes advantage of the way the pressure cooker mellows sour notes. That said, if you prefer sweet to the sour that is still present here, you might want to double (or even triple) the honey.
• Dredging the chicken in the flour mixture serves two purposes: (1) you can get a browner crust on the chicken before you braise it, and (2) some of that flour will melt into the sauce and thicken it a bit.

Serve It Up! Toss cauliflower florets with olive oil, salt, and pepper; bake on a rimmed baking sheet in a 375°F oven until browned and tender, about 20 minutes, stirring occasionally.

STEWED CHICKEN WITH **CHICKPEAS** AND TOMATOES

EFFORT: **A LOT** • PRESSURE: **HIGH** • TIME UNDER PRESSURE: **12 OR 18 MINUTES** • RELEASE: **QUICK** • SERVES: **4 TO 6**

2 tablespoons olive oil

6 ounces slab bacon, chopped

One 3$\frac{1}{2}$- to 4-pound whole chicken, cut into 8 or 9 pieces, the giblets and neck removed

1 large yellow onion, chopped

2 teaspoons minced garlic

One 28-ounce can diced tomatoes, drained but the liquid reserved

Up to $\frac{3}{4}$ cup rosé wine, such as Bandol

2 tablespoons all-purpose flour

1 tablespoon smoked paprika

1 tablespoon loosely packed fresh oregano leaves, minced

One 15-ounce can chickpeas, drained and rinsed (about 1$\frac{3}{4}$ cups)

1 tablespoon red wine vinegar

$\frac{1}{2}$ teaspoon ground black pepper

1 Heat the oil in a 6-quart stovetop pressure cooker set over medium heat or in a 6-quart electric pressure cooker turned to the browning function. Add the slab bacon; cook, stirring often, until browned and even crisp at the edges, about 4 minutes. Use a slotted spoon to transfer these bits to a large bowl.

2 Add half the chicken pieces and brown well, turning once, about 5 minutes. Transfer to the bowl, then repeat with the remaining chicken.

3 Add the onion to the pot; cook, stirring often, until translucent, about 4 minutes. Add the garlic and cook for about 20 seconds.

Stir in the drained tomatoes and ¾ cup wine in the stovetop model or ½ cup in the electric one.

4 Whisk the flour, smoked paprika, and oregano into the reserved tomato juice in a bowl until smooth, then pour this mixture into the pot. Cook, stirring often, until thickened, 3 to 5 minutes. Stir in the chickpeas; return the chicken pieces and bacon to the pot, layering the chicken pieces skin side up as much as possible. Pour any juices from their bowl into the cooker.

5 Lock on the lid.

STOVETOP: Raise the heat to high and bring the pot to high pressure (15 psi). Once this pressure has been reached, reduce the heat as much as possible while maintaining this pressure. Cook for 12 minutes.

········· OR ·········

ELECTRIC: Set the machine to cook at high pressure (9–11 psi). Set the machine's timer to cook at high pressure for 18 minutes.

6 Use the quick-release method to bring the pot's pressure back to normal.

7 Unlock and open the cooker. Transfer the chicken pieces to a deep serving bowl or individual bowls. Stir the vinegar and pepper into the sauce before ladling it over the meat.

TESTERS' NOTES

• The flavors here are modeled on those in classic Spanish braises. The vinegar at the end brightens everything. For a more authentic flavor, substitute sherry vinegar for the red wine vinegar.

• There's an important difference between stewing and braising. The former uses more liquid, sometimes almost submerging the meat in the sauce; the latter, much less, both steaming and stewing the meat as it cooks.

CHICKEN FRICASSEE

EFFORT: **A LOT** • PRESSURE: **HIGH** • TIME UNDER PRESSURE: **12 OR 18 MINUTES** • RELEASE: **QUICK** • SERVES: **4 TO 6**

1¼ **cups chicken broth**

2 **tablespoons all-purpose flour**

1 **tablespoon unsalted butter**

1 **tablespoon olive oil**

One 3½**- to 4-pound whole chicken, cut into 8 or 9 parts, the giblets and neck removed**

1½ **cups fresh pearl onions, peeled, or frozen pearl onions, thawed**

¾ **pound white button mushrooms, thinly sliced**

1 **large turnip (about 10 ounces), peeled and cubed**

1 **tablespoon loosely packed fresh sage leaves, minced**

1 **tablespoon stemmed fresh thyme leaves**

2 **teaspoons minced garlic**

½ **cup dry white wine, such as Chardonnay**

¼ **cup heavy cream**

1 Whisk the broth and flour in a small bowl until smooth; set aside.

2 Melt the butter in the oil in a 6-quart stovetop pressure cooker set over medium heat or in a 6-quart electric pressure cooker turned to the browning function. Add half the chicken pieces; brown lightly, just until golden, turning once, 3 to 4 minutes. Transfer to a large bowl and repeat with the remaining chicken.

3 Add the onions to the pot and cook, stirring often, just until pale brown, about

(continued)

3 minutes. Add the mushrooms and cook, stirring often, until they give off their liquid and it evaporates, about 6 minutes. Stir in the turnip, sage, thyme, and garlic just until aromatic, about 1 minute.

4 Pour in the wine and scrape up any browned bits in the cooker as the wine comes to a simmer. Whisk the broth mixture one more time and pour it into the cooker. Return the chicken pieces to the sauce, nestling them in skin side up and overlapping as necessary. Pour the juices from the bowl over the chicken.

5 Lock the lid onto the cooker.

STOVETOP: Raise the heat to high and bring the pot to high pressure (15 psi). Once this pressure has been reached, reduce the heat as much as possible while maintaining this pressure. Cook for 12 minutes.

······················ **OR** ······························

ELECTRIC: Set the machine to cook at high pressure (9–11 psi). Set the machine's timer to cook at high pressure for 18 minutes.

6 Use the quick-release method to return the pot's pressure to normal.

7 Unlock and open the cooker. Transfer the chicken pieces to a large serving bowl or individual bowls. Set the stovetop cooker over medium heat or turn the electric cooker to its browning function; bring the sauce to a simmer. Stir in the cream; cook for 1 minute, stirring all the while. Ladle the sauce over the chicken.

TESTERS' NOTES

• A fricassee is an Old World grandmotherly dish with a creamy mushroom sauce. We've added a turnip to give it more of that European feel, but the peppery notes in the vegetable will indeed calm down under pressure.

• If using frozen, make sure the pearl onions are completely thawed, preferably after spending two days in the refrigerator. Otherwise, they'll compromise the temperature as the dish comes up to high pressure, causing it to take longer and overcooking the chicken.

• Because of complex reactions in dairy products under high pressure, it's hard to braise in cream without its curdling. (Yes, you can do so by adding baking soda but we find the flavor is compromised in a dish like this one.) That said, we can create a rich, luscious sauce that we then enrich with cream.

CHICKEN PAPRIKASH

EFFORT: **A LITTLE** • PRESSURE: **HIGH** • TIME UNDER PRESSURE: **12 OR 18 MINUTES** • RELEASE: **QUICK** • SERVES: **4 TO 6**

2 tablespoons unsalted butter

One 3^1/$_2$- to 4-pound whole chicken, cut into 8 or 9 parts, any giblets removed

^{1}/$_2$ teaspoon salt

^{1}/$_2$ teaspoon ground black pepper

1 medium yellow onion, chopped

6 ounces white button mushrooms, thinly sliced

1 teaspoon dried thyme

^{2}/$_3$ cup chicken broth

2 medium Roma (plum) tomatoes, chopped

1^1/$_2$ tablespoons sweet paprika

^{1}/$_3$ cup regular or low-fat sour cream

1 Melt the butter in a 6-quart stovetop pressure cooker set over medium heat or in a 6-quart electric pressure cooker turned to the browning function. Season the chicken with the salt and pepper, then slip half the pieces into the pot. Brown lightly, 3 to 4 minutes, turning once; transfer to a big bowl. Repeat with the remaining chicken.

2 Add the onion to the pot; cook, stirring often, just until barely softened, about 2 minutes. Add the mushrooms and thyme; cook, stirring less frequently, until they give off their liquid and it reduces to a thick glaze, about 5 minutes. Pour in the broth and scrape up any browned bits in the pot.

3 Stir in the tomatoes and paprika. Return the chicken pieces to the pot, arranging them skin side up as much as possible and overlapping as little as possible. Pour the juices from their bowl into the cooker.

4 Lock the lid on the cooker.

STOVETOP: Raise the heat to high and bring the pot to high pressure (15 psi). Once this pressure has been reached, reduce the heat as much as possible while maintaining this pressure. Cook for 12 minutes.

························ **OR** ····························

ELECTRIC: Set the machine to cook at high pressure (9–11 psi). Set the machine's timer to cook at high pressure for 18 minutes.

5 Use the quick-release method to bring the pot's pressure back to normal.

6 Unlock and open the pot. Transfer the chicken pieces to a large serving bowl or individual bowls.

7 Set the stovetop cooker over medium heat or turn the electric one to its browning function; bring the sauce to a simmer. Cook, stirring occasionally, until the sauce is reduced to half its volume, 3 to 4 minutes. Remove the pot from the heat or unplug it; stir in the sour cream until smooth. Ladle the sauce over the chicken to serve.

TESTERS' NOTES

• No, it's not authentic paprikash. Instead, it's the American version, a family classic. The sour cream must not be boiled in the sauce; when you remove the pot from the heat or unplug it, make sure the sauce has stopped bubbling before you stir in the sour cream. Otherwise, it may curdle.

• Paprika is not just a coloring agent—it has a great, sweet and slightly sour flavor. If your bottle is over a year old, consider springing for a new bottle. The essential oils in paprika degrade rather quickly, even when you store the bottle in a cool, dry place.

Serve It Up! Ladle the chicken and sauce over cooked egg noodles.

Turkey, Game Hens, and Duck

The range in this section is as large as any in the book—not just because we move from workaday turkey sausage to sophisticated duck leg-and-thigh quarters, but because we can use more flavors across a wider swath. These three birds can be served in a straightforward sauce or a hearty braise loaded with chiles and aromatics.

We start with some simple suppers that use turkey sausage: kid-friendly recipes for casseroles and easy stews. Then we move to bigger and bigger fare, including a whole set of braises for turkey thighs, about our favorite cut of that bird. If you can't spot a package of turkey thighs at your supermarket, your butcher will often slice them off a whole bird for you (and repackage the breasts later).

By the way, some of these turkey cuts don't move quickly at the market. You're probably best off buying them frozen and thawing them in a bowl in your fridge for a couple of days. If you do buy them fresh, ask to smell them before purchasing if possible. Sure, they'll think you're a crank. But you shouldn't detect any acrid, rancid odor, a sign they've sat in the cabinet or case too long.

We then move on to game hens and duck. The flavors get even bigger with bold spices aplenty. If you haven't prepared duck at home, you're in for a treat. The pressure cooker mellows the meat considerably and renders it gorgeously tender. We've also got some ways to cut down on the fat in a duck recipe.

These are fairly simple recipes, very few bumping up into the "a lot of effort" category. We figured that the prize was the poultry, not some intricate stuffing or brining technique. We hope you'll agree: these birds make a fine supper without a lot of fuss.

TURKEY SAUSAGE AND MACARONI CASSEROLE

EFFORT: **NOT MUCH** · PRESSURE: **HIGH** · TIME UNDER PRESSURE: **5 OR 8 MINUTES** · RELEASE: **QUICK** · SERVES: **4 TO 6**

1¹/₂ cups regular or low-fat evaporated milk

1¹/₂ cups chicken broth

1¹/₂ tablespoons all-purpose flour

1 teaspoon dried sage

2 tablespoons unsalted butter

¹/₂ small red onion, chopped

1 pound turkey sausage, such as sweet Italian turkey sausage, cut into 1-inch pieces

8 ounces dried elbow macaroni

1¹/₂ cups shredded Swiss cheese (about 6 ounces)

1 cup shelled fresh peas, or frozen peas, thawed

¹/₄ teaspoon salt

¹/₄ teaspoon ground black pepper

1 Whisk the milk, broth, flour, and sage in a large bowl until the flour has dissolved; set aside.

2 Melt the butter in a 6-quart stovetop pressure cooker set over medium heat or in a 6-quart electric pressure cooker turned to the browning function. Add the onion and cook, stirring occasionally, just until softened, about 2 minutes.

3 Add the sausage pieces; cook, stirring occasionally, until browned, about 4 minutes. Stir in the milk mixture until smooth, then add the macaroni and toss well.

4 Lock the lid onto the pot.

STOVETOP: Raise the heat to high and bring the pot to high pressure (15 psi). Once this pressure has been reached, reduce the heat as much as possible while maintaining this pressure. Cook for 5 minutes.

·· OR ··

ELECTRIC: Set the machine to cook at high pressure (9–11 psi). Set the machine's timer to cook at high pressure for 8 minutes.

5 Use the quick-release method to bring the pot's pressure back to normal.

6 Unlock and open the pot. Stir in the cheese, peas, salt, and pepper. Set the lid loosely over the pot and set aside for 5 minutes to melt the cheese and warm through. Stir well before serving.

TESTERS' NOTES
• This simple casserole is a robust, weeknight meal. For a more complex flavor palette, add up to 1 teaspoon dried thyme, 1 teaspoon dried oregano, and/or ½ teaspoon red pepper flakes.
• Note the *evaporated* milk. Regular milk will curdle.
• Don't use turkey breakfast sausage, although you can substitute other turkey sausages, including turkey bratwurst or kielbasa.
• Leftovers may be even better! Spread them into a small baking pan, cover, and refrigerate for up to 3 days. Cut the leftovers into squares and fry in butter in a large nonstick skillet until crisp.

Serve It Up! Make **Carrot Almond Slaw** to go on the side: Shred 1 pound large carrots through a box grater and into a large bowl, then mix in ½ cup sliced almonds, 2 tablespoons apple cider vinegar, 2 tablespoons soy sauce, and 2 tablespoons canola or vegetable oil. Season with ground black pepper before serving.

TURKEY SAUSAGE AND RICE CASSEROLE

EFFORT: **A LITTLE** • PRESSURE: **HIGH** • TIME UNDER PRESSURE: **10 OR 15 MINUTES** • RELEASE: **MODIFIED QUICK** • SERVES: **4 TO 6**

2 tablespoons unsalted butter

1 large yellow onion, chopped

8 ounces white button mushrooms, thinly sliced

1 pound bulk mild Italian turkey sausage meat

1 teaspoon dried sage

1/2 teaspoon fennel seeds

1/2 teaspoon salt

1/2 teaspoon ground black pepper

1 1/2 cups long-grain white rice, such as basmati rice

1/4 cup dry but fruit-forward white wine, such as Pinot Grigio

2 3/4 cups chicken broth

1/4 cup finely grated Parmesan cheese (about 2 ounces)

Up to 1/4 cup packed fresh parsley leaves, chopped

1 Melt the butter in a 6-quart stovetop pressure cooker set over medium heat or in a 6-quart electric pressure cooker turned to the browning function. Add the onion and cook, stirring often, until softened, about 4 minutes.

2 Add the mushrooms and cook, stirring occasionally, until they give off their liquid and it evaporates to a thick glaze, about 5 minutes. Crumble in the sausage meat and cook, stirring occasionally, until it loses its raw, red color, about 4 minutes. Stir in the sage, fennel seeds, salt, and pepper until aromatic, about 20 seconds.

3 Add the rice; stir over the heat for 1 minute. Pour in the wine and scrape up any browned bits in the cooker as it comes to a simmer. Stir in the broth and make sure no rice grains are outside the liquid.

4 Lock the lid onto the pot.

STOVETOP: Raise the heat to high and bring the pot to high pressure (15 psi). Once this pressure has been reached, reduce the heat as much as possible while maintaining this pressure. Cook for 10 minutes.

·············· OR ··············

ELECTRIC: Set the machine to cook at high pressure (9–11 psi). Set the machine's timer to cook at high pressure for 15 minutes.

5 Use the quick-release method to bring the pot's pressure back to normal but do not open the pot. Remove or turn off the heat and set aside for 10 minutes to steam the rice.

6 Unlock and open the pot. Stir in the cheese and parsley. Cover loosely and set aside for 1 minute to blend the flavors before serving.

TESTERS' NOTES

• Here's an old-fashioned casserole that normally takes hours but is now faster and tastier.
• Bulk sausage meat is usually found at the meat counter of larger supermarkets. It's basically the ground meat with spices before that mixture is put into casings. If your supermarket doesn't carry the sausage meat in bulk, buy a similar amount of raw (not smoked) sausage in casings, then slice off the casings and remove the ground meat.
• For more complex flavors, substitute smoked turkey sausage, finely diced. You can also substitute aged Asiago or pecorino for the Parmesan.

Serve It Up! Drizzle an aged, syrupy balsamic vinegar over each helping for a bit of sweet-and-sour sophistication.

TURKEY SAUSAGE AND POTATO STEW

EFFORT: **NOT MUCH** • PRESSURE: **HIGH** • TIME UNDER PRESSURE:
10 OR 15 MINUTES • RELEASE: **QUICK** • SERVES: **4 TO 6**

2 tablespoons olive oil

1 medium yellow onion, chopped

1 pound mild Italian turkey sausage, cut
   into 2-inch pieces

2 teaspoons minced garlic

2 tablespoons white wine vinegar

One 28-ounce can whole tomatoes,
   drained and roughly chopped (about
   3$^{1}/_{2}$ cups)

$^{3}/_{4}$ cup chicken broth

1 tablespoon dried basil

$^{1}/_{2}$ teaspoon salt

$^{1}/_{2}$ teaspoon ground black pepper

1 pound small white potatoes, cut into
   $^{1}/_{2}$-inch-thick rounds

1 Heat the oil in a 6-quart stovetop pressure cooker set over medium heat or in a 6-quart electric pressure cooker turned to the browning function. Add the onion; cook, stirring often, until barely translucent, about 2 minutes.

2 Add the sausage and cook, stirring occasionally, until browned, 4 to 5 minutes. Stir in the garlic; cook for about 15 seconds, then stir in the vinegar and scrape up any browned bits in the pot as it comes to a boil.

3 Add the tomatoes, broth, basil, salt, and pepper. Toss well over the heat. Stir in the potatoes.

4 Lock the lid onto the pot.

STOVETOP: Raise the heat to high and bring the pot to high pressure (15 psi). Once this pressure has been reached, reduce the heat as much as possible while maintaining this pressure. Cook for 10 minutes.

························· **OR** ·····························

ELECTRIC: Set the machine to cook at high pressure (9–11 psi). Set the machine's timer to cook at high pressure for 15 minutes.

5 Use the quick-release method to return the pressure in the pot to normal.

6 Unlock the lid and open the pot. Stir the stew before serving.

TESTERS' NOTES
• The vinegar foregrounds the other flavors, an acidic pop to bring out sweet and savory notes.
• Use only white potatoes, not baking or Russet potatoes, which are too starchy and cloud the stew.
• Canned diced tomatoes are very small bits and would turn this stew into a pasta sauce. By chopping the canned tomatoes into pieces, you will have larger chunks in the stew.
• Cook the onion only a bit, not even until it's translucent. It will continue to cook as the sausage browns. You don't want it to brown (or worse, burn).

Serve It Up! Braise stemmed and chopped collard greens and minced garlic with some chicken broth in a covered skillet set over medium-low heat until tender, 15 to 20 minutes, stirring often.

GROUND TURKEY AND ZITI CASSEROLE

EFFORT: **NOT MUCH** • PRESSURE: **HIGH** • TIME UNDER PRESSURE:
5 OR 8 MINUTES • RELEASE: **QUICK** • SERVES: **6**

2 tablespoons olive oil

1 pound ground turkey

1/2 cup dry and bold red wine,
    such as Syrah

1 tablespoon dried basil

1 teaspoon dried oregano

1/2 teaspoon dried thyme

1/4 teaspoon red pepper flakes

1/4 teaspoon salt

2 cups chicken broth

One 14-ounce can diced tomatoes (about
    1 3/4 cups)

8 ounces dried ziti

1 cup shredded mozzarella cheese (about
    4 ounces)

1/2 cup finely grated Parmesan cheese
    (about 1 ounce)

1 Heat the oil in a 6-quart stovetop pressure cooker set over medium heat or in a 6-quart electric pressure cooker turned to the browning function. Crumble in the ground turkey; cook, stirring occasionally, until well browned, about 5 minutes.

2 Add the wine, basil, oregano, thyme, red pepper flakes, and salt; cook, stirring often, until bubbling and fragrant, about 1 minute. Stir in the broth, tomatoes, and ziti.

3 Lock the lid onto the pot.

STOVETOP: Raise the heat to high and bring the pot to high pressure (15 psi). Once this pressure has been reached, reduce the heat as much as possible while maintaining this pressure. Cook for 5 minutes.

·······················OR·······················
ELECTRIC: Set the machine to cook at high pressure (9–11 psi). Set the machine's timer to cook at high pressure for 8 minutes.

4 Use the quick-release method to bring the pot's pressure back to normal.

5 Unlock and open the pot. Mix the cheeses in a bowl. Stir the stew well, then sprinkle the cheese mixture over the top. Cover loosely and set aside for 4 to 5 minutes to melt the cheese. Serve by scooping up spoonfuls into bowls.

TESTERS' NOTES
• You can make this hearty casserole even more flavorful by using 1/2 pound ground turkey and 1/2 pound bulk mild Italian turkey sausage meat, any casings removed.
• You'll never get a crust on a casserole in the pressure cooker. To give this one some crunch, complete the recipe through step 4, then open the pot and pour the contents into a very large broiler-safe baking dish. Cover with the cheese mixture and broil 4 to 6 inches from the heat source until bubbling and brown, about 4 minutes, the cheese now a bit crunchy on top.

EASY TURKEY CHILI

EFFORT: **NOT MUCH** • PRESSURE: **HIGH** • TIME UNDER PRESSURE:
5 OR 8 MINUTES • RELEASE: **QUICK** • SERVES: **6 TO 8**

One 30-ounce can kidney beans, drained
    and rinsed (about 3 1/2 cups)

One 14-ounce can diced tomatoes (about
    1 3/4 cups)

One 14-ounce can crushed tomatoes
    (about 1 3/4 cups)

One 4 1/2-ounce can chopped mild green
    chiles (about 1/2 cup)

One 2-ounce jar diced pimientos

1 small yellow or white onion, chopped

$\frac{1}{2}$ cup beef broth

3 tablespoons chili powder

$\frac{1}{2}$ teaspoon ground cumin

$\frac{1}{2}$ teaspoon ground black pepper

$1\frac{1}{2}$ pounds ground turkey

1 Mix the beans, diced and crushed tomatoes, green chiles, pimientos, onion, broth, chili powder, cumin, and pepper in a 6-quart stovetop or electric pressure cooker. Crumble in the ground turkey and stir well.

2 Lock the lid onto the cooker.

STOVETOP: Set the pot over high heat and bring it to high pressure (15 psi). Once this pressure has been reached, reduce the heat as much as you can while still maintaining this pressure. Cook for 5 minutes.

·········· OR ··········

ELECTRIC: Set the machine to cook at high pressure (9–11 psi). Set the machine's timer to cook at high pressure for 8 minutes.

3 Use the quick-release method to drop the pot's pressure back to normal.

4 Unlock and open the pot. Stir the chili before serving.

TESTERS' NOTES

• There's nothing simpler than this full-flavored chili. The turkey doesn't add much fat and the resulting taste is surprisingly bright, even a little sweet. Frankly, it doesn't matter to the taste whether you use regular ground turkey or ground white-meat turkey, slightly drier and certainly less fatty.

• If you'd like some heat in the mix, use canned diced tomatoes with chiles.

• Drain the beans but not the tomatoes, chiles, or pimientos. The moisture of the latter three will become the basis of the sauce for the chili.

• There's no salt here because the canned ingredients carry plenty of sodium. Pass more at the table for those who miss it.

Serve It Up! Make a quick batch of **Honey Cornbread** to go alongside: Whisk $\frac{3}{4}$ cup buttermilk, 3 tablespoons melted unsalted butter, 2 tablespoons honey, and 1 large egg in a large bowl. Stir in $\frac{3}{4}$ cup yellow cornmeal, $\frac{2}{3}$ cup all-purpose flour, $\frac{1}{2}$ teaspoon baking powder, $\frac{1}{2}$ teaspoon baking soda, and $\frac{1}{2}$ teaspoon salt. Spread into a greased 8-inch square baking pan and bake in a 350°F oven until puffed and set, until a toothpick inserted into the center of the cornbread comes out clean, about 30 minutes. Cool on a wire rack for 10 minutes before cutting into squares.

SLOPPY TURKEY SUBS

EFFORT: **NOT MUCH** • PRESSURE: **HIGH** • TIME UNDER PRESSURE: **3 OR 5 MINUTES** • RELEASE: **QUICK** • SERVES: **6**

2 tablespoons olive oil

$1\frac{1}{2}$ pounds ground turkey

1 small red bell pepper, stemmed, cored, and chopped

$\frac{1}{2}$ cup chopped red onion

$\frac{1}{2}$ teaspoon onion powder

$\frac{1}{2}$ teaspoon dried oregano

$\frac{1}{2}$ teaspoon dried sage

$\frac{1}{2}$ teaspoon dried thyme

$\frac{1}{2}$ teaspoon ground cumin

$\frac{1}{2}$ teaspoon ground black pepper

1 cup canned crushed tomatoes

2 tablespoons packed dark brown sugar

2 tablespoons Worcestershire sauce

2 tablespoons canned tomato paste

6 hoagie buns

(continued)

1 Heat the oil in a 6-quart stovetop pressure cooker set over medium heat or in a 6-quart electric pressure cooker turned to the browning function. Add the ground turkey; cook, stirring often, until it's broken into small clumps and has lost its raw color, about 3 minutes.

2 Stir in the bell pepper, onion, onion powder, oregano, sage, thyme, cumin, and pepper until fragrant, about 1 minute. Add the tomatoes, brown sugar, and Worcestershire sauce along with ¼ cup water; stir well.

3 Lock the lid onto the pot.

STOVETOP: Raise the heat to high and bring the pot to high pressure (15 psi). Once this pressure has been reached, reduce the heat as much as possible while maintaining this pressure. Cook for 3 minutes.

·····················**OR**·····················

ELECTRIC: Set the machine to cook at high pressure (9–11 psi). Set the machine's timer to cook at high pressure for 5 minutes.

4 Use the quick-release method to drop the pot's pressure to normal.

5 Unlock and open the pot. Set the stovetop pot over medium heat or turn the electric model to its browning or simmer setting; bring to a simmer, stirring occasionally. Stir in the tomato paste until dissolved; cook for 1 or 2 minutes, stirring often, until slightly thickened. Cool a few minutes, then spoon the filling into hoagie buns to serve.

TESTERS' NOTES

• You'll need a knife and a fork to eat these stuffed sandwiches. And lots of napkins. If the sauce is too wet, simmer it a couple of minutes in step 5 to reduce it a bit more. We like it sloppy, but it may be too much so for your taste.
• You can use 1 tablespoon of your favorite dried spice grilling blend for all the dried spices.

Serve It Up! Spread the buns with pickle relish before adding the filling. Offer small romaine lettuce leaves, pickled jalapeño rings, cole slaw, and/or finely shredded Cheddar as toppings.

TURKEY PICADILLO with GREEN OLIVES, RAISINS, and CILANTRO

EFFORT: **A LITTLE** • PRESSURE: **HIGH** • TIME UNDER PRESSURE: **3 OR 5 MINUTES** • RELEASE: **QUICK** • SERVES: **6**

2 tablespoons olive oil

1 medium yellow onion, chopped

1 medium green bell pepper, stemmed, cored, and chopped

1 medium red bell pepper, stemmed, cored, and chopped

2 pounds ground turkey

2 teaspoons minced garlic

½ tablespoon ground cumin

½ tablespoon dried oregano

½ teaspoon ground coriander

½ teaspoon ground black pepper

1 bay leaf

One 28-ounce can tomato puree (about 3½ cups)

¼ cup chicken broth

½ cup chopped, pitted green olives

½ cup chopped golden raisins

¼ cup packed fresh cilantro leaves, chopped

2 tablespoons drained and rinsed capers, chopped

Boston lettuce leaves, rinsed for grit, for serving

1 Heat the oil in a 6-quart stovetop pressure cooker set over medium heat or in a 6-quart electric pressure cooker turned to the browning function. Add the onion and both bell peppers; cook, stirring often, until the onion turns translucent, about 4 minutes.

2 Crumble in the ground turkey; cook, stirring often, until it loses its raw color, 3 to 4 minutes. Stir in the garlic, cumin, oregano, coriander, pepper, and bay leaf. Cook about 1 minute, stirring all the while, until aromatic. Add the tomato puree, broth, olives, raisins, cilantro, and capers; stir well.

3 Lock the lid onto the pot.

STOVETOP: Raise the heat to high and bring the pot to high pressure (15 psi). Once this pressure has been reached, reduce the heat as much as possible while maintaining this pressure. Cook for 3 minutes.

························· OR ·························

ELECTRIC: Set the machine to cook at high pressure (9–11 psi). Set the machine's timer to cook at high pressure for 5 minutes.

4 Use the quick-release method to bring the pot's pressure to normal.

5 Unlock and open the pot. Set the stovetop cooker over medium heat or turn the electric cooker to its browning function; bring the stew to a full simmer. Cook, stirring occasionally, until thickened, 2 to 3 minutes, then discard the bay leaf. Serve by spooning the mixture into lettuce leaves and folding them closed.

TESTERS' NOTES

• A picadillo is a Latin American or Caribbean dish, often served on top of rice and beans. We've simplified it into a meal served in lettuce leaves, perfect for your summer deck. You could also stuff it into hollowed-out bell peppers for an easy lunch or take it back to its origins over white rice and black beans.

• Because of varying amounts of moisture in ingredients (based on seasonality, ambient humidity, and shelf life), you may have more or less moisture than we did in testing. Cook the stew in step 5 just until most of the liquid in the pot has evaporated.

• Save any leftovers in a sealed container in the fridge for up to 4 days, but moisten them with some more chicken broth before reheating in a covered saucepan.

• Use the leftovers for a pizza topping. Spread a purchased pizza crust with tomato sauce, then sprinkle on the picadillo. Top with shredded mozzarella and bake on a rimmed baking sheet until crunchy and bubbling in a 400°F oven, 15 to 17 minutes.

Serve It Up! Garnish the picadillo with pickled jalapeño rings, sour cream, and/or pico de gallo.

TURKEY "FRIED RICE" PILAF

EFFORT: **NOT MUCH** • PRESSURE: **HIGH** • TIME UNDER PRESSURE: **10 OR 15 MINUTES** • RELEASE: **MODIFIED QUICK** • SERVES: **4 TO 6**

2 tablespoons peanut oil

6 medium scallions, thinly sliced

2 tablespoons minced fresh ginger

2 teaspoons minced garlic

¾ pound ground turkey

3 tablespoons rice vinegar

3 tablespoons hoisin sauce

3 tablespoons soy sauce

1 cup long-grain white rice, such as jasmine rice

2 medium carrots, thinly sliced

2 cups chicken broth

1 Heat the oil in a 6-quart stovetop pressure cooker set over medium heat or in a 6-quart electric pressure cooker turned to the

(continued)

browning function. Add the scallions, ginger, and garlic; stir-fry for 30 seconds.

2 Crumble in the turkey; cook, stirring often, until lightly browned, about 5 minutes. Stir in the vinegar, hoisin sauce, and soy sauce until bubbling, about 30 seconds. Add the rice and carrots; stir well. Pour in the broth, making sure the rice grains are submerged.

3 Lock the lid onto the cooker.

STOVETOP: Raise the heat to high and bring the pot to high pressure (15 psi). Once this pressure has been reached, reduce the heat as much as possible while maintaining this pressure. Cook for 10 minutes.

························ **OR** ························

ELECTRIC: Set the machine to cook at high pressure (9–11 psi). Set the machine's timer to cook at high pressure for 15 minutes.

4 Use the quick-release method to return the pot's pressure to normal, but do not open the cooker. Set aside for 10 minutes to steam the rice.

5 Unlock and open the cooker. Stir well before serving.

TESTERS' NOTES
• We took the flavors of fried rice and packed them into a pilaf, a one-pot rice dish.
• There's no scrambled egg in this dish, as you might find in a Chinese restaurant, nor is there room in the cooker to scramble an egg. If you miss the egg, fry some eggs (sunny side up or over easy) and lay one on top of each serving.
• You can substitute 1½ tablespoons white wine vinegar and 1½ tablespoons additional broth for the rice vinegar and/or 1 tablespoon ketchup and 2 tablespoons unsweetened apple juice for the hoisin sauce.
• Lots of vegetables work in this dish—in lieu of the carrots, try thinly sliced celery, very finely diced and seeded butternut squash, or thinly sliced green beans.

TURKEY MEATBALLS IN A CREAMY TOMATO SAUCE

EFFORT: **A LITTLE** • PRESSURE: **HIGH** • TIME UNDER PRESSURE: **7 OR 10 MINUTES** • RELEASE: **QUICK** • SERVES: **4**

1 pound ground turkey
1 large egg, at room temperature and beaten in a small bowl
½ cup plain dried breadcrumbs
¼ cup finely grated Parmesan cheese (about ½ ounce)
½ teaspoon dried oregano
½ teaspoon dried rosemary
½ teaspoon ground black pepper
½ teaspoon salt
2 tablespoons unsalted butter
1 medium yellow onion, chopped
2 medium celery stalks, thinly sliced
One 28-ounce can whole tomatoes, drained and roughly chopped (about 3½ cups)
½ cup chicken broth
1 tablespoon packed fresh oregano leaves, minced
¼ cup heavy cream
¼ teaspoon grated nutmeg

1 Mix the ground turkey, egg, breadcrumbs, cheese, oregano, rosemary, pepper, and ¼ teaspoon salt in a large bowl until well combined. Form the mixture into 12 balls.

2 Melt the butter in a 6-quart stovetop pressure cooker set over medium heat or in a 6-quart electric pressure cooker turned to the browning function. Add the onion and celery; cook, stirring often, until the onion turns translucent, about 3 minutes.

3 Stir in the tomatoes, broth, oregano, and the remaining ¼ teaspoon salt. Drop the meatballs into the sauce.

4 Lock the lid onto the cooker.

STOVETOP: Raise the heat to high and bring the pot to high pressure (15 psi). Once this pressure has been reached, reduce the heat as much as possible while maintaining this pressure. Cook for 7 minutes.

······································ **OR** ·······························

ELECTRIC: Set the machine to cook at high pressure (9–11 psi). Set the machine's timer to cook at high pressure for 10 minutes.

5 Use the quick-release method to drop the pot's pressure to normal.

6 Unlock and open the cooker. Set the stovetop pot over medium heat or turn the electric model to its browning function. Stir in the cream and nutmeg; simmer, stirring all the while, for 1 minute to reduce the cream a little and blend the flavors.

TESTERS' NOTES
• When we were testing recipes, we had to put the leftovers from this one away lest we eat the entire batch *after* lunch. It's so creamy and luscious, with heavily spiced meatballs.
• Dried seasonings in these meatballs are better than fresh since they have a slightly duller, earthier flavor, a better match to the sweet turkey.

Serve It Up! Serve over cooked long-grain white rice, over cooked and drained spaghetti, or in hoagie buns as meatball subs with the sauce drizzled on top.

TURKEY MEATBALLS WITH BASIL AND PINE NUTS IN A VINEGARY BROTH

EFFORT: **A LITTLE** · PRESSURE: **HIGH** · TIME UNDER PRESSURE: **7 OR 10 MINUTES** · RELEASE: **QUICK** · SERVES: **4**

1 pound ground turkey

½ cup oil-packed sun-dried tomatoes, drained and chopped (about 4 ounces)

½ cup plain dried breadcrumbs

1 large egg, at room temperature and beaten in a small bowl

2 tablespoons pine nuts, chopped

1 tablespoon dried basil

½ teaspoon ground black pepper

¼ teaspoon salt

2 tablespoons olive oil

1 medium yellow onion, chopped

1 large green bell pepper, stemmed, cored, and chopped

2 teaspoons minced garlic

½ teaspoon fennel seeds

¼ teaspoon red pepper flakes

3 tablespoons balsamic vinegar

½ cup chicken broth

1 Mix the ground turkey, sun-dried tomatoes, breadcrumbs, egg, pine nuts, basil, pepper, and salt in a big bowl until uniform. Form into 12 meatballs.

2 Heat the oil in a 6-quart stovetop pressure cooker set over medium heat or in a 6-quart electric pressure cooker turned to the browning function. Add the onion, bell pepper, garlic, fennel seeds, and red pepper flakes; stir over the heat until aromatic,

(continued)

about 2 minutes. Pour in the vinegar and stir to get any browned bits off the bottom of the cooker. Add the broth and nestle in the meatballs.

3 Lock the lid onto the cooker.

STOVETOP: Raise the heat to high and bring the pot to high pressure (15 psi). Once this pressure has been reached, reduce the heat as much as possible while maintaining this pressure. Cook for 7 minutes.

·········· **OR** ··········

ELECTRIC: Set the machine to cook at high pressure (9–11 psi). Set the machine's timer to cook at high pressure for 10 minutes.

4 Use the quick-release method to return the pot's pressure to normal.

5 Unlock and open the pot. Stir gently before serving.

TESTERS' NOTES
• This meatball recipe is surprisingly savory, thanks to the vegetables and the balsamic vinegar. Consider it a comforting Italian dinner without much fuss.
• Pack the meatballs into the pot without crushing them. They need all the help they can get to stay together under pressure.
• Use only sun-dried tomatoes packed in olive oil, preferably not too heavily flavored. Their extra oil will add body and texture to the meatballs as they cook.

Serve It Up! Although you can serve these meatballs on their own in their soupy sauce, you can also ladle them over cooked and drained linguine with plenty of grated Parmesan on top.

CHEESY TURKEY-STUFFED BELL PEPPERS

EFFORT: **A LITTLE** · PRESSURE: **HIGH** · TIME UNDER PRESSURE: **5 OR 7 MINUTES** · RELEASE: **QUICK** · SERVES: **4**

2 tablespoons unsalted butter
1 medium yellow onion, chopped
1 pound ground turkey
2 teaspoons minced garlic
1 teaspoon dried oregano
1 teaspoon ground cumin
$1/4$ teaspoon salt
Up to $1/4$ teaspoon cayenne
$1/2$ cup fresh corn kernels, or frozen kernels, thawed
One $4^{1}/_{2}$-ounce can chopped mild green chiles (about $1/2$ cup)
1 cup shredded sharp Cheddar cheese (about 4 ounces)
4 large green or red bell peppers

1 Melt the butter in a 6-quart stovetop pressure cooker set over medium heat or in a 6-quart electric pressure cooker turned to the browning function. Add the onion and cook, stirring occasionally, until softened, about 3 minutes. Crumble in the ground turkey and cook, stirring occasionally, until it loses its raw color, about 3 minutes.

2 Stir in the garlic, oregano, cumin, salt, and cayenne; cook until aromatic, about 30 seconds. Transfer the contents of the cooker to a large bowl and cool for 20 minutes. Stir the corn, chiles, and cheese into the turkey mixture.

3 Slice the tops off the bell peppers and scrape out any membranes and seeds inside without breaking through the peppers' walls. Stuff each pepper with the ground turkey mixture. Wipe out the cooker; set the pressure cooker rack inside. Pour in 1 cup water, then stand the peppers cut side up on the rack.

4 Lock the lid onto the pot.

STOVETOP: Set the pot over high heat and bring it to high pressure (15 psi). Once this pressure has been reached, reduce the heat as much as possible while maintaining this pressure. Cook for 5 minutes.

························· **OR** ·························

ELECTRIC: Set the machine to cook at high pressure (9–11 psi). Set the machine's timer to cook at high pressure for 7 minutes.

5 Use the quick-release method to bring the pot's pressure back to normal.

6 Unlock and open the pot. Transfer the stuffed peppers to individual serving bowls or plates and serve.

TESTERS' NOTES
• The pressure cooker takes away much of the mess and work of stuffed peppers: no need to pre-steam or bake for hours (and very little cleanup). Plus, we bake the cheese right into the filling, rather than just leaving it as a coating on top.
• Red bell peppers are a little sweeter than green ones—and are perhaps a better match with this spiced and somewhat savory filling.
• Look for squat, large bell peppers, rather than the narrow, skinny ones that may be too tall for the cooker. If the bumps on the bottom of the pepper are too irregular for it to stand up straight, slice a little off to create a more stable base. Just don't cut through to the hollow inside.

TOMATO-BRAISED TURKEY MEATLOAF

EFFORT: **A LITTLE** • PRESSURE: **HIGH** • TIME UNDER PRESSURE: **20 OR 30 MINUTES** • RELEASE: **QUICK** • SERVES: **6**

2 medium carrots, thinly sliced

One 14-ounce can diced tomatoes (about 1³/₄ cups)

¹/₂ cup chicken broth

1 tablespoon Worcestershire sauce

1 tablespoon sweet paprika

1¹/₂ pounds ground turkey

1 large egg plus 1 large egg white, at room temperature and beaten in a small bowl

1 small white or yellow onion, finely chopped

³/₄ cup plain dried breadcrumbs

¹/₄ cup ketchup

1 tablespoon packed fresh thyme leaves

1 tablespoon packed fresh sage leaves, minced

¹/₂ teaspoon salt

¹/₂ teaspoon ground black pepper

1 Mix the carrots, tomatoes, chicken broth, Worcestershire sauce, and paprika in a 6-quart stovetop or electric pressure cooker.

2 Mix the ground turkey, egg and egg white, onion, breadcrumbs, ketchup, thyme, sage, salt, and pepper in a large bowl until well combined and uniform. Form into an oval loaf with a flat bottom. Transfer the meatloaf to the pressure cooker.

(continued)

3 Lock the lid onto the pot.

STOVETOP: Set the pot over high heat and bring it to high pressure (15 psi). Once this pressure has been reached, reduce the heat as much as possible while maintaining this pressure. Cook for 20 minutes.

·························· **OR** ··························

ELECTRIC: Set the machine to cook at high pressure (9–11 psi). Set the machine's timer to cook at high pressure for 30 minutes.

4 Use the quick-release method to return the pot's pressure to normal.

5 Unlock and open the pot. Cut the meatloaf into slices to serve with the sauce.

TESTERS' NOTES
• Form this meatloaf into a fairly compact bundle so it stays together as it cooks under pressure. The egg will give it some sticky binding, but you'll still have to make sure it's a cohesive, firmly packed loaf.
• It doesn't matter if there are some carrots and tomatoes underneath the meatloaf as it cooks. They'll just add more flavor!
• Measure the diameter of your cooker and then shape the meatloaf so it will fit.
• You might be able to transfer the cooked meatloaf to a carving board, provided you have two large, sturdy spatulas. However, to avoid messy spills, it's easier just to slice it into pieces right in the cooker and lift them out one by one. If you've got a nonstick-coated pressure cooker, you'll need to use nonstick-approved utensils to cut the meatloaf.

CREAMY TURKEY CUTLETS AND FUSILLI

EFFORT: **A LITTLE** • PRESSURE: **HIGH** • TIME UNDER PRESSURE: **5 OR 8 MINUTES** • RELEASE: **QUICK** • SERVES: **4**

1 tablespoon unsalted butter

1 small yellow onion, chopped

1 pound turkey breast cutlets, sliced into thin strips

1 teaspoon dried sage

1 teaspoon dried thyme

½ teaspoon salt

½ teaspoon ground black pepper

⅔ cup dry vermouth

2½ cups chicken broth

8 ounces dried fusilli

½ cup heavy cream

1½ tablespoons all-purpose flour

½ cup finely grated Parmesan cheese (about 4 ounces)

1 Melt the butter in a 6-quart stovetop pressure cooker set over medium heat or in a 6-quart electric pressure cooker turned to the browning function. Add the onion and cook, stirring often, until translucent, about 2 minutes.

2 Add the turkey and cook, stirring often, until it has lost its raw color, 4 to 5 minutes. Stir in the sage, thyme, salt, and pepper; cook until aromatic, about 20 seconds. Pour in the vermouth and scrape any browned bits off the bottom of the cooker as it comes to a simmer. Stir in the broth and pasta.

3 Lock the lid onto the pot.

STOVETOP: Raise the heat to high and bring the pot to high pressure (15 psi). Once this pressure has been reached, reduce the heat as much as possible while maintaining this pressure. Cook for 5 minutes.

·································· **OR** ··································

ELECTRIC: Set the machine to cook at high pressure (9–11 psi). Set the machine's timer to cook at high pressure for 8 minutes.

4 Use the quick-release method to bring the pot's pressure back to normal.

5 Unlock and open the pot. Set the stovetop cooker over medium heat or turn the electric cooker to its browning function. As the stew comes to a simmer, whisk the cream and flour in a small bowl until smooth. Whisk this mixture into the stew; stir until bubbling and somewhat thickened, about 1 minute. Stir in the cheese before serving.

TESTERS' NOTES
• Sort of like a pressure cooker version of tetrazzini, this rich casserole uses turkey cutlets, rather than ground turkey, for a milder, sweeter flavor. Fusilli—little twisted pasta shapes—will hold the sauce.
• Whisk—don't stir—in step 5. Yes, bits of turkey and the vegetables may get caught in the whisk. But you need to keep the sauce moving in the pot so it doesn't scorch.
• You can substitute dry sherry (bolder), dry white wine (sweeter), or unsweetened apple juice (much sweeter) for the dry vermouth.
• For a lighter dish, use half-and-half instead of the cream.

Serve It Up! Garnish the servings with minced parsley and grated nutmeg.

CHEESY TURKEY, PASTA, AND VEGGIE CASSEROLE

EFFORT: **A LITTLE** • PRESSURE: **HIGH** • TIME UNDER PRESSURE: **5 OR 8 MINUTES** • RELEASE: **QUICK** • SERVES: **4 TO 6**

1 cup heavy or light cream

3/4 cup whole milk

1 tablespoon Worcestershire sauce

1 tablespoon all-purpose flour

1 teaspoon dried sage

1/2 teaspoon ground black pepper

1 pound turkey breast cutlets, diced into 1/2-inch pieces

8 ounces dried ziti or penne

2 cups frozen peas and carrots (do not thaw)

2 tablespoons unsalted butter

1 small yellow onion, chopped

2 cups grated Gruyère cheese (about 8 ounces)

1 Whisk the cream, milk, Worcestershire sauce, flour, sage, and pepper in a large bowl until the flour dissolves; set aside.

2 Place the turkey, pasta, and 6 cups water in a 6-quart stovetop or electric pressure cooker.

3 Lock the lid onto the pot.

STOVETOP: Set the pot over high heat and bring it to high pressure (15 psi). Once this pressure has been reached, reduce the heat as much as possible while maintaining this pressure. Cook for 5 minutes.

·································· **OR** ··································

ELECTRIC: Set the machine to cook at high pressure (9–11 psi). Set the machine's timer to cook at high pressure for 8 minutes.

(continued)

4 Use the quick-release method to drop the pot's pressure to normal.

5 Place the peas and carrots in a large colander set in the sink. Unlock and open the pot, then pour its contents over the vegetables in the colander. Set aside for 5 minutes. Wipe out the cooker.

6 Melt the butter in the stovetop cooker set over medium heat or in the electric cooker turned to the browning function. Add the onion and cook, stirring often, until softened, about 3 minutes. Add the milk mixture and whisk until bubbling, about 2 minutes. Stir in the contents of the colander, then the cheese. Cover loosely and set aside off the heat for a few minutes to warm everything through and melt the cheese.

TESTERS' NOTES
• This easy casserole uses the pressure cooker both as a quick-cooking tool and as a saucepan to build a quick cheese sauce. This recipe is real comfort food, no fakes necessary.
• Gruyère (French, *gree-YAIR*) is the melty cheese familiar from French onion soup. It has a slightly sour, bright flavor with nutty accents, a sophisticated bump in this casserole. Any leftover Gruyère will be a marvel in grilled cheese sandwiches!

TURKEY BREAST WITH MUSHROOM GRAVY

EFFORT: **A LOT** • PRESSURE: **HIGH** • TIME UNDER PRESSURE: **25 OR 37 MINUTES** • RELEASE: **NATURAL** • SERVES: **6**

2 tablespoons unsalted butter

1 tablespoon olive oil

One 2- to 2½-pound boneless turkey breast

½ teaspoon salt

½ teaspoon ground black pepper

1 small yellow onion, chopped

8 ounces baby bella or cremini mushrooms, thinly sliced

½ cup dry white wine, such as Chardonnay

2 fresh thyme sprigs

¾ cup chicken broth

1 teaspoon potato starch or cornstarch

1 Melt the butter in the oil in a 6-quart stovetop pressure cooker set over medium heat or in a 6-quart electric pressure cooker turned to the browning function. Season the turkey breast with the salt and pepper, then brown on both sides, turning once, about 6 minutes. Transfer to a large plate.

2 Add the onion to the pot and cook, stirring occasionally, until translucent, about 3 minutes. Add the mushrooms and cook, stirring once in a while, until they give off their liquid and it reduces to a thick glaze, about 4 minutes.

3 Pour in the wine; add the thyme sprigs. Stir to get any browned bits up off the bottom of the cooker as the wine simmers. Pour in the broth and nestle the turkey breast into the sauce. Pour any juices from the plate into the cooker.

4 Lock the lid onto the pot.

STOVETOP: Raise the heat to high and bring the pot to high pressure (15 psi). Once this pressure has been reached, reduce the heat as much as possible while maintaining this pressure. Cook for 25 minutes.

·············· **OR** ··············

ELECTRIC: Set the machine to cook at high pressure (9–11 psi). Set the machine's timer to cook at high pressure for 37 minutes.

5 Reduce the pressure.

STOVETOP: Set the pot off the heat and let its pressure come back to normal naturally, about 15 minutes.

·············· **OR** ··············

ELECTRIC: Turn off the machine or unplug it so it doesn't flip to its keep-warm setting. Let its pressure return to normal naturally, 15 to 20 minutes.

6 Unlock and open the pot. Use kitchen tongs and a large spatula to transfer the turkey breast to a carving board. Whisk the potato or cornstarch with ½ tablespoon water in a small bowl until you have a loose slurry.

7 Set the stovetop pot over medium heat or turn the electric one to its browning or simmer function. Bring the sauce to a simmer. Stir in the slurry; cook for 1 minute, stirring occasionally, until thickened. Remove from the heat or turn off the machine; slice the breast and serve with the gravy on the side.

TESTERS' NOTES

• Don't wait for a holiday to prepare this favorite, especially since you can make the meal in no time flat.

• Although the turkey will surely be done after 40 minutes, err on the side of safety—take an instant-read meat thermometer and insert it into the thickest part of the meat; it

should register 160°F. If it doesn't, cover the pot and bring it back to high pressure, then cook for 2 to 3 minutes.

• To carve a turkey breast, start at one of the thinner ends and make ½-inch-thick slices widthwise through the meat.

Serve It Up! Serve with **Skillet-Blistered Green Beans**: Heat 2 tablespoons olive oil in a large skillet set over medium-high heat until rippling; add 1 pound trimmed green beans and cook, tossing often, until they begin to blister. Add ¼ cup water and 2 tablespoons lemon juice; stir until all the liquid has boiled away. Season with salt and pepper to taste and serve hot.

TURKEY BREAST WITH **PROSECCO** AND FENNEL

EFFORT: **A LITTLE** · PRESSURE: **HIGH** · TIME UNDER PRESSURE: **25 OR 37 MINUTES** · RELEASE: **NATURAL** · SERVES: **6**

2 tablespoons olive oil

One 2- to 2½-pound boneless turkey breast

½ teaspoon salt

½ teaspoon ground black pepper

1 large fennel bulb, trimmed and cut into ½-inch-thick slices

1 tablespoon minced fresh sage leaves

2 teaspoons finely grated lemon zest

½ teaspoon fennel seeds

1½ cups Prosecco or any other sparkling wine

1 Heat the oil in a 6-quart stovetop pressure cooker set over medium heat or in a 6-quart electric pressure cooker turned to the browning function. Season the turkey breast with the salt and pepper, slip it into

(continued)

the cooker, and brown on both sides, turning once, about 6 minutes.

2 Lay the fennel slices around the turkey breast; sprinkle in the sage, lemon zest, and fennel seeds. Pour the Prosecco around the meat.

3 Lock the lid onto the pot.

STOVETOP: Raise the heat to high and bring the pot to high pressure (15 psi). Once this pressure has been reached, reduce the heat as much as possible while maintaining this pressure. Cook for 25 minutes.

·····················OR·····················

ELECTRIC: Set the machine to cook at high pressure (9–11 psi). Set the machine's timer to cook at high pressure for 37 minutes.

4 Reduce the pressure.

STOVETOP: Set the pot off the heat and let its pressure come back to normal naturally, about 15 minutes.

·····················OR·····················

ELECTRIC: Turn off the machine or unplug it so it doesn't jump to its keep-warm setting. Let its pressure return to normal naturally, 15 to 20 minutes.

5 Unlock and open the cooker. Transfer the turkey breast to a carving board; slice widthwise into ½-inch-thick pieces. Serve in deep plates with the sauce and vegetables.

TESTERS' NOTES
• Prosecco is an Italian sparkling wine, a little sweeter than and not as yeasty as Champagne. As such, it's a great complement to turkey breast and offers a bit of sweet that is then balanced by the lemon zest.
• Browning the turkey breast will provide the major savory notes for the dish, so don't stint on that step. You want it to brown enough that the natural sugars caramelize across the meat until you can almost pop it off the cooker.

FRUIT-STUFFED TURKEY BREAST WITH WHITE WINE AND HONEY

EFFORT: **A LOT** • PRESSURE: **HIGH** • TIME UNDER PRESSURE: **25 OR 37 MINUTES** • RELEASE: **NATURAL** • SERVES: **6**

One 2- to 2½-pound boneless turkey breast, butterflied
¼ cup chopped glacéed fruit
¼ ounce dried porcini mushrooms
8 fresh sage leaves
¼ teaspoon salt
¼ teaspoon ground black pepper
2 tablespoons unsalted butter
1¼ cups dry, fruit-forward white wine, such as Sauvignon Blanc
2 tablespoons honey
2 fresh thyme sprigs

1 Lay the turkey breast smooth side down on a clean work surface or cutting board. Spread the glacéed fruit across it. Lay the dried mushrooms and sage leaves over the fruit. Starting with one short side, roll the meat into a tight, firm tube. Tie in three or four places with butcher's twine to secure. Season with salt and pepper.

2 Melt the butter in a 6-quart stovetop pressure cooker set over medium heat or in a 6-quart electric pressure cooker turned to the browning function. Set the tied turkey breast in the cooker and brown on all sides, turning occasionally, about 5 minutes.

3 Pour in the white wine; drizzle the honey on and around the turkey breast. Tuck in the thyme sprigs.

4 Lock the lid onto the pot.

STOVETOP: Raise the heat to high and bring the pot to high pressure (15 psi). Once this pressure has been reached, reduce the heat as much as possible while maintaining this pressure. Cook for 25 minutes.

·························· **OR** ··························

ELECTRIC: Set the machine to cook at high pressure (9–11 psi). Set the machine's timer to cook at high pressure for 37 minutes.

5 Reduce the pressure.

STOVETOP: Set the pot off the heat and let its pressure come back to normal naturally, about 15 minutes.

·························· **OR** ··························

ELECTRIC: Turn off the machine or unplug it so it doesn't jump to its keep-warm setting. Let its pressure return to normal naturally, 15 to 20 minutes.

6 Unlock and open the cooker. Transfer the stuffed turkey breast to a carving board; let stand for 5 minutes. Snip off the twine; slice the stuffed breast into ½-inch-thick rounds. Serve with the pot sauce ladled over the helpings.

TESTERS' NOTES

• Stuffing turkey with dried fruit brings out its natural sweetness—which is tamed with earthy dried mushrooms and sage.

• You'll need a quality wine to stand up to the honey in the sauce and the many aromatics. Figure on a moderately priced bottle, something you would drink with the meal.

• Chopped glacéed fruit is found most often in the baking aisle, and is familiar as the bits of color in fruit cakes. It adds a subtle, tangy sweetness to the dish. If you prefer, substitute chopped candied orange peel, often available near the nuts and dried fruit.

TURKEY POT ROAST WITH **PORT** AND CRANBERRIES

EFFORT: **A LITTLE** • PRESSURE: **HIGH** • TIME UNDER PRESSURE: **12 OR 18 MINUTES** • RELEASE: **NATURAL** • SERVES: **4**

2 tablespoons peanut oil

Two 1¼- to 1½-pound bone-in turkey thighs

¼ teaspoon salt

¼ teaspoon ground black pepper

2 medium yellow onions, halved and sliced into thin half-moons

1 tablespoon minced garlic

½ cup dried cranberries, chopped

1 tablespoon Dijon mustard

2 teaspoons dried thyme

2 bay leaves

One 14-ounce can diced tomatoes, drained (about 1¾ cups)

½ cup non-vintage tawny or ruby port

1 cup chicken broth

1½ tablespoons all-purpose flour

1 Heat the oil in a 6-quart stovetop pressure cooker set over medium heat or in a 6-quart electric pressure cooker turned to the browning function. Season the thighs with the salt and pepper; set them in the cooker. Brown well, turning once, about 6 minutes. Transfer to a large bowl.

2 Add the onions and cook, stirring often, just until softened, about 4 minutes. Add the garlic and stir until aromatic, less than 1 minute. Stir in the dried cranberries, mustard, thyme, and bay leaves.

3 Pour in the tomatoes and port; scrape up any browned bits on the bottom of the cooker as the liquid comes to a simmer. Tuck the

(continued)

turkey thighs into the onion mixture; pour any juice from their bowl into the cooker. Whisk the broth and flour in a small bowl until smooth; pour into the cooker around (but not over) the thighs.

4 Lock the lid onto the pot.

STOVETOP: Raise the heat to high and bring the pot to high pressure (15 psi). Once this pressure has been reached, reduce the heat as much as possible while maintaining this pressure. Cook for 12 minutes.

··················· **OR** ···················

ELECTRIC: Set the machine to cook at high pressure (9–11 psi). Set the machine's timer to cook at high pressure for 18 minutes.

5 Reduce the pressure.

STOVETOP: Set the pot off the heat and let its pressure return to normal naturally, about 15 minutes.

··················· **OR** ···················

ELECTRIC: Turn off the machine or unplug it so it doesn't flip to its keep-warm setting. Let its pressure return to normal naturally, 15 to 20 minutes.

6 Unlock and open the cooker. Discard the bay leaves. Transfer the thighs to a large cutting board; slice into thick chunks to serve in bowls with the sauce in the pot ladled on top.

TESTERS' NOTES
• Turkey thighs cook up gorgeously tender in the pressure cooker, a rich meal in minutes. This one mimics the tastes of a classic version of beef pot roast (but with leaner meat).
• We leave the skin on the thighs for richness in the sauce. If you're going to serve the meat with the skin on, brown it well, past golden, with dark bits across its surface. You may want to brown only one thigh at a time for better caramelization. If so, divide the oil between the two thighs as you brown them.
• In lieu of the port, you can use Madeira (sweeter) or a dry red wine plus 1 tablespoon dark brown sugar.

Serve It Up! Steam peeled and sliced parsnips until tender, then mash with unsalted butter, milk, salt, and pepper. Use this puree as a bed for the stew in the bowls.

TURKEY, BROWN RICE, AND MUSHROOM CASSEROLE

EFFORT: **A LITTLE** • PRESSURE: **HIGH** • TIME UNDER PRESSURE: **22 OR 33 MINUTES** • RELEASE: **MODIFIED QUICK** • SERVES: **4**

One 4-ounce pancetta chunk, chopped

Two 1¼- to 1½-pound bone-in turkey thighs, each cut in half

2 medium shallots, chopped

4 ounces baby bella or cremini mushrooms, thinly sliced

½ ounce dried mushrooms, preferably porcini

2 teaspoons minced garlic

2 teaspoons dried sage

1 teaspoon dried marjoram or thyme

1 cup plus 2 tablespoons long-grain brown rice, such as brown basmati

2 cups chicken broth

1 Set the pancetta in a 6-quart stovetop pressure cooker set over medium heat or in a 6-quart electric pressure cooker turned to the browning function; cook, stirring occasionally, until crisp, about 4 minutes. Use a slotted spoon to transfer the pancetta to a large bowl.

2 Set the turkey in the cooker; brown well, turning once, about 6 minutes. Transfer to the bowl as well.

3 Add the shallots to the pot; cook, stirring often, until softened, about 2 minutes. Add the fresh mushrooms and cook, stirring occasionally, until they give off their liquid and it has reduced to a thick glaze, about 5 minutes.

4 Crumble in the dried mushrooms; add the garlic, sage, and marjoram. Stir until aromatic, about 20 seconds. Add the rice and cook, stirring all the while, for 1 minute. Pour in the broth; return the pancetta, turkey thighs, and any juices in their bowl to the pot. Make sure no grains of rice and as little turkey as possible are sticking up above the liquid.

5 Lock the lid onto the cooker.

STOVETOP: Raise the heat to high and bring the pot to high pressure (15 psi). Once this pressure has been reached, reduce the heat as much as possible while maintaining this pressure. Cook for 22 minutes.

·············· **OR** ··············

ELECTRIC: Set the machine to cook at high pressure (9–11 psi). Set the machine's timer to cook at high pressure for 33 minutes.

6 Use the quick-release method to bring the pot's pressure back to normal but do not open the cooker. Set aside off the heat or turned off for 10 minutes to steam the rice before serving.

7 Unlock and open the cooker. Serve the casserole.

TESTERS' NOTES
• This satisfying casserole uses brown rice, rather than white, for a better textural contrast with the turkey and a sophisticated flavor, more in keeping with the mushrooms.
• To slice the thighs in half, lay them on a cutting board and slice down with your knife parallel to the bone running

through the meat, leaving you with a boneless half and a bone-in half. If possible, make the cut on the side of the bone with more meat on it, thereby making about equal parts to the thigh.
• While the baby bella mushrooms offer an appealing look and give some flavor to the dish, the workhorses are the dried mushrooms. Make sure the ones you've purchased are dry but not desiccated and have no mushy bits. Use every speck of dust in the package.

TURKEY THIGHS WITH MAPLE SYRUP, SAGE, AND PARSNIPS

EFFORT: **A LITTLE** • PRESSURE: **HIGH** • TIME UNDER PRESSURE: **25 OR 37 MINUTES** • RELEASE: **QUICK, THEN QUICK AGAIN** • SERVES: **4**

2 tablespoons unsalted butter

Two 1¼- to 1½-pound bone-in turkey thighs

1 medium red onion, halved and cut into thin half-moons

2 tablespoons loosely packed fresh sage leaves, minced

½ teaspoon ground cinnamon

½ teaspoon salt

½ teaspoon ground black pepper

¼ cup maple syrup

¼ cup chicken broth

4 large parsnips, peeled

1 Melt the butter in a 6-quart stovetop pressure cooker set over medium heat or in a 6-quart electric pressure cooker turned to the browning function. Add the turkey thighs and brown them well, particularly the skin, about 6 minutes, turning once. Transfer to a large bowl.

(continued)

2 Add the onion to the pot; cook, stirring often, until softened, about 4 minutes. Stir in the sage, cinnamon, salt, and pepper until aromatic, about 30 seconds. Pour in the maple syrup and broth; stir well to get any browned bits up off the bottom of the cooker. Return the thighs and any juices in the bowl to the cooker, nestling the meat into the onion.

3 Lock the lid onto the pot.

STOVETOP: Raise the heat to high and bring the pot to high pressure (15 psi). Once this pressure has been reached, reduce the heat as much as possible while maintaining this pressure. Cook for 15 minutes.

·········· **OR** ··········

ELECTRIC: Set the machine to cook at high pressure (9–11 psi). Set the machine's timer to cook at high pressure for 22 minutes.

4 Use the quick-release method to bring the pot's pressure to normal.

5 Unlock and open the pot. Lay the parsnips on top of the stew.

6 Lock the lid back onto the cooker.

STOVETOP: Raise the heat back to high and bring the pot back to high pressure (15 psi). Once this pressure has been reached, reduce the heat as much as possible while maintaining this pressure. Cook for 10 minutes.

·········· **OR** ··········

ELECTRIC: Set the machine to cook once again at high pressure (9–11 psi). Set the machine's timer to cook at high pressure for 15 minutes.

7 Use the quick-release method to return the pot's pressure in the pot to normal.

8 Unlock and open the pot. Transfer the thighs to a cutting board and slice each in

half, a boneless piece and a bone-in piece. Serve one piece of turkey in a bowl with a parsnip and the sauce ladled on top.

TESTERS' NOTES
• The combination of maple syrup and parsnips is an aromatic match-up with savory undertones.
• There's no need for expensive maple syrup here; use the more economical Grade B (or 2).

TURKEY THIGHS WITH BEER AND PEPPERS

EFFORT: **NOT MUCH** • PRESSURE: **HIGH** • TIME UNDER PRESSURE: **12 OR 18 MINUTES** • RELEASE: **NATURAL** • SERVES: **4**

2 tablespoons unsalted butter

Two 1¼- to 1½-pound bone-in turkey thighs

2 medium red bell peppers, stemmed, cored, and chopped

Up to 2 canned chipotles in adobo sauce, stemmed, cored, and minced

2 tablespoons adobo sauce from the can

½ teaspoon dried oregano

½ cup light-colored beer, preferably a pale ale

1 Melt the butter in a 6-quart stovetop pressure cooker set over medium heat or in a 6-quart electric pressure cooker turned to the browning function. Add the thighs and brown well, turning once, about 6 minutes. Transfer the thighs to a large bowl.

2 Add the bell peppers, chipotles, adobo sauce, and oregano to the pot; stir for about 1 minute. Pour in the beer, stir well, and nestle the thighs into the sauce. Pour any juice from their bowl into the cooker.

3 Lock the lid onto the cooker.

STOVETOP: Raise the heat to high and bring the pot to high pressure (15 psi). Once this pressure has been reached, reduce the heat as much as possible while maintaining this pressure. Cook for 12 minutes.

·· **OR** ··

ELECTRIC: Set the machine to cook at high pressure (9–11 psi). Set the machine's timer to cook at high pressure for 18 minutes.

4 Reduce the pressure.

STOVETOP: Set the pot off the heat and let its pressure come back to normal naturally, about 15 minutes.

·· **OR** ··

ELECTRIC: Turn off the machine or unplug it so it doesn't flip to its keep-warm setting. Let its pressure return to normal naturally, 15 to 20 minutes.

5 Unlock and open the pot. Transfer the thighs to a cutting board; slice each in half, a boneless and a bone-in section. Serve in bowls with the sauce and peppers spooned on top.

TESTERS' NOTES

• Control the heat in this spicy dish by adding as much of the chipotles and their sauce as you want. If you're uncertain, begin with about a quarter of the stated amount. But remember that a pressure cooker mutes capsaicin, the fiery chemical in the chiles, so you might be able to stand more than you think.
• For more flavor, throw in a few coriander seeds, yellow mustard seeds, and/or cumin seeds. The taste will get muskier, even earthier—and provide a sophisticated contrast to the sweet and hot peppers.

Serve It Up! Serve over a simple hominy salad: mix drained and rinsed hominy and black beans in a large bowl; toss with enough salsa verde to coat.

TURKEY THIGHS WITH WHITE WINE AND RED CURRANT JELLY

EFFORT: **NOT MUCH** • PRESSURE: **HIGH** • TIME UNDER PRESSURE: **12 OR 18 MINUTES** • RELEASE: **NATURAL** • SERVES: **4**

2 tablespoons unsalted butter

Two 1¼- to 1½-pound bone-in turkey thighs

1 large leek, white and pale green parts only, halved lengthwise, washed and thinly sliced

¼ cup dry, oaky white wine, such as Chardonnay

¼ cup red currant jelly

½ teaspoon dried thyme

½ teaspoon salt

¼ teaspoon ground black pepper

1 Melt the butter in a 6-quart pressure cooker set over medium heat or in a 6-quart electric pressure cooker turned to the browning function. Add the thighs and brown well, turning once, about 6 minutes. Transfer to a large bowl.

2 Add the leek to the pot; cook, stirring often, until softened, about 2 minutes. Stir in the wine, jelly, thyme, salt, and pepper until the jelly melts. Return the thighs to the pot; pour any juices from their bowl in as well.

(continued)

3 Lock the lid onto the cooker.

STOVETOP: Raise the heat to high and bring the pot to high pressure (15 psi). Once this pressure has been reached, reduce the heat as much as possible while maintaining this pressure. Cook for 12 minutes.

·················· **OR** ··················

ELECTRIC: Set the machine to cook at high pressure (9–11 psi). Set the machine's timer to cook at high pressure for 18 minutes.

4 Reduce the pressure.

STOVETOP: Set the pot off the heat and let its pressure come back to normal naturally, about 15 minutes.

·················· **OR** ··················

ELECTRIC: Turn off the machine or unplug it so it doesn't flip to its keep-warm setting. Let its pressure return to normal naturally, 15 to 20 minutes.

5 Unlock and open the pot. Transfer the thighs to a cutting board; slice each into two pieces along the bone. Serve with generous amounts of the sauce on each.

TESTERS' NOTES

• An oaky white wine will not only stand up to the sweet jelly but will also provide some mildly bitter and earthy notes for contrast.

• Make sure the jelly has thoroughly melted into the sauce before you return the turkey and its juices to the pot; otherwise, some of it can scorch under pressure.

• For a sweet-and-sour finish to the dish, add 1 tablespoon red wine vinegar to the sauce after cooking.

REAL-DEAL TURKEY CHILI

EFFORT: **A LOT** • PRESSURE: **HIGH** • TIME UNDER PRESSURE: **5 OR 8 MINUTES** • RELEASE: **NATURAL** • SERVES: **6 TO 8**

12 dried New Mexican red chiles, stemmed, seeded, and torn into large chunks

1 tablespoon minced garlic

¼ cup packed fresh sage leaves

2 teaspoons drained and rinsed capers

1 teaspoon ground cinnamon

½ teaspoon ground allspice

½ teaspoon salt

2 tablespoons olive oil

1 large yellow onion, chopped

3 pounds boneless skinless turkey thighs, cut into ½-inch pieces

1 cup chicken broth

½ cup dark beer, such as a brown ale

1 Place the chiles in a large bowl; cover with boiling water. Soak for 20 minutes. Save ¼ cup of the soaking liquid, then drain the chiles in a colander set in the sink.

2 Transfer the drained chiles to a large blender or food processor. Add the garlic, sage, capers, cinnamon, allspice, and salt. Process until you have a smooth paste, scraping down the inside of the canister once or twice and adding some of the soaking liquid in 1-tablespoon increments if necessary to keep the mixture blending.

3 Heat the oil in a 6-quart stovetop pressure cooker set over medium heat or in a 6-quart electric pressure cooker turned to the browning function. Add the onion and cook, stirring often, until translucent, about 4 minutes. Add the chile paste; cook for 1 minute, stirring all the while. Stir in the turkey, then pour in the broth and beer. Stir well to reduce the foaming.

4 Lock the lid onto the cooker.

STOVETOP: Raise the heat to high and bring the pot to high pressure (15 psi). Once this pressure has been reached, reduce the heat as much as possible while maintaining this pressure. Cook for 5 minutes.

·······················OR·······················

ELECTRIC: Set the machine to cook at high pressure (9–11 psi). Set the machine's timer to cook at high pressure for 8 minutes.

5 Reduce the pressure.

STOVETOP: Set the pot off the heat and let its pressure come back to normal naturally, about 20 minutes.

·······················OR·······················

ELECTRIC: Turn off the machine or unplug it so it doesn't flip to its keep-warm setting. Let its pressure return to normal naturally, 20 to 30 minutes.

6 Unlock and open the cooker. Stir the chili before serving.

TESTERS' NOTES
• We soak dried chiles to create an authentic paste that flavors this chili. Look for dried chiles that are fragrant, without brown or mushy bits (a sign of rot) and/or broken stems (a sign of sitting on the shelf too long).
• If you can find only bone-in turkey thighs, buy 5 pounds and then skin the thighs and cut the meat off the bone before slicing into the smaller pieces for the chili.
• Add a chopped green bell pepper with the onion.

Serve It Up! Have plenty of flour tortillas on hand, as well as chopped tomatoes and cilantro leaves, sour cream, and/or shredded Monterey jack for garnishes.

BEER-AND-MUSTARD PULLED TURKEY

EFFORT: **A LITTLE** • PRESSURE: **HIGH** • TIME UNDER PRESSURE: **30 OR 45 MINUTES** • RELEASE: **QUICK** • SERVES: **4 TO 6**

2 teaspoons ground coriander

1 teaspoon dry mustard

1 teaspoon salt

1 teaspoon ground black pepper

1/2 teaspoon garlic powder

Two 1 1/4 - to 1 1/2 -pound bone-in turkey thighs, skin removed

One 12-ounce bottle dark beer, preferably a porter

2 tablespoons packed dark brown sugar

2 tablespoons apple cider vinegar

1 tablespoon whole-grain mustard

1 tablespoon canned tomato paste

1 Mix the coriander, dry mustard, salt, pepper, and garlic powder in a small bowl; rub the mixture over the thighs, coating them evenly and thoroughly.

2 Pour the beer into a 6-quart stovetop or electric pressure cooker; nestle the thighs into the beer.

3 Lock the lid onto the pot.

STOVETOP: Set the pot over high heat and bring it to high pressure (15 psi). Once this pressure has been reached, reduce the heat as much as possible while maintaining this pressure. Cook for 30 minutes.

·······················OR·······················

ELECTRIC: Set the machine to cook at high pressure (9–11 psi). Set the machine's timer to cook at high pressure for 45 minutes.

(continued)

4 Use the quick-release method to drop the pot's pressure to normal.

5 Unlock and open the cooker. Transfer the thighs to a carving board; cool for a few minutes. Debone the meat and chop it into small bits.

6 Set the stovetop cooker over medium heat or turn the electric cooker to its browning function; bring the liquid inside to a simmer. Cook until reduced to about half its volume when you opened the pot in the previous step, about 4 minutes.

7 Stir in the brown sugar, vinegar, mustard, and tomato paste until smooth. Cook for 1 minute, stirring all the while. Add the chopped turkey, stir well, and set aside off the heat or unplugged for a couple of minutes to heat through.

TESTERS' NOTES

• Cooking spice-rubbed turkey in beer, then mixing it into a simple barbecue sauce—what could be better? Turkey thighs make the best pulled turkey. The meat is moist and flavorful, even after an intense braise.
• For more flavor, coat the thighs in the spice rub early in the day and set them, covered, on a plate in the fridge for up to 8 hours.
• If you want some heat, add up to ½ teaspoon cayenne to the spice rub.

Serve It Up! Rather than on buns, serve the pulled turkey like soft tacos in flour tortillas; top with some sour cream and pico de gallo.

BUTTERY TURKEY STEW WITH CELERY AND CHESTNUTS

EFFORT: **A LITTLE** • PRESSURE: **HIGH** • TIME UNDER PRESSURE: **25 OR 37 MINUTES** • RELEASE: **QUICK** • SERVES: **4**

1½ **cups chicken broth**
2 **tablespoons all-purpose flour**
½ **teaspoon salt**
½ **teaspoon ground black pepper**
4 **tablespoons (½ stick) unsalted butter**
Two 1¼- **to** 1½-**pound bone-in turkey thighs**
1 **medium yellow onion, chopped**
4 **medium celery stalks, cut into 1-inch pieces**
1½ **cups jarred steamed chestnuts**
⅓ **cup chopped celery leaves**

1 Whisk the broth, flour, salt, and pepper in a small bowl until the flour dissolves; set aside.

2 Melt 2 tablespoons butter in a 6-quart stovetop pressure cooker set over medium heat or in a 6-quart electric pressure cooker turned to the browning function. Put the thighs in the pot and brown well, turning once, about 6 minutes. Transfer to a large bowl.

3 Melt the remaining 2 tablespoons butter in the pot. Add the onion and cook, stirring often, until softened, about 4 minutes. Stir in the celery, chestnuts, and celery leaves; cook for 1 minute, stirring all the while. Stir the broth mixture into the pot; return the thighs and any juices to the sauce.

4 Lock the lid onto the cooker.

STOVETOP: Raise the heat to high and bring the pot to high pressure (15 psi). Once this pressure has been reached, reduce the heat as much as possible while maintaining this pressure. Cook for 25 minutes.

·············· OR ··············

ELECTRIC: Set the machine to cook at high pressure (9–11 psi). Set the machine's timer to cook at high pressure for 37 minutes.

5 Use the quick-release method to bring the pot's pressure back to normal.

6 Unlock and open the pot. Transfer the thighs to a cutting board; cool for a few minutes, then skin the thighs and take the meat off the bones. Chop the meat into chunks and stir them back into the stew in the pot before serving.

TESTERS' NOTES
• If you've never cooked with celery leaves, you're in for a treat! They add a grassy, sweet flavor to the sauce, a great foil to the generous amount of butter.
• Steamed chestnuts are a seasonal item in some supermarkets around the winter holidays. If so, consider this a holiday meal for one of those evenings without company in the house. Look for steamed chestnuts in jars in the baking aisle or near the stuffing mixes.

TURKEY STEW WITH APPLES AND THYME

EFFORT: **A LITTLE** • PRESSURE: **HIGH** • TIME UNDER PRESSURE: **25 OR 37 MINUTES** • RELEASE: **QUICK** • SERVES: **4**

1¼ cups chicken broth
1 tablespoon all-purpose flour
1 tablespoon unsalted butter
1 tablespoon olive oil
Two 1¼- to 1½-pound bone-in turkey thighs
½ teaspoon salt
½ teaspoon ground black pepper
1 small red onion, chopped
2 tablespoons apple jelly
2 fresh thyme sprigs
2 large tart green apples, such as Granny Smith, peeled, cored, and quartered
2 tablespoons apple cider vinegar

1 Whisk the broth and flour in a small bowl until the flour dissolves; set aside.

2 Melt the butter in the oil in a 6-quart stovetop pressure cooker set over medium heat or in a 6-quart electric pressure cooker turned to the browning function. Season the turkey thighs with the salt and pepper, then slip them into the pot. Brown on both sides, turning once, about 6 minutes, until the skin is a deep brown, certainly beyond golden. Transfer to a large bowl.

3 Add the onion to the pot; cook, stirring often, until softened, about 2 minutes. Stir in the jelly and thyme sprigs until bubbling. Pour the broth mixture into the pot; return the thighs and any juice in their bowl to the sauce. Scatter the apples around the pot; drizzle with the vinegar.

4 Lock the lid onto the cooker.

STOVETOP: Raise the heat to high and bring the pot to high pressure (15 psi). Once this pressure has been reached, reduce the heat as much as possible while maintaining this pressure. Cook for 25 minutes.

·············· OR ··············

ELECTRIC: Set the machine to cook at high pressure (9–11 psi). Set the machine's timer to cook at high pressure for 37 minutes.

(continued)

5 Use the quick-release method to bring the pot's pressure back to normal.

6 Unlock and open the cooker. Transfer the thighs to a large cutting board. Cool for a few minutes, then remove the skin and slice the meat off the bones. Cut the meat into chunks, stir them back into the sauce in the cooker, and serve in bowls.

TESTERS' NOTES
• More like a sweet-and-sour stew, this main course is great on a fall evening.
• We require a quick release in this recipe because we wanted the thighs to get falling-off-the-bone tender while keeping the apple quarters from turning into sauce.

Serve It Up! Serve over hash browns or crispy fried shredded potatoes.

TURKEY STEW WITH BACON AND POTATOES

EFFORT: **A LITTLE** • PRESSURE: **HIGH** • TIME UNDER PRESSURE: **25 OR 37 MINUTES** • RELEASE: **QUICK, THEN NATURAL** • SERVES: **4**

4 thin bacon slices, chopped

Two 1¼- to 1½-pound bone-in turkey thighs

½ teaspoon ground black pepper

1 small yellow onion, chopped

1 medium carrot, chopped

1 medium celery stalk, chopped

1 teaspoon dried oregano

¼ teaspoon ground allspice

1½ cups hard cider

1 pound small yellow potatoes, such as Yukon Gold

1 Lay the bacon in a 6-quart stovetop pressure cooker set over medium heat or in a 6-quart electric pressure cooker turned to the browning function. Fry until crisp, turning once, about 3 minutes. Transfer to a plate.

2 Season the thighs with the pepper and slip them into the cooker. Brown on both sides, turning once, about 6 minutes. Transfer to the plate with the bacon.

3 Add the onion, carrot, and celery to the cooker; cook, stirring often, until the onion softens, about 3 minutes. Stir in the oregano and allspice, then pour in the cider. Scrape any browned bits up off the bottom of the pot. Crumble the bacon into the pot; return the thighs and any juices to the cooker.

4 Lock the lid onto the cooker.

STOVETOP: Raise the heat to high and bring the pot to high pressure (15 psi). Once this pressure has been reached, reduce the heat as much as possible while maintaining this pressure. Cook for 20 minutes.

······································ OR ································

ELECTRIC: Set the machine to cook at high pressure (9–11 psi). Set the machine's timer to cook at high pressure for 30 minutes.

5 Use the quick-release method to drop the pot's pressure back to normal.

6 Unlock and open the pot. Scatter the potatoes on top of the other ingredients.

7 Lock the lid onto the pot again.

STOVETOP: Set the pot over high heat and bring it back to high pressure (15 psi). Once this pressure has been reached, reduce the heat as much as possible while maintaining this pressure. Cook for 5 minutes.

·························· **OR** ··························

ELECTRIC: Set the machine once again to cook at high pressure (9–11 psi). Set the machine's timer to cook at high pressure for 7 minutes.

8 Reduce the pressure.

STOVETOP: Set the pot off the heat and let its pressure come back to normal naturally, about 15 minutes.

·························· **OR** ··························

ELECTRIC: Turn off or unplug the machine so it doesn't flip to its keep-warm setting. Let its pressure return to normal naturally, 15 to 20 minutes.

Set the cooker aside, covered, for 5 minutes.

9 Unlock and open the pot. Transfer the thighs to a cutting board. Cool for a couple of minutes, then remove the skin and debone the meat. Chop the meat into chunks and stir back into the stew in the pot before serving in bowls.

TESTERS' NOTES
• Although we preferred this dish as a stew, you could serve it as whole thighs, carving them into halves at the table and then ladling the sauce over each helping.
• Hard cider has a slightly sweeter finish than standard apple juice. If you'd rather do without the alcohol, use unsweetened apple juice, but add up to ½ tablespoon light brown sugar with it to increase the sweetness a bit.
• The potatoes should be pretty small, no larger than 1½ inches in diameter. Small yellow fingerling potatoes would work, too.

SMOKY BRAISED TURKEY DRUMSTICKS

EFFORT: **A LITTLE** • PRESSURE: **HIGH** • TIME UNDER PRESSURE: **20 OR 30 MINUTES** • RELEASE: **NATURAL** • SERVES: **4**

4 thin bacon slices, preferably double-smoked, chopped

4 turkey drumsticks (about ¾ pound each)

1 cup frozen pearl onions, thawed

One 14-ounce can diced tomatoes (about 1¾ cups)

Up to 2 canned chipotles in adobo sauce, stemmed, seeded, and minced

2 teaspoons Worcestershire sauce

2 teaspoons smoked paprika

1 teaspoon dried oregano

1 Set a 6-quart stovetop pressure cooker pot over medium heat or turn a 6-quart electric pressure cooker pot to its browning mode. Add the bacon and fry until crisp, about 3 minutes, stirring occasionally. Use a slotted spoon to transfer the bacon to a large bowl, leaving the rendered fat behind.

2 Brown two turkey drumsticks in the fat in the cooker, turning occasionally, about 4 minutes. Transfer them to the bowl and repeat with the remaining drumsticks.

3 Add the pearl onions to the pot; cook, stirring often, until softened, about 3 minutes. Stir in the tomatoes, chipotles, Worcestershire sauce, smoked paprika, and oregano along with ¼ cup water. Stir well to get any browned bits up off the bottom of the pot. Return the drumsticks and any juices in their bowl to the cooker, stacking the small ends over the meaty ends (thus

(continued)

letting the thicker parts sit in as much liquid as possible).

4 Lock the lid onto the pot.

STOVETOP: Raise the heat to high and bring the pot to high pressure (15 psi). Once this pressure has been reached, reduce the heat as much as possible while maintaining this pressure. Cook for 20 minutes.

························ OR ························

ELECTRIC: Set the machine to cook at high pressure (9–11 psi). Set the machine's timer to cook at high pressure for 30 minutes.

5 Reduce the pressure.

STOVETOP: Set the pot off the heat and let its pressure come back to normal naturally, about 15 minutes.

························ OR ························

ELECTRIC: Turn off the machine or unplug it so it doesn't flip to its keep-warm setting. Let its pressure return to normal naturally, 15 to 20 minutes.

6 Unlock and open the cooker. Serve the drumsticks in bowls with the sauce ladled around each.

TESTERS' NOTES
• You'll need a knife and fork to eat this messy braise, with flavors like an intense, spicy barbecue sauce.
• Brown the drumsticks well so the skin isn't gummy after cooking. Working in batches, you'll be able to lay them both on the hot surface with full contact for the best caramelization.
• Turkey drumsticks are full of tendons and cartilage. You may need to cut the meat off the bones for children or picky eaters.

Serve It Up! Have sticky, short-grain white rice in the bowls so it can sop up every last bit of the sauce.

CIDER-BRAISED TURKEY DRUMSTICKS WITH CARROTS AND HERBS

EFFORT: **A LOT** • PRESSURE: **HIGH** • TIME UNDER PRESSURE: **27 OR 41 MINUTES** • RELEASE: **QUICK, THEN QUICK AGAIN** • SERVES: **4**

2 tablespoons olive oil

4 turkey drumsticks (about ³/₄ pound each)

1 medium yellow onion, chopped

2 medium celery stalks, chopped

³/₄ cup unsweetened apple cider

2 tablespoons packed light brown sugar

3 fresh thyme sprigs

2 fresh sage sprigs

¹/₂ teaspoon salt

¹/₂ teaspoon ground black pepper

1 bay leaf

4 large carrots, halved widthwise

1 Heat the oil in a 6-quart stovetop pressure cooker set over medium heat or in a 6-quart electric pressure cooker turned to the browning function. Add two turkey drumsticks and brown them well, turning occasionally, about 5 minutes. Transfer to a large bowl and repeat with the remaining drumsticks.

2 Add the onion and celery to the pot; cook, stirring occasionally, until softened, about 4 minutes. Pour in the cider; stir in the brown sugar, thyme, sage, salt, pepper, and bay leaf to get any browned bits up off the bottom of the pot and to dissolve the brown sugar. Return the drumsticks and any juices to the cooker, overlapping the smaller ends over the meatier bits so these latter sit in the sauce.

3 Lock the lid onto the pot.

STOVETOP: Raise the heat to high and bring the pot to high pressure (15 psi). Once this pressure has been reached, reduce the heat as much as possible while maintaining this pressure. Cook for 15 minutes.

·····················OR·····················

ELECTRIC: Set the machine to cook at high pressure (9–11 psi). Set the machine's timer to cook at high pressure for 23 minutes.

4 Use the quick-release method to return the pot's pressure to normal.

5 Unlock and open the cooker. Tuck the carrots into the sauce around the legs.

6 Lock the lid back onto the pot.

STOVETOP: Set the pot back over high heat and bring it back to high pressure (15 psi). Once this pressure has again been reached, reduce the heat as much as possible while maintaining this pressure. Cook for 12 minutes.

·····················OR·····················

ELECTRIC: Set the machine to cook once again at high pressure (9–11 psi). Set the machine's timer to cook at this pressure for 18 minutes.

7 Use the quick-release method to drop the pot's pressure to normal.

8 Unlock and open the pot. Discard the thyme sprigs, sage sprigs, and bay leaf. Serve the drumsticks and carrots in bowls with the sauce spooned over them.

TESTERS' NOTES
• Braising turkey drumsticks in apple cider renders them gorgeously sweet, rich, and tender.
• We wanted the carrots to stay slightly firm, so we added them later and in much bigger chunks.

TURKEY DRUMSTICKS WITH LEEKS, PINEAPPLE, AND JALAPEÑO

EFFORT: **A LITTLE** • PRESSURE: **HIGH** • TIME UNDER PRESSURE: **20 OR 30 MINUTES** • RELEASE: **NATURAL** • SERVES: **4**

2 tablespoons unsalted butter

4 turkey drumsticks (about ¾ pound each)

1 large leek, white and pale green parts only, halved lengthwise, washed and thinly sliced

1 medium red bell pepper, stemmed, cored, and chopped

1 medium fresh jalapeño chile, stemmed and chopped (seeded if you prefer less heat)

1 teaspoon dried thyme

½ teaspoon ground allspice

¼ teaspoon ground cloves

1½ tablespoons apple cider vinegar

¾ cup chicken broth

¼ cup pineapple jam or jelly

1 Melt the butter in a 6-quart stovetop pressure cooker set over medium heat or in a 6-quart electric pressure cooker turned to the browning function. Add two turkey drumsticks and brown well, turning occasionally, about 5 minutes. Transfer to a large bowl and repeat with the remaining drumsticks.

2 Add the leek, bell pepper, and jalapeño to the pot; cook, stirring often, until the leek softens, about 2 minutes. Stir in the thyme, allspice, and cloves until aromatic, just a few seconds. Pour in the vinegar and scrape up any browned bits on the bottom of the pot.

(continued)

Add the broth and jam; stir until the latter dissolves. Return the drumsticks and any juices in their bowl to the cooker, overlapping the thinner bits over the thicker.

3 Lock the lid onto the pot.

STOVETOP: Raise the heat to high and bring the pot to high pressure (15 psi). Once this pressure has been reached, reduce the heat as much as possible while maintaining this pressure. Cook for 20 minutes.

·························· **OR** ··························

ELECTRIC: Set the machine to cook at high pressure (9–11 psi). Set the machine's timer to cook at high pressure for 30 minutes.

4 Reduce the pressure.

STOVETOP: Set the pot off the heat and let its pressure come back to normal naturally, about 15 minutes.

·························· **OR** ··························

ELECTRIC: Turn off the machine or unplug it so it doesn't flip to its keep-warm setting. Let its pressure return to normal naturally, 15 to 20 minutes.

5 Unlock and open the pot. Serve the drumsticks in bowls with the sauce ladled over them.

TESTERS' NOTES
• We modeled these flavors on Jamaican jerk braises, sometimes fiery hot but here toned down a bit.
• The pineapple jam lends a sweet, appealing finish to the sauce, turning it a little sticky and a good match to that hot chile. For even more flavor, add up to ½ cup diced fresh pineapple with the jam.
• Of course, you can use more chile at will—or even minced habanero for a real kick.

TURKEY CACCIATORE

EFFORT: **A LITTLE** • PRESSURE: **HIGH** • TIME UNDER PRESSURE: **25 OR 37 MINUTES** • RELEASE: **NATURAL** • SERVES: **4**

2 tablespoons olive oil

4 turkey drumsticks (about ¾ pound each)

1 large yellow onion, chopped

1 large green bell pepper, stemmed, cored, and chopped

6 ounces baby bella or cremini mushrooms, thinly sliced

½ ounce dried mushrooms, preferably porcini

1½ cups canned crushed tomatoes

Up to 1¼ cups dry fruit-forward white wine, such as Pinot Grigio

2 teaspoons dried oregano

2 teaspoons dried rosemary

½ teaspoon salt

½ teaspoon ground black pepper

1 Heat the oil in a 6-quart stovetop pressure cooker set over medium heat or in a 6-quart electric pressure cooker turned to the browning function. Add two drumsticks and brown well, turning occasionally, about 5 minutes. Transfer to a large bowl and repeat with the other two drumsticks.

2 Add the onion and bell pepper to the pot; cook, stirring often, until the onion softens, about 4 minutes. Add the fresh mushrooms and cook, stirring often, until they give off their liquid and it evaporates, about 6 minutes.

3 Crumble in the dried mushrooms, stir over the heat for a few seconds, then pour in the tomatoes and 1¼ cups wine in a stovetop cooker or 1 cup wine in an electric model.

Stir to get any browned bits up off the bottom of the cooker, then add the oregano, rosemary, salt, and pepper. Return the drumsticks and any juices in their bowl to the cooker, laying the thinner ends of some over the thicker ends of others.

4 Lock the lid onto the pot.

STOVETOP: Raise the heat to high and bring the pot to high pressure (15 psi). Once this pressure has been reached, reduce the heat as much as possible while maintaining this pressure. Cook for 25 minutes.

·························**OR**·························

ELECTRIC: Set the machine to cook at high pressure (9–11 psi). Set the machine's timer to cook at this pressure for 37 minutes.

5 Reduce the pressure.

STOVETOP: Set the pot off the heat and let its pressure come back to normal naturally, about 15 minutes.

·························**OR**·························

ELECTRIC: Turn off the machine or unplug it so it doesn't flip to its keep-warm setting. Let its pressure return to normal naturally, 15 to 20 minutes.

6 Unlock and open the pot. Transfer the drumsticks to a carving board and cool for a couple of minutes. Shred the meat off the bones, removing any skin, cartilage, or tendons. Chop the meat and stir it back into the cooker before serving in bowls.

TESTERS' NOTES
• Turkey drumsticks make the best cacciatore, a tomato-rich Italian braise, because the bones and cartilage leach plenty of flavor into the liquids.
• Of course, if you don't want to go to such lengths in step 6, you could just serve the drumsticks as they are, in big bowls with the sauce poured over each helping.

• You can use 1 tablespoon bottled Italian dried seasoning blend instead of the oregano, rosemary, salt, and pepper.

Serve It Up! You *need* cooked polenta as a bed for this stew. There is nothing better.

WHITE WINE–BRAISED GAME HEN

EFFORT: **A LITTLE** • PRESSURE: **HIGH** • TIME UNDER PRESSURE: **10 OR 15 MINUTES** • RELEASE: **QUICK** • SERVES: **2 TO 4**

1/4 **cup dry white wine, such as Chardonnay**
1 1/2 **tablespoons all-purpose flour**
1 **teaspoon dried thyme**
1 **teaspoon dried oregano**
1 **tablespoon unsalted butter**
1 **tablespoon olive oil**
One 2 1/4-pound game hen, giblets and neck removed, the bird halved lengthwise
1/2 **teaspoon salt**
1/2 **teaspoon ground black pepper**
1/2 **cup chicken broth**
6 **ounces shiitake mushroom caps, thinly sliced**

1 Whisk the wine, flour, thyme, and oregano in a small bowl until the flour dissolves; set aside.

2 Melt the butter in the oil in a 6-quart stovetop pressure cooker set over medium heat or in a 6-quart electric pressure cooker turned to the browning function. Season the game hen halves with salt and pepper, set them in the cooker skin side down, and brown without turning, about 4 minutes. Transfer to a large bowl.

(continued)

3 Pour in the broth and scrape up any browned bits on the bottom of the pot as it comes to a simmer. Stir in the wine mixture, then add the mushrooms. Nestle the hen halves into the sauce skin side up; pour any juices from their bowl into the cooker.

4 Lock the lid onto the pot.

STOVETOP: Raise the heat to high and bring the pot to high pressure (15 psi). Once this pressure has been reached, reduce the heat as much as possible while maintaining this pressure. Cook for 10 minutes.

·····························**OR**·····························

ELECTRIC: Set the machine to cook at high pressure (9–11 psi). Set the machine's timer to cook at high pressure for 15 minutes.

5 Use the quick-release method to bring the pot's pressure back to normal.

6 Unlock and open the pot. Cut the meat into smaller pieces, if desired; serve in bowls with the sauce spooned on top.

TESTERS' NOTES

• Game hens are a natural for the pressure cooker: lots of bone to give flavor to the meat, which is pretty moist so it doesn't dry out under pressure.

• To cut a game hen in half, position the bird breast up so that the large opening is facing you, then slice down, large to small opening, on one side of the breast bone at the top and the spinal column at the bottom (or ask your butcher to do it for you).

• Only brown the game hens on one side to avoid overcooking them—but do get the skin quite brown, so it has good flavor and texture after cooking under pressure.

• The servings sizes for these game hens fluctuate a bit. We'd eat half a game hen each, but if you've got a few sides as well, you'll get up to four servings out of one bird.

RED WINE–BRAISED GAME HEN

EFFORT: **A LITTLE** • PRESSURE: **HIGH** • TIME UNDER PRESSURE: **10 OR 15 MINUTES** • RELEASE: **QUICK** • SERVES: **2 TO 4**

3 tablespoons unsalted butter

One 2¼-pound game hen, giblets and neck removed, the bird halved lengthwise

½ teaspoon salt

½ teaspoon ground black pepper

1 small yellow onion, chopped

1 medium carrot, sliced into thin coins

1 teaspoon minced garlic

Up to 1 cup dry red wine, such as Syrah

1 fresh tarragon sprig

¼ cup packed fresh parsley leaves, chopped

1 Melt the butter in a 6-quart stovetop pressure cooker set over medium heat or in a 6-quart pressure cooker turned to the browning function. Season the game hen halves with salt and pepper, set them in the pot skin side down, and brown without turning, about 4 minutes. Transfer to a large bowl.

2 Add the onion and carrot to the pot; cook, stirring often, until slightly softened, about 2 minutes. Add the garlic, stir for a few seconds, and then pour in 1 cup wine in a stovetop cooker or ¾ cup wine in an electric model. Stir to pick up any browned bits stuck to the bottom.

3 Return the hen halves skin side up to the cooker as well as any juices in their bowl. Tuck the tarragon into the sauce; sprinkle everything with the parsley.

4 Lock the lid onto the pot.

STOVETOP: Raise the heat to high and bring the pot to high pressure (15 psi). Once this pressure has been reached, reduce the heat as much as possible while maintaining this pressure. Cook for 10 minutes.

·························· **OR** ··························

ELECTRIC: Set the machine to cook at high pressure (9–11 psi). Set the machine's timer to cook at high pressure for 15 minutes.

5 Use the quick-release method to return the pressure in the pot to normal.

6 Unlock and open the cooker. Transfer the hen halves to a cutting board; cut them into smaller pieces, if desired. Discard the tarragon sprig from the sauce.

7 Set the stovetop pot over medium heat or turn the electric pot to its browning function; bring the sauce to a boil. Boil until reduced to half its original volume, about 3 minutes. Serve the meat in bowls with the sauce ladled on top.

TESTERS' NOTES
• This sauce is a complex mix of flavors: red wine, butter, and plenty of herbs. You'll want a crunchy baguette on hand to sop up every drop.
• You could make the sauce even bolder by stirring up to 1 tablespoon beef or poultry demi-glace into it as it reduces. Look for small demi-glace containers at the butcher counter or in the freezer section of high-end markets.
• Brown the game hen until the skin pops off the hot surface without much tearing.

Serve It Up! Cook egg noodles in a large pot of boiling water, then drain in a colander. Melt several tablespoons of unsalted butter in a large skillet, add the noodles, and cook, stirring occasionally, until crisp at the edges. Use these as a bed for the meat and sauce.

GAME HEN WITH APPLE, BRANDY, AND CREAM

EFFORT: **A LITTLE** • PRESSURE: **HIGH** • TIME UNDER PRESSURE: **10 OR 15 MINUTES** • RELEASE: **QUICK** • SERVES: **2 TO 4**

1 tablespoon unsalted butter

1 tablespoon olive oil

One 2¼-pound game hen, giblets and neck removed, the bird halved lengthwise

¼ teaspoon salt

¼ teaspoon ground black pepper

1 large tart apple, such as Granny Smith or Northern Spy, peeled, cored, and thinly sliced

1 small yellow onion, halved and sliced into thin half-moons

½ cup chicken broth

¼ cup brandy, preferably apple brandy

½ teaspoon dried sage

¼ teaspoon grated nutmeg

¼ cup heavy cream

1 Melt the butter in the oil in a 6-quart stovetop pressure cooker set over medium heat or in a 6-quart electric pressure cooker turned to the browning function. Season the game hen halves with the salt and pepper, set them skin side down in the pot, and brown well without turning, about 4 minutes. Transfer to a large bowl.

2 Add the apple and onion to the pot; cook, stirring often, until the onion is translucent, about 3 minutes. Pour in the broth and brandy; stir in the sage and nutmeg. Stir well to get any browned bits up off the bottom of the cooker. Return the hen halves skin side up to the sauce as well as any juices in their bowl.

(continued)

3 Lock the lid onto the pot.

STOVETOP: Raise the heat to high and bring the pot to high pressure (15 psi). Once this pressure has been reached, reduce the heat as much as possible while maintaining this pressure. Cook for 10 minutes.

·····················OR·····················

ELECTRIC: Set the machine to cook at high pressure (9–11 psi). Set the machine's timer to cook at high pressure for 15 minutes.

4 Use the quick-release method to return the pot's pressure to normal.

5 Unlock and open the cooker. Transfer the hen halves to a carving board.

6 Set the stovetop pot over medium heat or turn the electric pot to its browning or simmer function. Stir in the cream and bring the sauce to a simmer. Cook for 1 minute, stirring all the while, to blend the flavors. Divide the hen halves if desired; serve in bowls with the sauce spooned over each.

TESTERS' NOTES
• A rich dish with flavors from northern France, this recipe offers a sweet sauce for the tender game hen. The browning on the game hen provides the basic counterbalance of flavors (a few bitter notes, some savory ones)—so don't stint.
• Apple brandy will give the dish an even sweeter finish—but more apple flavor. (You can also use cognac or bourbon instead.)
• There's little chance the brandy will ignite, given the size of the pot. But if it does, cover the pot, take it off the heat or unplug it, and set it aside for a few minutes before continuing.

Serve It Up! Sprinkle pomegranate seeds over the servings.

GAME HEN WITH APRICOTS AND ALMONDS

EFFORT: **A LITTLE** • PRESSURE: **HIGH** • TIME UNDER PRESSURE: **10 OR 15 MINUTES** • RELEASE: **QUICK** • SERVES: **2 TO 4**

2 tablespoons olive oil

One 2¼-pound game hen, giblets and neck removed, the hen halved lengthwise

4 medium shallots, halved

8 dried apricots, halved

¼ cup toasted almonds, roughly chopped

½ teaspoon ground cumin

¼ teaspoon ground ginger

¼ teaspoon ground turmeric

¼ teaspoon salt

¼ teaspoon ground black pepper

⅛ teaspoon saffron threads

Up to 1 cup chicken broth

1 Heat the oil in a 6-quart stovetop pressure cooker set over medium heat or in a 6-quart electric pressure cooker turned to the browning function. Add the game hen halves skin side down; brown well without turning, about 4 minutes. Transfer the halves to a large bowl.

2 Add the shallots; cook, stirring often, for 2 minutes. Stir in the dried apricots, almonds, cumin, ginger, turmeric, salt, pepper, and saffron.

3 Set the hen halves skin side up in the sauce; pour any juice in their bowl over them. Pour 1 cup broth into a stovetop cooker or ¾ cup broth into an electric cooker.

4 Lock the lid onto the pot.

STOVETOP: Raise the heat to high and bring the pot to high pressure (15 psi). Once this pressure has been reached, reduce the heat as much as possible while maintaining this pressure. Cook for 10 minutes.

························ **OR** ························

ELECTRIC: Set the machine to cook at high pressure (9–11 psi). Set the machine's timer to cook at high pressure for 15 minutes.

5 Use the quick-release method to bring the pot's pressure back to normal.

6 Unlock and open the cooker. Slice each half into smaller pieces, if desired, to serve in bowls with the sauce.

TESTERS' NOTES
• With the flavors of a North African tagine, this dish is more savory than sweet, especially since the apricots give it a little sour pop that foregrounds the spices.
• The shallots will become the sweet notes after cooking under pressure. Peel them so their root ends stay intact—they'll then hold together as they cook.
• Substitute 1 teaspoon garam masala for the cumin, ginger, and turmeric.

GAME HEN WITH **BACON** AND **BRUSSELS SPROUTS**

EFFORT: **A LITTLE** • PRESSURE: **HIGH** • TIME UNDER PRESSURE: **10 OR 15 MINUTES** • RELEASE: **QUICK, THEN MODIFIED QUICK** • SERVES: **2 TO 4**

1 tablespoon unsalted butter

4 thin strips of bacon, chopped

One 2¼-pound game hen, giblets and neck removed, the bird halved lengthwise

Up to ¾ cup dry, fruit-forward white wine, such as Sauvignon Blanc

1 teaspoon sweet paprika

½ teaspoon dried sage

½ teaspoon ground black pepper

12 ounces medium Brussels sprouts, trimmed and quartered

1 Melt the butter in a 6-quart stovetop pressure cooker set over medium heat or in a 6-quart electric pressure cooker turned to the browning function. Add the bacon and cook until lightly browned, about 2 minutes, stirring occasionally.

2 Set the hen halves skin side down into the pot; cook until well browned without turning, about 4 minutes. Turn them over and add ¾ cup wine in a stovetop cooker or ½ cup wine in an electric cooker. Sprinkle the paprika, sage, and pepper over the hen halves.

3 Lock the lid onto the pot.

(continued)

STOVETOP: Raise the heat to high and bring the pot to high pressure (15 psi). Once this pressure has been reached, reduce the heat as much as possible while maintaining this pressure. Cook for 8 minutes.

·····························**OR**·····························

ELECTRIC: Set the machine to cook at high pressure (9–11 psi). Set the machine's timer to cook at high pressure for 12 minutes.

4 Use the quick-release method to bring the pot's pressure back to normal.

5 Unlock and open the cooker. Scatter the Brussels sprouts into the pot.

6 Lock the lid back onto the cooker.

STOVETOP: Set the pot back over high heat and bring it back to high pressure (15 psi). Once this pressure has been reached, reduce the heat as much as possible while maintaining this pressure. Cook for 2 minutes.

·····························**OR**·····························

ELECTRIC: Set the machine to cook once again at high pressure (9–11 psi). Set the machine's timer to cook at high pressure for 3 minutes.

7 Use the quick-release method to bring the pot's pressure back to normal but do not open the pot. Set aside, covered, for 2 minutes.

8 Unlock the lid and open the pot. Divide the hen halves into two smaller pieces each, if desired. Serve in bowls with the sauce and vegetables poured over each helping.

TESTERS' NOTES

• Here's our most savory preparation for game hen, stocked with Brussels sprouts in a fairly straightforward sauce with smoky notes from the bacon.

• The bacon will continue to cook after the hen halves have been added to the pot. It shouldn't burn but it will be quite dark and crunchy when the whole thing undergoes high pressure.

• If you want a sauce without any smoky notes, use 4 ounces chopped pancetta instead of bacon.

GAME HEN AND RICE CASSEROLE

EFFORT: **A LITTLE** • PRESSURE: **HIGH** • TIME UNDER PRESSURE: **8 OR 12 MINUTES** • RELEASE: **MODIFIED QUICK** • SERVES: **4**

2 tablespoons olive oil

8 ounces dried Spanish chorizo, chopped

One 2¼-pound game hen, giblets and neck removed, the hen quartered

1 medium yellow onion, chopped

1 medium green bell pepper, stemmed, cored, and chopped

2 teaspoons smoked paprika

1 teaspoon dried oregano

One 14-ounce can diced tomatoes (about 1¾ cups)

1 cup medium-grain white rice, such as Arborio

2 cups chicken broth

1 Heat the oil in a 6-quart stovetop pressure cooker set over medium heat or in a 6-quart electric pressure cooker turned to the browning function. Add the chorizo and cook, stirring often, until browned, about 3 minutes. Transfer to a large bowl.

2 Set the hen pieces skin side down into the cooker; brown well without turning, about 4 minutes. Transfer to the bowl.

3 Add the onion and bell pepper to the pot; cook, stirring often, until the onion turns translucent, about 4 minutes. Stir in the smoked paprika and oregano; cook a few seconds until aromatic. Pour in the tomatoes and add the rice; cook, stirring often, for 1 minute. Stir in the broth. Return the hen and chorizo to the sauce as well as any juices in the bowl. Make sure no grains of rice stick up outside the liquid.

4 Lock the lid onto the pot.

STOVETOP: Raise the heat to high and bring the pot to high pressure (15 psi). Once this pressure has been reached, reduce the heat as much as possible while maintaining this pressure. Cook for 8 minutes.

·················· **OR** ··················

ELECTRIC: Set the machine to cook at high pressure (9–11 psi). Set the machine's timer to cook at high pressure for 12 minutes.

5 Use the quick-release method to bring the pot's pressure back to normal but do not open the pot. Set aside, covered, for 10 minutes to steam the rice.

6 Unlock and open the pot. Serve the casserole in bowls.

TESTERS' NOTES

• These flavors are modeled after Spanish dishes like arroz con pollo. You can increase the heat (exponentially) by substituting hotter smoked paprika.

• If desired, stir up to 1 cup frozen peas, thawed, into the rice after bringing the pressure back to normal. Set aside, covered, for 10 minutes to steam the rice and warm the peas.

• Use only dried chorizo, not fresh Mexican chorizo. If you can't find dried chorizo, substitute spicy kielbasa or hot Italian sausage.

SOY AND HONEY– BRAISED GAME HENS

EFFORT: **A LITTLE** • PRESSURE: **HIGH** • TIME UNDER PRESSURE: **10 OR 15 MINUTES** • RELEASE: **QUICK** • SERVES: **4 TO 6**

2 tablespoons peanut oil

Two 2-pound game hens, giblets and neck removed, the birds halved lengthwise

4 medium scallions, thinly sliced

1 tablespoon minced fresh ginger

2 teaspoons minced garlic

$1/2$ cup chicken broth

$1/4$ cup soy sauce

2 tablespoons honey

1 tablespoon dry sherry

1 teaspoon Dijon mustard

$1/2$ teaspoon ground black pepper

1 Heat 1 tablespoon oil in a 6-quart stovetop pressure cooker set over medium heat or in a 6-quart electric pressure cooker turned to the browning function. Add two hen halves skin side down and brown well without turning, about 4 minutes. Transfer to a large bowl. Add the remaining tablespoon oil to the cooker and brown the remaining two hen halves skin side down as well before transfering to the bowl.

2 Add the scallions, ginger, and garlic to the pot; stir-fry for 30 seconds. Pour in the broth, soy sauce, honey, sherry, mustard, and pepper. Stir well to get any browned bits up off the bottom of the pot. Add the bird halves and any juice from their bowl; use kitchen tongs to turn them repeatedly to coat well in the sauce. Position them skin side up, overlapping thin parts on top of thick as necessary.

(continued)

3 Lock the lid onto the pot.

STOVETOP: Raise the heat to high and bring the pot to high pressure (15 psi). Once this pressure has been reached, reduce the heat as much as possible while maintaining this pressure. Cook for 10 minutes.

······················· **OR** ·······················

ELECTRIC: Set the machine to cook at high pressure (9–11 psi). Set the machine's timer to cook at high pressure for 15 minutes.

4 Use the quick-release method to bring the pot's pressure back to normal.

5 Unlock and open the pot. Serve the hens in bowls with the sauce drizzled over each helping.

TESTERS' NOTES

• These game hens are given a Chinese-inspired glaze that's sweet and aromatic. You can remove the game hens and boil the sauce for a minute or two to thicken it even more—although it will then need to be "painted" onto the birds when they're served.

• For heat, add up to 1 teaspoon red pepper flakes with the broth in step 2.

• The servings for these hens are stated in a wide range. If you're eating only the meat and its sauce, it'll make four servings. If you're offering this with a side dish of stir-fried bok choy and water chestnuts, you'll be able to stretch the recipe to eight servings.

• You can substitute ¾ teaspoon dry vermouth or dry white wine and ¼ teaspoon Worcestershire sauce for the dry sherry.

Serve It Up! Offer the pieces in bowls of long-grain white rice that can absorb every drop of the sauce.

BUTTERY VINEGAR-BRAISED GAME HENS

EFFORT: **A LITTLE** • PRESSURE: **HIGH** • TIME UNDER PRESSURE: **10 OR 15 MINUTES** • RELEASE: **QUICK** • SERVES: **4 TO 6**

2 tablespoons unsalted butter

One 6-ounce pancetta chunk, diced

Two 2-pound game hens, giblets and necks removed, the birds halved lengthwise

⅓ cup chicken broth

⅓ cup white balsamic vinegar

1 teaspoon dried oregano

½ teaspoon ground black pepper

1 Melt the butter in a 6-quart stovetop pressure cooker set over medium heat or in a 6-quart electric pressure cooker turned to the browning function. Add the pancetta and cook, stirring often, until browned and sizzling, about 3 minutes. Use a slotted spoon to transfer the pancetta to a large bowl.

2 Add two game hen halves skin side down and brown well without turning, about 4 minutes. Transfer these to the bowl before repeating with the other two halves.

3 Stir the broth, vinegar, oregano, and pepper into the pot. Return the game hen halves skin side up and the pancetta as well as any juices in their bowl, overlapping thinner parts over thicker as necessary.

4 Lock the lid onto the pot.

STOVETOP: Raise the heat to high and bring the pot to high pressure (15 psi). Once this pressure has been reached, reduce the heat as much as possible while maintaining this pressure. Cook for 10 minutes.

·············· **OR** ··············

ELECTRIC: Set the machine to cook at high pressure (9–11 psi). Set the machine's timer to cook at high pressure for 15 minutes.

5 Use the quick-release method to return the pot's pressure to normal.

6 Unlock and open the pot. Serve the hens in bowls with the sauce drizzled over each helping.

TESTERS' NOTES
• Braising poultry in a vinegary broth makes the meat impossibly tender—and actually a little sweeter, thanks to the way the sauce brings forward the natural sugars.
• White balsamic vinegar is a bit sweeter than regular balsamic and so will offer a more mellow, less pungent spike among the flavors.
• For a richer sauce, remove the hen halves after cooking under pressure and bring the sauce to a simmer by setting the stovetop pot over medium heat or turning the electric model to its browning function. Whisk in 2 tablespoons unsalted butter, cut into small bits, then ladle this sauce over the game hens when serving.

Serve It Up! Mix cooked white quinoa, corn kernels, and chopped roasted red peppers as a bed under the meat and sauce.

POMEGRANATE-BRAISED GAME HENS

EFFORT: **A LOT** · PRESSURE: **HIGH** · TIME UNDER PRESSURE: **10 OR 15 MINUTES** · RELEASE: **QUICK** · SERVES: **4 TO 6**

¼ **cup sliced almonds**
2 **tablespoons unsalted butter**
1 **tablespoon olive oil**
Two 2-pound game hens, giblets and necks removed, the hens halved lengthwise
2 **tablespoons minced fresh chives**
2 **teaspoons stemmed fresh thyme leaves**
½ **cup unsweetened pomegranate juice**
½ **cup chicken broth**
2 **tablespoons honey**
½ **teaspoon salt**
½ **teaspoon ground black pepper**
1 **teaspoon potato starch or cornstarch**

1 Toast the almonds in a dry skillet set over medium-low heat, stirring occasionally, about 3 minutes, until lightly browned. Pour into a small bowl and set aside.

2 Melt the butter in the oil in a 6-quart stovetop pressure cooker set over medium heat or in a 6-quart electric pressure cooker turned to the browning function. Add two of the hen halves skin side down and brown well without turning, about 4 minutes. Transfer to a large bowl and brown the other two halves without transferring them to the bowl.

3 Return the first two halves to the cooker, overlapping the thinner bits over the thicker as necessary. Sprinkle the chives and thyme over the meat, then pour in the juice, broth, and honey. Sprinkle in the salt and pepper as well.

(continued)

4 Lock the lid onto the pot.

5 Use the quick-release method to bring the pot's pressure back to normal.

6 Unlock and open the pot. Transfer the bird halves to a large serving platter. Set the stovetop cooker over medium heat or turn the electric cooker to its browning or simmer function. Bring the sauce to a simmer.

7 Whisk the potato starch or cornstarch with 2 teaspoons water in a small bowl until smooth. Whisk the slurry into the sauce; cook until thickened, whisking all the while, about 30 seconds. Pour the sauce over the hens and sprinkle the toasted almonds on top.

TESTERS' NOTES
• Tart pomegranate juice makes a wonderful if unexpected braising medium: full of berry flavors that will brighten up even a wintry dish like this one.
• Sprinkle the honey over the meat in step 3, so it has a chance to caramelize onto the hens as they cook.

DUCK WITH APPLE JELLY AND THYME

EFFORT: **A LITTLE** • PRESSURE: **HIGH** • TIME UNDER PRESSURE: **25 OR 37 MINUTES** • RELEASE: **QUICK** • SERVES: **4**

1 tablespoon unsalted butter
4 duck leg-and-thigh quarters (about 8 ounces each)
1/2 teaspoon salt
1/2 teaspoon ground black pepper
1/2 cup apple jelly
2/3 cup chicken broth
2 fresh thyme sprigs
1/4 teaspoon grated nutmeg

1 Melt the butter in a 6-quart stovetop pressure cooker set over medium heat or in a 6-quart electric pressure cooker turned to the browning function. Season the duck with the salt and pepper, then add two of the quarters skin side down and brown well, turning once, about 8 minutes. Transfer to a large bowl. Repeat with the second two leg quarters; transfer to the bowl. Drain off all but a tablespoon or so of fat in the cooker.

2 Stir the jelly into the duck fat in the cooker until it dissolves, then pour in the broth. Return the leg quarters and any juices to the pot, overlapping the legs onto the thighs as necessary. Tuck the thyme sprigs into the sauce; sprinkle the nutmeg over the meat.

3 Lock the lid onto the cooker.

ELECTRIC: Set the machine to cook at high pressure (9–11 psi). Set the machine's timer to cook at high pressure for 37 minutes.

4 Use the quick-release method to return the pot's pressure to normal.

5 Unlock and open the cooker. Transfer the duck leg quarters to a serving platter or individual serving bowls. Discard the thyme sprigs.

6 Set the stovetop cooker over medium heat or turn the electric cooker to its browning function. Bring the sauce to a simmer. Cook, stirring occasionally, until reduced to a thick glaze, 3 to 5 minutes. Drizzle over the duck before serving.

TESTERS' NOTES

• Duck breasts are a no-no in the pressure cooker: they cook too quickly and become unappealingly dry. However, duck leg-and-thigh quarters (that is, the leg and thigh together as one piece) are perfect: long stewers that turn gorgeously tender under pressure. Look for them in the freezer case of most supermarkets.

• You can't just tip the fat out of an electric cooker; the insert is very hot and could fall out. Instead, grasp a wad of paper towels with kitchen tongs and allow the towels to absorb the fat in the cooker. (Remember: the paper towels will get very hot!)

• Here's the great divide in cooking duck leg quarters in the pressure cooker: after 25 minutes stovetop or 37 minutes electric, with a quick release either way, they're still a knife-and-fork affair. If you'd like the meat falling-off-the-bone tender, a fork-and-spoon affair, use the natural release method after cooking.

DUCK WITH BRANDY AND BLACKBERRY JAM

EFFORT: **A LITTLE** • PRESSURE: **HIGH** • TIME UNDER PRESSURE: **25 OR 37 MINUTES** • RELEASE: **QUICK** • SERVES: **4**

1 tablespoon unsalted butter

1 tablespoon olive oil

4 duck leg-and-thigh quarters (about 8 ounces each)

1/2 teaspoon salt

1/2 teaspoon ground black pepper

2 medium shallots, halved and thinly sliced

1 medium carrot, thinly sliced

1/2 cup brandy

1/4 cup chicken broth

1/4 cup blackberry jam

1/2 teaspoon dried thyme

1/2 teaspoon ground allspice

1/4 teaspoon ground cloves

1/4 cup heavy cream

1 Melt the butter in the oil in a 6-quart stovetop pressure cooker set over medium heat or in a 6-quart electric pressure cooker turned to the browning function. Season the leg quarters with the salt and pepper, then put two of them skin side down in the pot and brown well, turning once, about 8 minutes. Transfer to a large bowl and repeat with the remaining two quarters; transfer to the bowl. Drain off all but a tablespoon or so of fat in the pot.

2 Add the shallots and carrot to the pot; cook, stirring often, until the shallots have softened, about 2 minutes. Pour in the brandy and scrape up any browned bits on the bottom of the pot as it bubbles.

(continued)

3 Pour in the broth; stir in the jam, thyme, allspice, and cloves. Return the duck skin side up to the cooker, overlapping the pieces by placing thinner parts over thick. Pour in any juices in their bowl.

4 Lock the lid onto the cooker.

STOVETOP: Raise the heat to high and bring the pot to high pressure (15 psi). Once this pressure has been reached, reduce the heat as much as possible while maintaining this pressure. Cook for 25 minutes.

············ **OR** ············

ELECTRIC: Set the machine to cook at high pressure (9–11 psi). Set the machine's timer to cook at high pressure for 37 minutes.

5 Use the quick-release method to return the pot's pressure to normal.

6 Unlock and remove the lid. Transfer the leg quarters to a serving platter or serving bowls.

7 Set the stovetop cooker over medium heat or turn the electric one to its browning function; bring the sauce to a bubble. Stir in the cream and cook, stirring often, for 2 minutes to blend the flavors and reduce a bit. Ladle the sauce over the duck before serving.

TESTERS' NOTES

• Rich and decadent, this preparation is good enough for Christmas Eve dinner. The sweet-and-sour blackberry jam will balance the cream and bring the spices to the fore to create wintry comfort food.
• If you want some heat, add up to ½ teaspoon red pepper flakes with the other spices.
• Slice the shallots as thin as possible so they begin to melt into the sauce, a counterbalance to the cream.
• To thaw frozen duck quarters, unwrap and place them in a large bowl in the refrigerator for about 2 days.

Serve It Up! Have glazed carrots on the side. Steam baby carrots until tender, then cook in melted butter with a little sugar until bubbling and shiny, just a few minutes, stirring all the while.

DUCK WITH RED ONION, ORANGE MARMALADE, AND CHIPOTLES

EFFORT: **A LITTLE** • PRESSURE: **HIGH** • TIME UNDER PRESSURE: **25 OR 37 MINUTES** • RELEASE: **QUICK** • SERVES: **4**

2 thick-cut strips of bacon, chopped

4 duck leg-and-thigh quarters (about 8 ounces each)

2 medium red onions, halved and sliced into thin half-moons

½ cup orange marmalade

Up to 2 canned chipotles in adobo sauce, stemmed, seeded, and chopped

Up to 2 teaspoons adobo sauce from the can

2 teaspoons minced garlic

1 teaspoon dried oregano

½ teaspoon ground black pepper

1 cup chicken broth

1 Heat a 6-quart stovetop pressure cooker over medium heat or a 6-quart electric pressure cooker turned to the browning function. Add the bacon and cook until crisp, stirring often, 3 to 4 minutes. Use a slotted spoon to transfer the bacon bits to a large bowl.

2 Add two of the duck quarters skin side down to the pot and brown them in the bacon fat, turning once, about 8 minutes. Transfer to the bowl with the bacon and repeat with the remaining duck quarters; transfer to the bowl. Drain off all but a tablespoon of fat.

3 Add the onions to the pot; cook, stirring occasionally, until softened, about 6 minutes. Stir in the marmalade, chipotles, adobo sauce, garlic, oregano, and pepper until the marmalade melts and the sauce begins to bubble. Stir in the broth, then return the leg quarters skin side up to the pot, stacking thinner ends over thicker. Pour any juice in their bowl over everything.

4 Lock the lid onto the cooker.

STOVETOP: Raise the heat to high and bring the pot to high pressure (15 psi). Once this pressure has been reached, reduce the heat as much as possible while maintaining this pressure. Cook for 25 minutes.

························ **OR** ····························

ELECTRIC: Set the machine to cook at high pressure (9–11 psi). Set the machine's timer to cook at high pressure for 37 minutes.

5 Use the quick-release method to bring the pot's pressure back to normal.

6 Unlock and open the cooker. Serve the duck in bowls with the sauce spooned on top.

TESTERS' NOTES
• Spicy and rich, the flavors of this braise are lightened up with orange marmalade. Use a high-quality marmalade, one with plenty of fruit in every tablespoonful.
• The chipotles will lose some of their punch under pressure; however, if you're unsure of your heat tolerance, use less than the full amount.
• The more you brown the duck, the better it will taste—and the more fat you'll pull off the meat before it undergoes pressure, leaving you with a lighter dish.

Serve It Up! Serve over cooked rice noodles.

DUCK WITH GINGER AND DRIED APPLES

EFFORT: **A LITTLE** · PRESSURE: **HIGH** · TIME UNDER PRESSURE: **25 OR 37 MINUTES** · RELEASE: **QUICK** · SERVES: **4**

1 tablespoon peanut oil

4 duck leg-and-thigh quarters (about 8 ounces each)

$1/4$ teaspoon ground ginger

$1/4$ teaspoon salt

$1/4$ teaspoon ground black pepper

1 medium yellow onion, chopped

$1^1/4$ cups dry, fruit-forward white wine, such as a dry Riesling

1 cup packed dried apples, chopped

2 tablespoons minced crystallized (candied) ginger

1 Heat the oil in a 6-quart stovetop pressure cooker set over medium heat or in a 6-quart stovetop pressure cooker turned to the browning function. Season the duck with the ground ginger, salt, and pepper. Add two of the quarters skin side down and brown well, turning once, about 8 minutes. Transfer to a large bowl and repeat with the remaining duck quarters; transfer to the bowl. Drain off all but a couple tablespoons of fat from the pot.

2 Add the onion to the pot; cook, stirring often, until softened, about 3 minutes. Pour in the wine and scrape up any browned bits in the bottom of the pot as it comes to a simmer. Stir in the apples and ginger. Return the duck quarters skin side up to the cooker, overlapping thinner bits over thicker. Pour in any juice from their bowl.

(continued)

3 Lock the lid onto the pot.

STOVETOP: Raise the heat to high and bring the pot to high pressure (15 psi). Once this pressure has been reached, reduce the heat as much as possible while maintaining this pressure. Cook for 25 minutes.

································ **OR** ································

ELECTRIC: Set the machine to cook at high pressure (9–11 psi). Set the machine's timer to cook at high pressure for 37 minutes.

4 Use the quick-release method to drop the pot's pressure to normal.

5 Unlock and open the cooker. Serve the quarters in bowls with the sauce spooned over each.

TESTERS' NOTES
• Although the flavors in duck meat take well to sweet preparations, that pairing must be counterbalanced in some way—with the onion's aromatic finish, of course, but here also with candied ginger that adds a spicy note to the sauce.
• Dried apples will not break down into a sauce the way fresh apples would, so we've used them here to give a textural contrast to the smooth sauce.

Serve It Up! To make a **cauliflower puree** to put under this stew: Steam cauliflower florets until tender, then place in a food processor fitted with the chopping blade. Add a little unsalted butter, salt, and pepper; cover and process, drizzling in heavy cream in 1-tablespoon increments, until you have a smooth, rich puree.

SPICED DUCK WITH SOUR CHERRIES AND PORT

EFFORT: **A LOT** • PRESSURE: **HIGH** • TIME UNDER PRESSURE: **25 OR 37 MINUTES** • RELEASE: **QUICK** • SERVES: **4**

1 tablespoon minced garlic
1 tablespoon red wine vinegar
2 teaspoons minced fresh ginger
1/2 teaspoon ground cardamom
1/2 teaspoon ground cinnamon
1/2 teaspoon ground coriander
1/2 teaspoon ground cumin
1/2 teaspoon salt
1/2 teaspoon cayenne
1/4 teaspoon ground cloves
4 tablespoons (1/2 stick) unsalted butter, cut into small bits
4 duck leg-and-thigh quarters (about 8 ounces each)
2 small red onions, halved and sliced into thin half-moons
1/4 cup dried sour cherries
2/3 cup chicken broth
1/4 cup non-vintage tawny port

1 Use a fork to mash the garlic, vinegar, ginger, cardamom, cinnamon, coriander, cumin, salt, cayenne, and cloves in a small bowl to make a coarse paste; set aside.

2 Melt the butter in a 6-quart stovetop pressure cooker set over medium heat or in a 6-quart stovetop pressure cooker turned to the browning function. Add two of the duck quarters skin side down and brown well, turning once, about 8 minutes. Transfer to a large bowl and repeat with the remaining quarters; transfer to the bowl. Pour off all but a tablespoon or two of fat from the cooker.

3 Add the onions and dried cherries to the pot; cook, stirring often, until the onion is beginning to brown and sweeten, until it is very soft, about 10 minutes. Add the spice paste; cook, stirring often, until fragrant and toasted, about 2 minutes. Return the duck quarters skin side down to the pot, stacking thinner bits over thicker as necessary. Pour in any juice from their bowl, then pour in the broth and port.

4 Lock the lid onto the pot.

STOVETOP: Raise the heat to high and bring the pot to high pressure (15 psi). Once this pressure has been reached, reduce the heat as much as possible while maintaining this pressure. Cook for 25 minutes.

·············· **OR** ··············

ELECTRIC: Set the machine to cook at high pressure (9–11 psi). Set the machine's timer to cook at high pressure for 37 minutes.

5 Use the quick-release method to bring the pot's pressure back to normal.

6 Unlock and open the pot. Serve the duck in bowls with the sauce ladled on each helping.

TESTERS' NOTES

• Sour cherries and a raft of spices—these make for one of the most aromatic recipes here. Make sure those dried sour cherries do taste like sour cherries, not just a vaguely sweet hint of cherry in a gummy candy.

• Duck with cherries is a bit of a cliché, so we created an intense, ginger-laced spice paste to reinvent the classic with layers of flavor. The vinegar bring the spices into balance and cuts through the richness of the duck.

DUCK RAGÙ

EFFORT: **A LOT** • PRESSURE: **HIGH** • TIME UNDER PRESSURE: **25 OR 37 MINUTES** • RELEASE: **NATURAL** • SERVES: **8**

2 tablespoons olive oil

1 medium yellow onion, chopped

1 medium green bell pepper, stemmed, cored, and chopped

1 medium carrot, chopped

2 tablespoons packed fresh oregano leaves, minced

2 tablespoons packed fresh rosemary leaves, minced

2 teaspoons minced garlic

1 cup full-bodied, dry red wine, such as Nebbiolo

One 28-ounce can diced tomatoes (about 3½ cups)

4 duck leg-and-thigh quarters (about 8 ounces each), skinned and excess fat removed

3 tablespoons canned tomato paste

1½ tablespoons balsamic vinegar

½ teaspoon salt

½ teaspoon ground black pepper

1 Heat the oil in a 6-quart stovetop pressure cooker set over medium heat or in a 6-quart electric pressure cooker turned to the browning function. Add the onion, bell pepper, and carrot; cook, stirring often, until the onion softens, about 4 minutes. Stir in the oregano, rosemary, and garlic; cook until aromatic, about 30 seconds.

2 Pour in the wine and scrape up any browned bits in the pot as it comes to a simmer. Stir in the tomatoes; nestle the duck down into the sauce.

(continued)

3 Lock the lid onto the pot.

STOVETOP: Raise the heat to high and bring the pot to high pressure (15 psi). Once this pressure has been reached, reduce the heat as much as possible while maintaining this pressure. Cook for 25 minutes.

·····················OR·····················

ELECTRIC: Set the machine to cook at high pressure (9–11 psi). Set the machine's timer to cook at high pressure for 37 minutes.

4 Reduce the pressure.

STOVETOP: Set the pot off the heat and let its pressure come back to normal naturally, about 25 minutes.

·····················OR·····················

ELECTRIC: Turn off the machine or unplug it so it doesn't flip to its keep-warm setting. Let its pressure fall to normal naturally, 25 to 30 minutes.

5 Unlock and open the cooker. Use kitchen tongs to transfer the leg quarters to a large cutting board. Cool for a few minutes, then debone the meat and chop it into bite-size bits.

6 Set the stovetop pot over medium heat or turn the electric cooker to its browning function. Stir in the duck meat, the tomato paste, vinegar, salt, and pepper. Simmer, stirring often, until slightly thickened, about like a pasta sauce, not soupy at all, 7 to 10 minutes.

TESTERS' NOTES

• This Italian pasta sauce uses duck meat as a somewhat sweet counterpoint to lots of herbs and aromatics. You could also call it "Duck Sunday Gravy."

• The sauce needs to be thickened properly in step 6. Depending on the residual moisture content of the ingredients, as well as the exact amount of pressure under which they cooked, it might take more time than stated but it's worth it.

• The ragù freezes well. Store it in sealed containers in the freezer for up to 4 months; reheat in a covered saucepan with a little extra broth before serving.

• Duck leg-and-thigh quarters can be difficult to skin. The skin will pull off the leg fairly easily but may adhere closely to the thigh, glued on by all the fat. You may need a paring knife to trim off the skin and fat, as though you were peeling the rind and pith from an orange.

Serve It Up! Ladle the ragù over pasta or polenta—or even over a buttery risotto for a truly luxurious dish. Grate Parmigiano-Reggiano, pecorino romano, or aged Asiago over each bowlful.

DUCK RAGOÛT

EFFORT: **A LITTLE** • PRESSURE: **HIGH** • TIME UNDER PRESSURE: **25 OR 37 MINUTES** • RELEASE: **QUICK** • SERVES: **4**

One 4-ounce pancetta chunk, chopped

4 duck leg-and-thigh quarters (about 8 ounces each)

1 cup fresh pearl onions, peeled, or frozen pearl onions, thawed

1 cup very dry white wine, such as a white Côtes-du-Rhône

1 ounce dried porcini mushrooms

1 cup jarred steamed chestnuts

1 teaspoon dried thyme

½ teaspoon ground allspice

½ teaspoon ground black pepper

2 tablespoons red currant jelly

1 Set a 6-quart stovetop pressure cooker over medium heat for a couple of minutes or turn a 6-quart electric pressure cooker to its browning function for a couple of minutes. Add the pancetta and cook, stirring often, until browned and even a little crunchy, about 4 minutes. Use a slotted spoon to transfer the pancetta to a big bowl.

2 Add two of the duck quarters skin side down and brown well, turning once, about 8 minutes. Transfer these to the bowl with the pancetta and repeat with the remaining quarters; transfer to the bowl. Drain off all but a couple tablespoons of rendered fat in the pot.

3 Add the onions to the pot; cook, stirring often, until softened, about 4 minutes. Pour in the wine and scrape up any browned bits off the bottom of the cooker. Crumble in the dried mushrooms, then add the chestnuts, thyme, allspice, and pepper. Stir well before returning the duck and pancetta to the cooker, as well as any juices in their bowl.

4 Lock the lid onto the pot.

STOVETOP: Raise the heat to high and bring the pot to high pressure (15 psi). Once this pressure has been reached, reduce the heat as much as possible while maintaining this pressure. Cook for 25 minutes.

······················ **OR** ····················

ELECTRIC: Set the machine to cook at high pressure (9–11 psi). Set the machine's timer to cook at high pressure for 37 minutes.

5 Use the quick-release method to return the pot's pressure to normal.

6 Unlock and open the pot. Use kitchen tongs to transfer the quarters to serving bowls. Use a flatware spoon to skim the excess fat from the sauce. Stir in the jelly until melted and spoon the sauce over the quarters.

TESTERS' NOTES

• A ragoût is a French stew, like an Italian ragù (pronounced the same) but with more vegetables, and is not just a sauce for pasta. It's usually not tomato-based, but instead uses aromatics and wine to create a braising liquid.

• The red currant jelly will give the sauce a necessary sweet spike to match the duck. For a bigger flavor, substitute sour cherry jam.

FISH AND SHELLFISH

WELCOME TO THE CHAPTER THAT'S ALL ABOUT SPEED. LET'S FACE IT: most of us choose tilapia, snapper, shrimp, or mussels for dinner because they are a culinary trifecta: fast, tasty, and healthy. We've got a hunch that the first member of this trio is the most important on a typical Tuesday night: fast. Well, guess what? Seafood just got even faster (while remaining tasty and healthy). With a pressure cooker, an ocean-fresh dinner can be cooked in a minute or two, sometimes (if you can believe it) even less.

It's tastier, too. The pressure cooker works with a quick blast of intense, uniform heat, rather than the more prolonged heat of a steamer, the more uneven heat of a grill grate, or the intensely localized heat of a skillet. If you follow the timings carefully, clams will retain their juicy fullness without shrinking into rubbery bits, snapper fillets won't dry out at the edges, and salmon will better retain more of its delicate flavor.

Not every piece of fish needs to undergo pressure cooking. Sometimes, we use the appliance to build a sauce, layering and balancing the flavors. Then we add the shrimp or fish to the pot and set it aside for a couple of minutes to cook these briny treats. But this chapter's not just about sauces. We've got some family-friendly noodle casseroles here, as well as some dinner-party–worthy interpretations of risotto. And given what we've said about clams (and mussels, too!), we've got a large set of recipes for our favorite mollusks.

But before we start cooking, we need to state the most important rule for fish or shellfish. Whatever you choose needs to smell clean, like the ocean on a spring morning at high tide. If you detect the murky stink of the tidal flats in August, or (worse still) if you smell gasoline, or if (worst of all) you notice a slimy film on the fish or shellfish, take your business elsewhere. If possible, never buy fish or shellfish under plastic wrap. If the smell test is the one right way to assure freshness, how can you tell that with a sealed container?

That said, frozen fish or shellfish are excellent choices. After all, most of the seafood sold at your supermarket came in frozen and was thawed in the back before it hit the ice out front. Economize and buy yours in the same way: thaw your selection in a bowl in the fridge for a day or two. Never put frozen or partially thawed seafood in a pressure cooker (it will alter the timings considerably). And never refreeze fish or shellfish—once it's thawed, you're committed.

Remember, too, that mussels and clams are live-food products—they should shut when tapped. Get them straight home, preferably on ice, then take them out of their wrapper and set them in a bowl in the fridge for no more than a day. And skip all that blather about submerging them in water with a little cornmeal so they'll expel their grit. These are saltwater creatures; fresh water will kill them. Do not cook any bivalves that will not close when tapped and avoid any that will not open after cooking.

Armed with this simple knowledge, you're ready for the fastest meals in this book—and maybe some of the best. You won't believe how high pressure keeps fish and shellfish tender and moist. You'll soon be hooked. We are.

SHRIMP RISOTTO

EFFORT: **NOT MUCH** · PRESSURE: **HIGH** · TIME UNDER PRESSURE: **7 OR 10 MINUTES** · RELEASE: **QUICK** · SERVES: **4 TO 6**

2 tablespoons unsalted butter

1 medium yellow onion, chopped

1 jarred roasted red bell pepper, chopped

1 tablespoon loosely packed fresh oregano leaves, minced

1 tablespoon sweet paprika

1/2 teaspoon salt

1/2 teaspoon ground black pepper

1 1/2 cups white Arborio rice (a medium-grain rice)

1/4 cup dry sherry

3 cups chicken broth

1 cup bottled clam juice

1 pound medium shrimp (about 30 per pound), peeled, deveined, and roughly chopped

1/2 cup finely grated Parmesan cheese (about 2 ounces)

1 Melt the butter in a 6-quart stovetop pressure cooker set over medium heat or in a 6-quart electric pressure cooker turned to the browning function. Add the onion and roasted pepper; cook, stirring often, until the onion turns translucent, about 4 minutes. Stir in the oregano, paprika, salt, and pepper until aromatic, less than a minute.

2 Add the rice and stir over the heat for 1 minute. Pour in the sherry and stir until absorbed, about 2 minutes. Stir in the broth and clam juice.

3 Lock the lid onto the pot.

STOVETOP: Raise the heat to high and bring the pot to high pressure (15 psi). Once this pressure has been reached, reduce the heat as much as possible while maintaining this pressure. Cook for 7 minutes.

···OR·····························

ELECTRIC: Set the machine to cook at high pressure (9–11 psi). Set the machine's timer to cook at high pressure for 10 minutes.

4 Use the quick-release method to bring the pot's pressure back to normal.

5 Unlock and open the cooker. Set the stovetop pot over medium heat or turn the electric cooker to its browning or simmer setting. Add the shrimp and cook, stirring often, until pink and firm, about 2 minutes. Stir in the cheese and set aside off the heat for a couple of minutes to blend the flavors before serving.

TESTERS' NOTES

• This elegant dinner may become a go-to weeknight staple. The rice becomes tender but a little chewy, while the delicate flavors give the dish a springtime feel, even if you make it in the dead of winter.

• We like risotto with a bit of bite in each grain of rice. If you prefer it softer, turn off the heat at the specific time, set the stovetop pot aside for 2 minutes or the electric pot aside for 3 minutes, and then use the quick-release method to reduce the pressure and carry on with step 5.

• Bottled clam juice is an acceptable if very salty substitute for fish stock. If you find the stock at a high-end market, use 4 cups and omit the chicken broth and clam juice. Otherwise, look for bottled clam juice in the canned good aisle, among the soups, or with the condiments. (If you can't find clam juice, you can substitute 1 cup additional broth.)

• Substitute dry vermouth for the dry sherry, if you prefer.

CREAMY SHRIMP AND CORN STEW

EFFORT: **A LITTLE** • PRESSURE: **HIGH** • TIME UNDER PRESSURE: **3 OR 5 MINUTES** • RELEASE: **QUICK** • SERVES: **4**

2 tablespoons unsalted butter

2 thin bacon slices, chopped

1 medium yellow onion, chopped

1 medium yellow bell pepper, stemmed, cored, and diced

1 tablespoon loosely packed fresh oregano leaves, minced

2 teaspoons finely grated lemon zest

$1/2$ teaspoon celery seeds

2 cups chicken broth

1 pound medium shrimp (about 30 per pound), peeled, deveined, and halved widthwise

1 cup fresh corn kernels (about 1 large ear), or frozen kernels, thawed

$1/2$ cup heavy cream

1 Melt the butter in a 6-quart stovetop pressure cooker set over medium heat or in a 6-quart electric pressure cooker turned to the browning function. Add the bacon and fry until crisp, about 3 minutes, stirring often.

2 Add the onion and bell pepper; cook, stirring often, until softened, about 3 minutes. Stir in the oregano, zest, and celery seeds until aromatic, about half a minute. Pour in the broth and stir well.

3 Lock the lid onto the pot.

STOVETOP: Raise the heat to high and bring the pot to high pressure (15 psi). Once this pressure has been reached, reduce the heat as much as possible while maintaining this pressure. Cook for 3 minutes.

························· OR ·························

ELECTRIC: Set the machine to cook at high pressure (9–11 psi). Set the machine's timer to cook at high pressure for 5 minutes.

4 Use the quick-release method to bring the pot's pressure back to normal.

5 Unlock and open the cooker. Set the stovetop pot over medium heat or turn the electric model to its browning or simmer function. Stir in the shrimp, corn, and cream. Cook, stirring often, until the shrimp are pink and firm, about 3 minutes. Serve at once.

TESTERS' NOTES

• Sort of like a potato-free chowder, this hearty stew uses the pressure cooker to create a rich and satisfying broth base. After that, it's merely a matter of cooking the shrimp, corn, and cream with all those layers of flavor.

• Save any shrimp shells in a sealed plastic bag in the freezer. Once you've got 6 cups, you can make shrimp stock by simmering them very slowly for 4 or 5 hours in an uncovered pot of water with onions, celery, and carrots, until reduced to at least half the original volume.

Serve It Up! Make **Mustard-Maple Vinaigrette** for a chopped salad on the side: Whisk $1/3$ cup maple syrup, 3 tablespoons coarse-grained mustard, 2 tablespoons white wine vinegar, 1 tablespoon canola oil, $1/4$ teaspoon salt, and $1/4$ teaspoon ground black pepper in a large bowl until creamy. Add chopped lettuce, cucumber, radishes, celery, carrots, and/or red onion; toss to combine.

SHRIMP AND LENTIL STEW

EFFORT: **A LITTLE** • PRESSURE: **HIGH** • TIME UNDER PRESSURE:
25 OR 37 MINUTES • RELEASE: **QUICK** • SERVES: **4**

2 tablespoons olive oil

1 small yellow onion, chopped

2 medium carrots, thinly sliced

1 teaspoon minced garlic

**8 ounces smoked pork or turkey sausage,
such as kielbasa, thinly sliced**

1/2 teaspoon smoked paprika

1/2 teaspoon dried thyme

1/4 teaspoon cayenne

**One 14-ounce can diced tomatoes (about
1 3/4 cups)**

1 1/2 cups chicken broth

**1/2 cup green lentils (French lentils or
lentils du Puy)**

**1 1/4 pounds medium shrimp (about 30 per
pound), peeled, deveined, and halved
widthwise**

1 Heat the oil in a 6-quart stovetop pressure cooker set over medium heat or in a 6-quart electric pressure cooker turned to the browning function. Add the onion and carrots; cook, stirring often, until the onion softens, about 3 minutes.

2 Add the garlic, cook for a few seconds, and then stir in the sausage, smoked paprika, thyme, and cayenne. Cook for about a minute, until aromatic, then pour in the tomatoes and broth. Add the lentils and stir well.

3 Lock the lid onto the pot.

STOVETOP: Raise the heat to high and bring the pot to high pressure (15 psi). Once this pressure has been reached, reduce the heat as much as possible while maintaining this pressure. Cook for 25 minutes.

························ **OR** ····························

ELECTRIC: Set the machine to cook at high pressure (9–11 psi). Set the machine's timer to cook at high pressure for 37 minutes.

4 Use the quick-release method to bring the pot's pressure back to normal.

5 Unlock and open the cooker. Set the stovetop model over medium heat or turn the electric one to its browning or simmer function. Stir in the shrimp; cook until pink and firm, about 2 minutes. Serve in bowls.

TESTERS' NOTES
• The earthy flavor of lentils balances the sweet-and-salty finish of shrimp to make a satisfying Spanish-inspired stew.
• There's not much liquid here because we wanted a thick stew, almost like a casserole. If you'd like it soupier, increase the broth to 2½ cups. Or use 1½ cups broth and 1 cup light-colored beer, such as a pale ale.

SHRIMP AND TOMATILLO CASSEROLE

EFFORT: **A LITTLE** • PRESSURE: **HIGH** • TIME UNDER PRESSURE:
6 OR 9 MINUTES • RELEASE: **QUICK** • SERVES: **4 TO 6**

2 tablespoons olive oil

1 medium yellow onion, chopped

**1 small fresh jalapeño chile, stemmed,
seeded, and minced**

2 teaspoons minced garlic

1½ pounds fresh tomatillos, husked and chopped

½ cup bottled clam juice

2 tablespoons fresh lime juice

1½ pounds medium shrimp (about 30 per pound), peeled and deveined

¼ cup loosely packed fresh cilantro leaves, chopped

1 cup shredded Monterey jack cheese (about 4 ounces)

1 Heat the oil in a 6-quart stovetop pressure cooker set over medium heat or in a 6-quart electric pressure cooker turned to the browning function. Add the onion and cook, stirring often, until translucent, about 3 minutes.

2 Add the jalapeño and garlic; cook until aromatic, stirring all the while, less than a minute. Stir in the tomatillos, clam juice, and lime juice.

3 Lock the lid onto the pot.

STOVETOP: Raise the heat to high and bring the pot to high pressure (15 psi). Once this pressure has been reached, reduce the heat as much as possible while maintaining this pressure. Cook for 6 minutes.

························ **OR** ·······························

ELECTRIC: Set the machine to cook at high pressure (9–11 psi). Set the machine's timer to cook at high pressure for 9 minutes.

4 Use the quick-release method to bring the pot's pressure back to normal.

5 Unlock and open the pot. Set the stovetop pot over medium heat or turn the electric one to its browning or simmer function. Stir in the shrimp and cilantro; cook for 2 minutes, stirring frequently. Sprinkle the cheese over the top of the casserole, cover the cooker, and lock the lid in place. Set aside off

the heat for 2 minutes to melt the cheese and blend the flavors.

6 Use the quick-release method (if necessary) to bring any pressure in the pot back to normal.

7 Unlock and open the pot. Stir gently before serving.

TESTERS' NOTES
• Stocked with big flavors, this casserole is modeled on the flavors of salsa verde, with a little melted cheese on top for good measure.
• The tomatillos should be firm and bright green, even a little sticky under their husks. They'll break down into most of the essential moisture in the dish. Look for them near the tomatoes in most large supermarkets.
• You can substitute chicken broth for the clam juice.

SHRIMP CURRY WITH LEEKS AND APPLES

EFFORT: **NOT MUCH** • PRESSURE: **HIGH** • TIME UNDER PRESSURE: **LESS THAN A MINUTE** • RELEASE: **QUICK** • SERVES: **4**

2 tablespoons unsalted butter

1 large leek, white and pale green parts only, halved lengthwise, washed, and thinly sliced

2 medium celery stalks, thinly sliced

2 tart green apples, such as Granny Smith, peeled, cored, and thinly sliced

2 teaspoons yellow curry powder

1 cup chicken broth

1½ pounds medium shrimp (about 30 per pound), peeled and deveined

2 teaspoons cornstarch or arrowroot

1 Melt the butter in a 6-quart stovetop pressure cooker set over medium heat or in a

(continued)

6-quart electric pressure cooker turned to the browning function. Add the leek and celery; cook, stirring frequently, until softened, about 2 minutes.

2 Stir in the apples and curry powder; cook until aromatic, less than a minute. Pour in the broth; add the shrimp.

3 Lock the lid onto the pot.

STOVETOP: Lock the lid onto the pot and bring the pot to high pressure (15 psi).

···················· **OR** ····················

ELECTRIC: Set the machine to cook at high pressure (9–11 psi).

4 The moment the pot's at high pressure, use the quick-release method to bring its pressure back to normal.

5 Unlock and open the pot. Set the stovetop model over medium heat or turn the electric one to its browning function. Mix the cornstarch or arrowroot with 2 teaspoons water until dissolved; stir the slurry into the pot. Cook, stirring all the while, until simmering and thickened, about 30 seconds.

TESTERS' NOTES

• The apples add sweetness to this otherwise savory curry, done in almost no time. If you prefer an even sweeter curry, use a sweet baking apple like Mutsu.
• Make sure you slice those apples into thin bits so they soften in the quick cooking time.
• Although there are standard bottlings of yellow curry powder in our supermarkets, you can find a vast array of flavorful alternatives from East Indian grocery stores online.

Serve It Up! Combine cooked long-grain white rice with sliced almonds and raisins to use as a bed for the curry.

SHRIMP CREOLE

EFFORT: **A LITTLE** • PRESSURE: **HIGH** • TIME UNDER PRESSURE: **5 OR 8 MINUTES** • RELEASE: **QUICK** • SERVES: **4 TO 6**

2 tablespoons peanut oil

1 large yellow onion, chopped

2 medium celery stalks, chopped

1 medium green bell pepper, stemmed, cored, and chopped

1 teaspoon sweet paprika

1 teaspoon dried thyme

1 teaspoon dried oregano

1 teaspoon ground black pepper

Up to 1/2 teaspoon onion powder

Up to 1/4 teaspoon garlic powder

2 cups chicken broth

One 14-ounce can diced tomatoes (about 1 3/4 cups)

1/2 cup dry but very fruit-forward white wine, such as Sauvignon Blanc

2 tablespoons canned tomato paste

1 tablespoon Worcestershire sauce

2 pounds medium shrimp (about 30 per pound), peeled and deveined

6 medium scallions, green and white parts, thinly sliced

1/4 cup loosely packed fresh parsley leaves, minced

1 Heat the oil in a 6-quart stovetop pressure cooker set over medium heat or in a 6-quart stovetop pressure cooker turned to the browning function. Add the onion, celery, and bell pepper; cook, stirring often, until the onion turns translucent, about 4 minutes. Stir in the paprika, thyme, oregano, pepper, onion powder, and garlic powder until aromatic, less than 1 minute.

2 Stir in the broth, tomatoes, wine, tomato paste, and Worcestershire sauce until the paste dissolves.

3 Lock the lid onto the cooker.

STOVETOP: Raise the heat to high and bring the pot to high pressure (15 psi). Once this pressure has been reached, reduce the heat as much as possible while maintaining this pressure. Cook for 5 minutes.

································ **OR** ································

ELECTRIC: Set the machine to cook at high pressure (9–11 psi). Set the machine's timer to cook at high pressure for 8 minutes.

4 Use the quick-release method to bring the pressure in the pot back to normal.

5 Unlock and open the pot. Set the stovetop pot over medium heat or turn the electric model to its browning function. Stir in the shrimp, scallions, and parsley. Cook, stirring often, until the shrimp are pink and firm, 2 to 3 minutes. Serve at once.

TESTERS' NOTES
• Look no further for the best quick version of this Louisiana favorite. (No, there's not a long simmer or a complex roux.)
• Serve the dish as soon as it's done; otherwise, the shrimp become rubbery and tough in the hot liquid.
• Use onion and garlic powders, not onion and garlic salts. You can substitute up to 2 tablespoons bottled Creole dried seasoning blend for the spices.
• If desired, add up to ½ pound chopped tasso ham or other spicy, smoked, ready-to-eat sausage with the onion and celery.

Serve It Up! You'll need cooked long-grain white rice in the bowls on which to add the shrimp creole.

SCALLOPS WITH TOMATOES AND FENNEL SEEDS

EFFORT: **A LITTLE** • PRESSURE: **HIGH** • TIME UNDER PRESSURE: **4 OR 6 MINUTES** • RELEASE: **QUICK** • SERVES: **4**

2 tablespoons olive oil
12 large sea scallops (1 to 1¼ pounds total)
¼ teaspoon salt
¼ teaspoon ground black pepper
2 tablespoons unsalted butter
1 small yellow onion, chopped
1 small fennel bulb, trimmed and chopped
One 14-ounce can diced tomatoes (about 1¾ cups)
3 tablespoons honey
1 teaspoon fennel seeds

1 Heat the oil in a 6-quart stovetop pressure cooker set over medium heat or in a 6-quart electric pressure cooker turned to the browning function. Season the scallops with salt and pepper, then add them to the cooker and brown on both sides, about 4 minutes, turning once. Transfer to a large plate. Set aside.

2 Melt the butter in the cooker, then add the chopped onion and fennel. Cook, stirring often, until softened, about 4 minutes. Pour in the diced tomatoes; stir in the honey and fennel seeds.

3 Lock the lid onto the pot.

(continued)

STOVETOP: Raise the heat to high and bring the pot to high pressure (15 psi). Once this pressure has been reached, reduce the heat as much as possible while maintaining this pressure. Cook for 4 minutes.

························· **OR** ·························

ELECTRIC: Set the machine to cook at high pressure (9–11 psi). Set the machine's timer to cook at high pressure for 6 minutes.

4 Use the quick-release method to return the pot's pressure to normal.

5 Unlock and open the cooker. Stir in the scallops and set aside for 1 minute to heat through before serving.

TESTERS' NOTES

• Here's a great way to use the pressure cooker to prepare scallops: use it to build a sauce, particularly taking advantage of the caramelized bits the scallops leave behind after browning. Stir them back into the sauce to absorb its flavor as they warm up again.

• The honey may be a bit of a surprise; it actually brings the tomatoes and fennel into balance, creating a luxurious sauce.

• Choose the largest scallops you can find. They should also be evenly sized so they cook at the same rate. When done, they should be firm and opaque, perhaps still a tinge pink inside.

Serve It Up! Toss cooked and drained spaghetti with plenty of olive oil, some minced parsley leaves, a little minced garlic, and a little salt; serve it on the side.

HEARTY SCALLOP CHOWDER

EFFORT: **A LITTLE** • PRESSURE: **HIGH** • TIME UNDER PRESSURE: **5 OR 7 MINUTES** • RELEASE: **QUICK** • SERVES: **4 TO 6**

3 thin bacon slices

2 tablespoons unsalted butter

1 large yellow onion, chopped

2 medium celery stalks, chopped

2 cups chicken broth

1 cup bottled clam juice

$1/2$ cup dry white wine, such as Chardonnay

2 pounds yellow potatoes, such as Yukon Gold, cut into $1/2$-inch pieces

1 tablespoon stemmed fresh thyme leaves

2 bay leaves

$1^1/2$ pounds bay scallops

1 cup heavy cream

$1/4$ cup loosely packed fresh parsley leaves, chopped

2 tablespoons minced chives

1 Fry the bacon until crisp in a 6-quart stovetop pressure cooker set over medium heat or in a 6-quart electric pressure cooker turned to the browning function, turning a couple of times, about 3 minutes. Transfer to a plate.

2 Melt the butter in the bacon fat. Add the onion and celery; cook, stirring occasionally, until softened, about 4 minutes. Pour in the broth, clam juice, and wine. Stir well, getting up any browned bits on the bottom of the pot. Stir in the potatoes, thyme, and bay leaves.

3 Lock the lid onto the cooker.

STOVETOP: Raise the heat to high and bring the pot to high pressure (15 psi). Once this pressure has been reached, reduce the heat as much as possible while maintaining this pressure. Cook for 5 minutes.

···············OR···············

ELECTRIC: Set the machine to cook at high pressure (9–11 psi). Set the machine's timer to cook at high pressure for 7 minutes.

4 Use the quick-release method to bring the pot's pressure back to normal.

5 Unlock and open the pot. Stir the stovetop cooker over medium heat or turn the electric model to its browning mode. Crumble in the bacon; stir in the scallops, cream, parsley, and chives. Cook until the scallops are firm and opaque, about 2 minutes, stirring almost constantly. Discard the bay leaves before serving.

TESTERS' NOTES
• We thicken this chowder with the natural starches from the potatoes. However, it's looser than some pasty New England chowders out there.
• Bay scallops are far smaller than sea scallops—and sweeter, too. They cook in no time, so watch carefully in step 5 to avoid overcooking them. If you can't find them, substitute calico scallops, a less seasonal product. Or cut larger sea scallops into quarters before adding them in step 5.
• You can substitute 1 additional cup broth for the clam juice, minced green parts of a scallion for the chives, and/or light cream (or half-and-half) for the heavy cream.

STEAMED SALMON WITH GARLIC-CITRUS BUTTER

EFFORT: **NOT MUCH** • PRESSURE: **HIGH** • TIME UNDER PRESSURE: **4 OR 6 MINUTES** • RELEASE: **QUICK** • SERVES: **4 TO 6**

4 tablespoons (1/2 stick) unsalted butter, at room temperature
2 teaspoons minced garlic
1 teaspoon finely grated orange zest
1 teaspoon finely grated lemon zest
1/2 teaspoon salt
1/2 teaspoon ground black pepper
Two 1-pound skin-on salmon fillets

1 Mash the butter, garlic, both zests, salt, and pepper in a small bowl until uniform.

2 Pour 2 cups water in a 6-quart stovetop or electric pressure cooker. Line a large steamer basket with parchment paper; set it in the cooker. Add the fillets skin side down; top with the butter mixture.

3 Lock the lid onto the pot.

STOVETOP: Set the pot over high heat and bring to high pressure (15 psi). Once this pressure has been reached, reduce the heat as much as possible while maintaining this pressure. Cook for 4 minutes.

···············OR···············

ELECTRIC: Set the machine to cook at high pressure (9–11 psi). Set the machine's timer to cook at high pressure for 6 minutes.

4 Use the quick-release method to drop the pot's pressure to normal.

5 Unlock and open the pot. Transfer the salmon to a large platter and slice each fillet into two or three pieces to serve.

(continued)

TESTERS' NOTES

- Steaming the salmon fillets in the pressure cooker keeps them moist and flavorful under the intense pressure.
- The butter will melt onto the fillets and even run into the water below. Honestly, you just want flavor on the fish, not a big dousing of fat. Spread and smear a thin layer of the butter over the salmon for even cooking.
- The skin must remain on the fillets or they'll fall apart as they steam.
- Use a large, flat, metal spatula to lift the fillets one by one out of the basket.

POACHED SALMON WITH SOUR CREAM AND CUCUMBER SAUCE

EFFORT: **A LITTLE** • PRESSURE: **HIGH** • TIME UNDER PRESSURE: **LESS THAN A MINUTE** • RELEASE: **MODIFIED NATURAL** • SERVES: **6**

6 cups vegetable broth

¼ cup white wine vinegar

1 tablespoon plus ½ teaspoon salt

1½ pounds skin-on salmon fillets

1 medium cucumber, peeled, seeded, and diced

½ teaspoon sugar

1 cup regular, low-fat, or fat-free sour cream

2 tablespoons chopped fresh dill fronds

2 teaspoons fresh lemon juice

1 Pour the broth, vinegar, and 1 tablespoon salt in a 6-quart stovetop set over medium heat or in a 6-quart electric pressure cooker turned to the browning function. Bring the liquid to a boil, stirring, until the salt dissolves. Slip the salmon fillets skin side down into the poaching liquid.

2 Lock the lid onto the pot.

STOVETOP: Raise the heat to high and cook for 1 minute. (The pot may not come fully up to pressure.) Set the pot off the heat for 8 minutes.
························· **OR** ·························
ELECTRIC: Set the machine to cook at high pressure. Cook for 1 minute. (The machine may not come fully up to high pressure.) Turn off the machine or unplug it; set aside for 8 minutes.

3 As the pressure cooker sits, stir the cucumber, sugar, and remaining ½ teaspoon salt in a large bowl; set aside.

4 Use the quick-release method to bring the pot's pressure back to normal as necessary. Unlock and open the pot. Line a cutting board with paper towels; transfer the salmon to the cutting board. Blot fillets dry with more paper towels. Cut each into 6 wedges or slices and transfer to a serving platter.

5 Drain any liquid from the bowl with the cucumber bits. Stir in the sour cream, dill, and lemon juice. Spoon this sauce on top of the salmon pieces to serve.

TESTERS' NOTES

- Atlantic salmon is by and large fattier while Pacific salmon is leaner. The choice is yours.
- To seed a cucumber, peel it and halve it lengthwise. Use a small flatware spoon, preferably a grapefruit spoon, to scrape the seeds out of each half. To dice it, slice these halves into long, thin spears, then slice these crosswise into ¼-inch bits.
- If desired, serve the salmon cold. Poach it as stated with the modified natural release, then transfer to a serving platter and refrigerate until cold, about 2 hours. Serve or cover and store in the fridge for up to 2 days.

SALMON STEAKS WITH CREAMY MUSTARD SAUCE

EFFORT: **A LITTLE** • PRESSURE: **HIGH** • TIME UNDER PRESSURE:
4 OR 6 MINUTES • RELEASE: **QUICK** • SERVES: **4**

Four 2-inch-thick salmon steaks (about 8 ounces each)

4 tablespoons Dijon mustard

1/2 teaspoon dried dill

1/4 teaspoon ground black pepper

1/2 cup dry white wine, such as Chardonnay

1/2 cup chicken broth

1 small yellow or white onion, minced

2 tablespoons heavy cream

1 teaspoon cornstarch or arrowroot

1 Smear one side of each salmon steak with the mustard; sprinkle with the dill and pepper.

2 Pour the wine and broth into a 6-quart stovetop or electric pressure cooker; stir in the onion. Set a large vegetable steamer in the pot; line the steamer with parchment paper. Lay the fillets coating side up in the steamer.

3 Lock the lid onto the pot.

STOVETOP: Set the pot over high heat and bring to high pressure (15 psi). Once this pressure has been reached, reduce the heat as much as possible while maintaining this pressure. Cook for 4 minutes.

························ **OR** ························

ELECTRIC: Set the machine to cook at high pressure (9–11 psi). Set the machine's timer to cook at high pressure for 6 minutes.

4 Use the quick-release method to drop the pot's pressure back to normal.

5 Unlock and open the pot. Lift out the vegetable steamer; transfer the steaks to serving plates or a serving platter.

6 Set the stovetop model over medium-high heat or turn the electric one to its browning or simmer function. Whisk the cream and cornstarch or arrowroot in a small bowl until smooth. Once the sauce is boiling, whisk in this slurry. Continue cooking, whisking all the while, until thickened, about 30 seconds. Pour or ladle the sauce over the fillets to serve.

TESTERS' NOTES

• Salmon steaks hold up well to the intense pressure in the pot, becoming infused with the flavors of this simple coating. A thickened, light sauce turns them into an elegant meal.

• If you don't want the alcohol in the sauce for dinner, use ¾ cup reduced-sodium chicken broth and ¼ cup unsweetened apple juice.

• Salmon steaks are quite bony—and probably not the best choice for kids at the table. But the steaks are indeed flavorful because they have that prime combination of skin and bone.

SWORDFISH STEAKS IN A SPICY TOMATO CURRY

EFFORT: **A LOT** · PRESSURE: **HIGH** · TIME UNDER PRESSURE: **5 OR 8 MINUTES** · RELEASE: **QUICK, THEN QUICK AGAIN** · SERVES: 6

2 tablespoons olive oil

Two 1¼-pound boneless and skinless swordfish steaks

½ teaspoon salt

1 medium yellow onion, chopped

1 tablespoon minced garlic

1 tablespoon sweet paprika

½ tablespoon ground coriander

1 teaspoon ground turmeric

1 teaspoon ground cumin

½ teaspoon ground cinnamon

½ teaspoon ground ginger

Up to ½ teaspoon cayenne

One 14-ounce can diced tomatoes (about 1¾ cups)

½ cup chicken broth

½ cup bottled clam juice

2 tablespoons red wine vinegar

1 Heat the oil in a 6-quart stovetop pressure cooker set over medium heat or in a 6-quart electric pressure cooker turned to the browning function. Season the fish with the salt, then slip the steaks into the pot. Brown on both sides, about 4 minutes, turning once. Transfer to a plate.

2 Add the onion and garlic to the pot; cook for 1 minute, stirring all the while. Stir in the paprika, coriander, turmeric, cumin, cinnamon, ginger, and cayenne until aromatic, less than a minute. Pour in the tomatoes, broth, clam juice, and vinegar; stir well.

3 Lock the lid onto the pot.

STOVETOP: Raise the heat to high and bring the pot to high pressure (15 psi). Once this pressure has been reached, reduce the heat as much as possible while maintaining this pressure. Cook for 3 minutes.

···················· **OR** ····················

ELECTRIC: Set the machine to cook at high pressure (9–11 psi). Set the machine's timer to cook at high pressure for 5 minutes.

4 Use the quick-release method to bring the pot's pressure back to normal.

5 Unlock and open the pot. Nestle the fish into the sauce; pour any juices on the plate over the fillets.

6 Lock the lid back onto the pot.

STOVETOP: Set the pot back over high heat and bring it back to high pressure (15 psi). Once this pressure has been reached, reduce the heat as much as possible while maintaining this pressure. Cook for 2 minutes.

···················· **OR** ····················

ELECTRIC: Set the machine to cook once again at high pressure (9–11 psi). Set the machine's timer to cook at high pressure for 3 minutes.

7 Use the quick-release method to drop the pot's pressure back to normal.

8 Unlock and open the pot. Serve the fish with the sauce.

TESTERS' NOTES

• Swordfish fillets are meaty enough to stand up to a big sauce—like this one, modeled on vindaloo.

• You can substitute 3 tablespoons purchased vindaloo spice paste for the garlic and all the dried spices. You can also swap in ½ cup broth for the clam juice.

HALIBUT WITH TOMATOES, OLIVES, AND JALAPEÑOS

EFFORT: **A LITTLE** • PRESSURE: **HIGH** • TIME UNDER PRESSURE:
4 OR 7 MINUTES • RELEASE: **QUICK, THEN MODIFIED NATURAL** •
SERVES: **4 TO 6**

2 tablespoons olive oil

1 medium yellow onion, chopped

1 tablespoon minced garlic

One 28-ounce can diced tomatoes (about
3½ cups)

16 large pitted green olives, chopped

2 tablespoons drained capers, chopped

2 tablespoons minced pickled jalapeño
rings

2 tablespoons brine from the jar of
pickled jalapeños

2 tablespoons fresh lime juice

Two 4-inch fresh rosemary sprigs

Two fresh oregano sprigs

Two 1-pound skinless halibut fillets

1 Heat the oil in a 6-quart stovetop pressure cooker set over medium heat, or in a 6-quart electric pressure cooker turned to the browning function. Add the onion and cook, stirring often, until translucent, about 3 minutes. Add the garlic and cook for less than 1 minute, just until aromatic. Stir in the tomatoes, olives, capers, jalapeños, brine, and lime juice; tuck in the herb sprigs.

2 Lock the lid onto the pot.

STOVETOP: Raise the heat to high and bring the pot to high pressure (15 psi). Once this pressure has been reached, reduce the heat as much as possible while maintaining this pressure. Cook for 3 minutes.

·········OR·········
ELECTRIC: Set the machine to cook at high pressure (9–11 psi). Set the machine's timer to cook at high pressure for 5 minutes.

3 Use the quick-release method to drop the pot's pressure to normal.

4 Unlock and open the cooker. Nestle the fish into the sauce.

5 Lock the lid back onto the pot.

STOVETOP: Set the pot back over high heat and bring it back to high pressure (15 psi). Once this pressure has been reached, reduce the heat as much as possible while maintaining this pressure. Cook for 1 minute.
·········OR·········
ELECTRIC: Set the machine to cook once again at high pressure (9–11 psi). Set the machine's timer to cook at high pressure for 2 minutes.

6 Reduce the pressure.

STOVETOP: Set the pot off the heat for 2 minutes.
·········OR·········
ELECTRIC: Turn off or unplug the machine so it doesn't flip to its keep-warm setting; set aside for 2 minutes.

Use the quick-release method to drop the pot's pressure to normal.

7 Unlock and open the pot. Divide each fish fillet into two or three pieces and serve with the sauce in bowls.

TESTERS' NOTES

• This dish is modeled on vera cruz, a classic Mexican braise for fish. The pressure cooker deepens the flavors of the sauce, and all that's left is to poach the fish in it.

• Use two larger fish fillets, rather than four or six smaller ones. The greater mass will help them stay together and cook more evenly under pressure.

(continued)

- You'll need a very large spatula to scoop the individual fillets into bowls without their breaking apart.
- If desired, substitute cod, haddock, or pollock for the halibut.

Serve It Up! Have lots of warmed flour tortillas on the side. If desired, garnish the bowls with chopped avocado.

MUSSELS WITH APPLES, BRANDY, AND SAGE

EFFORT: **NOT MUCH** • PRESSURE: **HIGH** • TIME UNDER PRESSURE: **1 OR 2 MINUTES** • RELEASE: **QUICK** • SERVES: **2 TO 4**

2 tablespoons unsalted butter

1 small leek, white and pale green parts only, halved lengthwise, washed and thinly sliced

2 medium celery stalks, thinly sliced

1 large tart green apple, such as Granny Smith, peeled, cored, and diced

1 teaspoon dried sage

1/2 teaspoon ground black pepper

1/4 teaspoon grated nutmeg

1/2 cup chicken broth

1/4 cup brandy

2 pounds mussels, scrubbed and debearded

1 Melt the butter in a 6-quart stovetop pressure cooker set over medium heat or in a 6-quart electric pressure cooker turned to the browning function. Add the leek and celery; cook, stirring often, until the leek softens, about 2 minutes. Add the apple, sage, pepper, and nutmeg; stir until aromatic, about 1 minute.

2 Pour in the broth and brandy; bring to a full simmer. Add the mussels and toss well.

3 Lock the lid onto the pot.

STOVETOP: Raise the heat to high and bring the pot to high pressure (15 psi). Once this pressure has been reached, reduce the heat as much as possible while maintaining this pressure. Cook for 1 minute.

·····························OR·····························

ELECTRIC: Set the machine to cook at high pressure (9–11 psi). Set the machine's timer to cook at high pressure for 2 minutes.

4 Use the quick-release method to bring the pot's pressure back to normal.

5 Unlock and open the cooker. Stir gently before serving in bowls. Discard any mussels that do not open.

TESTERS' NOTES
- Mussels make an easy dinner in a pressure cooker; their salty liquid is forced into the sauce to create a richer dish. Have some crunchy bread on hand to sop up the sauce.
- Mussels should be scrubbed under running water to get rid of any sand on their shells. They should also be "debearded" by pulling off any small, wiry threads that extend from their shells. Most mussels these days are farmed on ropes and may lack these wiry threads—making your job much easier.
- Mussels are a live food product: buy them on the day you plan to prepare them. Store them in a bowl in the refrigerator until just before you place them in the cooker. Discard any before cooking that are open and will not close when tapped shut. Mussels that don't open may be clogged shut with mud and debris, so toss these out just in case.
- You can substitute cognac, bourbon, or 1/4 cup additional broth for the brandy.

MUSSELS IN SPICY TOMATO SAUCE

EFFORT: **NOT MUCH** • PRESSURE: **HIGH** • TIME UNDER PRESSURE:
1 OR 2 MINUTES • RELEASE: **QUICK** • SERVES: **2 TO 4**

2 tablespoons olive oil

1 medium yellow onion, chopped

2 teaspoons minced garlic

1/2 teaspoon red pepper flakes

**One 14-ounce can diced tomatoes (about
    13/4 cups)**

1/2 cup chicken broth

2 teaspoons dried oregano

2 pounds mussels, scrubbed and debearded

1 Heat the oil in a 6-quart stovetop pressure cooker set over medium heat or in a 6-quart electric pressure cooker turned to the browning function. Add the onion and cook, stirring often, until softened, about 3 minutes. Stir in the garlic and red pepper flakes until aromatic, about 20 seconds.

2 Pour in the tomatoes and broth; stir in the oregano. Bring to a full simmer. Pour in the mussels and toss well.

3 Lock the lid onto the pot.

STOVETOP: Raise the heat to high and bring the pot to high pressure (15 psi). Once this pressure has been reached, reduce the heat as much as possible while maintaining this pressure. Cook for 1 minute.

································ **OR** ································

ELECTRIC: Set the machine to cook at high pressure (9–11 psi). Set the machine's timer to cook at high pressure for 2 minutes.

4 Use the quick-release method to return the pot's pressure to normal.

5 Unlock and open the pot. Stir gently before serving in bowls. Discard any mussels that do not open.

TESTERS' NOTES
• Mussels take to spicy preparations, partly because they're naturally so sweet. Make sure you scrub any grit off their shells and pull off those wiry threads before cooking.
• The dried oregano is added later, not with the garlic and red pepper flakes, to make sure it maintains a present, bright flavor in the final dish.
• If you like a more fiery sauce, double or even triple the amount of red pepper flakes in the mix.

Serve It Up! Add up to 8 ounces cooked fettuccini or linguine to the pot after cooking; toss well before serving.

MUSSELS IN CURRIED COCONUT SAUCE

EFFORT: **NOT MUCH** • PRESSURE: **HIGH** • TIME UNDER PRESSURE:
1 OR 2 MINUTES • RELEASE: **QUICK** • SERVES: **2 TO 4**

2 tablespoons peanut oil

1 large yellow onion, chopped

**1 large red bell pepper, stemmed, cored,
    and chopped**

2 tablespoons minced fresh ginger

1 tablespoon packed light brown sugar

2 teaspoons Thai yellow curry paste

1 cup canned coconut milk

1/2 cup chicken broth

**2 tablespoons fish sauce (such as nam
    pla or nuoc mam)**

2 tablespoons fresh lime juice

2 pounds mussels, scrubbed and debearded

1 Heat the oil in a 6-quart stovetop pressure cooker set over medium heat or in a 6-quart

(continued)

electric pressure cooker turned to the browning function. Add the onion, bell pepper, and ginger; cook, stirring often, until the onion turns translucent, about 4 minutes. Stir in the brown sugar and curry paste until aromatic, about 30 seconds.

2 Pour in the coconut milk, broth, fish sauce, and lime juice; bring to a full simmer, stirring often. Pour in the mussels and stir well.

3 Lock the lid onto the pot.

STOVETOP: Raise the heat to high and bring the pot to high pressure (15 psi). Once this pressure has been reached, reduce the heat as much as possible while maintaining this pressure. Cook for 1 minute.

························ **OR** ·······························

ELECTRIC: Set the machine to cook at high pressure (9–11 psi). Set the machine's timer to cook at high pressure for 2 minutes.

4 Use the quick-release method to bring the pot's pressure back to normal.

5 Unlock and open the cooker. Stir gently before serving in bowls. Discard any mussels that do not open.

TESTERS' NOTES
• This fiery Thai curry may well be our favorite preparation for mussels. Their sweet-and-salty brine balances the sauce's pungent aromatics, making this a terrific winter warmer.
• Some brands of packaged Thai yellow curry paste can be extraordinarily hot. Make sure chiles are not the first ingredient in the list (unless you like your dinner on fire).

Serve It Up! Ladle the stew over cooked short-grain white rice (sushi rice). If desired, toss the hot rice with a little rice vinegar before putting it in the bowls.

MUSSELS WITH SAUSAGE AND BEER

EFFORT: **NOT MUCH** • PRESSURE: **HIGH** • TIME UNDER PRESSURE: **1 OR 2 MINUTES** • RELEASE: **QUICK** • SERVES: **2 TO 4**

1 tablespoon olive oil

1 small yellow onion, chopped

8 ounces spicy sausage, such as Cajun, hot Italian, or spicy turkey sausage, chopped

1 tablespoon mild paprika

One 12-ounce bottle amber beer, such as an IPA

2 pounds mussels, scrubbed and debearded

1 Heat the oil in a 6-quart stovetop pressure cooker set over medium heat or in a 6-quart electric pressure cooker turned to the browning function. Add the onion and cook, stirring often, until softened, about 2 minutes. Add the sausage and cook until browned, stirring frequently, about 4 minutes.

2 Stir in the paprika until aromatic, about 30 seconds. Pour in the beer and stir down its foam. Add the mussels; toss well.

3 Lock the lid onto the pot.

STOVETOP: Raise the heat to high and bring the pot to high pressure (15 psi). Once this pressure has been reached, reduce the heat as much as possible while maintaining this pressure. Cook for 1 minute.

························ **OR** ·······························

ELECTRIC: Set the machine to cook at high pressure (9–11 psi). Set the machine's timer to cook at high pressure for 2 minutes.

4 Use the quick-release method to bring the pot's pressure back to normal.

5 Unlock and open the pot. Stir gently before serving in bowls. Discard any mussels that have not opened.

TESTERS' NOTES
• The large amount of paprika in the sauce will balance the beer and sausage, muting them a bit so they don't override the sweet (and more delicate) flavor of the mussels.
• The serving size among these mussel dishes varies depending on how you'll serve them. With no salad or sides, they'll probably serve 2. If you've got salad and maybe a green vegetable—or even rice or a whole grain as a bed for the stew—it can stretch to 4 servings. And if you're making a pot of mussels to put on the coffee table as an afternoon nibble while the game or a movie is on, you'll get 6 servings out of it.

MUSSELS WITH GARLIC, PROSCIUTTO, AND SWEET VERMOUTH

EFFORT: **NOT MUCH** • PRESSURE: **HIGH** • TIME UNDER PRESSURE: **1 OR 2 MINUTES** • RELEASE: **QUICK** • SERVES: **2 TO 4**

2 tablespoons olive oil
2 ounces thin prosciutto slices, chopped
2 teaspoons minced garlic
1/2 teaspoon fennel seeds
1/4 teaspoon red pepper flakes
1/2 cup chicken broth
1/2 cup sweet (red) vermouth
2 pounds mussels, scrubbed and debearded

1 Heat the oil in a 6-quart stovetop pressure cooker set over medium heat or in a 6-quart electric pressure cooker turned to the browning function. Add the prosciutto and cook, stirring often, until frizzled, about 2 minutes. Stir in the garlic, fennel seeds, and red pepper flakes until aromatic, about 20 seconds.

2 Pour in the broth and sweet vermouth; bring to a full simmer, stirring occasionally. Add the mussels and toss well.

3 Lock the lid onto the pot.

STOVETOP: Raise the heat to high and bring the pot to high pressure (15 psi). Once this pressure has been reached, reduce the heat as much as possible while maintaining this pressure. Cook for 1 minute.
·······OR·······
ELECTRIC: Set the machine to cook at high pressure (9–11 psi). Set the machine's timer to cook at high pressure for 2 minutes.

4 Use the quick-release method to return the pot's pressure to normal.

5 Unlock and open the pot. Stir gently before serving in bowls. Discard any mussels that do not open.

TESTERS' NOTES
• The sweet vermouth gives these mussels an aromatic finish—far less savory than dry (white) vermouth, but also a bit more herbaceous.
• For a brinier flavor, substitute bottled clam juice for the chicken broth.
• For a more aromatic flavor, add up to 1/2 teaspoon finely grated orange zest with the garlic and spices.

MARINATED MUSSEL SALAD

EFFORT: **A LITTLE** • PRESSURE: **HIGH** • TIME UNDER PRESSURE: **1 OR 2 MINUTES** • RELEASE: **QUICK** • SERVES: **4**

2 pounds mussels, scrubbed and debearded

2 tablespoons olive oil

2 tablespoons fresh lemon juice

1 tablespoon loosely packed fresh parsley leaves, minced

1 teaspoon drained and rinsed capers, chopped

1/2 teaspoon ground black pepper

1/4 teaspoon dry mustard

1 Bring 1½ cups water to a boil in a 6-quart stovetop pressure cooker set over high heat or in a 6-quart electric pressure cooker turned to the browning or simmer function. Add the mussels.

2 Lock the lid onto the pot.

STOVETOP: Raise the heat to high and bring the pot to high pressure (15 psi). Once this pressure has been reached, reduce the heat as much as possible while maintaining this pressure. Cook for 1 minute.

························ OR ························

ELECTRIC: Set the machine to cook at high pressure (9–11 psi). Set the machine's timer to cook at high pressure for 2 minutes.

3 Use the quick-release method to bring the pot's pressure back to normal.

4 Unlock and open the pot. Drain the mussels in a large colander set in the sink. Rinse with cool water to bring down their temperature, then shake the colander a few times to drain them well. Discard any mussels that have not opened. Remove the remainder of the mussels from their shells; discard those shells.

5 Whisk the oil, lemon juice, parsley, capers, pepper, and dry mustard in a large bowl. Add the mussels and toss well. Cover and refrigerate for at least 30 minutes or up to 6 hours before serving.

TESTERS' NOTES
• A cold mussel salad may well be the best lunch on a hot summer day. This dressing is a simple lemon vinaigrette with a few spiky ingredients (capers, dry mustard).
• Make sure the shelled mussels are drained well so they won't water down the dressing.
• Don't let the mussels sit in the marinade for more than 6 hours or they'll turn tough. But you can prepare them up to 2 days in advance, shelling and saving them in the fridge in a covered bowl before they hit the vinaigrette.

Serve It Up! Have a creamy dip like hummus or baba ghanouj on hand to serve on crackers with these mussels.

CLAMS WITH LINGUINE

EFFORT: **A LITTLE** • PRESSURE: **HIGH** • TIME UNDER PRESSURE: **2½ OR 4 MINUTES** • RELEASE: **QUICK** • SERVES: **4 TO 6**

1 pound dried linguine

1/2 cup olive oil

Up to 1½ tablespoons minced garlic

1/4 teaspoon red pepper flakes

1 cup dry white wine, such as Pinot Grigio

One 14-ounce can diced tomatoes (about 1¾ cups)

24 littleneck clams (8–9 per pound), scrubbed

1/2 cup loosely packed fresh parsley leaves, chopped

1 Fill a 6-quart stovetop or electric pressure cooker (or a large saucepan) about three-quarters with water and bring to boil by setting the stovetop model over high heat or by turning the electric cooker to its browning or simmer setting. Add the pasta and cook until firm but tender, between 4 and 8 minutes, as the package indicates. Drain the pasta in a colander set in the sink, saving ½ cup of the cooking liquid.

2 Heat the oil in the stovetop cooker set over medium heat or in the electric mode turned to its browning function. Add the garlic and red pepper flakes; cook, stirring all the while, for 1 minute, or until the garlic begins to brown. Add the wine and bring to a full boil, stirring frequently to get any browned bits of garlic up off the bottom of the pot.

3 Pour in the tomatoes; bring back to a boil. Add the clams; toss well.

4 Lock the lid onto the pot.

STOVETOP: Raise the heat to high and bring the pot to high pressure (15 psi). Once this pressure has been reached, reduce the heat as much as possible while maintaining this pressure. Cook for 2½ minutes.

························ **OR** ························

ELECTRIC: Set the machine to cook at high pressure (9–11 psi). Set the machine's timer to cook at high pressure for 4 minutes.

5 Use the quick-release method to bring the pot's pressure back to normal.

6 Unlock and open the cooker. Set the stovetop model over medium heat or turn the electric one to its browning setting. Stir in the pasta and parsley, tossing until heated through and adding a little of the cooking liquid if necessary to moisten the sauce.

TESTERS' NOTES
- You can prepare a rich pasta sauce with clams in no time. The tomatoes and wine will blend with the briny liquid from the clams, giving you a thick sauce with layers of flavor.
- The sauce may be a little thinner than you like. Add the pasta and see how it goes. If you feel it is too thin, cook it a minute or so to boil it down a bit without adding any extra cooking liquid.
- Clams can have sand and grit adhering to their shells. Make sure you scrub them clean under running water before cooking.

CLAMS WITH DILL, LEMON, AND BUTTER

EFFORT: **NOT MUCH** • PRESSURE: **HIGH** • TIME UNDER PRESSURE: **2½ OR 4 MINUTES** • RELEASE: **QUICK** • SERVES: **4**

½ cup dry white wine, such as Chardonnay

2 tablespoons fresh lemon juice

2 tablespoons unsalted butter, cut into small bits

1 tablespoon minced fresh dill fronds

1 tablespoon minced garlic

28 littleneck clams (8–9 per pound), scrubbed

1 Bring the wine, ¼ cup water, the lemon juice, butter, dill, and garlic to a simmer in a 6-quart stovetop pressure cooker set over medium heat or in a 6-quart electric pressure cooker turned to the browning function, stirring occasionally. Stir in the clams.

2 Lock the lid onto the pot.

(continued)

STOVETOP: Raise the heat to high and bring the pot to high pressure (15 psi). Once this pressure has been reached, reduce the heat as much as possible while maintaining this pressure. Cook for 2½ minutes.

························· **OR** ·························

ELECTRIC: Set the machine to cook at high pressure (9–11 psi). Set the machine's timer to cook at high pressure for 4 minutes.

3 Use the quick-release method to return the pressure in the pot to normal.

4 Unlock and open the cooker. Stir gently before serving in bowls. Discard any clams that do not open.

TESTERS' NOTES
• You'll want some crunchy bread on hand to soak up every bit of the sauce.
• Littleneck clams have the right weight and volume for the pressure cooker: they become soft and tender without shrinking or becoming rubbery. Because they have a thicker shell than mahogany clams or steamers, the pressure won't overcook the meat before the clam opens.

STEAMED CLAMS WITH TARTAR SAUCE

EFFORT: **NOT MUCH** • PRESSURE: **HIGH** • TIME UNDER PRESSURE:
2½ OR 4 MINUTES • RELEASE: **QUICK** • SERVES: **4**

½ cup regular or low-fat mayonnaise

4 small cornichon pickles, chopped

1 tablespoon drained and rinsed capers, chopped

1 tablespoon white wine vinegar

1 teaspoon Dijon mustard

½ teaspoon ground black pepper

28 littleneck clams (8–9 per pound), scrubbed

1 Stir the mayonnaise, cornichons, capers, vinegar, mustard, and pepper in a small bowl to create the tartar sauce; set aside.

2 Bring 1½ cups water to a boil in a 6-quart stovetop pressure cooker set over high heat or in a 6-quart electric pressure cooker turned to the browning or simmer function. Add the clams.

3 Lock the lid onto the pot.

STOVETOP: Raise the heat to high and bring the pot to high pressure (15 psi). Once this pressure has been reached, reduce the heat as much as possible while maintaining this pressure. Cook for 2½ minutes.

························· **OR** ·························

ELECTRIC: Set the machine to cook at high pressure (9–11 psi). Set the machine's timer to cook at high pressure for 4 minutes.

4 Use the quick-release method to bring the pot's pressure back to normal.

5 Unlock and open the pot. Drain the clams in a large colander set in the sink; discard any that have not opened. Serve with the tartar sauce on the side for dipping.

TESTERS' NOTES
• Gently pour the clams into the colander to keep the meat inside the shells.
• This timing will not work for large littlenecks, sometimes called cherrystones, about 2 inches across or bigger. If these are what you've got in hand, add an extra minute for the stovetop cooker (that is, 3½ minutes) and an extra 1½ minutes in the electric model (that is, 5½ minutes). But you can substitute the larger mahogany clams for the littlenecks.
• This tartar sauce is so piquant and delectable that you may be tempted to double the batch to save some back for another time. Don't. The mayonnaise will break with the vinegar in the mix. You'll just need to make a fresh batch.

SPICY STEAMED CLAMS

EFFORT: **NOT MUCH** • PRESSURE: **HIGH** • TIME UNDER PRESSURE: **2½ OR 4 MINUTES** • RELEASE: **QUICK** • SERVES: **4**

1 cup chicken broth

½ cup dry but light white wine, such as Fumé Blanc

3 tablespoons unsalted butter, cut into small bits

2 tablespoons canned tomato paste

2 teaspoons minced garlic

Up to ½ teaspoon red pepper flakes

28 littleneck clams (8–9 per pound), scrubbed

¼ cup loosely packed fresh parsley leaves, chopped

1 Mix the broth, wine, butter, tomato paste, garlic, and red pepper flakes in a 6-quart stovetop pressure cooker set over medium heat or in a 6-quart electric pressure cooker turned to the browning function until the tomato paste is dissolved. Bring to a simmer, stirring occasionally. Stir in the clams.

2 Lock the lid onto the pot.

STOVETOP: Raise the heat to high and bring the pot to high pressure (15 psi). Once this pressure has been reached, reduce the heat as much as possible while maintaining this pressure. Cook for 2½ minutes.

·········· OR ··········

ELECTRIC: Set the machine to cook at high pressure (9–11 psi). Set the machine's timer to cook at high pressure for 4 minutes.

3 Use the quick-release method to bring the pot's pressure back to normal.

4 Unlock and open the cooker. Stir in the parsley before serving in bowls. Discard any clams that do not open.

TESTERS' NOTES
• Buttery and spicy, this broth could also work well with mussels. Cook them for only 1 minute under high pressure in a stovetop cooker or 2 minutes under high pressure in an electric model (with a quick release afterward).
• The sauce won't reduce in the short cooking time. If you like a thicker sauce, remove the clams from the pot after cooking and boil down the remaining liquid for a few minutes.

Serve It Up! Pick out the clams; serve the warm broth with cooked rice noodles as a second dish.

CLAMS with WHITE WINE and GINGER

EFFORT: **NOT MUCH** • PRESSURE: **HIGH** • TIME UNDER PRESSURE: **2 OR 3 MINUTES** • RELEASE: **QUICK** • SERVES: **4**

¾ cup fruit-forward white wine, such as Riesling

¾ cup olive oil

2 tablespoons grated fresh ginger (see note)

1 teaspoon minced garlic

½ teaspoon ground black pepper

28 littleneck clams (8–9 per pound), scrubbed

1 Mix the wine, oil, ginger, garlic, and pepper in a 6-quart stovetop or electric pressure cooker. Add the clams and stir well.

(continued)

2 Lock the lid onto the pot.

STOVETOP: Set the pot over high heat and bring it to high pressure (15 psi). Once this pressure has been reached, reduce the heat as much as possible while keeping this pressure constant. Cook for 2 minutes.

···································· **OR** ······························

ELECTRIC: Set the machine to cook at high pressure (9–11 psi). Set the machine's timer to cook at high pressure for 3 minutes.

3 Use the quick-release method to bring the pot's pressure back to normal.

4 Unlock and open the pot. Stir gently before serving in bowls. Discard any clams that do not open.

TESTERS' NOTES
• The cooking time is slightly less than other clam recipes because of all that olive oil. It will superheat and cook the clams quickly.
• The ginger should be grated on the small holes of a box grater. There's no need to peel it if it's fresh and the papery hull is still soft. However, if the piece of ginger is more than a few days old, remove that hull with a vegetable peeler before grating.

CLAMS WITH MUSTARD AND CAPERS

EFFORT: **NOT MUCH** • PRESSURE: **HIGH** • TIME UNDER PRESSURE: **2½ OR 4 MINUTES** • RELEASE: **QUICK** • SERVES: **4**

4 tablespoons (½ stick) unsalted butter, cut into small pieces
Up to 2 tablespoons minced garlic
1 cup dry vermouth

2 tablespoons drained and rinsed capers
2 tablespoons Dijon mustard
1 tablespoon packed stemmed fresh thyme leaves
1 tablespoon packed fresh rosemary leaves, minced
28 littleneck clams (8–9 per pound), scrubbed
½ cup heavy cream

1 Melt the butter in a 6-quart stovetop pressure cooker set over medium heat or in a 6-quart electric pressure cooker turned to the browning function. Add the garlic and cook for a minute, stirring all the while, just until golden. Pour in the vermouth; stir in the capers, mustard, thyme, and rosemary. Bring to a full simmer, stirring occasionally. Add the clams and toss well.

2 Lock the lid onto the pot.

STOVETOP: Raise the heat to high and bring the pot to high pressure (15 psi). Once this pressure has been reached, reduce the heat as much as possible while keeping this pressure constant. Cook for 2½ minutes.

···································· **OR** ······························

ELECTRIC: Set the machine to cook at high pressure (9–11 psi). Set the machine's timer to cook at high pressure for 4 minutes.

3 Use the quick-release method to bring the pot's pressure back to normal.

4 Unlock and open the lid. Set the stovetop model over medium heat or turn the electric one to its browning function. Stir in the cream and simmer, stirring gently, for 1 minute to remove the cream's raw taste. Serve in bowls, discarding any unopened clams.

TESTERS' NOTES
• The best way to make a good cream sauce in a pressure cooker is (1) to build a layered sauce before you add the

cream, (2) to add that cream after cooking (not before), and (3) to add less than you might imagine.
• Dried herbs will have too earthy a flavor for this rich sauce. The fresh herbs will cut right through the richness.
• You can substitute dry white wine for the vermouth.

CLAM BAKE AT HOME

EFFORT: **NOT MUCH** • PRESSURE: **HIGH** • TIME UNDER PRESSURE: **4 OR 6 MINUTES** • RELEASE: **QUICK** • SERVES: **4**

1 tablespoon crab boil seasoning blend, such as Old Bay

6 medium garlic cloves

1 pound small red potatoes (about 6), halved

12 littleneck clams (8–9 per pound), scrubbed

2 frozen raw lobster tails, thawed and split in half lengthwise (but still in their shells)

8 large shrimp (about 10 per pound), peeled and deveined

4 large sea scallops

1 Mix the seasoning blend with 1½ cups water in a 6-quart stovetop or electric pressure cooker. Add everything else, layering the items in the pot in the order that they're listed above and packing them loosely together.

2 Lock the lid onto the cooker.

STOVETOP: Raise the heat to high and bring the pot to high pressure (15 psi). Once this pressure has been reached, reduce the heat as much as possible while maintaining this pressure. Cook for 4 minutes.

.... **OR** ....
ELECTRIC: Set the machine to cook at high pressure (9–11 psi). Set the machine's timer to cook at high pressure for 6 minutes.

3 Use the quick-release method to bring the pot's pressure back to normal.

4 Unlock and open the cooker. Drain it slowly and gently into a large colander set in the sink, letting the cooking liquid pour over everything and thereby coating all the ingredients in the spice mix. Pour the potatoes and seafood into a large bowl to serve—or just pour out onto a newspaper-lined table.

TESTERS' NOTES
• Forget digging a pit in the backyard! You can make a clam bake in the middle of the winter, so long as you've got a pressure cooker. The ingredients are layered as they are so that the potatoes and clams are mostly in the water and everything else, slightly above it.
• If you want to add corn to this clambake, husk and remove the silks from two or three ears, then cut them into 2-inch sections. Place these in the colander before you pour the contents of the cooker into it; set the full colander aside for a minute or so. The hot water and the steaming ingredients on top of the corn will warm it up and soften it just a bit.

Serve It Up! Make **Spicy Cocktail Sauce**: Whisk 1 cup ketchup, 2 tablespoons jarred prepared white horseradish, 1½ tablespoons fresh lemon juice, 1 tablespoon Worcestershire sauce, ½ teaspoon dried dill, and several dashes of hot red pepper sauce in a small bowl. Serve on the side.

CLAMS WITH SAUSAGE AND TEQUILA

EFFORT: **A LITTLE** • PRESSURE: **HIGH** • TIME UNDER PRESSURE: **2½ OR 4 MINUTES** • RELEASE: **QUICK** • SERVES: **4**

2 tablespoons unsalted butter

6 ounces spicy Italian sausage, cut into 1-inch pieces

1 medium yellow onion, chopped

1 tablespoon minced garlic

½ cup chicken broth

½ cup tequila, preferably a silver or blanco tequila

2 tablespoons fresh lime juice

28 littleneck clams (8–9 per pound), scrubbed

¼ cup loosely packed fresh cilantro leaves, chopped

1 Melt the butter in a 6-quart stovetop pressure cooker set over medium heat or in a 6-quart electric pressure cooker turned to the browning function. Add the sausage and brown well, stirring occasionally, about 4 minutes.

2 Add the onion and garlic; cook, stirring often, until the onion softens, about 2 minutes. Pour in the broth, tequila, and lime juice; bring to a full summer, stirring once in a while. Add the clams and cilantro; toss well.

3 Lock the lid onto the pot.

STOVETOP: Set the pot over high heat and bring it to high pressure (15 psi). Once this pressure has been reached, reduce the heat as much as possible while keeping this pressure constant. Cook for 2½ minutes.

......................................**OR**..................................
ELECTRIC: Set the machine to cook at high pressure (9–11 psi). Set the machine's timer to cook at high pressure for 4 minutes.

4 Use the quick-release method to return the pressure in the pot to normal.

5 Unlock and open the pot. Stir gently before serving in bowls. Discard any clams that do not open.

TESTERS' NOTES

• Tequila is an amazing braising medium, both herbaceous and bracing. Under pressure, it sweetens considerably—which is why the lime juice is a welcome addition here. It's also why we add the cilantro *before* cooking, not after (as in other recipes): we want to extract as much flavor from the herb as we can to balance the tequila.

• For a more margarita feel, add up to 1 tablespoon finely grated orange zest with the onion and garlic. You can also substitute raw Mexican chorizo for the spicy Italian sausage.

Serve It Up! Rather than bread, have warmed corn tortillas on the side.

RISOTTO WITH CLAMS, HAM, AND SCALLIONS

EFFORT: **A LITTLE** • PRESSURE: **HIGH** • TIME UNDER PRESSURE: **7 OR 10 MINUTES** • RELEASE: **QUICK** • SERVES: **4 TO 6**

2 tablespoons olive oil

6 ounces smoked ham, diced

1 medium yellow onion, chopped

1½ cups medium-grain white rice, such as Arborio

2 teaspoons minced garlic

¹/₄ cup bottled clam juice

4 cups (1 quart) chicken broth

1¹/₂ cups drained chopped shelled clams
    (about two 6¹/₂-ounce cans)

¹/₂ cup finely grated Parmesan cheese
    (about 1 ounce)

3 medium scallions, white and green
    parts, thinly sliced

¹/₂ teaspoon ground black pepper

1 Heat the oil in a 6-quart stovetop pressure cooker set over medium heat or in a 6-quart electric pressure cooker turned to the browning function. Add the ham and cook, stirring often, until crisp around the edges, about 4 minutes.

2 Add the onion and cook, stirring often, until translucent, about 3 minutes. Add the rice and garlic; cook for 1 minute, stirring all the while. Pour in the clam juice and stir until the rice has absorbed the liquid, about 2 minutes. Pour in the broth.

3 Lock the lid onto the pot.

STOVETOP: Raise the heat to high and bring the pot to high pressure (15 psi). Once this pressure has been reached, reduce the heat as much as possible while maintaining this pressure. Cook for 7 minutes.

·····················OR·····················

ELECTRIC: Set the machine to cook at high pressure (9–11 psi). Set the machine's timer to cook at high pressure for 10 minutes.

4 Use the quick-release method to bring the pot's pressure back to normal.

5 Unlock and open the cooker. Set the stovetop pot over medium heat or turn the electric one to its browning function. Add the clams, cheese, scallions, and pepper;

cook, stirring all the while, for 2 minutes, just to warm through and thicken a bit.

TESTERS' NOTES

• Ham is a better choice than bacon in this simple risotto because it has more tooth after cooking, a better match to the texture of the clams.

• Although canned clams are the standard for a dish like this one, higher-end supermarkets may carry shucked fresh clams in the refrigerator case. By all means, use these, chopping them into smaller bits before adding them to the risotto.

CLAM ROLLS

EFFORT: **A LITTLE** • PRESSURE: **HIGH** • TIME UNDER PRESSURE: **2¹/₂ OR 4 MINUTES** • RELEASE: **QUICK** • SERVES: **4**

24 littleneck clams (8–9 per pound),
    scrubbed

1 medium red bell pepper, stemmed,
    cored, and diced

3 medium celery stalks, thinly sliced

¹/₄ cup regular or low-fat mayonnaise

¹/₄ cup plain Greek yogurt

2 tablespoons fresh lemon juice

¹/₂ teaspoon dried dill

¹/₂ teaspoon freshly ground black pepper

A few dashes of hot red pepper sauce, to
    taste

4 hot dog buns

4 tablespoons unsalted butter, melted
    and cooled

8 red-leaf or romaine lettuce leaves

1 Mix the clams with 1¹/₂ cups water in a 6-quart stovetop or electric pressure cooker.

2 Lock the lid onto the pot.

(continued)

STOVETOP: Set the pot over heat high and bring it to high pressure (15 psi). Once this pressure has been reached, reduce the heat as much as possible while maintaining this pressure. Cook for 2½ minutes.

························ **OR** ·······························

ELECTRIC: Set the machine to cook at high pressure (9–11 psi). Set the machine's timer to cook at high pressure for 4 minutes.

3 Use the quick-release method to bring the pot's pressure back to normal.

4 Unlock and open the pot. Drain its contents into a large colander set in the sink. Set aside to cool for a few minutes.

5 Mix the bell pepper, celery, mayonnaise, yogurt, lemon juice, dill, pepper, and hot red pepper sauce in a large bowl. Pull the clam meat from the shells; chop the meat and stir into the mayonnaise mixture.

6 Brush the inside of the rolls with the melted butter. Heat a nonstick skillet or grill pan over medium heat; set the buns cut side down in the skillet or pan and grill until browned and toasty, about 1 minute. Line the buns with the lettuce leaves and pile a quarter of the clam salad into each.

TESTERS' NOTES
• With these clam rolls, a beach favorite on the East Coast of North America, you can turn the day into summer, even in the darkest winter.
• The vegetables need to be in small bits so no one piece dominates any bite of the salad.

Serve It Up! This clam salad mixture doesn't only belong in buns: You could also stuff it into hollowed-out large tomatoes or into radicchio leaf cups. Or serve it on its own with crunchy potato chips on the side.

CREAMY CRAB AND **TOMATO** CASSEROLE

EFFORT: **NOT MUCH** • PRESSURE: **HIGH** • TIME UNDER PRESSURE: **5 OR 8 MINUTES** • RELEASE: **QUICK** • SERVES: **4**

One 14-ounce can diced tomatoes (about 1³/₄ cups)
2½ cups chicken broth
8 ounces dried rotini or other spiral-shaped pasta
4 medium scallions, green and white parts, thinly sliced
¼ cup loosely packed fresh basil leaves, chopped
1 pound lump crabmeat, picked over for shell and cartilage
½ cup heavy cream
½ cup grated fontina cheese (about 3 ounces)

1 Mix the tomatoes, broth, pasta, scallions, and basil in a 6-quart stovetop or electric pressure cooker.

2 Lock the lid onto the pot.

STOVETOP: Set the pot over high heat and bring it to high pressure (15 psi). Once this pressure has been reached, reduce the heat as much as possible while maintaining this pressure. Cook for 5 minutes.

························ **OR** ·······························

ELECTRIC: Set the machine to cook at high pressure (9–11 psi). Set the machine's timer to cook at high pressure for 8 minutes.

3 Use the quick-release method to bring the pot's pressure back to normal.

4 Unlock and open the cooker. Set the stovetop pot over medium heat or turn the electric one to its browning function. Stir in the crabmeat, cream, and cheese; cook for 1 minute, until the cheese has melted. Stir well, cover loosely, and set aside for 5 minutes to set up a bit before serving.

TESTERS' NOTES

• This pasta casserole is a sophisticated dish, a great way to get the kids eating something beyond mac-and-cheese.
• Unless the fontina is cold, it may not grate well (depending on the variety you've purchased—Italian versions will definitely be too soft). You can crumble it into the pot; just make sure it's in tiny bits.
• The pasta will still be *al dente,* with a bit of chew at the center of each piece. If you prefer it softer, cook an additional minute at high pressure.

CRAB RISOTTO WITH LEMON AND ASPARAGUS

EFFORT: **A LITTLE** • PRESSURE: **HIGH** • TIME UNDER PRESSURE: **7 OR 10 MINUTES** • RELEASE: **QUICK** • SERVES: **4 TO 6**

1 pound thin asparagus spears, cut into ½-inch pieces

2 tablespoons unsalted butter

1 medium yellow onion, chopped

1½ cups medium-grain white rice, such as Arborio

¼ cup dry vermouth

2 teaspoons finely grated lemon zest

2 teaspoons packed fresh tarragon leaves, minced

4 cups (1 quart) chicken broth

¾ pound lump crabmeat, picked over for shell and cartilage

¼ cup loosely packed fresh parsley leaves, chopped

½ teaspoon ground black pepper

1 Bring a large saucepan of water to a boil over high heat. Add the asparagus and blanch for 2 minutes. Drain in a colander set in the sink, rinsing with cool water to stop the cooking. Drain well.

2 Melt the butter in a 6-quart stovetop pressure cooker set over medium heat or in a 6-quart electric pressure cooker turned to the browning function. Add the onion and cook, stirring often, until softened, about 4 minutes. Add the rice and cook for 1 minute, stirring all the while.

3 Add the vermouth, zest, and tarragon; stir until the rice has absorbed the liquid. Pour in the broth and stir well.

4 Lock the lid onto the pot.

STOVETOP: Raise the heat to high and bring the pot to high pressure (15 psi). Once this pressure has been reached, reduce the heat as much as possible while maintaining this pressure. Cook for 7 minutes.

···································· **OR** ····································
ELECTRIC: Set the machine to cook at high pressure (9–11 psi). Set the machine's timer to cook at high pressure for 10 minutes.

5 Use the quick-release method to bring the pot's pressure back to normal.

6 Unlock and open the pot. Set the stovetop pot over medium heat or turn the electric one to its browning mode. Stir in the crabmeat, parsley, pepper, and blanched asparagus. Stir over the heat for 1 minute to warm through before serving.

TESTERS' NOTES

• This light risotto would be a perfect dish for guests on a summer evening. The servings are for four as a main course with a salad on the side, or for six if it's a starter.

(continued)

- Rather than buying shelf-stable cans of crabmeat, look for pasteurized tins, usually in the refrigerator case of the seafood section at your market. The meat will have a more subtle, delicate flavor.
- Before using the crabmeat, you'll need to spread it out on a cutting board and run your fingers through it to make sure there are no bits of shell or cartilage in the mix. There's no call for jumbo lump crab here, but you do want whole pieces, not threads and shards.
- To add more heft to this dish, stir in up to ½ cup finely grated Parmesan or pecorino romano with the crabmeat.

CREAMY LOBSTER CASSEROLE

EFFORT: **A LITTLE** • PRESSURE: **HIGH** • TIME UNDER PRESSURE: **5 OR 8 MINUTES** • RELEASE: **QUICK** • SERVES: **4**

Three 6-ounce frozen raw lobster tails, thawed

8 ounces dried ziti

1 cup half-and-half

½ cup dry white wine, such as Chardonnay

1 tablespoon all-purpose flour

1 tablespoon loosely packed fresh tarragon leaves, chopped

1 tablespoon Worcestershire sauce

½ teaspoon ground black pepper

¾ cup grated Gruyère cheese (about 6 ounces)

1 Pour 6 cups water into a 6-quart stovetop or electric pressure cooker. Stir in the lobster tails and pasta.

2 Lock the lid onto the pot.

STOVETOP: Set the pot over high heat and bring it to high pressure (15 psi). Once this pressure has been reached, reduce the heat as much as possible while maintaining this pressure. Cook for 5 minutes.

·············· OR ··············

ELECTRIC: Set the machine to cook at high pressure (9–11 psi). Set the machine's timer to cook at high pressure for 8 minutes.

3 Use the quick-release method to bring the pot's pressure back to normal.

4 Unlock and open the cooker. Drain its contents into a large colander set in the sink. Cool for a few minutes, then remove the meat from the lobster tails. Chop the meat and put it back on top of the pasta in the colander.

5 Set the stovetop cooker over medium heat or turn the electric model to its browning function. Add the half-and-half, wine, flour, tarragon, Worcestershire sauce, and pepper. Bring to a simmer, whisking occasionally to dissolve the flour and then to keep it from scorching.

6 Add the pasta and lobster; cook for 30 seconds, stirring all the while. Add the cheese and stir over the heat for 1 minute, until melted. Loosely cover the pot and set aside, off the heat or with the heat turned off, for 3 minutes, or until thickened somewhat.

TESTERS' NOTES
- By cooking lobster and pasta together under pressure, we can force more flavor into the pasta—and so create a rich casserole.
- The pasta should be slightly firm to the bite after it comes out of the cooker but it will cook more in the sauce. So there's no need to rinse the pasta once it's been drained—it will hold on to the sauce better if it's slightly sticky. Pull it apart to get it into the sauce if it's really sticking together.

• Frozen lobster tails are usually rock lobster tails, not the tails of the Atlantic lobster—unless, of course, the guys have steamed lobsters at the fish counter and are selling the now fire-engine red tails by themselves. If you find these, take the meat out of the shells, chop it (but don't cook it), and stir it into the casserole in step 6 to warm it through.

CALAMARI PASTA SAUCE WITH TOMATOES AND GARLIC

EFFORT: **NOT MUCH** • PRESSURE: **HIGH** • TIME UNDER PRESSURE: **10 OR 15 MINUTES** • RELEASE: **QUICK** • SERVES: **4**

3 tablespoons olive oil

1 tablespoon minced garlic

¼ teaspoon red pepper flakes

One 14-ounce can diced tomatoes (about 1¾ cups)

½ cup dry white wine, such as Chardonnay

1 pound frozen calamari rings, thawed

½ cup loosely packed fresh parsley leaves, chopped

2 tablespoons balsamic vinegar

1 pound linguine, cooked and drained

1 Heat the oil in a 6-quart stovetop pressure cooker set over medium heat or in a 6-quart electric pressure cooker turned to the browning mode. Add the garlic and red pepper flakes; cook for 30 seconds, stirring all the while. Pour in the tomatoes and wine; stir in the calamari.

2 Lock the lid onto the pot.

STOVETOP: Raise the heat to high and bring the pot to high pressure (15 psi). Once this pressure has been reached, reduce the heat as much as possible while maintaining this pressure. Cook for 10 minutes.

·· OR ··

ELECTRIC: Set the machine to cook at high pressure (9–11 psi). Set the machine's timer to cook at high pressure for 15 minutes.

3 Use the quick-release method to bring the pot's pressure back to normal.

4 Unlock and open the cooker. Stir in the parsley and vinegar, then serve over the cooked pasta in bowls.

TESTERS' NOTES
• Talk about a great pasta sauce! The calamari gets tender as it flavors the sauce in ways it never could stovetop.
• Double or even triple the red pepper flakes at will for a spicier sauce.
• For a more aromatic sauce, add up to 2 tablespoons minced fresh oregano and 1 tablespoon minced fresh rosemary with the tomatoes and wine.

Serve It Up! Garnish with finely grated Parmesan cheese.

VEGETABLES, BEANS, AND GRAINS

IF FISH AND SHELLFISH MADE UP OUR FASTEST CHAPTER, OR IF BEEF and pork bolstered the economical chapter with less expensive cuts, you've now come to the easiest chapter. More of these recipes are rated "not much" effort than in any other group.

Although there are some recipes that are definitely main courses and others that are smaller side dishes, many ride the line between the two. For example, a well-stocked bean stew could be a full meal with a salad on the side or it could be a side dish to a larger meal off the grill. We've given suggestions throughout for how to turn the small- to moderate-scale recipes into full meals. Frankly, we've always thought a 7- or 10-minute risotto was the main reason anyone should buy a pressure cooker.

You might want to use the pressure cooker as a quick steaming tool for fresh fare you find at the market. Here's an easy guide. Place a steamer rack inside a 6-quart stovetop or electric pressure cooker; add about ¾ cup water, just so it comes to the bottom of the rack. Set the pot over high heat or turn the electric cooker to its browning function. Bring the water to a simmer. Place up to 1½ pounds vegetables on the rack, lock the lid onto the pot, and bring to high pressure (15 psi for the stovetop pot or 9–11 psi for the electric one). Reduce the heat as necessary to keep the pressure constant. Then cook at high pressure for the times listed in the table at right. Turn off the heat and set the pot aside or turn off the electric pot; let the pressure come back to normal naturally. Once at normal pressure, unlock the lid at once to prevent overcooking.

So here's the widest range in the book. Yes, we can add lots of herbs and spices to beef and chicken; and yes, we can build an intense sauce for fish. But vegetables, beans, lentils, rice, and whole grains bring a wider array of flavors themselves—before any flavorings or other additions—than the panoply of pork cuts or other savory fare. Our sincere hope is that we can put more fresh vegetables on your table. If only that happens, the cost of a pressure cooker will have been worth it.

VEGETABLE FOR STEAMING	STOVETOP METHOD	ELECTRIC METHOD
Asparagus (moderately large spears)	2 minutes	3 minutes
Beets, peeled and cut into ¼-inch thick rings	4 minutes	5 minutes
Broccoli florets	3 minutes	4 minutes
Brussels sprouts, medium	4 minutes	6 minutes
Brussels sprouts, large	7 minutes	9 minutes
Butternut squash, peeled, seeded, and cut into ½-inch-thick slices	4 minutes	5 minutes
Carrots, cut into 2-inch sections	5 minutes	7 minutes
Cauliflower florets	3 minutes	4 minutes
Celeriac, peeled and diced	4 minutes	6 minutes
Corn on the cob	2 minutes	3 minutes
Eggplant, peeled and cut into 1-inch cubes	1 minute	2 minutes
Parsnips, peeled and cut into 2-inch sections	4 minutes	5 minutes
Red potatoes (very small or cut into ½-inch pieces)	6 minutes	8 minutes
Rutabaga, peeled and cut into ½-inch-thick slices	6 minutes	8 minutes
Sweet potatoes, peeled and cut into ¼-inch-thick rings	3 minutes	4 minutes
Turnips, peeled cut into ½-inch-thick rings	3 minutes	4 minutes
Yellow crookneck squash, cut into ½-inch sections	2 minutes	3 minutes
Zucchini, cut into ½-inch sections	2 minutes	3 minutes

Vegetarian Main Courses and Vegetable Side Dishes

When you walk inside a supermarket, you usually start out in the pro-
duce section. And no wonder: that produce represents the healthiest, freshest, and often-
times most economical choice in the store. So here's a section of main courses *and* sides
to put all that produce to good work. There's an old adage: if you're going to eat meat, you
should plan on not eating meat. In other words, you should make sure there are vegetarian meals in your repertory. They bring balance, a wider range of nutrients, and a broader
set of flavors.

The vegetarian pasta casseroles and sauces in this chapter can easily become part of
your weekly routine. Beyond those, there's a set of vegetarian stews that can make spring
more festive or winter bearable. Since the pressure cooker intensifies sour, bitter, herbaceous, and sweet notes, it's best to add hits of so-called high notes—that is, acids like
lemon juice or vinegar—*after* cooking so they don't overwhelm the flavors. If not, it's like
having a piccolo screaming over a quiet orchestra.

After the main courses, there's a long list of vegetable sides. We focused on long-
cooking vegetables: potatoes, roots, winter squash, kale, and cabbage. We suspect many of
us don't cook these on a regular basis because they take so much time. But when you can
make mashed potatoes, start to finish, in minutes . . . well, why not?

Most of these sides come with fairly simple prompts for possible main courses. Now
there's a concept: treat the side dish as the main part of the meal and the chicken breast,
fish fillet, or pork chop as an afterthought. Your heart and your health will thank you.

So on to the recipes that use the fare found at the front of your supermarket—or better yet, at a farmers' market. Because of the way the pressure cooker holds in moisture
and preserves a greater range of flavors, vegetables just got better. Not just faster. Better.

MACARONI AND CHEESE

EFFORT: **A LITTLE** · PRESSURE: **HIGH** · COOK TIME: **5 OR 8 MINUTES** · RELEASE: **QUICK** · SERVES: **6**

4 tablespoons (½ stick) unsalted butter,
  cut into small pieces
¼ cup all-purpose flour
4 cups (1 quart) whole or low-fat milk
1½ cups chicken broth
1 tablespoon Dijon mustard
1 teaspoon dried thyme
½ teaspoon salt
½ teaspoon ground black pepper
1 pound dried penne pasta
1 cup grated Gruyère cheese
  (about 4 ounces)
1 cup finely grated Parmesan cheese
  (about 2 ounces)

1 Melt the butter in a 6-quart stovetop pressure cooker set over medium heat or in a 6-quart electric pressure cooker turned to the browning function. Sprinkle in the flour; whisk until dissolved and even bubbling but not browned.

2 Whisk in the milk in a slow but steady stream to dissolve the flour further. Pour in the chicken broth and whisk until the mixture is smooth. Whisk in the mustard, thyme, salt, and pepper. Stir in the penne until coated.

3 Lock the lid onto the cooker.

STOVETOP: Raise the heat to high and bring the pot to high pressure (15 psi). Once this pressure has been reached, reduce the heat as much as possible while maintaining this pressure. Cook for 5 minutes.

·············· **OR** ··············

ELECTRIC: Set the machine to cook at high pressure (9–11 psi). Set the machine's timer to cook at high pressure for 8 minutes.

4 Use the quick-release method to drop the pot's pressure back to normal.

5 Unlock and open the pot. Stir the cheeses into the pasta mixture. Cover without locking on the lid and set aside for a couple of minutes to melt the cheese. Open and stir again before serving.

TESTERS' NOTES
• No special baking dishes, no complicated sauces—this macaroni and cheese may well become a go-to recipe in your house when everyone wants dinner *now*. There are no secret or short-cut ingredients here; yet it's a superfast one-pot meal, as creamy as you can imagine.
• Whisk the milk into the flour and butter slowly to get it as smooth a mixture as possible. You don't want any flour to fall out of suspension and burn on the bottom of the pot.
• Instead of the Gruyère, try pepperjack, Havarti, mild American, Taleggio, or Comté.

Serve It Up! If you miss a crunchy topping, spoon and spread the contents of the cooker into a 9 x 13-inch broiler-safe baking dish. Top with a mixture of 3 parts plain dried breadcrumbs to 1 part finely grated Parmesan cheese, plus a little ground black pepper; broil 4 to 6 inches from a heated broiling element until browned and crunchy, 2 to 4 minutes.

CHEESY TOMATO AND MACARONI CASSEROLE

EFFORT: **NOT MUCH** • PRESSURE: **HIGH** • COOK TIME: **5 OR 8 MINUTES** • RELEASE: **QUICK** • SERVES: **6**

One 28-ounce can crushed tomatoes (about 3¹/₂ cups)

One 12-ounce can regular or low-fat evaporated milk

1¹/₂ cups chicken broth

1 tablespoon dried basil

1 teaspoon dried oregano

¹/₂ teaspoon salt

¹/₄ teaspoon red pepper flakes

1 pound dried rotini or other spiral-shaped pasta

6 ounces fresh mozzarella cheese, diced

1¹/₄ cups finely grated Parmesan cheese (about 2¹/₄ ounces)

1 Stir the tomatoes, milk, broth, basil, oregano, salt, and red pepper flakes in a 6-quart stovetop or electric pressure cooker until well combined. Stir in the pasta until coated.

2 Lock the lid onto the pot.

STOVETOP: Set the pot over high heat and bring to high pressure (15 psi). Once this pressure has been reached, reduce the heat as much as possible while maintaining this pressure. Cook for 5 minutes.

·······················OR·······················

ELECTRIC: Set the machine to cook at high pressure (9–11 psi). Set the machine's timer to cook at high pressure for 8 minutes.

3 Use the quick-release method to bring the pot's pressure back to normal.

4 Unlock and open the pot. Stir in both cheeses. Set the lid back on the pot without locking it; set aside for 2 minutes to melt the cheese. Open and stir again before serving.

TESTERS' NOTES
• Think of this as a casserole that's part mac-and-cheese, part pasta in a rich tomato sauce. Either way, it's an easy meal or a quick lunch when the kids are out of school.
• We found that fresh herbs offered a bash of flavor in this simple casserole. Dried herbs have a slightly duller, muskier flavor and don't override the cheeses.
• Use plain canned tomatoes, not seasoned ones—and certainly don't use jarred marinara sauce.
• Use only soft, fresh mozzarella for the brightest but also lightest flavor here. It's difficult to get an accurate volume measure of the cubed cheese in a cup, so we opt for the weight for better accuracy.
• Be wary of pre-grated Parmesan cheese. If it's in a plastic container in the cheese case, chances are it's real, but the canned, shelf-stable stuff may be more fake than not. You're better off buying a chunk with the name Parmigiano-Reggiano stamped right on the rind. Wrap it in plastic wrap and store in your cheese drawer for up to 2 months.

FRESH TOMATO SAUCE FOR PASTA

EFFORT: **NOT MUCH** • PRESSURE: **HIGH** • COOK TIME: **15 OR 23 MINUTES** • RELEASE: **QUICK** • SERVES: **4 TO 6, WITH PASTA**

2 tablespoons olive oil

3 tablespoons minced garlic

1/4 teaspoon red pepper flakes

1/2 cup dry white wine, such as Pinot Grigio

3 pounds Roma (plum) tomatoes, cored and quartered

1/4 cup packed fresh basil leaves, finely chopped

1/2 teaspoon salt

1/2 teaspoon ground black pepper

1 Heat the oil, garlic, and red pepper flakes in a 6-quart stovetop pressure cooker set over medium heat or a 6-quart electric pressure cooker turned to the browning function until the garlic begins to sizzle and even brown a bit, stirring occasionally, about 3 minutes.

2 Add the wine and stir well as it comes to a simmer. Add the tomatoes and basil; bring to a full simmer, stirring occasionally.

3 Lock the lid onto the cooker.

STOVETOP: Raise the heat to high and bring the cooker to high pressure (15 psi). Once this pressure has been reached, reduce the heat as much as possible while maintaining this pressure. Cook for 15 minutes.

································· OR ·································

ELECTRIC: Set the machine to cook at high pressure (9–11 psi). Set the machine's timer to cook at high pressure for 23 minutes.

4 Use the quick-release method to return the pressure in the pot to normal.

5 Unlock and open the cooker. Use an immersion blender to puree the mixture into a thick sauce. Set the stovetop pressure cooker back over medium heat or turn the electric pressure cooker to its browning function. Bring the sauce to a simmer, stirring occasionally, until thickened into a rather rustic pasta sauce, about 15 minutes. Stir in the salt and pepper before serving.

TESTERS' NOTES

• The flavors of this meatless sauce focus directly on the tomatoes—not a lot of herbs or other ingredients to mask their sweet-sour flavor.

• Plum tomatoes sometimes have a hard core. To core the tomato, cut it in half through the stem end and then cut out that core and any hard bits of flesh directly below it.

• The sauce freezes well, so consider making a batch or two in the summer when tomatoes are at their best. Ladle the sauce into sealable plastic containers and store in the freezer for up to 6 months.

• Although this is a sauce for 4 main-course servings with pasta, alternatively it can be part of a pasta side dish for a steak or veal chop off the grill, about as it would be served in an Italian-American restaurant. In that case, serve it over cooked spaghetti for 6 servings.

• If you don't have an immersion blender, cool the sauce about 10 minutes, then blend it in batches in a blender, with the center knob removed from the lid (cover the resulting hole with a clean kitchen towel). Return the sauce to the pot and continue with the recipe.

Serve It Up! A fairly wide flat noodle, like pappardelle, is the best for this simple sauce. Fresh pasta would be even better. Grate Parmesan cheese or aged Asiago over each serving—and add a little grated nutmeg for garnish.

SPRING VEGETABLE RAGÙ

EFFORT: **NOT MUCH** • PRESSURE: **HIGH** • COOK TIME: **2 OR 3 MINUTES** • RELEASE: **QUICK** • SERVES: **4, WITH PASTA**

$^1/_3$ cup olive oil

1 large yellow onion, chopped

1 tablespoon minced garlic

1 tablespoon minced fresh ginger

1 teaspoon ground coriander

1 teaspoon ground cumin

$^1/_2$ teaspoon ground cinnamon

$^1/_2$ teaspoon salt

$^1/_4$ teaspoon ground cloves

One 14-ounce can crushed tomatoes (about 1$^3/_4$ cups)

12 ounces baby zucchini, halved crosswise

2 tablespoons packed dark brown sugar

12 ounces sugar snap peas, trimmed and halved crosswise

1 cup shelled fresh peas, or frozen peas, thawed

1 Heat the oil in a 6-quart stovetop pressure cooker set over medium heat or in a 6-quart electric pressure cooker turned to the browning function. Add the onion and cook, stirring often, until soft, about 4 minutes.

2 Stir in the garlic, ginger, coriander, cumin, cinnamon, salt, and cloves until aromatic, less than a minute. Add the tomatoes, zucchini, and brown sugar; stir until the brown sugar dissolves.

3 Lock the lid onto the cooker.

STOVETOP: Raise the heat to high and bring the pot to high pressure (15 psi). Once this pressure has been reached, reduce the heat as much as possible while maintaining this pressure. Cook for 2 minutes.

······························ **OR** ······························

ELECTRIC: Set the machine to cook at high pressure (9–11 psi). Set the machine's timer to cook at high pressure for 3 minutes.

4 Use the quick-release method to bring the pot's pressure back to normal.

5 Unlock and open the pot. Set the stovetop cooker over medium heat or turn the electric cooker to its browning function. Bring the sauce to a simmer, then stir in the sugar snaps and peas. Simmer for 2 minutes, stirring occasionally, until the vegetables are crisp yet tender. Serve at once.

TESTERS' NOTES

• This springtime sauce has the hint of a curried palette, although the many vegetables mute the spices a bit. In culinary terms, the addition of the ground cloves keeps the flavors of the other spices in check, none overpowering another.

• If you're using frozen peas, they must be thawed before adding them in step 5. Otherwise, they'll cool down the sauce and the sugar snaps won't get crisp-tender.

• Unfortunately, this sauce doesn't freeze well; the vegetables break down when thawed and reheated. In fact, the sauce won't even sit around on the stove very well, since you want the sugar snaps to be as crunchy as possible.

Serve It Up! Ladle the sauce over cooked rice stick noodles. Follow the package instructions for preparing them; some are just soaked; others, soaked *and* boiled.

LENTIL SAUCE FOR PASTA

EFFORT: **NOT MUCH** • PRESSURE: **HIGH** • COOK TIME: **10 OR 15 MINUTES** • RELEASE: **NATURAL** • SERVES: **4, WITH PASTA**

2 tablespoons olive oil

1 large yellow onion, chopped

1 tablespoon minced garlic

1/2 teaspoon ground allspice

1/2 teaspoon ground coriander

1/2 teaspoon ground cumin

1/2 teaspoon salt

1/4 teaspoon red pepper flakes

2 cups vegetable broth

1 cup brown lentils

3 medium Roma (plum) tomatoes, chopped

2 tablespoons canned tomato paste

1 Heat the oil in a 6-quart stovetop pressure cooker set over medium heat or in a 6-quart electric pressure cooker turned to the browning function. Add the onion and cook, stirring often, until softened, about 4 minutes.

2 Stir in the garlic, allspice, coriander, cumin, salt, and red pepper flakes; cook until fragrant, stirring all the while, less than 1 minute. Add the broth, lentils, tomatoes, and tomato paste; stir well until the paste has coated everything.

3 Lock the lid onto the pot.

STOVETOP: Raise the heat to high and bring the pot to high pressure (15 psi). Once this pressure has been reached, reduce the heat as much as possible while maintaining this pressure. Cook for 10 minutes.

·······OR·······

ELECTRIC: Set the machine to cook at high pressure (9–11 psi). Set the machine's timer to cook at high pressure for 15 minutes.

4 Reduce the pressure.

STOVETOP: Set the pot off the heat and let its pressure come back to normal naturally, about 10 minutes.

·······OR·······

ELECTRIC: Turn off the machine or unplug it so it doesn't flip to its keep-warm setting. Let its pressure return to normal naturally, 10 to 15 minutes.

5 Unlock and open the pot. Stir well before serving.

TESTERS' NOTES

• Lentils cook up into a thick, rich pasta sauce, here given a Middle Eastern twist with all those earthy and "warming" spices.

• The tomatoes are the primary sweetener, so make sure they're as fresh as possible. When you smell them at the store, you should detect a good amount of tomato fragrance at the stem ends. There's no need to core them; they'll soften during the long, natural release.

• Use only dried brown lentils, not red lentils or the green or gray French lentils (sometimes called *lentils du Puy*). Brown lentils will partially melt into the sauce, giving the dish its heft.

• For more heft in the sauce (in a non-vegetarian adjustment), substitute chicken broth for the vegetable broth.

Serve It Up! Offer the sauce over cooked and drained egg noodles. Garnish with minced parsley leaves, balsamic vinegar, and even some plain Greek yogurt.

ONE-POT PASTA PUTTANESCA

EFFORT: **NOT MUCH** • PRESSURE: **HIGH** • COOK TIME: **5 OR 8 MINUTES** • RELEASE: **QUICK** • SERVES: **4**

2 tablespoons olive oil

1 small red onion, chopped

1 tablespoon drained and rinsed capers, minced

1 tablespoon minced garlic

1 pound eggplant (about 1 large), stemmed and diced (no need to peel)

2 medium yellow bell peppers, stemmed, cored, and chopped

One 28-ounce can diced tomatoes (about 3½ cups)

1¼ cups vegetable broth

2 tablespoons canned tomato paste

2 teaspoons dried rosemary

1 teaspoon dried thyme

½ teaspoon ground black pepper

8 ounces dried whole wheat ziti

1 Heat the oil in a 6-quart stovetop pressure cooker set over medium heat or in a 6-quart electric pressure cooker turned to the browning function. Add the onion, capers, and garlic; cook, stirring often, just until the onion first begins to soften, about 2 minutes.

2 Add the eggplant and bell peppers; cook, stirring often, for 1 minute. Mix in the tomatoes, broth, tomato paste, rosemary, thyme, and pepper, stirring until the tomato paste coats everything. Stir in the ziti until coated.

3 Lock the lid onto the pot.

STOVETOP: Raise the heat to high and bring the pot to high pressure (15 psi). Once this pressure has been reached, reduce the heat as much as possible while maintaining this pressure. Cook for 5 minutes.

·········· **OR** ··········

ELECTRIC: Set the machine to cook at high pressure (9–11 psi). Set the machine's timer to cook at high pressure for 8 minutes

4 Use the quick-release method to drop the pressure in the pot back to normal.

5 Unlock and open the cooker. Stir well before serving.

TESTERS' NOTES
• If you want to add more depth to the sauce, add 2 rinsed and minced tinned anchovy fillets with the onion, capers, and garlic. The anchovies will melt into the sauce, their flavors muted to a subtle savoriness.
• Whole wheat pasta has a better bite in this well-stocked sauce. You can use regular pasta, but the dish will be much sweeter and the pasta slightly gummier.

Serve It Up! Make **Green Goddess Salad**: For four servings, whisk together 6 tablespoons mayonnaise, 2 tablespoons sour cream, 2 smashed tinned anchovy fillets, 1 minced scallion (light green and white parts only), 1 tablespoon minced parsley leaves, 1 tablespoon minced dill fronds, 1 tablespoon minced basil leaves, and 1 teaspoon red wine vinegar in a large bowl. Add 6 to 8 cups chopped romaine and toss well.

ONE-POT FARFALLE WITH MUSHROOMS AND CREAM

EFFORT: **NOT MUCH** • PRESSURE: **HIGH** • COOK TIME: **5 OR 8 MINUTES** • RELEASE: **QUICK** • SERVES: **6**

3 cups vegetable broth

2¹/₂ tablespoons all-purpose flour

1 tablespoon unsalted butter

2 tablespoons olive oil

1 medium yellow onion, chopped

¹/₂ tablespoon minced garlic

¹/₂ tablespoon fresh thyme leaves

6 ounces baby bella or cremini mushrooms, thinly sliced

4 ounces white button mushrooms, thinly sliced

3¹/₂ ounces shiitake mushroom caps, thinly sliced

¹/₄ cup dry white wine, such as Chardonnay

8 ounces dried whole wheat farfalle (bow-tie) pasta

¹/₂ cup finely grated Parmesan cheese (about 1 ounce)

¹/₄ cup heavy cream

1 Whisk the broth and flour in a small bowl until the flour dissolves.

2 Melt the butter in the oil in a 6-quart stovetop pressure cooker set over medium heat or in a 6-quart electric pressure cooker turned to the browning function. Add the onion; cook, stirring often, until soft, about 4 minutes. Add the garlic and thyme; cook until aromatic, less than a minute, stirring all the while.

3 Stir in all the mushrooms. Cook just until they soften, about 3 minutes, stirring often.

Pour in the wine and scrape up any browned bits in the cooker as it comes to a simmer.

4 Whisk the broth mixture one more time, then pour it into the cooker. Add the pasta and stir until coated.

5 Lock the lid onto the pot.

STOVETOP: Raise the heat to high and bring the pot to high pressure (15 psi). Once this pressure has been reached, reduce the heat as much as possible while maintaining this pressure. Cook for 5 minutes.

·····OR·····

ELECTRIC: Set the machine to cook at high pressure (9–11 psi). Set the machine's timer to cook at high pressure for 8 minutes.

6 Use the quick-release method to bring the pot's pressure back to normal.

7 Unlock and open the pot. Stir in the cheese and cream. Cover without locking the lid and set aside for a couple of minutes to blend the flavor and melt the cheese. Stir again before serving.

TESTERS' NOTES

• This pasta main course is loaded with mushrooms. And luckily there's also no need to dirty more than one pot to make this decadent meal. For even more flavor, crumble up to ¼ ounce dried porcini or chanterelle mushrooms into the pot when you add the broth.

• For a slightly lighter dish, reduce the amount of cream to ¼ cup.

Serve It Up! Make **Raspberry Vinaigrette** for a chopped salad: For four servings (or 6 to 8 cups of chopped lettuce or vegetables), whisk ¹/₃ cup olive oil, 2 tablespoons raspberry vinegar, 1 tablespoon lemon juice, ¹/₂ teaspoon salt, and ¹/₄ teaspoon freshly ground black pepper in a small bowl.

SOUTHWESTERN MUSHROOM AND TORTILLA CASSEROLE

EFFORT: **A LOT** • PRESSURE: **HIGH** • TIME UNDER PRESSURE: **15 OR 23 MINUTES** • RELEASE: **NATURAL** • SERVES: **4**

2 tablespoons unsalted butter, plus more
  for dish

1 small yellow or white onion, chopped

8 ounces baby bella or cremini
  mushrooms, thinly sliced

2 tablespoons all-purpose flour

1 cup whole or low-fat milk

1 cup vegetable or chicken broth

One 4½-ounce can chopped mild green
  chiles (about ½ cup)

½ tablespoon dried oregano

½ teaspoon salt

½ teaspoon ground black pepper

Six 8-inch flour tortillas

1½ cups shredded Cheddar cheese (about
  6 ounces)

1 Melt 2 tablespoons butter in a large skillet set over medium heat. Add the onion and cook, stirring often, until softened, about 2 minutes. Add the mushrooms and cook, stirring occasionally, until they give off their liquid and it evaporates to a thick glaze, about 5 minutes.

2 Whisk in the flour, then whisk in the milk in a slow, steady stream until the flour has dissolved. Whisk in the broth, chiles, oregano, salt, and pepper until bubbling and thickened, about 1 minute. Remove from the heat.

3 Lightly butter the inside of a 2-quart round, high-sided baking or soufflé dish.

4 Place a tortilla in the dish, add a scant ½ cup sauce and about ¼ cup cheese in two even layers, and then continue building the casserole, one tortilla between the ongoing layers of sauce and cheese. End with a layer of sauce, then of cheese. Cover the baking dish with parchment paper, then with aluminum foil to seal it tightly closed.

5 Set the pressure cooker rack in the bottom of a 6-quart stovetop or electric cooker; pour in 2 cups water. Make an aluminum foil sling (see page 19) for the baking dish and use it to lower the dish onto the rack.

6 Lock the lid onto the pot.

STOVETOP: Set the pot over high heat and bring it to a high pressure (15 psi). Once this pressure has been reached, reduce the heat as much as possible while maintaining this pressure. Cook for 15 minutes.

·····························**OR**·····························

ELECTRIC: Set the machine to cook at high pressure (9–11 psi). Set the machine's timer to cook at high pressure for 23 minutes.

7 Reduce the pressure.

STOVETOP: Set the pot off the heat and let its pressure come back to normal, about 12 minutes.

·····························**OR**·····························

ELECTRIC: Turn off the machine or unplug it so it doesn't flip to its keep-warm setting. Let its pressure return to normal, 12 to 15 minutes.

8 Unlock and remove the lid. Use the foil sling to lift the casserole dish from the cooker and onto a wire rack for cooling. Remove the foil and the parchment paper; cool for 5 minutes before dishing up by the spoonful.

• Why would you go the trouble of building a casserole in a pressure cooker? Not just for the faster cooking time—this casserole also becomes gooey and rich but quite moist without condensing, sort of like a Southwestern version of mushrooms in cream sauce.
• Seal the baking dish tightly so no steam from the cooker gets into the casserole and renders it boggy.
• For more heat, use canned chopped hot green chiles. Or perhaps use a tablespoon or two of the hot green chiles with the rest of the volume filled out with mild chiles.
• For a firmer and somewhat heartier casserole, substitute whole wheat tortillas for the flour ones.

LENTIL SLOPPY JOES

EFFORT: **NOT MUCH** • PRESSURE: **HIGH** • COOK TIME: **18 OR 27 MINUTES** • RELEASE: **NATURAL** • SERVES: **6, WITH BUNS**

1 tablespoon olive oil

1 medium yellow onion, chopped

1 medium red bell pepper, stemmed, cored, and chopped

3 cups vegetable broth

2 cups green lentils (lentils du Puy)

One 14-ounce can crushed tomatoes (about 1³/₄ cups)

2 tablespoons soy sauce

1 tablespoon Dijon mustard

1 tablespoon packed dark brown sugar

1 teaspoon ground black pepper

1 Heat the olive oil in a 6-quart stovetop pressure cooker set over medium heat or in a 6-quart electric pressure cooker turned to the browning function. Add the onion and bell pepper; cook, stirring often, until the onion is translucent, about 3 minutes.

2 Pour in the broth; add the lentils, tomatoes, soy sauce, mustard, brown sugar, and pepper, stirring until the brown sugar dissolves.

3 Lock the lid onto the pot.

STOVETOP: Raise the heat to high and bring the pot to high pressure (15 psi). Once this pressure has been reached, reduce the heat as much as possible while maintaining this pressure. Cook for 18 minutes.

·····OR·····

ELECTRIC: Set the machine to cook at high pressure (9–11 psi). Set the machine's timer to cook at high pressure for 27 minutes.

4 Reduce the pressure.

STOVETOP: Set the pot off the heat and let its pressure come back to normal, about 18 minutes.

·····OR·····

ELECTRIC: Turn off the machine or unplug it so it doesn't jump to its keep-warm setting. Let its pressure fall back to normal, 18 to 22 minutes.

5 Unlock and open the cooker. Stir the mixture before serving.

TESTERS' NOTES
• These vegan sloppy joes get their oomph from the soy sauce. It provides a long-cooked, deep flavor underneath the lentils.
• Although there's some brown sugar in the mix, these sloppy joes are actually quite savory. If you need more sweetness, offer ketchup for the buns.

Serve It Up! Have toasted hamburger buns at the ready, as well as chopped lettuce, sliced tomatoes, pickle relish, chow-chow, and/or thin dill pickle sandwich slices. Or skip the buns and serve the lentil mixture in bowls with warmed corn tortillas on the side.

MIXED BEAN CHILI

EFFORT: **A LITTLE** • PRESSURE: **HIGH** • COOK TIME: **12 OR
18 MINUTES** • RELEASE: **QUICK** • SERVES: **8**

²/₃ **cup dried red kidney beans**

²/₃ **cup dried black beans**

²/₃ **cup pink (chili) beans**

2 **tablespoons olive oil**

1 **large yellow onion, chopped**

1 **large green bell pepper, stemmed,
    cored, and chopped**

3 **tablespoons chili powder**

**One 28-ounce can diced tomatoes (about
    3¹/₂ cups)**

4 **cups (1 quart) vegetable broth**

2 **cups fresh corn kernels, or frozen
    kernels, thawed**

¹/₂ **tablespoon dried oregano**

¹/₂ **tablespoon ground cumin**

¹/₂ **teaspoon salt**

1 Soak all the beans in a big bowl of water
overnight, at least 12 hours or up to 16 hours.

2 Heat the oil in a 6-quart stovetop pressure
cooker set over medium heat or in a 6-quart
electric pressure cooker turned to the
browning function. Add the onion and bell
pepper; cook, stirring often, until the onion is
translucent, about 4 minutes.

3 Stir in the chili powder; cook, stirring constantly, for 30 seconds. Add the tomatoes,
broth, corn, oregano, cumin, and salt. Stir
well and bring to a simmer. Drain the beans
in a colander set in the sink. Pour them into
the cooker and stir well again.

4 Lock the lid onto the pot.

STOVETOP: Raise the heat to high and bring to
high pressure (15 psi). Once this pressure has been
reached, reduce the heat as much as possible while
maintaining this pressure. Cook for 12 minutes.

························· OR ·······························

ELECTRIC: Set the machine to cook at high pressure (9–11 psi). Set the machine's timer to cook at
high pressure for 18 minutes.

5 Use the quick-release method to bring the
pot's pressure back to normal.

6 Unlock and open the pot. Stir the chili
before serving.

TESTERS' NOTES

• Here's a vegan chili that highlights one of the pressure
cooker's best tricks: it turns economical dried beans into
savory weeknight fare.

• Slim down the number of different beans in the chili,
as long as you have 2 cups total. You could use 1 cup
dried black beans and 1 cup dried pink beans—or for
a more Southwestern flair, substitute pinto beans for
the pink beans.

• Red kidney beans have been associated with phytohae-
magglutinin, a protein that can be rather pernicious in the
human digestive system. However, the problems occur most
often with slow cookers, which cook the beans at too low
a temperature to do away with the pesky lectin. Pressure
cookers work at a very high temperature, so there's not
much worry. However, if you have family members with sensitive stomachs, consider par-cooking the soaked kidney
beans in a large saucepan of simmering water for 5 minutes
before adding them in step 3.

• You can substitute 2¼ cups frozen chopped onion and
bell pepper mix, thawed, for the onion and bell pepper.

Serve It Up! Garnish the bowls with dollops
of sour cream and diced mango. Since there's
no real heat in the dish—the chili powder is
relatively mild—pass bottles of hot red pepper
sauce on the side.

RISOTTO WITH PEAS AND BRIE

EFFORT: **NOT MUCH** • PRESSURE: **HIGH** • COOK TIME: **7 OR 10 MINUTES** • RELEASE: **QUICK** • SERVES: **6**

3 tablespoons unsalted butter

1 large yellow onion, chopped

1¹/₂ cups white Arborio rice

¹/₄ cup unsweetened apple cider

1 tablespoon apple cider vinegar

4 cups (1 quart) vegetable broth

1 tablespoon minced fresh sage leaves

¹/₄ teaspoon grated nutmeg

1 cup shelled fresh peas, or frozen peas, thawed

4 ounces Brie cheese, rind removed and the cheese chopped

1 Melt the butter in a 6-quart stovetop pressure cooker set over medium heat or in a 6-quart electric pressure cooker turned to the browning function. Add the onion and cook, stirring often, until softened, about 4 minutes.

2 Add the rice and stir well until the grains are shiny and coated. Pour in the cider and vinegar; stir constantly until they have been absorbed into the rice, about 2 minutes. Add the broth, sage, and nutmeg; stir well.

3 Lock the lid onto the cooker.

STOVETOP: Raise the heat to high and bring the pot to high pressure (15 psi). Once this pressure has been reached, reduce the heat as much as possible while maintaining this pressure. Cook for 7 minutes.

·························· **OR** ··························

ELECTRIC: Set the machine to cook at high pressure (9–11 psi). Set the machine's timer to cook at high pressure for 10 minutes.

4 Use the quick-release method to drop the pot's pressure back to normal.

5 Unlock and open the cooker. Stir in the peas and Brie. Put the lid onto the pot without locking it and set aside for 5 minutes. Stir again before serving.

TESTERS' NOTES
• Use only medium-grain white rice, preferably Arborio rice, for all risottos.
• Brie can be sticky to chop; place the wedge in the freezer for 1 hour before removing the rind and chopping the remainder.
• For a heftier (and non-vegetarian) meal, cook 4 ounces chopped pancetta until crisp in the butter before adding the onion. (You might as well use chicken broth instead of vegetable broth.)

RISOTTO WITH BUTTERNUT SQUASH AND PORCINI

EFFORT: **NOT MUCH** • PRESSURE: **HIGH** • COOK TIME: **7 OR 10 MINUTES** • RELEASE: **QUICK** • SERVES: **6**

2 tablespoons unsalted butter

1 medium leek, white and pale green parts only, halved lengthwise, washed, and thinly sliced

1¹/₂ cups white Arborio rice

¹/₄ cup dry vermouth

4 cups (1 quart) vegetable broth

2 cups seeded, peeled, and finely chopped butternut squash

¹/₂ ounce dried porcini mushrooms, crumbled

1 teaspoon dried thyme

¹/₄ teaspoon saffron threads

¹/₂ cup finely grated Parmesan cheese (about 1 ounce)

(continued)

1 Melt the butter in a 6-quart stovetop pressure cooker set over medium heat or in a 6-quart electric pressure cooker turned to the browning function. Add the leek and cook, stirring often, until softened, about 2 minutes.

2 Add the rice; stir until coated in the butter. Pour in the vermouth; stir over the heat until fully absorbed into the grains, 1 to 2 minutes. Add the broth, squash, dried porcini, thyme, and saffron.

3 Lock the lid onto the pot.

STOVETOP: Raise the heat to high and bring the pot to high pressure (15 psi). Once this pressure has been reached, reduce the heat as much as possible while maintaining high pressure. Cook for 7 minutes.

································ **OR** ································

ELECTRIC: Set the machine to cook at high pressure (9–11 psi). Set the machine's timer to cook at high pressure for 10 minutes.

4 Use the quick-release method to bring the pot's pressure back to normal.

5 Unlock and open the cooker. Set the stovetop cooker over medium heat or turn the electric cooker to its browning function. Bring to a simmer, stirring until thickened, about 2 minutes.

6 Stir in the cheese. Put the lid onto the cooker without locking it in place. Set aside for 5 minutes to melt the cheese and blend the flavors. Stir again before serving.

TESTERS' NOTES
- Sure, it's a vegetarian main course. But also consider serving this risotto with T-bone steaks hot off the grill.
- To get tender, the butternut squash must indeed be finely chopped—that is, cut into ½-inch cubes. If you've bought prepared butternut squash, you may need to cut the larger cubes down to this required size.
- This risotto is stirred over the heat for a bit after cooking because the butternut squash will have leached moisture into the batch. It's hard to predict exactly how much; a little stirring will take care of any problem.
- The dried mushrooms will add both flavor and texture to the dish. Do not substitute fresh mushrooms.
- Other winter squashes may not work here: spaghetti squash is way too stringy; buttercup, turban, or acorn squash are too starchy.

Serve It Up! Yes, you'll want some crunchy bread on the side. Garnish each serving with plenty of ground black pepper.

EGGPLANT AND POTATO STEW

EFFORT: **A LITTLE** • PRESSURE: **HIGH** • TIME UNDER PRESSURE: **5 OR 7 MINUTES** • RELEASE: **QUICK** • SERVES: **4**

3 tablespoons olive oil

1 medium yellow onion, chopped

1 tablespoon minced garlic

¼ teaspoon red pepper flakes

3 large globe or beefsteak tomatoes

½ cup vegetable broth

2 tablespoons canned tomato paste

2 large potatoes, such as Yukon Gold (about 10 ounces each), cut into 1-inch pieces

1 large eggplant (about 1 pound), stemmed and cut into 1-inch pieces

½ cup packed celery leaves, chopped

½ teaspoon salt

1 Heat the oil in a 6-quart stovetop pressure cooker set over medium heat or in a 6-quart electric pressure cooker turned to the browning mode. Add the onion; cook, stirring often, until translucent, about 3 minutes. Stir in the garlic and red pepper flakes until aromatic, about 30 seconds.

2 Grate the tomatoes into the cooker, using the large holes of a box grater. Stir in the broth and tomato paste until the paste dissolves and the mixture comes to a simmer. Add the potatoes, eggplant, celery leaves, and salt; stir well.

3 Lock the lid onto the pot.

STOVETOP: Raise the heat to high and bring the pot to high pressure (15 psi). Once this pressure has been reached, reduce the heat as much as possible while maintaining this pressure. Cook for 5 minutes.

··················· **OR** ···················

ELECTRIC: Set the machine to cook at high pressure (9–11 psi). Set the machine's timer to cook at high pressure for 7 minutes.

4 Use the quick-release method to drop the pot's pressure back to normal.

5 Unlock and open the pot. Stir the stew before serving.

TESTERS' NOTES
• This stew has a silky, luxurious texture, thanks mostly to the combination of tomatoes and eggplant.
• Grating the tomatoes gives the stew a fresher taste than canned tomatoes. It also keeps the essential moisture from the tomato in the stew, rather than on the cutting board. Grate all of the tomato: seeds, skins, the works.

• Celery leaves offer a subtle but also slightly brighter flavor than chopped celery. If you want to go all out, substitute chopped fresh lovage leaves for the celery, which delivers a refined taste akin to a mash-up of tarragon, celery, and parsley.

Serve It Up! To make an easy pot pie, bake four small squares of frozen puff pastry on a large, rimmed baking sheet, following the package's instructions. Serve one square on top of each bowl of stew.

WHITE BEAN AND PUMPKIN STEW

EFFORT: **NOT MUCH** • PRESSURE: **HIGH** • TIME UNDER PRESSURE: **8 OR 12 MINUTES** • RELEASE: **QUICK** • SERVES: **4**

2 tablespoons unsalted butter

1 medium yellow onion, chopped

2 medium celery stalks, chopped

2 teaspoons minced garlic

8 cups peeled, seeded, and cubed pumpkin (about 1 medium pumpkin)

2 cups vegetable broth

One 15-ounce can white beans, drained and rinsed (about 1 3/4 cups)

1 teaspoon sweet paprika

1 teaspoon dried sage

1 teaspoon dried thyme

1/2 teaspoon salt

1/2 teaspoon ground black pepper

1 Melt the butter in a 6-quart stovetop pressure cooker set over medium heat or in a 6-quart electric pressure cooker turned to the browning mode. Add the onion and celery; cook, stirring frequently, until the onion has softened, about 4 minutes. Stir in the garlic until aromatic, about 20 seconds.

(continued)

2 Add the pumpkin, broth, beans, paprika, sage, thyme, salt, and pepper; stir well.

3 Lock the lid onto the cooker.

> **STOVETOP:** Raise the heat to high and bring the pot's pressure to high (15 psi). Once this pressure has been reached, reduce the heat as much as possible while maintaining this pressure. Cook for 8 minutes.
>
> ·························· **OR** ··························
>
> **ELECTRIC:** Set the machine to cook at high pressure (9–11 psi). Set the machine's timer to cook at high pressure for 12 minutes.

4 Use the quick-release method to bring the pot back to normal pressure.

5 Unlock and open the cooker. Stir the stew before serving.

TESTERS' NOTES

• White beans and pumpkin compete for delivering a creamy texture to this stew. Make sure the pumpkin is in 1-inch cubes so they cook quickly and evenly.

• To cube a pumpkin, first cut it in half through the stem end, then use a vegetable peeler to remove the tough skin. Use a serrated grapefruit spoon to remove the seeds and their sticky membranes. Chop the pumpkin into large bits, then cut each piece down to size.

• For a richer dish, bring the stew to a simmer after cooking by placing the opened stovetop pot over medium heat or turning the opened electric cooker to its browning function. Stir in up to ½ cup heavy cream and simmer for 1 minute, stirring all the while, just to remove the raw taste from the cream.

• You can substitute chopped butternut squash (which will be milder, and not as rich) for the pumpkin.

Serve It Up! Garnish the stew with toasted pumpkin seeds.

WHITE BEAN, CHICKPEA, AND RED LENTIL STEW

EFFORT: **NOT MUCH** • PRESSURE: **HIGH** • TIME UNDER PRESSURE: **7 OR 10 MINUTES** • RELEASE: **QUICK** • SERVES: **4 TO 6**

2 tablespoons olive oil

1 medium yellow onion, chopped

2 medium celery stalks, chopped

1½ tablespoons sweet paprika

½ teaspoon caraway seeds

½ teaspoon ground cinnamon

½ teaspoon salt

½ teaspoon ground black pepper

One 15-ounce can chickpeas, drained and rinsed (about 1¾ cups)

One 15-ounce can white beans, drained and rinsed (about 1¾ cups)

One 14-ounce can diced tomatoes (about 1¾ cups)

1 cup chicken broth

¼ cup red lentils

2 tablespoons canned tomato paste

1 Heat the oil in a 6-quart stovetop pressure cooker set over medium heat or in a 6-quart electric pressure cooker turned to the browning function. Add the onion and celery; cook, stirring often, until the onion turns translucent, about 4 minutes.

2 Stir in the paprika, caraway, cinnamon, salt, and pepper until aromatic, about 30 seconds. Add the chickpeas, beans, tomatoes, broth, lentils, and tomato paste, stirring until the tomato paste dissolves.

3 Lock the lid onto the cooker.

STOVETOP: Raise the heat to high and bring the pot to high pressure (15 psi). Once this pressure has been reached, reduce the heat as low as possible while maintaining this pressure. Cook for 7 minutes.

·· **OR** ··

ELECTRIC: Set the machine to cook at high pressure (9–11 psi). Set the machine's timer to cook at high pressure for 10 minutes.

4 Use the quick-release method to return the pot's pressure to normal.

5 Unlock and open the pot. Stir the stew before serving.

TESTERS' NOTES
• With canned beans and tomatoes, you'll still get a long-simmered taste in this spicy stew, reminiscent of those served in Eastern Europe and even Russia.
• The red lentils will break down and almost melt, thickening the stew—so do not substitute any other sort of lentil.

Serve It Up! Offer chunks of black bread and plenty of butter.

SPICY CHICKPEA STEW

EFFORT: **NOT MUCH** • PRESSURE: **HIGH** • TIME UNDER PRESSURE: **5 OR 7 MINUTES** • RELEASE: **QUICK** • SERVES: **4**

2 medium serrano chiles, stemmed, seeded, and minced

2 tablespoons minced garlic

2 tablespoons minced fresh ginger

1/4 cup peanut oil

3 medium yellow onions, chopped

1 tablespoon ground cumin

1 tablespoon ground coriander

One 28-ounce can chickpeas, drained and rinsed (about 3 1/2 cups)

One 14-ounce can diced tomatoes (about 1 3/4 cups)

1 Make a coarse, gritty paste from the chiles, garlic, and ginger by processing them in a mini food processor or grinding them in a mortar with a pestle.

2 Heat the oil in a 6-quart stovetop pressure cooker set over medium heat or in a 6-quart electric pressure set to the browning mode. Add the onions; cook, stirring often, until softened, about 6 minutes.

3 Scrape the chile paste into the pot; add the cumin and coriander. Stir well until the onions are evenly coated. Stir in the chickpeas and tomatoes.

4 Lock the lid onto the pot.

STOVETOP: Raise the heat to high and bring the pot to high pressure (15 psi). Once this pressure has been reached, reduce the heat as much as possible while maintaining this pressure. Cook for 5 minutes.

·· **OR** ··

ELECTRIC: Set the machine to cook at high pressure (9–11 psi). Set the machine's timer to cook at high pressure for 7 minutes.

5 Use the quick-release method to bring the pot's pressure back to normal.

6 Unlock and open the cooker. Stir the stew before serving.

TESTERS' NOTES
• The chile will add most of the flavor to this otherwise straightforward stew. It tastes as if it's cooked on a back burner for hours (instead of under pressure for less than 10 minutes).

(continued)

- If you're concerned about the heat, seed the serrano chiles, or only use one (or even less).
- Serrano chiles will add a fruity, bright heat to the dish. If you'd like a tart spark to brighten the flavors, stir up to 1 tablespoon lemon juice into the stew after cooking.

Serve It Up! Garnish the bowls with plain yogurt and chopped cilantro and have pita chips on hand. Or serve it in bowls alongside grilled cheese sandwiches.

CHICKPEA STEW WITH CARROTS, DATES, AND CRISP ARTICHOKES

EFFORT: **A LOT** • PRESSURE: **HIGH** • TIME UNDER PRESSURE: **8 OR 12 MINUTES** • RELEASE: **QUICK** • SERVES: **4**

1½ **cups dried chickpeas**

2 **cups chicken broth**

2 **tablespoons all-purpose flour**

2½ **tablespoons olive oil**

1 **medium red onion, halved and sliced into thin half-moons**

2 **teaspoons minced garlic**

1 **tablespoon sweet paprika**

½ **teaspoon ground cinnamon**

½ **teaspoon ground coriander**

½ **teaspoon ground cumin**

½ **teaspoon salt**

One 14-ounce **can diced tomatoes (about 1¾ cups)**

1 **pound "baby" carrots, cut into 1-inch pieces**

6 **pitted dates, preferably Medjool, chopped**

One 9-ounce **box frozen artichoke heart quarters, thawed and squeezed of excess moisture**

1 Soak the chickpeas in a big bowl of water for at least 12 hours or up to 16 hours.

2 Drain the chickpeas in a colander set in the sink. Whisk the broth and flour in a medium bowl until the flour dissolves.

3 Heat 1½ tablespoons oil in a 6-quart stovetop pressure cooker set over medium heat or in a 6-quart electric pressure cooker turned to the browning function. Add the onion and cook, stirring often, until softened, about 4 minutes.

4 Stir in the garlic, paprika, cinnamon, coriander, cumin, and salt until aromatic, about 30 seconds. Pour in the tomatoes as well as the broth mixture. Stir well, then add the carrots, dates, and drained chickpeas.

5 Lock the lid onto the pot.

STOVETOP: Raise the heat to high and bring the pot to high pressure (15 psi). Once this pressure has been reached, reduce the heat as much as possible while maintaining this pressure. Cook for 8 minutes.

························ **OR** ························

ELECTRIC: Set the machine to cook at high pressure (9–11 psi). Set the machine's timer to cook at high pressure for 12 minutes.

6 Use the quick-release method to drop the pot's pressure back to normal.

7 Unlock and open the cooker. Heat the remaining tablespoon oil in a large nonstick skillet set over medium-high heat. Add the artichoke heart quarters; fry until brown and crisp, stirring and turning occasionally, about 10 minutes. Dish up the chickpea mixture into big bowls and top with the crisp artichoke bits.

STOVETOP: Set the pot over high heat and bring to high pressure (15 psi). Once this pressure has been reached, reduce the heat as much as possible while maintaining this pressure. Cook for 15 minutes.

································ **OR** ································

ELECTRIC: Set the machine to cook at high pressure (9–11 psi). Set the machine's timer to cook at high pressure for 22 minutes.

3 Use the quick-release method to return the pot's pressure to normal.

4 Unlock and open the cooker. Drain the black-eyed peas in a colander; wipe out the cooker.

5 Melt the butter in the stovetop cooker set over medium heat or in the electric cooker turned to the browning function. Add the onions, celery, bell pepper, and garlic; cook, stirring often, until the onions turn translucent, about 3 minutes.

6 Sprinkle the flour over the vegetables and stir well. Add the sage, thyme, paprika, salt, celery seeds, and nutmeg; stir until the vegetables are coated in the spices. Stir over the heat for 1 minute to cook the flour a bit (without browning it), then whisk in the broth in a slow, steady stream to dissolve the flour. Stir in the black-eyed peas.

7 Lock the lid onto the cooker.

STOVETOP: Raise the heat to high and bring the pot to high pressure (15 psi). Once this pressure has been reached, reduce the heat as much as possible while maintaining this pressure. Cook for 2 minutes.

································ **OR** ································

ELECTRIC: Set the machine to cook at high pressure (9–11 psi). Set the machine's timer to cook at high pressure for 3 minutes.

TESTERS' NOTES

• Talk about vegetarian elegance! You can even make the stew in advance, then save it, covered, in the fridge for up to 2 days. Rewarm it before serving in a large saucepan over medium-low heat and fry the artichokes as directed in step 7.

• For a bigger burst of flavor, add up to 1 chopped preserved lemon with the carrots and dates.

Serve It Up! For a heartier meal, ladle the stew over cooked couscous.

CREAMY BLACK-EYED PEA STEW

EFFORT: **A LOT** • PRESSURE: **HIGH** • TIME UNDER PRESSURE: **17 OR 25 MINUTES** • RELEASE: **QUICK, THEN QUICK AGAIN** • SERVES: **6**

2 cups dried black-eyed peas

4 tablespoons (¹/₂ stick) unsalted butter

2 medium yellow onions, chopped

4 medium celery stalks, chopped

1 medium green bell pepper, stemmed, cored, and chopped

2 teaspoons minced garlic

3 tablespoons all-purpose flour

1 teaspoon dried sage

1 teaspoon dried thyme

1 teaspoon sweet paprika

¹/₂ teaspoon salt

¹/₄ teaspoon celery seeds

¹/₄ teaspoon grated nutmeg

2¹/₂ cups vegetable broth

¹/₂ cup heavy cream

1 Place the black-eyed peas in a 6-quart stovetop or electric pressure cooker. Cover them with cool tap water until they're submerged by 2 inches.

(continued)

8 Use the quick-release method to drop the pot's pressure back to normal.

9 Set the stovetop pressure cooker over medium heat or turn the electric pressure cooker to its brown function; bring the stew to a simmer. Stir in the cream and cook for 2 minutes, stirring frequently, to reduce the cream a little and get rid of its raw taste. Serve at once.

TESTERS' NOTES
• If you grew up in the South, this recipe is guaranteed to bring back childhood memories.
• There's plenty of butter and cream here—and also loads of vegetables. They'll balance the heavier flavors, especially since they begin to break down into the stew after so long under pressure.

BLACK-EYED PEA AND BROWN RICE STEW

EFFORT: **NOT MUCH** • PRESSURE: **HIGH** • TIME UNDER PRESSURE: **15 OR 22 MINUTES** • RELEASE: **NATURAL** • SERVES: **6**

4 cups (1 quart) **vegetable broth**

1 medium **yellow onion, chopped**

2 large **carrots, chopped**

2 medium **yellow potatoes, such as Yukon Gold (about 6 ounces each), cut into 1-inch pieces**

3 medium **celery stalks, chopped**

1 cup **dried black-eyed peas**

½ cup **medium-grain brown rice, such as brown Arborio rice**

¼ cup **minced fresh dill fronds**

1 teaspoon **salt**

½ teaspoon **ground black pepper**

1 Mix everything in a 6-quart stovetop or electric pressure cooker.

2 Lock the lid onto the pot.

STOVETOP: Set the pot over high heat and bring it to high pressure (15 psi). Once this pressure has been reached, reduce the heat as much as possible while maintaining this pressure. Cook for 15 minutes.

·····OR·····

ELECTRIC: Set the machine to cook at high pressure (9–11 psi). Set the timer to cook at this pressure for 22 minutes.

3 Reduce the pressure.

STOVETOP: Set the pot off the heat and let its pressure come back to normal naturally, about 14 minutes.

·····OR·····

ELECTRIC: Turn off the machine or unplug it so it doesn't flip to its keep-warm setting. Let its pressure return to normal naturally, 14 to 18 minutes.

4 Unlock and open the cooker. Stir the stew before serving.

TESTERS' NOTES
• This dish rides the line between a casserole and a stew since the brown rice will absorb much of the liquid. In fact, you may need to thin it out with more broth when you reheat leftovers.
• To brighten the flavors and take away some of their savory earthiness, add up to 1 teaspoon finely grated lemon zest with the other ingredients before cooking under pressure.

RICOTTA-STUFFED ZUCCHINI

EFFORT: **A LOT** • PRESSURE: **HIGH** • TIME UNDER PRESSURE: **3 OR 5 MINUTES** • RELEASE: **QUICK** • SERVES: **6**

1 cup regular ricotta

1/2 cup fresh breadcrumbs

1 large egg yolk

2 teaspoons fresh thyme leaves

1/4 teaspoon grated nutmeg

3 large zucchini

2 tablespoons olive oil

1 small yellow onion, chopped

2 teaspoons minced garlic

One 14-ounce can crushed tomatoes (about 1 3/4 cups)

1 tablespoon minced fresh oregano leaves

1/4 teaspoon salt

1/4 teaspoon ground black pepper

1 Mix the ricotta, breadcrumbs, egg yolk, thyme, and nutmeg in a medium bowl until uniform.

2 Cut the zucchini into 2-inch-long sections. Use a melon baller or a serrated grapefruit spoon to hollow out these sections, turning them into hollowed-out logs, leaving about 1/4 inch of flesh at the skin and perhaps 1/2 inch at the bottom for support. Stuff each of these sections with the ricotta mixture, about 2 tablespoons per section.

3 Heat the oil in a 6-quart stovetop pressure cooker set over medium heat or in a 6-quart electric pressure cooker turned to the browning function. Add the onion; cook, stirring often, until translucent, about 3 minutes. Stir in the garlic and cook until aromatic, about 30 seconds.

4 Stir in the tomato, oregano, salt, and pepper. Stand the stuffed zucchini filling side up in the sauce.

5 Lock the lid onto the cooker.

STOVETOP: Raise the heat to high and bring the pot to high pressure (15 psi). Once this pressure has been reached, reduce the heat as much as possible while maintaining this pressure. Cook for 3 minutes.

······· **OR** ·······

ELECTRIC: Set the machine to cook at high pressure (9–11 psi). Set the machine's timer to cook at high pressure for 5 minutes.

6 Use the quick-release method to bring the pot's pressure back to normal.

7 Unlock and open the pot. Spoon the stuffed zucchini and sauce into bowls to serve.

TESTERS' NOTES

• These cheese-filled zucchini logs would make a wonderful addition to a holiday table—or a first course at a dinner party before a roast from the oven.

• You'll need to pack the stuffed zucchini into the cooker—and the sauce is hot. Watch your fingers! But once packed in and standing up, the zucchini will have a better chance of staying upright during cooking.

• Use fresh breadcrumbs, not dried. The latter creates a grainy texture in the filling. Look for fresh breadcrumbs at the bakery of your supermarket, or grind up a day-old baguette to make your own.

SOUR CREAM-AND-CHIVE MASHED POTATOES

EFFORT: **A LITTLE** • PRESSURE: **HIGH** • TIME UNDER PRESSURE: **10 OR 15 MINUTES** • RELEASE: **QUICK** • SERVES: **6**

4 pounds medium yellow potatoes, such as Yukon Gold (about 6 ounces each), peeled and quartered

1/2 cup whole or low-fat milk

1/2 cup regular or low-fat sour cream

1 teaspoon salt

1/2 teaspoon ground black pepper

3 tablespoons minced fresh chives

1 Place the potatoes in a 6-quart stovetop or electric pressure cooker; add enough cool tap water so that they're submerged by 1 inch.

2 Lock the lid onto the cooker.

STOVETOP: Set the pot over high heat and bring it to high pressure (15 psi). Once this pressure has been reached, reduce the heat as much as possible while maintaining this pressure. Cook for 10 minutes.

·······································**OR**·······································

ELECTRIC: Set the machine to cook at high pressure (9–11 psi). Set the machine's timer to cook at high pressure for 15 minutes.

3 Bring the pot's pressure back to normal with the quick-release method.

4 Unlock and open the pot. Drain the potatoes in a colander, then return them to the cooker. Add the milk, sour cream, salt, and pepper. Use a potato masher to create smooth mashed potatoes right in the pot. Stir in the chives just before serving.

TESTERS' NOTES
• An old-fashioned potato masher will give you a smooth, velvety side dish in seconds. However, you can use an electric mixer at medium speed in the pressure cooker pot (in this case, the potatoes have to be peeled or the peels will gum up the mixer).
• For the creamiest mashed potatoes, put each cooked potato through a potato ricer, an old-fashioned tool that forces them through little holes to create tiny potato threads. Stir in the other ingredients with a wooden spoon.
• Keep the mashed potatoes warm for up to 30 minutes by setting the lid back on the cooker without locking it. Stir in the chives just before serving.
• You can substitute the green part of a scallion for the chives.

Serve It Up! There's no butter in the mashed potatoes, so you can put a little pat on each serving.

BISTRO MASHED POTATOES WITH MUSTARD AND TARRAGON

EFFORT: **A LITTLE** • PRESSURE: **HIGH** • TIME UNDER PRESSURE: **10 OR 15 MINUTES** • RELEASE: **QUICK** • SERVES: **6**

4 pounds medium yellow potatoes, such as Yukon Gold (about 6 ounces each), peeled and quartered

3/4 cup chicken broth

2 tablespoons Dijon mustard

2 tablespoons packed fresh tarragon leaves, minced

1 tablespoon Worcestershire sauce

1 teaspoon ground black pepper

1 Place the potatoes in a 6-quart electric or stovetop pressure cooker; add enough cool tap water that they're submerged by 1 inch.

2 Lock the lid onto the cooker.

STOVETOP: Set the pot over high heat and bring it to high pressure (15 psi). Once this pressure has been reached, reduce the heat as much as possible while maintaining this pressure. Cook for 10 minutes.

············ OR ············

ELECTRIC: Set the machine to cook at high pressure (9–11 psi). Set the machine's timer to cook at high pressure for 15 minutes.

3 Use the quick-release method to return the pot's pressure to normal.

4 Unlock and open the cooker. Drain the potatoes into a colander set in the sink, then return them to the pot. Add the broth, mustard, tarragon, Worcestershire sauce, and pepper. Press the mixture with a potato masher to create smooth mashed potatoes.

TESTERS' NOTES
• There's no dairy in these mashed potatoes, which are best with a hearty beef or chicken stew or next to grilled red snapper fillets.
• The combination of mustard and tarragon is a savory, slightly sour mix that calls to mind French bistro cooking.
• You can substitute stemmed fresh thyme leaves for the tarragon.

HERB-SMASHED POTATOES

EFFORT: **A LITTLE** • PRESSURE: **HIGH** • TIME UNDER PRESSURE: **6 OR 9 MINUTES** • RELEASE: **QUICK** • SERVES: **4**

2 pounds small red potatoes (about 4 ounces each), halved
3 tablespoons olive oil
1 teaspoon minced garlic
1 tablespoon minced fresh rosemary leaves
2 teaspoons fresh thyme leaves
2 teaspoons minced fresh oregano leaves
1/2 teaspoon salt
1/2 teaspoon ground black pepper

1 Place the potatoes in a 6-quart stovetop or electric pressure cooker; add enough cool tap water that they're submerged by 1 inch.

2 Lock the lid onto the cooker.

STOVETOP: Set the pot over high heat and bring it to high pressure (15 psi). Once this pressure has been reached, reduce the heat as much as possible while maintaining this pressure. Cook for 6 minutes.

············ OR ············

ELECTRIC: Set the machine to cook at high pressure (9–11 psi). Set the machine's timer to cook at high pressure for 9 minutes.

3 Use the quick-release method to drop the pot's pressure back to normal.

4 Unlock and open the pot. Drain the potatoes in a colander set in the sink. Set the stovetop cooker over medium heat or turn the electric cooker to its browning function. Swirl in the oil, then add the garlic and cook just until it begins to brown, less than 1 minute, stirring constantly.

(continued)

5 Add the rosemary, thyme, and oregano; cook for 10 seconds, stirring all the while. Remove the stovetop cooker from the heat or turn off the electric cooker. Return the potatoes to the cooker; add the salt and pepper. Stir with a wooden spoon until the potatoes are smashed without becoming a full-on puree.

TESTERS' NOTES

• Waxy red potatoes make the best smashed potatoes because they hold their shape better than higher-starch yellow or baking potatoes.

• Although the dish is highly flavored, you can put the lid onto the pot without engaging the lock and set it aside for 15 minutes, to further blend the flavors.

• Don't even think about using dried herbs. They won't have enough spiky flavor.

• For a bit of heat, add up to ½ teaspoon red pepper flakes with the herbs. For a sour spark, add ½ teaspoon finely grated lemon zest.

Serve It Up! For an elegant main course, pile the potatoes on plates and top with a grilled fish fillet. Drizzle the servings with **Lemon Tahini Vinaigrette**: for four servings, in a small bowl whisk ¼ cup olive oil, 1 tablespoon lemon juice, ½ tablespoon white balsamic vinegar, ½ tablespoon Dijon mustard, ½ tablespoon tahini, and ¼ teaspoon salt.

WARM POTATO AND GREEN BEAN SALAD

EFFORT: **A LITTLE** • PRESSURE: **HIGH** • COOK TIME: **4 OR 6 MINUTES** • RELEASE: **QUICK** • SERVES: **6**

2½ **pounds very small red potatoes (about 2 ounces each), halved**

¾ **pound green beans, trimmed and cut into ½-inch segments**

2 **tablespoons white wine vinegar**

2 **tablespoons packed fresh tarragon leaves, minced**

2 **teaspoons Dijon mustard**

½ **teaspoon salt**

½ **teaspoon ground black pepper**

6 **tablespoons olive oil**

1 Place the potatoes in a 6-quart stovetop or electric pressure cooker; cover them with cool tap water until they're submerged by 1 inch.

2 Lock the lid onto the cooker.

STOVETOP: Set the pot over high heat and bring to high pressure (15 psi). Once this pressure has been reached, reduce the heat as much as possible while maintaining this pressure. Cook for 4 minutes.

·························· **OR** ··························

ELECTRIC: Set the machine to cook at high pressure (9–11 psi). Set the machine's timer to cook at high pressure for 6 minutes.

3 Use the quick-release method to bring the pot's pressure back to normal.

4 Unlock and open the cooker. Place the green bean segments in a large colander set in the sink. Drain the hot potatoes over the green beans in the colander. Set aside for 5 minutes to steam the beans.

5 Whisk the vinegar, tarragon, mustard, salt, and pepper in a large serving bowl; whisk in the oil in a small, steady stream to make a creamy, velvety dressing. Add the warm potatoes and beans; toss before serving.

TESTERS' NOTES

• Consider this the best side for roast chicken: the acidic dressing on the vegetables will go perfectly with the meat.

• By draining the hot potatoes over the green beans, you cook those beans without, well, cooking them—the heat tenderizes them a bit while leaving their crunch intact.

• If you want to carry this dish to a potluck, store the vegetables and dressing in separate bowls. At the last moment, microwave the vegetables for 1 to 2 minutes on high to warm them, then toss them in the whisked dressing.

SMASHED SWEET POTATOES WITH PINEAPPLE AND GINGER

EFFORT: **NOT MUCH** • PRESSURE: **HIGH** • TIME UNDER PRESSURE: **8 OR 12 MINUTES** • RELEASE: **QUICK** • SERVES: **8**

4 pounds medium sweet potatoes (about 6 potatoes), peeled and cut into 1¹/₂-inch chunks

3 tablespoons unsalted butter

¹/₂ teaspoon ground ginger

¹/₄ teaspoon ground cinnamon

¹/₄ teaspoon grated nutmeg

2 tablespoons frozen unsweetened pineapple juice concentrate, thawed

1 teaspoon salt

1 Place the sweet potatoes and 3 cups water in a 6-quart stovetop or electric pressure cooker.

2 Lock the lid onto the cooker.

STOVETOP: Set the pot over high heat and bring to high pressure (15 psi). Once this pressure has been reached, reduce the heat as much as possible while maintaining this pressure. Cook for 8 minutes.

·······························**OR**·······························

ELECTRIC: Set the machine to cook at high pressure (9–11 psi). Set the machine's timer to cook at high pressure for 12 minutes.

3 Use the quick-release method to bring the pot's pressure back to normal.

4 Unlock and open the cooker. Drain the sweet potatoes in a colander set in the sink. Set the stovetop cooker over medium heat or turn the electric cooker to its browning function. Melt the butter in the cooker, then add the ginger, cinnamon, and nutmeg; cook until aromatic, stirring constantly, less than 1 minute.

5 Stir in the pineapple juice concentrate and salt, then take the stovetop model off the heat or turn off the electric cooker. Add the potatoes and stir well with a wooden spoon, smashing them a bit, until you have a vaguely smooth puree with chunks of sweet potato.

TESTERS' NOTES

• Look no further for the ultimate side dish with your holiday turkey. The pressure cooker will keep the sweet potatoes moist and very flavorful.

• Toasting the spices gives them more heft, a better finish against the sweet potatoes.

• If you miss the marshmallows in the standard holiday casserole, heat your broiler and spread the warm finished potatoes into a 9 x 13-inch baking dish and cover with mini-marshmallows. Broil until the marshmallows melt and brown a bit, 1 to 2 minutes.

CREAMY CHEESY ONIONS AND BRUSSELS SPROUTS

EFFORT: **NOT MUCH** • PRESSURE: **HIGH** • TIME UNDER PRESSURE:
5 OR 8 MINUTES • RELEASE: **QUICK** • SERVES: **4**

4 tablespoons (1/2 stick) unsalted butter

2 medium yellow onions, sliced into very
    thin rings

1 1/2 tablespoons all-purpose flour

1 cup whole or low-fat milk

3/4 cup chicken broth

1/2 teaspoon dried thyme

1/4 teaspoon grated nutmeg

1/4 teaspoon salt

1/4 teaspoon ground black pepper

3/4 pound small Brussels sprouts, halved

1 cup grated Cheddar cheese (about
    4 ounces)

1 Melt the butter in a 6-quart stovetop
pressure cooker set over medium heat or in
a 6-quart electric pressure cooker turned
to the browning function. Add the onions;
cook, stirring often, until softened, about
5 minutes. Sprinkle the flour over the
onions and stir over the heat for 30 seconds,
just to lose the raw taste of the flour without
browning it.

2 Whisk in the milk in a slow, steady stream
to dissolve the flour. Whisk in the broth,
thyme, nutmeg, salt, and pepper. Add the
Brussels sprouts and stir well.

3 Lock the lid onto the pot.

STOVETOP: Raise the heat to high and bring the
pot to high pressure (15 psi). Once this pressure
has been reached, reduce the heat as much as possible while maintaining this pressure. Cook for
5 minutes.

···························· **OR** ····························

ELECTRIC: Set the machine to cook at high pressure (9–11 psi). Set the machine's timer to cook at
high pressure for 8 minutes.

4 Use the quick-release method to return
the pressure in the pot to normal.

5 Unlock and open the cooker. Add the
cheese and stir well before serving.

TESTERS' NOTES
• This gooey casserole is a wonderful side dish for almost any roast or grilled fare. The slightly bitter Brussels
sprouts will mellow considerably with the warming flavor
of nutmeg.

• Use a whisk in step 2 to help the flour dissolve into the
milk. Pouring the milk into the cooker in a slow but steady
stream as you whisk will help avoid any lumps.

BRAISED RED CABBAGE WITH APPLES AND BACON

EFFORT: **NOT MUCH** • PRESSURE: **HIGH** • TIME UNDER PRESSURE:
10 OR 13 MINUTES • RELEASE: **QUICK** • SERVES: **6**

4 thin bacon slices, chopped

1 small red onion, chopped

1 medium tart green apple, such as
    Granny Smith, peeled, cored, and
    chopped

1 teaspoon dried thyme

¼ teaspoon ground allspice

¼ teaspoon ground mace

1 tablespoon packed dark brown sugar

1 tablespoon balsamic vinegar

1 medium red cabbage (about 2 pounds),
    cored and thinly sliced

½ cup chicken broth

1 Fry the bacon in a 6-quart stovetop pressure cooker set over medium heat or in a 6-quart electric pressure cooker turned to the browning function, stirring often, until crisp, about 4 minutes.

2 Add the onion to the pot; cook, stirring often, until soft, about 4 minutes. Add the apple, thyme, allspice, and mace. Cook about 1 minute, stirring all the while, until fragrant. Stir in the brown sugar and vinegar; keep stirring until bubbling, about 1 minute.

3 Add the cabbage; toss well to mix evenly with the other ingredients. Drizzle the broth over the cabbage mixture.

4 Lock the lid onto the cooker.

STOVETOP: Raise the heat to high and bring the pot to high pressure (15 psi). Once this pressure has been reached, reduce the heat as much as possible while maintaining this pressure. Cook for 10 minutes.

························ **OR** ························

ELECTRIC: Set the machine to cook at high pressure (9–11 psi). Set the machine's timer to cook at high pressure for 13 minutes.

5 Use the quick-release method to return the pot to normal pressure.

6 Unlock and open the pot. Stir well before serving.

TESTERS' NOTES

• The combination of allspice and thyme is particularly appealing, delivering an earthy savoriness underneath the sweet-and-sour flavors. The mace adds an autumnal comfort, welcome even in the middle of the summer.

• To prepare the cabbage, cut it in half through its root end, then cut out the tough, pyramidal bits of that core inside each half. Set the halves cut side down on your cutting board and slice them into ¼-inch-thick half-moons that can be separated into their individual shreds.

• Fry the bacon until it's crisp—it'll add more flavor and retain a better texture under pressure.

Serve It Up! You'll want sausages or pork chops off the grill to go along with this easy rendition of a beer garden favorite.

STEWED SAVOY CABBAGE WITH TOMATOES AND DILL

EFFORT: **NOT MUCH** • PRESSURE: **HIGH** • TIME UNDER PRESSURE: **5 OR 8 MINUTES** • RELEASE: **QUICK** • SERVES: **6**

4 tablespoons (½ stick) unsalted butter

1 large yellow onion, chopped

3 medium celery stalks, thinly sliced

One 14-ounce can diced tomatoes
    (1¾ cups)

¼ cup packed dark brown sugar

¼ cup dried currants

¼ cup fresh lemon juice

2 teaspoons smoked paprika

½ teaspoon celery seeds

½ teaspoon salt

½ teaspoon ground black pepper

1 medium savoy cabbage (about 2
    pounds), cored and shredded (about
    10 cups)

2 tablespoons minced fresh dill fronds

(continued)

1 Melt the butter in a 6-quart stovetop pressure cooker set over medium heat or in a 6-quart electric pressure cooker turned to the browning function. Add the onion and celery; cook, stirring often, until the onion has softened, about 4 minutes.

2 Stir in the tomatoes, brown sugar, currants, lemon juice, smoked paprika, celery seeds, salt, and pepper. Add the cabbage and dill; stir well to combine.

3 Lock the lid onto the pot.

STOVETOP: Raise the heat to high and bring the pot to high pressure (15 psi). Once this pressure has been reached, reduce the heat as much as possible while maintaining this pressure. Cook for 5 minutes.

······················· **OR** ·······················

ELECTRIC: Set the machine to cook at high pressure (9–11 psi). Set the machine's timer to cook at high pressure for 8 minutes.

4 Use the quick-release method to bring the pressure in the pot back to normal.

5 Unlock and open the pot. Stir well before serving.

TESTERS' NOTES
• Savoy cabbage has a pleasing, mild taste, sort of like a sweeter version of Belgian endive. It cooks more quickly than standard green or red cabbage.
• The smoked paprika adds an almost barbecue quality to the tomato sauce, taking the dish from Eastern Europe to the American Southwest. If you'd prefer a more straightforward dish, substitute sweet paprika.

Serve It Up! Stir 2 cups cooked wheatberries or spelt berries into the cabbage mixture after cooking, for an easy vegetarian entrée. Have some toasted pita rounds on hand as well.

ROSÉ-BRAISED KALE WITH FENNEL SEEDS

EFFORT: **A LITTLE** • PRESSURE: **HIGH** • TIME UNDER PRESSURE: **1 OR 2 MINUTES** • RELEASE: **QUICK** • SERVES: **6**

2 tablespoons olive oil
3 teaspoons minced garlic
1 teaspoon fennel seeds
2 pounds kale, such as curly leaf kale, washed (but not dried), stemmed, and chopped
1 cup rosé wine, such as Bandol
1 tablespoon sherry vinegar

1 Heat the oil in a 6-quart stovetop pressure cooker set over medium heat or in a 6-quart electric pressure cooker turned to the browning function. Add the garlic and fennel seeds; cook until fragrant and lightly browned, stirring often, about 1 minute. Add the kale and toss well. Pour in the wine.

2 Lock the lid onto the pot.

STOVETOP: Raise the heat to high and bring the pot to high pressure (15 psi). Once this pressure has been reached, reduce the heat as much as possible while maintaining this pressure. Cook for 1 minute.

······················· **OR** ·······················

ELECTRIC: Set the machine to cook at high pressure (9–11 psi). Set the machine's timer to cook at high pressure for 2 minutes.

3 Use the quick-release method to bring the pot's pressure back to normal.

4 Unlock and open the cooker. Transfer the kale to a serving bowl. Pour the vinegar into the pot and set the stovetop cooker over medium heat or turn the electric cooker to its browning function. Bring the sauce to a simmer. Cook, stirring often, until the liquid has reduced to about ½ cup, about 4 minutes. Pour the sauce over the kale and serve.

TESTERS' NOTES

• This fast, healthy side dish should be the last thing you make before you bring dinner to the table.

• Braising the kale in rosé wine gives it a slightly sweet finish, a perfect match for its mildly bitter earthiness. Almost any variety of kale will work, from the standard curly leaf to more exotic varietals.

• Kale leaves are often sandy or gritty. Make sure you wash them before chopping—but there's no need to dry them. The excess moisture will simply add more volume to the braising liquid.

• You can substitute ½ cup reduced-sodium vegetable broth and ½ cup unsweetened apple juice for the rosé wine.

STEWED KALE AND MUSHROOMS

EFFORT: **NOT MUCH** • PRESSURE: **HIGH** • TIME UNDER PRESSURE: **1 OR 2 MINUTES** • RELEASE: **QUICK** • SERVES: **4**

2 tablespoons olive oil

2 tablespoons minced garlic

8 ounces baby bella or cremini mushrooms, thinly sliced

¼ teaspoon salt

1 pound kale, such as curly leaf kale, washed (but not dried), stemmed, and chopped (about 5⅓ packed cups)

1 tablespoon white wine vinegar

½ teaspoon ground black pepper

1 Heat the oil in a 6-quart stovetop pressure cooker set over medium heat or in a 6-quart electric pressure cooker turned to the browning function. Add the garlic and cook,

stirring often, until lightly browned, about 2 minutes.

2 Add the mushrooms and salt; cook, stirring occasionally, until the mushrooms give off their liquid, 2 to 3 minutes. Add the kale and toss well.

3 Lock the lid onto the pot.

STOVETOP: Raise the heat to high and bring the pot to high pressure (15 psi). Once this pressure has been reached, reduce the heat as much as possible while maintaining this pressure. Cook for 1 minute.

OR

ELECTRIC: Set the machine to cook at high pressure (9–11 psi). Set the machine's timer to cook at high pressure for 2 minutes.

4 Use the quick-release method to drop the pressure in the pot back to normal.

5 Unlock and open the pot. Add the vinegar and pepper; stir well before serving.

TESTERS' NOTES

• Presliced fresh mushrooms vary wildly in quality. Some are a true convenience; others are nothing more than dried mushroom chips. Inspect the package before buying to make sure the ones you've got are moist, fresh, and free from boggy spots.

• There's a lot of garlic here. You can reduce the amount if you don't want such a hit.

• There's also no broth or wine in this preparation—the only liquid is either given off by the mushrooms or clinging to the kale.

Serve It Up! Make a main course out of this side dish by setting a poached egg or two on top of each serving, letting the soft yolks run down and enrich the sauce. You could even set the kale on top of pan-fried ham slices before adding those eggs.

COLLARD GREENS IN A SPICY TOMATO SAUCE

EFFORT: **NOT MUCH** · PRESSURE: **HIGH** · TIME UNDER PRESSURE:
4 OR 6 MINUTES · RELEASE: **QUICK** · SERVES: **6**

2 tablespoons olive oil

1 tablespoon minced garlic

$1/2$ teaspoon red pepper flakes

$1^{1/2}$ pounds collard greens, tough stems
 removed, the leaves chopped (about
 8 packed cups)

$1/2$ cup canned tomato puree

$1/2$ cup vegetable or chicken broth

$1/2$ cup moderately sweet white wine,
 such as a dry Riesling

$1/2$ teaspoon salt

1 Heat the oil in a 6-quart stovetop pressure cooker set over medium heat or in a
6-quart electric pressure cooker turned to
the browning function. Add the garlic and
red pepper flakes; cook, stirring all the while,
until aromatic, less than 1 minute.

2 Add the collards; toss over the heat for
2 minutes. Add the tomato puree, broth,
wine, and salt, and stir well.

3 Lock the lid onto the pot.

> **STOVETOP:** Raise the heat to high and bring the
> pot to high pressure (15 psi). Once this pressure
> has been reached, reduce the heat as much as pos-
> sible while maintaining this pressure. Cook for
> 4 minutes.
> ·· **OR** ··
> **ELECTRIC:** Set the machine to cook at high pres-
> sure (9–11 psi). Set the machine's timer to cook at
> high pressure for 6 minutes.

4 Use the quick-release method to bring the
pot's pressure back to normal.

5 Unlock and open the cooker. Stir well
before serving.

TESTERS' NOTES

• Here's a Southern favorite as a spicy side dish—but not
too spicy. If you're hankering for heat, up the red pepper
flakes to 1 teaspoon (or even more).

• The tough stem on larger collard greens can extend up
into the leaf itself. You want to get rid of any fibrous bits
that won't soften with this quick-cooking method.

• The collards will be soft but with a little chew. If you like
really soft collards, use a natural release after cooking, not
the suggested quick-release method.

• Make the prep easier by buying bagged chopped collard greens, available in the produce section of many
supermarkets.

Serve It Up! To make a main course out
of this side dish, serve it over cooked and
drained ziti and top with shaved pecorino
romano.

VINEGARY COLLARD GREENS WITH BACON

EFFORT: **A LITTLE** • PRESSURE: **HIGH** • TIME UNDER PRESSURE:
4 TO 6 MINUTES • RELEASE: **QUICK** • SERVES: **4**

4 ounces slab bacon, diced

1 small yellow onion, chopped

2 teaspoons minced garlic

**1½ pounds collard greens, tough stems
removed and the leaves chopped
(about 8 packed cups)**

½ cup chicken broth

3 tablespoons balsamic vinegar

2 tablespoons canned tomato paste

1 tablespoon packed dark brown sugar

1 Put the bacon in a 6-quart stovetop pressure cooker set over medium heat or in a 6-quart electric pressure cooker turned to the browning function; fry until crisp and well browned, stirring occasionally, about 4 minutes.

2 Add the onion; cook, stirring often, until translucent, about 2 minutes. Add the garlic, stir well, and add the collard greens. Stir over the heat for 2 minutes, then pour in the broth, vinegar, tomato paste, and brown sugar until the latter two items dissolve into the sauce. Stir well one more time.

3 Lock the lid onto the pot.

STOVETOP: Raise the heat to high and bring the pot to high pressure (15 psi). Once this pressure has been reached, reduce the heat as much as possible while maintaining this pressure. Cook for 4 minutes.

······················· **OR** ·······················

ELECTRIC: Set the machine to cook at high pressure (9–11 psi). Set the machine's timer to cook at high pressure for 6 minutes.

4 Use the quick-release method to bring the pot's pressure back to normal.

5 Unlock and open the pot. Stir well before serving.

TESTERS' NOTES
• By using somewhat sweeter balsamic vinegar (rather than, say, apple cider vinegar), we keep the sour notes muted in the dish. Use a standard bottling, not an aged, syrupy balsamic. However, if you like more spike, then substitute red wine vinegar for up to half the balsamic vinegar.
• Pass bottled hot red pepper sauce at the table, rather than adding red pepper flakes to the pot (these will add a dull heat, rather than complementing the vinegar in the sauce).

Serve It Up! For a simple dinner, split open large baked potatoes and ladle this stew on top.

SUGAR-GLAZED CARROTS

EFFORT: **NOT MUCH** • PRESSURE: **HIGH** • TIME UNDER PRESSURE: **2 OR 3 MINUTES** • RELEASE: **QUICK** • SERVES: **6**

8 moderately large carrots (about 6 ounces each), peeled and cut into 1-inch segments
2 tablespoons unsalted butter
1 tablespoon sugar
1 tablespoon unseasoned rice vinegar

1 Put the carrots in a 6-quart stovetop or electric pressure cooker; add enough cool tap water that they're submerged by 2 inches.

2 Lock the lid onto the pot.

STOVETOP: Set the cooker over high heat and bring to high pressure (15 psi). Once this pressure has been reached, reduce the heat as much as possible while maintaining this pressure. Cook for 2 minutes.

············ **OR** ············

ELECTRIC: Set the machine to cook at high pressure (9–11 psi). Set the machine's timer to cook at high pressure for 3 minutes.

3 Use the quick-release method to return the pot's pressure to normal.

4 Unlock and open the pot. Drain the carrots in a colander set in the sink. Set the stovetop cooker over medium heat or turn the electric cooker to its browning function. Add the butter; when it has melted, stir in the sugar and cook until it melts and becomes bubbly, stirring all the while, less than 1 minute.

5 Add the carrots and vinegar; toss over the heat for 1 minute to glaze the carrots evenly and thoroughly.

TESTERS' NOTES
• Although it's not necessary to peel carrots for braises and stews (just make sure they're well cleaned), peel them here because of the aesthetics of the final dish: those bright orange bits lacquered with a sweet glaze.
• The vinegar slightly mitigates the sweetness and so creates more sophisticated fare, not simply a dessert masquerading as a vegetable side.
• If desired, add some herbs with the vinegar: up to 2 teaspoons minced fresh oregano leaves or ½ tablespoon stemmed thyme leaves. You can also give the dish a little heat by adding up to 2 teaspoons Sichuan peppercorns or ½ teaspoon red pepper flakes with the sugar.

BUTTERY CARROTS WITH PANCETTA AND LEEKS

EFFORT: **A LOT** • PRESSURE: **HIGH** • TIME UNDER PRESSURE: **5 OR 7 MINUTES** • RELEASE: **QUICK** • SERVES: **4 TO 6**

4 ounces pancetta, diced
1 medium leek, white and pale green parts only, sliced lengthwise, washed, and thinly sliced
¼ cup moderately sweet white wine, such as a dry Riesling
1 pound baby carrots
½ teaspoon ground black pepper
2 tablespoons unsalted butter, cut into small bits

1 Put the pancetta in a 6-quart stovetop pres-sure cooker set over medium heat or in a 6-quart electric pressure cooker turned to the browning function. Fry until crisp and well browned, stirring occasionally, about 3 minutes.

2 Add the leek; cook, stirring often, until softened, about 1 minute. Pour in the wine and scrape up any browned bits at the bottom of the pot as it comes to a simmer.

3 Add the carrots and pepper; stir well. Scrape and pour the contents of the pressure cooker into a 1-quart, round, high-sided soufflé or baking dish. Dot with the bits of butter. Lay a piece of parchment paper on top of the dish, then a piece of aluminum foil. Seal the foil tightly over the baking dish.

4 Wipe out the (hot!) cooker, set the pressure cooker rack inside, and pour in 2 cups water. Use aluminum foil to build a sling (see page 19) for the baking dish; lower the baking dish into the cooker.

5 Lock the lid onto the pot.

STOVETOP: Set the pot over high heat and bring to high pressure (15 psi). Once this pressure has been reached, reduce the heat as much as possible while maintaining this pressure. Cook for 5 minutes.
······················ **OR** ····························
ELECTRIC: Set the machine to cook at high pressure (9–11 psi). Set the machine's timer to cook at high pressure for 7 minutes.

6 Use the quick-release method to return the pot's pressure to normal.

7 Unlock and open the pot. Use the foil sling to lift the baking dish out of the cooker. Uncover, stir well, and serve.

TESTERS' NOTES
• Like a baked casserole, this side dish offers luxurious carrots in a sweet, buttery sauce. The carrots are cooked in a baking dish to infuse them with the other flavors without a lot of liquid. They'll be slightly firmer with a deeper flavor.
• There'll be a little liquid in the baking dish, maybe more than you might like in a side dish. We prefer the sauciness here, but if you're concerned, use a slotted spoon to dish up the carrots.

Serve It Up! Sprinkle each serving with toasted white sesame seeds or chopped toasted pecans.

WINE-BRAISED ARTICHOKES

EFFORT: **A LITTLE** • PRESSURE: **HIGH** • TIME UNDER PRESSURE: **6 OR 10 MINUTES** • RELEASE: **QUICK** • SERVES: **8**

4 large globe artichokes
1 medium lemon, halved
One 4-inch fresh rosemary sprig
1 cup dry white wine, such as Pinot Grigio
1/4 cup olive oil
1/2 teaspoon salt
1/2 teaspoon ground black pepper

1 Prepare the artichokes by cutting the top third off each one; peel off the first few outer layers of leaves to reveal the more tender leaves inside. Trim the woody bits off the ends of the stems, then cut each artichoke in half through its stem. Scoop out the fuzzy choke and remove any pink, soft, inner leaves.

2 Place the eight halves in a 6-quart stovetop or electric pressure cooker. Squeeze the lemon halves over the artichokes, then drop the halves into the pressure cooker. Tuck the rosemary sprig among the artichokes; pour in the wine and oil. Sprinkle with salt and pepper.

3 Lock the lid onto the pot.

STOVETOP: Set the pot over high heat and bring it to high pressure (15 psi). Immediately reduce the heat as much as possible while still maintaining this pressure. Cook for 6 minutes.
······················ **OR** ····························
ELECTRIC: Set the machine to cook at high pressure (9–11 psi). Set the timer to cook at this pressure for 10 minutes.

(continued)

4 Use the quick-release method to bring the pot's pressure back to normal.

5 Unlock and open the pot. Transfer the artichoke halves from the cooker to serving plates.

TESTERS' NOTES
• If you love artichokes but don't make them because they have to steam for too long, the pressure cooker will revolutionize your menu choices.
• The stems of some artichokes are fibrous. If yours are more than ½ inch in diameter, shave them with a vegetable peeler to reveal the more tender, inner core. If the stem looks shriveled or wrinkled, remove it completely.
• The best tool for removing the choke and inner leaves is a serrated grapefruit spoon. You can get inside the vegetable and scrape away the bits you don't want.
• Larger artichokes will have a thorn at the end of each leaf. Snip these off before cooking.
• The oil adds flavor to the artichokes—and if you serve them at room temperature, it will function almost as a marinade.

Serve It Up! Artichokes can be served warm or at room temperature. For the latter, set the lid loosely on the pot and allow them to cool in the poaching liquid for up to 3 hours. Either way, they're most often served with melted butter. Dip the individual leaves in the butter, scraping off the softer inner flesh against your upper front teeth before slicing the stem and heart and dipping these bits in butter. But there's no reason to stand on ceremony. How about cocktail sauce? Or a lemony vinaigrette? Or a Caesar dressing? Or ranch dressing? Or even sour cream?

ARTICHOKES BRAISED WITH TOMATOES AND OLIVES

EFFORT: **A LITTLE** • PRESSURE: **HIGH** • TIME UNDER PRESSURE: **6 OR 10 MINUTES** • RELEASE: **QUICK** • SERVES: **8**

One 14-ounce can diced tomatoes (about 1³/₄ cups)
¹/₄ cup pitted oil-cured black olives
2 tablespoons minced fresh basil leaves
2 teaspoons minced garlic
Up to 2 tinned anchovy fillets, minced
¹/₄ teaspoon red pepper flakes
4 large globe artichokes, trimmed and halved

1 Stir the tomatoes, olives, basil, garlic, anchovy fillets, and red pepper flakes in a 6-quart stovetop or electric pressure cooker. Add the artichoke halves; toss well.

2 Lock the lid onto the pot.

STOVETOP: Set the pot over high heat and bring it to high pressure (15 psi). Once this pressure has been reached, reduce the heat as much as possible while maintaining this pressure. Cook for 6 minutes.

···································· **OR** ····································

ELECTRIC: Set the machine to cook at high pressure (9–11 psi). Set the machine's timer to cook at high pressure for 10 minutes.

3 Use the quick-release method to drop the pot's pressure back to normal.

4 Unlock and open the pot. Transfer the artichoke halves to serving plates or a large platter; ladle the warm sauce over the vegetables.

• Here's an Italian-inspired preparation that hits all the flavor notes: sweet, sour, salty, bitter, and umami. You could even consider it a vegetarian main course, provided you have a large tossed salad and some hearty bread on the side.
• Mince the anchovies into tiny bits so they melt into the sauce. Some larger salt-packed fillets will need to be deboned; most others won't. If you're concerned about a too-assertive flavor, use just one or even half an anchovy the first time you make this dish.
• For instructions on how to trim and prep the artichokes, see step 1 of the Wine-Braised Artichokes (page 407).

SMASHED PARSNIPS WITH CARAMEL ONIONS AND MASCARPONE

EFFORT: **A LITTLE** • PRESSURE: **HIGH** • TIME UNDER PRESSURE:
5 OR 7 MINUTES • RELEASE: **QUICK** • SERVES: **8**

2 pounds medium parsnips, peeled and cut into 1-inch pieces

4 tablespoons (1/2 stick) unsalted butter

1 medium yellow onion, chopped

1/4 cup sugar

1 cup mascarpone, at room temperature

1/2 teaspoon salt

1/2 teaspoon ground black pepper

1/4 cup packed fresh parsley leaves, chopped

1 Place the parsnips in a 6-quart stovetop or electric pressure cooker. Add enough cool tap water so they're submerged by 1 inch.

2 Lock the lid onto the pot.

STOVETOP: Set the pot over high heat and bring to high pressure (15 psi). Once this pressure has been reached, reduce the heat as much as possible while maintaining this pressure. Cook for 5 minutes.

·············· **OR** ··············

ELECTRIC: Set the machine to cook at high pressure (9–11 psi). Set the machine's timer to cook at high pressure for 7 minutes.

3 Use the quick-release method to return the pot's pressure to normal.

4 Drain the parsnips in a colander set in the sink. Melt the butter in the stovetop cooker set over medium heat or the electric cooker turned to its browning function. Add the onion and cook, stirring often, until softened, about 4 minutes. Add the sugar and cook, stirring constantly, until it dissolves and begins to turn golden, about 2 minutes.

5 Take the stovetop cooker off the heat or turn off the electric cooker. Pour the parsnips into the pot: add the mascarpone, salt, and pepper. Use a potato masher to turn the mixture into a somewhat smooth if still rustic puree—the cheese should be melted throughout and the onion evenly distributed. Stir in the parsley before serving.

TESTERS' NOTES
• No, these are not carameli*zed* onions. Rather, you'll make a caramel sauce for the onions and then use that to sweeten the parsnips, turning them into a glorious side dish fit for a holiday table.
• How smoothly you smash the parsnips is a matter of taste. We like some texture, some bits with chew, about like smashed potatoes.
• Mascarpone cheese is a delicate, soft cheese, popular in Italian desserts. Substitute softened cream cheese for a less sweet, slightly more aggressive flavor.

CREAMY PUREED PARSNIPS

EFFORT: **NOT MUCH** • PRESSURE: **HIGH** • TIME UNDER PRESSURE: **5 OR 7 MINUTES** • RELEASE: **QUICK** • SERVES: **8**

2 pounds medium parsnips, peeled and
    cut into $1/2$-inch sections (about
    7 medium parsnips)

6 medium garlic cloves

4 fresh thyme sprigs

1 cup heavy cream

4 tablespoons ($1/2$ stick) unsalted butter, at
    room temperature and cut into small bits

$1/2$ teaspoon salt

$1/2$ teaspoon ground black pepper

1 Place the parsnips, garlic cloves, and thyme sprigs in a 6-quart stovetop or electric pressure cooker. Add cool tap water until they're submerged by 1 inch.

2 Lock the lid onto the pot.

STOVETOP: Set the pot over high heat and bring to high pressure (15 psi). Once this pressure has been reached, reduce the heat as much as possible while maintaining this pressure. Cook for 5 minutes.

·········· OR ··········

ELECTRIC: Set the machine to cook at high pressure (9–11 psi). Set the machine's timer to cook at high pressure for 7 minutes.

3 Use the quick-release method to drop the pot's pressure back to normal.

4 Unlock and open the cooker. Drain the parsnips and garlic in a colander set in the sink; set aside the garlic cloves. Put the parsnips and thyme back in the cooker; add the cream and butter. Set the stovetop cooker over medium heat or turn the electric cooker to its browning function; bring the sauce to a simmer, uncovered, stirring occasionally. Simmer for 2 minutes, stirring often.

5 Discard the thyme sprigs. Add the reserved garlic as well as the salt and pepper. Use an immersion blender in the pot to create a thick puree.

TESTERS' NOTES
• Forget mashed potatoes! Here's a rich, creamy side dish, a good change from the usual.
• There's quite a bit of garlic flavor in the puree. For less, add all the cloves to the cooker but use fewer in the blender.
• For a silkier puree, use 3 pounds medium parsnips; peel them and cut them in half lengthwise. Cut the more tender flesh off the solid, white core; discard the cores. Proceed with the recipe as directed.
• For pitch-perfect aesthetics (and a slightly muskier flavor), substitute ground white pepper for the black pepper.
• If you don't have an immersion blender, you can make the puree in a large blender. Remove the center knob in the lid to avoid a pressure build-up, setting a clean towel over the hole to avoid splatters in the kitchen.

HARVARD BEETS

EFFORT: **A LITTLE** • PRESSURE: **HIGH** • TIME UNDER PRESSURE: **20 OR 30 MINUTES** • RELEASE: **QUICK** • SERVES: **6**

3 pounds large beets (about 8 large
    beets), trimmed

$1/3$ cup cider vinegar

2 tablespoons orange marmalade

2 teaspoons cornstarch

1 tablespoon unsalted butter

$1/2$ teaspoon salt

1 Place the beets and 2 cups water in a 6-quart stovetop or electric pressure cooker.

2 Lock the lid onto the pot.

STOVETOP: Set the pot over high heat and bring to high pressure (15 psi). Once this pressure has been reached, reduce the heat as much as possible while maintaining this pressure. Cook for 20 minutes.

·········· OR ··········

ELECTRIC: Set the machine to cook at high pressure (9–11 psi). Set the machine's timer to cook at high pressure for 30 minutes.

3 Use the quick-release method to bring the pot's pressure back to normal.

4 Drain the beets in a colander set in the sink; rinse with cool water so you can handle them. Slip off the skins and quarter the beets. Pour the vinegar into the cooker; set the stovetop pot over medium heat or turn the electric pot to its browning function. Bring the vinegar to a simmer, then whisk in the marmalade, cornstarch, butter, and salt. Continue whisking until thickened and bubbling, about 1 minute. Take the pot off the heat or turn it off, add the beets, and toss well to coat.

TESTERS' NOTES
• Harvard beets were a 1950s staple: a sweet-and-sour thickened sauce around tender, earthy beets. We've simplified the recipe, but added orange marmalade for a sweet pop against the sauce.
• The skins should come right off the beets after they've been cooked at high pressure. You can use a paring knife to get them started if they seem stubborn.
• To remove beet stains from yours hands, fill your palm with coarse salt, add some liquid soap, and rub your hands together under warm, running water to remove as much of the staining as possible. Rinse well, then moisturize afterward since the salt will dry out your skin. Or skip this whole process and wear latex gloves.

RATATOUILLE

EFFORT: **A LITTLE** • PRESSURE: **HIGH** • TIME UNDER PRESSURE: **4 OR 6 MINUTES** • RELEASE: **QUICK** • SERVES: **6**

2 tablespoons dry vermouth
1 tablespoon canned tomato paste
3 tablespoons olive oil
1 small red onion, chopped
1 tablespoon minced garlic
1 large eggplant (about 1 pound), stemmed and cut into 1-inch cubes (no need to peel)
2 medium red bell peppers, stemmed, cored, and chopped
2 medium zucchini, chopped
2 pounds Roma (plum) tomatoes, chopped
1 tablespoon packed fresh rosemary leaves, minced
1 tablespoon fresh thyme leaves
1/2 teaspoon salt
1/2 teaspoon ground black pepper

1 Whisk the vermouth and tomato paste in a small bowl until smooth.

2 Heat the oil in a 6-quart stovetop pressure cooker set over medium heat or in a 6-quart electric pressure cooker turned to the browning function. Add the onion and cook, stirring often, until softened, about 4 minutes.

3 Add the garlic and cook until aromatic, less than a minute. Stir in the eggplant, bell peppers, and zucchini. Cook, stirring often, for 1 minute; then add the tomatoes, rosemary, thyme, salt, and pepper. Stir over the heat until the tomatoes just begin to break down, about 2 minutes. Stir in the vermouth mixture until everything is coated.

(continued)

4 Lock the lid onto the pot.

STOVETOP: Raise the heat to high and bring the pot to high pressure (15 psi). Once this pressure has been reached, reduce the heat as much as possible while maintaining this pressure. Cook for 4 minutes.

·······································**OR**·······························

ELECTRIC: Set the machine to cook at high pressure (9–11 psi). Set the machine's timer to cook at high pressure for 6 minutes.

5 Use the quick-release method to return the pressure to normal.

6 Unlock and open the cooker. Stir well before serving.

TESTERS' NOTES
• The pressure cooker allows this classic side dish to become meltingly smooth. You won't end up with a thick, reduced ratatouille but instead with a velvety vegetable stew.
• You want fairly even, ¾-inch pieces among the bell peppers, zucchini, and tomatoes with slightly larger chunks for the eggplant.
• We like a slightly chunkier ratatouille, the vegetables maintaining some toothy texture. If you like a smoother side dish, use a natural release rather than the quick-release method.
• You can substitute dry white wine (a bit sweeter) for the dry vermouth.

CAPONATA

EFFORT: **A LITTLE** · PRESSURE: **HIGH** · TIME UNDER PRESSURE: **5 OR 8 MINUTES** · RELEASE: **QUICK** · SERVES: **8**

⅓ **cup red wine vinegar**
2 **tablespoons sugar**
½ **teaspoon red pepper flakes**
½ **teaspoon salt**

¼ **cup olive oil**
1 **large yellow onion, chopped**
2 **Roma (plum) tomatoes, chopped**
2 **medium eggplants (about ¾ pound each), stemmed and diced into ½-inch pieces (no need to peel)**
3 **medium celery stalks, diced**
¼ **cup pine nuts**
1 **tablespoon drained capers, rinsed**
½ **teaspoon ground cinnamon**
½ **teaspoon dried thyme**

1 Whisk the vinegar, sugar, red pepper flakes, and salt in a small bowl until the sugar dissolves.

2 Heat the oil in a 6-quart stovetop pressure cooker set over medium heat or in a 6-quart electric pressure cooker turned to the browning function. Add the onion; cook, stirring often, until soft, about 4 minutes.

3 Add the tomatoes; cook, stirring often, until they begin to break down, about 2 minutes. Add the eggplants, celery, pine nuts, capers, cinnamon, and thyme; stir well over the heat. Pour in the vinegar mixture; stir again.

4 Lock the lid onto the pot.

STOVETOP: Raise the heat to high and bring the pot to high pressure (15 psi). Once this pressure has been reached, reduce the heat as much as possible while maintaining this pressure. Cook for 5 minutes.

·······································**OR**·······························

ELECTRIC: Set the machine to cook at high pressure (9–11 psi). Set the machine's timer to cook at high pressure for 8 minutes.

5 Use the quick-release method to bring the pot's pressure back to normal.

6 Unlock and open the cooker. Stir well before serving.

- This classic Italian dish could also be a spread on slices of crunchy toast, a great appetizer before a festive meal.
- The cooking time is a little longer here than for Ratatouille (page 411) since we want the vegetables to break down even more into a smoother finish.
- Diced celery is different from thinly sliced celery. To dice the stalks, cut them lengthwise into three long pieces, then slice these into small bits.
- We added a pinch of cinnamon for a slightly sweet, warming taste in the final dish. You can omit it and substitute red pepper flakes for a spicier dish.

BUTTERNUT SQUASH PUREE

EFFORT: **A LITTLE** · PRESSURE: **HIGH** · TIME UNDER PRESSURE: **4 OR 6 MINUTES** · RELEASE: **NATURAL** · SERVES: **6**

1 large butternut squash (2¹/₂ pounds), peeled, seeded, and cut into 2-inch cubes
1 cup plain Greek yogurt
¹/₄ cup tahini
2 tablespoons olive oil
2 tablespoons honey
2 teaspoons minced garlic
¹/₂ teaspoon salt
2 tablespoons packed fresh cilantro leaves, minced

1 Place the squash and 2 cups water in a 6-quart stovetop or electric pressure cooker.

2 Lock the lid onto the pot.

STOVETOP: Set the pot over high heat and bring it to high pressure (15 psi). Once this pressure has been reached, reduce the heat as much as possible while maintaining this pressure. Cook for 4 minutes.

········· OR ·········

ELECTRIC: Set the machine to cook at high pressure (9–11 psi). Set the machine's timer to cook at high pressure for 6 minutes.

3 Reduce the pressure.

STOVETOP: Set the pot off the heat and let its pressure come back to normal naturally, about 8 minutes.

········· OR ·········

ELECTRIC: Turn off the machine or unplug it so it doesn't flip to its keep-warm setting. Let its pressure return to normal naturally, 8 to 12 minutes.

If the pressure hasn't return to normal within 12 minutes, use the quick-release method to bring it back to normal.

4 Unlock and open the pot. Drain the squash in a colander set in the sink. Add the squash to a large food processor fitted with the chopping blade; add the yogurt, tahini, olive oil, honey, garlic, and salt. Cover and process until smooth, scraping down the inside of the processor at least once. Scrape the puree into a large serving bowl. Stir in the cilantro before serving.

TESTERS' NOTES
- This is a Middle Eastern-inspired preparation, a sweet and tangy mix of spices and aromatics with the autumnal squash. Tahini and honey are a wonderful match-up: the earthy sesame seed paste matches well with some sweetness, taming it a bit so that it doesn't override the butternut squash.
- For an easier prep, buy 2 pounds precut butternut squash, then cut any larger cubes into the stated size here.
- Spoon the puree into a baking dish and chill for up to 3 days. It will become thicker and can be used as a spread in wraps or pita pockets (along with chopped tomatoes and lettuce), or as a dip for chips and cut-up vegetables.

DELICATA SQUASH PUREE WITH APPLES, WINE, AND CREAM

EFFORT: **A LITTLE** • PRESSURE: **HIGH** • TIME UNDER PRESSURE: **10 OR 15 MINUTES** • RELEASE: **QUICK** • SERVES: **6**

3 large delicata squash (about 1 pound each)

1/2 cup moderately dry white wine, such as Sauvignon Blanc

1/2 cup unsweetened smooth applesauce

2 tablespoons honey

1/2 teaspoon ground cinnamon

1/4 teaspoon salt

2 tablespoons unsalted butter

1/4 cup heavy cream

1 Halve the squash lengthwise, then use a spoon to scrape out the seeds and their membranes inside each half. Remove any woody stems and slice the squash in half widthwise.

2 Whisk the wine, applesauce, honey, cinnamon, and salt in a 6-quart stovetop or electric pressure cooker until smooth. Stand the squash pieces cut side down but against each other in the liquid.

3 Lock the lid onto the pot.

STOVETOP: Set the pot over high heat and bring it to high pressure (15 psi). Once this pressure has been reached, reduce the heat as much as possible while maintaining this pressure. Cook for 10 minutes.

···················· **OR** ····················

ELECTRIC: Set the machine to cook at high pressure (9–11 psi). Set the machine's timer to cook at high pressure for 15 minutes.

4 Use the quick-release method to return the pot's pressure to normal.

5 Unlock and open the cooker. Transfer the squash pieces to a large cutting board; cool the squash and the liquid separately for 10 minutes.

6 Working over the cooker's pot, use a spoon to scrape the squash flesh off the skin, letting the flesh fall into the pot; discard the skin. Set the stovetop cooker over medium heat or turn the electric cooker to its browning function. Whisk in the butter until melted, then whisk in the cream until smooth and bubbling. Serve at once.

TESTERS' NOTES
• This rich side dish may be perfect for your holiday table.
• The poaching ingredients actually become the basis of the dish itself, rather than a throwaway flavoring. Use a high-quality smooth applesauce to get plenty of flavor into the final dish.

SAGE-BUTTER SPAGHETTI SQUASH

EFFORT: **A LITTLE** • PRESSURE: **HIGH** • TIME UNDER PRESSURE:
8 OR 12 MINUTES • RELEASE: **QUICK** • SERVES: **6**

**One 3- to 3¹/₂-pound spaghetti squash,
halved lengthwise and seeded**

6 tablespoons unsalted butter

**2 tablespoons packed fresh sage leaves,
minced**

¹/₂ teaspoon salt

¹/₂ teaspoon ground black pepper

**¹/₂ cup finely grated Parmesan cheese
(about 1 ounce)**

1 Put the squash cut side up in the cooker;
add 1 cup water.

2 Lock the lid onto the pot.

> **STOVETOP:** Set the pot over high heat and bring
> it to high pressure (15 psi). Once this pressure has
> been reached, reduce the heat as much as possible
> while keeping this pressure constant. Cook for
> 8 minutes.
>
> ·······················**OR**························
>
> **ELECTRIC:** Set the machine to cook at high pres-
> sure (9–11 psi). Set the machine's timer to cook at
> high pressure for 12 minutes.

3 Use the quick-release method to bring the
pot's pressure back to normal.

4 Unlock and open the cooker. Transfer the
squash halves to a cutting board; cool for
10 minutes. Discard the liquid in the cooker.
Use a fork to scrape the spaghetti-like flesh
off the skin and onto the cutting board; discard the skins.

5 Melt the butter in the stovetop cooker over
medium heat or in the electric cooker turned
to its browning function. Stir in the sage,
salt, and pepper, then add all of the squash.
Stir and toss over the heat until well combined and heated through, about 2 minutes.
Add the cheese, toss well, and serve.

TESTERS' NOTES

• Spaghetti squash is something of a natural miracle: a
squash that turns into vegetable spaghetti when cooked. If
you haven't tried it before, here's a rather straightforward
recipe that could become a favorite in your home. And now
it's much faster than cooking it in the oven with a lot more
of its natural flavor intact.

• Stirring those spaghetti squash threads in the pot can
be a bit of a pain. Two large forks will get the job done a
little more efficiently.

Rice and Grains

The magic of the pressure cooker on grains is old news: a dish in minutes. But you may not know that the pressure cooker plumps those grains while retaining their essential chew. That's the true magic: faster cooking, better texture.

In this section, we often use the pressure cooker as a two-in-one appliance: itself plus a rice cooker. A rice cooker uses moisture to rehydrate and soften the grains, then drops the heat and steams them to become tender without turning mushy. We use the quick-release method to stop the cooking just before the grains are tender, then set the pot aside and let them steam for 10 minutes.

If you're interested in the basics of rice, consider these formulas:

- For 1 cup long-grain white rice (like white basmati or jasmine), add 1½ cups water, a little salt, and 1 tablespoon oil or butter, if desired; lock the lid onto the pot, bring it to high pressure, cook for 3 minutes in a stovetop pot or 4 minutes in an electric model; then let the pressure come back to normal naturally. Double or triple the servings at will but never go above the max-fill line.

- For 1 cup long-grain brown rice (like brown basmati), add 1¾ cups plus 1 tablespoon water, a little salt, and 1 tablespoon oil or butter (which will cut down on the foaming); lock the lid onto the pot, bring it to high pressure, and cook at high pressure for 25 minutes in a stovetop pot or 31 minutes in an electric one. Then turn off the heat and let the pressure come back to normal naturally. Double at will.

Most supermarkets carry a selection, rather than the full range of grains. Follow the instructions exactly. There can be foaming problems associated with whole grains. And wild rice comes in distinct varieties with distinct timing issues. For now, suffice it to say that you can get these satisfying side dishes on the table in minutes *and* they'll be better than if you had cooked them stovetop.

BUTTERY RICE WITH TOMATOES AND CINNAMON

EFFORT: **NOT MUCH** • PRESSURE: **HIGH** • TIME UNDER PRESSURE:
10 OR 15 MINUTES • RELEASE: **MODIFIED QUICK** • SERVES: **6**

2¹/₂ cups vegetable or chicken broth

One 14-ounce can diced tomatoes (about
   1³/₄ cups)

1¹/₂ cups long-grain white rice, such as
   basmati or jasmine

4 tablespoons (¹/₂ stick) unsalted butter,
   cut into small pieces

One 4-inch cinnamon stick

¹/₂ teaspoon salt

1 Mix the broth, tomatoes, rice, butter, cinnamon stick, and salt in a 6-quart stovetop or electric pressure cooker.

2 Lock the lid onto the pot.

STOVETOP: Set the pot over high heat and bring to high pressure (15 psi). Once this pressure has been reached, reduce the heat as much as possible while maintaining this pressure. Cook for 10 minutes.

·············· **OR** ··············

ELECTRIC: Set the machine to cook at high pressure (9–11 psi). Set the machine's timer to cook at high pressure for 15 minutes.

3 Use the quick-release method to reduce the pot's pressure to normal but do not open the pot. Set aside for 10 minutes to steam the rice.

4 Unlock and open the cooker. Remove the cinnamon stick and stir well before serving.

TESTERS' NOTES
• Here's a simplified version of Spanish rice—but way more buttery.
• Vegetable broth will give the dish a cleaner, sweeter finish; chicken broth, a bit more savory and certainly heftier.
• Basmati rice will be less aromatic than jasmine, which adds a fragrant herbal finish.
• For more heat, substitute a 14-ounce can of diced tomatoes with chiles for the regular tomatoes.

SAFFRON BASMATI RICE

EFFORT: **NOT MUCH** • PRESSURE: **HIGH** • TIME UNDER PRESSURE:
10 OR 15 MINUTES • RELEASE: **MODIFIED QUICK** • SERVES: **6**

¹/₄ teaspoon saffron threads

3 tablespoons unsalted butter

1 large yellow onion, finely chopped

¹/₂ teaspoon ground ginger

¹/₂ teaspoon salt

3 cups chicken broth

1¹/₂ cups long-grain white basmati rice

1 Mix the saffron with 1 tablespoon warm water in a small bowl. Set aside for 10 minutes.

2 Melt the butter in a 6-quart stovetop pressure cooker set over medium heat or in a 6-quart electric pressure cooker turned to the browning function. Add the onion and cook, stirring almost constantly, until golden and soft, about 4 minutes.

3 Stir in the ginger and salt, as well as the saffron and its soaking water; cook until aromatic, about 30 seconds. Pour in the broth; stir in the rice.

(continued)

4 Lock the lid onto the pot.

STOVETOP: Raise the heat to high and bring the pot to high pressure (15 psi). Once this pressure has been reached, reduce the heat as much as possible while maintaining this pressure. Cook for 10 minutes.

·················· **OR** ··················

ELECTRIC: Set the machine to cook at high pressure (9–11 psi). Set the machine's timer to cook at high pressure for 15 minutes.

5 Use the quick-release method to reduce the pot's pressure to normal but do not open the cooker. Set aside for 10 minutes to steam the rice.

6 Unlock and open the pot. Stir before serving.

TESTERS' NOTES
• If you've got a curry of any sort, even a curry rub on pork or chicken off the grill, you'll want to have this East Indian–inspired dish on the table. It offers a gentle balance of spices to complement the more complex blends in the curry rub.
• Cut the onion into bits fine enough to almost dissolve among the rice, flavoring it subtly under pressure. Stir constantly to ensure that those little bits of onion don't brown or (God forbid!) burn when they're first cooked.
• For more flavor, stir ½ cup chopped roasted pistachios into the rice after cooking.
• You can substitute ghee (clarified butter), which is a bit sweeter, for the butter.

YELLOW RICE WITH PEAS AND PEPPERS

EFFORT: **NOT MUCH** • PRESSURE: **HIGH** • TIME UNDER PRESSURE: **10 OR 15 MINUTES** • RELEASE: **MODIFIED QUICK** • SERVES: **6**

2 tablespoons canola or vegetable oil

1 medium yellow onion, chopped

1 medium red bell pepper, stemmed, cored, and chopped

½ teaspoon ground turmeric

Up to ¼ teaspoon saffron threads

1½ cups long-grain white rice, preferably jasmine

3 cups vegetable or chicken broth

¼ cup sliced pitted black olives

1 cup shelled fresh peas, or frozen peas, thawed

1 Heat the oil in a 6-quart stovetop pressure cooker set over medium heat or in a 6-quart electric pressure cooker turned to the browning function. Add the onion and bell pepper; cook, stirring often, until the onion has softened, about 4 minutes.

2 Add the turmeric and saffron; stir until aromatic, less than half a minute. Add the rice and stir over the heat for 1 minute. Stir in the broth and olives.

3 Lock the lid onto the cooker.

STOVETOP: Raise the heat to high and bring the pot to high pressure (15 psi). Once this pressure has been reached, reduce the heat as much as possible while maintaining this pressure. Cook for 10 minutes.

·················· **OR** ··················

ELECTRIC: Set the machine to cook at high pressure (9–11 psi). Set the machine's timer to cook at high pressure for 15 minutes.

4 Bring the pot's pressure back to normal using the quick-release method but do not open the cooker. Set aside for 5 minutes.

5 Unlock and open the lid. Stir in the peas. Cover again and set aside for 5 minutes to warm the peas.

TESTERS' NOTES
• Why buy those packages of yellow rice mix with all their chemical chicanery when you can make this dish quickly without any fake stuff?
• We stir the rice over the heat because we want to stain the rice with the turmeric to give the grains a vibrant yellow color.
• To skew the dish to an Italian palette, omit the saffron and add up to 1 tablespoon minced oregano leaves, as well as 1 teaspoon finely grated lemon zest with the turmeric.

RICE AND KALE

EFFORT: **NOT MUCH** • PRESSURE: **HIGH** • TIME UNDER PRESSURE: **10 OR 15 MINUTES** • RELEASE: **MODIFIED QUICK** • SERVES: **6**

1 tablespoon olive oil

1 tablespoon minced garlic

$\frac{1}{2}$ teaspoon cumin seeds

8 ounces kale, washed, stemmed, and chopped (about 2 cups packed)

3 cups vegetable, chicken, or beef broth

$1\frac{1}{3}$ cups long-grain white basmati rice

1 Heat the oil in a 6-quart stovetop pressure cooker set over medium heat or in a 6-quart electric pressure cooker turned to the browning function. Add the garlic and cumin; stir until aromatic, until the cumin seeds start to pop, about 1 minute.

2 Add the kale and stir until wilted, about 1 minute. Stir in the broth and scrape up any browned bits in the bottom of the cooker. Add the rice and stir well.

3 Lock the lid onto the pot.

STOVETOP: Raise the heat to high and bring the pot to high pressure (15 psi). Once this pressure has been reached, reduce the heat as much as possible while maintaining this pressure. Cook for 10 minutes.

······ **OR** ······

ELECTRIC: Set the machine to cook at high pressure (9–11 psi). Set the machine's timer to cook at high pressure for 15 minutes.

4 Bring the pot's pressure back to normal with the quick-release method but do not open the cooker. Set aside for 10 minutes to steam the rice.

5 Unlock and open the cooker. Stir before serving.

TESTERS' NOTES
• Vegetable broth will make the lightest dish, perhaps best with a roast chicken. Chicken broth will make a silkier and richer side, better with the bigger flavor of an Italian-spice–rubbed pork loin. And beef broth will offer a hefty, wintry side, almost a meal in itself.
• To take the dish over the top with a savory finish, use veal stock or a thinned-out veal demi-glace available at high-end supermarkets.

Serve It Up! Although a side dish, this recipe could become a great lunch with a fried egg on each serving.

RICE AND MUSHROOMS

EFFORT: **NOT MUCH** • PRESSURE: **HIGH** • TIME UNDER PRESSURE:
10 OR 15 MINUTES • RELEASE: **MODIFIED QUICK** • SERVES: **6**

2 tablespoons peanut oil

8 medium scallions, thinly sliced

8 ounces baby bella or cremini
mushrooms, thinly sliced

1½ cups long-grain white rice, preferably
jasmine

1 tablespoon minced fresh ginger

3 cups chicken broth

2 tablespoons soy sauce

2 tablespoons mirin

1 Heat the oil in a 6-quart stovetop pressure cooker set over medium heat or in a 6-quart electric pressure cooker turned to the browning function. Add the scallions and mushrooms; cook, stirring often, until both soften and the mushrooms give off their liquid, about 5 minutes.

2 Add the rice and ginger; stir for 1 minute. Pour in the broth, soy sauce, and mirin; scrape up any browned bits in the bottom of the cooker.

3 Lock the lid onto the pot,

STOVETOP: Set the machine to cook at high pressure (9–11 psi). Set the machine's timer to cook at high pressure for 10 minutes.

·························· **OR** ··························

ELECTRIC: Raise the heat to high and bring the pot to high pressure (15 psi). Once this pressure has been reached, reduce the heat as much as possible while maintaining this pressure. Cook for 15 minutes.

4 Use the quick-release method to return the pot's pressure to normal but do not open the cooker. Set aside for 10 minutes to steam the rice.

5 Unlock and open the cooker. Stir before serving.

TESTERS' NOTES
• This Asian-flavored side dish will make a hefty bed for aromatic stir-fries or braises, particularly those with chiles, chile paste, or other hot bits in the mix.
• Cook the mushrooms in step 1 until the pot is again dry. Their excess moisture can bog down the dish.
• You can substitute thinly sliced shiitake mushroom caps (for earthier flavor) for the baby bella mushrooms and/or dry white wine plus ½ tablespoon sugar for the mirin.

GREEN RICE

EFFORT: **NOT MUCH** • PRESSURE: **HIGH** • TIME UNDER PRESSURE:
22 OR 33 MINUTES • RELEASE: **MODIFIED QUICK** • SERVES: **6**

2 tablespoons unsalted butter

2 medium shallots, minced

2 cubanelle peppers (Italian frying
peppers), stemmed, cored, and minced

1½ cups long-grain brown rice, such as
brown basmati

3½ cups vegetable or chicken broth

1 cup packed fresh parsley leaves,
minced

⅓ cup packed fresh cilantro leaves,
minced

½ teaspoon salt

¼ teaspoon cayenne

1 Melt the butter in a 6-quart stovetop pressure cooker set over medium heat or in a 6-quart stovetop pressure cooker turned to the browning function. Add the shallots and peppers; cook, stirring often, until softened, no more than 2 minutes.

2 Add the rice and stir for 1 minute. Stir in the broth, parsley, cilantro, salt, and cayenne.

3 Lock the lid onto the pot.

STOVETOP: Raise the heat to high and bring the pot to high pressure (15 psi). Once this pressure has been reached, reduce the heat as much as possible while maintaining this pressure. Cook for 22 minutes.

·················· OR ··················

ELECTRIC: Set the machine to cook at high pressure (9–11 psi). Set the machine's timer to cook at high pressure for 33 minutes.

4 Use the quick-release function to drop the pot's pressure to normal but do not open the cooker. Set aside to steam the rice for 10 minutes.

5 Unlock and open the pot. Stir well before serving.

TESTERS' NOTES
• Green rice is a Latin American side, often served with grilled meat and beans. We prefer the dish with brown rice because its nutty taste and firmer texture work better against the herbs and peppers.
• Mince the vegetables into tiny bits, each smaller than a grain of rice, so that they'll keep the dish from becoming a pilaf (that is, a mélange of rice and chopped vegetables).
• You can substitute 2 medium poblano chiles (hotter) or 1 medium green bell pepper (milder) for the cubanelles.

BROWN RICE PILAF with TOMATOES, OLIVES, and FETA

EFFORT: **NOT MUCH** • PRESSURE: **HIGH** • TIME UNDER PRESSURE: **22 OR 33 MINUTES** • RELEASE: **MODIFIED QUICK** • SERVES: **6**

3 tablespoons olive oil

2 large globe or beefsteak tomatoes, chopped

1 tablespoon packed fresh oregano leaves, chopped

$1/2$ teaspoon salt

$1/2$ teaspoon ground black pepper

$1^1/_2$ cups long-grain brown rice, such as brown basmati

$2^1/_2$ cups chicken broth

$1/_3$ cup chopped pitted black olives

$1/_3$ cup packed fresh parsley leaves, chopped

$2^1/_2$ ounces feta cheese, crumbled

1 Heat the oil in a 6-quart stovetop pressure cooker set over medium heat or in a 6-quart electric pressure cooker turned to the browning function. Add the tomatoes, oregano, salt, and pepper; cook, stirring often, until the tomato begins to break down, about 3 minutes.

2 Stir in the rice and cook for 1 minute. Add the broth, olives, and parsley.

3 Lock the lid onto the cooker.

STOVETOP: Raise the heat to high and bring the pot to high pressure (15 psi). Once this pressure has been reached, reduce the heat as much as you can while maintaining this pressure. Cook for 22 minutes.

(continued)

ELECTRIC: Set the machine to cook at high pressure (9–11 psi). Set the machine's timer to cook at high pressure for 33 minutes.

4 Return the pot's pressure to normal using the quick-release method, but do not open the cooker. Set aside to steam the rice for 10 minutes.

5 Unlock and open the pot. Crumble in the cheese, and stir gently to incorporate it throughout the rice without breaking it up.

TESTERS' NOTES

• A pilaf is like a well-stocked rice casserole, sometimes baked. The pressure cooker keeps the rice plump and moist, a good match for the olives and tomatoes.
• There's no need to skin or seed the tomatoes; you want every drop of flavor in the final dish.

Serve It Up! Lay a piece of grilled fish or a grilled chicken breast over the rice and garnish with aromatic olive oil and plenty of freshly ground black pepper.

BROWN RICE PILAF WITH **CASHEWS** AND **LEEKS**

EFFORT: **NOT MUCH** • PRESSURE: **HIGH** • TIME UNDER PRESSURE: **22 OR 33 MINUTES** • RELEASE: **MODIFIED QUICK** • SERVES: **6**

3 tablespoons unsalted butter

1 large leek, white and pale green parts only, halved lengthwise, washed, and thinly sliced

$1/2$ teaspoon dried thyme

$1/2$ teaspoon salt

$1/8$ teaspoon ground turmeric

$1^1/2$ cups long-grain brown rice, such as brown basmati

3 cups vegetable or chicken broth

$1/2$ cup chopped roasted unsalted cashews

1 Melt the butter in a 6-quart stovetop pressure cooker set over medium heat or in a 6-quart electric pressure cooker turned to the browning function. Add the leek and cook, stirring often, until softened, about 2 minutes.

2 Stir in the thyme, salt, and turmeric until fragrant, less than half a minute. Add the rice and cook for 1 minute, stirring all the while. Pour in the broth and stir well to get any browned bits off the bottom of the cooker.

3 Lock the lid onto the pot.

STOVETOP: Raise the heat to high and bring the pot to high pressure (15 psi). Once this pressure has been reached, reduce the heat as much as possible while maintaining this pressure. Cook for 22 minutes.

ELECTRIC: Set the machine to cook at high pressure (9–11 psi). Set the machine's timer to cook at high pressure for 33 minutes.

4 Use the quick-release method to return the pot's pressure to normal but do not open the cooker. Set aside for 10 minutes to steam the rice.

5 Unlock and open the pot. Stir in the chopped cashews before serving.

TESTERS' NOTES

• Make sure you use *roasted* unsalted cashews, not raw unsalted cashews (which are not very tasty). If you can find only salted cashews, omit the additional salt.
• The dried thyme gives the dish a slightly musky earthiness, a better match to the sweet cashews and rice.

BROWN RICE AND LENTILS WITH CARAMELIZED ONIONS

EFFORT: **A LITTLE** · PRESSURE: **HIGH** · TIME UNDER PRESSURE: **23 OR 35 MINUTES** · RELEASE: **NATURAL** · SERVES: **8**

5 tablespoons olive oil

3 large onions, halved through the root (flatter) end, then sliced into thin half-moons

1 teaspoon coriander seeds

1 teaspoon cumin seeds

$1/2$ teaspoon ground turmeric

$1/2$ teaspoon ground allspice

$1/2$ teaspoon ground cinnamon

2 cups long-grain brown rice, preferably basmati

1 teaspoon sugar

1 teaspoon ground black pepper

$1/2$ teaspoon salt

$4^1/2$ cups vegetable or chicken broth

$1/2$ cup green lentils (French lentils or lentils de Puy)

1 Heat 1½ tablespoons oil in a 6-quart stovetop pressure cooker set over medium heat or in a 6-quart electric pressure cooker turned to the browning function. Add half the onions and cook until well browned and crisp at the edges, at least 10 minutes, stirring occasionally. Transfer the cooked onions to a large bowl; repeat with 1½ tablespoons more oil and the rest of the onions.

2 Add the remaining 2 tablespoons oil to the cooker; stir in the coriander, cumin, turmeric, allspice, and cinnamon until aromatic, about 1 minute. Add the rice, sugar, pepper, and salt; stir for 1 minute. Stir in the broth, scraping up any brown bits in the cooker. Stir in the lentils.

3 Lock the lid onto the pot.

STOVETOP: Raise the heat to high and bring the pot to high pressure (15 psi). Once this pressure has been reached, reduce the heat as much as possible while maintaining this pressure. Cook for 23 minutes.

······································ OR ································

ELECTRIC: Set the pot to cook at high pressure (9–11 psi). Set the machine's timer to cook at high pressure for 35 minutes.

4 Reduce the pressure.

STOVETOP: Set the pot off the heat and let its pressure come back to normal naturally, about 14 minutes.

······································ OR ································

ELECTRIC: Turn off the machine or unplug it so it doesn't flip to the keep-warm setting. Let its pressure return normal naturally, 14 to 20 minutes.

5 Unlock and open the cooker. Spoon the caramelized onions on top of the rice; set the lid back on the cooker without locking it in place, and set aside for 10 minutes to warm the onions. Serve by scooping up big spoonfuls with onions and rice in each.

TESTERS' NOTES

• Here's a quick take on mujadarra, a highly spiced Middle Eastern rice dish. It would be great with any roast or grilled meat, like a tenderloin off the grill or roasted game hens.

• Although white rice is most often used for this dish, brown offers a more nutty flavor and a better texture after cooking under pressure. It sure stands up to the spices!

BROWN RICE AND BARLEY WITH SWEET POTATOES AND CHESTNUTS

EFFORT: **NOT MUCH** · PRESSURE: **HIGH** · TIME UNDER PRESSURE: **25 OR 40 MINUTES** · RELEASE: **NATURAL** · SERVES: **6**

3 tablespoons peanut oil

8 medium scallions, thinly sliced

2 tablespoons minced fresh ginger

2 teaspoons minced garlic

1 cup medium-grain brown rice, such as brown Arborio

$1/2$ cup pearled barley

$1/4$ cup soy sauce

$1/4$ cup mirin

$2^{1}/2$ cups vegetable broth

1 large sweet potato (about 1 pound), peeled and cut into $1^{1}/2$-inch cubes

$1^{1}/2$ cups jarred roasted chestnuts

1 Heat the oil in a 6-quart stovetop pressure cooker set over medium heat or in a 6-quart electric pressure cooker turned to the browning function. Add the scallions, ginger, and garlic; cook, stirring often, until the scallions soften, about 2 minutes.

2 Add the rice and barley; cook for 1 minute, stirring constantly, to coat the grains in the aromatics and oil. Pour in the soy sauce and mirin; stir well to scrape up any browned bits in the cooker. Pour in the broth; stir in the sweet potato and chestnuts.

3 Lock the lid onto the cooker.

STOVETOP: Raise the heat to high and bring the pot to high pressure (15 psi). Once this pressure has been reached, reduce the heat as much as possible while maintaining this pressure. Cook for 25 minutes.

·············· OR ··············

ELECTRIC: Set the machine to cook at high pressure (9–11 psi). Set the machine's timer to cook at high pressure for 40 minutes.

4 Reduce the pressure.

STOVETOP: Set the pot off the heat and let its pressure come back to normal naturally, about 13 minutes.

·············· OR ··············

ELECTRIC: Turn off the machine or unplug it so it doesn't flip to its keep-warm setting. Let its pressure return to normal naturally, 13 to 18 minutes.

5 Unlock and open the pot. Stir well before serving.

TESTERS' NOTES

• This dish is modeled after autumn rice, a Japanese favorite served at the harvest of the rice crop. The medium-grain rice gives the dish a slight stickiness overall, but with a great, firm chew in each grain.

• Natural release allows the sweet potatoes to continue to soften with the rice. Make sure the vegetable is cut into small cubes so they're not too mushy or too hard after cooking.

• You can substitute dry white wine, dry vermouth, or dry sherry plus 1 tablespoon sugar for the mirin.

Serve It Up! Stir in chopped ham after cooking for a hearty meal.

WILD RICE PILAF WITH PEARS AND PECANS

EFFORT: **A LITTLE** · PRESSURE: **HIGH** · TIME UNDER PRESSURE:
28 OR 43 MINUTES · RELEASE: **QUICK** · SERVES: **6**

1 cup black wild rice (about 5¼ ounces)

2 tablespoons unsalted butter

½ cup chopped pecans

1 large ripe pear, preferably Bartlett,
    cored and chopped

2 medium scallions, thinly sliced

1 medium celery stalk, thinly sliced

1 tablespoon packed fresh sage leaves,
    minced

½ teaspoon salt

1 Pour the wild rice into a 6-quart stovetop or electric pressure cooker; add enough cool tap water so that the wild rice is submerged by 2 inches.

2 Lock the lid onto the cooker.

STOVETOP: Set the pot over high heat and bring it to high pressure (15 psi). Once this pressure has been reached, reduce the heat as much as possible while maintaining this pressure. Cook for 28 minutes.

·············· **OR** ··············

ELECTRIC: Set the machine to cook at high pressure (9–11 psi). Set the machine's timer to cook at high pressure for 43 minutes.

3 Use the quick-release method to drop the pot's pressure back to normal.

4 Unlock and open the cooker. Drain the wild rice in a fine-mesh colander set in the sink. Wipe out the cooker.

5 Melt the butter in the stovetop cooker set over medium heat or in the electric cooker turned to the browning function. Add the pecans; cook, stirring often, until lightly browned, about 2 minutes. Add the pear, scallion, celery, sage, and salt; stir over the heat for 1 minute.

6 Pour in the cooked rice; set the stovetop pot off the heat or turn the electric cooker off. Cover and set aside for 5 minutes to blend the flavors. Uncover and stir well before serving.

TESTERS' NOTES

• Wild rice gets unexpectedly creamy in the pressure cooker, preserving its plump texture without waterlogging the natural, grassy flavors.

• Make sure the pear is fragrant: if it doesn't smell like anything, it won't taste like anything. That sweet pear balances the other, subtle flavors in the rice, celery, and sage.

• Black wild rice is a cultivar grown specifically for modern rice production. It is the most common form of wild rice sold in North American supermarkets. If you find gray or green hand-harvested wild rice—probably at a gourmet store or a farmers' market—the cooking times will vary wildly, from half this stated time to up to 25 percent more, depending on the varietal. You'll need to use a quick-release method and take the lid off the pot occasionally as this hand-harvested wild rice cooks to see how done it is.

WILD RICE WITH SWEET POTATOES AND CRANBERRIES

EFFORT: **A LOT** • PRESSURE: **HIGH** • TIME UNDER PRESSURE: **30 OR 45 MINUTES** • RELEASE: **QUICK, THEN QUICK** • SERVES: **6**

2 tablespoons olive oil

1 medium yellow onion, chopped

2 medium celery stalks, chopped

1 tablespoon packed fresh sage leaves, minced

2 teaspoons fresh thyme leaves

1½ cups black wild rice (about 8 ounces)

3 cups vegetable or chicken broth

1 large sweet potato (about 1 pound), peeled and diced

¼ cup dried cranberries

½ teaspoon salt

½ teaspoon ground black pepper

1 Heat the olive oil in a 6-quart stovetop pressure cooker set over medium heat or in a 6-quart electric pressure cooker turned to the browning function. Add the onion and celery; cook, stirring often, until the onion softens, about 4 minutes.

2 Mix in the sage and thyme; cook until fragrant, about 30 seconds. Stir in the rice and toss well to coat. Pour in the broth; stir well to get up any browned bits in the bottom of pot.

3 Lock the lid onto the cooker.

STOVETOP: Raise the heat to high and bring the pot to high pressure (15 psi). Once this pressure has been reached, reduce the heat as much as possible while maintaining this pressure. Cook for 20 minutes.

·······························OR·······························
ELECTRIC: Set the machine to cook at high pressure (9–11 psi). Set the machine's timer to cook at high pressure for 30 minutes.

4 Use the quick-release method to return the pot's pressure to normal.

5 Unlock and open the cooker. Stir in the sweet potato, cranberries, salt, and pepper.

6 Lock the lid back onto the cooker.

STOVETOP: Set the pot back over high heat and bring it back to high pressure (15 psi). Once this pressure has been reached, reduce the heat as much as possible while maintaining this pressure. Cook for 10 minutes.

·······························OR·······························
ELECTRIC: Set the machine to cook at high pressure (9–11 psi). Set the machine's timer to cook at high pressure for 15 minutes.

7 Use the quick-release method to return the pot's pressure to normal.

8 Unlock and open the cooker. Stir well before serving.

TESTERS' NOTES

• Although orange sweet potatoes are the North American standard and will give the dish a good amount of sweet notes, you can substitute white sweet potatoes. They are a little drier and starchier, offering a more complex contrast to the wild rice. Also, the overall feel of the dish won't be as sticky.

• Dice the sweet potatoes into small bits, no more than ½-inch cubes. These will cook quickly in the final stage to get tender without melting into the dish.

Serve It Up! To impress unexpected guests, use this dish as the bed for a cut-up purchased rotisserie chicken.

CHEESY CHORIZO AND HOMINY CASSEROLE

EFFORT: **A LOT** • PRESSURE: **HIGH** • TIME UNDER PRESSURE: **12 OR 18 MINUTES** • RELEASE: **NATURAL** • SERVES: **8**

1 pound dried Spanish chorizo, chopped

1 large yellow onion, chopped

1 large green bell pepper, stemmed, seeded, and chopped

1 large red bell pepper, stemmed, seeded, and chopped

1/4 cup packed fresh cilantro leaves, minced

1 teaspoon dried oregano

1 teaspoon ground cumin

Three 15-ounce cans hominy, drained and rinsed (about 5 cups)

1/2 cup heavy cream

1 1/2 cups shredded Manchego cheese, shredded (about 6 ounces)

1 Fry the chorizo bits in a 6-quart stovetop pressure cooker set over medium heat or in a 6-quart electric pressure cooker turned to the browning function until lightly browned and lots of fat has been given off into the cooker, about 4 minutes, stirring often.

2 With the chorizo still in the pot, add the onion and both bell peppers; cook, stirring often, until the onion softens, about 4 minutes. Stir in the cilantro, oregano, and cumin. Scrape the mixture in the cooker into a large bowl. Stir in the hominy, cream, and 1 cup of the shredded cheese.

3 Lightly oil the inside of a 2-quart, round, high-sided soufflé or baking dish. Scrape the contents of the bowl into this baking dish. Top with the remaining 1/2 cup cheese. Lay parchment paper over the baking dish, then seal with foil. Wipe out the cooker.

4 Set the pressure cooker rack inside the cooker and add 2 cups water. Make a sling out of aluminum foil (see page 19) and use it to lower the baking dish onto the rack. Fold down the sling a bit over the edges.

5 Lock the lid onto the pot.

STOVETOP: Set the pot over high heat and bring it to high pressure (15 psi). As soon as this pressure has been reached, reduce the heat as much as possible while maintaining this pressure. Cook for 12 minutes.

······································· **OR** ·······································

ELECTRIC: Set the machine to cook at high pressure (9–11 psi). Set the machine's timer to cook at high pressure for 18 minutes.

6 Reduce the pressure.

STOVETOP: Set the pot aside off the heat and let its pressure come back to normal naturally, about 10 minutes.

······································· **OR** ·······································

ELECTRIC: Turn off the machine or unplug it so it doesn't flip to its keep-warm setting. Let its pressure come back to normal naturally, 10 to 15 minutes.

7 Unlock and open the cooker. Use the foil sling to transfer the baking dish to a wire rack for cooling. Uncover and cool for 5 minutes before dishing up by the spoonful.

TESTERS' NOTES

• Although there's plenty of sausage in this casserole, it's really a side dish for a Tex-Mex meal. Or try this dish instead of baked beans with your next burger cookout.

• The chorizo will give off plenty of red-stained fat; if you'd like a somewhat healthier dish, you can drain off up to three-fourths of it before adding the vegetables.

• You can substitute pecorino romano or aged Asiago for the Manchego.

CREAMY CHEESY POLENTA

EFFORT: **NOT MUCH** • PRESSURE: **HIGH** • TIME UNDER PRESSURE:
8 OR 12 MINUTES • RELEASE: **QUICK** • SERVES: **6**

5 cups chicken or vegetable broth

1 cup medium-ground polenta (not instant polenta)

1 tablespoon fresh thyme leaves

1/2 teaspoon salt

1/8 teaspoon saffron threads (optional)

4 tablespoons (1/2 stick) unsalted butter, cut into small pieces

1/2 cup finely grated Parmesan cheese (about 1 ounce)

1 Mix the broth, polenta, thyme, salt, and saffron, if desired, in a 6-quart stovetop or electric pressure cooker.

2 Lock the lid onto the pot.

STOVETOP: Set the pot over high heat and bring it to high pressure (15 psi). Once this pressure has been reached, reduce the heat as much as possible while maintaining this pressure. Cook for 8 minutes.

························ **OR** ························

ELECTRIC: Set the machine to cook at high pressure (9–11 psi). Set the machine's timer to cook at high pressure for 12 minutes.

3 Use the quick-release method to return the pressure in the pot to normal.

4 Unlock and open the cooker. Whisk in the butter and cheese until the polenta is creamy. Serve at once.

TESTERS' NOTES

• Unfortunately, you need pretty good timing for polenta in the pressure cooker. If it sits more than a few minutes, it'll start to harden. But when it all works out, the reward is some of the creamiest—and certainly the easiest—polenta you've ever made.

• The saffron will make the polenta's flavor both more sophisticated (floral and herbaceous) and also earthier (a slight muskiness). Omitting it will yield an overall cleaner palate.

• For an even richer dish, add up to 1/4 cup heavy cream with the butter and cheese.

POLENTA PUDDING WITH BRIE AND APPLES

EFFORT: **A LOT** • PRESSURE: **LOW OR HIGH** • TIME UNDER
PRESSURE: **18 OR 20 MINUTES** • RELEASE: **NATURAL** • SERVES: **6**

2 cups vegetable or chicken broth

1/2 cup quick-cooking (or instant) polenta

1 cup fresh corn kernels, or frozen kernels, thawed

1 medium, moderately sweet apple, such as Gala or Fuji, peeled, cored, and chopped

2 large eggs, at room temperature and lightly beaten in a small bowl

6 ounces Brie, rind removed and broken into small pieces

1 teaspoon dried oregano

1/2 teaspoon onion powder

1/2 teaspoon salt

1/2 teaspoon ground black pepper

1 Bring the broth to a boil in a 6-quart stovetop pressure cooker over medium-high heat or in a 6-quart electric pressure cooker turned to the browning function. Add the polenta and whisk until thick and smooth, about 5 minutes. Transfer the mixture to a large bowl; cool for 10 minutes. Meanwhile, butter the inside of a high-sided 2-quart soufflé or baking dish.

2 Clean and dry the inside of the cooker. Set the pressure cooker rack in the cooker; pour in 2 cups water. Make an aluminum foil sling for the baking dish (see page 19).

3 Stir the corn, apple, eggs, and Brie into the polenta mixture. Add the oregano, onion powder, salt, and pepper. Stir well, then spoon and spread the mixture into the prepared baking dish. Use the foil sling to lower the baking dish onto the rack. Tuck the ends of the sling into the pot.

4 Lock the lid onto the cooker.

STOVETOP: Set the pot over high heat and bring to low pressure (8 psi). Once this pressure has been reached, reduce the heat as much as possible while maintaining this pressure. Cook for 18 minutes.
························ OR ························
ELECTRIC: Set the machine to cook at high pressure (9–11 psi). Set the machine's timer to cook at high pressure for 20 minutes.

5 Reduce the pressure.

STOVETOP: Set the pot off the heat and let its pressure come back to normal naturally, about 10 minutes.
························ OR ························
ELECTRIC: Turn off the machine or unplug it so it doesn't flip to its keep-warm setting. Let its pressure return to normal naturally, 10 to 12 minutes.

6 Unlock and open the cooker. Use the foil sling to lift the baking dish out of the cooker; transfer to a wire rack. Cool for 10 minutes before scooping up by the big spoonful.

TESTERS' NOTES
• You've probably never had corn pudding this creamy. The apple bits almost melt into the polenta, sweetening it a bit to further balance the Brie. You can also use Taleggio (creamier) or Camembert (stronger flavor) instead of the Brie.
• The stovetop method requires you to cook the dish at *low* pressure. If your stovetop model has only a high setting (15 psi), and no ability to adjust down to low pressure, cook for 13 minutes and then use a natural release (as stated here). At this higher pressure, the pudding will rise up high, especially along the sides of the dish, and then fall back into a concave center—not the best texture or look, but a fine dish to spoon up nonetheless.

LEMONY WHEATBERRIES AND BRUSSELS SPROUTS

EFFORT: **A LITTLE** • PRESSURE: **HIGH** • TIME UNDER PRESSURE: **25 OR 40 MINUTES** • RELEASE: **QUICK** • SERVES: **6**

1 cup wheatberries, preferably soft white

3/4 pound Brussels sprouts, thinly sliced

1 small shallot, halved and sliced into thin half-moons

3 tablespoons olive oil

2 tablespoons fresh lemon juice

2 teaspoons finely grated lemon zest

1 teaspoon fennel seeds

1/2 teaspoon salt

1/2 teaspoon ground black pepper

1 Put the wheatberries in a 6-quart stovetop or electric pressure cooker. Add enough cool tap water so that they're submerged by 2 inches.

(continued)

2 Lock the lid onto the pot.

STOVETOP: Set the pot over high heat and bring it to high pressure (15 psi). As soon as this pressure has been reached, reduce the heat as much as possible while maintaining this pressure. Cook for 25 minutes.

···············**OR**···············

ELECTRIC: Set the machine to cook at high pressure (9–11 psi). Set the machine's timer to cook at high pressure for 40 minutes.

---

3 Use the quick-release method to return the pot's pressure to normal.

4 Unlock and open the pot. Stir in the Brussels sprouts. Set the lid back on the pot without locking it; set aside for 10 minutes.

5 Unlock and open the pot. Drain the contents of the pot into a colander set in the sink. Place the wheatberries and Brussels sprouts in a large serving bowl; add the shallot, olive oil, lemon juice, lemon zest, fennel seeds, salt, and pepper. Toss well; serve warm or at room temperature.

TESTERS' NOTES
• This refreshing whole-grain side dish salad takes advantage of the unbeatable combo of Brussels sprouts and lemon. (You can also use spelt berries instead of the wheatberries.)
• The fennel seeds provide a small spark of flavor that will help the dish from becoming monotonous after the second bite. (But you can substitute caraway seeds or celery seeds for the fennel seeds.)
• There's really no need to whisk the dressing in a separate bowl for a salad this simple. Just make sure you toss the salad well before serving so that the dressing evenly coats all the ingredients.

Serve It Up! Make the wheatberries and Brussels sprouts up to 2 days in advance, storing them tightly covered in the fridge. When ready to serve, let them come back to room temperature before stirring in the dressing ingredients. For a main course, crumble up to 1 pound plain grilled salmon onto the salad; toss gently before serving.

WHEATBERRY TABBOULEH

EFFORT: **A LITTLE** • PRESSURE: **HIGH** • TIME UNDER PRESSURE: **25 OR 40 MINUTES** • RELEASE: **QUICK** • SERVES: **6**

1½ cups wheatberries, preferably hard red winter

1 large globe or beefsteak tomato, finely chopped

½ cup packed fresh parsley leaves, minced

1 small shallot, minced

3 tablespoons olive oil

2 tablespoons fresh lemon juice

1 teaspoon finely grated lemon zest

1 teaspoon salt

1 teaspoon ground black pepper

1 Place the wheatberries in a 6-quart stovetop or electric pressure cooker; add enough cool tap water so they're submerged by 2 inches.

2 Lock the lid onto the cooker.

STOVETOP: Set the pot over high heat and bring to high pressure (15 psi). Once this pressure has been reached, reduce the heat as much as possible while maintaining this pressure. Cook for 25 minutes.

·························· OR ··························

ELECTRIC: Set the machine to cook at high pressure (9–11 psi). Set the machine's timer to cook at high pressure for 40 minutes.

3 Use the quick-release method to drop the pot's pressure back to normal.

4 Unlock and open the lid. Drain the grains in a colander set in the sink. Transfer the grains to a food processor. Cover and pulse until roughly chopped.

5 Scrape the chopped grains into a serving bowl. Stir in the tomato, parsley, shallot, olive oil, lemon juice and zest, salt, and pepper.

TESTERS' NOTES

• No, you can't use traditional bulgur to make tabbouleh with a pressure cooker. You can use something better! The wheatberries offer a wheatier flavor once they've been processed into smaller bits. Plus, you'll end up with a chewy, slightly firmer tabbouleh, a better texture all around. You may never go back to the old way.

• If the holes in your colander are large, the wheatberries may slip through. Line the colander with a very large coffee filter or a layer of paper towels.

• For an Italian-inspired tabbouleh, substitute basil for the parsley and white balsamic vinegar for the lemon juice.

• You can use dried spelt berries, Kamut, or whole-grain farro for the wheatberries.

BEET TABBOULEH

EFFORT: **A LITTLE** • PRESSURE: **HIGH** • TIME UNDER PRESSURE: **20 OR 30 MINUTES** • RELEASE: **QUICK** • SERVES: **6**

1 pound medium red beets (about 8), any greens or roots trimmed

4 cups (1 quart) chicken or vegetable broth

6 medium scallions

4 fresh dill sprigs

2 cups medium-grind, quick-cooking bulgur

1/2 cup packed parsley leaves, finely chopped

3 tablespoons fresh lemon juice

2 tablespoons olive oil

1/2 teaspoon salt

1 Wash the beets but do not peel them. Place them in a 6-quart stovetop or electric pressure cooker with the broth, scallions, and dill.

2 Lock the lid onto the pot.

STOVETOP: Set the pot over high heat and bring it to high pressure (15 psi). Immediately reduce the heat as much as possible while maintaining this pressure. Cook for 20 minutes.

·························· OR ··························

ELECTRIC: Set the machine to cook at high pressure (9–11 psi). Set the machine's timer to cook at high pressure for 30 minutes.

3 Use the quick-release method to return the pot's pressure to normal.

4 Unlock and open the cooker. Set a large bowl underneath a colander set in the sink. Drain the contents into the colander, catching the cooking liquid below. Cool for 10 minutes.

(continued)

5 Discard the scallions and dill; slip the skins off the beets and chop the beets into small bits. Measure 3 cups of the caught cooking liquid into the cooker.

6 Set the stovetop model over medium heat or turn the electric cooker to its browning function; bring the liquid to a simmer. Stir in the bulgur and chopped beets. Turn off the heat or unplug the electric cooker. Set the lid onto the cooker without locking it; set aside for 30 minutes or until the water has been absorbed.

7 Uncover the pot; fluff the bulgur with a fork. Stir in the parsley, lemon juice, olive oil, and salt before serving.

TESTERS' NOTES
• Tabbouleh is said to be a prized dish in the Middle East because parsley requires water to grow, something of a luxury in the desert. We've added beets for sweetness and increased the grains because we like the wheat flavor to balance (and tame) all the parsley.
• Depending on the day's humidity (and how much ambient moisture the bulgur has absorbed), there may be a little broth left in the pot after 30 minutes of soaking. Use a large spoon to hold back the beets and bulgur as you drain the liquid out of the cooker.
• You can substitute yellow beets plus 1 teaspoon sugar for the red beets.

Serve It Up! Offer hummus and whole wheat crackers on the side.

FARRO AND PEAS

EFFORT: **A LITTLE** • PRESSURE: **HIGH** • TIME UNDER PRESSURE: **12 OR 17 MINUTES** • RELEASE: **QUICK** • SERVES: **4 TO 6**

1 cup semi-perlato farro

1 cup shelled fresh peas, or frozen peas, thawed

2 tablespoons olive oil

2 tablespoons fresh lemon juice

2 teaspoons minced fresh rosemary leaves

1 teaspoon finely grated lemon zest

$1/2$ teaspoon salt

$1/2$ teaspoon ground black pepper

1 Place the farro in a 6-quart stovetop or electric pressure cooker. Add enough cool tap water so the grains are submerged by 2 inches.

2 Lock the lid onto the pot.

STOVETOP: Set the pot over high heat and bring it to high pressure (15 psi). Once this pressure has been reached, reduce the heat as much as possible while maintaining this pressure. Cook for 12 minutes.

························· **OR** ·························

ELECTRIC: Set the machine to cook at high pressure (9–11 psi). Set the machine's timer to cook at high pressure for 17 minutes.

3 Use the quick-release method to return the pot's pressure to normal.

4 Unlock and open the cooker. Stir in the peas and set the lid back on the pot without locking it. Set aside for 2 minutes.

5 Drain the grains and peas in a colander set in the sink; rinse with cool tap water to bring them to room temperature. Drain well, shaking the colander a few times. Pour into a large serving bowl. Stir in the oil, lemon juice, rosemary, lemon zest, salt, and pepper to serve.

TESTERS' NOTES

• Semi-perlato farro (semi-pearled farro) is a compromise between the fairly non-nutritious perlato farro (with no bran or germ left on the grain) and the more time-consuming whole-grain farro (which hasn't been denuded). In this case, the germ and bran have been scored (but not removed) to promote quicker cooking.

• If you want to cook whole-grain farro in the pressure cooker, increase the cooking time to 25 minutes in a stovetop cooker at high pressure or 40 minutes in an electric cooker at high pressure.

• The rosemary and lemon juice balance each other well, the acid taking some of the hard edge off the herb's fragrance. If you're leery, substitute thyme or oregano but cut the amounts of the lemon juice and zest in half.

FARRO WITH FENNEL AND SMOKED TROUT

EFFORT: **A LITTLE** • PRESSURE: **HIGH** • TIME UNDER PRESSURE: **12 OR 17 MINUTES** • RELEASE: **QUICK** • SERVES: **4**

1 cup semi-perlato farro

1 large fennel bulb, trimmed and shaved into thin strips

1/2 cup regular or low-fat mayonnaise

1/4 cup regular or low-fat sour cream

3 tablespoons lemon juice

2 tablespoons Dijon mustard

1 teaspoon sugar

1 teaspoon ground black pepper

12 ounces smoked trout, skinned and chopped

1 Pour the farro into a 6-quart stovetop or electric pressure cooker; pour in enough water that the grains are submerged by 2 inches.

2 Lock the lid onto the cooker.

STOVETOP: Set the pot over high heat and bring it to high pressure (15 psi). Once this pressure has been reached, reduce the heat as much as possible while maintaining high pressure. Cook for 12 minutes.

·······**OR**·······

ELECTRIC: Set the machine to cook at high pressure (9–11 psi). Set the machine's timer to cook at high pressure for 17 minutes.

3 Use the quick-release method to drop the pot's pressure to normal.

4 Unlock and open the cooker. Place the fennel strips in a colander set in the sink and drain the farro into the colander over the fennel. Toss well, then let cool for 30 minutes in the colander.

5 Whisk the mayonnaise, sour cream, lemon juice, mustard, sugar, and pepper in a large serving bowl until creamy. Add the farro, fennel, and smoked trout; toss gently to coat well.

TESTERS' NOTES

• By pouring the hot liquid from the cooker onto the fennel, it blanches without your needing to dirty a saucepan.

• To shave the fennel bulb, remove the stalks and any fronds, as well as any tough or discolored outside sections of the bulb. Run the fennel bulb over a mandoline with the blade set at 1/8 inch (or 2 millimeters). You can also feed the prepared fennel bulb into the tube of a food processor fitted with the 2-millimeter slicing blade. Failing all that, cut the bulb in half, set it cut side down on your cutting board, and slice it into paper-thin strips.

• You can substitute smoked salmon for the smoked trout, but then omit the sugar.

KAMUT AND KALE

EFFORT: **A LITTLE** • PRESSURE: **HIGH** • TIME UNDER PRESSURE:
31 OR 47 MINUTES • RELEASE: **QUICK, THEN QUICK AGAIN** •
SERVES: **4 TO 6**

1 cup Kamut berries

1 pound kale, preferably curly, stemmed
    and chopped

2 tablespoons unsalted butter

1 medium yellow onion, chopped

2 tablespoons white balsamic vinegar

¹/₂ teaspoon salt

1 Place the Kamut in a 6-quart stovetop or
electric pressure cooker; add enough cool
tap water so that the grains are submerged
by 2 inches.

2 Lock the lid onto the pot.

STOVETOP: Set the pot over high heat and bring
it to high pressure (15 psi). Once this pressure has
been reached, reduce the heat as much as possible while maintaining this pressure. Cook for
30 minutes.
·······························OR······························
ELECTRIC: Set the machine to cook at high pressure (9–11 psi). Set the machine's timer to cook at
high pressure for 45 minutes.

3 Use the quick-release method to bring the
pot's pressure back to normal.

4 Unlock and open the cooker. Stir in the
chopped kale.

5 Lock the lid back onto the pot.

STOVETOP: Set the pot back over high heat and
bring it back to high pressure (15 psi). Once this
pressure has been reached, reduce the heat as
much as possible while maintaining this pressure.
Cook for 1 minute.
·······························OR······························
ELECTRIC: Set the machine to cook at high pressure once again (9–11 psi). Set the timer to cook at
high pressure for 2 minutes.

6 Use the quick-release method to bring the
pot's pressure back to normal.

7 Unlock and open the cooker. Drain the
Kamut and kale in a colander set in the sink.

8 Melt the butter in the stovetop cooker set
back over medium heat or in the stovetop
cooker turned to the browning function.
Add the onion and cook, stirring often, until
softened, about 5 minutes. Stir in the Kamut
and kale; cook for 2 minutes, stirring almost
constantly. Stir in the vinegar and salt before
serving.

TESTERS' NOTES

• A pressure cooker can double as a saucepan and thus
makes this a one-pot affair.

• Kamut is an ancient strain of khorasan wheat, trade-
marked so it can only be grown organically in the United
States and western Canada. It has a distinct fragrance, like
hot buttered popcorn. It pairs exceptionally well with kale,
giving the slightly bitter green a sweet finish that is balanced by the vinegar.

• You can substitute wheatberries for the Kamut.

KAMUT WITH PEARS, ARTICHOKES, AND PARMESAN

EFFORT: **A LITTLE** • PRESSURE: **HIGH** • TIME UNDER PRESSURE:
30 OR 45 MINUTES • RELEASE: **QUICK** • SERVES: **6**

1¼ cups Kamut

**One 9-ounce package frozen artichoke
heart quarters, thawed (about 2 cups)**

**2 large ripe pears, preferably Comice,
peeled, cored, and chopped**

2 tablespoons olive oil

2 tablespoons fresh lemon juice

1 tablespoon white balsamic vinegar

1 tablespoon finely grated lemon zest

1 teaspoon ground black pepper

**2½ ounces Parmesan cheese, shaved
(about ¾ cup)**

1 Place the Kamut in a 6-quart stovetop or electric pressure cooker; pour in enough cool tap water so that the grains are submerged by 2 inches.

2 Lock the lid onto the pot.

STOVETOP: Set the pot over high heat and bring it to high pressure (15 psi). As soon as this pressure has been reached, reduce the heat as much as possible while keeping this pressure constant. Cook for 30 minutes.

··············· **OR** ···············

ELECTRIC: Set the machine to cook at high pressure (9–11 psi). Set the machine's timer to cook at high pressure for 45 minutes.

3 Use the quick-release method to return the pot's pressure to normal.

4 Unlock and open the pot. Add the artichoke heart quarters; stir gently. Set the lid

back on the pot without locking it. Set aside for 5 minutes.

5 Open the pot and drain the Kamut and artichoke quarters in a large colander set in the sink. Transfer them to a large bowl. Add the pears, oil, lemon juice, vinegar, zest, and pepper; stir gently. Add the cheese and stir gently just to combine.

TESTERS' NOTES

• With some baba ghanouj and crunchy bread on the table, this might well be an easy supper one evening.

• If you can't find frozen artichoke heart quarters, use canned artichoke hearts packed in water. Drain them well and cut them into quarters. Add these with the pears—no need to blanch them beforehand.

• Use a cheese plane or a vegetable peeler to shave the cheese into paper-thin strips. For a more assertive flavor, use an aged dry Asiago instead of the Parmigiano-Reggiano.

• There's no salt in the dish because the cheese adds plenty of sodium. Pass more at the table for those who want it.

KASHA VARNISKES

EFFORT: **A LITTLE** • PRESSURE: **HIGH** • TIME UNDER PRESSURE:
4 OR 7 MINUTES • RELEASE: **QUICK** • SERVES: **4**

8 ounces dried farfalle (bow-tie) pasta

¾ cup kasha (roasted buckwheat)

5 tablespoons unsalted butter

2 medium red onions, chopped

1 tablespoon fresh thyme leaves

1 teaspoon sweet paprika

½ teaspoon salt

½ teaspoon ground black pepper

1 Place the pasta and kasha in a 6-quart stovetop or electric pressure cooker; add

(continued)

enough cool tap water that they're covered by 2 inches of water.

2 Lock the lid onto the pot.

STOVETOP: Set the pot over high heat and bring to high pressure (15 psi). Once this pressure has been reached, reduce the heat as much as possible while maintaining this pressure. Cook for 4 minutes.

·······························OR·······························

ELECTRIC: Set the machine to cook at high pressure (9–11 psi). Set the machine's timer to cook at high pressure for 7 minutes.

3 Use the quick-release method to bring the pot's pressure back to normal.

4 Unlock and open the pot. Drain the pasta and kasha into a large colander set in the sink. Wipe out the cooker.

5 Melt the butter in the stovetop cooker set over medium heat or in the electric cooker turned to the browning function. Add the onions and cook, stirring quite often, until beyond golden, even browned, and very soft, about 20 minutes.

6 Transfer the pasta and buckwheat to a large serving bowl; scrape the contents of the cooker into that bowl. Add the thyme, paprika, salt, and pepper; toss well to serve.

TESTERS' NOTES
• Here's an Old World side dish, once a favorite in New York delis. You'll need to search out toasted buckwheat, sometimes available in the world foods aisle of your supermarket and always available from a variety of online grocery stores.
• If you can't find roasted buckwheat, toast regular buckwheat in a large, dry skillet set over medium-low heat, stirring often, until lightly browned and very aromatic, about 5 minutes.

• The pasta will be slightly less done than you might like. Taste a piece after cooking under high pressure. If you want it softer, set the lid on the pot without locking it and set aside for 5 minutes before continuing with the recipe.

Serve It Up! Don't even think about serving this without a brisket, pastrami, corned beef, or turkey sandwich on the side!

BUCKWHEAT POLENTA

EFFORT: **NOT MUCH** • PRESSURE: **HIGH** • TIME UNDER PRESSURE: **5 OR 7 MINUTES** • RELEASE: **QUICK** • SERVES: **4 TO 6**

2 tablespoons unsalted butter
1 medium yellow or white onion, chopped
2 medium celery stalks, thinly sliced
1 tablespoon sweet paprika
2 teaspoons fresh thyme leaves
$1/2$ teaspoon salt
$1/2$ cup dry white wine, such as Pinot Grigio
$1^3/4$ cups chicken broth
1 cup kasha (roasted buckwheat)
2 tablespoons regular or low-fat sour cream

1 Melt the butter in a 6-quart stovetop pressure cooker set over medium heat or in a 6-quart electric pressure cooker turned to the browning function. Add the onion and celery; cook, stirring often, until the onion has softened, about 4 minutes.

2 Stir in the paprika. thyme, and salt until fragrant, less than a minute. Pour in the wine and scrape up any browned bits in the bottom of the cooker as it comes to a simmer. Stir in the broth and kasha.

3 Lock the lid onto the cooker.

STOVETOP: Raise the heat to high and bring the pot to high pressure (15 psi). Once this pressure has been reached, reduce the heat as much as possible while maintaining this pressure. Cook for 5 minutes.

································ **OR** ································

ELECTRIC: Set the machine to cook at high pressure (9–11 psi). Set the machine's timer to cook at high pressure for 7 minutes.

4 Use the quick-release method to bring the pot's pressure back to normal.

5 Unlock and open the pot. Stir in the sour cream. Cover without locking and set aside for 5 minutes to set up into a polenta-like texture.

TESTERS' NOTES

• Not a traditional polenta, this side dish offers a more assertive flavor, grassy and even a little bitter, so it's better with beef or game cuts.
• Buckwheat has a natural stickiness that is somewhat mitigated once it's been roasted. However, you may find the side dish clumps before it's tender. If so, add a little more broth and set aside for another 5 minutes or so to give the groats more moisture.

Serve It Up! Mound spoonfuls onto plates and garnish them with plenty of minced fresh dill fronds (and maybe a little extra butter).

WARM RYE BERRY AND WHITE BEAN SALAD WITH SMOKED VINAIGRETTE

EFFORT: **A LITTLE** • PRESSURE: **HIGH** • TIME UNDER PRESSURE: **25 OR 40 MINUTES** • RELEASE: **QUICK** • SERVES: **6**

1 cup rye berries

One 15-ounce can white beans, such as cannellini or great northern beans (about 1³/₄ cups)

2 jarred roasted red peppers, chopped

¹/₂ cup roasted almonds, chopped

1 medium shallot, minced

1 medium celery stalk, minced

¹/₄ cup olive oil

2 tablespoons sherry vinegar

1 teaspoon smoked paprika

1 teaspoon dried oregano

¹/₂ teaspoon salt

¹/₂ teaspoon ground black pepper

1 Place the rye berries in a 6-quart stovetop or electric pressure cooker. Add enough cool tap water that they are submerged by 2 inches.

2 Lock the lid onto the pot.

STOVETOP: Set the pot over high heat and bring to high pressure (15 psi). Once this pressure has been reached, reduce the heat as much as possible while maintaining this pressure. Cook for 25 minutes.

································ **OR** ································

ELECTRIC: Set the machine to cook at high pressure (9–11 psi). Set the machine's timer to cook at high pressure for 40 minutes.

3 Use the quick-release method to bring the pot's pressure back to normal.

(continued)

4 Unlock and open the pot. Pour the beans into a colander set in the sink; drain and rinse them thoroughly. Pour the rye berries over the beans, warming them up.

5 Transfer the beans and berries to a large bowl; mix in the roasted red peppers, almonds, shallot, and celery. Add the oil, vinegar, smoked paprika, oregano, salt, and pepper; toss well before serving.

TESTERS' NOTES

• Rye berries are the whole grain from which rye flour is milled. They have a slightly sour, earthy flavor, more savory than many other whole grains.

• The smoked paprika gives the dressing the flavor of a smoker without any of the work. If you want even more smoky flavor, use smoked olive oil (which you can find online and at various high-end supermarkets).

• The raw shallot and celery can have a too-aggressive taste in this salad. Make sure they're truly minced into ⅛-inch bits so they soften (and mellow) against the warm ingredients.

• If you want to make the salad in advance and serve at room temperature, make it through step 3, then set aside, lightly covered, on the counter for up to 3 hours.

• You can substitute triticale berries or hard red winter wheatberries for the rye berries.

• Never soak whole grains before they go in a pressure cooker. They can foam and clog the pressure release valve.

Serve It Up! Shave some Manchego or aged Asiago over each helping.

BUTTERY RYE BERRY AND CELERY ROOT SALAD

EFFORT: **A LITTLE** • PRESSURE: **HIGH** • TIME UNDER PRESSURE: **25 OR 40 MINUTES** • RELEASE: **QUICK** • SERVES: **4 TO 6**

¾ **cup rye berries**
1 **medium celeriac (celery root), peeled and shredded through the large holes of a box grater**
2 **tablespoons unsalted butter**
2 **tablespoons honey**
2 **tablespoons apple cider vinegar**
½ **teaspoon salt**
½ **teaspoon ground black pepper**

1 Place the rye berries in a 6-quart stovetop or electric pressure cooker; pour in enough cool tap water so the grains are submerged by 2 inches.

2 Lock the lid onto the pot.

STOVETOP: Set the pot over high heat and bring to high pressure (15 psi). Once this pressure has been reached, reduce the heat as much as possible while maintaining this pressure. Cook for 25 minutes.

······················· **OR** ·······················

ELECTRIC: Set the machine to cook at high pressure (9–11 psi). Set the machine's timer to cook at high pressure for 40 minutes.

3 Use the quick-release method to bring the pot's pressure back to normal.

4 Unlock and open the cooker. Stir in the shredded celeriac. Cover the pot without locking it and set aside for 1 minute. Drain the pot into a large colander set in the sink. Wipe out the cooker.

5 Melt the butter in the stovetop cooker set over medium heat or in the electric model turned to its browning function. Add the honey and cook for 1 minute, stirring constantly. Add the drained rye berries and celeriac; cook, stirring constantly, for 1 minute. Stir in the vinegar, salt, and pepper to serve.

TESTERS' NOTES

• Nothing beats a buttery dressing on whole grains! Cooking the honey for just a minute in the butter allows it to mellow, so it doesn't override the other ingredients.

• Sliced celeriac can brown when exposed to the air for too long. If you grate the root ahead of time, drop the pieces into a large bowl, cover with water, and stir in the juice of half a lemon.

• For an easier but less sophisticated salad, substitute 3 medium celery stalks for the celeriac; slice the stalks into almost-paper-thin slices. No need to add them to the hot water in the pot; simply add them in step 5.

BARLEY WITH SHIITAKES AND CARROTS

EFFORT: **A LITTLE** • PRESSURE: **HIGH** • TIME UNDER PRESSURE: **18 OR 25 MINUTES** • RELEASE: **QUICK, THEN QUICK AGAIN** • SERVES: **4**

1 cup pearled barley

2 medium carrots, thinly sliced

4 tablespoons (½ stick) unsalted butter

1 medium yellow or white onion, chopped

12 ounces shiitake mushroom caps, thinly sliced

2 tablespoons white wine vinegar

1 tablespoon fresh thyme leaves

½ teaspoon salt

½ teaspoon ground black pepper

1 Place the barley in a 6-quart stovetop or electric pressure cooker; fill with cool tap water until the grains are submerged by 2 inches.

2 Lock the lid onto the pot.

STOVETOP: Set the pot over high heat and bring it to high pressure (15 psi). Once this pressure has been reached, reduce the heat as much as possible while maintaining this pressure. Cook for 16 minutes.

······················ OR ······················

ELECTRIC: Set the machine to cook at high pressure (9–11 psi). Set the machine's timer to cook at high pressure for 22 minutes.

3 Use the quick-release method to bring the pot's pressure back to normal.

4 Unlock and open the cooker. Stir in the carrots.

5 Lock the lid back onto the cooker.

STOVETOP: Set the pot over high heat and bring back to high pressure (15 psi). Once this pressure has been reached, reduce the heat as much as possible while maintaining this pressure. Cook for 2 minutes.

······················ OR ······················

ELECTRIC: Set the machine to cook once again at high pressure (9–11 psi). Set the machine's timer to cook at high pressure for 3 minutes.

6 Unlock and open the cooker. Drain the barley and carrots into a large colander set in the sink. Wipe out the cooker.

7 Set the stovetop cooker over medium heat or turn the electric cooker to its browning function. Melt the butter in the pot; add the onion and cook, stirring often, until softened, about 4 minutes. Add the mushrooms; cook,

(continued)

stirring frequently, until they begin to soften, about 2 minutes. Add the vinegar, thyme, salt, and pepper to the pot; stir well. Add the barley and carrots; cook until warmed through, about 1 minute, stirring often.

TESTERS' NOTES

• This easy barley dish is like a salad *and* a mixed vegetable side.

• There's plenty of butter here, but you could use olive oil instead for a cleaner, brighter flavor—perhaps better with a fish or chicken main course.

• There's a vaguely Asian palette among these flavors. For an even more Asian profile, substitute unseasoned rice vinegar for the white wine vinegar and add up to ¼ teaspoon five-spice powder with the salt and pepper.

SWEET AND SPICY BARLEY WITH BEANS AND BACON

EFFORT: **A LITTLE** • PRESSURE: **HIGH** • TIME UNDER PRESSURE: **18 OR 25 MINUTES** • RELEASE: **QUICK** • SERVES: **6 TO 8**

1 cup dried navy beans

8 ounces slab bacon, diced

1 medium yellow onion, chopped

3 cups chicken broth

One 14-ounce can diced tomatoes (about 1³/₄ cups)

1 cup pearled barley

¹/₃ cup molasses

¹/₃ cup packed dark brown sugar

2 tablespoons balsamic vinegar

2 tablespoons Worcestershire sauce

Up to 2 tablespoons chopped pickled jalapeño rings

1 Soak the beans in a big bowl of water overnight, at least 12 hours or up to 16 hours. Drain them in a colander set in the sink.

2 Fry the bacon just until it begins to render its fat, stirring occasionally, in a 6-quart stovetop pressure cooker set over medium heat or in a 6-quart electric pressure cooker turned to the browning function, about 3 minutes.

3 Add the onion; cook until both the onion and the bacon have browned a bit, stirring often, about 4 more minutes. Pour in the broth and scrape up any browned bits in the bottom of the pot.

4 Add the drained beans, tomatoes, pearled barley, molasses, brown sugar, vinegar, Worcestershire sauce, and jalapeño rings. Stir well.

5 Lock the lid onto the pot.

STOVETOP: Raise the heat under the pot to high and bring it to high pressure (15 psi). Once this pressure has been reached, reduce the heat as much as possible while maintaining high pressure. Cook for 18 minutes.

············· OR ·············

ELECTRIC: Set the machine to cook at high pressure (9–11 psi). Set the machine's timer to cook at high pressure for 25 minutes.

6 Use the quick-release method to bring the pot's pressure back to normal.

7 Unlock and open the pot. Stir well before serving.

• Consider this an even heartier version of baked beans, almost a barbecue-flavored stew. The beans will get soft, almost meltingly so. You'll have a rich, thick side dish to be served in small bowls.

• The flavors here skew sweet with the molasses and brown sugar, not to mention the natural sweetness of the beans and barley. If you'd like a little more spike in the dish, substitute red wine vinegar for the balsamic—add up to 1 additional tablespoon, if desired.

• For a smoky finish, substitute up to 1 canned chipotle in adobo sauce, stemmed, seeded, and minced for the jalapeño chile.

BARLEY AND FENNEL RISOTTO

EFFORT: **A LITTLE** • PRESSURE: **HIGH** • TIME UNDER PRESSURE: **18 OR 25 MINUTES** • RELEASE: **QUICK** • SERVES: **4 TO 6**

4 tablespoons (¹/₂ stick) unsalted butter

1 large leek, white and pale green parts only, halved lengthwise, washed and thinly sliced

1 medium fennel bulb, trimmed and chopped

1 teaspoon fennel seeds

1¹/₄ cups pearled barley

¹/₃ cup moderately sweet white wine, such as Riesling

3 cups chicken broth

¹/₄ teaspoon salt

Up to ¹/₄ teaspoon saffron threads

¹/₃ cup finely grated Parmesan cheese (about ³/₄ ounce)

1 Melt the butter in a 6-quart stovetop or electric pressure cooker set over medium heat. Add the leek, chopped fennel, and fennel seeds; cook, stirring often, until the leek softens, about 3 minutes.

2 Pour in the barley; stir until coated, about 1 minute. Add the wine and cook, stirring often, until it has been absorbed, about 1 minute. Pour in the broth; add the salt and saffron, and stir well.

3 Lock the lid onto the pot.

STOVETOP: Raise the heat to high and bring the pot to high pressure (15 psi). Once this pressure has been reached, reduce the heat as much as possible while maintaining this pressure. Cook for 18 minutes.

·····**OR**·····

ELECTRIC: Set the machine to cook at high pressure (9–11 psi). Set the machine's timer to cook at high pressure for 25 minutes.

4 Use the quick-release method to bring the pot's pressure back to normal.

5 Unlock and open the cooker. Stir in the Parmesan. Set the stovetop pot over medium-low heat or turn the electric cooker to its browning function; cook, stirring often, until most of the liquid has been absorbed and the dish is like a thick porridge, 2 to 5 minutes, depending on the residual moisture content of the barley. Serve at once.

TESTERS' NOTES
• With barley, you can make an aromatic dish that mimics risotto but has bolder flavors.

• If you want to increase the flavor profile, crumble up to ½ ounce dried mushrooms into the pot when you add the broth.

• If you like, substitute unsweetened apple juice for the white wine.

BARLEY SALAD WITH PARSLEY, ALMONDS, AND LEMON

EFFORT: **A LITTLE** · PRESSURE: **HIGH** · TIME UNDER PRESSURE:
18 OR 25 MINUTES · RELEASE: **QUICK** · SERVES: **6**

1 cup pearled barley

$1/3$ cup roasted almonds, chopped

2 cups packed fresh parsley leaves, chopped

4 medium scallions, thinly sliced

3 tablespoons olive oil

3 tablespoons fresh lemon juice

1 teaspoon dried oregano

$1/2$ teaspoon ground allspice

$1/2$ teaspoon salt

$1/2$ teaspoon ground black pepper

1 Place the barley in a 6-quart stovetop or electric pressure cooker; fill with cool tap water until the grains are covered by 2 inches of water.

2 Lock the lid onto the cooker.

STOVETOP: Set the pot over high heat and bring it to high pressure (15 psi). Once this pressure has been reached, reduce the heat as much as possible while maintaining this pressure. Cook for 18 minutes.

·······················**OR**·····························

ELECTRIC: Set the machine to cook at high pressure (9–11 psi). Set the machine's timer to cook at high pressure for 25 minutes.

3 Use the quick-release method to return the pot's pressure to normal.

4 Unlock and open the pot. Drain the barley into a large colander set in the sink and run the grains under cool tap water to bring them to room temperature. Drain well, shaking the colander several times.

5 Transfer the barley to the bowl of a food processor fitted with the chopping blade; add the almonds. Cover and process until coarsely ground. Scrape the contents of the processor canister into a large bowl. Stir in the parsley, scallions, oil, lemon juice, oregano, allspice, salt, and pepper.

TESTERS' NOTES

• A hearty salad for a weekday lunch, this recipe can be made up to 3 days in advance, stored in a covered container in the fridge. If the salad sits at room temperature before serving, the parsley will wilt and soften, offering a slightly more muted flavor in the overall dish.

• The dish is somewhat like tabbouleh, but barley adds a more subtle sweetness than wheat and can stand up to a wider array of chopped vegetables.

• The allspice will add a slightly earthy warmth, a gentle nod to the wheaty bulgur that usually makes up tabbouleh.

Serve It Up! Use this salad as a bed for plump steamed shrimp.

QUINOA AND APPLES

EFFORT: **NOT MUCH** • PRESSURE: **HIGH** • TIME UNDER PRESSURE:
6 OR 9 MINUTES • RELEASE: **QUICK** • SERVES: **6**

1$\frac{1}{2}$ **tablespoons unsalted butter**

1 large yellow onion, chopped

2 teaspoons minced garlic

$\frac{1}{2}$ **tablespoon fresh thyme leaves**

$\frac{1}{2}$ **teaspoon ground allspice**

$\frac{1}{2}$ **teaspoon ground black pepper**

$\frac{1}{4}$ **teaspoon ground cloves**

1$\frac{1}{2}$ **cups white (or blond) quinoa**

$\frac{3}{4}$ **cup chopped dried apple**

3 cups chicken broth

1 tablespoon apple cider vinegar

1 tablespoon honey

$\frac{1}{2}$ **teaspoon salt**

1 Melt the butter in a 6-quart stovetop pressure cooker set over medium heat or in a 6-quart electric pressure cooker turned to the browning function. Add the onion and cook, stirring frequently, until softened, about 4 minutes.

2 Stir in the garlic, thyme, allspice, pepper, and cloves until aromatic, less than 1 minute. Add the quinoa and dried apple; stir until the grains are well coated. Add the broth, vinegar, honey, and salt; stir until the honey dissolves.

3 Lock the lid onto the pot.

STOVETOP: Raise the heat to high and bring the pot to high pressure (15 psi). Once this pressure has been reached, reduce the heat as much as possible while maintaining this pressure. Cook for 6 minutes.

·······································OR·······································

ELECTRIC: Set the machine to cook at high pressure (9–11 psi). Set the machine's timer to cook at high pressure for 9 minutes.

4 Use the quick-release method to bring the pot's pressure back to normal.

5 Unlock and open the pot. Stir well before serving.

TESTERS' NOTES
• Dried apples retain more of their texture than fresh apples in this simple side dish.
• Rinse the quinoa before cooking if the package directs you to.
• There may be a little liquid left in the pot after cooking, depending on how much moisture the quinoa has absorbed while sitting on the shelf. If you find the dish too soupy, set the stovetop pot over medium heat, or turn the electric cooker to its browning function; cook a few minutes, stirring all the while, until the dish is much drier.

Serve It Up! There may be no better accompaniment to this than pan-seared pork chops!

QUINOA RISOTTO WITH BACON, TOMATOES, AND PARMESAN

EFFORT: **A LITTLE** • PRESSURE: **HIGH** • TIME UNDER PRESSURE:
6 OR 9 MINUTES • RELEASE: **QUICK** • SERVES: **4**

3 ounces slab bacon, diced

6 medium scallions, thinly sliced

12 cherry tomatoes, halved

¼ cup dry vermouth

3½ cups chicken broth

1½ cups white or red quinoa, rinsed if
  necessary

3 fresh thyme sprigs

¼ cup finely grated Parmesan cheese
  (about ½ ounce)

½ teaspoon ground black pepper

1 Place the bacon in a 6-quart stovetop pressure cooker set over medium heat or in a 6-quart electric pressure cooker turned to the browning function. Fry until crisp, stirring occasionally, about 4 minutes.

2 Add the scallions; stir over the heat until softened, about 1 minute. Put in the tomatoes; cook just until they begin to break down, about 2 minutes, stirring occasionally. Pour in the vermouth; as it comes to a simmer, scrape up any browned bits in the bottom of the cooker. Stir in the broth, quinoa, and thyme sprigs.

3 Lock the lid onto the pot.

STOVETOP: Raise the heat to high and bring the pot to high pressure (15 psi). Once this pressure has been reached, reduce the heat as much as possible while maintaining this pressure. Cook for 6 minutes.

··· **OR** ···

ELECTRIC: Set the machine to cook at high pressure (9–11 psi). Set the machine's timer to cook at high pressure for 9 minutes.

4 Return the pot's pressure to normal with the quick-release method.

5 Unlock and open the cooker. Set the stovetop pot over medium heat or turn the electric model to its browning function. Discard the thyme sprigs. Bring the mixture in the pot to a simmer; cook, stirring often, until thickened, 2 to 3 minutes. Stir in the cheese and pepper to serve.

TESTERS' NOTES

• This easy, whole-grain, nontraditional risotto takes advantage of the more assertive flavor palette of quinoa: grassy, sweet, and even a little sour.

• The tomatoes should break down just a bit, releasing their juice into the pot. They'll provide essential moisture to the cooker so the quinoa can soften properly.

WARM QUINOA AND POTATO SALAD

EFFORT: **A LITTLE** • PRESSURE: **HIGH** • TIME UNDER PRESSURE:
7 OR 10 MINUTES • RELEASE: **QUICK** • SERVES: **6**

$1/4$ **cup white balsamic vinegar**

1 tablespoon Dijon mustard

1 teaspoon sweet paprika

$1/2$ **teaspoon ground black pepper**

$1/4$ **teaspoon celery seeds**

$1/4$ **teaspoon salt**

$1/4$ **cup olive oil**

$1^1/2$ **pounds tiny white potatoes, halved**

1 cup blond (white) quinoa

1 medium shallot, minced

2 medium celery stalks, thinly sliced

1 large dill pickle, diced

1 Whisk the vinegar, mustard, paprika, pepper, celery seeds, and salt in a large serving bowl until smooth; whisk in the olive oil in a thin, steady stream until the dressing is fairly creamy.

2 Place the potatoes and quinoa in a 6-quart stovetop or electric pressure cooker; add enough cool tap water so that the ingredients are submerged by 3 inches (some of the quinoa may float).

3 Lock the lid onto the cooker.

STOVETOP: Set the pot over high heat and bring it to high pressure (15 psi). Once this pressure has been reached, reduce the heat as much as possible while maintaining this pressure. Cook for 7 minutes.

·······································**OR**·······························

ELECTRIC: Set the machine to cook at high pressure (9–11 psi). Set the machine's timer to cook at high pressure for 10 minutes.

4 Use the quick-release method to bring the pot's pressure back to normal.

5 Unlock and open the pot. Drain the contents of the pot into a colander lined with paper towels or into a fine-mesh sieve in the sink. Do not rinse.

6 Transfer the potatoes and quinoa to the large bowl with the dressing. Add the shallot, celery, and pickle; toss gently and set aside for a minute or two to warm up the vegetables.

TESTERS' NOTES
• Quinoa takes well to potatoes—a bit of bitter grassiness against the spud's sweet starch. Use only white potatoes, such as Irish creamers, not Russets or baking potatoes.
• Use *small* potatoes, none larger than 2 inches long, so they become tender in the cooking time. If you can only find small potatoes 3 to 4 inches long, then quarter them.
• The cooking time is a little longer than other quinoa recipes so that the potatoes can get tender.

Beans and Lentils

Yes, pressure cookers, beans, lentils, faster, better, plumper—by now, you know the drill. Or maybe you only think you do. We're about to slow down the process. Not with lentils. They're easy: they cook in minutes. But almost every other bean in this section is soaked overnight before it hits the pressure cooker.

No, we didn't soak whole grains because (1) they'd foam in the cooker and create a kitchen mess, and (2) their texture is actually better without it. But beans are another story: they need as much moisture under their skins as possible. So our timings here for anything non-canned are for *soaked* dried beans.

Sure, dried beans are a pantry staple. Nevertheless, they can sit in our supermarkets month after month; they continue to dry out, to lose internal moisture, even to crack and split. Soaking is the one true test of their "freshness." When soaked, they should double or even triple in volume. If not, they may never get tender, no matter how long they're under pressure.

But you can still use a quick-soak method for dried beans: place them in a 6-quart pressure cooker and fill it with cool tap water until they're submerged by about 1 inch. Lock the lid onto the pot and bring it to high pressure, either by putting it over high heat or turning it to the high-pressure setting. Cook at high pressure for 4 minutes on the stovetop (15 psi) or 6 minutes in an electric pot (9–11 psi). Set the pot off the heat or unplug the electric one; let the pressure come back to normal naturally. Unlock the lid and drain the beans in a colander set in the sink. Now prepare the recipe as stated, skipping (of course) that soaking step.

Economical, hearty, satisfying, abundant—we don't have to sell you on beans and lentils. You surely know *that* drill, too. Otherwise, you probably wouldn't be here.

FRANKS AND BEANS

EFFORT: **NOT MUCH** • PRESSURE: **HIGH** • TIME UNDER PRESSURE:
5 OR 7 MINUTES • RELEASE: **QUICK** • SERVES: **4**

3 ounces slab bacon, chopped

1 medium yellow onion, chopped

2 teaspoons minced garlic

Two 15-ounce cans pinto beans, drained
    and rinsed (about 3^1/$_2$ cups)

^{1}/$_2$ cup ketchup

^{1}/$_4$ cup maple syrup, preferably Grade B
    or 2

2 tablespoons Dijon mustard

2 tablespoons packed dark brown sugar

^{1}/$_2$ teaspoon ground black pepper

^{1}/$_4$ teaspoon ground cloves

1 pound hot dogs, cut into 2-inch pieces

1 Fry the bacon until brown and crisp, stirring occasionally, in a 6-quart stovetop pressure cooker set over medium heat or in a
6-quart electric pressure cooker turned to
the browning function, about 3 minutes.

2 Add the onion and cook until softened,
about 4 minutes, stirring occasionally. Add
the garlic and cook until aromatic, less than
1 minute. Stir in the beans, ketchup, maple
syrup, mustard, brown sugar, pepper, and
cloves until the brown sugar dissolves; then
stir in the hot dogs.

3 Lock the lid onto the pot.

STOVETOP: Raise the heat to high and bring the
pot to high pressure (15 psi). Once this pressure
has been reached, reduce the heat as much as possible while maintaining this pressure. Cook for
5 minutes.

········ OR ········
ELECTRIC: Set the machine to cook at high pressure (9–11 psi). Set the machine's timer to cook at
high pressure for 7 minutes.

4 Use the quick-release method to bring the
pot's pressure back to normal.

5 Unlock and open the pot. Stir well before
serving.

TESTERS' NOTES
• There's not an easier dish than this kid-friendly casserole, a fast lunch or dinner any day of the week.
• The secret is in the quality of the hot dogs. Consider buying all-meat hot dogs, maybe even beef hot dogs that have
somewhat bigger flavors in each bite.
• For smokier flavor, use double-smoked slab bacon. You
can also swap in barbecue sauce for the ketchup.

Serve It Up! Garnish with pickle relish or
chow-chow and have warmed flour tortillas
on the side.

REFRIED BEANS

EFFORT: **A LITTLE** • PRESSURE: **HIGH** • TIME UNDER PRESSURE:
14 OR 21 MINUTES • RELEASE: **QUICK** • SERVES: **8**

1^1/$_2$ pounds (3 cups) dried pinto beans

One 3-ounce salt pork chunk

1 tablespoon minced garlic

^{1}/$_4$ cup vegetable or canola oil

Up to 2 cups finely shredded smoked
    Cheddar cheese (about 8 ounces)

1 Soak the beans in a big bowl of water on
the counter overnight, for at least 12 hours or
up to 16 hours.

(continued)

2 Drain the beans in a colander set in the sink; pour them into a 6-quart stovetop or electric pressure cooker. Add the salt pork and garlic; pour in enough cool tap water so that the ingredients are covered by 2 inches of water (the garlic will float).

3 Lock the lid onto the pot.

STOVETOP: Set the pot over high heat and bring it to high pressure (15 psi). Once this pressure has been reached, reduce the heat as much as possible while maintaining this pressure. Cook for 14 minutes.

························ **OR** ························

ELECTRIC: Set the machine to cook at high pressure (9–11 psi). Set the machine's timer to cook at high pressure for 21 minutes.

4 Use the quick-release method to drop the pot's pressure back to normal.

5 Unlock and open the cooker. Discard the salt pork. Scoop out 1 cup of the soaking water and set aside. Drain the remaining contents of the cooker into a colander set in the sink.

6 Transfer the beans and garlic to a large bowl. Use a potato masher to create a thick paste, adding the soaking water in small bits until you've added just enough to get a smooth but not wet paste.

7 Heat the oil in a large pot over medium heat. Add the bean paste and cook, stirring often, until hot and bubbling, about 5 minutes. Spread the mixture on a large serving platter or individual plates and top with the shredded cheese.

TESTERS' NOTES
• This dish is your go-to side with tacos, burritos, or enchiladas. The pressure cooker keeps the beans creamy with a much better texture than those boiled in a saucepan.

• The smoked cheese gives the beans a great campfire feel, like beans made at a ranch cookout. Finely shredding the cheese ensures it melts over the hot beans.
• For a more authentic version, substitute lard or rendered bacon fat for the oil.

CHEESY BEANS WITH PICO DE GALLO

EFFORT: **A LOT** • PRESSURE: **HIGH** • TIME UNDER PRESSURE: **15 OR 23 MINUTES** • RELEASE: **NATURAL** • SERVES: **6**

2 tablespoons olive oil

1 small yellow or white onion, chopped

Up to 1 fresh jalapeño chile, stemmed, seeded, and chopped

1 tablespoon minced garlic

1 teaspoon dried oregano

1 teaspoon ground cumin

$1/2$ teaspoon ground cloves

$1/2$ teaspoon salt

$1/2$ teaspoon ground black pepper

Two 15-ounce cans pinto beans, drained and rinsed (about $3^1/2$ cups)

2 tablespoons packed dark brown sugar

2 tablespoons canned tomato paste

$1/2$ cup dark beer, such as Negra Modelo

$1^1/2$ cups shredded Monterey jack cheese (about 6 ounces)

2 large globe or beefsteak tomatoes, chopped

1 small shallot, minced

$1/4$ cup packed fresh cilantro leaves, minced

Up to 6 jarred pickled jalapeño rings, minced

1 tablespoon fresh lime juice

1 teaspoon minced garlic

$1/4$ teaspoon salt

1 Heat the oil in a 6-quart stovetop pressure cooker set over medium heat or in a 6-quart electric pressure cooker turned to the browning function. Add the onion and cook, stirring often, until softened, about 2 minutes.

2 Stir in the jalapeño, garlic, oregano, cumin, cloves, salt, and pepper until aromatic, less than 1 minute. Add the beans, brown sugar, and tomato paste; stir until the brown sugar has melted and the tomato paste coats everything evenly. Pour in the beer and mix well.

3 Spoon a third of the bean mixture into a 2-quart, high-sided, round soufflé or baking dish; top with ½ cup cheese. Spoon half the remaining bean mixture into the dish; sprinkle on another ½ cup cheese. Finally, top with the remaining bean mixture and the remaining ½ cup cheese. Cover the baking dish with parchment paper, then seal with aluminum foil.

4 Clean and dry the pressure cooker pot. Set the pressure cooker rack inside the pot; add 2 cups water. Make a foil sling for the baking dish (see page 19) and lower it onto the rack, tucking in the ends of the sling.

5 Lock the lid onto the pot.

STOVETOP: Set the pot over high heat and bring it to high pressure (15 psi). Once this pressure has been reached, reduce the heat as much as possible while maintaining this pressure. Cook for 15 minutes.

·············· **OR** ··············

ELECTRIC: Set the machine to cook at high pressure (9–11 psi). Set the machine's timer to cook at high pressure for 23 minutes.

6 Reduce the pressure.

STOVETOP: Set the pot off the heat and let its pressure come back to normal naturally, about 12 minutes.

·············· **OR** ··············

ELECTRIC: Turn off the machine or unplug it so it doesn't flip to its keep-warm setting. Let its pressure return to normal naturally, 12 to 15 minutes.

7 Unlock and open the pot. Use the foil sling to transfer the baking dish to a wire cooling rack; uncover the dish and set aside for about 5 minutes.

8 Make the pico de gallo: mix the tomatoes, shallot, cilantro, pickled jalapeño, lime juice, garlic, and salt in a big bowl. Serve by scooping up large spoonfuls of the bean casserole and topping them with the pico de gallo.

TESTERS' NOTES

• Here's a rich, gooey main course, truly a winter warmer. Although black beans are more common in some Latin American dishes like this one, we think pinto beans give it a Tex-Mex flare. They've also got an earthy flavor and a mild chewiness, two things black beans lack.

• Pack leftovers into small, sealable, microwavable containers that you can store in the fridge and then take for lunch in the days ahead.

• You can use purchased, chunky salsa, although the flavor will be cooked, not bright; squeeze a lime section over each serving to give it some pop.

PINTO BEANS WITH BACON, PECANS, AND CHILES

EFFORT: **A LITTLE** • PRESSURE: **HIGH** • TIME UNDER PRESSURE:
12 OR 18 MINUTES • RELEASE: **QUICK** • SERVES: **4**

1 cup dried pinto beans
1 tablespoon unsalted butter
3 thin bacon slices, chopped
$1/2$ cup chopped pecans
1 medium yellow or white onion, chopped
$1/2$ teaspoon dried oregano
$1/2$ teaspoon ground cumin
$1/4$ teaspoon ground coriander
One $4^1/2$-ounce can chopped mild green
    chiles (about $1/2$ cup)

1 Soak the beans in a large bowl of water on the counter overnight, for at least 12 hours or up to 16 hours.

2 Drain the beans in a colander set in the sink; pour them into a 6-quart stovetop or electric pressure cooker. Add enough cool tap water that they're submerged by 2 inches.

3 Lock the lid onto the pot.

STOVETOP: Set the pot over high heat and bring it to high pressure (15 psi). Once this pressure has been reached, reduce the heat as much as possible while maintaining this pressure. Cook for 12 minutes.

························ **OR** ························

ELECTRIC: Set the machine to cook at high pressure (9–11 psi). Set the machine's timer to cook at high pressure for 18 minutes.

4 Use the quick-release method to bring the pot's pressure back to normal.

5 Unlock and open the cooker. Scoop out 1 cup of the cooking liquid and reserve it. Drain the beans in a colander set in the sink. Wipe out the cooker.

6 Melt the butter in the stovetop cooker set over medium heat or in the electric cooker turned to its browning function. Add the bacon and pecans; fry until both are lightly browned, stirring occasionally, about 3 minutes. Add the onion and cook, stirring often, until softened, about 3 minutes.

7 Stir in the oregano, cumin, and coriander until aromatic, about 20 seconds. Then pour in the drained beans, green chiles, and $1/4$ cup of the reserved cooking liquid. Cook, stirring often, until the beans are just heated through, adding more of the reserved cooking liquid in $1/4$-cup increments when the mixture gets too dry.

TESTERS' NOTES
• Control how soupy you want these beans: adding more soaking liquid at the end will give you a dish fit for bowls. If you add less, it's better on a plate (or even inside burritos).
• Butter is the unexpected balance among the flavors: it offers a slightly sour richness that foregrounds the sweet beans and pecans—and also brings out the spices.
• There's a lot of foodie chatter about not salting the water when you cook beans on the stovetop because of the way the sodium toughens their skins. In this book, fuhgettaboutit! The pressure cooker will keep the skins soft, even with salt in the mix. There's no time for exterior dehydration—and no way it can happen under pressure anyway.
• Beans can cause, to put it politely, gastric distress. You can cut down on that problem by (1) never using the soaking water as your cooking water, (2) changing the soaking water at least once during the process, and (3) rinsing the beans well after soaking. If you're really sensitive, use the quick-soak method outlined above to rehydrate the beans; drain and rinse well. You'll cut down on the problem sugars dramatically.

BOURBON PORK AND PINTO BEANS

EFFORT: **A LITTLE** • PRESSURE: **HIGH** • TIME UNDER PRESSURE:
12 OR 18 MINUTES • RELEASE: **QUICK** • SERVES: **8**

2 cups dried pinto beans

1 medium navel orange

2 tablespoons olive oil

12 ounces cooked ham, any seasoning on
   the rind removed, the meat chopped

1 medium red onion, chopped

2 fresh red cherry peppers, stemmed,
   cored, and chopped

1 tablespoon minced garlic

1 teaspoon dried rosemary, crumbled

1/2 teaspoon ground cloves

1/4 teaspoon ground cinnamon

1/4 cup bourbon

1/2 cup packed dark brown sugar

6 tablespoons canned tomato paste

3 cups chicken broth

1 Soak the beans in a large bowl of water on the counter overnight, for at least 12 hours or up to 16 hours.

2 Remove half the zest from the orange with a vegetable peeler, taking it off in shallow strips. Mince the zest, then peel the remainder of the orange, removing as much white pith as possible. Chop the flesh of the orange, removing any seeds. Set aside with the prepared zest.

3 Heat the oil in a 6-quart stovetop pressure cooker set over medium heat or in a 6-quart electric pressure cooker turned to the browning function. Add the ham and cook, stirring often, until crisp at the edges, about 4 minutes.

4 Add the onion and peppers; cook, stirring often, until the onion becomes translucent, about 3 minutes. Stir in the garlic until aromatic, less than a minute; then add the rosemary, cloves, and cinnamon. Pour in the bourbon; add the brown sugar, tomato paste, minced zest, and chopped orange. Stir until the tomato paste covers everything evenly.

5 Drain the beans in a colander set in the sink; add them to the cooker. Pour in the broth and stir well.

6 Lock the lid onto the cooker.

STOVETOP: Raise the heat to high and bring the pot to high pressure (15 psi). Once this pressure has been reached, reduce the heat as much as possible while maintaining this pressure. Cook for 12 minutes.

························· **OR** ·························

ELECTRIC: Set the machine to cook at high pressure (9–11 psi). Set the machine's timer to cook at high pressure for 18 minutes.

7 Use the quick-release method to drop the pot's pressure back to normal.

8 Unlock and open the pot. Set the stovetop cooker over medium heat or turn the electric model to its browning option. Use a wooden spoon to smash a few of the cooked beans against the side of the pot. Cook, stirring often, until thickened slightly, about 2 minutes.

TESTERS' NOTES

• Look no further for the ultimate baked beans to serve at your next barbecue! These are rich and sweet, a gorgeous complement to smoky ribs or brisket off the grate.

• The combination of orange and bourbon is reminiscent of an Old Fashioned cocktail. Maybe that's what you should drink at your next barbecue.

BEEFY PINTO BEANS

EFFORT: **A LOT** · PRESSURE: **HIGH** · TIME UNDER PRESSURE: **32 OR 48 MINUTES** · RELEASE: **NATURAL, THEN QUICK** · SERVES: **6**

1¹/₂ cups dried pinto beans

2 meaty beef ribs

2 large yellow onions, one halved and one chopped

1 large carrot, halved widthwise

1 medium celery stalk, halved widthwise

2 tablespoons olive oil

1 tablespoon minced garlic

1 tablespoon chili powder

1 teaspoon dried oregano

2 tablespoons canned tomato paste

2 tablespoons balsamic vinegar

¹/₂ teaspoon salt

¹/₂ teaspoon ground black pepper

1 Soak the beans in a large bowl of water on the counter overnight, for at least 12 hours or up to 16 hours.

2 Place the ribs, halved onion, carrot, and celery with 4 cups water in a 6-quart stovetop or electric pressure cooker.

3 Lock the lid onto the cooker.

STOVETOP: Set the pot over high heat and bring it to high pressure (15 psi). Once this pressure has been reached, reduce the heat as much as possible while maintaining this pressure. Cook for 20 minutes.

············· **OR** ·············

ELECTRIC: Set the machine to cook at high pressure (9–11 psi). Set the machine's timer to cook at high pressure for 30 minutes.

4 Reduce the pressure.

STOVETOP: Set the pot aside off the heat and let its pressure come back to normal naturally, about 15 minutes.

············· **OR** ·············

ELECTRIC: Turn off the machine or unplug it so it doesn't flip to its keep-warm setting. Let its pressure return to normal naturally, 14 to 18 minutes.

5 Unlock and open the cooker. Drain the soaked beans in a large colander set in the sink. Add them to the cooker, making sure they're all submerged.

6 Lock the lid back onto the pot.

STOVETOP: Set the pot back over high heat and bring it back to high pressure (15 psi). Once this pressure has been reached, reduce the heat as much as possible while maintaining this pressure. Cook for 12 minutes.

············· **OR** ·············

ELECTRIC: Set the machine to cook once again at high pressure (9–11 psi). Set the machine's timer to cook at high pressure for 18 minutes.

7 Use the quick-release method to bring the pot's pressure back to normal.

8 Unlock and open the cooker. Scoop out and reserve 2 cups of the cooking liquid. Remove the ribs with kitchen tongs; drain the remainder of the cooker's contents in a large colander set in the sink. Discard the onion halves, carrot, and celery. Slice any meat off the bones and chop into small pieces; discard the bones. Wipe out the cooker.

9 Heat the oil in the stovetop pot set over medium heat or in the electric pot set over medium heat. Add the chopped onion and cook, stirring often, until softened, about

4 minutes. Stir in the garlic, chili powder, and oregano until aromatic, less than 1 minute.

10 Add the tomato paste, vinegar, salt, and pepper, as well as 1 cup of the reserved liquid, stirring until the tomato paste coats everything evenly. Stir in the beans and meat. Cook, stirring often, for 5 minutes, until heated through, adding more soaking liquid as necessary to make sure the dish doesn't dry out.

TESTERS' NOTES
• Here's a version of baked beans with the most flavor of any other baked bean recipe in this book. It's a lot of work but the complex flavor will show off your culinary skills!
• Buy beef ribs with plenty of meat adhering to the bones. If you don't see any meaty enough, ask the butcher at the supermarket to cut you a couple. Don't use any undissolved cartilage, but you want every other speck of meat you can find.
• The vinegar is crucial to the dish's success. You don't need an aged, syrupy balsamic, just a sturdy bottling with plenty of sweet-and-sour notes.

SPICY BLACK-EYED PEAS

EFFORT: **NOT MUCH** • PRESSURE: **HIGH** • TIME UNDER PRESSURE: **15 OR 22 MINUTES** • RELEASE: **QUICK** • SERVES: **6**

4 ounces slab bacon, chopped

1 medium yellow onion, chopped

2 cups dried black-eyed peas

One 14-ounce can diced tomatoes (about 1³/₄ cups)

One 4¹/₂-ounce can chopped hot green chiles (about ¹/₂ cup)

1 tablespoon dried oregano

1 Fry the bacon in a 6-quart stovetop pressure cooker over medium heat or a 6-quart electric pressure cooker turned to its browning function, until it begins to brown and give off its fat, about 2 minutes.

2 Add the onion and cook, stirring often, until it turns translucent, about 4 minutes. Pour in 3 cups water; add the black-eyed peas, tomatoes, chiles, and oregano, and stir well.

3 Lock the lid onto the cooker.

STOVETOP: Raise the heat to high and bring the pot to high heat (15 psi). Once this pressure has been reached, reduce the heat as much as possible while maintaining this pressure. Cook for 15 minutes.

······· **OR** ·······

ELECTRIC: Set the machine to cook at high pressure (9–11 psi). Set the machine's timer to cook at high pressure for 22 minutes.

4 Use the quick-release method to bring the pot's pressure back to normal.

5 Unlock and open the cooker. Stir well before serving.

TESTERS' NOTES
• Black-eyed peas don't need to be soaked before they undergo pressure. In fact, they actually stay firmer if they go into the cooker without any preliminary fandango.
• For an even spicier side dish, pass bottled hot red pepper sauce at the table.

Serve It Up! Put a spoonful of sour cream on each serving, and garnish with minced cilantro leaves.

BLACK-EYED PEAS WITH GINGER AND TURMERIC

EFFORT: **NOT MUCH** • PRESSURE: **HIGH** • TIME UNDER PRESSURE: **15 OR 22 MINUTES** • RELEASE: **QUICK** • SERVES: **6**

2 tablespoons unsalted butter

2 medium yellow onions, chopped

1 tablespoon minced garlic

1 tablespoon minced fresh ginger

Up to 1 fresh jalapeño chile, stemmed and minced

1/2 teaspoon ground turmeric

1/2 teaspoon salt

1 large globe or beefsteak tomato, chopped

3 cups vegetable or chicken broth

1 1/2 cups dried black-eyed peas

1 Melt the butter in a 6-quart stovetop pressure cooker set over medium heat or in a 6-quart electric pressure cooker turned to the browning function. Add the onions and cook, stirring often, until translucent, about 5 minutes.

2 Stir in the garlic, ginger, jalapeño, turmeric, and salt until aromatic, less than 1 minute. Add the tomato and cook, stirring often, until it begins to break down, about 3 minutes. Pour in the broth and scrape up any browned bits in the bottom of the cooker. Add the black-eyed peas.

3 Lock the lid onto the pot.

STOVETOP: Raise the heat to high and bring the cooker to high pressure (15 psi). Once this pressure has been reached, reduce the heat as much as possible while maintaining this pressure. Cook for 15 minutes.

···········OR···········

ELECTRIC: Set the machine to cook at high pressure (9–11 psi). Set the machine's timer to cook at high pressure for 22 minutes.

4 Use the quick-release method to drop the pot's pressure to normal.

5 Unlock and open the cooker. Stir well before serving.

TESTERS' NOTES
• With a flavor profile like a simplified curry, this quick side dish would be a great addition to any roast chicken or grilled pork loin.
• Seed the jalapeño for less heat.
• If you find the dish too soupy, set the stovetop pot over medium heat or turn the electric pot to its browning function; stir over the heat for a minute or two until somewhat thickened.
• Turn the dish into a vegetarian main course by stirring 4 packed cups of chopped kale leaves into the finished stew. Lock the lid back onto the pot and bring to high pressure again. Cook for 2 minutes in the stovetop or 3 minutes in an electric cooker, then use the quick-release method to stop the cooking before opening the pot.

HOPPIN' JOHN

EFFORT: **NOT MUCH** • PRESSURE: **HIGH** • TIME UNDER PRESSURE: **10 OR 15 MINUTES** • RELEASE: **MODIFIED QUICK** • SERVES: **6 TO 8**

2 tablespoons olive oil

1 pound smoked sausages, preferably Cajun andouille, cut into 1-inch pieces

1 medium yellow onion, chopped

1 medium green bell pepper, stemmed, cored, and chopped

3 medium celery stalks, chopped

1 tablespoon minced garlic

Two 15-ounce cans black-eyed peas, drained and rinsed (about 3½ cups)

1 cup long-grain white rice, such as basmati rice

1 teaspoon dried thyme

1 teaspoon ground cumin

¼ teaspoon celery seeds

¼ teaspoon cayenne

2 bay leaves

2½ cups chicken broth

⅓ cup packed fresh parsley leaves, chopped

1 Heat the oil in a 6-quart stovetop pressure cooker set over medium heat or in a 6-quart electric pressure cooker turned to the browning function. Add the sausages and brown on all sides, turning occasionally, about 8 minutes. Transfer to a large bowl.

2 Add the onion, bell pepper, and celery; cook, stirring often, until the onion turns translucent, about 4 minutes. Stir in the garlic until aromatic, less than a minute.

3 Add the black-eyed peas, rice, thyme, cumin, celery seeds, cayenne, and bay leaves; stir well. Add the sausage, any juices in its bowl, the broth, and parsley; again stir well, this time to get any browned bits up off the bottom of the pot.

4 Lock the lid onto the cooker.

STOVETOP: Raise the heat to high and bring the pot to high pressure (15 psi). Once this pressure has been reached, reduce the heat as much as possible while maintaining this pressure. Cook for 10 minutes.

································ OR ································

ELECTRIC: Set the machine to cook at high pressure (9–11 psi). Set the machine's timer to cook at high pressure for 15 minutes.

5 Use the quick-release method to bring the pot's pressure back to normal, but do not open the pot. Set aside, off the heat or unplugged, for 10 minutes to steam the rice.

6 Unlock and open the pot. Discard the bay leaves. Stir gently before serving.

TESTERS' NOTES
• Traditionally eaten in the South on New Year's Day as a harbinger of good luck, this side dish would be welcome with a roast turkey or baked ham.
• We've stocked this dish so well that it could pass as a main course, particularly with a big salad on the side.
• Put out an array of bottled hot sauces with this dish— a hot sauce bar, as it were.

BLACK BEAN AND CORN SALAD

EFFORT: **A LITTLE** · PRESSURE: **HIGH** · TIME UNDER PRESSURE: **12 OR 18 MINUTES** · RELEASE: **QUICK** · SERVES: **8**

2 cups dried black beans

2 tablespoons olive oil

2 teaspoons cumin seeds

2 teaspoons minced garlic

1 medium fresh jalapeño chile, stemmed and split lengthwise

2 cups fresh corn kernels (about 2 large ears), or frozen kernels, thawed

1 large globe or beefsteak tomato, chopped

Up to 6 medium scallions, thinly sliced

1 medium yellow bell pepper, stemmed, cored, and diced

¼ cup fresh lime juice

3 tablespoons olive oil

1 tablespoon sherry vinegar

1 tablespoon honey

1 teaspoon salt

(continued)

1 Soak the beans in a large bowl of water on the counter overnight, for at least 12 hours or up to 16 hours. Drain them in a colander set in the sink.

2 Heat the oil in a 6-quart stovetop pressure cooker set over medium heat or in a 6-quart electric pressure cooker turned to the browning function. Add the cumin seeds and garlic; cook for 1 minute, stirring constantly, just until the garlic begins to brown. Pour in the drained beans; add the jalapeño. Add enough cool tap water so that the ingredients are submerged by 2 inches (the seeds will float).

3 Lock the lid onto the cooker.

STOVETOP: Raise the heat to high and bring the pot to high pressure (15 psi). Once this pressure has been reached, reduce the heat as much as possible while maintaining this pressure. Cook for 12 minutes.

·······································**OR**·······································

ELECTRIC: Set the machine to cook at high pressure (9–11 psi). Set the machine's timer to cook at high pressure for 18 minutes.

4 Use the quick-release method to bring the pot's pressure back to normal.

5 Unlock and open the cooker. Drain the contents of the cooker into a colander set in the sink. Discard the jalapeño.

6 Transfer the bean mixture to a large bowl; stir in the corn, tomato, scallions, and bell pepper. Whisk the lime juice, olive oil, vinegar, honey, and salt in a small bowl until smooth; pour over the salad and toss well.

TESTERS' NOTES

• This quick side salad is the perfect thing to bring to a potluck or a barbecue. The corn and tomatoes will sweeten the dish considerably, pushing back against all that tart lime juice.

• The jalapeño gives a surprisingly subtle heat; if you'd like more, add some red pepper flakes to the dressing.

• The garlic and cumin seeds are just there to flavor the beans under pressure, so we don't have to worry about catching them in a fine-mesh sieve after cooking. If a few remain, they'll just add a little extra flavor to the salad.

CUBAN-STYLE BLACK BEANS WITH HAM

EFFORT: **A LITTLE** • PRESSURE: **HIGH** • TIME UNDER PRESSURE: **12 OR 18 MINUTES** • RELEASE: **QUICK** • SERVES: **6 TO 8**

2 cups dried black beans

2 tablespoons olive oil

$1/2$ pound smoked ham, any rind removed, the meat chopped

2 medium yellow onions, chopped

1 large green bell pepper, stemmed, cored, and chopped

1 tablespoon finely grated orange zest

2 teaspoons minced garlic

$1/2$ tablespoon dried oregano

$1/2$ teaspoon red pepper flakes

2 bay leaves

One 4-inch cinnamon stick

3 tablespoons sherry vinegar

1 tablespoon packed dark brown sugar

4 cups (1 quart) chicken broth

$1/4$ cup packed fresh cilantro leaves, chopped

1 Soak the beans in a big bowl of water on the counter overnight, for at least 12 hours or up to 16 hours. Drain in a colander set in the sink.

2 Heat the oil in a 6-quart stovetop pressure cooker set over medium heat or in a 6-quart electric pressure cooker turned to the browning function. Add the ham and fry until well browned, about 5 minutes, stirring occasionally.

3 Add the onions and pepper; cook, stirring often, until the onion turns translucent, about 4 minutes. Stir in the orange zest, garlic, oregano, red pepper flakes, bay leaves, and cinnamon stick until aromatic, less than 1 minute.

4 Add the vinegar and brown sugar; stir until the brown sugar melts. Pour in the broth and scrape up any browned bits in the bottom of the cooker. Stir in the beans and cilantro.

5 Lock the lid onto the cooker.

STOVETOP: Raise the heat to high and bring the pot to high pressure (15 psi). Once this pressure has been reached, reduce the heat as much as possible while maintaining this pressure. Cook for 12 minutes.

································· OR ·································

ELECTRIC: Set the machine to cook at high pressure (9–11 psi). Set the machine's timer to cook at high pressure for 18 minutes.

6 Use the quick-release method to return the pot's pressure to normal.

7 Unlock and open the cooker. Discard the bay leaves and cinnamon stick. Set the stovetop pot over medium heat or turn the electric cooker to its browning function. Bring to a simmer; cook, uncovered and stirring often, until the remaining liquid in the pot is reduced by half, between 5 and 10 minutes.

TESTERS' NOTES

• This dish is not a Cuban black bean soup; rather, it's a somewhat stewy side dish, a sophisticated mix of flavors. The orange zest and cinnamon serve as a background to the other flavors, the better to highlight them individually.

• Sherry vinegar may seem like an obscure ingredient here, but it gives the dish a Spanish flair with a medium level of acidity.

• If you use ham from the deli case, look for the house-roasted one, rather than a salty water-pumped, extruded deli ham.

Serve It Up! For a main-course meal, spoon it up over bowls of long-grain white rice.

SMOKY BLACK BEAN TOSTADOS

EFFORT: **A LOT** • PRESSURE: **HIGH** • TIME UNDER PRESSURE: **12 OR 18 MINUTES** • RELEASE: **QUICK** • SERVES: **6**

2 cups dried black beans

1 medium yellow onion, halved

1 medium carrot

Up to 1 fresh medium jalapeño chile, stemmed and halved lengthwise

2 bay leaves

2 tablespoons olive oil

3 thin bacon slices, finely chopped

1 medium shallot, minced

Up to 1 canned chipotle chile in adobo sauce, stemmed, seeded, and minced

2 teaspoons minced garlic

2 teaspoons smoked paprika

1 teaspoon ground cumin

1/2 teaspoon salt

1/2 cup corn oil

12 corn tortillas

1 cup regular or low-fat sour cream

12 radishes, shredded through the large holes of a box grater

(continued)

1 Soak the beans in a large bowl of water on the counter overnight, for at least 12 hours or up to 16 hours. Drain in a colander set in the sink.

2 Combine the drained beans, onion, carrot, jalapeño, and bay leaves in a 6-quart stovetop or electric pressure cooker. Add enough cool tap water to submerge them all by 2 inches.

3 Lock the lid onto the pot.

STOVETOP: Set the cooker over high heat and bring it to high pressure (15 psi). Once this pressure has been reached, reduce the heat as much as possible while maintaining this pressure. Cook for 12 minutes.

······················ OR ···························

ELECTRIC: Set the machine to cook at high pressure (9–11 psi). Set the machine's timer to cook at high pressure for 18 minutes.

4 Use the quick-release method to drop the pot's pressure to normal.

5 Unlock and open the pot. Scoop out and reserve 1 cup of the cooking liquid. Discard the vegetables and bay leaves; drain the beans into a large colander set in the sink. Wipe out the cooker.

6 Pour the beans into a large bowl; use a potato masher to create a chunky paste, adding the reserved cooking liquid in dribs and drabs to keep the paste wet without becoming soupy.

7 Heat the olive oil in the stovetop cooker set over medium heat or in the electric model turned to the browning function. Add the bacon and cook, stirring often, until crisp, about 3 minutes. Add the shallot, chipotle, garlic, smoked paprika, cumin, and salt; stir until aromatic, about 1 minute. Pour in

the bean puree and stir for 1 minute to heat through. Remove from the heat or turn off the machine, cover without locking, and set aside.

8 Heat the corn oil in a large nonstick skillet set over medium heat until shimmering. Add the tortillas one at a time; fry until crisp, turning once, about 2 minutes. Transfer the finished tostados to a wire cooling rack as you make more. Serve by mounding the bean paste on each and topping with the sour cream and radishes.

TESTERS' NOTES

• Like refried beans on steroids, this creamy bean filling for tostados is full of complex flavors—and pretty fiery to boot. Tame the heat by adding less chipotle or by using a little less jalapeño (or none at all). For more oomph, top the tostados with shredded Monterey jack.

• You can buy fried tostado shells if you prefer, but they may not be as crisp as the ones you make fresh. Or you can skip the tostados and use the bean puree in lavash with chopped lettuce and tomatoes for wraps.

CRANBERRY BEAN SALAD

EFFORT: **A LITTLE** · PRESSURE: **HIGH** · TIME UNDER PRESSURE: **10 OR 15 MINUTES** · RELEASE: **QUICK** · SERVES: **6**

1 cup dried cranberry beans

12 cherry tomatoes, quartered

2 medium yellow bell peppers, stemmed, cored, and diced

2 medium celery stalks, diced

1 medium shallot, diced

¼ cup roasted pepitas (shelled pumpkin seeds)

3 tablespoons fresh lime juice

2 tablespoons toasted pumpkin seed oil (or other toasted nut oil)

¹/₂ teaspoon salt

¹/₂ teaspoon ground black pepper

¹/₄ teaspoon ground caraway

1 Soak the beans in a large bowl of water on the counter overnight, for at least 12 hours or up to 16 hours.

2 Drain the beans in a colander set in the sink. Pour them into a 6-quart stovetop or electric pressure cooker; add enough cool tap water that they're covered by 2 inches.

3 Lock the lid onto the cooker.

STOVETOP: Set the pot over high heat and bring it to high pressure (15 psi). Once this pressure has been reached, reduce the heat as much as possible while maintaining this pressure. Cook for 10 minutes.

·····················**OR**·····················

ELECTRIC: Set the machine to cook at high pressure (9–11 psi). Set the machine's timer to cook at high pressure for 15 minutes.

4 Use the quick-release method to drop the pot's pressure back to normal.

5 Unlock and open the pot. Drain the beans into a colander set in the sink; rinse with cool water to stop the cooking and bring the beans to room temperature. Drain well, shaking the colander a few times. Pour the beans into a large bowl; stir in the tomatoes, bell peppers, celery, shallot, and pepitas.

6 Add the lime juice, oil, salt, pepper, and caraway; toss to combine and coat.

TESTERS' NOTES

• Cranberry beans are prized for their delicate sweetness and mildly creamy texture.

• Our favorite version of this easy bean salad uses toasted pumpkin seed oil and ground caraway to balance the

natural sweetness in the beans and vegetables, putting everything on an even keel.

• Green pepitas (shelled pumpkin seeds) are common ingredients in Latin American cooking, and are now found at large supermarkets across the United States. If you can only find salted pepitas, omit the salt in the dressing. If you find shelled but untoasted pepitas, toast them in a dry skillet over medium heat, shaking constantly, until they brown lightly and pop open, about 2 minutes.

• To make the salad ahead, complete the recipe through step 5 up to 2 days in advance; cover the bowl and store the salad in the refrigerator. Dress the salad at the last minute.

• Substitute dried borlotti beans (a bit creamier) for the cranberry beans and/or chopped walnuts or unsalted sunflower seeds for the pepitas.

WARM CRANBERRY BEANS WITH BLACK OLIVES AND TOMATOES

EFFORT: **A LITTLE** • PRESSURE: **HIGH** • TIME UNDER PRESSURE: **10 OR 15 MINUTES** • RELEASE: **QUICK** • SERVES: **6**

1¹/₂ cups dried cranberry beans

2 tablespoons olive oil

¹/₂ tablespoon minced garlic

1 large globe or beefsteak tomato, chopped

¹/₂ cup packed pitted black olives, chopped

¹/₂ teaspoon dried thyme

¹/₂ teaspoon ground black pepper

¹/₂ cup packed fresh basil leaves, chopped

1 Soak the beans in a big bowl of water on the counter overnight, for at least 12 hours or up to 16 hours.

(continued)

2 Drain the beans in a colander set in the sink. Pour them into a 6-quart stovetop or electric pressure cooker. Add enough cool tap water so that they're submerged by 2 inches.

3 Lock the lid onto the cooker.

STOVETOP: Set the pot over high heat and bring to high pressure (15 psi). Once this pressure has been reached, reduce the heat as much as possible while maintaining this pressure. Cook for 10 minutes.

······························**OR**······························

ELECTRIC: Set the machine to cook at high pressure (9–11 psi). Set the machine's timer to cook at high pressure for 15 minutes.

4 Use the quick-release method to drop the pressure in the pot back to normal.

5 Unlock and open the cooker. Drain the beans in a colander set in the sink. Rinse them with cool tap water to stop the cooking and bring them to room temperature. Drain well. Wipe out the cooker.

6 Heat the oil in the stovetop cooker set over medium heat or in the electric model turned to the browning function. Add the garlic and cook until lightly browned, less than 1 minute. Add the tomato, olives, thyme, and pepper; stir well, just until the tomato begins to break down, about 3 minutes. Stir in the drained beans and basil; cook, stirring often, until warmed through, about 2 minutes.

TESTERS' NOTES
• This comfort-food side dish would be a welcome addition to your holiday table—or any wintry meal with roasted or pan-sautéed chicken, pork, beef, or fish.
• For the best flavor, look for oil-cured or brine-soaked olives.
• For a bit more heft in the side dish, stir in diced feta cheese before serving.

• You can substitute dried borlotti or romano beans for a creamier finish.

Serve It Up! For an easy main-course lunch, open a can of Italian oil-packed tuna and crumble some over each serving.

BUTTERY CURRIED RED KIDNEY BEANS

EFFORT: **A LITTLE** • PRESSURE: **HIGH** • TIME UNDER PRESSURE: **10 OR 15 MINUTES** • RELEASE: **QUICK** • SERVES: **6**

2 cups dried red kidney beans
4 tablespoons (1/2 stick) unsalted butter
1 medium red onion, chopped
1 tablespoon minced fresh ginger
1 tablespoon minced garlic
Up to 1 serrano chile, stemmed, seeded, and minced
4 cups (1 quart) vegetable or chicken broth
1/4 cup canned tomato paste
1 tablespoon cumin seeds
1 teaspoon salt
1/2 teaspoon ground turmeric
1/4 cup packed fresh cilantro leaves, minced

1 Soak the beans in a big bowl of water on the counter overnight, for at least 12 hours or up to 16 hours.

2 Melt the butter in a 6-quart stovetop pressure cooker set over medium heat or in a 6-quart electric pressure cooker turned to the browning function. Add the onion and cook, stirring often, until softened, about 4 minutes. Stir in the ginger, garlic, and chile until aromatic, less than 1 minute.

3 Add the broth, tomato paste, cumin seeds, salt, and turmeric; stir until the tomato paste coats everything evenly. Drain the beans in a colander set in the sink; stir them into the pot as well.

4 Lock the lid onto the pot.

STOVETOP: Raise the heat to high and bring the pot to high pressure (15 psi). Once this pressure has been reached, reduce the heat as much as possible while maintaining this pressure. Cook for 10 minutes.

···················· **OR** ····························

ELECTRIC: Set the machine to cook at high pressure (9–11 psi). Set the machine's timer to cook at high pressure for 15 minutes.

5 Use the quick-release method to drop the pot's pressure to normal.

6 Unlock and open the cooker. Add the cilantro and stir well before serving.

TESTERS' NOTES
• Consider this an East Indian version of baked beans, given its flavor from the ginger, turmeric, and cumin.
• Although the kidney beans will hold their shape, the other ingredients will begin to melt into the sauce under high pressure, leaving you with a satisfying side that's best served in bowls.
• There's no pop of tartness here, but you could squeeze lemon wedges over the servings for a little brightness.

Serve It Up! Make an East Indian barbecue. Buy a jar of tandoori paste and spread some on chicken breasts or thighs as a marinade; grill the pieces and serve this recipe as your side dish. Have plain yogurt and diced cucumbers as the garnish.

RED BEANS AND RICE

EFFORT: **A LITTLE** • PRESSURE: **HIGH** • TIME UNDER PRESSURE: **10 OR 15 MINUTES** • RELEASE: **MODIFIED QUICK** • SERVES: **6 TO 8**

$1^1/_2$ **cups red kidney beans**

4 cups (1 quart) vegetable broth

1 cup long-grain white rice, such as white basmati

$^1/_2$ **cup packed fresh cilantro leaves, chopped**

One $4^1/_2$-ounce can chopped mild green chiles (about $^1/_2$ cup)

1 tablespoon Worcestershire sauce

$^1/_2$ **tablespoon dried oregano**

$^1/_4$ **teaspoon ground black pepper**

1 Soak the beans overnight in a big bowl on the counter, for at least 12 hours or up to 16 hours.

2 Drain the beans in a colander set in the sink. Pour them into a 6-quart stovetop or electric pressure cooker. Add the broth, rice, cilantro, chiles, Worcestershire sauce, oregano, and pepper.

3 Lock the lid onto the cooker.

STOVETOP: Set the pot over high heat and bring to high pressure (15 psi). Once this pressure has been reached, reduce the heat as much as possible maintaining this pressure. Cook for 10 minutes.

···················· **OR** ····························

ELECTRIC: Set the machine to cook at high pressure (9–11 psi). Set the machine's timer to cook at high pressure for 15 minutes.

4 Use the quick-release method to bring the pot's pressure back to normal but do not open the cooker. Set aside for 10 minutes to steam the rice.

(continued)

5 Unlock and open the cooker. Stir well before serving.

TESTERS' NOTES

• Here's a vegetarian version of the Louisiana favorite—with quite a few more green things in the mix! We pumped up the flavors to make a dish more worthy of steaks or chops.

• If you want a more traditional version of this dish, cut up as much as 1 pound of pork sausage (preferably Louisiana andouille) into 1-inch segments and brown them in some olive oil before adding the remaining ingredients. Reduce the cilantro by as much as half.

• And if you want to turn that heartier version into a main course, stir peeled and deveined medium shrimp into the dish after cooking under pressure, place the lid on the pot, engage the lock, and set aside for 5 minutes, until the shrimp are pink and firm.

BUTTERY NAVY BEAN PUREE

EFFORT: **A LITTLE** • PRESSURE: **HIGH** • TIME UNDER PRESSURE: **8 OR 12 MINUTES** • RELEASE: **QUICK** • SERVES: **6 TO 8**

2 cups dried navy beans

1 medium yellow or white onion, halved

1 large carrot, halved widthwise

2 medium celery stalks, halved widthwise

One 4-inch fresh rosemary sprig

2 fresh thyme sprigs

1 bay leaf

$1/3$ cup heavy cream

3 tablespoons unsalted butter, melted and cooled

$1/2$ teaspoon salt

$1/2$ teaspoon ground black pepper

$1/4$ teaspoon grated nutmeg

1 Soak the beans in a large bowl on the counter overnight, for at least 12 hours or up to 16 hours. Drain them in a colander set in the sink.

2 Pour the beans into a 6-quart stovetop or electric pressure cooker. Add the onion, carrot, celery, rosemary, thyme, and bay leaf. Add enough cool tap water so that everything can be submerged by 2 inches (some onion pieces may float).

3 Lock the lid onto the cooker.

STOVETOP: Set the pot over high heat and bring to high pressure (15 psi). Once this pressure has been reached, reduce the heat as much as possible while maintaining this pressure. Cook for 8 minutes.

······················ **OR** ························

ELECTRIC: Set the machine to cook at high pressure (9–11 psi). Set the machine's timer to cook at high pressure for 12 minutes.

4 Use the quick-release method to bring the pot's pressure back to normal.

5 Unlock and open the cooker. Reserve 1 cup of the cooking liquid and drain everything else into a large colander set in the sink. Discard the vegetables, herbs, and bay leaf.

6 Pour the beans into a food processor fitted with the chopping blade. Add the cream, butter, salt, pepper, and nutmeg. Cover and process until a smooth, thick puree forms, adding additional soaking liquid in 2-tablespoon increments as necessary, scraping down the inside of the canister once or twice. Spoon it onto plates as a side dish to grilled pork, chicken, fish, or beef.

TESTERS' NOTES

• Here's a great alternative to mashed potatoes, a side dish with lots of flavor and a creamy texture.

• Add just enough soaking liquid to keep the processor working on the beans. Too much and the side dish will turn soupy. Err on the safe side and don't add any liquid until you see how the ingredients are blending on their own.

NAVY BEAN AND PARSNIP PUREE WITH LEMON AND SAGE

EFFORT: **A LOT** · PRESSURE: **HIGH** · TIME UNDER PRESSURE: **8 OR 12 MINUTES** · RELEASE: **QUICK** · SERVES: **6**

1½ cups dried navy beans

2 large carrots, halved widthwise

3 large parsnips, peeled, halved lengthwise, and cored

2 medium garlic cloves

1 dried chile de Àrbol or small dried red chile

1 bay leaf

1 medium lemon

1 tablespoon unsalted butter

2 tablespoons olive oil

1 medium shallot, minced

1 tablespoon packed fresh sage leaves

2 tablespoons fresh lemon juice

1 teaspoon ground black pepper

½ teaspoon salt

1 Soak the beans in a large bowl of water on the counter overnight, for at least 12 hours or up to 16 hours.

2 Drain the beans in a colander set in the sink. Combine them in a 6-quart stovetop or electric pressure cooker with the carrots, parsnips, garlic, chile, and bay leaf. Use a vegetable peeler to remove the peel from the lemon; drop the peel into the pot. Add enough cool water so that everything can be submerged by 2 inches (the peel and chile will float).

3 Lock the lid onto the cooker.

STOVETOP: Set the pot over high heat and bring it to high pressure (15 psi). Once this pressure has been reached, reduce the heat as much as possible while maintaining this pressure. Cook for 8 minutes.

·······OR·······

ELECTRIC: Set the machine to cook at high pressure (9–11 psi). Set the machine's timer to cook at high pressure for 12 minutes.

4 Use the quick-release method to drop the pot's pressure to normal.

5 Unlock and open the cooker. Reserve 1 cup of the cooking liquid and drain the contents of the cooker into a large colander set in the sink. Discard all but the beans and parsnips. Place these in a food processor fitted with the chopping blade. Wipe out the cooker.

6 Melt the butter in the oil in the stovetop cooker set over medium heat or in the electric cooker turned to its browning function. Add the shallot and sage leaves; cook for 1 minute, stirring often, until the shallot is softened. Scrape the contents of the cooker into the food processor.

7 Add the lemon juice, pepper, and salt. Cover and process into a thick, rich puree, like mashed potatoes, adding the reserved cooking liquid in 2-tablespoon increments *only* as needed to form this puree and scraping down the inside of the canister once in a while.

TESTERS' NOTES

• Here's another alternative to mashed potatoes, a little more complicated than the Buttery Navy Bean Puree (page 462), but better for a spring or summer barbecue.

• To core a parsnip, lay the lengthwise halves on your work surface and chop the slightly darker bits off the core, turning the segments to reveal more that can be taken off the core. If the parsnip pieces are long, it may be easier to cut them into 3- or 4-inch segments.

NAVY BEANS WITH EGGPLANT, FETA, AND LEMON

EFFORT: **A LITTLE** • PRESSURE: **HIGH** • TIME UNDER PRESSURE: **8 OR 12 MINUTES** • RELEASE: **QUICK** • SERVES: **4**

½ cup dried navy beans

¼ cup olive oil

1 large yellow onion, preferably sweet onion, chopped

1 pound thin Japanese eggplants, trimmed and chopped into ½-inch cubes

2 tablespoons packed fresh sage leaves, minced

1 teaspoon packed fresh oregano leaves, minced

1 cup vegetable or chicken broth

2 tablespoons fresh lemon juice

1 to 2 ounces feta cheese

1 Soak the beans in a big bowl of water on the counter overnight, for at least 12 hours or up to 16 hours. Drain in a colander set in the sink.

2 Heat the oil in a 6-quart stovetop pressure cooker set over medium heat or in a 6-quart stovetop pressure cooker turned to the browning function. Add the onion and cook, stirring often, until translucent, about 4 minutes. Add the eggplants, sage, and oregano; cook, stirring constantly, for 1 minute. Stir in the broth and lemon juice; add the beans.

3 Lock the lid onto the cooker.

STOVETOP: Raise the heat to high and bring to high pressure (15 psi). Once this pressure has been reached, reduce the heat as much as possible while maintaining this pressure. Cook for 8 minutes.

························· **OR** ·····························

ELECTRIC: Set the machine to cook at high pressure (9–11 psi). Set the machine's timer to cook at high pressure for 12 minutes.

4 Use the quick-release method to drop the pot's pressure back to normal.

5 Unlock and open the pot. Stir well. Serve by mounding onto plates and topping with crumbled feta.

TESTERS' NOTES

• This one's a luxurious side, vaguely Greek inspired, being full of rich eggplant and topped with feta.

• If you want to go over the top, stir in a little plain Greek yogurt before serving.

• Japanese eggplants are long and tubular, with a milder flavor and a more tender skin than more common Italian eggplants. That said, if you can't find these specialty eggplants, you can go with the standard but you'll need to peel the eggplant before cutting it into correctly sized pieces.

NAVY BEANS WITH FENNEL AND GREEN OLIVES

EFFORT: **A LITTLE** • PRESSURE: **HIGH** • TIME UNDER PRESSURE:
8 OR 12 MINUTES • RELEASE: **QUICK** • SERVES: **6**

1½ cups dried navy beans

1 large fennel bulb, trimmed, halved,
    and thinly sliced (preferably with a
    mandoline)

1 large red bell pepper, stemmed, cored,
    and very thinly sliced

½ cup packed pitted green olives, thinly
    sliced

¼ cup golden raisins, chopped

3 tablespoons packed fresh basil leaves,
    minced

1 tablespoon packed fresh mint leaves,
    minced

¼ cup olive oil

3 tablespoons fresh lemon juice

½ teaspoon salt

½ teaspoon ground black pepper

1 Soak the beans in a big bowl of water on
the counter overnight, for at least 12 hours
or up to 16 hours.

2 Drain the beans in a colander set in the
sink. Put them in a 6-quart stovetop or
electric pressure cooker. Add enough
cool tap water that they're submerged by
2 inches.

3 Lock the lid onto the cooker.

STOVETOP: Set the pot over high heat and bring
it to high pressure (15 psi). Once this pressure has
been reached, reduce the heat as much as possible while maintaining this pressure. Cook for
8 minutes.

·· **OR** ····································

ELECTRIC: Set the machine to cook at high pressure (9–11 psi). Set the machine's timer to cook at
high pressure for 12 minutes.

4 Use the quick-release method to drop the
pot's pressure to normal.

5 Unlock and open the cooker. Stir in the
fennel and set aside, uncovered, for 2 minutes. Drain the contents of the pot in a colander set in the sink; rinse with cool tap water
until room temperature. Drain well.

6 Pour the beans and fennel into a large
bowl; stir in the bell pepper, olives, raisins,
basil, and mint. Add the oil, lemon juice, salt,
and pepper and toss well until combined and
coated.

TESTERS' NOTES
• This easy side dish gets much of its flavor from the *fresh*
vegetables and herbs (rather than a cooked mixture). Only
the fennel is parcooked in the hot liquid in the cooker—and
that's so it doesn't overpower the other, more subtle
ingredients.
• Frankly, nothing tastes as much like summer as the combination of mint and basil.
• For a brighter, less aromatic taste, substitute white wine
vinegar for the lemon juice.

CANNELLINI BEANS AND TOMATOES

EFFORT: **A LITTLE** • PRESSURE: **HIGH** • TIME UNDER PRESSURE:
10 OR 15 MINUTES • RELEASE: **QUICK** • SERVES: **6**

2 cups dried cannellini beans

1 small red onion, chopped

1 small red bell pepper, stemmed, cored, and chopped

One 14-ounce can diced tomatoes (about 1 3/4 cups)

1 cup chicken broth

1/4 cup olive oil

1 tablespoon Worcestershire sauce

1 teaspoon dried dill

1 teaspoon dried sage

1 teaspoon dried thyme

1/2 teaspoon fennel seeds

1/2 teaspoon ground black pepper

1 Soak the beans in a large bowl of water on the counter overnight, for at least 12 hours or up to 16 hours.

2 Drain the beans in a colander set in the sink. Pour them into a 6-quart stovetop or electric pressure cooker. Stir in the onion, bell pepper, tomatoes, broth, olive oil, Worcestershire sauce, dried herbs, fennel seeds, and pepper.

3 Lock the lid onto the pot.

STOVETOP: Set the pot over high heat and bring it to high pressure (15 psi). Once this pressure has been reached, reduce the heat as much as possible while maintaining this pressure. Cook for 10 minutes.

····························· OR ·····························

ELECTRIC: Set the machine to cook at high pressure (9–11 psi). Set the machine's timer to cook at high pressure for 15 minutes.

4 Return the pot to normal pressure using the quick-release method.

5 Unlock and open the cooker. Set the stovetop cooker over medium heat or turn the electric one to its browning function. Bring to a simmer; cook for 5 minutes, stirring often, to thicken somewhat.

TESTERS' NOTES

• This classic Italian-American side dish delivers a wide range of flavors. Dried herbs (rather than fresh) will give the dish an earthier finish.

• A quick release will yield slightly firm beans with a little chew at the center. If you like softer beans, use the natural-release method after cooking under high pressure.

Serve It Up! Serve this side in small bowls and have some crunchy bread on hand for dipping.

CANNELLINI BEANS WITH CARAMELIZED ONIONS AND PARMESAN

EFFORT: **A LITTLE** • PRESSURE: **HIGH** • TIME UNDER PRESSURE:
10 OR 15 MINUTES • RELEASE: **QUICK** • SERVES: **6 TO 8**

1 1/2 cups dried cannellini beans

6 tablespoons olive oil

2 large yellow onions, halved and sliced into thin half-moons

1 tablespoon chopped fresh rosemary leaves

1/4 teaspoon red pepper flakes

1/2 teaspoon salt

1/2 teaspoon ground black pepper

2 tablespoons packed fresh parsley leaves, minced

1/2 cup finely grated Parmesan cheese (about 1 ounce)

1 Soak the beans in a big bowl of water on the counter overnight, for at least 12 hours or up to 16 hours.

2 Drain the beans in a colander set in the sink. Add them to a 6-quart stovetop or electric pressure cooker. Pour in enough cool tap water that they're submerged by 2 inches.

3 Lock the lid onto the cooker.

STOVETOP: Set the pot over high heat and bring it to high pressure (15 psi). Once this pressure has been reached, reduce the heat as much as possible while maintaining this pressure. Cook for 10 minutes.

·······················OR·······················

ELECTRIC: Set the machine to cook at high pressure (9–11 psi). Set the machine's timer to cook at high pressure for 15 minutes.

4 Use the quick-release method to bring the pot's pressure back to normal.

5 Unlock and open the cooker. Drain the beans in a colander set in the sink. Rinse them with cool water to stop the cooking and bring them to room temperature. Wipe out the cooker.

6 Heat the oil in the stovetop model set over medium-low heat or in the electric cooker turned to its browning function. Add the onions; cook, stirring often, until golden, even browned in places, about 12 minutes in the electric cooker or up to 25 minutes in the stovetop model.

7 Stir in the rosemary, red pepper flakes, salt, and pepper. Cook for a couple of

minutes, stirring often, to blend the flavors. Add the beans and parsley; stir well. Spoon onto plates and top with the cheese.

TESTERS' NOTES
• Although we can't caramelize onions in the traditional method with an electric cooker (the heat's simply too high, even on the browning function), we can turn those onions soft and golden for a sophisticated finish in this hearty side dish.
• For a richer flavor, use half butter and half olive oil to caramelize the onions.
• You can substitute dried great northern beans for the cannellini beans.

Serve It Up! Instead of chili burgers, use this side as a topping on the patties!

WHITE BEAN, SAUSAGE, AND ESCAROLE STEW

EFFORT: **A LITTLE** • PRESSURE: **HIGH** • TIME UNDER PRESSURE: **10 OR 15 MINUTES** • RELEASE: **QUICK** • SERVES: **6**

2 cups dried great northern beans

2 tablespoons olive oil

1 pound mild Italian sausage, cut into 1-inch pieces

4 cups (1 quart) chicken broth

2 small escarole heads, cored and chopped

2 tablespoons white wine vinegar

1/2 cup finely grated Parmesan cheese (about 1 ounce)

1 Soak the beans in a big bowl of water on the counter overnight, for at least 12 hours or up to 16 hours. Drain them in a colander set in the sink.

(continued)

2 Heat the oil in a 6-quart stovetop pressure cooker set over medium heat or in a 6-quart electric pressure cooker turned to the browning function. Add the sausage and brown on all sides, turning occasionally with kitchen tongs, about 6 minutes. Pour in the broth and the drained beans.

3 Lock the lid onto the pot.

STOVETOP: Set the pot over high heat and bring to high pressure (15 psi). Once this pressure has been reached, reduce the heat as much as possible while maintaining this pressure. Cook for 10 minutes.

························· **OR** ·························

ELECTRIC: Set the machine to cook at high pressure (9–11 psi). Set the machine's timer to cook at high pressure for 15 minutes.

4 Use the quick-release function to bring the pot's pressure back to normal.

5 Unlock and open the pot. Stir in the escarole and vinegar. Cover and lock the lid onto the pot. Set aside for 3 minutes. (If the pressure lock has become engaged, use the quick-release method to bring the pressure back to normal, then open the pot.) Stir well and serve with the cheese sprinkled over each bowlful.

TESTERS' NOTES
• This bean stew couldn't be easier—the beans are creamy and the escarole is still a tad crunchy, making for great texture.
• Unwashed escarole can be quite sandy: fill a sink with cool water, add all the leaves before chopping, and agitate them a bit. Leave them alone for 5 to 10 minutes, then lift them out without disturbing any of the grit that will have fallen to the bottom. Drain, wash out the sink, and chop the leaves.
• If you've grated fresh Parmesan cheese, cut off the rind and toss it into the soup with the beans. Fish it out at the end and scrape any gooey bits of cheese onto bread slices.

• You can substitute cannellini beans for the great northern beans.

Serve It Up! For brighter notes in the soup, grate lemon zest onto the cheese in each serving.

GREAT NORTHERN BEANS AND SUN-DRIED TOMATOES WITH GREEN OLIVE PESTO

EFFORT: **A LITTLE** • PRESSURE: **HIGH** • TIME UNDER PRESSURE: **10 OR 15 MINUTES** • RELEASE: **QUICK** • SERVES: **8**

2 cups dried great northern beans
1 large yellow onion, chopped
2 teaspoons minced garlic
1 fresh oregano sprig
1 fresh sage sprig
1 teaspoon salt
1 teaspoon ground black pepper
1/2 cup sun-dried tomatoes packed in oil, drained and chopped
2 tablespoons balsamic vinegar
2 cups packed fresh basil leaves
1/2 cup sliced pitted green olives
1/4 cup toasted pine nuts
1/2 cup finely grated Parmesan cheese (about 1 ounce)
1/4 cup olive oil

1 Soak the beans in a big bowl of water on the counter for 12 hours or up to 16 hours. Drain them in a colander set in the sink.

2 Pour the beans into a 6-quart stovetop or electric pressure cooker. Add enough cool tap water so that the beans are covered by 2 inches. Stir in the onion, garlic, oregano, sage, salt, and pepper.

3 Lock the lid onto the cooker.

STOVETOP: Set the pot over high heat and bring it to high pressure (15 psi). Once this pressure has been reached, reduce the heat as much as possible while maintaining this pressure. Cook for 10 minutes.

·········· **OR** ··········

ELECTRIC: Set the machine to cook at high pressure (9–11 psi). Set the machine's timer to cook at high pressure for 15 minutes.

4 Use the quick-release method to drop the pot's pressure to normal.

5 Unlock and open the cooker. Discard the herb sprigs. Transfer the beans to a large bowl; stir in the sun-dried tomatoes and balsamic vinegar. Set aside.

6 Place the basil, olives, pine nuts, and cheese in a food processor fitted with the chopping blade. Cover and process the contents, dribbling the oil through the feed tube, until you have a coarse pesto. Scrape down the inside of the canister once or twice to make sure nothing misses the blades. Serve by spooning the bean mixture onto plates or bowls and topping with the olive pesto.

TESTERS' NOTES
• Perhaps the most elegant dish in our bean line-up, this one would make a great addition to a dinner party with roast chicken, duck, pork loin, or rib roast.
• The olives can easily overpower the other ingredients in the pesto. Don't pack them into the measuring cup—a couple fewer olives is better than a few too many.

CASSOULET-STYLE BEANS

EFFORT: **A LITTLE** • PRESSURE: **HIGH** • TIME UNDER PRESSURE: **10 OR 15 MINUTES** • RELEASE: **QUICK** • SERVES: **8**

2 cups dried great northern beans
2 tablespoons olive oil
6 ounces pancetta, diced
1 large yellow onion, chopped
2 medium carrots, diced
1 tablespoon minced garlic
One 28-ounce can diced tomatoes (about 3½ cups)
4 fresh thyme sprigs
One 4-inch fresh rosemary sprig
1 dried chile de Àrbol or small dried red chile
1 bay leaf
Up to 2 cups chicken broth

1 Soak the beans in a big bowl of water on the counter for at least 12 hours or up to 16 hours. Drain them in a colander set in the sink.

2 Heat the oil in a 6-quart stovetop pressure cooker set over medium heat or in a 6-quart electric pressure cooker turned to the browning function. Add the pancetta and fry until crisp, stirring occasionally, about 4 minutes. Use a slotted spoon to transfer the pancetta to a small bowl.

3 Add the onion and carrots to the cooker. Cook, stirring often, until the onion turns translucent, about 4 minutes. Stir in the garlic until aromatic, less than 1 minute.

4 Add the tomatoes, thyme, rosemary, chile, and bay leaf; stir to get up any browned bits on the bottom of the cooker. Add the beans,

(continued)

pancetta, and any juice in their bowl; stir well. Add just enough broth to submerge the ingredients.

5 Lock the lid onto the cooker.

STOVETOP: Raise the heat to high and bring the pot to high pressure (15 psi). Once this pressure has been reached, reduce the heat as much as possible while maintaining this pressure. Cook for 10 minutes.

····················· **OR** ·····················

ELECTRIC: Set the machine to cook at high pressure (9–11 psi). Set the machine's timer to cook at high pressure for 15 minutes.

6 Use the quick-release method to bring the pot's pressure back to normal.

7 Unlock and remove the lid. Discard the thyme, rosemary, chile, and bay leaf. Stir well before serving.

TESTERS' NOTES
• These firm but tender beans have the flavor of the French classic, a hearty main course that usually includes plenty of meat and even a breadcrumb topping. We've simplified the ingredients to morph the dish into a hearty side, best with burgers or brats.
• You can substitute dried cannellini or flageolet beans for the dried great northern beans.

Serve It Up! Brown up to ½ pound sausage, cut into 1-inch sections, with the pancetta; remove it, then stir back into the dish with the pancetta. Submerge one or two duck confit legs into the stew before locking on the lid. (You may need to use a little more broth—but never more than the maximum fill line indicated on the inside of the pot.) After cooking, shred the meat off the duck legs and stir it back into the bean mixture before serving. For the breadcrumb topping, fry fresh breadcrumbs in a large skillet with a little olive oil with minced capers and red pepper flakes until lightly browned, stirring often; add some finely grated Parmigiano-Reggiano and sprinkle over each serving.

WARM FLAGEOLET AND CELERY ROOT SALAD

EFFORT: **A LITTLE** • PRESSURE: **HIGH** • TIME UNDER PRESSURE: **12 OR 18 MINUTES** • RELEASE: **QUICK** • SERVES: **6**

1 cup dried flageolet beans

1 medium celery root, peeled and shredded through the large holes of a box grater

1 medium yellow bell pepper, stemmed, cored, and chopped

3 medium scallions, thinly sliced

1 small frisée lettuce head, cored and chopped

1½ tablespoons white wine vinegar

1 tablespoon Dijon mustard

1 tablespoon lemon juice

½ teaspoon sugar

½ teaspoon salt

½ teaspoon ground black pepper

⅓ cup almond or olive oil

1 Soak the beans in a large bowl of water on the counter for at least 12 hours or up to 16 hours.

2 Drain the beans in a colander set in the sink. Pour them into a 6-quart stovetop or electric pressure cooker. Add enough cool tap water so that they're submerged by 2 inches.

3 Lock the lid onto the pot.

STOVETOP: Set the pot over high heat and bring it to high pressure (15 psi). Once this pressure has been reached, reduce the heat as much as possible while maintaining this pressure. Cook for 12 minutes.

·························· **OR** ··························

ELECTRIC: Set the machine to cook at high pressure (9–11 psi). Set the machine's timer to cook at high pressure for 18 minutes.

4 Use the quick-release method to return the pot's pressure to normal.

5 Unlock and open the pot. Stir in the celery root. Set aside for 2 minutes, covered but without the pressure lock engaged, to blanch the vegetable.

6 Drain the contents of the pressure cooker into a colander set in the sink, then transfer the beans and vegetable to a large bowl. Stir in the bell pepper, scallions, and lettuce.

7 Whisk the vinegar, mustard, lemon juice, sugar, salt, and pepper in a medium bowl until smooth. Whisk in the oil in a slow, steady stream until the dressing is creamy. Pour over the bean mixture; toss well to coat.

TESTERS' NOTES
• Frisée, a mop head of curly leaves, can get quite bitter. For the mildest flavor, look for heads that are *not* all green but instead include very pale green and even stark white bits. Wash the leaves carefully to remove any grit.
• Flageolet beans, a French favorite, may well be both the creamiest and firmest bean on the market. They're actually immature kidney beans. You can substitute dried navy beans in a pinch, but cook them under high pressure for 8 minutes in a stovetop model or for 12 minutes in an electric one.

FLAGEOLET BEANS
WITH PORK BELLY

EFFORT: **A LITTLE** • PRESSURE: **HIGH** • TIME UNDER PRESSURE: **12 OR 18 MINUTES** • RELEASE: **QUICK** • SERVES: **4**

2 cups dried flageolet beans
One 8-ounce skinless pork belly chunk
1 large yellow onion, chopped
4 medium carrots, cut into 1-inch pieces
4 medium garlic cloves
4 cups (1 quart) chicken broth
Several dashes of hot red pepper sauce
1 tablespoon packed fresh sage leaves, chopped
1 tablespoon fresh thyme leaves
$1/2$ teaspoon salt
$1/2$ teaspoon ground black pepper
2 bay leaves

1 Soak the beans in a large bowl of water on the counter overnight, for at least 12 hours or up to 16 hours. Drain them in a colander set in the sink.

2 Heat a 6-quart stovetop pressure cooker over medium heat or a 6-quart electric pressure cooker turned to its browning mode for a few minutes. Add the pork belly; brown on all sides, turning occasionally, about 6 minutes. Transfer to a large plate.

3 Put the onion, carrots, and garlic in the pot; cook, stirring often, until the onion softens, about 4 minutes. Pour in the broth and hot red pepper sauce to taste; stirring to get up any browned bits on the bottom of the cooker.

4 Stir in the sage, thyme, salt, pepper, and bay leaves. Return the beans to the pot, stir well, then nestle the pork belly into the

(continued)

mixture. Pour any juices from its plate into the pot.

5 Lock the lid onto the cooker.

STOVETOP: Raise the heat to high and bring the pot to high pressure (15 psi). Once this pressure has been reached, reduce the heat as much as possible while maintaining this pressure. Cook for 12 minutes.

························· **OR** ·························

ELECTRIC: Set the machine to cook at high pressure (9–11 psi). Set the machine's timer to cook at high pressure for 18 minutes.

6 Use the quick-release method to bring the pot's pressure back to normal.

7 Unlock and open the cooker. Transfer the pork belly to a cutting board; cool for a couple of minutes. Discard the bay leaves in the pot. Slice the pork belly into eight ½-inch-thick strips and stir them back into the bean mixture before serving.

TESTERS' NOTES
• If you want the most over-the-top bean main course imaginable, you've come to the right place. You don't need much more, other than some hunks of hearty, rustic bread.
• The pork belly must be skinless to soften properly under pressure. (You can ask the butcher at your supermarket to skin it for you.) You'll need about a 10-ounce chunk to get the right amount once the skin has been removed.
• Do not confuse salt pork for the pork belly; this is fresh pork, not cured.
• Of course, to make an over-the-top dish even more so, stir in up to ¼ cup heavy cream with the pork belly.

SUCCOTASH

EFFORT: **A LITTLE** • PRESSURE: **HIGH** • TIME UNDER PRESSURE: **6 OR 9 MINUTES** • RELEASE: **QUICK** • SERVES: **6**

1½ cups dried lima beans

2 cups chicken or vegetable broth

One 14-ounce can diced tomatoes (about 1¾ cups)

1½ cups fresh corn kernels (about 1½ large ears), or frozen kernels, thawed

1 medium green bell pepper, stemmed, cored, and chopped

1 small red onion, chopped

One 4½-ounce can chopped mild green chiles (about ½ cup)

1 teaspoon minced garlic

1 teaspoon dried thyme

1 teaspoon dried sage

¼ teaspoon salt

1 Soak the beans in a big bowl of water on the counter overnight, for at least 12 hours or up to 16 hours. Drain them in a colander set in the sink.

2 Mix the beans and all the remaining ingredients in a 6-quart stovetop or electric pressure cooker.

3 Lock the lid onto the pot.

STOVETOP: Set the pot over high heat and bring it to high pressure (15 psi). Once this pressure has been reached, reduce the heat as much as possible while maintaining this pressure. Cook for 6 minutes.

························· **OR** ·························

ELECTRIC: Set the machine to cook at high pressure (9–11 psi). Set the machine's timer to cook at high pressure for 9 minutes.

4 Use the quick-release method to bring the pot's pressure back to normal.

5 Unlock and open the pot. Stir well before serving.

TESTERS' NOTES
• This Southern favorite of beans and corn in an aromatic stew just got a whole lot easier! Consider it for your next barbecue.
• Chop the bell pepper and onion into ½- to 1-inch pieces, fairly large, so they stay whole in the final dish, rather than melting into the sauce.

LIMA BEANS WITH FORTY CLOVES OF GARLIC

EFFORT: **A LOT** • PRESSURE: **HIGH** • TIME UNDER PRESSURE: **16 OR 24 MINUTES** • RELEASE: **QUICK, THEN QUICK AGAIN** • SERVES: **6 TO 8**

2 cups dried lima beans

40 medium cloves of garlic, unpeeled (about 5 garlic heads)

Up to 2 dried red chiles de Àrbol or small dried red chiles

2 fresh thyme sprigs

¼ teaspoon ground cloves

2 tablespoons unsalted butter

2 medium shallots, minced

½ cup packed fresh parsley leaves, chopped

¼ teaspoon salt

½ teaspoon ground black pepper

1 Soak the lima beans in a big bowl of water set on the counter for at least 12 hours or up to 16 hours. Drain in a colander set in the sink.

2 Place the garlic into a piece of cheesecloth and tie closed with butcher's twine; place the bag in a 6-quart stovetop or electric pressure cooker. Pour in 6 cups water.

3 Lock the lid onto the pot.

STOVETOP: Set the pot over high heat and bring it to high pressure (15 psi). Once this pressure has been reached, reduce the heat as much as possible while maintaining this pressure. Cook for 10 minutes.

································ **OR** ································

ELECTRIC: Set the machine to cook at high pressure (9–11 psi). Set the machine's timer to cook at high pressure for 15 minutes.

4 Use the quick-release method to bring the pot's pressure back to normal.

5 Unlock and open the pot. Stir in the drained beans, chiles, thyme, and ground cloves.

6 Lock the lid onto the pot again.

STOVETOP: Set the pot back over high heat and bring it back to high pressure (15 psi). Once this pressure has been reached, reduce the heat as much as possible while maintaining this pressure. Cook for 6 minutes.

································ **OR** ································

ELECTRIC: Set the machine to cook again on high pressure (9–11 psi). Set the machine's timer to cook at high pressure for 9 minutes.

7 Use the quick-release method to bring the pot's pressure back to normal.

8 Unlock and open the pot. Reserve 2 cups of the liquid. Drain the contents of the cooker into a large colander set in the sink. Discard the chiles, thyme sprigs, and the bag of garlic cloves. Wipe out the cooker.

(continued)

9 Melt the butter in the stovetop cooker set over medium heat or in the electric model turned to its browning mode. Add the shallots and cook, stirring often, until softened, about 2 minutes.

10 Stir in the parsley, salt, and pepper; then stir in the beans. Pour in ¼ cup of the reserved liquid and cook, stirring often, until hot and bubbling, 2 to 4 minutes, adding more soaking liquid in ¼-cup increments to make sure the dish never dries out. Serve at once.

TESTERS' NOTES
• By cooking the garlic cloves in a small bag, we can infuse their flavor into the beans without overseasoning the dish.
• To make the cheesecloth bag, lay a 10-inch strip of cheesecloth on your work surface, then pile all the garlic cloves in its center. Gather up the sides and tie them with butcher's twine to make a secure but not packed pouch. You want some room inside so that water can flow between the cloves, extracting more of their flavor.
• Yes, you can eat the garlic. Squeeze the soft cloves out of their hulls and spread on bread—or mix into olive oil for a dip—or save, covered, in the fridge for up to 2 weeks to add to soups and stews for a less pungent garlic flavor.

HUMMUS

EFFORT: **A LOT** • PRESSURE: **HIGH** • TIME UNDER PRESSURE: **8 OR 12 MINUTES** • RELEASE: **QUICK** • SERVES: **8**

2 cups dried chickpeas
1 teaspoon baking soda
¼ cup olive oil
¼ cup tahini
6 tablespoons fresh lemon juice
2 or 3 medium garlic cloves
½ teaspoon ground cumin
½ teaspoon dried oregano
½ teaspoon dried sage
½ teaspoon salt
½ teaspoon ground black pepper

1 Soak the chickpeas in a big bowl of water on the counter for at least 12 hours or up to 16 hours.

2 Drain the chickpeas in a colander set in the sink, then pour them into a 6-quart stovetop or electric pressure cooker. Add enough cool tap water so they're submerged by 2 inches. Stir in the baking soda.

3 Lock the lid onto the pot.

STOVETOP: Set the pot over high heat and bring it to high pressure (15 psi). Once this pressure has been reached, reduce the heat as much as possible while maintaining this pressure. Cook for 8 minutes.

················· OR ·················

ELECTRIC: Set the machine to cook at high pressure (9–11 psi). Set the machine's timer to cook at high pressure for 12 minutes.

4 Use the quick-release method to bring the pot's pressure back to normal.

5 Unlock and open the cooker. Drain the chickpeas into a colander set in the sink; rinse with cool water to bring them back to room temperature. Pour the chickpeas into a large bowl and cover with cool tap water; agitate the water to loosen their skins. Rub off and discard the skins. (You should have about 4 cups of peeled chickpeas.)

6 Pour the peeled chickpeas into a food processor fitted with the chopping blade. Add the olive oil, tahini, lemon juice, garlic, cumin, oregano, sage, salt, and pepper. Cover and process until a thick, velvety spread, scraping down the inside of the canister at least once and adding a tablespoon or more of water if the paste is too thick. Scrape into a serving bowl, cover, and refrigerate for at least 2 hours or up to 3 days.

TESTERS' NOTES

• Once you taste how impossibly creamy and savory this real-deal hummus is, you may never go back to making it (or buying it) any other way.

• Skinning the chickpeas may well be the hardest part of this task, although the baking soda helps loosen those skins during cooking. Deal with the cooked chickpeas in small, palm-sized batches so you can see the skins that can be pulled off. You needn't get every last one—but the more you get, the creamier the dip will be.

Serve It Up! Drizzle toasted pumpkin seed oil or a toasted nut oil over the hummus before serving. Or spread the hummus into a wrap, add plenty of chopped romaine and sprouts, and roll it up for a quick lunch on the go.

RICH AND CREAMY LENTILS

EFFORT: **NOT MUCH** • PRESSURE: **HIGH** • TIME UNDER PRESSURE: **10 OR 15 MINUTES** • RELEASE: **QUICK** • SERVES: **6**

2 tablespoons olive oil

1 large yellow onion, chopped

1 tablespoon minced garlic

1 tablespoon minced fresh ginger

1 tablespoon garam masala

2 cups brown lentils

1½ cups chicken broth

¾ cup canned crushed tomatoes

2 bay leaves

1 cup plain whole-milk yogurt

1 Heat the oil in a 6-quart stovetop pressure cooker set over medium heat or in a 6-quart electric pressure cooker turned to the browning function. Add the onion and cook, stirring often, until softened, about 4 minutes. Add the garlic and ginger; cook, stirring constantly, until aromatic, about 1 minute.

2 Stir in the garam masala until aromatic, less than a minute; then add the lentils, broth, tomatoes, and bay leaves. Stir well.

3 Lock the lid onto the cooker.

STOVETOP: Raise the heat to high and bring the pot to high pressure (15 psi). Immediately reduce the heat as much as possible while keeping this pressure constant. Cook for 10 minutes.

······················ **OR** ······················

ELECTRIC: Set the machine to cook at high pressure (9–11 psi). Set the timer to cook at high pressure for 15 minutes.

4 Use the quick-release method to bring the pot's pressure back to normal.

5 Unlock and open the cooker. Set the stovetop cooker over medium heat or turn the electric cooker to its browning function. Bring to a simmer, stirring often. Cook, stirring almost constantly, until the liquid has evaporated, 5 to 10 minutes. Discard the bay leaves. Stir in the yogurt before serving.

TESTERS' NOTES

• Brown lentils break down under pressure, becoming almost porridge-like—a good match for the creamy yogurt.

• Simmering the dish in step 5 helps keep it from being too soupy. However, the electric pressure cooker will heat quite high even on its browning function; you'll need to stir regularly and pay close attention to how quickly it thickens.

• Garam masala means "warm spices," and it is a blend of comforting spices without any heat in the mix. Look for bottled blends at the supermarket—or make your own: toast 3 tablespoons coriander seeds, 1½ tablespoons

(continued)

cumin seeds, 1½ tablespoons black peppercorns, 4 green cardamom pods, a 2-inch piece of cinnamon stick, about 8 whole cloves, and a bay leaf in a dry skillet over low heat, stirring often, until aromatic and lightly browned, about 3 minutes. Pour the contents of the skillet into a mini-food processor, add ½ tablespoon ground ginger, and process until a fine powder. Store in a jar in a dark place at room temperature for up to 1 year.

WARM LENTIL SALAD WITH BACON VINAIGRETTE

EFFORT: **A LITTLE** · PRESSURE: **HIGH** · TIME UNDER PRESSURE: **20 OR 30 MINUTES** · RELEASE: **NATURAL** · SERVES: **8**

2 cups green lentils (French lentils or lentils du Puy)

2 large carrots, diced

2 tablespoons olive oil

8 ounces slab bacon, diced

2 medium shallots, minced

1 medium celery stalk, minced

1 tablespoon Dijon mustard

1 tablespoon Worcestershire sauce

1 teaspoon dried thyme

1 teaspoon ground black pepper

¹/₃ cup white wine vinegar

1 Place the lentils in a 6-quart stovetop or electric pressure cooker. Add enough cool tap water that they're submerged by 2 inches.

2 Lock the lid onto the cooker.

STOVETOP: Set the pot over high heat and bring it to high pressure. Immediately reduce the heat as much as possible while maintaining this pressure. Cook for 20 minutes.

···················· OR ····················
ELECTRIC: Set the machine to cook at high pressure (9–11 psi). Set the machine's timer to cook at high pressure for 30 minutes.

3 Reduce the pressure.

STOVETOP: Set the pot aside off the heat and let its pressure come back to normal naturally, about 14 minutes.

···················· OR ····················
ELECTRIC: Turn off the machine or unplug it so it doesn't flip to its keep-warm setting. Let its pressure return to normal naturally, 14 to 16 minutes.

4 Unlock and open the cooker. Stir in the carrots. Set the lid back on the pot without locking it; set aside for 4 minutes to blanch the carrots.

5 Remove the lid and drain the lentils and carrots into a colander set in the sink. Rinse with warm water to remove the lentils' muddy film without cooling them down. Transfer to a large bowl. Wipe out the cooker.

6 Heat the oil in the stovetop cooker over medium heat or in an electric cooker turned to the browning function. Add the bacon and fry until crisp, stirring occasionally, between 3 and 6 minutes, depending on the heat levels.

7 Add the shallots and celery; cook, stirring often, for 1 minute. Stir in the mustard, Worcestershire sauce, thyme, and pepper until aromatic, about 15 seconds. Pour in the vinegar and scrape up any browned bits in the bottom of the cooker as it comes to a simmer. Pour and scrape the contents of the cooker over the lentils and carrots; toss well to coat.

• Almost hearty enough to be a meal, these lentils become luxuriously soft with just a bit of chew at their centers. Their earthiness provides a good balance with the full-flavored dressing (and the salty bacon).
• Fry the bacon until it's truly crisp; it's the dominant bit of firm texture in the final dish. Plus, its flavor needs lots of caramelization to stand up to so many other ingredients.

Serve It Up! For a main-course meal, mound the lentil mixture onto plates and top each with a poached or fried egg. Garnish with plenty of freshly ground black pepper.

CREAMY RED LENTILS WITH POTATOES, SPINACH, AND FRIED MUSTARD SEEDS

EFFORT: **A LITTLE** • PRESSURE: **HIGH** • TIME UNDER PRESSURE:
6 OR 9 MINUTES • RELEASE: **QUICK** • SERVES: **6**

6 cups (1¹/₂ quarts) vegetable or chicken broth

2 cups red lentils

1 medium yellow onion, chopped

1 tablespoon minced garlic

1 teaspoon ground coriander

1 teaspoon ground cumin

¹/₂ teaspoon ground cinnamon

¹/₂ teaspoon ground ginger

1¹/₂ pounds small yellow potatoes, such as Yukon Gold, cut into 1¹/₂-inch pieces

3 cups chopped stemmed spinach leaves

2 tablespoons unsalted butter

2 tablespoons yellow or brown mustard seeds

1 Mix the broth, lentils, onion, garlic, coriander, cumin, cinnamon, and ginger in a 6-quart stovetop or electric pressure cooker. Set the potatoes into the mixture.

2 Lock the lid onto the cooker.

STOVETOP: Set the pot over high heat and bring the pot to high pressure (15 psi). Once this pressure has been reached, reduce the heat as much as possible while maintaining this pressure. Cook for 6 minutes.

·········· **OR** ··········

ELECTRIC: Set the machine to cook at high pressure (9–11 psi). Set the machine's timer to cook at high pressure for 9 minutes.

3 Use the quick-release method to bring the pot's pressure back to normal.

4 Unlock and open the pot. Set the stovetop cooker over medium heat or turn the electric cooker to the browning function. Add the spinach and cook, stirring often, until the spinach has wilted, about 3 minutes. Set aside off the heat or turn off the machine.

5 Melt the butter in a medium nonstick skillet set over medium heat. Add the mustard seeds and cook until they pop, about 1 minute, stirring often. Spoon the red lentil mixture onto plates and top with a little of the butter and fried mustard seeds.

TESTERS' NOTES
• Red lentils will break down into almost a puree as they cook, giving you a thick and rich dish. You'll need to stir them quite a bit in step 4 as you wilt the spinach.
• For an easier task, use 3 cups bagged baby spinach leaves (no need to stem them).

DESSERTS

IF A FISH CHAPTER IS SOMETHING OF A SURPRISE IN A PRESSURE
cooker book, a dessert chapter is downright shocking. And we'll admit it right up front: you're not saving much time when it comes to desserts. In fact, some require the same amount of effort that they would in the oven. So don't make desserts in a pressure cooker because you're trying to shave minutes off your work load. Make them because you love desserts.

Cheesecakes come out denser and firmer; compotes, more intensely flavored; and cakes, moister. Puddings become like softened frosting; custards, rich and silky. True, we can't make an airy sponge cake or a crisp crust. So we won't try. Instead, let's focus on the velvety, the dense, and the intensely flavored.

Almost all of these recipes require some sort of special equipment: a certain size baking dish or ramekins, a rack in the pressure cooker, or an aluminum foil sling so you can get the baking dish in and out of the cooker without burning your fingers (see page 19). Follow the instructions exactly for the equipment you need: baking is more precise; the tools are part of the precision. And use good ingredients, the best that you can comfortably afford. Make sure your chocolate doesn't include fake flavorings. Stick to pure, not imitation, vanilla extract. And choose fruits that smell luscious.

Here's one more important ingredient note for all our recipes: use only full-fat dairy products unless the recipe specifically states that you can use low-fat or fat-free. Because of the intense pressure environment, as well as certain thickeners and stabilizers that low-fat or fat-free dairy products may contain, they can break while cooking, leaving your dessert a soupy mess.

And please note this: many of these desserts are cooked over *low* pressure in a *stovetop* cooker. Simply put, these desserts are best at 8 psi, the lowest setting for most stovetop models. Check your manufacturer's instructions for exact specifications.

That said, many stovetop cookers do not have a low setting. Yes, you can cook the cheesecakes and such under high pressure (15 psi); but you need to cut the time by a third and understand that although the flavor will be fine, the texture and appearance won't win any awards.

Additionally, the low pressure setting on some *electric* machines is simply too low to get the cake to properly set before it turns into a gummy mess. So you have to resort to high pressure (9–11 psi) for the electric models and realize you're going to end up with a somewhat compromised look (but not taste), more bumps and squiggles on top of the cake as well as many more holes inside it.

That all said, digging into a cheesecake or pudding will convince you that this appliance can do just about anything. So whip up a batter, pull together a pudding, or poach some fruit in a sweet, aromatic syrup. You'll soon discover that a pressure cooker can do even these things exceptionally well.

CHOCOLATE PUDDING

EFFORT: **A LITTLE** • PRESSURE: **HIGH** • TIME UNDER PRESSURE:
10 OR 15 MINUTES • RELEASE: **NATURAL** • SERVES: **6**

6 ounces semisweet or bittersweet chocolate, chopped

$1/2$ ounce unsweetened chocolate, chopped

6 tablespoons sugar

$1^1/2$ cups light cream

4 large egg yolks, at room temperature and whisked in a small bowl

1 tablespoon vanilla extract

$1/4$ teaspoon salt

1 Place all the chopped chocolate and the sugar in a large bowl. Heat the cream in a saucepan over low heat until small bubbles fizz around the inside edge of the pan.

2 Pour the warmed cream over the chocolate; whisk until the chocolate has completely melted. Cool a minute or two, then whisk in the yolks, vanilla, and salt. Pour the mixture into six $1/2$-cup heat-safe ramekins, filling each about three-quarters full. Cover each with foil.

3 Set the rack in a 6-quart stovetop or electric pressure cooker; pour in 2 cups water. Set the ramekins on the rack, stacking them as necessary without any one ramekin sitting directly on top of another.

4 Lock the lid onto the pot.

STOVETOP: Set the pot over high heat and bring it to high pressure (15 psi). Once this pressure has been reached, reduce the heat as much as possible while maintaining this pressure. Cook for 10 minutes.

·····OR·····

ELECTRIC: Set the machine to cook at high pressure (9–11 psi). Set the machine's timer to cook at high pressure for 15 minutes.

5 Reduce the pressure.

STOVETOP: Set the pot aside off the heat and let its pressure come back to normal naturally, about 10 minutes.

·····OR·····

ELECTRIC: Turn off the machine or unplug it so it doesn't flip to its keep-warm setting. Let its pressure return to normal naturally, 10 to 14 minutes.

6 Unlock and open the cooker. Transfer the hot ramekins to a cooling rack, uncover, and cool for 10 minutes before serving—or chill in the refrigerator for up to 3 days, covering again once the puddings have chilled.

TESTERS' NOTES

• Talk about rich! Because of the way the pressure works on the fat and chocolate, these puddings end up more like French pot de crème, dense custards almost like soft icing. You'll probably need whipped cream to cut the richness!
• Chop the chocolate into small bits so they melt quickly.
• Stack the ramekins so that the second layer sits on the rim of at least two ramekins below, rather than right on top of (and thus into) the ramekins below. It's also better to stack the ramekins in the pot once it's at the stove.
• Heavy cream is just too, well, heavy. Light cream is about 20 percent butterfat and yields a better texture. You can also use half-and-half for a less rich dessert.

Serve It Up! To make **Sweetened Whipped Cream**, beat 1 cup chilled heavy cream, 2 tablespoons confectioners' sugar, and $1/2$ teaspoon vanilla in a large bowl with an electric mixer at high speed until thick and soft. For better texture, refrigerate the bowl and beaters for 2 hours before using.

WHITE CHOCOLATE LEMON PUDDING

EFFORT: **A LITTLE** • PRESSURE: **HIGH** • TIME UNDER PRESSURE:
10 OR 15 MINUTES • RELEASE: **NATURAL** • SERVES: **6**

6 ounces white chocolate, chopped

1 cup heavy cream

1 cup half-and-half

**4 large egg yolks, at room temperature
and whisked in a small bowl**

1 tablespoon sugar

**1 tablespoon finely grated lemon zest
(about 1 medium lemon)**

¼ teaspoon lemon extract

1 Put the chopped white chocolate in a large bowl. Mix the cream and half-and-half in a small saucepan and warm over low heat until bubbles fizz around the edges of the pan.

2 Pour the warm mixture over the white chocolate and whisk until melted. Whisk in the egg yolks, sugar, zest, and extract. Pour the mixture into six ½-cup heat-safe ramekins; cover each tightly with aluminum foil.

3 Set the pressure cooker rack in a 6-quart stovetop or electric pressure cooker; pour in 2 cups water. Set the ramekins on the rack, stacking them as necessary without any one ramekin sitting directly on top of another.

4 Lock the lid onto the pot.

STOVETOP: Set the pot over high heat and bring it to high pressure (15 psi). Once this pressure has been reached, reduce the heat as much as possible while maintaining this pressure. Cook for 10 minutes.

·················· **OR** ··················

ELECTRIC: Set the machine to cook at high pressure (9–11 psi). Set the machine's timer to cook at high pressure for 15 minutes.

5 Reduce the pressure.

STOVETOP: Set the pot off the heat and let its pressure come back to normal naturally, about 10 minutes.

·················· **OR** ··················

ELECTRIC: Turn off the machine or unplug it so it doesn't jump to its keep-warm setting. Let its pressure return to normal naturally, 10 to 14 minutes.

6 Unlock and open the cooker. Transfer the (hot!) ramekins to a cooling rack; uncover each and cool for a few minutes before serving—or store in the refrigerator for up to 3 days, covering the ramekins again after they have chilled.

TESTERS' NOTES

• These are dense, almost chewy puddings laced with lemon to help counteract the richness. The puddings condense a bit as they chill, so if you like very soft pudding, enjoy them warm.

• There's a wide range of white chocolate on the market, some of it little more than sweetened and flavored shortening. Check the label carefully to make sure cocoa fat is the primary ingredient. As a general rule, better-quality white chocolate is found in bars, not chips.

Serve It Up! Crumble gingersnaps over the puddings.

ESPRESSO PUDDING

EFFORT: **NOT MUCH** • PRESSURE: **HIGH** • TIME UNDER PRESSURE: **10 OR 15 MINUTES** • RELEASE: **NATURAL** • SERVES: **6**

1 cup heavy cream
1 cup half-and-half
1 tablespoon instant espresso powder
1/2 cup sugar
1 large egg plus 4 large egg yolks, at room temperature and whisked in a small bowl

1 Whisk the cream, half-and-half, and espresso powder in a large bowl until the powder dissolves. Whisk in the sugar, whole egg, and egg yolks until smooth. Ladle the mixture into six 1/2-cup heat-safe ramekins; cover each tightly with aluminum foil.

2 Set the pressure cooker rack in a 6-quart stovetop or electric cooker; pour in 2 cups water. Stack the ramekins on the rack, no one ramekin sitting directly on top of another below.

3 Lock the lid onto the pot.

STOVETOP: Set the pot over high heat and bring it to high pressure (15 psi). Once this pressure has been reached, reduce the heat as much as possible while maintaining this pressure. Cook for 10 minutes.

·······························OR·······························

ELECTRIC: Set the machine to cook at high pressure (9–11 psi). Set the machine's timer to cook at high pressure for 15 minutes.

4 Reduce the pressure.

STOVETOP: Set the pot aside off the heat and let its pressure come back to normal naturally, about 10 minutes.

·······························OR·······························

ELECTRIC: Turn off the machine or unplug it so it doesn't flip to its keep-warm setting. Let its pressure return to normal naturally, 10 to 14 minutes.

5 Unlock and open the pot. Transfer the hot ramekins to a wire rack, uncover, and cool for a few minutes before serving. Or set them in the fridge and cool completely, covering again once when they're no longer hot; store them there for up to 3 days.

TESTERS' NOTES

• Like a rich coffeehouse drink turned into a pudding, these custards set to a firm texture, the better to hold up to some whipped cream (see page 480).
• Instant espresso powder should dissolve quickly in the liquids, so forgo any of the stuff with coarse grains. Once opened, tightly seal and store the powder for up to 1 year in the freezer.
• For a chocolate espresso flavor, sprinkle a pinch of cocoa powder over each pudding before cooking under pressure.
• Removing the hot ramekins from the cooker can be a challenge. Silicone-based oven mitts work best; cloth oven mitts or hot pads can get wet and transfer hot steam directly to your fingers.

PUMPKIN PIE PUDDING

EFFORT: **A LITTLE** • PRESSURE: **HIGH** • TIME UNDER PRESSURE: **15 OR 22 MINUTES** • RELEASE: **NATURAL** • SERVES: **4**

1½ cups canned pumpkin
½ cup packed dark brown sugar
½ cup heavy cream
2 large eggs, at room temperature
2 tablespoons unsulphured molasses
1 teaspoon vanilla extract
2 tablespoons all-purpose flour
1 teaspoon ground cinnamon
¼ teaspoon salt

1 Lightly butter the inside of a 1-quart round, high-sided soufflé or baking dish; set aside.

2 Whisk the pumpkin, brown sugar, cream, eggs, molasses, and vanilla in a large bowl until the brown sugar has dissolved. Whisk in the flour, cinnamon, and salt until smooth.

3 Pour the mixture into the prepared baking dish. Butter one side of a 10-inch piece of aluminum foil and set it buttered side down over the baking dish; seal well.

4 Set the pressure cooker rack in a 6-quart stovetop or electric cooker; pour in 2 cups water. Make an aluminum foil sling for the baking dish (see page 19), then set the dish on it and use that foil sling to lower the dish onto the rack. Crimp the ends of the sling to fit inside the cooker.

5 Lock the lid onto the pot.

STOVETOP: Set the pot over high heat and bring it to high pressure (15 psi). Once this pressure has been reached, reduce the heat as much as possible while maintaining this pressure. Cook for 15 minutes.

··· **OR** ···

ELECTRIC: Set the machine to cook at high pressure (9–11 psi). Set the machine's timer to cook at this pressure for 22 minutes.

6 Reduce the pressure.

STOVETOP: Set the pot off the heat and let its pressure come back to normal naturally, about 10 minutes.

··· **OR** ···

ELECTRIC: Turn off the machine or unplug it so it doesn't flip to its keep-warm setting. Let its pressure return to normal naturally, 10 to 14 minutes.

7 Unlock and open the cooker. Use the foil sling to transfer the baking dish to a wire cooling rack; uncover and set aside for a few minutes, until the pudding is firm and set. Serve by dishing it up warm by the spoonful.

TESTERS' NOTES
• Consider this dessert a pumpkin pie without the crust. The pudding is firm, almost cutable. It cries out for whipped cream (page 480) or vanilla ice cream on top.
• Because of varying moisture content in canned pumpkin, there's a slight chance the pudding may not be fully set when uncovered. If so, cover the baking dish again, lower it in its sling onto the rack over the water, lock the lid onto the cooker, and cook at high pressure for 2 or 3 more minutes to set completely.
• Use solid-pack canned pumpkin, not pumpkin pie filling.
• While we prefer this pudding warm, it condenses some more when cold to make it even more pumpkin-pie like. If this texture is your preference, make the pudding up to 3 days in advance; once cooled, cover it again and store in the fridge.
• You can use honey (sweeter) instead of molasses.

COCONUT FLAN

EFFORT: **A LOT** • PRESSURE: **HIGH** • TIME UNDER PRESSURE: **25 OR 37 MINUTES** • RELEASE: **NATURAL** • SERVES: **8**

1 cup unsweetened shredded coconut

²/₃ cup granulated sugar

1³/₄ cups coconut milk

1 cup sweetened condensed milk

2 large eggs plus 4 large egg yolks, at room temperature and whisked in a small bowl

3 tablespoons packed light brown sugar

1¹/₂ tablespoons dark rum, such as Myers's

1 teaspoon vanilla extract

¹/₄ teaspoon salt

1 Position the rack in the center of the oven; heat the oven to 350°F. Spread the coconut on a large rimmed baking sheet; bake until golden brown, tossing occasionally, about 10 minutes. Set aside on a wire rack to cool completely. (If desired, pour the coconut into a small bowl, seal with plastic wrap, and store at room temperature for up to 2 days.)

2 Cook the sugar and ¼ cup water in a small saucepan over medium-low heat, stirring until the sugar dissolves. Let the syrup simmer undisturbed until it turns amber, 3 to 4 minutes. Pour the hot sugar syrup into an 8-inch round cake pan. Swirl to coat the bottom and about three-fourths of the way up the sides of the pan.

3 Whisk the coconut milk, condensed milk, eggs and egg yolks, brown sugar, rum, vanilla, and salt in a large bowl until the sugar dissolves and the mixture is smooth. Pour the batter into the cake pan and cover tightly with aluminum foil.

4 Set the rack inside a 6-quart stovetop or electric pressure cooker; pour in 2 cups water. Make an aluminum foil sling (see page 19) and use it to lower the cake pan onto the rack. Crimp the ends of the sling inside the pot.

5 Lock the lid onto the cooker.

STOVETOP: Set the pot over high heat and bring it to high pressure (15 psi). Once this pressure has been reached, reduce the heat as much as possible while maintaining this pressure. Cook for 25 minutes.

·················· **OR** ··················

ELECTRIC: Set the machine to cook at high pressure (9–11 psi). Set the machine's timer to cook at this pressure for 37 minutes.

6 Reduce the pressure.

STOVETOP: Set the pot off the heat and let its pressure come back to normal naturally, about 10 minutes.

·················· **OR** ··················

ELECTRIC: Turn off the machine or unplug it so it doesn't flip to its keep-warm setting. Let its pressure return to normal naturally, 10 to 14 minutes.

7 Unlock and open the pot. Use the foil sling to transfer the hot baking dish to a wire rack. Uncover and cool to room temperature, about 2 hours. Cover the dish and chill in the refrigerator for at least 6 hours or up to 2 days.

8 Unmold the flan by setting a rimmed serving platter over the baking dish, then carefully flipping the whole thing upside down. Tap the baking dish to release the flan. Once you're confident it has released, remove the cake pan, letting the sugar syrup pour over the custard. Top with the toasted coconut before slicing into wedges to serve.

• Why make a flan in a pressure cooker rather than in a water bath in the oven? Besides a quicker baking time, the flan becomes denser with a gorgeously rich consistency.

• Don't use fat-free condensed milk or low-fat ("lite") coconut milk. The flan needs fat to set up properly.

• Once you've poured the hot sugar syrup into the cake pan, that pan is too hot to touch with bare hands. Handle it with hot pads or baking mitts.

• It's imperative that the flan cool and set up before you try to unmold it. There's a slight possibility, especially in the lower pressure of an electric cooker, that the flan will not be fully set by the time it's out of the cooker. If you uncover it while cooling on the wire rack and notice that it's still liquid at its center; cover again and give it 1 to 2 minutes at high pressure on a rack over water, followed by a quick release.

• The caramel may harden enough in the fridge that you can't unmold the flan. If so, set the pan in a bowl of hot water without immersing it, to remelt the sugar.

RICE PUDDING

EFFORT: **A LITTLE** • PRESSURE: **HIGH** • TIME UNDER PRESSURE: **10 OR 16 MINUTES** • RELEASE: **NATURAL** • SERVES: **6**

1 tablespoon unsalted butter

3/4 cup medium-grain white rice, such as Arborio

1 1/2 cups whole milk

1/2 cup sugar

1 tablespoon vanilla extract

1/2 teaspoon salt

1/2 teaspoon ground cinnamon (optional)

1 large egg plus 1 large egg yolk, at room temperature

1/4 cup heavy cream

1 Melt the butter in a 6-quart stovetop pressure cooker set over medium heat or in a 6-quart electric pressure cooker turned to the browning function. Add the rice and cook, stirring all the while, for 1 minute. Stir in the milk, sugar, vanilla, salt, and cinnamon, if using, along with 1 1/2 cups water, until the sugar dissolves. Cook for 1 minute, stirring constantly, to heat through and make sure no grains of rice are sticking to the bottom of the pot.

2 Lock the lid onto the pot.

STOVETOP: Set the pot over high heat and bring it to high pressure (15 psi). Once this pressure has been reached, reduce the heat as much as possible while maintaining this pressure. Cook for 10 minutes.

························ **OR** ························

ELECTRIC: Set the machine to cook at high pressure (9–11 psi). Set the machine's timer to cook at high pressure for 16 minutes.

3 Reduce the pressure.

STOVETOP: Set the pot off the heat and let its pressure come back to normal naturally, about 10 minutes.

························ **OR** ························

ELECTRIC: Turn off the machine or unplug it so it doesn't flip to its keep-warm setting. Let its pressure return to normal naturally, 10 to 16 minutes.

4 Unlock and open the cooker. Whisk the egg, egg yolk, and cream in a large bowl until smooth and creamy. Whisk about 2 cups of the hot pudding mixture into the egg mixture until creamy, then whisk this combined mixture into the pudding in the cooker until uniform.

5 Set the stovetop model over medium heat or turn the electric model to its browning setting. Whisk the pudding constantly until thickened, about 30 seconds, never letting the mixture come to a bubble (or the eggs will curdle). Remove from the heat or turn off the machine. Serve warm.

(continued)

• We're unabashed fans of this rice pudding, a lot creamier than the standard because the rice grains do not have the time to dry out. What's more, we used medium-grain rice, turning this dish into something like a dessert risotto.
• The egg and egg yolks will cook in the hot pudding. But if you're concerned about salmonella, set the stovetop pot over medium-low heat or turn the electric one to its browning function and whisk the combined mixture over the heat for about 1 minute, just until you see the first bubble. Immediately remove the pot from the heat or turn off the electric model to avoid scrambling the eggs.
• Although this rice pudding is best served warm, it can be stored in a sealed container in the fridge for a couple of days. It will firm up—but still make a good snack.

RICE CUSTARD

EFFORT: **A LITTLE** • PRESSURE: **LOW OR HIGH** • TIME UNDER PRESSURE: **38 OR 30 MINUTES** • RELEASE: **NATURAL** • SERVES: **6**

2²/₃ **cups whole or 2% milk**

2 **large eggs plus 2 large egg yolks, at room temperature**

2 **cups cooked long-grain white rice**

¹/₃ **cup sugar**

¹/₃ **cup golden raisins**

1¹/₂ **tablespoons vanilla extract**

¹/₄ **teaspoon salt**

1 Butter the inside of a 2-quart round, high-sided soufflé or baking dish. Set a rack inside a 6-quart stovetop or electric pressure cooker; pour in 2 cups water.

2 Whisk the milk, eggs, and egg yolks in a large bowl until smooth and creamy, no bits of egg white floating in the mix. Whisk in the rice, sugar, raisins, vanilla, and salt; pour into the prepared baking dish. Cover tightly with aluminum foil.

3 Make an aluminum foil sling (see page 19) and set the baking dish on top of it. Use the sling to lower the dish onto the rack in the cooker. Crimp the ends of the sling to fit into the pot.

4 Lock on the lid.

STOVETOP: Set the pot over high heat and bring it to low pressure (8 psi). Once this pressure has been reached, reduce the heat as much as possible while maintaining this pressure. Cook for 38 minutes.

······················ **OR** ······················

ELECTRIC: Set the machine to cook at high pressure (9–11 psi). Set the machine's timer to cook at this pressure for 30 minutes.

5 Reduce the pressure.

STOVETOP: Set the pot off the heat and let its pressure come back to normal naturally, about 8 minutes.

······················ **OR** ······················

ELECTRIC: Turn off the machine or unplug it so it doesn't flip to its keep-warm setting. Let its pressure return to normal naturally, 8 to 12 minutes.

6 Unlock and open the cooker. Use the foil sling to transfer the baking dish to a wire rack; uncover the dish. The custard should be loosely set, thickened but still jiggly when the baking dish is tapped. Cool for 1 hour before dishing up by the spoonful.

TESTERS' NOTES
• This custard tastes more decadent than standard rice pudding. It's also slightly firmer than rice pudding while still being loose enough to be eaten with a spoon, not a fork.
• If the custard is not fully set, cover it again, lower it onto the rack over the water, and cook at low pressure in the stovetop model for 2 more minutes, or at high in the electric cooker for 1 minute.
• The raisins will swell under pressure. If that bothers you, chop them first.

- We use cooked rice here so it will get softer as the custard sets for a luxurious dessert. For a shortcut, stop by a Chinese restaurant and pick up a container.
- The *stovetop* method must be cooked at *low* pressure. Check your manufacturer's instructions to determine the exact method of doing this in your model. The lower pressure will give you a smoother top and a better set overall.

CHERRY CLAFOUTI

EFFORT: **A LITTLE** • PRESSURE: **LOW OR HIGH** • TIME UNDER PRESSURE: **20 OR 18 MINUTES** • RELEASE: **NATURAL** • SERVES: **6**

2 cups pitted sour cherries

3/4 cup regular or low-fat sour cream (not fat-free)

4 large egg yolks, at room temperature

1/3 cup honey

1/4 cup whole or 2% milk

1 tablespoon vanilla extract

1/2 teaspoon salt

1/2 cup all-purpose flour

1 Butter the inside of a 2-quart round, high-sided baking or soufflé dish. Set the rack inside a 6-quart stovetop or electric pressure cooker; pour in 2 cups water.

2 Place the cherries in the bottom of the prepared baking dish. Whisk the sour cream, egg yolks, honey, milk, vanilla, and salt in a large bowl until smooth and creamy. Whisk in the flour until completely dissolved. Pour the batter over the cherries in the baking dish.

3 Make an aluminum foil sling (see page 19) and set the baking dish on top of it. Use the sling to lower the baking dish onto the rack in the cooker; crimp the ends of the sling so they'll fit inside the cooker.

4 Lock the lid onto the pot.

STOVETOP: Set the pot over high heat and bring it to low pressure (8 psi). Once this pressure has been reached, reduce the heat as much as possible while maintaining this pressure. Cook for 20 minutes.

·········· **OR** ··········

ELECTRIC: Set the machine to cook at high pressure (9–11 psi). Set the machine's timer to cook at this pressure for 18 minutes.

5 Reduce the pressure.

STOVETOP: Set the pot off the heat and let its pressure come back to normal naturally, about 8 minutes.

·········· **OR** ··········

ELECTRIC: Turn off the machine or unplug it so it doesn't flip to its keep-warm setting. Let its pressure return to normal naturally, 8 to 12 minutes.

6 Unlock and open the pot. Use the foil sling to transfer the hot baking dish to a wire cooling rack. Let stand for 10 minutes. If desired, unmold onto a serving platter before slicing into wedges to serve.

TESTERS' NOTES

- A clafouti (French, *clah-foo-TEE*) is a cake-like custard baked over fruit—and it makes a fine breakfast, too. Honey's not traditional, but we feel it adds a floral richness.
- A traditional cherry clafouti is made with cherries that have their pits, the slightly bitter flavor of which helps to balance the sweet custard. However, we found the flavor became too pronounced under pressure, so we opted for pitted cherries. (You can also substitute 8 ripe apricots, halved and pitted, for the cherries.)
- The texture here is more like a cake than a custard, so cut it into slices.

Serve It Up! Sweeten sour cream with confectioners' sugar and flavor it with a little vanilla extract. Serve dollops on each wedge.

PINEAPPLE UPSIDE-DOWN CAKE

EFFORT: **A LITTLE** • PRESSURE: **LOW OR HIGH** • TIME UNDER PRESSURE: **35 OR 25 MINUTES** • RELEASE: **NATURAL** • SERVES: **6**

1 cup all-purpose flour

³/₄ teaspoon baking powder

¹/₄ teaspoon salt

¹/₄ teaspoon ground cinnamon

¹/₄ cup packed dark brown sugar

4 canned pineapple rings packed in syrup

2 large eggs, at room temperature

¹/₂ cup regular or low-fat sour cream

¹/₂ cup granulated sugar

3 tablespoons unsalted butter, melted and cooled

2 teaspoons vanilla extract

1 Generously butter the inside of a 2-quart round, high-sided soufflé or baking dish. Place a rack inside a 6-quart stovetop or electric pressure cooker; pour in 2 cups water. Whisk the flour, baking powder, salt, and cinnamon in a small bowl; set aside.

2 Sprinkle the brown sugar evenly over the bottom of the prepared dish. Lay the pineapple rings in the baking dish. Whisk the eggs, sour cream, sugar, butter, and vanilla in a large bowl until smooth. Whisk in the flour mixture until moistened and uniform; pour into the baking dish. Do not cover.

3 Make an aluminum foil sling (see page 19), set the baking dish on it, and lower it onto the rack in the cooker. Crimp the ends of the sling to fit into the pot.

4 Lock on the lid.

STOVETOP: Set the pot over high heat and bring it to low pressure (8 psi). Once this pressure has been reached, reduce the heat as much as possible while maintaining this pressure. Cook for 35 minutes.

·····················OR·····················

ELECTRIC: Set the machine to cook at high pressure (9–11 psi). Set the machine's timer to cook at high pressure for 25 minutes.

5 Reduce the pressure.

STOVETOP: Set the pot off the heat and let its pressure come back to normal naturally, about 8 minutes.

·····················OR·····················

ELECTRIC: Turn off the machine or unplug it so it doesn't flip to its keep-warm setting. Let its pressure return to normal naturally, 8 to 12 minutes.

6 Unlock and open the cooker. Use the foil sling to transfer the hot baking dish to a wire rack. Cool for 10 minutes, then set a serving platter over the baking dish, invert it all, and remove the baking dish, thereby unmolding the cake. Serve warm or at room temperature.

TESTERS' NOTES

• This buttery cake has a moist, chewy consistency, halfway between a sponge cake and a steamed pudding. The results are irresistible, sweet yet not cloying.

• If your *stovetop* machine does not have a *low* pressure setting, cook this cake at high pressure (15 psi) for 15 minutes. The results will be gummier and not nearly so refined, but the cake will have the old-fashioned flavors intact.

Serve It Up! Make a pot of coffee to serve with the cake.

CHERRY ALMOND PUDDING CAKE

EFFORT: **A LITTLE** · PRESSURE: **HIGH** · TIME UNDER PRESSURE:
20 OR 35 MINUTES · RELEASE: **NATURAL** · SERVES: **6**

¹/₃ **cup cherry jam**

8 **tablespoons (1 stick) unsalted butter**

¹/₄ **cup packed dark brown sugar**

¹/₄ **cup granulated white sugar**

2 **large eggs, at room temperature**

3 **tablespoons almond liqueur, such as
   Amaretto**

1 **tablespoon vanilla extract**

³/₄ **cup finely ground almonds**

¹/₂ **cup all-purpose flour**

¹/₄ **teaspoon salt**

1 Generously butter the inside of a 2-quart
round, high-sided soufflé or baking dish.
Spread the jam across the bottom of the baking dish. Set the pressure cooker rack inside
a 6-quart stovetop or electric cooker; pour in
2 cups water.

2 Use an electric mixer at medium speed
to beat the butter and both sugars in a large
bowl until creamy and pale yellow, about
5 minutes, scraping down the inside of the
bowl occasionally with a rubber spatula.

3 Beat in the eggs one at a time until smooth,
then beat in the liqueur and vanilla. Add the
almonds, flour, and salt; beat at low speed
until uniform. Pour the batter into the
prepared baking dish. Butter one side
of a 12-inch piece of aluminum foil and set
it buttered side down on the baking dish.
Seal well.

4 Make an aluminum foil sling (see page 19)
and set the baking dish on it. Use the sling to

lower the dish onto the rack; crimp the ends
to fit into the pot.

5 Lock the lid onto the cooker.

STOVETOP: Set the pot over high heat and bring
it to high pressure (15 psi). Once this pressure has
been reached, reduce the heat as much as possible while maintaining this pressure. Cook for
20 minutes.

······················ **OR** ······················

ELECTRIC: Set the machine to cook at high pressure (9–11 psi). Set the machine's timer to cook at
this pressure for 35 minutes.

6 Reduce the pressure.

STOVETOP: Turn off the heat and let the pot's
pressure come back to normal naturally, about
12 minutes.

······················ **OR** ······················

ELECTRIC: Turn off the machine or unplug it so it
doesn't flip to its keep-warm setting. Let its pressure return to normal naturally, 12 to 16 minutes.

7 Unlock and open the pot. Use the foil sling
to transfer the hot baking dish to a wire rack.
Uncover the dish and cool for 5 minutes.
Invert the dish over a rimmed serving platter
and release the cake onto the platter. Remove
the baking dish and serve warm.

TESTERS' NOTES

• This sweet and nutty pudding cake has the texture of an
old-fashioned steamed pudding: moist, dense, and chewy.
The cake can be cut into wedges but the edges won't be
clean, given the "pudding" nature of the cake. It's best to
serve it with forks *and* spoons.

• The liquor will add lots of almond flavor but the cake
will retain much of its alcohol. If desired, substitute flavored almond syrup, available in the coffee aisle of many
supermarkets.

RICOTTA LEMON PUDDING CAKES

EFFORT: **A LOT** • PRESSURE: **HIGH** • TIME UNDER PRESSURE: **15 OR 22 MINUTES** • RELEASE: **NATURAL** • SERVES: **6**

1 pound whole-milk ricotta (not low-fat or fat-free)

4 large eggs, at room temperature

¹⁄₂ cup sugar

2 tablespoons fresh lemon juice

2 teaspoons finely grated lemon zest

¹⁄₂ teaspoon lemon extract (optional)

¹⁄₄ cup all-purpose flour

1 Set the rack inside a 6-quart stovetop or electric pressure cooker; pour in 2 cups water. Generously butter the inside of a 7-inch springform baking pan or a 2-quart round, high-sided soufflé or baking dish.

2 Place the ricotta, eggs, sugar, lemon juice, lemon zest, and lemon extract, if using, in a food processor fitted with the chopping blade. Cover and process until smooth, stopping the machine once or twice to scrape down the inside of the canister. Add the flour and pulse until uniform and smooth. Scrape the batter into the prepared baking pan; cover tightly with foil.

3 Make an aluminum foil sling (see page 19) and set the baking dish on top of it. Use the sling to lower the dish onto the rack in the pot; crimp the sling's ends to fit inside the pot.

4 Lock the lid onto the cooker.

STOVETOP: Set the pot over high heat and bring it to high pressure (15 psi). Once this pressure has been reached, reduce the heat as much as possible while maintaining this pressure. Cook for 15 minutes.

······························ OR ·····························
ELECTRIC: Set the machine to cook at high pressure (9–11 psi). Set the machine's timer to cook at this pressure for 22 minutes.

5 Reduce the pressure.

STOVETOP: Set the pot off the heat and let its pressure come back to normal naturally, about 12 minutes.

······························ OR ·····························
ELECTRIC: Turn off the machine or unplug it so it doesn't flip to its keep-warm setting. Let its pressure return to normal naturally, 10 to 16 minutes.

6 Unlock and open the pot. Use the foil sling to transfer the hot baking dish to a wire cooling rack; uncover the dish and cool for 30 minutes. If you used a springform pan, unlatch the sides and serve warm by scooping out chunks with a big spoon.

TESTERS' NOTES
• The water content of ricotta keeps this cake from being a cheesecake and turns it into a fairly loose pudding cake, best eaten with a spoon.
• The lemon extract—that is, diluted lemon oil—will add a deeper flavor to the cake.
• For a sophisticated cake, add up to 1 tablespoon minced fresh basil with the lemon extract.

Serve It Up! Have a scoop of chocolate sorbet on the side.

CHRISTMAS PUDDING

EFFORT: **A LOT** · PRESSURE: **HIGH** · TIME UNDER PRESSURE:
1 HOUR 10 MINUTES OR 1 HOUR 45 MINUTES · RELEASE: **NATURAL**
· SERVES: **8–10**

7 ounces golden raisins (about 1¼ cups)

7 ounces raisins (about 1¼ cups)

7 ounces dried cranberries
    (about 1¼ cups)

3 ounces candied orange peel
    (about ½ cup)

1 medium tart green apple, peeled

½ cup dark beer, such as porter or stout

2 tablespoons brandy

1 teaspoon ground cinnamon

½ teaspoon ground ginger

½ teaspoon ground cloves

¼ teaspoon salt

1 cup plain dried breadcrumbs

¾ cup all-purpose flour

½ cup packed dark brown sugar

2 large eggs, whisked in a small bowl

6 ounces coconut oil

1 Place the rack inside a 6-quart stovetop or electric pressure cooker; pour in 2 cups water. Generously butter the inside of a 2-quart round, high-sided baking or soufflé dish.

2 Put all the dried fruit and candied peel in a food processor fitted with the chopping blade; cover and process until coarsely chopped. Scrape the fruit into a large bowl. Use the large holes of a box grater to shred the apple into this mixture, stopping at the core on each side. Stir in the beer, brandy, cinnamon, ginger, cloves, and salt. Set aside for 1 hour while the dried fruit absorbs the liquids.

3 Stir in the breadcrumbs, flour, brown sugar, and eggs. Grate the coconut oil through the large holes of a box grater into the mixture; stir well. Pour the mixture into the prepared baking dish. Cover tightly with aluminum foil.

4 Make an aluminum foil sling (see page 19) and set the baking dish on top of it. Use the sling to lower the baking dish onto the rack in the cooker; crimp the ends of the foil sling so they fit inside the pot.

5 Lock the lid onto the cooker.

STOVETOP: Set the pot over high heat and bring it to high pressure (15 psi). Once this pressure has been reached, reduce the heat as much as possible while maintaining this pressure. Cook for 1 hour 10 minutes.

··········· **OR** ···········

ELECTRIC: Set the machine to cook at high pressure (9–11 psi). Set the machine's timer to cook at high pressure for 1 hour 45 minutes.

6 Reduce the pressure.

STOVETOP: Set the pot off the heat and let its pressure come back to normal naturally, about 20 minutes.

··········· **OR** ···········

ELECTRIC: Turn off the machine or unplug it so it doesn't flip to its keep-warm setting. Let its pressure return to normal naturally, 20 to 30 minutes.

7 Unlock and open the pot. Use the foil sling to transfer the hot baking dish to a wire cooling rack. Uncover the baking dish and cool for 20 minutes. Invert the warm dish onto a serving plate or platter, tap out the cake, and remove the dish. Serve warm or at room temperature.

(continued)

• Like an old-fashioned steamed pudding, this dense cake will be a welcome holiday treat with a moist yet crumbly texture. It will not slice into neat pieces, but that's pretty much in keeping with the traditional form of this cake.

• Look for candied orange peel in the baking aisle or in the dried fruit part of the produce section. The candied orange peel is sometimes labeled "chopped glacéed orange peel." In fact, you can substitute a mixture of candied (or glacéed) rinds like orange and citron, often available in small packages.

• Coconut fat is solid at room temperature. Grating it lets it get evenly distributed throughout the cake (and takes the place of suet, a rather unpleasant addition for some). Unfortunately, if it's in a jar with a narrow opening, you'll need to scrape it out of that jar with a fork, about like scraping a candle out of a jar. Doing so may grate the fat into tiny bits and thus save you the trouble of using a box grater.

Serve It Up! Make a **quick hard sauce** by beating 8 tablespoons (1 stick) unsalted butter at room temperature with 1½ cups confectioners' sugar in a large bowl with an electric mixer at medium speed until creamy and smooth, with no trace of undissolved sugar in the mix. Beat in 1 tablespoon vanilla extract and 1 to 2 tablespoons brandy or whisky. Spoon the sauce onto each serving.

NEW YORK–STYLE CHEESECAKE

EFFORT: **A LOT** • PRESSURE: **LOW OR HIGH** • TIME UNDER PRESSURE: **35 OR 25 MINUTES** • RELEASE: **NATURAL** • SERVES: **8**

1¼ cups graham cracker crumbs

5 tablespoons unsalted butter, melted and cooled

1 pound regular cream cheese

½ cup sugar

2 large eggs, at room temperature

¼ cup sour cream

1½ tablespoons all-purpose flour

1 tablespoon fresh lemon juice

2 teaspoons finely grated lemon zest

½ teaspoon vanilla extract

1 Set a rack inside a 6-quart stovetop or electric pressure cooker; pour in 2 cups water.

2 Mix the graham cracker crumbs and melted butter in a small bowl until moistened and uniform. Lightly butter the inside of a 2-quart round, high-sided soufflé or baking dish or a 7-inch springform pan. Pour the crumb mixture into the dish or pan; press gently to form an even crust across the bottom and about halfway up the sides.

3 Place the cream cheese and sugar in a food processor fitted with the chopping blade; cover and process until creamy and smooth, stopping the machine a couple of times to scrape down the inside of the canister. With the machine running, add the eggs one at a time through the feed tube, processing each until smooth.

4 Add the sour cream and process until smooth, then add the flour and process for 1 minute. Finally, process in the lemon juice, zest, and vanilla until creamy and smooth, again stopping the machine at least once to scrape down the inside of the canister. Pour the batter into the prepared dish or pan, taking care not to dislodge the crumb crust. Do not cover.

5 Make an aluminum foil sling (see page 19) and set the baking dish in it; use the sling to lower the baking dish onto the rack in the cooker. Crimp the ends of the sling to fit inside the pot.

6 Lock the lid onto the pot.

STOVETOP: Set the pot over high heat and bring it to low pressure (8 psi). Once this pressure has been reached, reduce the heat as much as possible while maintaining this pressure. Cook for 35 minutes.

························· **OR** ·························
ELECTRIC: Set the machine to cook at high pressure (9–11 psi). Set the machine's timer to cook at this pressure for 25 minutes.

7 Reduce the pressure.

STOVETOP: Set the pot off the heat and let its pressure come back to normal naturally, about 10 minutes.

························· **OR** ·························
ELECTRIC: Turn off the machine or unplug it so it doesn't flip to its keep-warm setting. Let its pressure return to normal naturally, 12 to 15 minutes.

8 Unlock and open the pot. Use the foil sling to transfer the dish or pan to a wire cooling rack. Cool for 1 hour. If using a soufflé or baking dish, refrigerate for 3 hours; then unmold onto a cutting board, invert onto a serving platter, and refrigerate for another 6 hours before slicing. If using a springform pan, unfasten, loosen, and remove the collar; refrigerate for at least 6 hours before slicing.

TESTERS' NOTES
• Dense and firm, with just the right amount of give in each bite, this cheesecake may well lure you away from ever making another one in the oven.
• The cheesecake is creamier and has a smoother top if made at *low* pressure in a *stovetop* cooker. If your model doesn't allow you to cook at low pressure, you can use high pressure: cook only 18 minutes with a natural release. The cake will be denser and less creamy with a rocky, uneven top but the flavors will be just as good.
• We find the food processor yields a denser cheesecake. If beaten with a mixer, the batter becomes airier and the

cake less firm and chewy, the way a New York cheesecake should be.
• If there's any water condensed on top of the cake, you can dip the corner of a paper towel in it to wick up the moisture.

Serve It Up! Spread strawberry or apricot preserves (or even an all-fruit spread) over the top of the cake after it has cooled and set.

CHOCOLATE CHEESECAKE

EFFORT: **A LOT** • PRESSURE: **LOW OR HIGH** • TIME UNDER PRESSURE: **35 OR 25 MINUTES** • RELEASE: **NATURAL** • SERVES: **8**

1¼ cups chocolate cookie or chocolate graham cracker crumbs
5 tablespoons unsalted butter, melted and cooled
1 pound regular cream cheese
¼ cup packed dark brown sugar
¼ cup granulated white sugar
1 large egg plus 2 large egg yolks, at room temperature
8 ounces dark chocolate (at least 60% but no more than 80% cocoa solids), melted and cooled for 10 minutes
¼ cup regular or low-fat sour cream
1 tablespoon all-purpose flour
1 teaspoon vanilla extract

1 Set the rack inside a 6-quart stovetop or electric pressure cooker; pour in 2 cups water.

2 Mix the crumbs and melted butter in a small bowl. Butter the inside of a 2-quart, high-sided, round soufflé or baking dish or a 7-inch springform pan. Pour the crumb mixture into the dish or pan; press gently to form

(continued)

an even crust across the bottom and about halfway up the sides.

3 Place the cream cheese and both sugars in a food processor fitted with the chopping blade; cover and process until smooth, scraping down the inside of the canister a couple of times. With the machine running, add the whole egg through the feed tube, then the egg yolks one a time, processing each until smooth. Scrape down the canister; add the melted chocolate, sour cream, flour, and vanilla; process again until very creamy, almost velvety. Pour the mixture into the prepared dish or pan. Do not cover.

4 Make an aluminum foil sling (see page 19), set the dish or pan on it, and use the sling to lower the dish or pan onto the rack in the cooker. Crimp the sling's ends inside.

5 Lock on the lid.

STOVETOP: Set the pot over high heat and bring it to low pressure (8 psi). Once this pressure has been reached, reduce the heat as much as possible while maintaining this pressure. Cook for 35 minutes.

···············OR···············

ELECTRIC: Set the machine to cook at high pressure (9–11 psi). Set the machine's timer to cook at high pressure for 25 minutes.

6 Reduce the pressure.

STOVETOP: Set the pot off the heat and let its pressure come back to normal naturally, about 10 minutes.

···············OR···············

ELECTRIC: Turn off the machine or unplug it so it doesn't flip to its keep-warm setting. Let its pressure return to normal naturally, 12 to 16 minutes.

7 Unlock and open the pot. Use the foil sling to transfer the dish or pan to a wire cooling

rack and cool for 1 hour. If using a soufflé or baking dish, refrigerate for 3 hours; then unmold onto a cutting board, invert onto a serving platter, and refrigerate for another 6 hours before slicing. If using a springform pan, unfasten, loosen, and remove the collar; refrigerate for at least 6 hours before slicing.

TESTERS' NOTES

• This cheesecake is loaded with chocolate—even the crust. To make the crust, look for thin chocolate wafer cookies in the baking aisle of most supermarkets. Grind them in a food processor until they're about like graham cracker crumbs.

• To melt the chocolate, chop it into small bits, then set it in the top half of a double boiler over about 1 inch of simmering water and stir until halfway melted, then remove the top half of the double boiler from the heat and keep stirring until fully melted. Or set the chopped chocolate in a large bowl and microwave on high in 10-second increments, stirring after each, until the chocolate is about two-thirds melted, then remove the bowl and continue stirring until fully melted.

• If your *stovetop* model does not have a *low* setting, cook the cheesecake at high pressure (15 psi) for 18 minutes with a natural release. The top will be uneven with deep declivities; the texture, less creamy, but the taste will still be gorgeously rich.

WHITE CHOCOLATE CHEESECAKE WITH RASPBERRY SAUCE

EFFORT: **A LOT** • PRESSURE: **LOW OR HIGH** • TIME UNDER PRESSURE: **35 OR 25 MINUTES** • RELEASE: **NATURAL** • SERVES: **8**

1¼ cups graham cracker crumbs

5 tablespoons unsalted butter, melted and cooled

1 pound regular cream cheese

7 tablespoons regular or low-fat sweetened condensed milk

2 large eggs plus 1 large egg yolk, at room temperature

4 ounces white chocolate, melted and cooled

1 tablespoon all-purpose flour

1 teaspoon vanilla extract

1½ cups fresh raspberries

½ cup seedless raspberry jam

2 teaspoons cornstarch

1 Set the pressure cooker rack inside a 6-quart stovetop or electric cooker; pour in 2 cups water.

2 Mix the graham cracker crumbs and melted butter in a small bowl. Butter the inside of a 2-quart round, high-sided soufflé or baking dish or a 7-inch springform pan. Pour in the crumb mixture; press gently to form an even crust across the bottom and halfway up the sides.

3 Put the cream cheese and condensed milk in a food processor fitted with the chopping blade; cover and process until smooth, scraping down the inside of the canister once or twice. With the machine running, add the whole eggs and egg yolk one at a time through the feed tube, processing each until smooth before adding the next. Scrape down the canister; add the white chocolate, flour, and vanilla; process until creamy and rich. Pour the batter into the prepared dish or pan. Do not cover.

4 Make an aluminum foil sling (see page 19), set the dish or pan on it, and use the sling to lower the dish onto the rack in the cooker. Crimp the ends of the sling so they fit inside the pot.

5 Lock the lid onto the pot,

STOVETOP: Set the pot over high heat and bring it to low pressure (8 psi). Once this pressure has been reached, reduce the heat as much as possible while maintaining this pressure. Cook for 35 minutes.

·· OR ··

ELECTRIC: Set the machine to cook at high pressure (9–11 psi). Set the machine's timer to cook at high pressure for 25 minutes.

6 Reduce the pressure.

STOVETOP: Set the pot off the heat and let its pressure come back to normal naturally, about 10 minutes.

·· OR ··

ELECTRIC: Turn off the machine or unplug it so it doesn't flip to its keep-warm setting. Let its pressure return to normal naturally, 12 to 16 minutes.

7 Unlock and open the pot. Use the foil sling to transfer the dish or pan to a wire cooling rack. Cool for 1 hour. If using a soufflé or baking dish, refrigerate for 3 hours; then unmold onto a cutting board, invert onto a serving platter, and refrigerate for another 6 hours before slicing. If using a springform pan, unfasten, loosen, and remove the collar; refrigerate for at least 6 hours before slicing.

8 As the cheesecake cools, place the raspberries in a fine-mesh sieve set over a large bowl; use a rubber spatula to wipe them back and forth across the mesh, pushing the juice and puree through to the bowl below and leaving the seeds and skins in the sieve. Pour the puree into a small saucepan, stir in the jam, and set over medium-low heat until simmering, stirring occasionally.

9 Whisk the cornstarch and 2 teaspoons water in a small bowl and stir into the simmering raspberry mixture. Cook until

(continued)

thickened, stirring all the while, less than 1 minute. Cool off the heat until room temperature, then pour onto the top of the cooled cheesecake so the sauce runs down the sides. Or pour the sauce onto individual serving plates and set a slice of cheesecake on top of each pool.

TESTERS' NOTES

• Smooth and luscious, this creamy cheesecake uses condensed milk for more body and a subtle, caramelized flavor, plus all the sugar the cake needs. Do not use low-fat or fat-free condensed milk.

• If possible, look for "non-deodorized white chocolate," a specialty product available online and through gourmet stores. It has a much more pronounced flavor, with hints of dark chocolate as well as an earthy finish.

• For more raspberry flavor, substitute a raspberry-flavored liqueur, such as Chambord, for the water in the cornstarch slurry used to thicken the raspberry puree.

• For a quicker topping, just spread 1½ cups raspberry jam over the top of the cake. Whisk it first in a small bowl, so it's smooth and spreadable. You won't have a sauce, but you'll save lots of effort.

MAPLE CHEESECAKE

EFFORT: **A LOT** • PRESSURE: **LOW OR HIGH** • TIME UNDER PRESSURE: **35 OR 25 MINUTES** • RELEASE: **NATURAL** • SERVES: **8**

1¼ **cups gingersnap crumbs**

5 **tablespoons unsalted butter, melted and cooled**

1 **pound regular cream cheese**

½ **cup maple syrup, preferably Grade B or 2**

1 **large egg plus 2 large egg yolks, at room temperature**

2 **tablespoons all-purpose flour**

1 **teaspoon vanilla extract**

¼ **teaspoon salt**

1 Place the pressure cooker rack inside a 6-quart stovetop or electric cooker; pour in 2 cups water.

2 Mix the cookie crumbs and melted butter in a small bowl until moist and uniform. Butter the inside of a 2-quart round, high-sided soufflé or baking dish or a 7-inch springform pan. Pour in the crumb mixture; press to form an even crust across the bottom and halfway up the sides.

3 Process the cream cheese and maple syrup in a food processor fitted with the chopping blade, stopping the machine a couple of times to scrape down the inside of the canister. With the machine running, add the whole egg and egg yolks one at a time, processing each until smooth before adding the next. Scrape down the canister again, then add the flour, vanilla, and salt. Process until smooth and creamy; pour the batter into the prepared dish or pan.

4 Make an aluminum foil sling (see page 19), set the dish or pan on it, and use the sling to lower the dish onto the rack in the cooker. Crimp the ends of the sling so they fit inside the pot.

5 Lock the lid onto the pot.

STOVETOP: Set the pot over high heat and bring it to low pressure (8 psi). Once this pressure has been reached, reduce the heat as much as possible to keep the pot at this pressure. Cook for 35 minutes.

······················· OR ·······················

ELECTRIC: Set the machine to cook at high pressure (9–11 psi). Set the machine's timer to cook at this pressure for 25 minutes.

6 Reduce the pressure.

STOVETOP: Set the pot off the heat and let its pressure come back to normal naturally, about 10 minutes.

···························· **OR** ····························

ELECTRIC: Turn off the machine or unplug it so it doesn't flip to its keep-warm setting. Let its pressure return to normal naturally, 12 to 16 minutes.

7 Unlock and open the pot. Use the foil sling to transfer the dish or pan to a wire cooling rack. Cool for 1 hour. If using a soufflé or baking dish, refrigerate for 3 hours; then unmold onto a cutting board, invert onto a serving platter, and refrigerate for another 6 hours before slicing. If using a springform pan, unfasten, loosen, and remove the collar; refrigerate for at least 6 hours before slicing.

TESTERS' NOTES
• Only Grade B or 2 maple syrup will have enough oomph to stand up to the pressure and add plenty of flavor to this rich cheesecake.
• We've added a little salt, a missing bit from most cheesecakes because of the sodium in the cream cheese, because we feel it brings the maple flavor more to the fore.
• Look for fairly thin gingersnaps that you can grind in the food processor until the consistency of graham cracker crumbs. Or just use 1¼ cups graham cracker crumbs mixed with ½ teaspoon ground ginger as an easy shortcut.

Serve It Up! Grind some peanut brittle in a food processor and sprinkle over each serving.

APRICOT CHEESECAKE

EFFORT: **A LOT** • PRESSURE: **LOW OR HIGH** • TIME UNDER PRESSURE: **35 OR 25 MINUTES** • RELEASE: **NATURAL** • SERVES: **8**

½ cup dried apricots, preferably California
1¼ cups graham cracker crumbs
5 tablespoons unsalted butter, melted and cooled
1 pound regular cream cheese
¼ cup honey
¼ cup sugar
2 large eggs, at room temperature
1½ tablespoons all-purpose flour
1 teaspoon vanilla extract

1 Place the rack inside a 6-quart stovetop or electric pressure cooker; add 2 cups water.

2 Cover the apricots with boiling water in a large bowl; set aside to soak for 20 minutes.

3 Mix the graham cracker crumbs and melted butter in a small bowl until moist and uniform; pour into a 2-quart round, high-sided soufflé or baking dish or a 7-inch springform pan. Press to form an even crust across the bottom and halfway up the sides.

4 Drain the apricots in a colander set in the sink. Put them in a food processor fitted with the chopping blade; add the cream cheese, honey, and sugar. Cover and process until creamy, scraping down the inside of the canister several times to make sure the apricots are pureed. With the machine running, add the eggs one at a time, making sure the first is thoroughly incorporated before adding the next. Scrape down the canister, add the flour and vanilla, and process until velvety smooth. Pour the mixture into the prepared dish or pan. Do not cover.

(continued)

5 Make an aluminum foil sling (see page 19), set the dish or pan on it, and use the sling to lower the dish onto the rack in the cooker. Crimp the ends of the sling so they fit inside the pot.

6 Lock the lid onto the pot.

STOVETOP: Set the pot over high heat and bring it to low pressure (8 psi). Once this pressure has been reached, reduce the heat as much as possible while maintaining this pressure. Cook for 35 minutes.

·············· **OR** ··············

ELECTRIC: Set the machine to cook at high pressure (9–11 psi). Set the machine's timer to cook at this pressure for 25 minutes.

7 Reduce the pressure.

STOVETOP: Set the pot off the heat and let its pressure come back to normal naturally, about 10 minutes.

·············· **OR** ··············

ELECTRIC: Turn off the machine or unplug it so it doesn't flip to its keep-warm setting. Let its pressure return to normal naturally, 12 to 16 minutes.

8 Unlock and open the pot. Use the foil sling to transfer the dish or pan to a wire cooling rack. Cool for 1 hour. If using a soufflé or baking dish, refrigerate for 3 hours; then unmold the cake onto a cutting board, invert onto a serving platter, and refrigerate for another 6 hours before slicing. If using a springform pan, unfasten, loosen, and remove the collar; refrigerate for at least 6 hours before slicing.

TESTERS' NOTES
• Dried California apricots (actually apricot halves, and deep orange in color) give this cheesecake a sour, pronounced flavor, a great way to cut through its richness.
• You really can't scrape down the inside of that food processor too many times. You need a smooth puree for the best consistency.

RICOTTA GINGER CHEESECAKE

EFFORT: **A LOT** • PRESSURE: **LOW OR HIGH** • TIME UNDER PRESSURE: **35 OR 25 MINUTES** • RELEASE: **NATURAL** • SERVES: **8**

1¼ cups gingersnap crumbs (about 15 thin cookies)

5 tablespoons unsalted butter, melted and cooled

8 ounces regular cream cheese

8 ounces regular ricotta

½ cup packed light brown sugar

2 large eggs, at room temperature

2 tablespoons plain whole-milk yogurt (not Greek yogurt)

¼ cup minced crystallized (candied) ginger

1 tablespoon all-purpose flour

1 teaspoon vanilla extract

1 Put the pressure cooker rack in a 6-quart stovetop or electric cooker; pour in 2 cups water.

2 Mix the cookie crumbs and melted butter in a small bowl until uniform and moist. Butter the inside of a 2-quart round, high-sided soufflé or baking dish or a 7-inch springform pan. Pour in the cookie crumb mixture; press into an even crust across the bottom and about halfway up the sides.

3 Process the cream cheese, ricotta, and brown sugar in a food processor fitted with the chopping blade until creamy and smooth, scraping down the inside of the canister once or twice. With the machine running, add the eggs one at a time, making sure the first is completely incorporated before adding the second. Scrape down the canister again, add the yogurt, and process well.

4 Press the ginger through a garlic press and into the food processor; process until smooth. Scrape down the canister one more time before processing in the flour and vanilla until rich and velvety. Pour the mixture into the prepared dish or pan. Do not cover.

5 Make an aluminum foil sling (see page 19), set the dish or pan on it, and use the sling to lower the dish onto the rack in the cooker. Crimp the ends of the sling so they fit inside the pot.

6 Lock the lid onto the pot.

STOVETOP: Set the pot over high heat and bring it to low pressure (8 psi). Once this pressure has been reached, reduce the heat as much as possible while maintaining this pressure. Cook for 35 minutes.

·······OR·······

ELECTRIC: Set the machine to cook at high pressure (9–11 psi). Set the machine's timer to cook at high pressure for 25 minutes.

7 Reduce the pressure.

STOVETOP: Set the pot off the heat and let its pressure come back to normal naturally, about 10 minutes.

·······OR·······

ELECTRIC: Turn off the machine or unplug it so it doesn't flip to its keep-warm setting. Let its pressure return to normal naturally, 12 to 16 minutes.

8 Unlock and open the pot. Use the foil sling to transfer the dish or pan to a wire cooling rack. Cool for 1 hour. If using a soufflé or baking dish, refrigerate for 3 hours; then unmold the cake onto a cutting board, invert onto a serving platter, and refrigerate for another 6 hours before slicing. If using a springform pan, unfasten, loosen, and remove the collar; refrigerate for at least 6 hours before slicing.

TESTERS' NOTES
• Ricotta isn't as sweet as cream cheese, so this cheesecake is not quite as sweet as some of the others. Ricotta is also not as creamy, so there's a slight graininess in the texture—like the crumb of a cake.
• Use the ricotta found in the dairy case rather than the more expensive ricotta found in the cheese case.

TIRAMISÙ CHEESECAKE

EFFORT: **A LOT** • PRESSURE: **LOW OR HIGH** • TIME UNDER PRESSURE: **35 OR 25 MINUTES** • RELEASE: **NATURAL** • SERVES: **8**

1¼ cups vanilla wafer cookie crumbs (about 35 cookies)

5 tablespoons unsalted butter, melted and cooled

8 ounces regular cream cheese

8 ounces mascarpone cheese

¼ cup packed light brown sugar

¼ cup granulated white sugar

2 large eggs plus 1 large egg yolk, at room temperature

2 tablespoons all-purpose flour

2 tablespoons coffee-flavored liqueur, such as Kahlua

1 tablespoon instant espresso powder

½ teaspoon vanilla extract

¾ cup heavy cream

2 tablespoons confectioners' sugar

1 tablespoon unsweetened cocoa powder

1 Place the pressure cooker rack inside a 6-quart stovetop or electric cooker; add 2 cups water.

2 Mix the cookie crumbs and melted butter in a small bowl until moist and uniform. Butter the inside of a 2-quart round,

(continued)

high-sided soufflé or baking dish or a 7-inch springform pan. Pour in the crumb mixture and press into an even crust across the bottom and about halfway up the sides.

3 Process the cream cheese, mascarpone cheese, and both sugars in a food processor fitted with the chopping blade until smooth, scraping down the inside of the canister several times. With the machine running, add the whole eggs and egg yolk one at a time, letting each get thoroughly incorporated before adding the next. Scrape down the canister, add the flour, and process until smooth.

4 Stir the liqueur, espresso powder, and vanilla in a small bowl until the powder dissolves. Add the coffee mixture to the food processor and process until you have a smooth, creamy batter. Pour the batter into the prepared dish or pan. Do not cover.

5 Make an aluminum foil sling (see page 19), set the dish or pan on it, and use the sling to lower the dish onto the rack in the cooker. Crimp the ends of the sling so they fit inside.

6 Lock the lid onto the pot.

STOVETOP: Set the pot over high heat and bring it to low pressure (8 psi). Once this pressure has been reached, reduce the heat as much as possible while maintaining this pressure. Cook for 35 minutes.

························· **OR** ·························

ELECTRIC: Set the machine to cook at high pressure (9–11 psi). Set the machine's timer to cook at high pressure for 25 minutes.

7 Reduce the pressure.

STOVETOP: Set the pot off the heat and let its pressure come back to normal naturally, about 10 minutes.

························· **OR** ·························

ELECTRIC: Turn off the machine or unplug it so it doesn't flip to its keep-warm setting. Let its pressure return to normal naturally, 12 to 16 minutes.

8 Unlock and open the pot. Use the foil sling to transfer the dish or pan to a wire cooling rack. Cool for 1 hour. If using a soufflé or baking dish, refrigerate for 3 hours, then unmold the cake onto a cutting board, invert onto a serving platter, and refrigerate for another 6 hours before slicing. If using a springform pan, unfasten, loosen, and remove the collar; refrigerate for at least 6 hours before slicing.

9 As the cheesecake cools, use an electric mixer at high speed to whip the cream and confectioners' sugar in a medium bowl until soft, luscious peaks form. Spread the whipped cream over the top of the cooled cheesecake; dust with cocoa powder before serving.

TESTERS' NOTES

• The combination of cream cheese and mascarpone makes this cheesecake irresistibly light. Although the name means "pick me up" in Italian (since it's an afternoon snack to get you going again), you might want to serve this at the end of a big meal, a little bit of creamy bliss to conclude the evening.

• Tiramisù is traditionally made with *savoiardi* (ladyfingers). They turn gummy under pressure, so vanilla wafers make a better crust.

• The espresso powder needs to be dissolved so it is incorporated evenly into the batter. The trick here is to create the smoothest, most uniform puree possible to get the best texture in the finished dessert.

SPICED APPLES

EFFORT: **NOT MUCH** • PRESSURE: **HIGH** • TIME UNDER PRESSURE: **4 OR 6 MINUTES** • RELEASE: **QUICK** • SERVES: **4**

2 cups moderately dry white wine, such as Riesling

1/2 cup sugar

1/4 teaspoon grated nutmeg

One 4-inch cinnamon stick

8 whole cloves

4 large, firm apples, such as Granny Smith, Honeycrisp, Mutsu, or Rome, peeled, halved, and cored

1 Bring the wine, sugar, nutmeg, cinnamon stick, and cloves to a boil in a 6-quart stovetop pressure cooker set over medium heat or in a 6-quart electric pressure cooker turned to the browning function, stirring occasionally, particularly until the sugar dissolves. Drop in the apple halves.

2 Lock the lid onto the pot.

STOVETOP: Set the pot over high heat and bring it to high pressure (15 psi). Once this pressure has been reached, reduce the heat as much as possible while maintaining this pressure. Cook for 4 minutes.

························ OR ························

ELECTRIC: Set the machine to cook at high pressure (9–11 psi). Set the machine's timer to cook at high pressure for 6 minutes.

3 Use the quick-release method to bring the pot's pressure back to normal.

4 Unlock and open the pot. Transfer the apple halves to a large bowl or individual serving bowls.

5 Bring the sauce to a boil in the stovetop cooker set over medium heat or in the electric one turned to its browning function. Cook, stirring occasionally, until it reduces to a thick syrup, about 5 minutes. Discard the cinnamon stick and cloves; pour the syrup over the apples to serve.

TESTERS' NOTES
• These stewed apples are aromatic and sweet, great on a fall evening. They'd also be terrific for a weekend lunch, served with their syrup over crunchy, whole-grain waffles.
• Add a slightly sour note to the sauce by including 1/2 teaspoon finely grated lemon zest with the spices.

Serve It Up! Dollop plain yogurt or crème fraîche over each serving.

POACHED PEARS IN RED WINE

EFFORT: **NOT MUCH** • PRESSURE: **HIGH** • TIME UNDER PRESSURE: **4 OR 6 MINUTES** • RELEASE: **QUICK** • SERVES: **4**

2 cups dry, fruit-forward red wine, such as Zinfandel

2 cups sugar

1 tablespoon vanilla extract

One 4-inch cinnamon stick

Two 1/2-inch-wide, 2-inch-long strips of orange zest

4 firm, ripe Bosc pears, peeled, halved, and cored

1 Mix the wine, sugar, vanilla, cinnamon stick, and zest in a 6-quart stovetop pressure cooker set over medium heat or in a 6-quart electric pressure cooker turned to the browning function. Bring to a simmer, stirring occasionally, particularly until the sugar dissolves. Add the pears and stir well to coat.

(continued)

2 Lock the lid onto the pot.

STOVETOP: Raise the heat to high and bring the pot to high pressure (15 psi). Once this pressure has been reached, reduce the heat as much as possible while maintaining this pressure. Cook for 4 minutes.

·························· **OR** ··························

ELECTRIC: Set the machine to cook at high pressure (9–11 psi). Set the machine's timer to cook at high pressure for 6 minutes.

3 Use the quick-release method to drop the pot's pressure to normal.

4 Unlock and open the pot. Use a slotted spoon to transfer the pear halves to a large sealable bowl. Discard the cinnamon stick and orange peels; pour the pan syrup into a large bowl. Cover and store the syrup and pears separately in the fridge until cooled.

5 Add the syrup to the pears, cover, and store in the fridge for at least 2 more hours before serving or store for up to 4 days.

TESTERS' NOTES

• Pears and red wine are a classic combination and couldn't be faster or easier with this preparation. But plan ahead: the fruit needs to cool and the flavors to ripen.

• The easiest way to core pear halves is with a melon baller. Set the pear cut side up on a cutting board and use the baller to scoop out the seeds and tough, fibrous bits around them, leaving a little, round indentation in the fruit.

• Use a vegetable peeler to create even, long strips of zest from an orange.

• If you want to double the servings, remove the cooked pears from the syrup, drop more raw pears in, and cook again as directed before continuing with the recipe.

Serve It Up! Crumble blue cheese over each pear or put a little crème fraîche or softened mascarpone cheese in the indentation of each.

DRIED FRUIT COMPOTE

EFFORT: **NOT MUCH** • PRESSURE: **HIGH** • TIME UNDER PRESSURE: **4 OR 6 MINUTES** • RELEASE: **QUICK** • SERVES: **6**

2 cups unsweetened apple juice

$1/2$ cup sugar

1 teaspoon whole cloves

$1/4$ teaspoon salt

One 4-inch cinnamon stick

9 ounces dried apricots, preferably Turkish (about $1^1/3$ cups)

3 ounces dried apples, chopped (about 1 cup)

$2^1/2$ ounces dried cranberries (about $1/2$ cup)

8 dried figs, stemmed and halved

1 Stir the juice, sugar, cloves, salt, and cinnamon stick in a 6-quart stovetop or electric cooker until the sugar dissolves. Stir in the dried fruit.

2 Lock the lid onto the pot.

STOVETOP: Set the pot over high heat and bring it to high pressure (15 psi). Once this pressure has been reached, reduce the heat as much as possible while maintaining this pressure. Cook for 4 minutes.

·························· **OR** ··························

ELECTRIC: Set the machine to cook at high pressure (9–11 psi). Set the machine's timer to cook at high pressure for 6 minutes.

3 Use the quick-release method to bring the pot's pressure back to normal.

4 Unlock and open the cooker. Set the stovetop model over medium heat or turn the electric one to its browning setting. Bring the mixture to a full simmer and cook, uncovered and stirring occasionally, for 2 minutes to reduce the syrup a bit. Cool for a few minutes in the pot, then pour into a large container, seal, and refrigerate for at least 6 hours or up to 4 days. Discard the cinnamon stick and cloves before serving.

TESTERS' NOTES

• Here's a great ending to a large meal: a sweet, aromatic compote that's best over a bowl of plain Greek yogurt or frozen vanilla yogurt.
• Remember the rule of dried fruit: it should smell like its fresh counterpart. If it's hard or brittle, or if it has no aroma (or worse, a musty aroma), it won't make a successful compote.

DRIED FIGS IN WHITE WINE SYRUP

EFFORT: **NOT MUCH** • PRESSURE: **HIGH** • TIME UNDER PRESSURE: **5 OR 8 MINUTES** • RELEASE: **QUICK** • SERVES: **8**

2½ **cups fairly sweet white wine, such as Gewürztraminer**
¾ **cup sugar**
One 4-inch cinnamon stick
1 vanilla bean, halved lengthwise
1½ **pounds dried white Turkish or Calimyrna figs**

1 Stir the wine, sugar, cinnamon stick, and vanilla bean in a 6-quart stovetop or electric pressure cooker until the sugar dissolves. Stir in the dried figs.

2 Lock the lid onto the pot.

STOVETOP: Set the pot over high heat and bring it to high pressure (15 psi). Once this pressure has been reached, reduce the heat as much as possible while maintaining this pressure. Cook for 5 minutes.

······································ OR ······································

ELECTRIC: Set the machine to cook at high pressure (9–11 psi). Set the machine's timer to cook at high pressure for 8 minutes.

3 Use the quick-release method to drop the pot's pressure to normal.

4 Unlock and open the cooker. Cool for 15 minutes, then pour into a large bowl or container. Cover and refrigerate for at least 6 hours or up to 4 days. Discard the cinnamon stick and vanilla bean before serving.

TESTERS' NOTES

• You'll want to make sure you have some leftovers of this sweet dessert because it'll go so well over plain yogurt for breakfast.
• For the best dried figs, the stems should still be attached and the fruit itself should have no soft or bruised bits. Dried Mission (or black) figs are generally too small and soft for a successful compote with this technique.
• There's no need to throw out the vanilla bean. Let it dry on the counter overnight, then pack it into a small jar of granulated sugar and store in a cool, dark place for about 2 weeks. After that, you'll have ridiculously good vanilla sugar that will keep in its jar for up to 1 year.

INDEX